2

Encyclopedia of
Early Television Crime Fig]

Encyclopedia of Early Television Crime Fighters

All Regular Cast Members in American Crime and Mystery Series, 1948–1959

EVERETT AAKER

Volume 2
(Players M–Z; Appendices;
Bibliography; Index)

McFarland & Company, Inc., Publishers
Jefferson, North Carolina, and London

Volume 2

Library of Congress Cataloguing-in-Publication Data

Aaker Everett.
Encyclopedia of early television crime fighters : all regular cast members in American crime and mystery series, 1948–1959 / Everett Aaker.
p.   cm.
Includes bibliographical references and index.

2 volume set—
ISBN 978-0-7864-6409-8   ∞
softcover : 50# alkaline paper

1. Detective and mystery television programs—United States—Encyclopedias.   2. Television actors and actresses—United States—Biography—Encyclopedias.   I. Title.
PN1992.8.D48A25   2011   791.45'65503—dc22   2006003232

British Library cataloguing data are available

© 2006 Everett Aaker. All rights reserved

No part of this book may be reproduced or transmitted in any form or by any means, electronic or mechanical, including photocopying or recording, or by any information storage and retrieval system, without permission in writing from the publisher.

Cover image © 2011 Photodisc

Manufactured in the United States of America

*McFarland & Company, Inc., Publishers
Box 611, Jefferson, North Carolina 28640
www.mcfarlandpub.com*

TABLE OF CONTENTS

• Volume 1 •

Acknowledgments xi
Introduction 1

The Players

Jack Albertson	5	Edward Binns	54	John Cassavetes	122
Lola Albright	6	Paul Birch	56	Lonny Chapman	126
Robert Alda	8	Honor Blackman	58	Eduardo Ciannelli	127
Ben Alexander	10	Lee Bowman	61	Dane Clark	129
Florenz Ames	12	William Boyett	63	Tristram Coffin	133
Judith (Rachel) Ames	13	Raymond Bramley	64	Lois Collier	135
Warner Anderson	14	George Brent	64	Ray Collins	137
Keith Andes	16	David Brian	68	John Compton	138
Tige Andrews	18	Lloyd Bridges	70	Mike Connors	139
Tod Andrews	19	Barbara Britton	76	Robert Conrad	143
Robert Arden	20	James Broderick	78	Richard Conte	147
Doe Avedon	23	Charles Bronson	79	Russ Conway	150
Tol Avery	24	Roxane Brooks	84	Tom Conway	151
Barbara Bain	24	James Burke	85	Wendell Corey	154
Carla Balenda	26	Paul Burke	86	Hazel Court	157
Michael Balfour	27	Bart Burns	89	Broderick Crawford	159
Lynn Bari	28	Raymond Burr	90	Donald Curtis	164
Joanna Barnes	31	Anthony Bushell	99	Dan Dailey	166
Vince Barnett	32	Herb Butterfield	101	James Daly	171
Harry Bartell	34	Ralph Byrd	102	Lisa Daniely	172
Tod Barton	34	Edd Byrnes	104	Helmut Dantine	173
Charles Bateman	35	King Calder	108	Claude Dauphin	175
Robert Beatty	35	Rod Cameron	108	Rupert Davies	177
Jacqueline Beer	39	Macdonald Carey	111	Diana Decker	179
Ralph Bellamy	40	Olive Carey	115	Richard Denning	181
Harry Bellaver	44	Philip Carey	116	Francis De Sales	184
John Bentley	45	Richard Carlson	118	Vittorio De Sica	185
Herschel Bernardi	48	Richard Carlyle	121	Joe Devlin	189
Lyle Bettger	49	Grace Carney	121	Patricia Donahue	190
Charles Bickford	51	Robert Carroll	122	Brian Donlevy	191

vi Table of Contents

John Doucette	194	James Gregory	240	Jay Jostyn	296
Melvyn Douglas	196	Reed Hadley	242	Louis Jourdan	297
Len Doyle	200	Don Haggerty	244	Boris Karloff	300
Ken Drake	201	Alan Hale, Jr.	246	Robert Karnes	306
Paula Drew	201	Barbara Hale	248	Roscoe Karns	307
Wendy Drew	201	Cliff Hall	251	Todd Karns	309
Andrew Duggan	202	Earl Hammond	251	Mike Keene	310
Archie Duncan	204	Jonathan Harris	252	Andrew Keir	310
Anthony Eisley	206	Stacy Harris	255	Brian Keith	312
Dick Elliott	209	Richard Hart	256	Byron Keith	316
Evan Elliott	210	Jack Hawkins	257	Barry Kelley	316
Herb Ellis	211	Margaret (Maggie)		Brian Kelly	317
Hope Emerson	211	Hayes	263	Walter Kinsella	318
Clifford Evans	212	Louis Hayward	264	Phyllis Kirk	319
Lee Farr	214	David Hedison	268	Charles Korvin	321
Abel Fernandez	214	Chuck Henderson	272	Duncan Lamont	323
James Flavin	215	Gloria Henry	272	Rusty Lane	325
Arthur Fleming	217	Fred Hillebrand	273	Keith Larsen	326
James Franciscus	219	Edd Hinton	273	Peter Lawford	327
William Gargan	222	Patrick Holt	274	Cloris Leachman	332
Beverly Garland	226	James Hong	276	William Leslie	335
Rian Garrick	229	William Hopper	278	Peggy Lobbin	336
Lisa Gastoni	230	Ronald Howard	279	Richard Long	336
John George	231	Clark Howat	282	Phillips H. Lord	339
Nick Georgiade	232	Arlene Howell	282	Jackie Loughery	340
John Gibson	233	Harold Huber	283	Frank Lovejoy	341
Bruce Gordon	233	Lizabeth Hush	285	Edmund Lowe	343
Glen Gordon	234	Conrad Janis	285	Laurette Luez	346
Bernie Gozier	236	David Janssen	286	Ken Lynch	347
Donald Gray	236	Frank Jenks	291	Gene Lyons	348
Walter Greaza	238	Diane Jergens	292		
Angela Greene	239	Victor Jory	293		

• Volume 2 •

James Maloney	349	Neil McCallum	366	Adolphe Menjou	386
Ralph Manza	349	Mercedes		Gary Merrill	390
Howard Marion-		McCambridge	367	Ray Milland	394
Crawford	350	Donald McClelland	371	Marvin Miller	400
Hugh Marlowe	352	Darren McGavin	371	Jan Miner	401
Joan Marshall	354	Charles McGraw	375	Gerald Mohr	402
Lee Marvin	355	John McIntire	377	Mary Tyler Moore	403
Sydney Mason	359	Horace McMahon	379	Dennis Morgan	406
Raymond Massey	359	John McQuade	381	Patricia Morison	410
Murray Matheson	363	Patrick McVey	382	Patricia Morrow	412
Lester Matthews	364	Ralph Meeker	383	Doug Mossman	412

Lionel Murton	413	Ewan Roberts	477	Colin Tapley	543
George Nader	414	Lynne Roberts	479	Kent Taylor	545
J. Carrol Naish	418	Cesar Romero	480	Robert Taylor	548
Russell Napier	421	Anthony Ross	485	Frank Thomas	552
Barry Nelson	422	Gena Rowlands	486	Jerome Thor	553
Paul Newlan	425	Mel Ruick	488	June Thorburn	554
Jane Nigh	426	Howard St. John	489	Russell Thorson	556
Lloyd Nolan	427	George Sanders	489	Regis Toomey	556
Gene O'Donnell	430	Gloria Saunders	495	Lee Tracy	559
Kevin O'Morrison	431	Nicholas Saunders	495	Richard Travis	562
Patrick O'Neal	432	Simon Scott	496	Les Tremayne	563
Jack Orrison	434	Sydna Scott	497	Tom Tully	565
Frank Orth	434	Bruce Seton	497	Tim Turner	566
Luciana Paluzzi	435	Michael Shepley	499	Beverly Tyler	568
Jerry Paris	437	Louis Sirgo	500	Minerva Urecal	569
Judy Parrish	438	Everett Sloane	501	Vicki Vola	571
Lee Philips	438	Archie Smith	503	Skip Ward	571
Barney Phillips	439	Roger Smith	503	Debbie Watling	572
Eric Pohlmann	440	Arthur Space	506	Richard Wattis	574
Poncie Ponce	442	Robert Stack	508	Jack Webb	576
Mel Prestidge	443	Lynn Stalmaster	515	Richard Webb	580
Robert Preston	443	Virginia Stefan	516	Mary K. Wells	582
Anne Préville	447	Connie Stevens	516	Nina Wilcox	582
William Prince	447	Craig Stevens	519	Hugh Williams	582
Denver Pyle	449	Julie Stevens	523	Van Williams	585
Louis Quinn	451	Mark Stevens	523	Lewis Wilson	587
George Raft	452	Paul Stewart	527	Roland Winters	587
Ron Randell	459	Harold J. Stone	528	John Witty	589
William (Billy) Redfield	463	Suzanne Storrs	530	Anna May Wong	590
		Ludwig Stossel	530	George Woodbridge	594
Brian Reece	464	Randy Stuart	532	Donald Woods	596
Marshall Reed	465	Barry Sullivan	533	Trudy Wroe	598
Michael Rennie	467	Frank Sully	537	Fred Wynn	598
Stafford Repp	472	Lyle Talbot	538	Barton Yarborough	599
Addison Richards	473	Nita Talbot	540	John Zaremba	599
Grant Richards	475	William Talman	541	Efrem Zimbalist, Jr.	600
Edwin Richfield	476	Gordon Tanner	543		

Appendix 1. Television Series Catalog 607
Appendix 2. Players Too Late for Date Range 619
Bibliography 621
Index 625

JAMES MALONEY

James Maloney was born on June 27, 1915. He made his Broadway debut in March 1949 in the play *Detective Story* which he appeared in until August 1950. The film version marked his screen debut in 1951. He had a two year run on Broadway in the play *Inherit the Wind* which he appeared in between April 1955 and June 1957. In the television detective series *21 Beacon Street* he played Jim who was a master of disguise and dialects attached to the staff of Dennis Chase (Dennis Morgan). Once the series finished, Maloney's appearances were minimal. He died in obscurity in New Britain, Connecticut on August 19, 1978 aged 63.

Filmography

1951: *The Detective Story.*
1952: *Wait Till the Sun Shines Nellie.*
1955: *Seminole Uprising.*
1957: *Lure of the Swamp, Hell Canyon Outlaws.*
1959: *A Lust to Kill.*
1962: *Third of a Man.*
1963: *The Two Little Bears.*

Television Series

1959: *21 Beacon Street* as Jim.

Sources

Brooks, Tim. *The Complete Directory to Prime Time TV Stars, 1946–Present.* New York: Ballantine, 1987.

Tibballs, Geoff. *TV Detectives.* London: Boxtree, 1992.

RALPH MANZA

Ralph Manza was born in San Francisco on December 1, 1921. He was a premed student at Berkeley when he was drafted into the Army during World War II. When he was assigned to a troupe of entertainers as a medic, he discovered his flair for acting. One of his earliest roles was in the crime series *The D.A.'s Man* in which he played Assistant District Attorney Al Bonacorsi. It was the task of the title character Shannon (John Compton) to infiltrate organized crime. Bonacorsi was his contact in the District Attorney's office. Much later Manza co-starred with George Peppard in another crime series *Banacek*. In this he played his chauffeur and sidekick, Jay Drury. He also played Stanke, the ambulance driver, in the short-lived comedy series *A.E.S. Hudson Street* and was Padre Guardiano in the *Mama Malone* series. He had a recurring role in the sitcom *Newhart* which ran throughout the latter part of the 1980s. In real life he lived in Leucadia. In early January 2000 he was filming a Budweiser commercial when he suffered a heart attack. He died at Scripps Hospital in Encinitas, California on January 31, 2000 aged 78, of complications from the heart attack, survived by his wife Catherine, four children and three grandchildren.

Filmography

1957: *The Enemy Below.*
1958: *Gang War, The Hunters.*
1960: *Too Soon to Love.*
1961: *Secret of Deep Harbor.*
1962: *That Touch of Mink, This Is Not a Test.*
1964: *Dear Heart.*

Left to right: Murray Matheson, George Peppard and Ralph Manza in *Banacek*. Earlier Matheson costarred in *Harbormaster* and Manza costarred in *The D.A.'s Man*.

HOWARD MARION-CRAWFORD

Howard Francis Marion-Crawford was born in Marylebone, London, England on January 17, 1914, the grandson of the writer Francis Marion Crawford. His parents were Harold Marion-Crawford, a rubber planter, and Nina Wood, an actress. His father, who served in the Irish Guards, was killed in World War I. He was an only child. He came from a military family background. He was educated at Clifton College, Bristol, England, and in France and Austria. Trained for the stage at the Royal Academy of Dramatic Art in London, he began his film career at Gaumont-British in 1935 with whom he stayed for two years. In 1938 he went to America where he entertained in a nightclub, but returned to England when war broke out and

1966: *What Did You Do in the War, Daddy?*, *Dragnet* (TV).
1968: *Three Guns for Texas* (TV), *The Smugglers* (TV).
1972: *Banacek: Detour to Nowhere* (TV).
1973: *Cops and Robbers.*
1974: *Blazing Saddles.*
1975: *A Cry for Help* (TV), *The Wild Party.*
1977: *Terraces* (TV).
1978: *The One and Only*, *Perfect Gentlemen* (TV), *The Cat from Outer Space.*
1979: *Love at First Bite*, *Samurai* (TV), *The Apple Dumpling Gang Rides Again.*
1980: *Little Miss Marker*, *Fatso.*
1984: *The Philadelphia Experiment.*
1985: *Beer.*
1988: *Retribution.*
1991: *9½ Ninjas.*
1992: *Mission of Justice.*
1993: *Dave.*
1995: *Get Shorty.*
1996: *Her Last Chance.*
1998: *Godzilla*, *Lookin' Italian.*
2000: *What's Cookin'?*, *Can't Be Heaven.*

TELEVISION SERIES

1959: *The D.A.'s Man* as Assistant District Attorney Al Bonacorsi.
1963: *General Hospital* as Mike Costello.
1972–1974: *Banacek* as Jay Drury.
1978: *A.E.S. Hudson Street* as Ambulance Driver Stanke.
1984: *Mama Malone* as Padre Guardiano.
1985–1990: *Newhart* as Bud.

SOURCES

Lentz, Harris M. III. *Obituaries in the Performing Arts, 2001.* Jefferson, NC: McFarland, 2002.
Tibballs, Geoff. *TV Detectives.* London: Boxtree, 1992.
Ward, Jack. *The Supporting Players of Television 1959–1986.* Cleveland, OK: Lakeshore West, 1996.

Left to right: Ronald Howard, Howard Marion-Crawford, Paulette Goddard (guest), and Peter Copley (guest) in *Sherlock Holmes.*

joined the army. Subsequently he transferred to the RAF in which he served as a night-fighter observer until injured in the leg and invalided out in 1944 with the rank of sergeant.

His hearty tones made him a natural for radio where he made his debut in 1935. He broadcast regularly in a variety of roles and after the war enthralled listeners to the BBC when he regularly read *A Book at Bedtime* and served as narrator on such radio serials as *The Pickwick Papers*. The first film in which he really made his presence felt was *The Hasty Heart* (1949). His most successful decade was the fifties when he was seen in several films and on television. His sole regular role in a television series was *Sherlock Holmes* which was shot in Paris in 1954 by executive producer Sheldon Reynolds. In this he played the role of Dr. Watson. Although there were reservations about Ronald Howard's portrayal of Holmes, Marion-Crawford's Watson was considered to be inspired casting. His fruity tones, bristling moustache and physical attributes were Watson to the life. A decade later he was considered to be equally good as Dr. Petrie in the *Fu Manchu* film series which started out extremely brightly, but quickly deteriorated in quality. Marion-Crawford was one of only three players who played the same role throughout the series. Christopher Lee as Fu Manchu and Tsai Chin as Fu's daughter were the others.

For reasons known only to himself on November 22, 1969 Marion-Crawford embarked on a marathon drinking spree going from one London drinking establishment to another. Two days later on November 24, still imbibing he arrived back at his rented Chelsea apartment where he took a couple of sleeping pills and collapsed. He was rushed to hospital, but found to be dead on arrival. He was 55 years old. The inquest established that he had asphyxiated on his own vomit. The pathologist described him as normally in quite good health, but a heavy social drinker. He was married and divorced from actresses Jeanne Scott-Gunn and Mary Wimbush. He had a son by both marriages: Harold (1942–1975) and Charles born in 1947. He had 8 grandchildren. While the gross value of his estate was £1,609, the net value was nil.

Filmography

1935: *Brown on Resolution* (a.k.a. *Forever England* and *Born for Glory*), *The Guv'nor* (a.k.a. *Mister Hobo*), *Music Hath Charms*.
1936: *Secret Agent*.
1938: *13 Men and a Gun*.
1941: *Freedom Radio* (a.k.a. *A Voice in the Night*).
1945: *The Rake's Progress* (a.k.a. *Notorious Gentleman*).
1947: *The Phantom Shot*.
1948: *Man on the Run*.
1949: *The Hasty Heart, Stage Fright*.
1950: *Mr. Drake's Duck*.
1951: *The Man in the White Suit, His Excellency*.
1952: *Where's Charley, Top of the Form*.
1953: *Star of India, Gilbert Harding Speaking of Murder, Don't Blame the Stork!*
1954: *West of Zanzibar, The Rainbow Jacket, Knights of the Round Table, Five Days* (a.k.a. *Paid to Kill*).
1956: *The Silken Affair, Man in the Sky* (a.k.a. *Decision Against Time*), *Reach for the Sky*.
1957: *Don Kikhot* (dubbed voice only), *The Birthday Present*.
1958: *Nowhere to Go, The Silent Enemy, Virgin Island* (a.k.a. *Our Virgin Island*), *Gideon's Day* (a.k.a. *Gideon of Scotland Yard*), *Next to No Time!*
1959: *North West Frontier* (a.k.a. *Flame Over India*), *Model for Murder, Life in Danger*.
1960: *Othello, Foxhole in Cairo, Two Way Stretch* (voice only).
1961: *Carry on Regardless*.
1962: *Lawrence of Arabia*.
1963: *Tamahine, Man in the Middle*.
1965: *The Face of Fu Manchu*.
1966: *The Brides of Fu Manchu, The Singing Princess* (voice only), *Secrets of a Windmill Girl*.
1967: *Smashing Time, The Vengeance of Fu Manchu*.
1968: *Blood of Fu Manchu* (a.k.a. *Kiss and Kill*), *The Charge of the Light Brigade, Castle of Fu Manchu*.

Television Series

1954: *Sherlock Holmes* as Dr. Watson

Sources

Andrews, Cyrus. *Radio and Television Who's Who*. 3rd ed. London: George Young, 1954.
McFarlane, Brian. *The Autobiography of British Film*. London: Methuen/BFI, 2003.
Picture Show. January 17, 1959.
Quinlan, David. *Illustrated Directory of Film Character Actors*. 2nd ed. London: Batsford, 1995.
Speed, F. Maurice. *Film Review, 1970–1971*. London: WH Allen, 1970.
Who's Who on the Screen. London: Amalgamated, 1956.

Hugh Marlowe

Hugh Marlowe was born Hugh Herbert Hipple in Philadelphia, PA on January 30, 1911. He was the son of George W. Hipple, advertising and real estate executive and his wife Mildred Schroeder. Raised in Chicago, he became interested in the stage as a career after appearing in school plays. Once he left high school, he had a number of mundane jobs, but was simultaneously gaining experience in Little Theater plays. His first job was selling chairs in a department store. His father tried to persuade him to go into real estate, but he had his heart set on acting. In 1932 he landed a job as a radio announcer in Davenport, Iowa. At one time he even ran a disc jockey show from a funeral parlor! After twelve months he left and went to California where he joined the Pasadena Playhouse. He appeared in about 75 plays there over a three year period.

He made his screen debut in a poverty row quickie *It Couldn't Have Happened* (1936). He was invited to take a screen test by MGM. Hearing nothing further from the studio, he ventured to New York where he made his Broadway debut at the National on September 18, 1936 as Donald Duke in *Arrest That Woman*. It led nowhere so he returned to the Playhouse. A few months went by before he heard from MGM who stated that they would like to give him another screen test. This test resulted in a couple of film roles, but when they were followed by six months without a part, he decided to return to New York. Over the following years he appeared in a number of stage plays until 1944.

MGM approached him again and he signed with them making appearances in three films in 1944. The parts were all small so eventually he left Hollywood for the second time to concentrate on stage work. Five years went by before he received a call from 20th Century–Fox to test for a role as Robert Masen in *Come to the Stable* (1949). His work in this film was so good that he was awarded a seven year contract. The next few years were the halcyon ones of his film career when he landed plum roles in some excellent films. During the Fox years he lived in a small house set in three acres of land at Malibu. He also had a workshop building where his hobby was carpentry. There he made some of the furniture for his house.

His television debut came in "Her Kind of Honor" an episode of *Schlitz Playhouse of the Stars* originally aired in 1954 on CBS. He continued on television to play the lead as Ellery Queen in *The New Adventures of Ellery Queen* which was also known as *Mystery Is My Business*. Marlowe was the first actor to play Ellery Queen in the long running radio series from 1939 to 1947. The series was derived from the celebrated literary sleuth created by cousins Frederic Dannay and Manfred B. Lee in 1929. The character had featured in several earlier movies and a live television series. In 1954 the Pincus brothers who owned the rights decided to resurrect the property as a filmed television series. Hugh Marlowe was chosen to play Ellery Queen with Florenz Ames reprising the role from the earlier series as Inspector Richard Queen of the police department who frequently called on his son to solve his most difficult cases.

There were 32 half hour, black and white episodes shot in this syndicated series. Purists were disappointed that none of them derived from the novels by Ellery Queen. The series however represented a definite improvement over the original one because it was filmed. The mysteries were intriguing and allowed for plenty of exteriors which were missing from the live series. The series also combined elements of deductive reasoning with scenes which were pure action. Of all the actors who played the role, Marlowe is reckoned to have been physically the closest to the character as described in the novels.

Once asked as primarily a film actor the reason for moving into television, Marlowe replied, "A film company spends $2,000,000 making and promoting a feature. It comes into town, stays three or four days and then moves out. A lot of people miss it. I didn't realize how you could miss a picture so quickly until I found that I'd never seen the last film I made. If I didn't see it, certainly a lot of fans didn't either. TV is different. Millions of viewers get to know you regularly each week."

Few decent film parts came his way after his stint in *The New Adventures of Ellery Queen*. He shot two low budget science fiction films during the fifties. In *World Without End* (1956) he was not the first choice for the leading role; he proved difficult on the set; and the producers were dissatisfied with his performance. The only reasons he was chosen were the quality of his acting in *All About Eve* (1950) together with the fact that his services could be bought very cheaply. The latter may have been a reflection of his declining status within the film industry after doing a television series. The irony was that both these science fiction films made a mint of money and were probably seen by more fans than some of his more prestigious movies.

After a decade away from the theater he reappeared on the stage at the Alcazar, San Francisco in April 1956 as Bud Walters in *Anniversary Waltz*. He continued to make regular stage appearances for the next twelve years. His last stage appearance was as Joe Keller in *All My Sons* at the Roundabout Stage One in October 1974. He was also a familiar face in guest starring roles on television. He maintained that he preferred character roles because they provided the friction that moved the story along. He basically abandoned both the stage and prime time television when he accepted the role of Jim Matthews in the day time soap opera *Another World* from 1968 onwards. He continued to play this role happily until he died suddenly at age 71 in New York of a heart attack on May 2, 1982 survived by his third wife and three sons. He is buried at Ferncliff Cemetery and Mausoleum at Hartsdale, New York.

Firstly he was married and divorced from actress Edith Atwater (1909–1986). His second wife was actress and union activist K.T. Stevens (1919–1994). She was the daughter of the director Sam Wood. They originally met while they were appearing in *The Land is Bright* (1941) on stage. They met again and fell in love during the 22 months when they were appearing in the Chicago company of *Voice of the Turtle*. They married in San Francisco on May 7, 1946. With her he had two sons who were Jeffrey who was born on July 7, 1948 and Christian who was born in 1951. They costarred in 20 summer stock productions, several television dramas and the Broadway production of *Laura* (1947). One of the reasons for agreeing to shoot *The New Adventures of Ellery Queen* was so that his sons could see him in the role because neither was old enough to hear him on the radio version. Nevertheless he went for long periods without seeing his wife and sons. He was shooting the series and films in Hollywood, while she was living with the boys in a New York apartment doing live television during the fifties. They eventually divorced in 1967. He married thirdly another actress Rosemary Tory in 1968. With her he had another son named Hugh Michael who was born in 1969.

Filmography

1936: *It Couldn't Have Happened.*

Hugh Marlowe, who starred in *The New Adventures of Ellery Queen.*

1937: *Married Before Breakfast, Between Two Women.*
1944: *Marriage is a Private Affair, Meet Me in St. Louis, Mrs. Parkington.*
1949: *Come to the Stable, Twelve O'Clock High.*
1950: *All About Eve, Night and the City.*
1951: *The Day the Earth Stood Still, Rawhide (a.k.a. Desperate Siege), Mr. Belvedere Rings the Bell.*
1952: *Monkey Business, Wait 'Til the Sun Shines Nellie, Way of a Gaucho, Bugles in the Afternoon.*
1953: *The Stand at Apache River, Casanova's Big Night.*
1954: *Garden of Evil.*
1955: *Illegal.*
1956: *World Without End, Earth Vs. The Flying Saucers.*
1957: *The Black Whip.*
1960: *Elmer Gantry.*
1961: *The Long Rope.*
1962: *Bird Man of Alcatraz.*
1963: *13 Frightened Girls!*
1964: *Seven Days in May.*
1966: *Castle of Evil.*
1968: *The Last Shot You Hear.*

Television Series

1954–1955: *The New Adventures of Ellery Queen* (a.k.a. *Mystery Is My Business*) as Ellery Queen.
1968–1982: *Another World* as Jim Matthews.

Sources

Herbert, Ian. *Who's Who in the Theatre*. 16th ed. London: Pitman, 1977.
Inman, David. *The TV Encyclopedia*. New York: Perigee, 1991.
Lamparski, Richard. *Whatever Became Of?* 11th Series. New York: Crown, 1989.
Lance, Steven. *Written Out Of Television*. Lanham, MD: Madison, 1996.
Nevins Francis M., Jr. "Ellery Queen on the Small Screen." *The Golden Years of TV and Radio*. No. 1 Winter 1983.
Picture Show. "Life Story." August 23, 1952.
Picture Show Annual. London: Amalgamated, 1951, 1952 and 1953.
Quinlan, David. *Film Stars*. 5th ed. London: Batsford, 2000.
Ragan, David. *Who's Who in Hollywood, 1900–1976*. New Rochelle, NY: Arlington, 1976.
Ryder, C.C. "Marlowe, Man of Mystery." *TV Times*. August 15, 1958.
Ward, Jack. *The Supporting Players of Television, 1959–1983*. Cleveland, OK: Lakeshore West, 1996.
Weaver, Tom. *Interviews with B Science Fiction and Horror Movie Makers*. Jefferson, NC: McFarland, 1988.

Joan Marshall

Joan Marshall was born Jean Schrepfermann in Chicago, ILL. on June 6, 1931. She was raised on Chicago's North Side and educated at St. Clements School there. At the age of 17 she suffered a bout of polio which paralyzed her vocal chords, spine, neck and face and she was hospitalized for seven weeks. She took up dancing as a form of remedial exercise and became extremely good at it. When she was only a teenager, she was hired as a showgirl at Chicago's Chez Paree, a leading nightclub of the era. She moved to Las Vegas where she danced in the line-up of various shows.

From there she relocated to Hollywood where she landed the female lead in the Ziv television series *Bold Venture* which was syndicated in 1959. This was set in the Bahamas and ran for 39 half hour, black and white episodes. She played Sailor Duval the ward of tough mariner cum hotelier Slate Shannon (Dane Clark). No one could explain why at her age, Sailor Duval needed a guardian. Marshall was a prolific television guest star during the late fifties and early sixties.

Her biggest film chance came when she played the lead in the William Castle production of *Homicidal* (1961) which was a blatant rip off of *Psycho*. She played the strange, pitiless, killer nurse who in the finale turned out to be a man! To disguise her identity from those who knew her under the Marshall name, she was billed as Jean Arless in this movie. Her hair was also shortened and dyed. What on the face of it seemed like a career making role turned to dust and ashes when most of the movie roles she was offered afterwards were as a male. This probably reflected that film executives were left as confused as audiences about her role in *Homicidal*.

Marshall gave up acting after a few more film and television roles in the sixties billed under the Marshall name. She appeared on stage in Hollywood in 1962 in *A Cold Wind in August*. During the seventies she became a writer of episodes of situation comedies using the name Jean Ashby frequently in tandem with childhood friend writer, Dirk Wayne Summers. Allegedly incidents from her own life provided the basis of the film *Shampoo* (1975).

Some sources indicate that she may have been married as many as five times, but if so history has only recorded three of them. Her first husband's name was Sanders whom she met and married in Las Vegas in the fifties. With him she had a son Steven born in 1954 and a daughter Shari who was born in 1957. Around 1970 she married writer-director Hal Ashby who preferred a hippie type lifestyle even though he was certainly prominent for a while in the industry. She was widowed in 1988. In 1989 she married businessman Mel Bartfield. She was also a close friend of actor Richard Chamberlain and guested in episodes of his television series *Dr. Kildare*.

On a visit to Jamaica she fell in love with the island and bought a property there. She died in obscurity in Jamaica on June 28, 1992 aged 61 of lung cancer. Her ashes were scattered beneath her favorite tree in the grounds of her home there.

Filmography

1958: *Live Fast Die Young*.
1961: *Homicidal*.

Dane Clark and Joan Marshall in *Bold Venture*.

1963: *Tammy and the Doctor.*
1964: *Looking for Love.*
1967: *The Happiest Millionaire.*
1968: *The Horse in the Gray Flannel Suit.*
1969: *The Great Sex War* (a.k.a. *Make Love Not War*).
1975: *Shampoo.*

Television Series

1959: *Bold Venture* as Sailor Duval.

Sources

Brode, Douglas. *Once Was Enough.* Secaucus, NJ: Citadel, 1997.
Brooks, Tim. *The Complete Directory to Prime Time TV Stars, 1946–Present.* New York: Ballantine, 1987.
Erickson, Hal. *Syndicated Television: The First Forty Years, 1947–1987.* Jefferson, NC: McFarland, 1989.

Lee Marvin

The film stars of the fifties were usually either extraordinarily handsome men like Rock Hudson or veterans with character in their faces like Randolph Scott. In the harsher climate of the sixties once these types were swept aside, there remained some villainous actors like Lee Marvin and Lee Van Cleef who became stars. Lee Marvin was a hard man and a hell raiser in real life. His military service in the U.S. Marines gave him convincing credentials to play soldiers on screen. He deserved credit for establishing himself as top flight star at a time when the American cinema was in steep decline. The critics were then trying to find an actor to fill Humphrey Bogart's shoes. They are still searching. Bogart was an icon whose stardom derived from a mixture of on-screen bravado and cynicism. He was fortified by delivering some of the brightest dialogue ever written for motion pictures and the sexual chemistry with players like Ingrid Bergman and Lauren Bacall. No actress bonded with Marvin like that. Bogart's best films were romantic and exciting. Although Marvin made some good films, others were ruined by gratuitous violence in which his personality emerged as a dangerous, grouchy slob. At one time he was respected as an actor, but his drunken antics which held up productions on which he worked alienated him from the directors of his films and many of his more sober costars.

Lee Marvin was born in New York City on February 19, 1924. He was the son of Lamont Waltman Marvin and Courtenay Davidge Washington. His father was a successful advertising executive for the New York and New England Apple Institute and from 1940 onwards the Florida Citrus Commission. His mother was a fashion writer and editor. He had one brother Robert who was seventeen months older. The family was an affluent one. When his mother refused to leave her job and New York, his father lived part of the year in Manhattan and part of the year in Florida. He was a rebellious child who attended eleven different schools and was expelled from several exclusive eastern boarding schools. Finally in desperation he was sent to St. Leo College Preparatory School, Benedictine Monastery and Priory in Florida in 1940 where he fared somewhat better although he only lasted about eighteen months there before being expelled. Much later in 1969 he was awarded a doctorate in fine arts from there which caused him some mirth.

On August 12, 1942 he enlisted in the Marine Corps in New York with his father's permission. During his service in the South Pacific he participated in 21 island landings as a scout sniper and made several hit and run raids on the Marshall Islands. His military service came to an abrupt end on June 18, 1944. His company had stormed a beach at Saipan and, while trying to advance, was caught in a deadly Japanese crossfire. There were 241 soldiers serving in I Company, Third Battalion, 24th Marines. Marvin, who was shot in the base of the spine and narrowly avoided being paralyzed, was one of only six survivors which gave him a sense of guilt thereafter. After 13 months in hospital, he was given an honorable discharge at Marine Barracks, Philadelphia on July 24, 1945 as a Private First Class. He was awarded battle ribbons including the Purple Heart, back pay and a disability pension of $40 a month. The legacy of his wound was a ten inch scar running the length of his back. His other problem was how to make a living.

His father and brother had both served in World War II and were suffering severe psychological problems connected with it. Marvin's mother relocated the family to Woodstock, New York to recuperate. He tried his hand at a variety of jobs, the last of which was as a plumber's mate. In this capacity he was sent to repair a leaky tap at the Maverick Playhouse in Woodstock. He became friendly with the other actors, so when one of them was too ill to appear in the production of *Roadside* (1947) one night, the director asked Marvin to replace him. The other actor did not return so he stayed with the play. He studied with other members of the cast learning as much about acting as he could. He remained throughout the 1947 season and did four other plays with them. In the final one he had the male lead. He went to North Carolina and joined the Vagabond Players where they did ten plays in summer stock. He went to New York in 1948 where he landed roles in "off Broadway" plays. At the American Theater Wing, New York in 1948 he undertook formal training, his tuition fees being paid for under the G.I. Bill of Rights. Afterwards he joined national touring companies of *A Streetcar Named Desire* and *The Hasty Heart*.

He waited three days at an open casting session held by film director Henry Hathaway, muscled his way in and landed a role at $175 a week which led to him making his screen debut in *You're in the Navy Now* (1951). Hathaway told him he belonged in movies, but he still had the traditional snobbery of stage actors against films. Instead he made his Broadway debut in *Billy Budd* (1951) which earned him great reviews in a subordinate role. When it flopped, he reconsidered his options and decamped to Hollywood. Once there he looked up Hathaway who introduced him to an agent. He found work mainly in villainous roles right from the start. The one which exploded upon the public consciousness was *The Big Heat* (1953) directed by Fritz Lang. In this film Marvin played Vince Stone, a thuggish gangster, who threw scalding coffee in the face of Dora, the character played by Gloria Grahame. Although he appeared in several other films over the next three years, none made quite the same impact. He did however contribute several chilling studies in savage brutality.

Marvin made his television debut in "The Big Cost" episode of *Dragnet* in 1952. He became a television star as Lt. Frank Ballinger, a plainclothes inspector of the Chicago Police Department, in *M Squad* which was shown on the NBC network for three seasons between September 20, 1957 and September 13, 1960 and lasted for a total of 115 half hour, black and white episodes. The last original episode was shown on June 28, 1960. Ballinger was a street wise, hard nosed cop who headed up an elite unit fighting organized crime in the Windy City. His superior officer was Captain Grey (Paul Newlan) who assigned him most of his cases. In the first season the theme for the series was composed by Stanley Wilson. It was succeeded in the second and third seasons by a more memorable jazzy composition written by Count Basie. Jack Webb began the trend for this sort of series with *Dragnet* which was located in Los Angeles. When *M Squad* tried to do likewise in Chicago, the Chicago cops wanted none of it. They refused to assist the producers because in 1953, a film crew had filmed in the city for a feature film. The police were pleased to cooperate and assisted the production company in every way possible. They believed it was going to show them in a very positive light as an honest and brave force. Instead it turned out to be an exposé of the corruption within the Chicago Police Department. No one would state whether the "M" in *M Squad* actually stood for murder, but it was whispered on the set that it stood for Marvin. It was a Latimer production for Revue which was Universal's television arm. Marvin received 50 per cent of the profits. Latimer was his company so named after the street on which he then lived in Santa Monica. This series contained some of his best work because it fell between the early period of violent, one dimensional characters and the later period of the bibulous buffoon. He also narrated *Lawbreakers* a factual series about real life gangsters.

His most acclaimed performance on television was as a war veteran in "People Need People," a segment of *Alcoa Premiere* aired in 1961 for which he received an Emmy award nomination for Outstanding Single Performance by an Actor in a Leading Role. Unlike many actors who become hopelessly typed by television, *M Squad* gave Marvin high visibility and increased the demand for his services in feature films. He made three films in the early sixties with John Wayne of which his best remembered role was as the pitiless killer Liberty Valance in *The Man Who Shot Liberty Valance* (1962). Marvin played a hit man in *The Killers* (1964) Don Siegal's adaptation of Ernest Hemingway's short story. Originally intended as the first movie shot directly for television, it was considered too violent and was released theatrically instead.

In *Cat Ballou* (1965) he played the dual roles of the whisky fuelled, but stout hearted gunfighter Kid Shelleen and his evil twin brother Tim Straun who dressed all in black and wore a silver nose because his own had been bitten off in a brawl. Marvin greatly enjoyed playing the characters and it brought him a Best Actor Oscar. Initially the roles offered him showed him in a more heroic light. In *The Professionals* (1966) he was Henry Rico Fardman, the leader of the group and the one who assembled them. In *The Dirty Dozen* (1967) he was Major John Reisman, the commando who assembled the bunch of violent criminals and deadbeats for the special mission. Both of these ranked at the forefront of his best and most popular movies.

The wayward trend surfaced when he chose to ally himself with director John Boorman who helmed his next two features. In *Point Blank* (1967) he played a vengeful gangster in a neo noir thriller although the film was a commercial success. In *Hell in the Pacific* (1968) which was reputedly his personal favorite of his own films, he and Toshiro Mifune played World War II soldiers stranded on a Pacific island who enact their own version of the war. Marvin then played Ben Rumson in the musical about the Goldrush *Paint Your Wagon* (1969), a film noted for its excesses in the making and for Marvin's deep, tuneless, apprehensive rendition of "I Was Born Under a Wandering Star" which surprisingly became a number one hit single. Director Joshua Logan observed, "Not since Attila the Hun swept across Europe leaving five hundred years of total blackness has there been a man like Lee Marvin." Marvin continued to shoot films regularly throughout the seventies, few of which earned much in the way of critical plaudits or were big commercial successes. Probably the one which was closest to his heart was *The Big Red One* (1979), a war movie directed by Sam Fuller, which utilized some of his war experiences. Marvin tutored the rest of the cast in guns and drilled them in how to behave like proper marines.

On July 9, 1979 he became the subject and target of one of the most famous legal battles in Hollywood history. On the set of *Ship Of Fools* (1965) he met Michelle Triola, a 31 year old extra and would be entertainer. They became lovers and lived together until they parted company in 1970. Although they were never married, she had legally changed her name to Marvin a mere four days before they split up. Marvin gave Triola money for eighteen months thereafter and then stopped whereupon she sued. Triola claimed that they had made a pact to share his earnings during the six years they were together. His earnings during this period were $3,800,000 and her claim for $1,800,000 became known as palimony. It is likely that if the case had involved anyone other than a top Hollywood star, it would have been thrown out of court at a very early stage or never reached there in the first place. The court found that there was no contract, but ordered Marvin to pay $104,000 at the rate of $1,000 a week for two years to assist her in becoming an independent woman. This was revoked on appeal.

He played Jack Osbourne, a dodgy dealer

Lee Marvin, who starred in *M Squad*.

in furs, in *Gorky Park* (1983). He first became ill prior to shooting this film and was hospitalized with what was diagnosed as an asthma attack in Helsinki in 1983. In the same year he contracted pneumonia while shooting *Canicule* in Paris. He reprised his role as Reisman in an expensive television movie *The Dirty Dozen—Next Mission* shot in London in the winter of 1984 where he developed a bad cough which was treated with antibiotics. His final film role was heroic as the leader of *The Delta Force* (1986) in which he costarred with Chuck Norris. This was shot in Israel in September 1985 where he was ill with pulmonary disease. He was set to reprise his role in *The Delta Force II*, but it is likely that his health was no longer up to it. His final work was as narrator of a training film for Marine recruits called *Combat Leadership—The Ultimate Challenge* for which he was paid minimum scale and turned his check over to a Marine Corps charity.

Marvin's main hobby was deep sea fishing which he pursued with tremendous zeal for decades. His favorite fishing grounds were off the Great Barrier Reef of Australia. He also had a big collection of guns. Years of hard living seriously undermined his health. In December 1986 he underwent intestinal surgery in Tucson. Officials stated that there was inflammation of the colon, but detected no cancer. On August 13, 1987 he was admitted to hospital in a weakened condition from a severe case of flu. On August 29, 1987 he died of a heart attack at Tucson Arizona Medical Center aged 63. According to his widow the actual cause of death was septicemia, peritonitis which had caused a heart attack. He was cremated and his ashes buried in an urn at Arlington National Cemetery near Washington D.C. on October 7, 1987. His grave is next to that of boxer Joe Louis.

Marvin married Betty Edeling in Las Vegas on February 5, 1952. With her he had a son Christopher who was born in 1952; a daughter Courtenay who was born in 1954; a daughter Cynthia who was born in 1956; and a daughter Claudia who was born in 1958. They lived in Santa Monica in a house he had bought from Johnny Weissmuller. He separated from his wife in 1964 and divorced in Santa Monica on January 4, 1967. She obtained custody of all four children. On October 18, 1970 in Las Vegas he married Pamela Feeley, who was born in 1930, and whom he had originally met in Woodstock in 1945. They lived in Malibu until 1974 when they relocated to property which he owned in Tucson, Arizona. He was survived by his widow and all four of his children. After his death his widow wrote an interesting, affectionate, but white-washed account of his life entitled simply *Lee A Romance*.

FILMOGRAPHY

1951: *You're in the Navy Now* (a.k.a. *USS Teakettle*), *Teresa, Hong Kong, Down Among the Sheltering Palms* (released 1953).
1952: *We're Not Married, Diplomatic Courier, Duel at Silver Creek, Eight Iron Men, Hangman's Knot.*
1953: *Gun Fury, The Stranger Wore a Gun, The Wild One, The Big Heat, The Glory Brigade, Seminole.*
1954: *The Caine Mutiny, The Raid, Gorilla at Large, Bad Day at Black Rock.*
1955: *Not As a Stranger, A Life in the Balance, Violent Saturday, Pete Kelly's Blues, Shack Out on 101, I Died a Thousand Times.*
1956: *Pillars of the Sky* (a.k.a. *The Tomahawk and the Cross*), *Seven Men From Now, The Rack, Attack!*
1957: *Raintree County.*
1958: *The Missouri Traveler.*
1961: *The Comancheros.*
1962: *The Man Who Shot Liberty Valance.*
1963: *Donovan's Reef.*
1964: *The Killers.*
1965: *Ship of Fools, Cat Ballou.*
1966: *The Professionals.*
1967: *The Dirty Dozen, Point Blank.*
1968: *Hell in the Pacific.*
1969: *Paint Your Wagon.*
1970: *Monte Walsh.*
1971: *Pocket Money.*
1972: *Prime Cut.*
1973: *The Iceman Cometh, The Emperor of the North Pole* (a.k.a. *Emperor of the North*).
1974: *The Spikes Gang, The Klansman.*
1976: *Shout at the Devil, The Great Scout and Cathouse Thursday.*
1979: *Avalanche Express, The Big Red One.*
1980: *Death Hunt.*
1983: *Gorky Park.*
1984: *Canicule* (a.k.a. *Dogsday*).
1985: *The Dirty Dozen: Next Mission* (TV).
1986: *The Delta Force.*

TELEVISION SERIES

1957–1960: *M Squad* as Det. Lt. Frank Ballinger.
1963: *Lawbreakers* Narrator.

Sources

The Annual Obituary. Chicago: St. James, 1987.
Cameron, Ian, and Elisabeth Cameron. *The Heavies*. London: Studio Vista, 1967.
Donnelly, Paul. *Fade to Black*. London: Omnibus, 2000.
Houseman, Victoria. *Made in Heaven: Unscrambling the Marriages and Children of Hollywood Stars*. Chicago: Bonus, 1991.
Inman, David. *The TV Encyclopedia*. New York: Perigee, 1991.
Laing, Nora. "A Leaky Tap Made a Star of Lee Marvin." *TV Times*. February 21, 1958.
Marvin, Pamela. *Lee: A Romance*. London: Faber and Faber, 1997.
Robinson, Robert. "Lee Marvin Dies Of Heart Attack: Rugged Actor In Nearly 60 Pics." *Variety*. September 2, 1987.
Skinner, John Walter. *Who's Who On The Screen*. Worthing, England: Madeleine. , 1983.
Tibballs, Geoff. *TV Detectives*. London: Boxtree, 1992.
Ward, Jack. *Television Guest Stars*. Jefferson, NC: McFarland, 1993.
Wise, James E., and Anne Collier Rehill. *Stars in the Corps*. Annapolis, MD: Naval Institute, 1999.
Zec, Donald. *Marvin: The Story of Lee Marvin*. London: New English Library, 1980.

SYDNEY MASON

Sydney Mason was born in New York on June 27, 1905. In the early crime television series, *Craig Kennedy Criminologist,* he was Inspector J.J. Burke, the friend and police contact of the title character played by Donald Woods. This was his sole regular role on television, but he was quite an active player during the 1950s. Mason died in Los Angeles on April 11, 1976 aged 70 of a heart attack.

Filmography

1950: *Between Midnight and Dawn, Emergency Wedding, The Killer That Stalked New York.*
1951: *Three Guys Named Mike, Bright Victory, The Mob.*
1952: *Hoodlum Empire, Paula, Apache Country, Somebody Loves Me.*
1953: *The Lady Wants Mink, The War of the Worlds, The Glass Web.*
1954: *The Creature from the Black Lagoon.*
1955: *Revenge of the Creature, Teen-age Crime Wave.*
1956: *Blackjack Ketchum Desperado, A Day of Fury.*
1957: *Guns Don't Argue.*
1958: *Frontier Gun.*
1962: *Secret File: Hollywood.*

Television Series

1952: *Craig Kennedy Criminologist* as Inspector J.J. Burke.

Source

Truitt, Evelyn Mack. *Who Was Who on Screen*. New York: Bowker, 1984.

RAYMOND MASSEY

The tall, lean, saturnine appearance of Raymond Massey enabled him to play both noble men and scoundrels with equal effect. Although he was a Canadian by birth, he was able to play men of many nationalities very convincingly. Nor was he restricted by genre. In films his name did not always head the cast, but he frequently counted for more than the nominal leads. Although he made frequent appearances in films, radio and television, he was primarily a man of the theater. Actress Virginia Mayo described him in her memoirs as being pompous. Since he had been on good terms professionally with many of the theatrical titans of the twentieth century, perhaps he was entitled to be. He was an early example of the truly international actor since he appeared on stage, television and in films on both sides of the Atlantic.

His roots lay both in Canada and America. On his mother's side, ancestors fought in both the Revolutionary War and the Civil War. On his father's side Geoffrey Massey, a puritan, fled from persecution in England to the New World and landed in 1630. Other paternal ancestors emigrated to Canada in 1810. The Massey-Harris Agricultural Implement Company was founded by them in 1847 and later became one of the biggest in the world.

Raymond Hart Massey was born in Toronto, Canada on August 30, 1896. His parents were Chester Daniel Massey (1850–1926) and Anna Vincent. His father was head of the family firm. His mother died in London while on vacation when Raymond was a child. He had one brother Vincent (1887–1967) who became the first Canadian born Governor-General of

Canada. He was raised in Toronto. Between 1910 and 1914 he was educated at Appleby School, Ontario, Canada.

Between 1915 and 1919 he served as a lieutenant in the Canadian Field Artillery. He was a member of the Canadian Expeditionary Force in 1916, but was twice wounded at the battle of Ypres. Shell shocked he was shipped home. During 1917 and 1918 he was a gunnery and riding instructor at Yale University Reserve Officers Training Corps. He recovered sufficiently from his wounds to participate in the invasion of Siberia from 1918 to 1919. While there he organized an all male minstrel and vaudeville show as an antidote to the boredom of the troops. After war service he went to study history at Balliol College, Oxford, England between 1919 and 1921 but went down without a degree because he showed no flair at the subject. He was only briefly involved in drama at Oxford.

For a year he was active in the family business as a trainee in Toronto, a period which he found frustrating and disillusioning. After hours he acted in three plays at a little theater at the University of Toronto sponsored by the Massey Foundation funded by the residual estate of his grandfather. The notion of becoming a professional actor burgeoned in his mind. On a visit to see famous stage actor John Drew in a play in Toronto, he sought Drew out after the play to obtain advice. Drew told him to go to London to obtain experience where his chances would be better, since his Canadian accent would qualify him to play Americans there. On the strength of this he sailed from New York to Liverpool to begin his career.

He invented some theatrical credits, but was nevertheless rejected by several theatrical managers. Three weeks after landing in England, he obtained an acting job as an American named Jock in the play *In the Zone* (1922) which opened at the Winter Gardens Theater, New Brighton, Merseyside before moving on to the Everyman, a small theater just outside London. He made his West End debut in a weak, short-lived play *The Heart of Doris* (1922). He scored a big hit at the Royalty in April 1923 with a theatrical boardinghouse comedy *At Mrs. Beams*. He scored another notable hit in two roles in the world premiere of *Saint Joan* by George Bernard Shaw at the New Theater in March 1924. His involvement with this play made him a friend of Shaw.

In January 1926 in conjunction with two other associates he became the manager of the Everyman Theater, directing a few plays and acting in others. Although this was a difficult task, his stewardship kept it afloat. Staging plays by George Bernard Shaw proved to be their economic salvation. They even persuaded Shaw to accept a reduced royalty which was unheard of. This period was punctuated by the General Strike of 1926 which paralyzed the country and left the theaters dark. During the strike Massey tried to help the lot of his fellow man by driving a bus.

From the Everyman he moved smoothly back to the West End playing Khan Aghaba in *The Transit of Venus* at the Ambassadors in April 1927. The play was short-lived, but it proved to be a personal triumph for Massey and led to some of the most productive years of his theatrical career. He made his screen debut in *The Crooked Billet* (1929) which was a part talkie oddly shot at night to avoid noise. When Sir Gerald du Maurier declined the role of Sherlock Holmes in *The Speckled Band* (1931) he recommended Massey for the part. This film was shot in seven weeks and was a hit. It deviated so much from author Sir Arthur Conan Doyle's version, that Massey regarded it as a travesty.

He made his Broadway debut at the Broadhurst Theater on November 5, 1931 in the title role of a weird expressionistic version of *Hamlet* to a mixed critical reaction and a short run. Unemployed for once, he ill-advisedly signed a general film contract at Universal where he was extremely unhappy. His contribution as a writer was two lines to a movie and a role in *The Old Dark House* (1932) now revered as a cult classic, but reviled at the time. The offer of a play caused him to walk out on his contract. In the event the play did not run and he returned to London. There he became as busy in the West End as he had been before the American sojourn.

For legendary producer Sir Alexander Korda he played Chauvelin in the film *The Scarlet Pimpernel* (1934) which starred Leslie Howard in the title role and was an immense success worldwide. This was his personal favorite of his own films. He shot this while simultaneously appearing in the West End play *The Shining Hour* which opened at the St. James on September 4, 1934. His most difficult film shoot was the twelve months he spent playing John Cabal and his grandson Oswald in the film *Things to Come* (1936) based on the novel by H.G. Wells. Wells wrote the script and his contract allowed total control over the production. Massey regarded the initial script as appalling and Wells' input into the production as a disaster. Eventually some of the problems with the script were rectified, but Wells' ignorance of film was still so great that he had to leave it to Alexander Korda and his creative production team. It was another big hit and highly regarded for its technical wizardry.

In Hollywood Massey spent nine months working on two films. He played the villainous Black Michael in *The Prisoner of Zenda* (1937). Then he and two of his costars, Mary Astor and C. Aubrey Smith, switched lots to appear together again in *The Hurricane* (1937). Massey returned to England to direct and star as Harry Van in the play *Idiot's Delight* by Robert E. Sherwood which opened at the Apollo, London in March 1938. He then quit one Sherwood play for another. At the Plymouth Theater on Broadway on October 17, 1938 he opened as Abraham Lincoln in *Abe Lincoln in Illinois* to outstanding critical reviews and smash box office. This was his greatest American theatrical triumph. He recreated this role in the film version in 1940 at RKO Radio for which he received an Oscar nomination as Best Actor. He played Lincoln on film again in a cameo in *How the West Was Won* (1962).

Following his performance as Lincoln in 1940 he gave an excellent account of himself as the abolitionist John Brown in the film *Santa Fe Trail* (1941). He recreated the role again on film in *Seven Angry Men* (1955) to equally fine effect. Against the advice of his wife, he signed a lucrative two picture a year deal with Warner Bros. in 1940. It was extended for various reasons and lasted for fourteen years. He felt miscast in many of his films for them. The only one which he particularly enjoyed was *Action in the North Atlantic* (1943), a salute to the Merchant Marines, which was the first of two films in which he costarred with Humphrey Bogart. He interspersed these films with appearing in plays which he found much more satisfying. During World War II between 1942 and 1943 he served as a major on the office staff of the Adjutant-General in the Canadian Royal Artillery. He had been anxious to serve his country, but he proved hopelessly inept at sifting paperwork. Some sources indicate that he was invalided out of the service. In any event he returned to Hollywood and the theater where he was considerably more use. In March 1944 he became a naturalized American citizen. Professionally he was rescued from the doldrums when Katharine Cornell asked for him as her leading man in the play *Lovers and Friends*. In 1945 he did a U.S.O. tour of *Our Town* by Thornton Wilder in France and Germany which was probably the kind of war service contribution which he was more suitable for.

The immediate post war period was a boom for him since within twelve months he appeared in a major Hollywood movie; acted in a Broadway play; started the *Harvest of Stars* radio program; and made two appearances in the fledging medium of television on CBS. Being active in all media in a year put him in the record books.

He wrote one play *Hanging Judge* in 1951 adapted from a book by Bruce Hamilton. This was staged and later televised in England and America where it was well received on all counts. In 1952 he joined Judith Anderson and Tyrone Power for a tour of staged readings of *John Brown's Body*, Stephen Vincent Benet's epic poem about the Civil War. They finished on Broadway where it played to standing room only and outstanding critical notices. On a second tour the following year, Judith Anderson was replaced by Anne Baxter. These were under the direction of Charles Laughton and the management of Laughton and his partner Paul Gregory. On each

Raymond Massey, who hosted *I Spy*.

tour they played more than 80 separate venues, traveling over 30,000 miles.

His personal favorite of the films which he shot for Warner Bros. was *East of Eden* (1955) which was actually lensed after his contract had expired. He played Adam Trask, the father of James Dean and Richard Davalos. Massey regarded Dean as arrogant and unprofessional. He stormed off the set after Dean's off screen use of profanity ruined a take when Massey was having a close-up. The crew and the director sided with Massey and Dean later apologized.

Massey's first brush with series television came with *I Spy* shot for Guild Films in 1955. Massey served as host, narrator and occasional star of this anthology spy series. He introduced each episode as Anton, the Spymaster. The arresting start of each segment had the camera zooming in on a staring human eye. There were 39 half hour, black and white episodes some of which had historic settings. Massey had scant regard for this series to the extent that he did not mention it in either volume of his memoirs. Oddly although it was shot in England, it does not ever appear to have been seen there.

He appeared in the "Roadhog" episode of the television series *Alfred Hitchcock Presents* in 1959. The actor who played his son was Richard Chamberlain. Massey developed a rapport with him. A year later a meeting with producer Norman Felton led to Massey verbally agreeing to play Dr. Leonard Gillespie, Chief Medical Officer of Blair General Hospital, in the television series *Dr. Kildare*. This had originally been a series of dime novels by Max Brand. The novels evolved into a single film at Paramount and later a film series at MGM. In the MGM series Lionel Barrymore played the irascible Gillespie. Massey was delighted when Richard Chamberlain was assigned the role of James Kildare in the television version. This very popular series was shown on NBC between September 28, 1961 and August 30, 1966. During the entire run of the series Massey never had a formal written contract. It was all agreed on the strength of a handshake.

After the series was finished he spent more leisure time traveling and polishing his golf handicap. His final Broadway appearance had been as God in *JB* which opened at the ANTA Theater on December 11, 1958 for a successful run of 364 performances. Massey was forced to leave after 196 performances to fulfill a movie commitment. His final West End play was as Tom Garrison in *I Never Sang for My Father* at the Duke of York's Theater in May 1970 for seven weeks to excellent notices, but poor box office. Massey continued to make regular television appearances in anthology series and movies for television until 1973. His final acting appearances came in a revival of Tennessee Williams *The Night of the Iguana* at the Ahmanson Theater in Los Angeles in December 1975. Massey played the 93 year old, wheelchair bound poet, Nonno. He was delighted to find that Richard Chamberlain was in it as the defrocked Reverend T. Lawrence Shannon. When he forgot his last speech in the play on opening night for a few minutes, Massey realized that his acting days were over. The revival was a success, but he left the play before it went to New York and retired.

During his retirement he wrote two well received volumes of memoirs which were *When I Was Young* (1976) and *A Hundred Different Lives* (1979). During his lifetime he had received six honorary degrees and had been very active in the Actors Equity Association. Politically he was a staunch Republican. For the first ten years of his American residence, he lived on East 80th Street in New York. In 1948 he moved to an estate in Wilton, Connecticut. In 1959 he moved permanently to his last home in Beverly Hills.

Massey married firstly Margery (Peggy) Freemantle in 1921. She was the daughter of Admiral Sir Sydney Freemantle and an art student whom he met on vacation in Cornwall. With her he had a son named Geoffrey who was born in London in October 1924. They divorced in London in 1929 and after an initial period he was given custody of his son in 1930. The son later became an architect in Canada. He married secondly actress Adrianne Allen (1907–1993) at Westminster Registry Office, London on October 30, 1929. With her he had an actor son Daniel who was born in London on October 10, 1933 and died in London on March 25, 1998 of Hodgkin's Disease. Massey father and son appeared together in one film *The Queen's Guards* (1961). With Allen he had a daughter, actress Anna who was born in Thakeham, Surrey on August 11, 1937. Allen divorced him in Carson City, Nevada on July 6, 1939 on the grounds of mental cruelty, although they remained friends. She was awarded custody of both children. Massey married thirdly Dorothy Ludington Whitney in New York City on July 10, 1939. She was a theatrical lawyer and a divorcee with two daughters. They remained happily wed until she died in July 1982.

During his last years Massey suffered from a degenerative arthritic condition. He died at Cedars Sinai Hospital, Los Angeles on July 29, 1983 aged 86 from pneumonia. He is buried at Beaverdale Memorial Park, New Haven, CT. He was survived by all three of his children and six grandchildren.

Filmography

1929: *The Crooked Billet* (a.k.a. *International Spy*).
1931: *The Speckled Band.*
1932: *The Face at the Window, The Old Dark House.*
1934: *The Scarlet Pimpernel.*
1936: *Things to Come, Fire over England.*
1937: *Dreaming Lips, Under the Red Robe, The Prisoner of Zenda, The Hurricane.*
1938: *The Drum* (a.k.a. *Drums*), *Black Limelight.*
1940: *Abe Lincoln in Illinois* (a.k.a. *Spirit of the People*), *Santa Fe Trail.*
1941: *49th Parallel* (a.k.a. *The Invaders*), *Dangerously They Live, Arsenic and Old Lace* (released 1944).
1942: *Desperate Journey, Reap the Wild Wind.*
1943: *Action in the North Atlantic.*
1944: *The Woman in the Window.*
1945: *Hotel Berlin, God is My Co-Pilot.*
1946: *A Matter of Life and Death* (a.k.a. *Stairway to Heaven*).
1947: *Possessed, Mourning Becomes Electra.*
1949: *The Fountainhead, Roseanna McCoy.*
1950: *Chain Lightning, Barricade, Dallas.*
1951: *Sugarfoot, Come Fill the Cup, David and Bathsheba.*
1952: *Carson City.*
1953: *The Desert Song.*
1955: *Battle Cry, Prince of Players, East of Eden, Seven Angry Men.*
1957: *Omar Khayyam.*
1958: *The Naked and the Dead.*
1960: *The Great Impostor.*
1961: *The Fiercest Heart, The Queen's Guards.*
1962: *How the West Was Won.*
1968: *Mackenna's Gold.*
1971: *The President's Plane Is Missing* (TV).
1972: *All My Darling Daughters* (TV).
1973: *My Darling Daughters' Anniversary* (TV).

Television Series

1955: *I Spy* Host and narrator.
1961–1966: *Dr. Kildare* as Dr. Leonard Gillespie.

Sources

Agan, Patrick. *Where Are They Now?* London: Everest, 1977.
The Annual Obituary. Chicago: St. James, 1983.
DeLong, Thomas A. *Radio Stars.* Jefferson, NC: McFarland, 1996.
Donnelly, Paul. *Fade to Black.* London: Omnibus, 2000.
Erickson, Hal. *Syndicated Television: The First Forty Years, 1947–1987.* Jefferson, NC: McFarland, 1989.
Hayward, Anthony. *TV Unforgettables.* London: Guinness, 1993.
Herbert, Ian. *Who's Who in the Theatre.* 16th ed. London: Pitman, 1978.
Inman, David. *The TV Encyclopedia.* New York: Perigee, 1991.
Lamparski, Richard. *Whatever Became Of?* 9th ed. New York: Crown, 1985.
Massey, Raymond. *A Hundred Different Lives.* London: Robson, 1979.
The Picturegoer's Who's Who and Encyclopedia. 1st ed. London: Odhams, 1933.
Picture Show Annual. London: Amalgamated, 1936, 1941, 1942, 1947 and 1957.
Quinlan, David. *Film Stars.* 5th ed. London: Batsford, 2000.
TV Times. "Hanging Judge." May 9, 1958.
Winchester, Clarence. *Screen Encyclopedia.* London: Winchester, 1948.
_____. *The World Film Encyclopedia.* London: Amalgamated Press, 1933.

Murray Matheson

Murray Matheson was born in Casterton, Victoria, Australia on July 1, 1912. He began his career in little theaters in Melbourne in 1933 where he acted until he moved to London in 1935. In 1937 he made his debut there in the revue *And On We Go.* He toured Great Britain in a couple of plays and appeared in other revues over the next three years. Between 1940 and 1945 he served in the Royal Air Force. For three years he was attached to the British Embassy in Moscow. He was still serving with the R.A.F. when he was chosen to play an Australian in his screen debut *Journey Together* (1945). Afterwards he returned to the stage and toured Britain and Canada as well as appearing in a few other British films.

In 1950 he moved to America where he appeared in two short-lived Broadway plays in 1950

Murray Matheson, who costarred in *Harbormaster*.

and 1953. He appeared in a number of films in Hollywood. In the crime adventure series *Harbormaster* he played the part of Professor Wheeler, one of the friends of the title character played by Barry Sullivan. Although he continued to work on the stage in straight plays and in *Kismet* in the San Francisco Light Opera, he was most active on television. His best remembered television role was as Felix Mulholland, the book store owner and friend of the Polish-American insurance investigator played by George Peppard in *Banacek*. He appeared in numerous guest starring roles on television and sometimes was quite outstanding in them. An example was Talbot, the suave head of an unusual murder for payment organization, in the "Why Wait Until Uncle Kevin Dies?" episode of *Hawaii Five-0* originally telecast in 1973.

Murray Matheson died in Woodland Hills, California on April 25, 1985 of heart failure aged 72. He was survived by a sister.

Filmography

1945: *Journey Together, Way to the Stars* (a.k.a. *Johnny in the Clouds*).
1946: *School for Secrets* (a.k.a. *Secret Flight*).
1948: *The Fool and the Princess*.
1952: *Hurricane Smith, Plymouth Adventure*.
1953: *Botany Bay, Jamaica Run, Flight to Tangier, King of the Khyber Rifles*.
1954: *The Bamboo Prison*.
1955: *Love Is a Many-Splendored Thing*.
1963: *Wall of Noise*.
1965: *Signpost to Murder*.
1966: *Assault on a Queen*.
1967: *How to Succeed in Business Without Really Trying*.
1968: *Star!, In Enemy Country*.
1969: *Explosion*.
1972: *Banacek: Detour to Nowhere* (TV), *Lieutenant Schuster's Wife* (TV).
1977: *Tail Gunner Joe* (TV).
1978: *Rabbit Test*.
1979: *Mary and Joseph: A Story of Faith* (TV).
1980: *Angel on My Shoulder*.
1981: *The Million Dollar Face* (TV).
1983: *Twilight Zone: The Movie*.

Television Series

1957–1958: *Harbormaster* as Professor Wheeler.
1972–1974: *Banacek* as Felix Mulholland.

Sources

Meyers, Richard. *TV Detectives*. San Diego, CA.: Barnes, 1981.
Picture Show's Who's Who on the Screen. London: Amalgamated, 1956.
Tibballs, Geoff. *TV Detectives*. London: Boxtree, 1992.
Variety. Obituary, May 1, 1985.
Ward, Jack. *Television Guest Stars*. Jefferson, NC: McFarland, 1993.

Lester Matthews

Lester Matthews was born in Nottingham, England on December 3, 1900. He was educated at Waverly, Nottingham and Paston, North Walsham. He ran away from home at the age of fifteen. He made his stage debut at the Theater Royal, Nottingham in a walk-on part in 1916. Fifteen years stage experience followed before he made his screen debut in a couple of shorts. His first feature film was *Creeping Shadows* (1931). Over the next few years he became moderately popular in British films, but scuttlebutt in the industry stated that he was not fortunate with the parts allotted to him on the screen nor in the directors chosen to guide his work. This made him decide to emigrate to Hollywood in 1935.

Once there he had some leading roles, but by the late thirties slipped into character roles or small parts in Hollywood lensed films located in England or where there were British expatriates in various outposts throughout the world. Despite a receding hairline, he occasionally still cropped up as heroes in the forties. One of his better efforts was *The Mysterious Doctor* (1943) in which he played the title role of Dr. Frederick Holmes who prevented an English squire Sir Henry Leland (John Loder), in league with the Nazis, from stopping the ore from mines being used to make arms for the British war effort. Some of Matthews' character work was also good. He made a sprightly King Charles II in *Lorna Doone* (1951) and bore a strong facial resemblance to that English monarch.

He had one regular role in a television mystery series namely that of Assistant Commissioner Sir Denis Nayland Smith of the Secret Service in *The Adventures of Dr. Fu Manchu*. Much of his job consisted of foiling the plots concocted by Dr. Fu Manchu (Glen Gordon) for world domination. He wore a grey wig for the role. He frequently worked in tandem with Dr. John Petrie (Clark Howat). He was quite old for an action series of this kind, but in a decidedly second division cast, he nevertheless acquitted himself quite well. His clipped, well modulated British accent was a decided asset in the series. He must have been disappointed that the much hyped series did not last beyond thirteen episodes.

He was married and divorced from Frances Elizabeth Walper and from 1931 to 1938 to Anne Grey (1907–1987?) who was his frequent leading lady in England. He died in Los Angeles on June 6, 1975 aged 74.

Filmography

1931: *Creeping Shadows* (a.k.a. *The Limping Man*), *The Man at Six* (a.k.a. *The Gables Mystery*), *The Wickham Mystery*, *Gypsy Blood* (a.k.a. *Carmen*), *The Old Man*.

1932: *Her Night Out, Fires of Fate, The Indiscretions of Eve*.

1933: *The Stolen Necklace, Called Back, On Secret Service* (a.k.a. *Secret Service*), *House of Dreams, Their Night Out, Out of the Past, She Was Only a Village Maiden, The Melody Maker, Facing the Music, The Song You Gave Me*.

1934: *Borrowed Clothes, Boomerang, Song at Eventide, Blossom Time* (a.k.a. *April Romance*), *Irish Hearts* (a.k.a. *Norah O'Neale*), *The Poisoned Diamond*.

1935: *The Werewolf of London, The Raven*.

1936: *Thank You Jeeves, Professional Soldier, Spy 77, Song and Dance Man, 15 Maiden Lane, Lloyds of London, Too Many Parents, Tugboat Princess, Crack-up*.

1937: *Lancer Spy, The Prince and the Pauper*.

1938: *There's Always a Woman, Three Loves Has Nancy, Mysterious Mr. Moto, If I Were King, Time Out for Murder, The Adventures of Robin Hood, I Am a Criminal*.

1939: *The Three Musketeers, Susannah of the Mounties, Should a Girl Marry?, Conspiracy, Mr. Moto in Danger Island, Rulers of the Sea, Everything Happens at Night*.

1940: *Northwest Passage, British Intelligence, The Sea Hawk, Gaucho Serenade, The Biscuit Eater, Women in War, Sing Dance Plenty Hot*.

1941: *Man Hunt, A Yank in the RAF, The Lone Wolf Keeps a Date, Life Begins for Andy Hardy, Scotland Yard*.

1942: *Son of Fury, Now Voyager, Across the Pacific, The Pied Piper, Sunday Punch, Desperate Journey, Manila Calling, London Blackout Murders*.

1943: *The Mysterious Doctor, Northern Pursuit, Appointment in Berlin, Ministry of Fear, Two*

Lester Matthews, who costarred in *The Adventures of Dr. Fu Manchu*.

Tickets to London, Corvette K-225, Tonight We Raid Calais.
1944: *Nine Girls, Between Two Worlds, Four Jills in a Jeep, The Invisible Man's Revenge, Gaslight, The Story of Dr. Wassell, Shadows in the Night, A Wing and a Prayer.*
1945: *The Beautiful Cheat, I Love a Mystery, Son of Lassie, Jungle Queen* (serial), *Objective Burma!, Salty O'Rourke, Two O'Clock Courage.*
1946: *Three Strangers.*
1947: *Dark Delusion, The Paradine Case, Bulldog Drummond at Bay, The Exile.*
1948: *Fighting Father Dunne.*
1949: *Free For All, I Married a Communist* (a.k.a. *The Woman on Pier 13*).
1950: *Tyrant of the Sea, Her Wonderful Lie, Montana, Rogues of Sherwood Forest.*
1951: *Anne of the Indies, Corky of Gasoline Alley, The Desert Fox* (a.k.a. *Rommel—Desert Fox*), *The Lady and the Bandit* (a.k.a. *Dick Turpin's Ride*), *The Son of Dr. Jekyll, Tales of Robin Hood.*
1952: *The Brigand, Against All Flags, Five Fingers, Captain Pirate* (a.k.a. *Captain Blood Fugitive*), *Jungle Jim in the Forbidden Land, Lady in the Iron Mask, Les Miserables, Savage Mutiny, Stars and Stripes Forever.*
1953: *Bad for Each Other, Jamaica Run, Fort Ti, Niagara, Trouble Along the Way, Rogue's March, Sangaree, Young Bess, Charge of the Lancers.*
1954: *Desiree, Jungle Man-Eaters, King Richard and the Crusaders, Man in the Attic.*
1955: *The Far Horizons, Moonfleet, Ten Wanted Men, Flame of the Islands, The Seven Little Foys.*
1957: *Something of Value.*
1959: *The Miracle.*
1960: *Song Without End.*
1963: *A Global Affair, The Prize.*
1964: *Mary Poppins.*
1966: *Assault on a Queen.*
1967: *The Scorpio Letters* (TV).
1968: *Star!*
1970: *Comeback* (a.k.a. *Hollywood Horror House*).

TELEVISION SERIES

1955–1956: *The Adventures of Dr. Fu Manchu* as Assistant Commissioner Sir Denis Nayland Smith.

SOURCES

Gifford, Denis. *The Illustrated Who's Who in British Films.* London: Batsford, 1978.
The Picturegoer's Who's Who and Encyclopedia. 1st ed. London: Odham's Press Limited, 1933.
Picture Show Annual. London: Amalgamated, 1933 and 1937.
Quinlan, David. *The Illustrated Directory of Film Character Actors.* 2nd ed. London: Batsford, 1995.
Ross, J.R. *Stars of the Screen 1934.* 4th ed. London: Herbert Joseph, 1934.
Winchester, Clarence. *The World Film Encyclopedia.* London: Amalgamated, 1933.

NEIL MCCALLUM

Neil John McCallum was born in Hanley, Canada on May 20, 1929. He was raised on a farm in Saskatchewan. His early life was remote from cities and theaters. The highlight of his life was the Saturday night film show in the village fifteen miles from his home. The singing lessons which he took when young led to him entering and winning a provincial music festival. As he recalled, "They were for no special reason. I just enjoyed singing." This in turn led to him trying his luck professionally. Of his singing he later admitted, "Hundreds of people sang ten times better, so I went over to acting instead."

In 1949 he came to England to study for the theater. When he left drama school in 1952, a short period of starvation followed. Afterwards he worked his way through provincial theater to London's West End. Then he worked in Canada for a time before returning to England to shoot the television series *Saber of London* in which he played Pete Paulson, the assistant of one armed detective Mark Saber (Donald Gray). McCallum had a distaste for series television. He dreaded watching *Saber of London* and said, "I think they're terrible." He was replaced in the series by another Canadian actor Gordon Tanner as Larry Nelson, who was less charismatic and presumably less temperamental.

The independent television companies had tremendous faith in McCallum and he was the first male actor to be signed to a seven year contract by ABC as part of their plan to create television stars of the future in 1957. He had television plays on *ABC Armchair Theatre* especially written for him such as *The Leather Jungle* (1960) in which he played Dave Burke, a tough former boxer reduced to being a removal man, who is intending to make a comeback in the ring. As with many others the momentum of McCallum's career was severely disrupted by the notorious actors' strike of 1962–1963 when the actors' trade union Equity went head to head with the independent television company ATV over better pay and conditions for actors.

Afterwards, although he continued to act, McCallum turned his talents towards producing and writing. He produced the minor films *The Eyes of Annie Jones* (1963) and *Catacombs* (1964) and wrote the screenplay of the film *Walk a Tightrope* (1964). In 1965 he was cast in one of the leading roles in another television series this time for the BBC called *Vendetta*. This dealt with the attempts of two gangbusters Danny Scipio (Stelio Candelli) and Angelo James (Neil McCallum) to infiltrate and expose Mafia gangs operating in Britain. The series was a hit and McCallum in particular scored excellent personal notices. Again however his dislike of series television surfaced and he insisted on his character being killed off part way through the run of 36 hour length episodes. He was replaced by Kieron Moore as Mike Hammond. McCallum went on acting until the early 1970s after which he largely abandoned appearing in front of the camera in favor of television production. The last serial which he produced was an Australian western for the BBC, *Ben Hall*, with Jon Finch in 1975.

McCallum married actress Judith Whittaker. With her he had two sons Mark who was born in 1958 and another son born in 1960. He was shooting the film *The Siege of Pinchgut* in Australia before the birth of his first child and arrived back just two days ahead of the baby. On the second occasion he had been doing a television play in Toronto and could not get an earlier flight so his second son was born half an hour before he landed at London airport. His wife said, "He seems fated to cut things a bit fine like this." McCallum also owned St. Georges Farm, a working farm at Newbury in Berkshire, which he ran to tide him over during the lean periods. His sons grew up believing him to be a farmer.

He died prematurely on April 26, 1976 aged 46 at Reading, Berkshire, England of a brain hemorrhage.

FILMOGRAPHY

1958: *On the Run*.
1959: *The Siege of Pinchgut* (a.k.a. *Four Desperate Men*), *The Devil's Disciple*, *Jet Storm*.

Neil McCallum (left) and Donald Gray in *Saber of London*.

1960: *Foxhole in Cairo*.
1961: *Night Without Pity*.
1962: *Lisa* (a.k.a. *The Inspector*), *The Longest Day*, *The War Lover*.
1965: *Walk a Tightrope*, *Dr. Terror's House of Horrors*, *The Woman Who Wouldn't Die* (a.k.a. *Catacombs*), *The Hill*.
1966: *Thunderbirds Are Go!* (voice only).
1968: *The Lost Continent*.
1969: *Moon Zero Two*.
1971: *Quest for Love*.

TELEVISION SERIES

1956: *Space School* as Sam Scroop.
1957–1958: *Saber of London* as Pete Paulson.
1965–1966: *Vendetta* as Angelo James.

SOURCES

Greener, Len. *Picturegoer*. April 2, 1960.
Noble, Peter. *The British Film and Television Year Book, 1965–1966*. London: BA, 1966.
Snow, Sarah. "Play Bill False Witness" *TV Times*. August 7, 1960.
Thirkell, Arthur. "TV Can Make Its Own Stars." *TV Mirror*. January 25, 1958.
TV Times. "The Leather Jungle." April 10, 1960.
Vahimagi, Tise. *British Television: An Illustrated Guide*. Oxford: Oxford University Press, 1994.

MERCEDES McCAMBRIDGE

Orson Welles once described Mercedes McCambridge as, "the world's greatest living radio actress." The feature of this actress which almost immediately comes to mind was the power, range and timbre of her voice. This was all the more remarkable in that throughout her adult life she suffered from bronchitis. Although her big screen roles were not large in number, she made them count through the sheer spirit and intensity of her acting. Even in her most famous screen roles *All the King's Men* and *Giant,* she did not have much onscreen time. Nevertheless the characters remain vivid, even when they not physically there. It is hard to imagine her in a conventional heroine's role. The closest she ever came was a pot-boiler series *Wire Service* which marked her only regular starring role in a network television show, but is seldom recalled today. Whenever she guest starred on a top rated series however, she was frequently the most memorable character.

Carlotta Mercedes McCambridge was born in Joliet, Illinois on March 16, 1916. She later took Agnes as her confirmation name. She was the daughter of John Patrick McCambridge and Marie Mahaffry. Her father was a farmer. She had two younger brothers, one of whom was called John Valerian. Neither seemed to figure too prominently in her life. Her ancestry was Irish and she was raised as a Roman Catholic. She spent the early part of her life in Kinman, Illinois. As a child she moved to Chicago where she was raised and attended high school. She attended Mundelein College on a church scholarship from where she graduated in English and Drama with a B.A. Degree in 1937 and the drama school's award, the Golden Rose. While there she was a member of a Verse Speaking Choir. At the age of eighteen she was heard by a vice-president from NBC who signed the members of the choir to a one year radio contract and McCambridge to a five year term.

Most of the soap operas were broadcast from Chicago and for eighteen months she acted in many of them. She married William Fifield, a radio announcer turned writer, in Chicago in 1940 after a whirlwind three week courtship. They moved to California where their son John Lawrence was born on December 25, 1941. Fifield was a conscientious objector who nevertheless went away during World War II. In his absence she moved to New York where she continued to be active in radio dramas. This proved to be her salvation and paid the bills while she made fruitless attempts to conquer Broadway. She was cast in a couple of Broadway bound plays, but was fired once for inexperience and the second time for not being physically attractive enough. When her husband returned, they were strangers and divorced in 1946.

She made her first appearance on television in an experimental broadcast in 1945. She eventually made her Broadway debut as Mary Lorimer in *A Place of Our Own* at the Royale Theater on April 2, 1945. This was a flop. After these failures she went to England where she made a doomed attempt to establish herself as a theatrical actress there. Once this fiasco was over she returned to New York and yet more radio work. Orson Welles hired her as part of his radio Mercury Theater in 1948, one of the high points of her career. She also found the perfect radio soul mate in Everett Sloane. She had a regular supporting role in a very early television soap opera *One Man's Family.*

She was persuaded by a female friend to attend an open audition for the role of Sadie Burke in the feature film *All the King's Men* (1949). This took place at the New York offices of Columbia Pictures. She was so incensed at the treatment she and her fellow thespians were receiving that her aggressive streak surfaced and she rounded on the executives there. These turned out to be Robert Rossen, the director and Max Arnow, Columbia's head of casting. This impressed them so much that they offered her the role on the spot. For her screen debut in which she played a manipulative campaign manager to Governor Willie Stark (Broderick Crawford), she received the Best Supporting Actress Oscar of 1949. This gave her more visibility and a higher salary than she had ever enjoyed before. She moved to Hollywood where she led a hectic social life with much imbibing. Off screen she was a committed Democrat who campaigned aggressively for Adlai Stevenson. *The Scarf* (1951) was a routine crime film notable for the fact that she did her own singing and was a rare starring role.

Johnny Guitar (1954) was a splendidly bizarre western directed by Nicholas Ray in which she played crazed banker Emma Small who dressed all in black. She menaced Vienna (Joan Crawford) and there was more than a hint of sexual depravity in the way she played her role. Off screen there was a feud between the two women every bit as dramatic as the events which unfolded on screen. When McCambridge was applauded by the crew for her dynamic acting during the lynch mob sequence, Crawford withdrew to her trailer and sulked. Later a drunken, out-of-control Crawford allegedly went on a rampage in which she cut McCambridge's clothes to ribbons and left them strewn on a highway close to the location in Arizona where they were filming. When she returned from location shooting, McCambridge told *Picturegoer* magazine, "In front of the whole company Crawford told me that she never wanted me in the picture in the first place.... I tried to be friends and five times I went to her dressing room and was ordered out. My conscience is clear except that I am ashamed I lacked the courage to fight back and tell the world what a difficult job I had. I learned a lot from the experience and I only hope it never happens to me again." In her memoirs McCambridge described her as, "Poor old rotten egg Joan." McCambridge received a second Best Supporting Actress Oscar nomination as Luz Benedict, domineering older sister of Bick Benedict (Rock Hudson), in *Giant* (1956).

Rather surprisingly she did not capitalize on these achievements. Instead she starred in *Wire Service* in which she played the part of Katherine Wells. Her costars were Dane Clark and George Brent. The three of them played roving reporters working for the Trans-Globe wire service. They each traveled to the various trouble spots of the world where they became involved in international intrigue and skullduggery. Contemporary world events would probably give them even more scope nowadays than they had at the time. Their crime busting adventures were seen on a rotational basis with each of the stars appearing in thirteen segments. The series was originally aired on ABC between October 1956 and September 1957. An indication of the low regard McCambridge had for the series is that she omitted all mention of it in her memoirs.

She married the radio producer Fletcher Markle on February 19, 1950. With him she had a child who was stillborn. They divorced in Los Angeles on June 7, 1962. With her life at a low ebb in 1963 she took an overdose but survived. During the middle and latter part of the sixties she had a highly successful theatrical career notably in the title role in *Who's Afraid of Virginia Woolf?* at the Billy Rose Theater on Broadway in 1964. Her career declined after her July 1969 testimony before the Senate Subcommittee on Alcoholism and Narcotics and her admission that she was a recovering alcoholic.

She provided the voice and vocal effects of the Demon in the Warner Bros. film *The Exorcist* (1973) which she admitted was some of the hardest work of her career. Orson Welles persuaded her to take the role when she was originally reluctant to do it. When an agreement to give her special billing was reneged upon and her name missing from the credits at the preview, The Screen Actors' Guild came to her aid and managed to restore her billing. It has been said that it was probably the controversy surrounding this which prevented Linda Blair from winning an Oscar for her role in the film.

McCambridge was an artist-in-residence at American colleges and was awarded seven honorary degrees. She continued to be active on stage well into the 1980s in both regional theaters and in national touring companies. She earned a Tony nomination for Best Supporting Actress in *The Love Suicide at Schofield Barracks* (1972). Her last stage role was on Broadway as a tough German-Jewish grandmother in the play *Lost in Yonkers* (1991).

Her autobiography *The Quality of Mercy* was published in 1981. This was an unusual memoir in that it does not go forward chronologically

Left to right: **Dane Clark, Mercedes McCambridge, and George Brent in** *Wire Service.*

from beginning to end. Instead it deals with diverse themes which have shaped her existence illustrated with incidents from her own life and others. There are some passages in this book which relate to the pride she had in her granddaughters and how she looked forward to them growing up. These passages are especially poignant in view of what followed.

On November 11, 1987 tragedy struck when her only child John shot and killed his wife, two daughters and then himself at his home in Little Rock, Arkansas. The probable reason was because of financial problems. Her son, who had a Doctorate in Economics, was formerly Vice-president of Stephens Inc., an investment bank which claimed to be the largest brokerage house off Wall Street and the fifteenth largest in America. He had worked there since 1980, but shortly before the killings he had either resigned or been fired. Three weeks later his father, William Fifield, died of a broken heart.

Understandably after this McCambridge was little seen, but did some voiceovers and narration. One of her final public appearances was at an Academy Award ceremony where she was highlighted as a previous winner. From the mid–1980s onwards, she lived in La Jolla, California where she eventually died at an assisted living facility on March 2, 2004 aged 87. There were no reported surviving family members.

FILMOGRAPHY

1949: *All the King's Men.*
1951: *Inside Straight, Lightning Strikes Twice, The Scarf.*
1954: *Johnny Guitar.*
1956: *Giant.*
1957: *A Farewell to Arms.*
1958: *Touch of Evil.*
1959: *Suddenly Last Summer.*
1960: *Cimarron.*
1961: *Angel Baby.*
1965: *Run Home Slow.*
1968: *The Counterfeit Killer* (TV).
1969: *Marquis de Sade: Justine* (a.k.a. *Deadly Sanctuary, Justine and Juliet*), *99 Women* (a.k.a. *Isle of Lost Women, Island of Despair*).
1971: *The President's Plane is Missing* (TV).
1972: *Two for the Money* (TV), *Killer by Night* (TV), *Sixteen* (a.k.a. *Like a Crow on a June Bug, The Young Prey*), *The Last Generation.*
1973: *The Girls of Huntingdon House* (TV), *The Exorcist* (voice only).
1975: *Who Is the Black Dahlia?* (TV).
1977: *Thieves.*
1979: *The Concorde—Airport '79* (a.k.a. *Airport '80—The Concorde*), *The Sacketts* (TV).
1980: *Echoes.*

Notes: (1) Mercedes McCambridge was also featured in Orson Welles' *The Other Side of the Wind* which was shot over a period of several years, was never finished and never appears to have had a public showing.
(2) Every reference book with a biography of McCambridge states that she was born on St. Patrick's Day, 1918. It was only after her death that it was revealed that she was actually born on St. Patrick's Eve, 1916.

TELEVISION SERIES

1949–1950: *One Man's Family* as Beth Holly.
1956–1957: *Wire Service* as Katherine Wells.

SOURCES

Adair, Gilbert. *The Independent*. Obituary, March 19, 2004.
Cameron, Ian, and Elisabeth Cameron. *Broads* London: Studio Vista, 1969.
Daily Mail. Obituary, March 19, 2004.
Daily Post. Obituary, March 22, 2004.
Daily Telegraph. Obituary, March 19, 2004.
DeLong, Thomas A. *Radio Stars*. Jefferson, NC: McFarland, 1996.
Hagen, Ray, and Laura Wagner. *Killer Tomatoes*. Jefferson, NC: McFarland, 2004.
The International Directory of Film and Filmmakers: Actors and Actresses. Vol. III. Chicago: St. James, 1986.
Jones, Ken D., Arthur F. McClure, and Alfred E. Twomey. *Character People*. Secaucus, NJ: Citadel, 1979.
Lentz, Harris M. III. *Obituaries in the Performing Arts, 2004*. Jefferson, NC: McFarland, 2005.
McCambridge, Mercedes *The Quality of Mercy*. New York: Times, 1981.
Pedelty, Donovan. "Crawford's in Another Row." *Picturegoer*. July 3, 1954.
Picture Show Annual. London: Amalgamated, 1952 and 1956.
Quinlan, David. *Illustrated Directory of Film Character Actors*. 2nd ed. London: Batsford, 1995.
_____. *Wicked Women of the Screen*. London: Batsford, 1987.
Variety. "Actress McCambridge's Son Kills Family, Self." November 18, 1987.
Ward, Jack. *The Supporting Players of Television*. Cleveland, OK.: Lakeshore West, 1996.

DONALD McCLELLAND

Donald McClelland was born in New York City on September 29, 1903. He was a child actor who first appeared on Broadway in *Peter Pan* in 1915. For the remainder of his career he was a fairly frequent Broadway performer. In the early crime series *Crime Photographer* he played Captain Logan who was the police contact of "Flash" Casey (Darren McGavin). McClelland made his final Broadway appearance in *Mid-Summer* in 1953. He died in New York on November 15, 1955 aged 52.

FILMOGRAPHY

1917: *Knights of the Square Table*.

TELEVISION SERIES

1951–1952: *Crime Photographer* as Captain Bill Logan.

SOURCES

Tibballs, Geoff. *TV Detectives*. London: Boxtree, 1992.
Truitt, Evelyn Mack. *Who Was Who on Screen*. 2nd ed. New York: Bowker, 1977.

DARREN McGAVIN

There is an old saying about acting, "Television is where the recognition lies, movies are where megabucks can be earned and the stage is where the actor finds greatest satisfaction." Darren McGavin strove to prove this by being active in all media. He had an aggressive acting style which was usefully deployed at times. He was one of the most ubiquitous players on the small screen in the past 50 years leading one critic to describe him as "The Gene Hackman of TV." McGavin's quotes, often tinged with irony, and some of his actions lead one to suppose that he did not believe that he fulfilled his potential as an actor. He was underrated and no doubt his talent was abused and exploited at times. He once expressed his personal philosophy as, "Do nothing you are ashamed of, honor all commitments and hope for the best."

Darren McGavin was born William Richardson McGaveran in Spokane, Washington on May 7, 1922 son of Reid Delano Richardson McGaveran and Grace Bogart. The actor himself shortened his family name to his stage one. When his parents vanished, he became a constant runaway by the age of ten. As a teenager he lived in warehouses in Tacoma, Washington. He relocated to in the small town of Galt in the San Joaquin Valley not far from San Francisco and attended the College Of The Pacific for one year, making his first stage appearance in a college production of *Lady Windermere's Fan* in 1941. He gate-crashed Hollywood a couple of times without making much impact. On the first occasion he retired to a lumber camp in north-west California to work and nurse his wounds after numerous rebuffs by agents. When he returned it was as a scene painter at Paramount Studios, working in his spare time in small theater productions, such as playing the Judge Advocate in *Liliom* for the controversial but acclaimed Actors Lab in Hollywood in 1945.

He recalled, "When I saw all the activity at Paramount, the costumes and most especially the warm lights—it was cold where I was—I knew that I wanted to be not only in the scene, but in the centre of it." He landed a contract with Columbia Pictures where he made his screen debut in *A Song To Remember* (1945). He made three other appearances for them before being abruptly dropped from contract. Smarting he disappeared from Hollywood. In 1946 he did a U.S.O. tour in *The Late Christopher Bean* playing the juvenile. Then he went East to work as a drug store assistant, truck driver and messenger.

In 1948 he studied acting for six months at the Neighborhood Playhouse and made an inauspicious return doing a walk-on in *The Old Lady Says No* at the Mansfield Theater, New York City. After a few more modest acting parts, he was cast as one of the leads in a production of *Death of a Salesman*. Initially he played the role of Happy at the Morosco Theater, New York City in 1949, but was subsequently in the national tour until 1951. He decided that he needed more study which was when he joined the Actors' Studio for six months. Amongst his fellow students were Marlon Brando, Rod Steiger and James Dean. He simultaneously began the hunt for television roles which paid the tuition fees and allowed him and his family to eat regularly.

Parts began to come his way after that. After several successful stage parts in New York, Philadelphia and playing the King in *The King and I* at the St. Louis Municipal Opera in 1955, he headed back to Hollywood. He played the part of Russ Peters, a family friend of Gary Cooper, in *The Court-Martial of Billy Mitchell* (1955) and the young painter, Eddie Yaeger, in *Summertime* (1955). By far his best remembered film part was as the flashy drug pusher Louie in *The Man with the Golden Arm* (1956).

His television career had begun with the live *Crime Photographer* series broadcast from New York in which he played "Flashgun" Casey. The character was created by George Harmon Coxe and originally appeared in the pulp fiction magazine *Black Mask*. As originally depicted, he was a disheveled, fast talking, two fisted crime photographer with a nose for trouble and a sure-fire talent for taking the big picture. This character was featured in a couple of "B" pictures and a very successful radio series which starred Staats Cotsworth. By the time the character came to television he had been sanitized and made more respectable.

In the television series Casey was to be found propping up the bar of the Blue Note Cafe where he related his cases to a sympathetic bartender Ethelbert. When the series originally aired in April 1951 Richard Carlyle played Casey with John Gibson as Ethelbert. The location had also been altered from Boston to New York so Casey worked for the New York Morning Express. The CBS network were unhappy with this combination and replaced them with Darren McGavin as Casey and Cliff Hall as Ethelbert from May 3, 1951 to June 1952. There were 40 half hour, black and white episodes originally shown live. Casey acquired a girl friend, Ann Williams (Jan Miner) who was a reporter. Later there was also a colleague Jack Williams (Archie Smith) who wrote copy to go with Casey's photographs. Music was supplied by the Tony Mottola Trio who played the Blue Note Cafe Musicians. McGavin had little enthusiasm for this series.

McGavin was the original tough television detective Mike Hammer and then landed the main starring role in *Riverboat*. When he starred in *Mickey Spillane's Mike Hammer,* he found himself rushing between the *Hammer* soundstage and the *Riverboat* set, working in both series simultaneously. The former derived from the novels by Mickey Spillane and the series was as violent as its pedigree. It was a syndicated series of 78 half hour, black and white episodes shot for Revue Productions between 1957 and 1959 and set in New York. McGavin breathed a sigh of relief when he had fulfilled his quota of *Hammer* episodes. Although he enjoyed the part, he never felt it was quite his type of characterization.

Riverboat was a weekly, one hour, black and white series which told of the adventures aboard "The Enterprise," one of the riverboats which traveled the length of the Mississippi during the 1840s. Among its passengers were gamblers, merchants, lawbreakers and immigrants, some seeking a new life, others trying to escape from the past, many in search of a fortune. For this was a time when the Mississippi was one of the world's great highways, a chief artery of trade for the southern states of North America and the gateway to many vast, newly opened territories. Historical research was carried out for two years before production of *Riverboat* began. A full sized replica of a two funneled stern wheel riverboat, complete with engine room and machinery was built for the series.

Darren McGavin starred as Grey Holden, a polished gentleman adventurer, who was captain and part owner of the riverboat "Enterprise" which he won in a poker game. Burt Reynolds costarred as Ben Frazer, the tough and experienced river pilot, who was Grey Holden's partner. The content of the series has been overshadowed by the highly publicized feud which developed between the two stars. It seems apparent that

Darren McGavin, who starred in *Crime Photographer* and *Mike Hammer*.

McGavin wanted to undermine permanently Reynolds's confidence as an actor, for he rode roughshod over the fledgling star. Before a take he would make disparaging remarks about Reynolds' performance. After a take he would belittle him in front of the crew and other actors. In their scenes together he ran the entire repertoire of tricks to upstage his costar. If it were time for a Reynolds close-up, he would rampage to such a degree that the shot was either ruined or never filmed. In the end it had become so bad that McGavin did not show up for work and the studio substituted Dan Duryea as Captain Brad Turner in two episodes "The Wichita Arrows" and "Fort Epitaph." McGavin found that little sympathy accrued to him on account of this. There was a general feeling that McGavin was such a gifted actor anyway that he scarcely need to indulge in these tricks to assert himself.

By the time of the second season, the series had been revamped. Burt Reynolds had departed and was replaced by another veteran Noah Beery, Jr. The list of guest stars on this series was extremely impressive and included names who previously had avoided television altogether. There were 44 episodes of *Riverboat* shown on NBC between September 13, 1959 and January 16, 1961 with most of the shooting being done on the backlot lake at Universal Studios. The series was set to emulate *Wagon Train* and *Rawhide* as one of the classiest shows on television and would no doubt have run much longer if the two original stars had been more harmonious.

In 1956 he purchased an old farmhouse in the mountains near Liberty, New York. It consisted of 250 acres of orchards and grazing land which he called Meladare. Initially he saw a lot of it. The farmhouse lacked electricity and running water. For more than a year he worked on the house installing modern equipment and putting a huge vegetable garden into shape. When acting roles became more numerous, his success prevented him from seeing too much of the place. The family home was a large modern house in the Beverly Hills.

McGavin continued to be very active and was a frequent guest star on numerous action orientated series during the 1960s and 1970s. Once the movie-for-television became a genre in itself, he embraced this and the frequency with which he turned up on these indicates that he was trying to compensate for all of the years of relative obscurity and anonymity. He came very close to hitting the jackpot when he starred in the telemovie *The Night Stalker* (1972), a unique blend of horror and humor, in which he played the cynical, hard boiled reporter Carl Kolchak.

The character was created by author Jeff Rice in the novel *The Kolchak Papers* (1970). ABC bought the rights, but did nothing with it until producer Dan Curtis handed it to writer Richard Matheson to adapt as a television movie. It told of reporter Carl Kolchak tracking down the mysterious Janos Skorzeny (Barry Atwater) who turns out to be a vampire in Las Vegas. When it was originally broadcast on March 17, 1972, it was a ratings bonanza. This prompted a follow-up the following year called *The Night Strangler* (1973) in which Kolchak confronts Dr. Malcolm Reynolds (Richard Anderson), an alchemist who lives in the city beneath the streets of Seattle. This was even more witty and there were plenty of thrills along the way. It was another ratings winner.

Although the ABC network were initially somewhat ashamed of such a lowbrow concept being such a success, they were convinced that a series would be a ratings grabber. McGavin agreed and coproduced it with his own Francy Productions, filming being done at Universal Studios. Each week Kolchak tackled a monster, but most of these were cleverly suggested rather than explicitly shown; many times they skulked in the shadows. The blend of scares and comedy, along with eerie photography and atmospheric music, was adroitly balanced in the same way as in the two telemovies, but oddly the series failed to repeat their success. It disappeared without a ripple in 1974 after only twenty episodes were shot. Network programming head Fred Silverman, who personally disliked sci-fi and horror series, zapped *Kolchak: The Night Stalker* in a way that none of the monsters ever could.

McGavin's film *Hangar 18* (1980), which dealt with UFOs, was another big hit in this genre. His experience on *The Natural* (1984) in which he played the leading heavy, was rather characteristic of this actor and his place in the Hollywood galaxy. His name was inexplicably missing from the credits. Initially critics speculated that this was an in-joke, until McGavin publicly admitted that after the producers refused to accede to his salary and billing demands, his reaction was to insist that his name be removed. He appeared on stage many times during the 1960s both on Broadway and on tour, re-emerging after a long absence as Vern in *California Dog Fight* at the Manhattan Theater Club at the New

York City Center in 1985. He later appeared in *The Night Hank Williams Died* in 1989 and *Greetings* in 1994. He directed a considerable number of stage plays and helmed episodes of such television series as *Buckskin*, *Riverboat* and *Death Valley Days*, all dating from the 1959–1960 period. He did not appear to have too many ambitions in that direction. In 1990 he received an Emmy award nomination as Outstanding Guest Actor in a Comedy Series for his work as the father of Murphy Brown (Candice Bergen).

McGavin married actress Melanie York on March 20, 1944. They had four children who are a son York born in 1950; a daughter Megan born in 1957, another daughter Bridget who was born in 1958; and Bogart. They originally met when they worked on stage together. Trivia buffs may note that they appeared together in the film *Queen For A Day* (1951), but in different episodes. They separated in 1966 and divorced in 1969. Secondly he married actress Kathie Browne on December 31, 1969. She was born in San Luis Obispo on September 19, 1939. She made a solid contribution to television and they first appeared together in an episode of *The Outsider* originally shown in 1968. She was particularly memorable as a police chief in "The Sentry" episode of *Kolchak: The Night Stalker*.

From 1998 onwards he played Arthur Dales, a retired FBI agent, in *The X-Files*. He had been working on the series during the last week of March 1999 when he was felled by a serious stroke at his Beverly Hills home and rushed to the UCLA Medical Center. He was later transferred to a rehabilitation unit where he made considerable progress towards a full recovery. He was hit by a further tragedy on April 8, 2003 when Kathie Browne died at their Beverly Hills home at age 63. She died of natural causes after surviving a bout of breast cancer.

Darren McGavin died in a Los Angeles hospital on February 25, 2006 aged 83 of natural causes. He is buried at Hollywood Forever Cemetery.

Filmography

1945: *A Song to Remember, Kiss and Tell, She Wouldn't Say Yes, Counter-Attack.*
1946: *Fear.*
1951: *Queen for a Day.*
1955: *Summertime* (a.k.a. *Summer Madness*), *The Court-Martial of Billy Mitchell* (a.k.a. *One Man Mutiny*)
1956: *The Man with the Golden Arm.*
1957: *Beau James, The Delicate Delinquent.*
1958: *The Case Against Brooklyn.*
1964: *Bullet for a Badman.*
1965: *The Great Sioux Massacre, Ride the High Wind.*
1967: *The Outsider* (TV).
1968: *The Challengers* (TV), *Mission Mars.*
1969: *Anatomy of a Crime.*
1970: *Mrs. Pollifax—Spy, The Challenge* (TV), *Berlin Affair* (TV), *Tribes* (a.k.a. *The Soldier Who Declared Peace*) (TV), *The 48 Hour Mile.*
1971: *The Birdmen* (a.k.a. *Escape Of The Birdmen*) (TV), *Banyon* (TV), *The Death of Me Yet* (TV).
1972: *The Night Stalker* (TV), *Something Evil* (TV), *The Rookies* (TV), *Say Goodbye Maggie Cole* (TV), *Smash-Up Alley* (a.k.a. *43: The Petty Story*).
1973: *The Night Strangler* (TV), *B Must Die, Happy Mother's Day Love George* (a.k.a. *Run Stranger Run* also produced and directed), *The Six Million Dollar Man* (TV).
1976: *No Deposit No Return, Brinks: The Great Robbery* (TV), *Law and Order* (TV).
1977: *Airport '77.*
1978: *Zero to Sixty, The Users* (TV), *Hot Lead and Cold Feet.*
1979: *Love For Rent* (TV).
1980: *Waikiki* (TV), *Hangar 18.*
1981: *Firebird 2015 A.D.*
1983: *A Christmas Story.*
1984: *The Natural, The Return Of Marcus Welby M.D.* (TV), *The Baron And The Kid* (TV), *Turk 182!*
1985: *My Wicked Wicked Ways: The Legend of Errol Flynn* (TV).
1986: *Raw Deal.*
1987: *From The Hip.*
1988: *Dead Heat, Inherit the Wind* (TV), *The Diamond Trap* (TV).
1989: *Captain America.*
1990: *By Dawn's Early Light* (TV), *Grand Tour* (a.k.a. *Disaster In Time* (TV), *A Child in the Night* (TV).
1991: *Blood and Concrete, Perfect Harmony* (TV).
1993: *The American Clock* (TV).
1994: *A Perfect Stranger* (TV).
1995: *Fudge-A-Mania* (TV), *Derby* (TV), *Billy Madison.*
1996: *Still Waters Burn, Perfect Crimes, Waiting for the Man* (a.k.a. *Small Time*).
1999: *Pros and Cons.*

CHARLES McGRAW

Charles McGraw was a belligerent, hell-raising actor with a rasping voice who was not conventionally handsome enough to succeed as the star of major films, but whose personality was well used in film noir. One of his films *The Narrow Margin* has passed into film classic folklore. He remains a memorable if not particularly likeable figure, whose real life personality mirrored much the same traits as those shown in his films. His idea of a good social life was to fly to some distant location where he was shooting a movie, find the nearest brothel and debauch himself to the full. He was very active in television both as a guest and as the star of two largely forgotten series.

Charles McGraw was born Charles Butters in Iowa on May 10, 1914 the son of Frank P. Butters and Beatrice Crisp. His father was born in Ohio of parents who came from Ireland. His mother was English. Raised in Akron, Ohio, he served in the U.S. Navy and attended Akron University. Prior to being an actor, he was a boxer. He worked in nightclubs in New York before joining a little theater company in 1935. He appeared in the London version of *Boy Meets Girl* in 1938. Subsequently he appeared on Broadway in such plays as *Dead End, Brother Rat* and *Native Son*. He was also a very active radio actor in New York until 1946.

Some authorities indicate that he made his screen debut as early as 1938, but this has never been verified. More likely he made his screen debut in 1942, but his attempt to establish himself in films between 1942 and 1944 met with failure. The first film in which he registered strongly was as one of the title characters, along with William Conrad, in *The Killers* (1946). From then onwards he frequently played ruthless underworld characters. He signed a contract with RKO Radio where he did most of his best work. RKO signed him as a threat to Robert Mitchum. Initially Mitchum was scared, but when he met McGraw and found out that he was of slight build, he treated him with good humor. McGraw's best film role was as wary Detective Walter Brown in the thriller *The Narrow Margin* (1952) in which he verbally sparred with Marie Windsor, unaware that she is an undercover cop. Off screen he was known to be very antagonistic towards directors and sometimes when he showed up on set for his work, he was obviously inebriated. When his tenure at RKO Radio ended, he successfully free-

TELEVISION SERIES

1951: *Crime Photographer* as "Flashgun" Casey.
1957–1959: *Mickey Spillane's Mike Hammer* as Mike Hammer.
1959–1961: *Riverboat* as Grey Holden.
1968–1969: *The Outsider* as David Ross.
1974–1975: *Kolchak: The Night Stalker* as Carl Kolchak.
1983: *Small And Frye* as Nick Small.
1998: *The X Files* as Agent Arthur Dales.

MINISERIES

1979: *Ike*.
1980: *The Martian Chronicles*.
1989: *Around The World In 80 Days*.

SOURCES

Anwen, D.N. "The Captain's Timber." *TV Times*. August 21, 1960.
Bird, Leslie. "Riverboat on a Stream of Adventure." *TV Times*. June 12, 1960.
Butterfield, Alan. "Night Stalker Darren McGavin Felled by Stroke." *National Enquirer*. July 27, 1999.
Brooks, Tim. *The Complete Directory to Prime Time TV Stars*. New York: Ballantine Books, 1987.
Cameron, Ian, and Elisabeth Cameron. *The Heavies*. London: Studio Vista, 1967.
Daily Post Obituary, Feruary 26, 2006.
Gerani, Gary. *Fantastic Television*. New York: Harmony, 1977.
Hayward, Anthony. *The Independent* Obituary, February 28, 2006.
Nelson, Valerie J. *L.A. Times* Obituary, February 27, 2006.
Picture Show Annual. London: Amalgamated, 1953 and 1959.
Lentz, Harris M. III. *Obituaries in the Performing Arts, 2003*. Jefferson, NC: McFarland, 2004.
Post, Kathleen. "Port of Dreams." *TV Radio Mirror*. January 1960.
Quinlan, David. *Film Stars*. 5th ed. London: Batsford, 2000.
Risling, Greg. *Washington Post* Obituary, February 26, 2006.
Skinner, John Walter. *Who's Who on the Screen*. Worthing, England: Madeleine, 1983.
Speed, F. Maurice. *The Western Film and Television Annual*. London: MacDonald, 1961.
Stallings, Penny. *Forbidden Channels*. New York: HarperPerennial, 1991.
Ward, Jack. *Television Guest Stars*. Jefferson, NC: McFarland, 1993.

Charles McGraw, who starred in *Adventures of the Falcon.*

lanced. Although he remained active, his subsequent film roles were all character parts. He was particularly effective as Marcellus, the gladiator trainer, in *Spartacus* (1960).

McGraw made his television debut in 1952 and starred in two television series. He played Michael Waring in a syndicated series *Adventures of the Falcon*. "The Falcon" was a crimebuster created by Michael Arlen in a short story *Gay Falcon* in 1940. He appeared in four films played by George Sanders. In the fourth film he was killed and replaced by his brother played by Sanders' real life brother, Tom Conway. He went on to play the role in a further nine films. John Calvert played the role in the final three films. The 39 episode, black and white, television series was produced by Federal Telefilms Incorporated during 1954–1955. As played by McGraw, the character was changed to being active during the Cold War. He was now Michael Waring, former private eye turned international secret agent, whose code name was "The Falcon." As he expressed it tersely, "I work for Uncle Sam." This series had some very good ideas for stories, but they were poorly developed because they were too ambitious for the budgets. Too much footage was consumed with senseless brawls. It was also virtually studio bound with no external shooting except for a few stock shots. Waring was however quite charming when dealing with the ladies.

McGraw then tried to fill Humphrey Bogart's shoes when he was cast in *Casablanca*, Warners doomed attempt to replicate the success of the classic movie on television. The producers of this series wanted Anthony Quinn for the lead and initially Jack Warner was prepared to cut a deal to secure his services, but Warner later reneged on the agreement and McGraw was cast instead. McGraw was not regarded by the producer as a suitable substitute for Bogart or Quinn. Poor casting and dismal scripts quickly sank the series. McGraw later had the regular role of Henry Fonda's superior officer in the series *The Smith Family*.

McGraw died at his private residence on 11727 Blix Street in North Hollywood on July 29, 1980 aged 66 when he accidentally crashed through the glass door of a shower. He was believed to be intoxicated at the time. He suffered severe lacerations of his left arm which resulted in a massive hemorrhage which paramedics were unable to stem. His accident was made worse by the fact that he was suffering from heart disease. There were no funeral services carried out for him. Funeral arrangements were undertaken by the Neptune Society and he was cremated at Los Angeles Abbey Crematorium in Compton, California on August 6, 1980. He was survived by his wife, Freda Choy Kitt, a Chinese fashion designer, whom he wed in London in 1938, together with a daughter named Jill who was born in 1941. Since his wife was resident at a different address, they were understood to be separated.

FILMOGRAPHY

1942: *The Moon is Down, The Undying Monster* (a.k.a. *The Hammond Mystery*).
1943: *They Came to Blow Up America, The Mad Ghoul, Corvette K-225, Destroyer.*
1944: *The Imposter.*
1946: *The Killers, The Big Fix.*
1947: *The Long Night, Brute Force, The Farmer's Daughter, The Gangster, Roses are Red, T-Men, On the Old Spanish Trail.*
1948: *Hazard, The Hunted, Blood on the Moon, Berlin Express.*
1949: *Reign of Terror* (a.k.a. *The Black Book*), *Border Incident, Once More My Darling, The Story of Molly X, Side Street, Ma and Pa Kettle Go to Town, The Threat.*
1950: *Armored Car Robbery, Double Crossbones, I Was a Shoplifter.*
1951: *His Kind of Woman, Road Block.*
1952: *The Narrow Margin, One Minute to Zero.*
1953: *Thunder over the Plains, Loophole, War Paint.*

1954: *The Bridges at Toko-Ri.*
1956: *Away All Boats, Toward the Unknown, The Cruel Tower.*
1957: *Joe Dakota, Joe Butterfly, Slaughter on 10th Avenue.*
1958: *Saddle the Wind, The Defiant Ones, Twilight for the Gods.*
1959: *The Man in the Net, The Wonderful Country.*
1960: *Spartacus, Cimarron.*
1962: *The Horizontal Lieutenant.*
1963: *The Birds, It's a Mad, Mad, Mad, Mad World.*
1965: *Nightmare in Chicago.*
1966: *The Busy Body.*
1967: *Hang 'em High, In Cold Blood.*
1968: *Pendulum, Perilous Voyage* (TV) (first shown 1976).
1969: *Tell Them Willie Boy is Here.*
1971: *O'Hara United States Treasury: Operation Cobra* (TV), *Johnny Got His Gun, The Devil and Miss Sarah* (TV), *Chandler.*
1972: *The Longest Night* (TV), *The Night Stalker* (TV).
1973: *Money to Burn* (TV), *Hawkins on Murder: Death and the Maiden* (TV).
1974: *A Boy and His Dog.*
1975: *The Killer Inside Me.*
1977: *Twilight's Last Gleaming.*

TELEVISION SERIES

1954–1955: *Adventures of the Falcon* as Mike Waring.
1955–1956: *Casablanca* as Rick Jason.
1971–1972: *The Smith Family* as Captain Hughes.

SOURCES

Cameron, Ian, and Elisabeth Cameron. *The Heavies.* London: Studio Vista, 1967.
Death Certificate.
Hyatt, Wesley. *Short-Lived Television Series, 1948–1978.* Jefferson, NC: McFarland, 2003.
Mitchum, John. *Them Ornery Mitchum Boys.* Pacifica, California: Creatures at Large, 1989.
Quinlan, David. *Film Stars.* 5th ed. London: Batsford, 2000.
Ward, Jack. *Television Guest Stars.* Jefferson, NC: McFarland, 1993.

JOHN MCINTIRE

"I've never been under contract for any length of time mainly because it interferes with my family's life on our ranch. We've made the place self-supporting now and enjoy cooking on a wood stove and swimming in our 135 acre lake." So spoke John McIntire. He was an unpretentious actor who proved to be equally versatile whether cast as villains or upstanding citizens. He frequently played older than his years. His craggy features equipped him well to play cops and westerners on television. He was one of a select band of actors who achieved stardom on television in a way which would have been impossible in films given that they usually featured handsome heroes.

John Herrick McIntire was born in Spokane, Washington on June 27, 1907 the son of an attorney. His childhood was mainly spent in Montana where he learned to ride bucking broncos and to punch cows. Later the family resided in Santa Monica, California. He studied at the University of California for two years before dropping out.

Next he went to sea on a cargo ship for a couple of years before going to New York where he became active on radio. There he met the actress Jeanette Nolan (1911–1998) whom he married in 1936. Before World War II he narrated the national radio news show *The March of Time* and did hundreds of radio broadcasts in the thirties and forties.

McIntire commenced his motion picture career in 1948 when he auditioned for the role of a clergyman. Instead he was hired to play a cattle owner in *Black Bart.* Over the next forty years he contributed a rich variety of characterizations in numerous motion pictures, but mainly in the western and crime genres. He was particularly praised for his performances in three westerns directed by Anthony Mann namely as Joe Lamont in *Winchester '73* (1950); as Gannon in *The Far Country* (1954); and as Dr. McCord in *The Tin Star* (1957). One of his most harrowing experiences was when shooting *The Phenix City Story* (1955) in which he played Albert Patterson. The movie told the true story in semi-documentary fashion of the town in Alabama where the main industry was crime and corruption and the way in which it was eventually ended. The film was shot on the actual locations where it happened against the wishes of the local politicians and mobsters. McIntire received threats daily that he would be killed unless he quit the film. He finished it however and survived. He made his television debut in "The Windmill" an episode of *General Electric Theater* in 1955.

His first television series was *The Naked City*

John McIntire, who starred in *The Naked City*.

which made its debut on the ABC network on September 30, 1958. This derived from an original story by Mark Hellinger which became the basis of the classic film thriller in 1948. In a sense the city of New York was as much the focal point of the stories in the television series as the actors. The series took maximum advantage of the city itself for location shooting. There was also a very gritty look to the show which emphasized that the drama originated in the streets, tenements and shops of New York and not in a studio.

It was the first television series to be shot entirely on location in New York. This included the interior photography which was lensed at the old Biograph Studios. The score and theme music for the half hour segments of *The Naked City* was composed by George Duning and Ned Washington. Each episode concluded with the famous line enunciated by producer Herbert B. Leonard, "There are eight million stories in the Naked City. This has been one of them." The series was made by Shelle Productions Incorporated for Screen Gems, Columbia's television wing.

McIntire played the part of the veteran Irish cop Det. Lt. Dan Muldoon complete with brogue. Widower Muldoon operated out of Manhattan's 65th Precinct and kept racing pigeons as a hobby. In the premiere episode "Meridian," Det. Jim Halloran (James Franciscus) was assigned as his partner. Together they tracked down assorted criminals who populated this urban jungle. The series was universally praised and won a high audience rating. McIntire himself was desperately unhappy however. The bitterly cold New York winter upset his constitution and he wanted out. His real estate holdings had made him an extremely wealthy man and he even offered to buy his way out of his contract. The producer, Herbert B. Leonard, agreed but insisted that the character be written out in such a way that McIntire could not return and that there should be a transitional episode introducing his successor. McIntire appeared in 25 episodes. In the last of these "The Bumper" which was originally aired on March 17, 1959, Muldoon's squad car crashed into a gas truck during a high speed chase. The explosion instantly killed the cop. This was probably the first time that the leading actor in a crime series had been killed off in this fashion and it created a sensation both among the viewers and in the press. McIntire was replaced by Horace McMahon as Det. Lt. Parker. In spite of McIntire's defection, the series won an Emmy award nomination as Best Dramatic Series—Less Than One Hour during the 1958–1959 season. McIntire and Franciscus were later reunited in the pilot to the short-lived television crime series *Longstreet* (1971).

Off screen ranching was McIntire's passion and he owned a 640 acre ranch in Montana. As he explained, "Even my wife, a product of Los Angeles, really goes for the frontier life, although we are so far cut off from civilization that we don't even have electricity.... If I'm lucky I might manage to spend four months of the year in it."

When Ward Bond died in 1960, McIntire eventually took over from him playing wagonmaster Chris Hale in the highly successful western series *Wagon Train*. He starred in this series from 1961 until it ended in 1965. He mused, "I've a fine outdoor life and I hate to give it up for any length of time, but I was offered a good deal of money by the makers of *Wagon Train* with time off to return to the ranch, so I accepted." A similar situation occurred later with the western series *The Virginian*. When Charles Bickford who played John Grainger died in 1967, McIntire took over for a season as his brother Clay. His real wife played his screen wife Holly in the series.

McIntire remained a jobbing actor until the late eighties. He eventually died on January 30, 1991 in Pasadena, California aged 83 of cancer and emphysema. With his wife he had two children who were daughter Holly born in 1942 and son Tim (1943–1986). His son was an actor and musician, but he became an alcoholic and died prematurely. McIntire was survived by his widow, daughter and grandson, Luke Savin Wright.

Filmography

1948: *Black Bart, The Street with No Name, Call Northside 777.*
1949: *Top o' the Morning, Scene of the Crime, Red Canyon, Johnny Stool Pigeon, Francis, Ambush.*
1950: *Winchester '73, Walk Softly Stranger, Saddle Tramp, Shadow on the Wall, No Sad Songs for Me, The Asphalt Jungle, Under the Gun.*
1951: *You're in the Navy Now* (a.k.a. *USS Teakettle*), *Westward the Women, That's My Boy, The Raging Tide.*
1952: *The World in his Arms, Sally and Saint Anne, The Lawless Breed, Horizon's West, Glory Alley.*
1953: *War Arrow, The President's Lady, Mississippi Gambler, A Lion Is in the Streets.*
1954: *The Far Country, Yellow Mountain, Four Guns to the Border, Apache, There's No Business Like Show Business.*
1955: *Stranger On Horseback, The Spoilers, The Scarlet Coat, The Phenix City Story, The Kentuckian, To Hell and Back* (narrator).
1956: *World in My Corner, I've Lived Before, Backlash, Away All Boats.*
1957: *The Tin Star.*
1958: *Sing Boy Sing, The Mark of the Hawk, The Light in the Forest.*
1959: *The Gunfight at Dodge City.*
1960: *Who Was That Lady? Seven Ways from Sundown, Psycho, Flaming Star, Elmer Gantry.*
1961: *Two Rode Together, Summer and Smoke.*
1967: *Rough Night in Jericho.*
1971: *Powderkeg* (TV), *Longstreet* (TV).
1972: *Challenge to Be Free* (narrator).
1973: *Linda* (TV).
1974: *Herbie Rides Again, The Healers* (TV).
1975: *Rooster Cogburn.*
1976: *The New Daughters of Joshua Cabe* (TV).
1977: *The Rescuers* (voice only), *Crisis in Sun Valley* (TV).
1978: *Lassie: The New Beginning* (TV), *The Jordan Chance* (TV).
1979: *Mrs. R's Daughter* (TV).
1981: *The Fox and the Hound* (voice only).
1982: *Honkytonk Man.*
1984: *Cloak and Dagger, The Cowboy and the Ballerina* (TV).
1986: *As Summers Die* (TV).
1989: *Dream Breakers* (a.k.a. *The O'Connors*) (TV), *Turner and Hooch.*

Television Series

1958–1959: *The Naked City* as Det. Lt. Dan Muldoon.
1961–1965: *Wagon Train* as Chris Hale.
1967–1968: *The Virginian* as Clay Grainger.
1979–1980: *Shirley* as Ethan "Dutch" McHenry.
1981: *The American Dream* as Sam Whittier.

Miniseries

1977: *Aspen* (a.k.a. *The Innocent and the Damned*).
1981: *Goliath Awaits.*

Sources

Cameron, Ian, and Elisabeth Cameron. *The Heavies.* London: Studio Vista, 1967.
De Long, Thomas A. *Radio Stars.* Jefferson, NC.: McFarland, 1996.
Inman, David. *The TV Encyclopedia.* New York: Perigee, 1991.
Laing, Nora. "John McIntire—Wagonmaster." *TV Times.* June 2, 1961.
Lance, Steven. *Written Out of Television.* Jefferson, NC: McFarland, 1993.
Perry, Jeb H. *Screen Gems: A History of Columbia Pictures Television from Cohn to Coke (1948–1983).* Metuchen, NJ: Scarecrow, 1991.
Quinlan, David. *The Illustrated Directory of Film Character Actors.* 2nd ed. London: Batsford, 1995.
Variety. Obituary, February 1991.
Ward, Jack. *Television Guest Stars.* Jefferson, NC: McFarland, 1993.

Horace McMahon

"My face has been my fortune. Although in *Naked City,* I am playing a lawman for the first time in many years." So spoke Horace McMahon who played Det. Lt. Mike Parker in that series. He had a lived-in face with beetle brows and a gravel voice which initially typed him in Hollywood as a gangster. He was one of the blue collar actors whom television viewers sometimes take to their hearts as a result of a characterization which registers strongly with them. He was very convincing as a hard nosed cop.

Horace McMahon was born in South Norwalk, Connecticut on May 17, 1906 the son of a toolmaker. His nose was broken in high school when playing football and again later while boxing. He attended Fordham University Law School with the aim of a becoming a lawyer. Simultaneously he wrote articles for newspapers and magazines. Sensing that his future did not lie as a lawyer, a friend obtained a job for him with a winter stock company in 1927. He made his Broadway debut with a one line bit in *Wonder Boy* in 1931. He played small roles in a number of other plays and appeared in vaudeville. His biggest theatrical success came with the Broadway play *Three Men on a Horse* (1936) which ran for 43 weeks. Joining the cast the same day was a pretty young actress named Louise Campbell (1911–1997) who was born Louise Weisbecker. When the play closed she went to California where she became one of Paramount's rising stars of the late thirties.

"As I was out of work I thought I'd take a look at the California sun. We were married less than two years later," he recalled. He worked his way into movies making his screen debut in 1937. Prior to war service he made small appearances in dozens of films. Louise Campbell was a much photographed actress of the period, but it is interesting that magazine layouts seldom if ever referred to her marriage possibly because screen roughneck McMahon was not quite the suave, gentlemanly type the studio thought the public expected her to be married to. She retired in 1941 to raise a family.

He scored a personal triumph as Lt. Monaghan in the play *The Detective Story* (1949). He repeated his role in the film version in 1951. He appeared only infrequently in films thereafter, but he became an increasingly familiar television actor. His first regular role on television was as a police captain in the crime series *Martin Kane, Private Eye* for a single season. For another season he played the agent of Danny Thomas in *Make Room for Daddy*. When *The Naked City* started on ABC on September 30, 1958 the stars were John McIntire as the veteran cop Det. Lt. Dan Muldoon and James Franciscus as his young assistant, Det. Jim Halloran. When McIntire was killed off in the series, he was replaced by McMahon as Det. Lt. Mike Parker. He operated out of Manhattan's 65th Precinct. The first episode which Parker appeared in was the same one which featured Muldoon's death namely "The Bumper" originally shown on ABC on March 17, 1959.

The Naked City was a gritty crime series which effectively used New York as the background for some very absorbing human dramas. Many of the early stories derived from the pen of Stirling Silliphant who literally walked all over Manhattan eavesdropping with pen and paper. Some of the conversations which he overheard found their way into scripts he wrote. In the character of Lt. Mike Parker, he found an ideal character to voice his words. McMahon stayed with the series until the end of the original series of 39 episodes on September 29, 1959. The series was nominated for an Emmy award during the 1958–1959 season as "Best Dramatic Series—Less Than One Hour," but failed to win.

The series proved to be so successful that when it returned on ABC on October 12, 1960, it had been extended to an hour which provided the opportunity for dramatic stories with even more depth. The title was shortened to *Naked City*. McMahon returned as Parker. James Franciscus had gone. He was replaced by Paul Burke in the role of Det. Adam Flint who assisted Parker. Another old pro who appeared in the original series Patrolman Frank Arcaro (Harry Bellaver) was back, now promoted to Sergeant. Together these three kept the streets of New York safe for a further three seasons and 99 black and white episodes until September 11, 1963. The series received three further Emmy award nominations for "Outstanding Program Achievement in the Field of Drama" in each of its seasons, but failed to win on any occasion. McMahon himself received a single Emmy award nomination as "Outstanding Performance in a Supporting Role by an Actor" during the 1961–1962 season.

Once the series ended, McMahon stayed active in occasional films, on stage and television. His final regular series role was as assistant to *Mr. Broadway* (Craig Stevens) in the short-lived series of that name. His last television appearance is believed to have been an episode of *Family Affair* in 1969. In the late sixties he retired to his home in Rowayton, Connecticut. He had been active in the Lamb's Club and wrote stories for the show business magazine *Variety*. A devout Catholic, he had served as President of the Catholic Actors Guild. He died in a Norwalk, Connecticut hospital on August 17, 1971 aged 65 of a heart ailment. He had been hospitalized a few times in the year prior to his death. He was survived by his widow; two daughters Kate and Missy both of whom became actresses; and a son Thomas. He is buried at Saint Mary's Cemetery, Norwalk, Connecticut.

Filmography

1937: *The Wrong Road, Bad Guy, Navy Blues, Exclusive, A Girl with Ideas, Double Wedding, Paid to Dance, The Last Gangster, They Gave Him a Gun, Kid Galahad.*

1938: *Tenth Avenue Kid, When G-Men Step In, I Am the Law, Fast Company, Ladies in Distress, King of the Newsboys, Secrets of a Nurse, The Crowd Roars, Broadway Musketeers, Pride of the Navy, Alexander's Ragtime Band, Gangs of New York, Marie Antoinette, Federal Man Hunt.*

1939: *Rose of Washington Square, Sergeant Madden, The Gracie Allen Murder Case, I Was a Convict, Big Town Czar, Laugh It Off, Quick Millions, Sabotage, She Married a Cop, For Love or Money, That's Right—You're Wrong, Newsboys' Home, Pirates of the Skies, Another Thin Man, 60,000 Enemies, Calling Dr. Kildare.*

1940: *Gangs of Chicago, Dr. Kildare's Crisis, The Marines Fly High, I Can't Give You Anything But Love Baby, Margie, Millionaires in Prison, Oh Johnny How You Can Love, Dr. Kildare's Strangest Case, The Ghost Comes Home, The Leather Pushers, Melody Ranch, We Who Are Young, Dr. Kildare Goes Home, My Favorite Wife.*

1941: *Come Live With Me, Dangerous Blondes, Rookies on Parade, Lady Scarface, Dr. Kildare's Wedding Day, The Bride Wore Crutches, Birth of the Blues, The Stork Pays Off, Buy Me That Town.*

1942: *Jail House Blues.*

1944: *The Navy Way, Timber Queen, Roger Touhy Gangster.*

1946: *13 Rue Madeleine.*

1948: *Fighting Mad, The Return of October, Smart Woman, Waterfront at Midnight.*

1951: *Detective Story.*

1953: *Abbott and Costello Go to Mars, Fast Company, Champ For a Day, Man in the Dark.*

1954: *Duffy of San Quentin, Susan Slept Here.*

1955: *My Sister Eileen, Blackboard Jungle, Texas Lady.*

1957: *Beau James, The Delicate Delinquent.*

1959: *Never Steal Anything Small.*

1966: *The Swinger.*

1968: *The Detective.*

Television Series

1950–1951: *Martin Kane, Private Eye* as Captain Willis.

1953–1954: *Make Room For Daddy* as Phil Arnold.

1959–1963: *Naked City* as Det. Lt. Mike Parker.

1963–1964: *The Jackie Gleason Show.*

1964: *Mr. Broadway* as Hank McClure.

Note: Early on his name was spelled MacMahon which is the way it appears in some reference sources.

Sources

Inman, David. *The TV Encyclopedia.* New York: Perigee, 1991.

Horace McMahon, who costarred in *Martin Kane Private Eye* **and** *Naked City.*

Lance, Steven. *Written Out of Television.* Lanham, MD: Madison, 1996.

Perry, Jeb H. *Screen Gems: A History of Columbia Pictures Television from Cohn to Coke, 1948–1983.* Metuchen, NJ: Scarecrow, 1991.

Picture Show Annual. London: Amalgamated, 1940.

Preston, Jim. "New York with the Lid Off." *TV Times.* December 16, 1962.

Quinlan, David. *Illustrated Directory of Film Character Actors.* 2nd ed. London: Batsford, 1995.

Variety. Obituary, August 25, 1971.

John McQuade

John McQuade was born in Pittsburgh, PA on July 9, 1912. He studied music at Duquesne University at Pittsburgh and at Columbia University. He was a radio singer prior to becoming an actor. A protégé of George M. Cohan, he began his theatrical career understudying Maurice Evans. He appeared with Evans in *Hamlet* (1939) as well as other Shakespeare plays. During the forties he appeared in a number of Broadway plays which were sometimes revivals of earlier hits. He made his screen debut in a bit role as Detective Constantino in *The Naked City* (1948).

He did a great deal of experimental television during the forties.

He was the second actor to play the title role in the television crime series *Charlie Wild, Private Detective*. This series started on American radio as *The Adventures of Sam Spade* where it became very popular. Its creator Dashiell Hammett fell foul of the House UnAmerican Activities Committee so the title character was changed to Charlie Wild. The name derived from Wildroot Hair Oils which was the show's sponsor. It continued to be a radio hit. When it came to television on CBS on December 22, 1950 the lead was played by Kevin O'Morrison. The CBS series ended on June 27, 1951. On September 11, 1951 it resumed on ABC until March 4, 1952. On March 13, 1952 it resumed again on DuMont and was last broadcast on June 19, 1952. When the series switched networks in 1951, McQuade assumed the lead and stayed with it until the end. Charlie Wild was a hardboiled private eye who lived up to his name. He enjoyed giving crooks and suspects a hard time usually with flying fists. He did not appear to have heard of civil liberties. He was assisted by his efficient secretary Effie Perrine (Cloris Leachman). There were 78 half hour, black and white episodes shown live.

Afterwards McQuade resumed his career without conspicuous success. Between 1953 and 1959 he acted in films in South America. His final Broadway appearances dated from 1962. McQuade died in New York City on September 21, 1979 aged 67.

FILMOGRAPHY

1948: *The Naked City*.
1973: *Serpico*.

TELEVISION SERIES

1951–1952: *Charlie Wild, Private Detective* as Charlie Wild.

SOURCES

Geoff Tibballs. *TV Detectives*. London: Boxtree, 1992.
Variety. Obituary, October 3, 1979.

PATRICK MCVEY

Born in Fort Wayne, Indiana on March 17, 1910, Patrick McVey graduated from Indiana University in 1931 and later from its law school. In 1938 he joined the Pasadena Playhouse which

Jane Nigh and Patrick McVey in *Big Town*. McVey later costarred in *Manhunt*.

was the start of a successful career. He was later a member of The Actors Studio and The Players. After World War II service he became a successful Broadway actor from 1947 onwards and appeared in such plays as *Detective Story* and *Bus Stop*. His final Broadway appearances were in 1970.

He had leading roles in three successful television series of which two qualified as crime and mystery series. From 1950 to 1954 he played crusading editor Steve Wilson in the newspaper series *Big Town*. This series originated on radio where it ran from 1937 to 1948. There was also a short-lived film series at Paramount in the late forties. In 1950 it moved to television where it became immediately popular. Production started as a live show on the CBS network out of New York where it remained until 1952. Then it moved from New York to Hollywood where it became a filmed series on CBS until 1954. Steve Wilson was the driving force behind "The Illustrated News" a powerful newspaper in a large urban metropolis. One of his main aims was to prevent the spread of organized crime. His star reporter was Lorelei Kilbourne. While McVey remained with the series until 1954 when he was replaced by Mark Stevens, several actresses played Lorelei Kilbourne. McVey's characterization was much more breezy and lighthearted than his successor.

While it was being shown on CBS, the DuMont network were simultaneously broadcasting repeats of the McVey episodes under the title *City Assignment*. His episodes were also later syndicated under another title *Heart of the City*. He virtually repeated his characterization in the syndicated series *Manhunt* as "Chronicle" reporter Ben Andrews, ally of Det. Lt. Finucane (Victor Jory) of the San Diego Police Department. McVey was also a prolific television performer from 1954 onwards in other series including multiples of *Perry Mason*.

McVey, who lived in Manhattan, died at Lenox Hill hospital, New York on July 6, 1973 aged 63 of a heart attack. He was survived by his wife and brother.

Filmography

1941: *They Died with Their Boots On, The Man Who Came to Dinner, Navy Blues*.
1942: *Calling Dr. Gillespie, To the Shores of Tripoli, Pierre of the Plains, The Mummy's Tomb, Snuffy Smith Yard Bird, Moonlight in Havana, The Invisible Agent, Juke Girl, The Talk of the Town, Murder in the Big House*.
1943: *No Time for Love*.
1946: *OSS, No Leave No Love, The Brute Man, Two Guys from Milwaukee, Swell Guy, The Show-Off*.
1947: *Suddenly It's Spring, Dark Passage, Welcome Stranger, Easy Come Easy Go*.
1957: *The Big Caper*.
1958: *Party Girl*.
1959: *North by Northwest*.
1968: *The Detective*.
1971: *Desperate Characters*.
1972: *The Visitors, Top of the Heap*.
1973: *Bang the Drum Slowly*.

Television Series

1950–1954: *Big Town* as Steve Wilson.
1957–1958: *Boots And Saddles—The Story Of The Fifth Cavalry* as Lt. Col. Hayes.
1959–1961: *Manhunt* as Ben Andrews.

Sources

Brooks, Tim. *The Complete Directory to Prime Time TV Stars, 1946–Present*. New York: Ballantine, 1987.
Inman, David. *The TV Encyclopedia*. New York: Perigee, 1991.
Jones, Ken D., Arthur F. McClure, and Alfred E. Twomey. *Character People*. Secaucus, NJ: Citadel, 1979.
Perry, Jeb H. *Screen Gems: A History of Columbia Pictures Television from Cohn to Coke, 1948–1983*. Metuchen, NJ: Scarecrow, 1991.
Truitt, Evelyn Mack. *Who Was Who on Screen*. New York: Bowker, 1984.
Variety. Obituary, July 11, 1973.

Ralph Meeker

It is curious how an actor can give a performance in a movie which is not much appreciated at the time, but as the years roll by becomes much more revered. This happened to Ralph Meeker who in retrospect gave the definitive interpretation of Mike Hammer in *Kiss Me Deadly*. Meeker was a respected stage actor who came to film and television. Although he did occasionally play romantic leads, he was one of the least sympathetic of heroes. In later years he had extreme difficulty controlling his weight. He much preferred the stage and liked to live in New York, commuting to Hollywood for acting assignments. Amongst his leading roles was a television mystery series called *Not For Hire*.

Ralph Meeker was born Ralph Rathgeber Jr. on November 21, 1920 in Minneapolis, Minnesota, the son of Ralph Meeker Rathgeber and Mayme Haavidsen. Some authorities state that his mother's maiden name was Magnhild Senovia Haavig. At the age of three he moved with his family to Chicago. After graduating from Leelanau School for Boys in Glen Arbor, Michigan, he attended Northwestern University in Evanston, Illinois from 1938 to 1942. He had always had a love for the theater, and this University is famous for its drama courses. Jean Hagen and Patricia Neal were two of his classmates. When he starred in the University drama club's stage presentations, it was often with the two girls as leading ladies. He was a very popular addition to any college party for he could play the piano, guitar, accordion, cornet and drums as well as being a song and dance man of no mean ability. He was also a splendid athlete.

When America entered World War II he joined the Navy, but after serving a year he received a medical discharge after a shipboard accident in which he injured his cervix. Back in civilian life, he made his professional debut in 1943 as the bellboy in the national company of *The Doughgirls*, opening at the Selwyn Theater, Chicago. When the production closed, he moved to New York with $35 in his pocket and was forced to work as a soda jerk. His goal was either Broadway or films, but he realized that he would have to serve an apprenticeship in stock. He once figured that he had appeared in no less than seventy plays during this period. Some were for one night only, while the longest run of all was three months. He also went to Italy to play Anthony Marston in a USO production of *Ten Little Indians*.

Back in New York in 1945, he took an assistant stage manager job with *Strange Fruit*, later playing the role of Chuck in the production which marked his Broadway debut. In 1946 he served as both assistant stage manager and understudy for a production of *Cyrano de Bergerac* which starred Jose Ferrer. His next big break was a small but important role as Mannion in the original 1947 production of *Mr. Roberts* for which he received a Theatre World award as a "Promising Personality." Meeker also served as understudy for the star of the show, Henry Fonda, but he never had the chance to take Fonda's place.

When Marlon Brando was about to leave the cast of the Broadway play *A Streetcar Named Desire* in 1949, there was an intense search for an actor to replace him. The director of *Mr. Roberts* introduced Ralph Meeker to *Streetcar's* producer and the part of Stanley Kowalski was filled. Meeker played the top role for three months in New York and then went on tour with the play for another nine months. It was when it was playing at a theater in San Francisco that the producer happened to be talking in New York to Fred Zinneman who was making plans to direct the film *Teresa* which was to be made in Italy and New York. The producer told Zinneman of the excellent young actor who was in the touring company of *A Streetcar Named Desire* and a meeting was arranged with the result that Meeker left for Italy almost immediately to play the part of Sgt. Dobbs in *Teresa* (1951). Dobbs dies early on. He had his first starring role in the Swiss lensed *Four in a Jeep* (1951) and next came *Shadow in the Sky*. He was only half way through the last named film when MGM decided to sign him to a long-term contract. The films in which he appeared for MGM, with the exception of the excellent western *The Naked Spur*, were minor but good. On loanout to Paramount he costarred opposite Betty Hutton in *Somebody Loves Me* (1952) as Benny Fields. This was the only film he appeared in which made use of his considerable musical ability, although his singing was dubbed.

In 1953 he returned to New York for his greatest stage triumph, starring as Hal Carter in the original Broadway production of *Picnic* by William Inge. Meeker and his leading lady Janice Rule were understudied by Paul Newman and Joanne Woodward. For his performance in *Picnic*, Meeker was awarded the New York Critics' Circle Award in 1954. When *Picnic* was filmed in 1955, William Holden and Kim Novak replaced Meeker and Rule. Meeker later stated that he was offered the starring role in the film version, but rejected it because he did not wish to sign a long term contract with Columbia Pictures. Meeker and Rule instead appeared in a minor film *A Woman's Devotion* (1956) in which he played Trevor Stevenson, a disturbed war veteran. This was one of his weakest films. He and Rule were constantly bickering when they appeared on Broadway together, but they got along famously when shooting the movie. They also appeared together in an episode of *Playhouse 90* on television called "Four Women in Black."

In his most famous film *Kiss Me Deadly* (1955) Meeker played ruthless private eye Mike Hammer in a movie which was directed by Robert Aldrich and based on a novel by Mickey Spillane. The film enjoyed only minor success in America and none in Europe. In recent years however it has enjoyed a revival and is currently regarded as the most satisfactory example of Spillane captured on film. Much of the credit must go to Meeker for his characterization. He continued to enjoy good roles in Sam Fuller's western *Run of the Arrow* (1957) as Lt. Driscoll and as Corporal Paris, one of three French soldiers sentenced to the firing squad in *Paths of Glory* (1958) directed by Stanley Kubrick.

Throughout the fifties Meeker starred frequently on television and substituted for Ed Sullivan on several occasions as host of the *Talk of the Town* series. Meeker starred in four half hour productions for *The Alfred Hitchcock Presents* series including the first episode "Revenge" directed by Hitchcock himself. In 1959 Meeker starred for California National Productions as Sgt. Steve Dekker in a television series *Not For Hire*. There were 39 half hour, black and white episodes of this series which was lensed in Hawaii. He played an operative for the Army Criminal Investigations Division and was therefore "not for hire" as a conventional P.I. The series was considered to be quite hard hitting for its time and dealt with some controversial themes. Lizabeth Hush played Sonica Zametoo, his W.A.C. aide and girlfriend, while Ken Drake played his aide, Corporal Zimmerman.

Between 1961 and 1967 Meeker appeared in only one film *Wall of Noise* (1963). The bulk of his time he spent appearing in short-lived plays both on Broadway and in California, but none of them enjoyed his former success. He returned to renewed film activity after 1967 notably in *The Dirty Dozen* (1967) as Captain Stuart Kinder, another film directed by Robert Aldrich. Although he remained busy throughout the seventies on television and film, his movies became increasingly minor or else he only had small roles in the more prestigious ones. For instance he played Captain Moretti, John Wayne's superior officer, in the thriller *Brannigan* (1975), but his only scene was prior to the opening credits. He also appeared in some television movies in which he became increasingly listless, overweight and out of condition.

He was the executive producer as well as star of the film *My Boys are Good Boys* (1976) which was coproduced by his second wife. His final film appearance was in *Without Warning* (1980). His final television appearance was in an episode of *The Eddie Capra Mysteries* in 1978, while his final stage appearance was in *Streamers* at the Westwood Playhouse in Los Angeles and the Cannery Theater in San Francisco both in 1977.

Meeker dropped out of sight after these and it was only revealed much later that he had suffered a series of strokes which had left him in an extremely poorly condition. He was placed in a series of rest homes, but the best care he received was at his last residence at the Motion Picture Country Home and Hospital in Woodland Hills, California. He died there on August 5, 1988 aged 67 after a heart attack complicated by generalized arteriosclerosis and dementia. He was cremated on August 16, 1988 at the Chapel of the Pines Crematory in Los Angeles.

Meeker was long regarded as a confirmed bachelor. He married actress Salome Jens on July 20, 1964, but they divorced in 1966. He then wed Colleen Rose Neary, but that marriage too ended in divorce. His third wife was Mildred Henson who survived him. He was a member of Actors' Equity Association; Screen Actors Guild; American Federation of Television and Radio Artists; and the Rosicrucians.

Ralph Meeker (right), who starred in *Not for Hire*.

It was a director of another generation Quentin Tarantino who particularly appreciated Meeker's abilities and gave him an appropriate epitaph when he said in 1997, "I was thinking about Ralph Meeker.... He fell on hard times, doing bad guy roles in really bad movies. I mean, he was not even the big boss guy, but rather his stupid deputy in *Hi-Riders*, this movie about drag racers. This was Ralph Meeker! Where were the filmmakers of the seventies? If I had been making movies back then, I'd have cast him in a great role. He's dead now and that opportunity has gone forever."

FILMOGRAPHY

1951: *Teresa, Four in a Jeep, Shadow in the Sky.*
1952: *Glory Alley, Somebody Loves Me.*
1953: *Code Two, Jeopardy, The Naked Spur.*
1955: *Big House USA, Kiss Me Deadly, Desert Sands.*
1956: *A Woman's Devotion.*
1957: *Run of the Arrow, The Fuzzy Pink Nightgown.*
1958: *Paths of Glory.*
1961: *Ada, Something Wild.*
1963: *Wall of Noise.*
1967: *The Dirty Dozen, The St. Valentines Day Massacre, Gentle Giant.*
1968: *The Devil's 8, The Detective.*
1969: *Lost Flight* (TV).
1970: *I Walk the Line.*
1971: *The Anderson Tapes, The Reluctant Heroes* (TV), *The Night Stalker* (TV).
1972: *The Happiness Cage* (a.k.a. *The Mind Snatchers*).

1973: *Birds of Prey* (TV), *Police Story* (TV), *You'll Never See Me Again* (TV).
1974: *Cry Panic* (TV), *The Girl on the Late Late Show* (TV), *Night Games* (TV), *The Dead Don't Die* (TV).
1975: *Johnny Firecloud, Brannigan*.
1976: *Love Comes Quietly, The Food of the Gods, My Boys are Good Boys, The Alpha Incident* (a.k.a. *Gift from a Red Planet*).
1977: *Hi-Riders, Winter Kills* (released 1979).
1980: *Without Warning*.

TELEVISION SERIES

1959–1960: *Not for Hire* as Sgt. Steve Dekker.

SOURCES

Cameron, Ian, and Elizabeth Cameron. *The Heavies*. London: Studio Vista, 1967.
Death Certificate.
Fleming, Michael. "Tarantino's Rediscovery Net." *Variety*. September 1, 1997.
Henreid, Paul. *Ladies Man*. New York: St. Martin's, 1984.
Herbert, Ian. *Who's Who in the Theatre*. 16th ed. London: Pitman, 1977.
Picture Show. "Life Story." February 14, 1953.
Picture Show Annual. London: Amalgamated, 1954.
Skinner, John Walter. *Who's Who on the Screen*. Worthing, England: Madeleine, 1983.
Variety. Obituary, August 1988.
Ward, Jack. *Television Guest Stars*. Jefferson, NC: McFarland, 1993.

ADOLPHE MENJOU

Adolphe Menjou was one of the few actors whose career began in the silent days, but who remained active into the television era. His trademark was his moustache which was instrumental in establishing him as a sophisticated scoundrel and man-about-town. During the fifties he sometimes appeared without it. His taste in clothes was impeccable and he frequently received the accolade of the best dressed star in movies. After sound took over Hollywood, he floundered for a while. Later he re-established himself as a star character actor whose portrayals were sometimes of impoverished men who could therefore not afford a decent wardrobe. He fell from favor once again because of his outspoken political views which were somewhere to the right of Attila the Hun. Television came to his rescue, although his work in that medium was amongst his least distinguished. One illusion which many of his admirers were under was that he was French, but Menjou was in fact an American. He suffered from chronic ulcers all his adult life.

Adolph Jean Menjou was born in Pittsburgh, Pennsylvania on February 18, 1890. In adulthood he added an extra "e" to his Christian name. He was the son of Jean Adolph Menjou, a French born restaurateur and hotelier, who died in 1917. His father used the Christian name Albert most of his life. His mother was Nora Joyce, an Irish born hotel worker. His parents were married in 1889. He had one brother Henry Menjou (1892–1956). His father's businesses caused them to move around, so he was mainly raised in Cleveland, Ohio. He was educated at St. Joseph's Seminary, Rockwell Public School and East High School, all of them in Cleveland. Even as a child he played bits on stage in Cleveland, but when his father found out he was incensed and sent him to Culver Military Academy in Indiana to learn discipline.

He went to Cornell University where he embarked on a course of study in mechanical engineering at which he was a hopeless failure, so he switched to liberal arts, but he did not graduate. He entertained in college as part of the Carroll Theatrical Group. In 1912 he decided he wanted to be an actor so he went to New York. After three months he ran out of funds and briefly became a farm hand and a salesman. Then his father moved to New York to open a restaurant so Menjou became his assistant. One of the patrons of the restaurant was a scene painter at the old Vitagraph studios who gave him some advice. This enabled him to become a bit player at Vitagraph during the day while helping at the restaurant in the evenings. He made his debut as a circus ringmaster in *The Man Behind the Door* (1915). Over the next couple of years he played bits and did a third rate vaudeville act. Gradually the parts became bigger. *The Moth* (1917) was his final film before World War I intervened.

He enlisted in 1917. Instead of being sent overseas, he was commissioned a lieutenant and assigned to direct an army show in New York. This turned out to be such a big success that he was promoted to captain. Subsequently as part of the ambulance corps, he was sent overseas to Italy in 1918 and later to France. He returned to the States and was demobilized in 1919. He decided to quit acting so he obtained a job in a steamship company, but it went bust. He then became a production manager with an entrepreneur who made short films, but quit in disgust. At length he became a motion picture unit manager and production supervisor of a film called *The Silent Barrier* (1920). He found the job so stressful that he decided to go to Hollywood and become an actor again.

In Hollywood he did the rounds of the studios without success. Through a friend comedian Roscoe "Fatty" Arbuckle, he met Mabel Normand who liked him sufficiently to have him cast in two of her films. This gave his career a boost and he played a variety of interesting parts thereafter. He became a household name when he costarred with Edna Purviance under the direction of Charles Chaplin in *A Woman of Paris* (1923). The movie was notable as the only serious drama directed by Chaplin. Chaplin himself did not appear in the film except a cameo as a railway baggageman. The reviews of the film and Menjou's personal notices were glowing. He played Pierre Ravel and this film typed him as a sophisticated man-about-town. As a result of this he spent the next few years in quality films with an increasing salary.

He signed a contract with Paramount in 1924 for $1,000 a week. At one point he went on strike for fewer films with better scripts and star billing. Eventually he returned to make peace at his home lot. Paramount did not meet his demands, but raised his salary to $3,000 a week. *The Grand Duchess and the Waiter* (1926) placed him amongst the top stars of the era and was the first film in which he was top billed. The final scene was shot in color. Its success sent his salary rocketing and won him stardom. Another source of income were commercial endorsements primarily for clothes.

When sound became the rage of Hollywood in 1928, he was in the last year of his contract earning $7,500 a week. He was however regarded as a silent star who could not talk. He lobbied studio brass for a voice test which proved beyond question that his speaking voice matched his appearance. He shot a talkie *Fashions in Love* (1929) which was a qualified success and his personal

Ginger Rogers and Adolphe Menjou in *Roxie Hart*. Menjou hosted *Target*.

notices were excellent. In spite of this when his Paramount contract expired in May 1929, the studio did not renew it. With the stock market buoyant, he decided to take a vacation in France. On the ship across he met two producers who signed him to a lucrative two picture deal to make simultaneous French/English versions of the same film in France.

While in France in 1929, he was warned about the volatile state of the stock exchange. He insisted on his brother, who was then his business manager, selling all his holdings. He had to undergo removal of his appendix at an American hospital in France. As he was recovering in October 1929, the stock market crashed, but he was sitting pretty. He shot the first film *My Adolescent Father* and its French version *Mon Gosse de Pere* in six grueling weeks. The finances of the film company were so shaky that he settled the contract and returned to Hollywood which was in a slump.

He was financially well afloat, but regarded as finished in the film business. He was reduced to shooting foreign language versions of American films being shot in Hollywood. Tired of this he went to MGM where he agreed to drop his salary by half and accept costarring billing in exchange for a contract. In spite of this the MGM pact did nothing for him. It was his old studio Paramount which borrowed him for the hit *Morocco* (1930) in which he was billed below stars Gary Cooper and Marlene Dietrich.

Fortune smiled on him once again when he went to buy some cigarettes in the Brown Derby restaurant. There he had an accidental encounter with director Howard Hawks who told him that director Lewis Milestone was looking all over town for him. Louis Wolheim who had been assigned an important role in *The Front Page* (1931) had been taken seriously ill and subsequently died. Milestone wanted Menjou to replace him. The part was that of the tough, aggressive, motor mouth newspaper editor, Walter Burns. MGM loaned him to United Artists who released the film. The film was a smash hit, won him great reviews and garnered him his only Oscar nomination as Best Actor. He enjoyed a highly successful decade notably costarring with Shirley Temple in *Little Miss Marker* (1934) and with Deanna Durbin in *100 Men and a Girl* (1937).

Throughout the remainder of his career he was a freelance, but Fox used him a great many times. Many of the parts were especially tailored for his talents. One film *Sing Baby Sing* (1936) was based on an episode in the life of John Barrymore. As a result he inherited several roles intended for Barrymore which he was too drunk to play. When Barrymore heard that Menjou was about to play the title role in *The Great Profile* (1940), a film loosely based on his life, he objected. That was Barrymore's nickname and he had no intention of letting anyone else play the role. So he sobered up sufficiently and played the part himself. Since Fox did not want to be involved in litigation, they chose to use Barrymore. Menjou had however already been signed for the film. He was paid his full salary for not appearing in it.

During World War II he made broadcasts for the Office of War Information in French, Italian, Spanish, German and Russian. In 1943 he did a USO tour of army bases in England, North Africa and Sicily for six months. Menjou was a Republican. Jean Pierre Aumont recalled, "I had been making *Heartbeat* (1946) with Ginger Rogers and Adolphe Menjou. Menjou had assumed a one man battle against Communism long before Senator Joseph McCarthy. At a time when we had hardly won the battle against Fascism, Menjou—also an Adolphe—was drawing up lists of suspects while putting the finishing touches to his make-up!" Menjou testified in the sensational trials of 1947 before H.U.A.C. (House UnAmerican Activities Committee). He feared that a Communist take-over of the country was imminent. He declared that he was moving to Texas because the Texans will shoot all Communists on sight. In the odium that followed, Menjou became something of a pariah. He reckoned that his stand cost him two dozen film roles in Hollywood. The dearth of parts may also have had something to do with advancing age. Clark Gable, whose political opinions were probably not too far apart from Menjou's, was one of his greatest friends in Hollywood. It is probably not a coincidence that Menjou had featured roles in three of Gable's post war MGM films. Menjou's memoirs *It Took Nine Tailors* were published in 1948, but mercifully steered clear of political dogma.

Menjou served as host, narrator and occasional star of two syndicated television series both of which were made by ZIV. *My Favorite Story* started out as a radio anthology series from 1946 onwards hosted by Ronald Colman. Celebrities introduced their favorite yarns mainly from classical literature. Colman passed on the television version. Instead ZIV hired Menjou who at the time was hardly working. Acting as host in this television series between 1952 and 1953 did his career the world of good. He was magically transformed from no good snitch to goody twoshoes within a remarkably short period of time.

Target, which started in March 1958, was a suspense series in which ordinary individuals found themselves the target of violent malevolent forces over which they had no control. The emphasis in this anthology series was definitely on crime and mystery. There were 39 half hour, black and white episodes. Scuttlebutt in the industry doomed this series to extinction almost before it had started. Stories circulated that no matter how successful the series was, no more than 39 episodes would ever be filmed. This was a complete fabrication, but before ZIV could issue a denial, sponsors had abandoned the series as if it were jinxed. Menjou had acquired enemies in the industry who knew the pressure points. It is likely that Menjou himself was the biggest target of all! Aside from these two television series, he was not a particularly frequent television performer.

In spite of this he did land some good roles in Hollywood films even in the fifties. He played a police lieutenant in the exciting thriller *The Sniper* (1952). This was particularly intriguing because the director was Edward Dmytryk who had served time in prison as one of the notorious Hollywood Ten for refusing to name names before H.U.A.C. Producer Stanley Kramer chose

Menjou because although he was past his prime, he was still an excellent actor. Menjou had built his reputation on being a sartorially splendid dresser, but in this film he was a slovenly, sloppily dressed man. The irony appealed to Kramer. He did however call both star and director together before shooting to admonish them about being professional. Filming proceeded harmoniously and if Menjou and Dmytryk discussed politics at all, it has not been recorded. The film received excellent notices and was highly regarded by the few people that saw it, but lack of sufficient promotion and publicity doomed it to failure.

Menjou married firstly Katherine Tinsley, an actress, in New York in April 1920, but they divorced in Los Angeles on October 20, 1927 on the grounds of his desertion. He wed secondly actress Kathryn Carver (1899–1947), a leading lady in two of his silent films, in Paris on May 16, 1928, but they divorced in Los Angeles on August 14, 1933. Some sources indicate that they adopted a son named Harold. Menjou married thirdly stylish actress Verree Teasdale (1903–1987). They met at the home of actor Frank Morgan and married in Los Angeles on August 25, 1934. Their union was one of Hollywood's happiest and they adopted a son Peter Adolphe in 1937.

Adolphe Menjou died in Beverly Hills on October 29, 1963 of chronic hepatitis aged 73, survived by his widow and son. He is buried at Hollywood Memorial Park Cemetery. His widow is buried alongside him.

Filmography

1915: *The Man Behind the Door.*
1916: *A Parisian Romance, The Habit of Happiness, Manhattan Madness, Nearly a King, The Crucial Test, The Devil at His Elbow, The Blue Envelope Mystery, The Reward of Patience, The Scarlet Runner* (serial).
1917: *The Amazons, The Valentine Girl, The Moth.*
1920: *What Happened to Rosa?, Head Over Heels* (released 1922).
1921: *The Sheik, The Three Musketeers, Through the Back Door, The Faith Healer, Courage, Queenie.*
1922: *The Fast Mail, Clarence, Is Matrimony a Failure?, Singed Wings, The Eternal Flame, Pink Gods, Arabian Love.*
1923: *A Woman of Paris, The World's Applause, The Spanish Dancer, Bella Donna, Rupert of Hentzau.*
1924: *The Fast Set, Broadway After Dark, For Sale, The Marriage Cheat, Shadows of Paris, Broken Barriers, Forbidden Paradise, The Marriage Circle, Open All Night, Sinners in Silk.*
1925: *Are Parents People?, A Kiss in the Dark, The King on Main Street, Lost—a Wife, The Swan.*
1926: *A Social Celebrity, The Grand Duchess and the Waiter, Fascinating Youth, The Sorrows of Satan, The Ace of Cads.*
1927: *Service for Ladies, A Gentleman of Paris, Blonde or Brunette, Serenade, Evening Clothes.*
1928: *His Tiger Lady, His Private Life, A Night of Mystery.*
1929: *Bachelor Girl, Marquis Preferred, Fashions in Love.*
1930: *Mon gosse de pere, My Adolescent Father, Soyons Gais, Wir shalten um auf Hollywood!, L'enigmatique Monsieur Parkes, The Parisian, New Moon, Morocco.*
1931: *The Front Page, Men Call It Love, Friends and Lovers, The Great Lover, The Easiest Way.*
1932: *Two White Arms* (a.k.a. *Wives Beware*), *Diamond Cut Diamond* (a.k.a. *Blame the Woman*), *Prestige, Bachelor's Affairs, A Farewell to Arms, Forbidden, Night Club Lady.*
1933: *Worst Woman in Paris?, The Circus Queen Murder, Morning Glory, Convention City.*
1934: *The Trumpet Blows, Journal of a Crime, Little Miss Marker, The Mighty Barnum, The Human Side, The Great Flirtation, Easy to Love.*
1935: *Goldiggers of 1935, Broadway Gondolier.*
1936: *Sing Baby Sing, Wives Never Know, The Milky Way, One in a Million.*
1937: *Café Metropole, A Star is Born, Stage Door, 100 Men and a Girl.*
1938: *Thanks for Everything, The Goldwyn Follies, A Letter of Introduction.*
1939: *That's Right—You're Wrong, King of the Turf, Golden Boy, The Housekeeper's Daughter.*
1940: *A Bill of Divorcement, Turnabout, Road Show.*
1941: *Father Takes a Wife.*
1942: *Roxie Hart, Syncopation, You Were Never Lovelier.*
1943: *Sweet Rosie O'Grady, Hi Diddle Diddle.*
1944: *Step Lively.*
1945: *Man Alive.*
1946: *Heartbeat, The Bachelor's Daughters.*
1947: *I'll Be Yours, The Hucksters, Mr. District Attorney.*
1948: *State of the Union.*
1949: *My Dream is Yours, Dancing in the Dark.*
1950: *To Please a Lady.*
1951: *The Tall Target, Across the Wide Missouri.*
1952: *The Sniper.*

1953: *Man on a Tightrope.*
1954: *Timberjack.*
1956: *Bundle of Joy, The Ambassador's Daughter, I Married a Woman.*
1957: *The Fuzzy Pink Nightgown, Paths of Glory.*
1960: *Pollyanna.*

TELEVISION SERIES

1952–1953: *Favorite Story* Host and narrator.
1958: *Target* Host and narrator.

SOURCES

Bermingham, Cedric Osmond. *Stars of the Screen.* 2nd and 3rd eds. London: Herbert Joseph, 1932 and 1933.
Donnelly, Paul. *Fade to Black.* London: Omnibus, 2000.
Erickson, Hal. *Syndicated Television: The First Forty Years, 1947–1987.* Jefferson, NC: McFarland, 1989.
Inman, David. *The TV Encyclopedia.* New York: Perigee, 1991.
Jones, Ken D., Arthur F. McClure, and Alfred E. Twomey. *Character People.* Secaucus, NJ: Citadel, 1979.
Kramer, Stanley. *A Mad, Mad, Mad, Mad World.* London: Aurum, 1997.
McClelland, Doug. *Forties Film Talk.* Jefferson, NC: McFarland, 1992.
Menjou, Adolphe. *It Took Nine Tailors.* London: Sampson Low, 1950.
The Picturegoer's Who's Who and Encyclopedia. London: Odhams, 1933.
Picture Show Annual. London: Amalgamated, 1933.
Quinlan, David. *Film Stars.* 5th ed. London: Batsford, 2000.
Ross, J.S. *Stars of the Screen.* 4th ed. London: Herbert Joseph, 1934.
Slide, Anthony. *Silent Portraits.* New York: Vestal, 1989.
Stuart, Ray. *Immortals of the Screen.* Los Angeles: Sherbourne, 1965.
Winchester, Clarence. *Screen Encyclopedia.* London: Winchester, 1948.
_____. *The World Film Encyclopedia.* London: Amalgamated, 1933.

GARY MERRILL

The chief interest in Gary Merrill lies less in his acting than in the fact that he was the fourth husband of the legendary Bette Davis. Despite the fact that they had a volatile relationship, of all her husbands, Merrill was the only one whose photograph still hung on her wall by the eighties. His off-screen personality was described as eccentric. For a man who had a reputation in real life for being a wild card, his acting tended to be humorless and his characters grimly determined. Craggy faced and bushy browed, he was not an inspired actor, but he was never less than competent. His best asset was a deep, resonant voice which netted him several jobs particularly on radio and doing voiceovers.

Gary Franklin Merrill was born in Hartford, CT on August 2, 1915, the son of Benjamin Gary Merrill and Hazel May Andrews. He had a twin sister who died at birth. He had one younger brother named Jerry who was born in 1926. His father was employed as a clerk by the Royal Typewriter Company and later worked for the AETNA Life Insurance Company. His mother was a former schoolteacher. His parents divorced in 1940. He had a fairly comfortable middle class upbringing. He grew up in Connecticut, but his summers were spent in Maine which gave him a lifelong love of that place.

He was educated at Loomis School, one of the top prep schools in Maine where he excelled in football, cross country running and hockey. The school encouraged a well rounded education and outside activities so he joined the Dramatic Club of which he eventually became President. He did not ever receive a graduation certificate from Loomis. Nevertheless he passed the entrance exam for Bowdoin College, Maine which he attended between 1933 and 1934. His intention was to become a professional actor, but he attended college to please his parents. He did not excel there and left to pursue his ambition.

He joined the Guy Hedlund Players, a group of radio actors in Hartford. His father however insisted that he give college another try, so he attended Trinity College at Hartford from 1934 to 1935 where he spent more time in escapades involving female students than actively studying. So he dropped out of college because of his poor grades. He was screen tested by Paramount in New York. Although he failed the test through lack of experience, they were not negative about his ability. Instead he joined the Hilda Spong School of Acting and Dramatic Arts in New York. At the end of the first year he did summer stock in New Jersey. A couple of friends from the drama school were going to Hollywood so he accompanied them. The idea was for him to obtain an acting job, but none materialized so disheartened he returned to New York.

After some months of unemployment he landed a job as the male lead in a play *Squaring the Circle* at Brighton Beach, New York in October 1936. Afterwards he appeared as an extra in a Jewish play *The Eternal Road* which lasted for 128 performances at the Manhattan Center from December 1936 onwards at a salary of $15 a week. From 1937 to 1938 he appeared briefly in New York and later in a road company of *Brother Rat* for nine months at a starting salary of $75 a week. When this finished he had saved enough money to tide him over, but aside from some acting classes with Berno Schneider everything was quiet.

He landed a job doing summer stock in Deer Lake, PA in 1940. He then returned to New York where he played a lawyer in a successful play *See My Lawyer* in 1941 on Broadway. He married actress Barbara Leeds at the Little Church Around the Corner in New York in 1942. In the spring of 1942 he was drafted into the US Army Air Force. Stationed at Camp Upton on Long Island as a private, he became part of a group that improvised sketches. Ezra Stone, a well known actor, arrived and established a legitimate theater company. From this evolved a touring company of *Brother Rat* which played at various army bases. Merrill, who was promoted to corporal, and his wife were part of the cast.

Irving Berlin created a show about World War II called *This Is the Army* which opened in New York on July 4, 1942 with Merrill in the cast. He later toured with this show. Eventually they wound up in Hollywood where Warner Bros. decided to make a film of it which marked his screen debut in 1943. Towards the end of shooting Merrill heard of another show called *Winged Victory* by Moss Hart which was designed as a tribute to the Air Force. Merrill's wife went to audition, but while there made an impassioned plea to Hart to cast her husband in the show rather than have him go overseas. Hart still had a few small roles to cast so he gave Merrill one of them for which Merrill felt grateful and relieved. He stayed with the show in New York, toured with it and again trekked to Hollywood to appear in the film version in 1944. Through friends he found a post with a radio unit in New York which broadcast radio dramas for the army. He was honorably discharged from the Army Airforce in 1945 as a sergeant. While in the services

Gary Merrill, who starred in *The Mask* and *Justice*.

he and his wife were apart much of the time unless they were acting in a show together. He had a trial separation from her in 1945, but they later patched their marriage up. During the interim he had a wild fling with actress Mercedes McCambridge.

They resided in a small apartment in New York for a while where he earned a decent living as a radio actor before landing a role as Paul Verrall in the play *Born Yesterday* by Garson Kanin which he played in tryouts at Boston and Philadelphia and then at the Lyceum, New York from 1946 onwards. Initially Billie Dawn was played by Jean Arthur, but she clashed with Kanin and was replaced by Judy Holliday in a star making performance. Merrill's notices were splendid. After a few months in the play he wanted to head for Hollywood, but the success of the play prevented this for a while. He played in radio soap operas during the day and in the play at night. Altogether he appeared in the play for a year and a half before quitting.

As a freelance he was hired by 20th Century–Fox to play Richard Widmark's commanding officer in a movie *Slattery's Hurricane* (1948), a thriller lensed in Florida. He became a good friend of Widmark's through this film. He landed a seven year contract with Fox starting out at $750 a week. Between shooting the film and signing the contract, he appeared in another play

At War With the Army initially in Boston and then at the Booth Theatre, New York in 1948 for two weeks. Next he went to Hollywood where he was initially hot and went from one film to another. He was frequently cast as military men of which the best known was Colonel Davenport in the classic *12 O' Clock High* (1949).

Originally the role of the bitchy fading actress, Margo Channing, in *All About Eve* (1950) was to have been played by Claudette Colbert, but when she broke her back, Bette Davis inherited her role. Joseph L. Mankiewicz who wrote and directed the film was the one who pushed for Merrill to be cast as Bill Sampson. Despite the differences in temperament and background of the cast, it was an extremely happy shoot. They were a harmonious combination possibly because they were all close to the peak of their careers and they probably knew that the script was about as good as they would appear in. In the course of shooting this film Merrill became infatuated with Davis. At the time Merrill was living with his wife in a modest apartment off Laurel Canyon in Malibu. After his involvement with Davis, their marriage ended in divorce in Juarez, Mexico on the morning of July 28, 1950. He paid Barbara Leeds $1,000 a month in alimony for years. In the same place that afternoon he married Bette Davis (1908–1989). He adopted Barbara, her daughter by a previous husband. In 1950 they adopted a baby girl named Margot and in February 1952 a baby boy named Michael. Their son eventually became a successful Massachusetts lawyer and had two sons. Margot was later found to be mentally retarded and had to be placed in a special school permanently. After the marriage Merrill and Davis initially lived in a large beach house in Malibu, but later they relocated to an older wooden house in the heart of Hollywood.

They then journeyed to England where they shot a dreadful British film *Another Man's Poison* (1951). In between whiles he enjoyed socializing with the leading British thespians of the day. Back in Hollywood he starred in *Phone Call From a Stranger* (1952) in which he played a lawyer who is the only survivor of a plane crash. He goes round visiting the various relatives of those who perished, giving comfort to them. Bette Davis talked the producers into letting her do a cameo in the film. She replaced a far lesser actress who was to be paid $1,500. The fee paid to Davis was $35,000.

Davis did a revue in New York called *Two's Company* in 1953 which earned bad reviews, but did great business. Unfortunately she became ill with a debilitating malady of the jaw which necessitated surgery. This illness closed the show. She and Merrill retreated to Maine to give her a chance to recuperate where they bought a house called "Witch Way." Not long after the move to Maine, Fox terminated his contract which he was not too upset about. He shot "B" pictures like *The Black Dakotas* (1954) in ten days for $15,000. He also turned to television making his television debut in the "Family Jewels" episode of the anthology series *Danger* in 1953.

He became the star of two crime and mystery series. The first of these was *The Mask*. It depicted the cases of two brothers who were legal partners in the firm of Guilfoyle and Guilfoyle. Walter was played by Gary Merrill, while Peter was played by William Prince. The series was shown live and later on kinescope and was the first hour length mystery series to feature regular characters. This made it expensive to produce and as it was unable to find a sponsor, it was axed after four months. An ABC production of 15 black and white episodes, it was originally aired on the ABC network between January 10, 1954 and May 16, 1954. An indication of the scant regard which Merrill had for this series is that he fails to mention it in his memoirs.

The second series which was called *Justice* dramatized early case files of the National Legal Aid Society. These were cases of people involved in either civil or criminal proceedings who could not afford an attorney. Initially it was an anthology series, but gradually two regular Legal Aid attorneys began to appear. Jason Tyler was played by Merrill, while Richard Adam was played by Dane Clark and later by William Prince. This highly regarded live, half hour, black and white series of 88 episodes was shown on NBC between April 8, 1954 and March 25, 1956. It was a David Susskind production. Merrill featured in episodes between September 1954 and June 1955. He flew to New York on Wednesday for rehearsals and then did the show live on a Thursday evening. He was back in Maine by midnight of the same day. Thus he actively worked for two days a week and had five days off.

Many assumed that they were millionaires, but this was far from the truth. Although they had a reasonable income, they had an extravagant lifestyle and no fiscal sense. Eventually he found a business manager who told them that they were virtually broke and had better head back to Hollywood to earn some money. They returned to

California in 1957 where they endured a trial separation. He went to Maine, but after Davis was injured in a fall down some cellar steps, they reconciled. They moved into a large house in the Beverly Hills. Merrill, who had a liking for alcohol, upset the movers and shakers of the industry at Hollywood parties with his plain speaking and his career suffered setbacks as a result. He was conspicuously absent from films for a while, but was a frequent guest star on many of the anthology series of the period. To compound matters the IRS hounded him for $50,000 worth of back taxes and threatened to seize his one asset, the house in Maine. He borrowed money from a friend to cover the payment, but thereafter placed his finances in good hands. The marriage fell apart in 1959 when they signed for a grueling tour of one and two night stands in a production called *The World of Carl Sandburg*. This was a three hander consisting of Davis and Merrill, with the backing of a guitarist, reading and responding to the works of the poet Carl Sandburg. They toured 67 cities in 17 weeks. It garnered excellent notices and was Merrill's personal favorite of his own work. By the time it ended in San Francisco he was drinking heavily and lit into Davis the following day at a party. She fled to Los Angeles, but when he followed he was unable to locate her. She divorced him in Maine on July 6, 1960 on the grounds of his cruel and abusive treatment. She also sold "Witch Way."

Smarting from his wounds, Merrill deliberately went to Spain to shoot a film. He later had an intimate relationship with sex symbol Rita Hayworth whom he met when he drove her children home one day from a mutual friend's house. They traveled a lot together and were very companionable until they eventually split up because she did not want to live in Maine. He and Hayworth appeared in a disastrous play together *Step on a Crack* in 1961. He appeared in another television series, *The Reporter*, as a city editor which came and went in three months on CBS in 1964. He was living alone in a small apartment in New York in a state of depression. He was boozing and his life had reached its lowest ebb. He found a focus in politics. In the spring of 1965 he took part in a civil rights march at Selma, Alabama which involved Martin Luther King. In 1967 he did a USO tour of Vietnam, in the company of actress Susan Oliver, to boost the morale of American servicemen. In 1970 he made another USO tour with Mercedes McCambridge visiting GI bases in Europe. Although he had been a lifelong Democrat, he made an unsuccessful bid for the Republican nomination of the Maine legislature in 1968. Although heavily defeated, he polled quite a large number of votes mainly on the strength of his personality. This virtually ended his serious attempts to enter the political arena, but during the sixties and seventies he spent a lot of time in Washington as a spectator at the Senate and House of Representatives. Even as late as 1986 when he became concerned about American policy in Central America, he flew to Nicaragua to find out the truth for himself.

He tried business with Gary Merrill Import Motors which was a foreign car franchise, but the lack of availability of spare parts caused it to close within three years and he lost money in the venture. More successfully he invested in a travel agency which gave him a small annual return. He obtained a real estate license at one point. His final television series was *Young Dr. Kildare* which was a doomed attempt to revive the original popular television and film character. He played Kildare's mentor Dr. Leonard Gillespie in 24 episodes of this syndicated series which was marred by poor production values. He played in summer stock. His final stage appearance was in a revival of the play *Mornings at Seven* which opened at the Lyceum Theater on Broadway in 1980 and was a hit. He played in it for eighteen months. He became a commercial spokesperson on television which only occupied him for short periods, but was very lucrative.

In 1985 he read a book called *My Mother's Keeper* by Bette Davis' daughter, Barbara under her married name of B.D. Hyman. This depicted her mother as a drunk and child abuser. Since he considered the book grossly inaccurate, he placed ads in the New York Times and elsewhere denouncing it. He also demonstrated against it with a placard outside a Falmouth, Maine bookstore which sold the book. His own memoirs were published in 1988. He had returned to Maine to live permanently. His final home was an abandoned nineteenth century cast iron lighthouse at Port Elizabeth which he had bought and renovated. It boasted a glassed-in bedroom at the top with a 360 degree view of the Atlantic.

Merrill died at Falmouth, Maine on March 6, 1990 aged 74 of lung cancer. He was survived by his adopted son, two grandsons and his adopted daughter. He is buried at Pine Grove Cemetery, Falmouth Foreside, Cumberland County, Maine.

Filmography

1943: *This is the Army.*
1944: *Winged Victory.*
1948: *The Quiet One* (narrator only).
1949: *Slattery's Hurricane, Twelve O' Clock High.*
1950: *Mother Didn't Tell Me, Where the Sidewalk Ends, All About Eve.*
1951: *The Frogmen, Decision Before Dawn, Another Man's Poison.*
1952: *The Girl in White, Night Without Sleep, Phone Call From a Stranger.*
1953: *A Blueprint for Murder.*
1954: *Witness to Murder, The Human Jungle, The Black Dakotas.*
1956: *Navy Wife, Bermuda Affair.*
1958: *Crash Landing, The Missouri Traveler.*
1959: *The Wonderful Country, The Savage Eye.*
1960: *The Great Impostor.*
1961: *Mysterious Island, The Pleasure of His Company.*
1962: *A Girl Named Tamiko, Hong Kong Farewell.*
1964: *The Woman Who Wouldn't Die* (a.k.a. *Catacombs*).
1965: *Run Psycho Run.*
1966: *Around the World Under the Sea, Ride Beyond Vengeance, Cast a Giant Shadow, The Dangerous Days of Kiowa Jones* (TV), *Destination Inner Space.*
1967: *Hondo and the Apaches* (TV), *The Power, Clambake, The Incident, New York chiama Superdrago, The Last Challenge.*
1969: *Loving Badly* (a.k.a. *The Wrong Kind of Love, Amarsi male*), *Then Came Bronson* (TV).
1971: *Earth II* (TV).
1974: *Huckleberry Finn.*
1977: *Thieves.*
1979: *The Seekers* (TV).

Television Series

1954: *The Mask* as Walter Guilfoyle.
1954–1955: *Justice* as Jason Tyler.
1960–1961: *Winston Churchill—The Valiant Years* Narrator.
1964: *The Reporter* as Lee Sheldon.
1972: *Young Dr. Kildare* as Dr. Leonard Gillespie.

Sources

The Annual Obituary, 1990. Chicago: St. James, 1991.
The Daily Telegraph. Obituary, March 7, 1990.
The Echo. Obituary, March 7, 1990.
Houseman, Victoria. *Made in Heaven: Unscrambling the Marriages and Children of Hollywood Stars.* Chicago: Bonus, 1991.
Inman, David. *The TV Encyclopedia.* New York: Perigee, 1991.
Lance, Stephen. *Written Out of Television.* Lanham, MD: Madison, 1996.
Merrill, Gary. *Bette, Rita and the Rest of My Life.* New York: Berkley, 1990.
Picture Show Annual. London: Amalgamated, 1952.
Quinlan, David. *Film Stars.* 5th ed. London: Batsford, 2000.
Tibballs, Geoff. *TV Detectives.* London: Boxtree, 1993.
Variety. Obituary, March 1990.
Ward, Jack. *Television Guest Stars.* Jefferson, NC: McFarland, 1993.

Ray Milland

Ray Milland was the urbane, charming leading man of the thirties who shocked his fans and the Hollywood community on two occasions. The first time was when he abandoned his familiar on screen persona to play an alcoholic in *The Lost Weekend*. His performance was so realistic that the studio was forced to issue a statement denying Milland was an alcoholic in real life. The second time was when he discarded his toupee in *Love Story* and so started another successful career as a character actor.

Milland admitted that he had virtually no experience of acting when he started and learned on the job from old pro actors like Sir Guy Standing and sympathetic directors like Frank Lloyd and Sam Wood. It was however a baptism of fire. As he expressed it, "In one film I spent two whole days trying to walk naturally through a door." Much later character actor Raymond Huntley who worked with him on *So Evil My Love* expressed it, "He was technically superb, although as an actor I would say he was quite limited."

Milland was a competitive type. His greatest rival was Cary Grant and Milland was not slow to make his dislike known. Which of them came out on top is open to debate. Cary Grant retained his debonair personality and lithe physique much longer. He continued to star in big budget films. Milland's overall film career was longer and he won a Best Actor Oscar, an accolade which was denied to Grant. When Milland's career as an actor started to decline, he extended his career not only by becoming a director, but also by starring in two radically different television series.

Ray Milland was born Reginald Alfred John Truscott-Jones in Neath, Glamorganshire, Wales on January 3, 1907, the son of Alfred Jones and Elizabeth Truscott-Jones. He was one of five children. He had a brother who drowned at the age of three. The other children were all girls. His father was an engineer, while his mother was the daughter of a steamship company owner. His parents divorced when he was a child. His mother remarried to a Welsh steel mill supervisor named Mullane who adopted Reginald.

His summers were mainly spent at an aunt's horse breeding farm in Wales where he became a proficient horseman, a skill which stood him in good stead when it came to an acting career. One summer he was employed as a cabin boy on a tramp steamer which visited some exotic places. He was educated at Radyr school at Taff Vale, Wales and undertook secretarial studies for a year at King's College, Cardiff. He sat and passed the entrance exam for the University of Wales and was there for a year before dropping out. He obtained a job as a clerk in the offices of a steel mill where he was employed for a year before becoming bored.

On a visit to his father, he decided to go to London at the age of eighteen. He joined the Household Cavalry, a very prestigious regiment, whose main responsibility was to guard the Royal Family. He passed the tests, acquired a commission as a lieutenant and became a crack shot. Simultaneously he enjoyed the London social life to the full. While at a party he met Estelle Brody, an American actress in British films, who asked him if he had ever considered becoming an actor.

On his twenty first birthday, he received a check for £500 from his aunt which he used to buy himself out of the Household Cavalry. When he was free, he called Estelle Brody who invited him to Elstree Studios. While there she introduced him to a casting director and suggested him for crowd work. The first film in which he appeared was *The Plaything* (1929), although it was not the first to be released. Next rather appropriately he played a sharpshooter in *The Informer* (1929). When the original leading man Cyril McLaglen broke a leg, he replaced him in *The Flying Scotsman* (1929) which was being filmed on a neighboring soundstage. This was a part talkie with sound effects and is the best remembered of his early films. It was also the first time that he received billing under the name of Raymond Milland. His stage surname he derived from Mill Land on his aunt's farm where he swam as a child. His Christian name was chosen by publicity people on the film. He followed this up with *The Lady From the Sea* (1929) in which he played the son of a fisherman.

He was seen at a dance studio by Andre Charlot of *Charlot's Revue* and given a lead in his new show. He went out to celebrate with friends to a hotel where he was spotted by MGM Vice President Robert Rubin who had seen him in *The Flying Scotsman*. Rubin suggested he should go to Hollywood where he might make the grade as a light leading man. Since he had not signed a contract for the revue, MGM were able to extricate him from the commitment.

He signed a nine month contract with MGM for $175 a week and received a steamer ticket for New York. From there he continued to California where he had unbilled bit parts in two MGM films, the first of which was *Way of a Sailor* (1930). At the studio's suggestion he adopted a shorter screen Christian name of Ray for *The Bachelor Father* (1930) which was the first American film in which he received billing. He was also loaned to Fox and Warners. His biggest role was in *Payment Deferred* (1932) in which he costarred with Charles Laughton and Maureen O'Sullivan. By coincidence the same three leads were reunited in *The Big Clock* (1948) which was one of his best forties films.

He moved in some decent social circles where he was usually in demand as a bridge and tennis partner. At one such event in the Beverly Hills he met Malvina Muriel Webber known as "Mal," a nineteen year old student teacher, whom he married at the Riverside Mission Inn on September 30, 1932. MGM had done little to advance his career so he decided to return to England. MGM obligingly paid his fare. To gain some stage experience he landed the juvenile lead in a touring version of a West End success called *The Woman in Room 13*, but was fired after five weeks for general incompetence. Some accounts of his life state that he briefly became a steeple chaser until a nasty spill from a horse put paid to that. Milland himself denied this. He did ride a horse but it belonged to a friend and the injury he sustained resulted from a fall off it.

He decided to return to California. His ticket was paid for by appearing in an advertising film. Shortly afterwards he was on his way back to California on a passenger freighter via the Panama Canal. He had a wardrobe from his previous experience and $150 in cash. Initially he did not live with his wife, but rented a room in a cheap apartment on Sunset Boulevard. Finances quickly ran out and in his search for movie work, he became so frustrated that he decided to give it up in favor of a more secure existence.

On his way to an interview at the Shell Oil Company, he disembarked from the bus close to Paramount Studios. A casting director Joe Egli saw him and rushed out to meet him, saying that he had been trying to find him for months. Egli had previously known him and wanted him to play a titled character in the film *Bolero* (1934) which starred George Raft and Carole Lombard. Milland was to be paid $300 a week for two weeks work. The producer of *Bolero*, Barney Glaser, cast him as Prince Michael Stofani in *We're Not Dressing* (1934). On the strength of these two films Paramount signed him to a seven year contract at $175 a week in February 1934. He moved into a large modern apartment joined by his wife.

He appeared in a succession of films at Paramount of varying prestige and billing. Universal borrowed him a couple of times. The film which really elevated him to stardom was when he played leading man to sarong clad Dorothy Lamour in *Jungle Princess* (1936). This caused an avalanche of fan mail. Universal borrowed him for a couple more films. At Paramount he was persuaded to appear in the comedy *Easy Living* (1937), one of several of his films to be directed by Mitchell Leisen. This film, in which he played the romantic lead opposite Jean Arthur, is widely regarded as one of the milestones of film comedy of the thirties and did much for his career. He reappeared with Dorothy Lamour in *Her Jungle Love* (1938), another smash hit.

In 1938 he and his wife built their first home which was in Coldwater Canyon. Milland became a naturalized American Citizen the same year. He played John Geste, the brother of Beau (Gary Cooper) and Digby (Robert Preston), in Paramount's exciting version of *Beau Geste* (1939). With the outbreak of World War II, Paramount dispatched him to England to head the cast of the comedy *French Without Tears* (1939). After this he returned to the States where he tried to enlist in the Air Force. He was rejected because of an accident to his left hand which left it impaired after an accident with hand tools at his home. Instead between film assignments he served as a civilian contract primary flight instructor for the army. He was active entertaining the troops at USO camp shows; made regular appearances at the Hollywood Canteen; and as a fluent Spanish speaker was the narrator in government sponsored radio broadcasts to Latin American countries.

He was skiing in Idaho when on March 6, 1940 word reached him that his son had been born a couple of weeks ahead of schedule. He was named Daniel David. On November 18, 1949 he and his wife officially adopted a six year old American girl Victoria Francesca who had lived with them for about a year.

Arise My Love (1940), a film role which he inherited from Joel McCrea, teamed him with Claudette Colbert. This was a contemporary drama directed by Mitchell Leisen in which he played an American flyer during the Spanish Civil War. It contained a potent message for Americans that isolationism was no longer an option. By this time Milland was regarded by the public and exhibitors as a top rank star. His position was consolidated when Cecil B. De Mille was persuaded to use him in the epic *Reap the Wild Wind* (1942) in which he battled a giant squid. This film was notable as the first one in which Milland began to take an active interest in what went on behind the cameras. This was of immense use when he became a director. He was extremely well cast in the comedy *The Major and the Minor* (1942) opposite Ginger Rogers; the thriller *Ministry of Fear* (1944); and the supernatural classic *The Uninvited* (1944).

Milland then went on to play the role of failed writer Don Birnam in the starkly realistic *Lost Weekend* (1945). This was scripted by Billy Wilder and Charles Brackett from the novel by Charles Jackson and directed by Wilder. It was the deeply disturbing case history of an alcoholic. It was completely different from the escapist fare of the period and was unique in Milland's filmography up to that time. The actor did an extensive amount of research on the subject including observing drunks and interviewing doctors. While he never became an alcoholic, his intensity and drive frightened his wife and made him impossible to live with so on March 31, 1945 they had a trial separation. By June 28, 1945 however they were back together.

Whilst most of the New York interiors were carefully replicated on studio soundstages in Hollywood, there were three weeks location shooting in New York which gave the film added authenticity. The film won him the critical reviews of a lifetime and was a commercial success as well. Paramount rewrote his contract so that he earned $200,000 a year plus an additional $60,000 through radio broadcasts. Throughout the remainder of the forties, his income remained as high as this. The greatest accolade however came when he won the Best Actor Oscar for his performance. He did not want to attend the ceremony, but his wife browbeat him into going. The award was presented to him by Ingrid Bergman.

Milland's films immediately following his triumph were not a particularly distinguished bunch. They did however include *Golden Earrings* (1947) in which he played a British intelligence officer opposite Marlene Dietrich as a gypsy. The film which was directed by Mitchell Leisen was a big box office hit, but the stars were antagonistic towards one another. Milland was at his best in *Alias Nick Beal* (1949) in which he played the devil in human form. This was reputed to be his personal favorite of his own films. This was his final film under his existing Paramount contract. He was suspended for refusing to shoot *Bride of Vengeance* which turned out to be a turkey and destroyed a number of careers.

Nevertheless he signed a fresh contract with them at slightly more money, but was loaned out as often as he shot films on his home lot. Of the films he made on loan *The Thief* (1952) was probably the one most recalled. Milland played a nuclear scientist who is persuaded to sell out to foreign agents, leading to murder and him going on the lam. The gimmick of the film was that there was no dialogue. Whilst this was too offbeat a movie to win much public favor, it did give him the opportunity to act with just his face and eyes.

With a declining film career and a number of stalled projects, Milland turned to television where he starred as a college professor in a CBS sitcom *Meet Mr. McNutley* from September 17, 1953 onwards. Simultaneously he did a radio version. He claimed he did the series because his agent talked him into it and he disliked the last batch of films in which he appeared. The original premise was to make the character a buffoon. In April 1954 the premise was changed to make the professor more of a hapless victim of the situation. The name of his character was changed to McNulty. On September 16, 1954 his television series survived for a second season under the title *The Ray Milland Show*. His character had the same name, but was now more restrained. The series ended on September 30, 1955 at the star's rather than the network's insistence.

He briefly separated from his wife again on October 20, 1953, but reconciled on November 17, 1953. The reason was widely believed to be his infatuation for Grace Kelly who was his costar in *Dial M For Murder* (1954) directed by Alfred Hitchcock. It was based on the highly successful Broadway play by Frederick Knott. The film was originally shot in 3-D, but shown flat.

One aspect of his career which he did lay emphasis on in his memoirs was his long frustrated desire to direct which was accomplished when he signed a one-sided contract with horrific penalties with Republic studios in 1954. The contract called for him to direct between two and four features providing that he also starred. A little surprisingly he chose a western *A Man Alone* (1955) as his first venture. As both star and director, he wore both hats very well. The second film was a medium crime thriller *Lisbon* (1956) which was filmed on location in the Portuguese capital. He both produced and directed this effort as well as starred.

After two lackluster British films in 1958 *The Safecracker* (which he also directed) and *High Flight*, he decided to retire but was so irritable that his wife became desperate to return him to work. He decided to try television again with a different type of series. On May 2, 1959 CBS television introduced a new program called simply *Markham* in which he played Roy Markham, a wealthy criminal lawyer turned private investigator, who lived on Sutton Place in New York. The series derived from an episode of the anthology series *Suspicion* aired on NBC in 1958 entitled "Eye for an Eye." In the first few episodes Markham employed a legman John Riggs (Simon Scott) to assist him, but he soon disappeared leaving Markham to do his own sleuthing. His cases covered all manner of crime including fraud, arson and murder. Although his base was New York, his cases involved him traveling all over the world. His character was usually seen wearing tweeds and sipping scotch and soda. *Markham* was a Miranda/Revue Production which lasted for 60 half hour, black and white episodes on the CBS network until September 22, 1960.

There was a general feeling that Milland gave it a veneer of class which it would otherwise have lacked. He produced and directed several segments. When the series threatened to fall apart because of the inability of several directors to bring their episodes in on time, Milland turned

Ray Milland, who starred in *Markham*.

to his old colleague Mitchell Leisen to direct fourteen segments which he did with considerable efficiency. Initially it was intended to do a great deal of location shooting, but time and budgetary considerations nixed the idea and foreign locales were created on the backlot of Revue studios. It was said that the character had the same initials as the star so he could wear his own monogrammed shirts on the show. An indication of his scant regard for television was that he makes no mention of either of his television series in his autobiography.

Milland again announced retirement to concentrate on production in 1960, but none of his plans came to fruition. When Vincent Price proved unavailable, he accepted an offer from American International Pictures to substitute for him in *The Premature Burial* (1962) directed by Roger Corman and loosely derived from an idea by Edgar Allan Poe. The film was sufficiently successful for him to ink a deal with American International for two more. Although they were well received, there was a general feeling that these were a comedown for an actor of his stature. These did however look like masterpieces compared with the Jamaica lensed *The Confession* (1964) which reunited with him with Ginger Rogers. This was an ill-advised attempt on the part of Rogers and her then husband William Marshall to create a film industry in Jamaica.

In 1965 Milland toured for twenty weeks in the United States in *My Fair Lady* as Henry Higgins to good notices. Whilst he had never been a stage star, the experience so fired his enthusiasm that he embarked on a new play. This was a courtroom thriller *Hostile Witness* which opened at the Music Box Theater on February 17, 1966 to good business and excellent reviews. This play marked his Broadway debut. He later toured with this play and took it to Australia. He starred and directed a low budget film version which was shot in England in black and white. In 1969 he toured in a musical *Take Me Along*.

He was doing an eight week tour of *The Front Page* when he received a call in Florida from Howard Minsky who was going to produce a film called *Love Story* (1970) and wanted Milland to appear in it as Ryan O'Neal's father. It was derived from Erich Segal's novella of two young students (O'Neal and Ali MacGraw) who meet, marry and then she dies. It was a character role, but Milland's instinct was that it was a surefire hit. He played the part simultaneously with appearing in the play by commuting between Florida and Hollywood. The film turned out to be one of the biggest grossers of all time. He reprised the role in the less successful *Oliver's Story* (1978).

His hobby was writing and several of his stories and articles appeared in various magazines under pen names. This culminated in his autobiography *Wide-Eyed in Babylon* (1974) a somewhat superficial memoir in which Milland strove to emulate the witty style of David Niven. His later films tended to be low budget shockers, but he admitted that he enjoyed working. The best of his later film assignments was *Gold* (1974) lensed in South Africa which was based on the Wilbur Smith novel. Roger Moore and Susannah York were the stars. He played the tough manager Harry Hirschfeld. He made several appearances in made-for-television movies and miniseries. For his appearance as Duncan Calderwood in the miniseries *Rich Man, Poor Man Book I* he received an Emmy award nomination as Outstanding Supporting Actor in a Drama Series in 1976.

Milland died in Torrance, California on March 10, 1986 aged 79 of cancer. He had fought a losing battle against the illness for the previous few months, said officials at the Torrance Memorial Hospital on the outskirts of Los Angeles.

Knowing that he was dying he had made a final nostalgic visit to Britain in December 1985. He was survived by his wife, daughter and two grandsons. His only son Daniel died in Los Angeles on March 27, 1981 in his Los Angeles apartment of a gunshot wound to the head. A Los Angeles coroner's court ruled his death a suicide. Milland, himself, was cremated and his ashes scattered over the Pacific Ocean at Redondo Beach, California.

Filmography

1929: *The Flying Scotsman, The Lady From the Sea, The Plaything, The Informer.*
1930: *Way for a Sailor, Passion Flower.*
1931: *The Bachelor Father, Just a Gigolo, Bought, Ambassador Bill, Blonde Crazy, Strangers May Kiss.*
1932: *The Man Who Played God, Polly of the Circus, Payment Deferred.*
1933: *Orders is Orders, This is the Life.*
1934: *Bolero, We're Not Dressing, Many Happy Returns, Charlie Chan in London, Menace, One Hour Late.*
1935: *The Gilded Lily, Four Hours to Kill, The Glass Key, Alias Mary Dow.*
1936: *Next Time We Love, The Return of Sophie Lang, The Big Broadcast of 1937, The Jungle Princess, Three Smart Girls.*
1937: *Wings Over Honolulu, Easy Living, Ebb Tide, Bulldog Drummond Escapes, Wise Girl.*
1938: *Her Jungle Love, Tropic Holiday, Men With Wings, Say It in French.*
1939: *Hotel Imperial, Beau Geste, Everything Happens at Night, French Without Tears.*
1940: *Irene, The Doctor Takes a Wife, Untamed, Arise My Love.*
1941: *I Wanted Wings, Skylark.*
1942: *The Lady Has Plans, Reap the Wild Wind, Are Husbands Necessary?, The Major and the Minor, Star Spangled Rhythm* (cameo).
1943: *The Crystal Ball, Forever and a Day* (cameo).
1944: *The Uninvited, Lady in the Dark, Till We Meet Again, Ministry of Fear.*
1945: *The Lost Weekend, Kitty.*
1946: *The Well Groomed Bride, California, The Imperfect Lady, The Trouble With Women.*
1947: *Golden Earrings, Variety Girl* (cameo).
1948: *The Big Clock, So Evil My Love, Miss Tatlock's Millions* (cameo), *Sealed Verdict.*
1949: *Alias Nick Beal, It Happens Every Spring.*
1950: *A Woman of Distinction, A Life of Her Own, Copper Canyon.*
1951: *Night Into Morning, Circle of Danger, Rhubarb, Close to My Heart.*
1952: *Bugles in the Afternoon, Something to Live For, The Thief.*
1953: *Jamaica Run, Let's Do It Again.*
1954: *Dial M For Murder.*
1955: *The Girl in the Red Velvet Swing, A Man Alone* (also directed).
1956: *Lisbon* (also produced and directed).
1957: *Three Brave Men, The River's Edge.*
1958: *The Safecracker* (also directed), *High Flight.*
1962: *The Premature Burial, Panic in the Year Zero* (also directed).
1963: *X* (a.k.a. *The Man With the X-Ray Eyes*).
1964: *The Confession* (a.k.a. *Quick Let's Get Married, Seven Different Ways*).
1968: *Hostile Witness* (also directed), *Red Roses for the Fuehrer.*
1969: *Daughter of the Mind* (TV).
1970: *Company of Killers* (TV), *Love Story.*
1971: *River of Gold* (TV), *Black Noon* (TV).
1972: *The Big Game, Frogs, The Thing With Two Heads, Embassy, The Screaming Lady* (TV).
1973: *The House in Nightmare Park, Terror in the Wax Museum.*
1974: *Gold, The Student Connection, Escape to Witch Mountain.*
1975: *The Swiss Conspiracy, The Dead Don't Die* (TV), *Oil: the Billion Dollar Fire, Ellery Queen: Too Many Suspects* (TV).
1976: *The Last Tycoon, Aces High, Mayday at 40,000 Feet* (TV), *Look What's Happened to Rosemary's Baby* (TV).
1977: *Slavers, The Uncanny, I gabiani volcano bassi.*
1978: *Spree, Oliver's Story, Battlestar Galactica* (TV), *Cruise into Terror* (TV), *Blackout.*
1979: *The Concorde Affair, Game for Vultures, Cave In!* (TV), *La ragazza in pigiama gialli, The Darker Side of Terror* (TV).
1980: *The Attic, Survival Run.*
1981: *Our Family Business* (TV).
1982: *Starflight One—The Plane That Couldn't Land* (TV), *The Royal Romance of Charles and Diana* (TV).
1983: *Cocaine: One Man's Seduction* (TV).
1984: *The Masks of Death* (TV).
1985: *The Sea Serpent, The Gold Key* (Video).

Television Series

1953–1954: *Meet Mr. McNutley* as Professor Ray McNutley/McNulty.
1954–1955: *The Ray Milland Show* as Professor Ray McNulty.
1959–1960: *Markham* as Roy Markham.

MINISERIES

1976: *Rich Man Poor Man Book I*
1977: *Seventh Avenue, Testimony of Two Men.*
1980: *The Dream Merchants.*

SOURCES

The Annual Obituary, 1986. Detroit, MI.: St. James, 1987.
Barrowclough, Anne. "Milland's Final Homecoming." *Daily Mail.* March 12, 1986.
Daily Post. "Ladies' Man Milland Dies at 79." March 12, 1986.
Daily Post. "Milland's Shooting Suicide." March 27, 1981.
Donnelly, Paul. *Fade to Black.* London: Omnibus, 2000.
Inman, David. *The TV Encyclopedia.* New York: Perigee, 1991.
McFarlane, Brian. *An Autobiography of British Cinema.* London: Methuen, 1997.
Milland, Ray. *Wide-Eyed in Babylon.* London: Bodley Head, 1974.
Parish, James Robert, and Don E. Stanke. *The Debonairs*Don E. New Rochelle, NY: Arlington, 1975.
Picture Show Annual. London: Amalgamated, 1936, 1937, 1938, 1947 and 1953.
Quinlan, David. *Film Stars.* 5th ed. London: Batsford, 2000.
Variety. "Ray Milland, Urbane Film Lead, Oscar Winner, Dies from Cancer." March 12, 1986.
Winchester, Clarence. *Screen Encyclopedia.* London: Winchester, 1948.

MARVIN MILLER

Marvin Miller was born Marvin Mueller in St. Louis, Missouri on July 18, 1913. His mother was Teresa Kiemast who died in 1951. Even as a student at Washington University he was active in radio. After graduating he became an in-demand radio performer both as an announcer and as an actor. He made his motion picture debut in 1945. He was frequently cast as Orientals. On screen he provided the voice of Robby the Robot in the film *Forbidden Planet* (1956) and its sequel *The Invisible Boy* (1957).

He was the star of *Mysteries of Chinatown* which was a primitive, live television mystery series shown on ABC between December 4, 1949 and October 23, 1950. Miller played Dr. Yat Fu whose main occupation was running a natural health and curio store in San Francisco's Chinatown district. His avocation however was dabbling in sleuthing and crime solving. In this capacity he was assisted by his niece Ah Toy (Gloria Saunders). There were only two standing sets for the series. One was their residence, while the other was the antique shop from which he traded. There was no commercial break and therefore no sponsor which led to its cancellation. There were 39 black and white, half hour episodes of this series.

By far his best remembered role was in the CBS television series *The Millionaire* which ran between June 1955 and September 1960. Miller was a regular on the series as Michael Anthony, personal secretary to unseen billionaire John Beresford Tipton. Each week Tipton would instruct his secretary Anthony to give an unsuspecting individual a check for $1,000,000. The drama then unfolded as to what happened to the individual after receiving such a windfall.

Rather surprisingly Miller found himself typecast and few acting assignments came his way afterwards. This hardly worried him however because he remained active as a commercial spokesperson; radio announcer; voicing cartoons; and as very effective television narrator (notably of *The FBI*). He once recorded the entire King

Marvin Miller, who starred in *The Mysteries of Chinatown*.

James version of The Bible for Audio Books. In 1965 and 1966 he won back-to-back Grammy awards as "Best Recordings for Children" for his readings of Dr. Seuss stories. One of his hobbies was cars and he owned a prize winning, custom made Mercedes Benz. His other hobbies were listed as painting, guitar playing and book binding.

Miller died in Santa Monica, California on February 8, 1985 aged 71 of a heart attack. He married artist Elizabeth Dawson (1919–1999) in 1938. With her he had a son named Anthony who was born in 1942 and a daughter named Melissa who was born in 1952. He was survived by all of them plus three grandchildren. He is buried with his wife at Westwood Village Memorial Park in Los Angeles.

Filmography

As Actor Only:

1945: *Blood on the Sun, Johnny Angel.*
1946: *Deadline at Dawn, Just Before Dawn, A Night in Paradise, The Phantom Thief, Without Reservations.*
1947: *The Brasher Doubloon* (a.k.a. *The High Window*), *Dead Reckoning, The Corpse Came C.O.D., Intrigue.*
1951: *Smuggler's Island, Peking Express, The Prince Who Was a Thief, The Golden Horde, Hong Kong.*
1952: *Red Planet Mars.*
1953: *Forbidden, Off Limits.*
1954: *Jivaro, The Shanghai Story.*
1957: *The Story of Mankind.*
1962: *When the Girls Take Over.*
1972: *Where Does It Hurt?*
1973: *The Naked Ape.*
1975: *I Wonder Who's Killing Her Now.*
1980: *American Raspberry* (a.k.a. *Prime Time*).
1981: *Kiss Daddy Goodbye, Evita Peron* (TV).
1984: *Swing Shift.*
1985: *Hell Squad* (a.k.a. *Commando Girls*).

Television Series

1949–1950: *Mysteries of Chinatown* as Dr. Yat Fu.
1951–1952: *Space Patrol* as Mr. Proteus.
1955–1960: *The Millionaire* as Michael Anthony.

Sources

DeLong, Thomas A. *Radio Stars*. Jefferson NC: McFarland, 1996.

Hyatt, Wesley. *Short-Lived Television Series, 1948–1978.* Jefferson, NC: McFarland, 2003.
Inman, David. *The TV Encyclopedia*. New York: Perigee, 1991.
Sackett, Susan. *Prime Time Hits*. New York: Billboard, 1993.
Geoff Tibballs. *TV Detectives*. London: Boxtree, 1992.
TV Star Annual. No. 7. 1959.
Variety. Obituary, February 13, 1985.

Jan Miner

Janice Miner was born in Boston, Massachusetts on October 15, 1917. She was the daughter of Walter Curtis Miner and Ethel Lindsey Chase. Her father was a dentist, while her mother was a painter. She was educated at Beaver County Day School, Chestnut, Massachusetts and the Vesper George School of the Arts in Boston.

She made her stage debut in *Street Scene* at the Copley Theater in Boston in 1945. Between 1945 and 1948 she was resident at this theater training and playing a variety of roles. She went to New York where she studied for the stage with inter alia Lee Strasberg and she became a foremost radio actress. Her outstanding work on radio was recognized when she was voted Best Dramatic Actress for nine consecutive years during the fifties.

When television came along she studied movement with various drama coaches. One of her radio roles was transferred to television when she played Ann Williams, reporter and girlfriend of Casey, in the early crime series *Crime Photographer*. Her best known television work was as Madge the Manicurist in the Palmolive's Dish Detergent commercials for 26 years commencing in 1965.

She made her Broadway debut as Maria Louvin in *Obligato* at the Marquee Theater in 1958. For the next thirty years she was a busy stage actress mainly in New York and Connecticut. She resided in Southbury, Connecticut until she died on February 15, 2004 aged 86 at the Bethel Health Care Facility in Bethel, Connecticut.

She was married to writer Richard Merrell from May 5, 1963 until he died in September 1998. She was survived by a brother, Donald Miner of Concord, New Hampshire.

Filmography
1968: *The Swimmer.*
1974: *Lenny.*
1980: *F.D.R.: The Last Year* (TV), *Willie and Phil.*
1981: *Endless Love.*
1986: *Heartbreak House* (TV).
1989: *Used Innocence.*
1990: *Mermaids.*

Television Series
1951–1952: *Crime Photographer* as Ann Williams.

Sources
Associated Press. Obituary, February 20, 2004.
DeLong, Thomas A. *Radio Stars.* Jefferson, NC: McFarland, 1996.
Herbert, Ian. *Who's Who in the Theatre.* 16th ed. London: Pitman, 1977.
Inman, David. *The TV Encyclopedia.* New York: Perigee, 1991.
Lentz, Harris M. III. *Obituaries in the Performing Arts, 2004.* Jefferson, NC: McFarland, 2005.
Tibballs, Geoff. *TV Detectives.* London: Boxtree, 1992.

GERALD MOHR

Gerald Mohr was born in New York on June 11, 1914. His parents were Gerald Mohr Sr. and Henrietta Noustadt, a Viennese singer. He was educated at Dwight Preparatory School in New York. While a premedical student at Columbia University, he was hospitalized in his teens. Announcer Andre Baruch overheard him speaking and persuaded him to audition for radio. CBS hired Mohr as an announcer. When aged only 20 he covered the Morro Castle ship disaster off the New Jersey coast. He auditioned for the Broadway stage and made his stage debut in *The Petrified Forest* (1936). From 1937 onwards he was a member of Orson Welles' Mercury Theatre. Through this connection he secured work in movies making his debut in 1939.

World War II interrupted the momentum of his career. After his honorable discharge, he became a very active radio lead notably playing the title characters in *The Lone Wolf* and *The Adventures of Philip Marlowe.* He signed a contract with Columbia pictures and appeared as the title character in three *Lone Wolf* films. Allegedly when the series ended, he had become so typecast that he underwent plastic surgery to alter his appearance. Since he looked much the same as before, this story may be apocryphal.

His sole starring role in a television series was the fourth and final season of *Foreign Intrigue* (1954–1955) in which he played Christopher Storm, a two fisted and resourceful American hotelier in Vienna. His hotel was a refuge for political exiles and victims of crime. He appeared in 39 episodes of this black and white syndicated series which was produced by Sheldon Reynolds. These episodes were later reissued under the title *Cross Current.* Mohr made comparatively few films after the fifties, but he became a prolific television guest star mainly in westerns and crime series in which he specialized in playing suave villains. He provided the voice for many cartoon characters. In real life he was a close friend from radio of Jeff Chandler, helped him decide on his screen name and was a pallbearer at his funeral. In spite of this however when Chandler had a hand in producing his own films, he did not choose to cast Mohr.

During the sixties Mohr alternated television in America with spending much time in Sweden because his second wife was Swedish. Mohr died suddenly of natural causes in Stockholm on November 10, 1968 aged 54. He went there to shoot a television series which he was coproducing with his wife. He married firstly in 1939 Rita Deneau from whom he was divorced in 1957. With her he had a son. He then wed Mai Dietrich in 1958. She survived him as did his son. He is buried at Lydingo, Kyrkogard near Stockholm, Sweden.

Gerald Mohr, who starred in *Foreign Intrigue*.

In a tribute to him actor Will Hutchins said, "I enjoyed working with Gerald immensely on two episodes of *Sugarfoot*. Between scenes he regaled us with stories about W.C. Fields whom he had known personally and I loved hearing him tell tall tales of the Great One. I think Gerald really wanted to be Humphrey Bogart."

FILMOGRAPHY

1939: *Panama Patrol, Love Affair, Charlie Chan at Treasure Island.*
1940: *The Sea Hawk.*
1941: *We Go Fast, The Monster and the Girl, Jungle Girl* (serial), *The Reluctant Dragon, The Adventures of Captain Marvel* (serial voice only), *Woman of the Year* (voice only).
1942: *The Lady Has Plans.*
1943: *Murder in Times Square, Lady of Burlesque, One Dangerous Night, The Desert Song, King of the Cowboys, Redhead from Manhattan.*
1946: *A Guy Could Change, Passkey to Danger, Dangerous Business, Young Widow, The Truth About Murder, The Invisible Informer, Catman of Paris, The Magnificent Rogue, Gilda, The Notorious Lone Wolf.*
1947: *The Lone Wolf in London, The Lone Wolf in Mexico, Heaven Only Knows* (a.k.a. *Montana Mike*).
1948: *The Emperor Waltz, Two Guys from Texas.*
1949: *The Blonde Bandit.*
1950: *Hunt the Man Down, Undercover Girl.*
1951: *Sirocco, Detective Story, Ten Tall Men.*
1952: *The Duel at Silver Creek, Son of Ali Baba, The Sniper, The Ring.*
1953: *Raiders of the Seven Seas, Invasion USA, Money from Home, The Eddie Cantor Story.*
1954: *Dragonfly Squadron.*
1957: *The Buckskin Lady.*
1958: *Guns, Girls and Gangsters, My World Dies Screaming* (a.k.a. *Terror in the Haunted House*).
1959: *A Date With Death, The Angry Red Planet.*
1960: *This Rebel Breed.*
1964: *Wild West Story.*
1968: *Funny Girl.*

TELEVISION SERIES

1954–1955: *Foreign Intrigue* as Christopher Storm.

SOURCES

Correspondence between the author and Will Hutchins.
DeLong, Thomas A. *Radio Stars.* Jefferson, NC: McFarland, 1996.
Erickson, Hal. *Syndicated Television: The First Forty Years, 1947–1987* Jefferson, NC: McFarland, 1989.
Quinlan, David. *Illustrated Directory of Film Character Actors.* 2nd ed. London: Batsford, 1995.
Twomey, Alfred E., and Arthur F. McClure. *The Versatiles.* South Brunswick, NJ: Barnes, 1969.
Variety. Obituary, November 13, 1968.

MARY TYLER MOORE

Mary Tyler Moore became a leading exponent of the art of situation comedy during the sixties and seventies. In her early days the image of some of the characters she played was lighthearted, but her own private life revealed more than her fair share of drama. Her career reached its zenith when she and her then husband Grant Tinker ran MTM, their own production company, which turned out a lot of quality television. Since then her television career has strayed into the realms of drama in which she has revealed a lot of angst since 1980. She was inducted into the Television Hall of Fame in 1985. Although some of her more recent television movies have had interesting premises, she has not been well cast in a few of them.

Mary Tyler Moore was born in Brooklyn Heights, New York on December 29, 1936. Her parents were George Tyler Moore and Marjorie Hackett. Her father was a clerk with Con Edison and later at the Southern California Gas Company. She had one brother John who was born on June 13, 1943. He became an alcoholic and died prematurely of kidney cancer. She had a sister Elizabeth who was born in April 1956. She died in 1978 of a drug and alcohol overdose aged 21 after a relationship went sour.

Mary Tyler Moore was raised in Flushing as a Catholic. She was educated at St. Rose of Lima School in Brooklyn. With a cousin she formed a song and dance act in childhood. In September 1945 the family moved to Hollywood where she was educated at St. Ambrose School and Immaculate Heart High School, both of which were in Los Angeles. Outside of school she attended the Ward Sisters Studio of Dance Arts and danced at local events for retired people and church clubs. An aunt was an assistant production manager at the local CBS television station. Through a friend of her aunt's, who was an advertising executive, she auditioned for and won the role of the *Happy Hotpoint Elf.* Hotpoint was the sponsor of *The Adventures of Ozzie and Harriet* television series in 1955. She performed in the commercials between the show.

She married Dick Meeker, a salesman, in Los Angeles in August 1955. With him she had a son Richard Carlton Meeker, Jr., who was born in Los Angeles on July 3, 1956. After the birth of her son she went back to work appearing as a dancer on all the top rated musical variety television shows of the fifties. She also appeared in commercials. She had a highly unusual role on a television crime series of the fifties when she played Sam, the answering service operator, on *Richard Diamond Private Detective* in 1959. Only her voice was heard and her shapely legs were shown. Her face and figure were never seen as she constantly warned Diamond (David Janssen) of impending danger and simultaneously boosted his self esteem. The show was a hit. For each episode she was paid only $80 however. She was the subject of constant speculation with viewers as to what Sam looked like. With the resulting publicity, she asked for a raise in salary and was promptly fired. Her agents and casting directors were able to make the most of her fleeting fame by having her cast in television shows where the viewers were informed in advance that they could see what Sam really looked like by tuning in. So she began to amass some television acting credits. She outgrew her husband and obtained a Mexican divorce from him in February 1962. She married Grant Tinker, then an advertising executive, in Las Vegas on June 1, 1962. He had four children by a previous marriage.

She unsuccessfully auditioned for the role of Danny Thomas's daughter on his television series. Although she did not win the part, Thomas remembered her a year later when he, Sheldon Leonard and Carl Reiner were searching for an actress to play Laura Petrie, the wife of Rob Petrie (Dick Van Dyke), on *The Dick Van Dyke Show.* In this groundbreaking situation comedy Van Dyke played Rob Petrie, comedy writer for a variety show. Laura Petrie wore Capri pants and flat shoes which caused a sensation and was a first for television. Moore was so successful in the series that the focus shifted from Rob Petrie's work to his home life. She initially earned $450 per show which slowly increased. She was nominated for an Emmy award in 1962– 1963. In 1963–1964 she won an Emmy award for Outstanding Continued Performance by an Actress in a Series (Lead). During 1965–1966 she won another Emmy award for Outstanding Continued Performance by an Actress in a Leading Role in a Comedy Series. The show ran on CBS between October 1961 and September 1966. The surviving members of the cast were reunited for a special in 2004 which proved that it is better to leave fans with fond memories of the originals rather than try to resurrect them when the spark has gone.

She then relocated to New York to try Broadway playing Holly Golightly in *Breakfast at Tiffany's* which was critically panned and a commercial disaster of 1966. She was paired with Julie Andrews in a movie musical *Thoroughly Modern Millie* (1967) in which she felt miscast. She was under contract to Universal and made some inconsequential movies for them. She became pregnant, but suffered a miscarriage at an early stage. In the course of her recovery she was discovered to be a Type 1 or insulin dependent diabetic. She later became and remains the International Chairman of the Juvenile Diabetes Foundation (JDF).

In 1969 she and Dick Van Dyke were reunited in a musical variety special *Dick Van Dyke*

Mary Tyler Moore in her first film, *X-15* (1961). She costarred in the television series *Richard Diamond Private Detective*.

and the Other Woman which did well in the ratings for CBS. On the strength of this CBS offered her a half hour show on the network with a firm commitment for 24 episodes and no pilot. She and Grant Tinker formed their own production company MTM to package the show. MTM later became known in the industry as the "Camelot" of independent television production. Their logo was an orange kitten meowing.

In *The Mary Tyler Moore Show* she played Mary Richards, a young single career woman who came to Minneapolis after the breakup of a long term relationship. She was looking for a new life and became a production assistant on a local news show for a television station. The character and the series captured the mood of the period perfectly. She won an Emmy award for Outstanding Continued Performance by an Actress in a Leading Role in a Comedy Series in 1973; Best Lead Actress in a Comedy Series and Actress of the Year in a Series in 1974; and Outstanding Lead Actress in a Comedy Series in 1976 all for *The Mary Tyler Moore Show*. She was also nominated in 1971, 1972, 1975 and 1977. She also directed an episode of the series. It was shown on CBS between September 1970 and September 1977. It was still riding high in the ratings when the decision was made to end it. She was the hostess of *Mary* on CBS in 1978 which was a tired musical variety format which was axed after only three segments. Another musical show within a sitcom format *The Mary Tyler Moore Hour* flopped on CBS in 1979.

Her film career received a big boost when she was chosen to play Beth Jarrett in *Ordinary People* (1980) directed by Robert Redford. In spite of receiving a Best Actress Oscar nomination, it remained her only film role of any consequence. In a sex switch she replaced Tom Conti in the play *Whose Life Is It Anyway?*, at the Royale Theater on Broadway in 1980. She did this for four months to mainly sellout audiences and standing ovations. While doing this she had a stalker, but he was apprehended. The job obviously dictated her living in New York. This virtually signaled the end of her second marriage from Tinker whom she divorced in 1980. In 1980 her son, who had a history of emotional problems but who appeared to have turned his life around, died aged 24 of a self inflicted gunshot wound from a gun with a hair trigger. His death was ruled accidental by a Los Angeles coroner. After the play ended she lived in New York for a while eventually buying an apartment in Central Park West.

Her only other major Broadway appearance was as Susan at the Music Box Theater in *Sweet Sue* in 1987 which was judged a middling success.

She made other attempts to return to series television. *Mary*, in which she played Mary Brenner, was shown on CBS during 1985 and 1986. It was a sitcom set in a Chicago newspaper office which flopped largely because the supporting characters were so mean spirited. She then played the title character in the CBS sitcom *Annie McGuire*. She played a divorced mother who married a construction contractor. This one had warmth, humor and imagination but not enough of any to keep it afloat so it came and went in 1988.

She fared much better in movies-for-television. She received an Emmy award nomination for Outstanding Lead Actress in a Limited Series or a Special for *First You Cry* (1978). In *Heartsounds* (1984) she played Martha Lear. James Garner played a man dying of heart failure. She received an Emmy nomination as Outstanding Lead Actress in a Limited Series or a Special. She was not obvious casting, but was reckoned to have turned in an excellent performance as Mary Todd Lincoln opposite Sam Waterston in *Gore Vidal's Lincoln* (1988) for which she received an Emmy award nomination as Outstanding Actress in a Miniseries or a Special. She also received an Emmy award as Outstanding Supporting Actress in a Miniseries or a Special for *Stolen Babies* (1993).

Grant Tinker quit MTM in the late seventies, but Mary Tyler Moore stayed on the Board of Directors until 1988 when the company was finally sold to TVS. She received a handsome severance package. Unfortunately she elected to take a third of it in TVS stock which subsequently hit rock bottom. Although she made a lot of money from the deal, she did not become as rich as many imagined. She gradually became an alcoholic and checked in for a spell at the Betty Ford Clinic in Palm Springs. She later became a regular attendee at Alcoholics Anonymous meetings which helped her recovery considerably. She eventually quit smoking too.

She married Dr. Robert Levine at the Pierre Hotel in New York on November 23, 1983. He was a cardiologist whom she met when her mother was taken ill in New York and is several years her junior. Their marriage has proved to be a very happy one. She resides with him at Greenawn, a 122 acre estate in New York State. She is very active in animal rights issues.

FILMOGRAPHY

1961: *X-15.*
1967: *Thoroughly Modern Millie.*
1968: *What's So Bad About Feeling Good?, Don't Just Stand There!*
1969: *Change of Habit, Run a Crooked Mile* (TV).
1978: *First You Cry* (TV).
1980: *Ordinary People.*
1982: *Six Weeks.*
1984: *Heartsounds* (TV).
1985: *Finnegan Begin Again* (TV).
1986: *Just Between Friends.*
1988: *Gore Vidal's Lincoln* (TV).
1990: *Thanksgiving Day* (a.k.a. *The Good Family*) (TV), *The Last Best Year* (TV).
1993: *Stolen Babies* (TV).
1995: *Stolen Memories: Secrets from the Rose Garden* (a.k.a. *Forbidden Memories*) (TV).
1996: *Flirting with Disaster, The Blue Arrow* (voice only).
1997: *Payback* (TV), *Keys to Tulsa.*
1999: *Labor Pains.*
2000: *Mary & Rhoda* (TV).
2001: *Like Mother Like Son: The Strange Story of Sante and Kenny Kimes* (TV), *Cheats* (a.k.a. *Cheaters*).
2002: *Miss Lettie and Me* (TV).
2003: *The Gin Game* (TV), *Blessings* (TV).
2004: *The Dick Van Dyke Show Revisited* (TV).
2005: *Snow Wonder* (TV).

TELEVISION SERIES

1959: *Richard Diamond Private Detective* as "Sam."
1961–1966: *The Dick Van Dyke Show* as Laura Meehan Petrie.
1970–1977: *The Mary Tyler Moore Show* as Mary Richards.
1978: *Mary* Hostess.
1979: *The Mary Tyler Moore Hour* as Mary McKinnon.
1985–1986: *Mary* as Mary Brenner.
1988: *Annie McGuire* as Annie McGuire.

SOURCES

Bryers, Chris. *The Real Mary Tyler Moore.* New York: Pinnacle, 1976
Inman, David. *The TV Encyclopedia.* New York: Perigee, 1991.
Moore, Mary Tyler. *After All.* New York: Dell, 1995.
Quinlan, David. *Film Stars.* 5th ed. London: Batsford, 2000.

DENNIS MORGAN

Dennis Morgan was unusual in that he was a dedicated family man in an industry where promiscuity was rife. He had a golden voice which made him a solid commercial asset in the days when musicals proliferated. He had a handsome face and a cheerful personality. He did appear in a number of dramatic roles. Although he made his name at RKO, the majority of his films date from his long years at Warner Bros. where he was a top box office draw. His career declined sharply when musicals began to go out of fashion. He was not one of the most likely players to star in a crime and mystery series, but the fact that he did star in a short-lived series *21 Beacon Street* is indicative of the low ebb his career had reached by then.

Dennis Morgan was born Stanley Morner in Prentice, Wisconsin on December 20, 1908. His father Frank Morner, a banker and lumber merchant, was of Swedish extraction, while his mother Grace Van Dusen was of Pennsylvania-Dutch and Scottish origins. He was one of three children. His older brother Kenneth died a few days before he was born. He also had a younger sister named Dorothy. He derived his musical talent from his mother. Another relative gave him singing lessons from childhood. He sang in church; at social events; and played trombone in the school band.

His family moved to Marshfield, Wisconsin where he attended high school. While there he met physician's daughter, Lillian Vedder, whom he later married in Wisconsin on September 5, 1933. They had three children who were Stanley, Jr., born in 1934; Kristin born in 1937; and James Irving born in 1943. As a result of meeting his future wife they both attended Carroll College in Waukesha where he acted in college plays and played on the football team. He sang between shows at the local movie theater and became an active member of the College Glee Club, performing with them around the Midwest. Even then his singing was so good that he won the Atwater, Kent radio contest in 1930 and 1931. In 1930 he graduated; played semiprofessional baseball in the Northern Wisconsin League; and toured the Midwest in a production of *Faust.*

He secured a job at radio station WTMJ in Milwaukee singing and reading poetry which he did for a year. From there he moved to Chicago in 1933 where he sang with Vernon Black's Orchestra at the Palmer House for seven months. He did a couple of seasons in stock. He was appearing with an opera company when diva Mary Garden heard him. She was so impressed that she arranged an audition with MGM who signed him to a contract.

His first contract stipulated that he arrive in Hollywood by a certain date in 1935. To this end he bought a big second hand car which he fitted with second hand tires, loaded his young wife, baby and luggage into it and set off. Stranded in New Mexico with no money and the deadline looming up, a rancher lent him $50 to tide him over. In Hollywood he made another unpleasant discovery. His standard contract paid him 40 weeks of the year. There was a three months holiday without pay. The contract was set to commence with the unpaid leave. When the time came for him to report to the studio for work, he wandered around like a lost sheep. Nobody seemed to know who he was or why he was there.

During the two years he was under contract to MGM he did virtually nothing but draw a good salary. They had no plans for him except to act as a threat to Nelson Eddy. Instead they loaned him to the Halperin brothers who ran Academy Pictures, an independent production company. They starred him in *I Conquer the Sea* (1936), a cheap drama about fishermen. A rare opportunity to sing at MGM occurred in a short *Annie Laurie* (1937). He appeared in a big production number "A Pretty Girl Is Like a Melody" in the prestigious MGM film *The Great Ziegfeld* (1936), but was amazed to discover that his singing voice was dubbed by Allan Jones. Simultaneously Morgan was playing leads in stage concerts and operas. He begged for his contract release from MGM who let him go.

He signed with Paramount in 1938 on a six month contract. They changed his name to Richard Stanley, gave him some bit roles in their features and then dropped him from contract. He was seen and heard by producer Charles Rogers who recommended him to Warner Bros. They signed him, but Jack Warner disliked his real name because of its funereal quality and insisted on giving him an Irish one instead, Dennis Morgan. Warners treated him slightly better, giving him leads in a few of their fast moving B features. *Tear Gas Squad* (1940) was notable as the first film which allowed him to sing using his natural voice.

He was considered for leads in *The Sea Hawk* and *The Santa Fe Trail*, but Errol Flynn and Ronald Reagan were assigned the roles instead. He fought like a tiger to play the role of the rich playboy in *Kitty Foyle* (1940). Since it was being shot at RKO, a rival studio, he had to convince Jack Warner to loan him which he did by saying that if he made a hit, it would enhance his box office at Warners. Then he had to win over director Sam Wood. Originally he was offered the part of the young intern, but he desperately wanted to play the other character which he eventually did. Ginger Rogers played the title role and won the Best Actress Oscar. Morgan became a star and Warner Bros. found themselves deluged with fan mail for him. Since they had worked together so harmoniously on screen, Rogers and Morgan wanted to work together again but it was a decade later before they found a decent script *Perfect Strangers* (1950). It failed to replicate the earlier success both critically and at the box office.

Throughout the greater part of his career he lived in La Canada, a rural community 20 miles from Hollywood, where he had the biggest swimming pool in the neighborhood. He definitely did not let success go to his head. His children attended the local public school. He was known by his real name in that locality and sang in the choir at the Hollywood Presbyterian Church.

After *Kitty Foyle*, Warners gave him decent roles in A features. At one point he was even announced for the role of Victor Lazlo in *Casablanca* which Paul Henreid played. Instead Morgan costarred opposite strong stars like James Cagney in *Captains of the Clouds* (1942), a story of the Royal Canadian Air Force, and *In This Our Life* (1942) opposite Bette Davis and Olivia de Havilland. *Wings for the Eagle* (1942) was notable because it marked his first on-screen appearance with Jack Carson who became his off-screen buddy and his most frequent co-star. *The Hard Way* (1942) in which he costarred with Carson, Ida Lupino and Joan Leslie was an uncompromising show business story. Although few had much faith in it at the time, it is one of the most honest backstage films and has stood the test of time well.

He featured prominently with Joan Leslie again in *Thank Your Lucky Stars* (1943), Warners' all star war time extravaganza. His first total musical was *The Desert Song* (1943) in which he starred as the Red Shadow. It was derived from the musical opera by Sigmund Romberg cleverly updated to World War II so that the Nazis be-

Dennis Morgan, who starred in *21 Beacon Street*.

came villains. It opened to brisk business and glowing reviews. Irene Manning costarred. This success warranted more musicals so Morgan, Manning and Ann Sheridan starred in *Shine on Harvest Moon* (1944). This was a fictionalized but commercially successful version of the life of musical theater stars Jack Norworth and Nora Bayes. The ubiquitous Jack Carson costarred. *Christmas in Connecticut* (1945), a personal favorite of his, which costarred him with Barbara Stanwyck was Warners' biggest grosser of that year. By this time he was allegedly receiving more fan mail than any other Warners' star.

Morgan and Carson had previously costarred in four films together, but *Two Guys From Milwaukee* (1946) marked their first official teaming as a comedy duo, while *The Time, the Place and the Girl* (1946) was their first proper musical. In *My Wild Irish Rose* (1947) he played real life, turn of the century, Irish musical star Chauncey Olcott (1858–1932), but sang in his own style a wonderful repertoire of Irish songs. This was the tragic backstage story of the rivalry between Olcott and Billy Scanlan (1856–1898) played by William Frawley. It broke all records at the box office and was Morgan's personal favorite of his own films. Following this he wanted to make a biopic of the life of Scottish poet Robert Burns, but Jack Warner nixed the idea. Morgan went on to costar with Carson again in *Two Guys from Texas* (1948) and the cameo laden *It's a Great Feeling* (1949). Regarding the last of these, Morgan was on suspension and no one at the studio noticed that his contract had lapsed. Jack Warner had promised the exhibitors another Morgan-Carson film. To appease Morgan he had to sign him to another contract at three times his former salary.

Warners and Morgan did not really patch up their differences. Morgan was the highest paid actor under contract to Warners. Jack Warner wanted him to break his contract so he sent him the worst scripts he could find. Morgan however had a family to support so he worked the remainder of his contract in generally poor films rather than face another lengthy suspension. *This Woman is Dangerous* (1952) which starred Joan Crawford was his last film of any worth. Throughout the fifties he appeared in anthology shows on television. He actively campaigned to win the role of the Reverend Peter Marshall who became U.S. Senate Chaplain in the film version of his life *A Man Called Peter* (1955) at 20th Century–Fox. Even though he was a dead ringer for the real life minister and the personal choice of Catherine Marshall, the chaplain's widow, executives at Fox would not even test him for the role. Richard Todd was cast as Marshall. Instead Morgan found himself in quickies produced by such characters as Sam Katzman and Benedict Bogeaus. In the mid fifties he set up his own production company with a view to producing a musical for which he had a script, but was unable to secure backing.

In the television series *21 Beacon Street* Morgan played Dennis Chase, a Boston based private eye, who headed a team of crime solving investigators. His team consisted of Girl Friday Lola (Joanna Barnes) who used her natural charms to extract information from reluctant witnesses; Brian (Brian Kelly) a young law school graduate; and Jim (James Maloney) who was a special effects wizard and master of dialects and disguise. *21 Beacon Street* was their base of operations. This was a Filmways Production which lasted for 13 half hour, black and white episodes shown between July 2 and September 24, 1959 on the NBC network. It was a summer replacement series for *The Ford Show*. Episodes were later rerun on the ABC network. The series made interesting early use of forensic science and electronic gadgets as techniques in aiding criminal investigations. There were however no false heroics in this series. The crime was committed prior to the investigation by the team and once the investigation was complete, Chase and his associates turned their findings over to the police for them to apprehend the culprits.

His final film was a bit in the cameo laden *Won Ton Ton the Dog Who Saved Hollywood* (1975). His last television appearance was a guest shot on *The Love Boat* in 1980. As a member of the Campus Community Players during the seventies, he continued to perform on stage in Wisconsin in musicals and straight plays for many years. In 1963 when pal Jack Carson died of cancer, Morgan became a traveling spokesman for The American Cancer Society giving lectures and fundraising. He had a working ranch at Awahnee between Fresno and Yosemite where he spent much of his time.

He died in Fresno, CA hospital on September 7, 1994 aged 85 of heart trouble. His wife was at the bedside when he died. He is buried at Oakhurst Cemetery, Madera County, California. Irene Manning, his co-star in two films, recalled of him, "I kept in touch with Dennis and his wife, Lillian, through the years. Working with him was wonderful. He was a delightful human being. We enjoyed very much working together."

Filmography

1936: *I Conquer the Sea, Suzy, The Great Ziegfeld, Piccadilly Jim, Down the Stretch, Old Hutch.*
1937: *Song of the City, Mama Steps Out, Navy Blue and Gold.*
1938: *Persons in Hiding, Illegal Traffic, Men with Wings, King of Alcatraz.*
1939: *Waterfront, The Return of Dr. X, No Place to Go.*
1940: *Three Cheers for the Irish, Tear Gas Squad, Flight Angels, River's End, The Fighting 69th, Kitty Foyle.*
1941: *Affectionately Yours, Bad Men of Missouri, Kisses for Breakfast.*
1942: *Captains of the Clouds, In This Our Life, Wings for the Eagle* (JC), *The Hard Way* (JC).
1943: *Thank Your Lucky Stars* (JC), *The Desert Song.*
1944: *The Very Thought of You, Hollywood Canteen* (JC) (cameo), *Shine On Harvest Moon* (JC).
1945: *God Is My Co-Pilot, Christmas in Connecticut.*
1946: *One More Tomorrow* (JC), *Two Guys from Milwaukee* (JC), *The Time, the Place and the Girl* (JC).
1947: *Cheyenne, My Wild Irish Rose, Always Together* (JC) (cameo).
1948: *To the Victor, Two Guys from Texas* (JC), *One Sunday Afternoon.*
1949: *It's a Great Feeling* (JC), *The Lady Takes a Sailor.*
1950: *Perfect Strangers, Pretty Baby.*
1951: *Raton Pass, Painting the Clouds With Sunshine.*
1952: *This Woman is Dangerous, Cattle Town.*
1955: *Pearl of the South Pacific, The Gun That Won the West.*
1956: *Uranium Boom.*
1968: *Rogue's Gallery.*
1975: *Won Ton Ton the Dog Who Saved Hollywood* (cameo).

Note: Films in which both Morgan and Jack Carson appeared are marked (JC) in the filmography.

Television Series

1959: *21 Beacon Street* as Dennis Chase.

Sources

Applebaum, Stanley. *Stars of the American Musical Theatre*. New York: Dover, 1981.
Brown, David. "Remembering Dennis Morgan, Parts I and II." *Movie Memories*. Nos. 38 and 39. Spring and Summer 2000.
Daily Mail. "Hollywood Stalwart Dies at 85." September 9, 1994.
Daily Telegraph. Obituary, September 1994.
Houseman, Virginia. *Made in Heaven: Unscrambling the Marriages and Children of Hollywood Stars*. Chicago: Bonus Books, 1992.
Inman, David. *The TV Encyclopedia*. New York: Perigee, 1991.
Lamparski, Richard. *Whatever Became Of?* 2nd and 8th Series. New York: Crown, 1968 and 1982.
Lentz, Harris M. III. *Obituaries in the Performing Arts, 1994*. Jefferson, NC: McFarland, 1995.
McClelland, Doug. *Forties Film Talk*. Jefferson, NC: McFarland, 1992.
McClure, Arthur F., and Ken D. Jones. *Star Quality*. South Brunswick, NJ: Barnes, 1974.
Picture Show Annual. London: Amalgamated, 1941, 1942, 1943, 1947, 1948 and 1954.
Quinlan, David. *Film Stars*. 5th ed. London: Batsford, 2000.
Ragan, David. *Movie Stars of the '40s*. Englewood Cliffs, NJ: Prentice-Hall, 1985.
Rogers, Ginger. *Ginger—My Story*. London: Headline, 1992.
Tibballs, Geoff. *TV Detectives*. London: Boxtree, 1992.
Wagner, Laura. "Dennis Morgan: Warner Bros.

Regular Guy." *Classic Images*. Nos. 277 and 278. July/August 1998.
Warner Bros. Biographical Questionnaire. February 13, 1939.
Wilson, Ivy Crane. *The Third Hollywood Album*. London: Sampson Low, 1949.
Winchester, Clarence. *Screen Encyclopedia*. London: Winchester, 1948.

PATRICIA MORISON

When Alfred Drake, who later costarred with Patricia Morison in *Kiss Me Kate*, first heard that she had signed a contract with Paramount in the late thirties, he was horrified and exclaimed, "You should not go to Hollywood! You belong to the theater!" More specifically he should have said, "The musical theater!" Time proved him correct. Patricia Morison appeared in several films at Paramount which few film buffs remember. Her delightful singing voice was heard in only one film, *Sofia*, which is quite possibly her worst movie. Fortunately Cole Porter came to her rescue professionally and made her an enduring star.

Eileen Patricia Augusta Fraser Morison was born in New York City on March 19, 1915. She was the daughter of William R. Morison (a.k.a. Norman Rainey) and Selena Carson. Her parents were both English. Her father was a playwright, actor and artist. He had served in the army in World War I. Her mother had been an intelligence officer in World War I. She later became a theatrical agent. She had one brother who was born in England during a Zeppelin raid.

She was educated at Public School No. 9 and Washington Irving High School in New York. Her original ambition was to become an artist and according to different sources she either won a scholarship to the Metropolitan Museum of Art or L'Ecole des Beaus Arts in Paris. Instead of going to either she studied drama at the Neighborhood Playhouse and dance and movement with Martha Graham. She had an early job working as a dress designer in a shop on Fifth Avenue.

She gave this up when she made her Broadway debut in *Growing Pains* as Helen which opened at the Ambassador Theater in November 1933 and lasted 28 performances. From December 26, 1935 at the Broadhurst Theater she understudied Helen Hayes in *Victoria Regina* which was an enormous success, although she never actually went on for the star. Nevertheless Morison found the experience rewarding. On May 31, 1938 at the Windsor Theater she played Laura Rivers in *The Two Bouquets* which starred Alfred Drake. Even though it only lasted 55 performances, it was an important role for her.

She was seen by a talent scout from Paramount who signed her to a contract in 1939 initially as a threat to "The Sarong Girl" Dorothy Lamour. Publicity layouts from the period compared and contrasted the two leading ladies as if they were prizefighters. Particular attention was paid to Morison's 39 inch tresses compared to Lamour's 36 inch length hair. Morison usually wore hers in a bun with a centre parting which made her look rather severe. In fact she did not usurp Lamour's throne. Although the two did appear together in one film *Beyond the Blue Horizon* (1942), they played cousins. Most of the footage was devoted to toplined, sarong clad, Lamour while Morison stayed aloof and fully clothed in a relatively small role.

The time Morison spent at Paramount was generally regarded as a total waste of her time and talent. There was considerable friction at Paramount between herself and the big brass. She was announced for a number of roles at the studio which eventually went to other actresses. She

Patricia Morison arriving at London airport in 1964. She costarred in *The Cases of Eddie Drake*.

deliberately contrived to obtain her release from Paramount by a combination of gluttony, not working out in the gym and the consequent loss of her svelte figure. Having cast herself adrift she shed the excess weight and went overseas with the first U.S.O. group to entertain American troops which was a very hazardous journey.

Upon her return to Hollywood she freelanced. She played the heroic Jarmila in *Hitler's Madman* (1943) which dealt with the assassination of demented Nazi Reinhard Heydrich (John Carradine) by Czech patriots and the Nazi retaliation by obliterating the village of Lidice on June 9, 1942. This was an independent film which was released by MGM after they had shot some extra scenes. It is possibly her best known movie and one of the few in which she had a starring role. She is also well remembered by film buffs as femme fatale Hilda Courtney in *Dressed to Kill* (1946), the final film in the Universal series of *Sherlock Holmes* films.

She continued in movies until 1948 when she became a television star. She received an Emmy award nomination in 1948 at the first awards ceremony as Most Outstanding Television Personality. In the early crime series *The Cases of Eddie Drake* she played psychologist Karen Gayle who is doing a thesis on criminal behavior. As part of her research, hardboiled private eye Eddie Drake (Don Haggerty) dictated his cases to her. This was reckoned to be the first filmed television series and was loosely derived from the radio series *The Cases of Eddie Ace* which starred George Raft. Her salary was only reckoned to be $250 a week. Nevertheless she was admired by the producers for her professionalism in that she was not temperamental, knew her lines and seldom needed a retake. The series was aired briefly in 1949 and then withdrawn only to emerge in syndication from March 1952 onwards in its entirety where it proved to be a modest hit.

While she was appearing in this series, she auditioned for and won the roles of Lilli Vanessi and Katherine in the Cole Porter stage musical *Kiss Me Kate*. She had appeared in half the projected series of 26 when she landed the part, so she had to be bought out of *The Cases of Eddie Drake* because of conflicting schedules. She was replaced by Lynne Roberts. *Kiss Me Kate* opened at the New Century Theater on Broadway on December 30, 1948 and was a smash hit. Morison continued with this role through 686 performances until 1950. Then she went with the show to London where she opened at the Coliseum Theater on March 8, 1951 making her the toast of the West End.

In February 1954 she opened at the St. James Theater, New York as Anna Leonowens in the Rodgers and Hammerstein musical *The King and I* opposite Yul Brynner and later toured American cities in this show. The combined success of *Kiss Me Kate* and *The King and I* made her one of the most acclaimed musical stars of the period. After this she continued to perform in Broadway musicals, the theater, television and toured the light opera circuit for decades. The only arena in which she lacked success was motion pictures where she was seldom in demand. Her only subsequent film role of any note was a cameo as George Sand in *Song Without End* (1960).

In later years she reverted back to her original ambition which was to be a professional oil painter. She has had several successful exhibitions of her work which she sells. Morison, who never married, continues to reside in a Los Angeles apartment.

Filmography

1939: *Persons in Hiding, I'm from Missouri, The Magnificent Fraud.*
1940: *Rangers of Fortune, Untamed.*
1941: *Romance of the Rio Grande, The Roundup, One Night in Lisbon.*
1942: *Beyond the Blue Horizon, Are Husbands Necessary?, A Night in New Orleans.*
1943: *Silver Skates, The Song of Bernadette, Hitler's Madman, The Fallen Sparrow, Calling Doctor Death, Where Are Your Children?*
1945: *Without Love, Lady on a Train.*
1946: *Dressed to Kill, Danger Woman.*
1947: *Queen of the Amazons, Tarzan and the Huntress, Song of the Thin Man.*
1948: *The Walls of Jericho, The Prince of Thieves, The Return of Wildfire, Sofia.*
1960: *Song Without End.*
1975: *Won Ton Ton the Dog Who Saved Hollywood* (cameo).
1985: *Mirrors* (TV).

Note: Patricia Morison was cast in the important role of Victor Mature's suicidal wife in *Kiss of Death* (1947), but her scenes ended up on the cutting room floor.

Television Series

1949: *The Cases of Eddie Drake* as Karen Gayle.

Sources

Appelbaum, Stanley. *Stars of the American Musical Theatre in Historic Photographs*. New York: Dover, 1981.
Lamparski, Richard. *Whatever Became Of?* 11th Series. New York: Crown, 1989.
Mank, Gregory. "Danger Woman." *Midnight Marquee*. Issue 56. Spring 1998.
Movie Memories. No. 46. "Patricia Morison Remembers Broadway's *Kiss Me Kate*" 2003.
Parish, James Robert, and Lennard DeCarl. *Hollywood Players: The Forties*. New Rochelle, NY: Arlington, 1976.
Picture Show Annual. London: Amalgamated, 1940, 1941 and 1942.
Quinlan, David. *Film Stars*. 5th ed. London: Batsford, 2000.
Springer, John, and Jack Hamilton. *They Had Faces Then*. Secaucus NJ: Citadel, 1974.
Who's Who in the Theatre. 15th ed. London: Pitman, 1972.
Winchester, Clarence. *Screen Encyclopedia*. London: Winchester, 1948.

PATRICIA MORROW

Patricia Anne Morrow was born in Los Angeles on February 17, 1944. Her father was an attorney. She was educated at UCLA where she was a political science major. She commenced her career at four months in the film *Marriage Is a Private Affair* (1944). In the television series *I Led 3 Lives* she had the recurring role of Constance Philbrick, the older daughter of Herbert Philbrick (Richard Carlson). Her best known television role occurred a decade later when she played Rita Jacks Harrington in the soap opera *Peyton Place*. In real life she married Lance Brisson, the son of actress Rosalind Russell and producer Frederick Brisson. She later quit show business and became a qualified attorney. Her hobbies were listed as wildlife and sailing.

Filmography

1944: *Marriage Is a Private Affair*.
1953: *Roar of the Crowd*.
1954: *Ma and Pa Kettle at Home*.
1956: *The Kettles in the Ozarks*, *The Bad Seed*, *The Wrong Man*.
1957: *The Kettles on Old MacDonald's Farm*.
1964: *Surf Party*.
1985: *Peyton Place: The Next Generation* (TV).

Patricia Morrow, who costarred in *I Led 3 Lives*.

Television Series

1953–1956: *I Led 3 Lives* as Constance Philbrick.
1965–1969: *Peyton Place* as Rita Jacks Harrington.
1972–1974: *Return to Peyton Place* as Rita Jacks Harrington.

Sources

Who's Who on Television London: Independent Television Publications, 1970.
Ragan, David *Who's Who in Hollywood* New York: Facts on File, 1992.

DOUG MOSSMAN

Doug Mossman was born in Honolulu in 1934. He was on stage from childhood. He continued his acting at Kamehameha Schools, the University of Hawaii and in the army where he performed in numerous special services productions overseas. He recalled, "Whenever I had the chance, I trotted out my ukulele and did the Hawaiian thing."

After his discharge in 1956, he became the first person from Hawaii to study at the Pasadena Playhouse from which he graduated in 1958. He recalled, "There were no parts for Hawaiians. I read for everything ethnic." He was working in a restaurant when he was called to audition for the role of an Indian in a western series, *Broken Arrow*. Even though he had never been on a horse before, he read his lines so well that he was given the part. A stuntman was hired for the riding scenes.

In 1959 three weeks after answering a casting call for a new Warner Bros. television series called *Hawaiian Eye*, he went from being a waiter to acting in a studio in Burbank. He played the part of Moke, the security guard at the Hawaiian Village hotel, from where the firm of private eyes headed by Tracy Steele (Anthony Eisley) and Tom Lopaka (Robert Conrad) operated in *Hawaiian Eye*. Most sources indicate that he only started in the series in 1960, but he was present in the earliest episodes. The name of his character was initially Marty, but he was still the security guard. He also became the show's technical adviser. He spent hundreds of hours screening old movies, looking for island scenes. His job was to ensure that the series was as authentic as possible.

After the series ended he went to New York where he coproduced the Hawaiian exhibit at the 1964 World's Fair. He returned to Los Angeles for several years, then went to Hawaii where he worked in television and radio. He tested for *Hawaii Five-0* and was cast in small parts for six seasons. His personal favorite of these episodes was the third season "The Bomber and Mrs. Moroney" in which he played himself. During the seventh season he was seen in the regular role of a new character Lt. Frank Kemana, a bomb disposal expert, who transferred to the Five-O unit from H.P.D. Between 1970 and 1990 he worked for one of the luau companies in Honolulu, but Jack Lord assured him there would be no conflict if he did both jobs.

He quit *Hawaii Five-0* to develop *West Wind* starring Van Williams, a television show produced in Hawaii, but it only lasted a season. Later between 1991 and 1999 he became Director of Sales and Marketing for the Hawaiian Imax Theater in Waikiki. He still does some acting when the opportunity arises, but tends to think of himself as mainly retired. His most recent appearance to date was in an episode of the short-lived series *Hawaii* in 2004. He is currently arranging to erect a memorial statue to Jack Lord in Honolulu and developing a performing arts center in Mililani-Mauka.

Doug Mossman is married to Judee and has a daughter, Heilee, and grandchildren. He and his family lived for over two decades in Hawaii Kai on the east side of Honolulu. Later he moved to Mililani up on the central part of the island.

TELEVISION SERIES

1959–1963: *Hawaiian Eye* as Marty/Moke.
1974–1975: *Hawaii Five-0* as Det. Lt. Frank Kemana.

SOURCES

Brooks, Tim. *The Complete Directory to Prime Time TV Stars, 1946–Present*. New York: Ballantine, 1987.
Honolulu Star Bulletin News. "Whatever Happened to Doug Mossman?" January 25, 2003.
Jacobs, Ron. "Five-O Forever." *Hawaii*. February 1993.
Pickard, Jerry. "Some Musings with Mossman." *Central Dispatch*. Vol. 5, Issue 18. January 2003.
Rhodes, Karen. *Booking Hawaii Five-0*. Jefferson, NC: McFarland, 1997.

LIONEL MURTON

Lionel Murton was born in London on June 2, 1915. His parents emigrated to Canada when he was a baby where he was brought up and educated in Montreal. He began his career with Montreal Repertory Company and did many radio broadcasts in Canada. He came to Britain as a wartime naval lieutenant where he joined the Canadian Navy Show *Meet the Navy* during World War II.

Immediately after the war he became a textile sales manager in Montreal before giving this up to reenter show business. In 1946 he returned to England where he subsequently appeared on the West End stage. In the wartime set thriller series *O.S.S.* Major Frank Hawthorne (Ron Randell) received his assignments from a character known simply as the Chief. Lionel Murton played this role.

Murton regarded his biggest show business break meeting Dickie Henderson while appear-

Lionel Murton (right), who costarred in *O.S.S.*

ing on the London stage in *Teahouse of the August Moon* in 1954. Years later when Henderson had his long running situation comedy series *The Dickie Henderson Show*, Murton played his musical manager neighbor. Murton's personal favorite of his own films was *The Battle of the River Plate* (1956) because it took him on location to Montevideo in South America where he had always wanted to go.

He lived in a basement flat at Ladbroke Grove, off Holland Park, in London and a country cottage in Hampshire both of which had an extensive garden. He also liked cats. He married Marie Anita Alexandrine D'Allaire, an acrobatic adagio dancer, whom he met while they were both appearing in the wartime review in London.

Filmography

1946: *Meet the Navy.*
1948: *Brass Monkey* (a.k.a. *Lucky Mascot*), *Trouble in the Air.*
1949: *I Was a Male War Bride.*
1950: *The Girl Is Mine, Dangerous Assignment.*
1951: *The Long Dark Hall.*
1952: *The Pickwick Papers, Down Among the Z Men.*
1953: *Our Girl Friday* (a.k.a. *The Adventures of Sadie*), *The Runaway Bus.*
1954: *Night People.*
1955: *Raising a Riot.*
1956: *The Battle of the River Plate, The Baby and the Battleship* (narrator only).
1957: *Interpol* (a.k.a. *Pickup Alley*), *Fire Down Below, Carry on Admiral.*
1958: *Virgin Island* (a.k.a. *Our Virgin Island*), *Up the Creek, The Captain's Table, Further Up the Creek.*
1959: *The Mouse That Roared, Northwest Frontier* (a.k.a. *Flame Over India*), *A Touch of Larceny, Make Mine a Million, Our Man in Havana.*
1960: *Surprise Package.*
1961: *Petticoat Pirates.*
1962: *On the Beat, The Main Attraction, Summer Holiday.*
1963: *Man in the Middle.*
1965: *The Truth About Spring, Carry on Cowboy.*
1966: *Doctor in Clover.*
1967: *The Dirty Dozen.*
1968: *The Last Shot You Hear, Nobody Runs Forever* (a.k.a. *The High Commissioner*).
1969: *Patton.*
1970: *Zeta One, The Revolutionary, Cannon for Cordoba, Welcome to the Club.*
1974: *Confessions of a Window Cleaner.*
1976: *Seven Nights in Japan.*
1977: *Twilight's Last Gleaming.*
1979: *The London Connection* (a.k.a. *The Omega Connection*).

Television Series

1958–1959: *O.S.S.* as the Chief.
1960–1965: *The Dickie Henderson Show* as Jack.

Sources

Noble, Peter *British Film and Television Year Book 1962/1963* London: British and American Press, 1963.
Picture Show Who's Who on the Screen London: Amalgamated Press, c1956.
Quinlan, David *The Illustrated Directory of Film Character Actors Second Edition* London: Batsford, 1995.
Scott, Esmé *TV Times* magazine "I Owe Everything to My Cat" December 10, 1961.
Vahimagi, Tise *BFI British Television* Oxford, England: Oxford University Press, 1994.
Who's Who on Television London: Independent Television Publications Limited, 1970.

George Nader

George Nader was a handsome, muscular hunk who was one of the leading male pinups of the fifties. Rather disappointingly for his army of female fans, he was also a homosexual. His private life and career were inextricably bound up with those of Universal's most successful male star, Rock Hudson. The degree to which Nader's career was adversely affected by his sexual preferences is a subject for speculation. Considering that he was extremely well qualified and trained for a career on the stage, Nader really should have been a better actor. At times with the right script and direction, he was capable of giving a good performance. The rest of the time he was barely adequate in the acting stakes. He extended his career by moving into television with some success and by achieving more popularity in Europe with a series of action movie thrillers notably playing FBI agent, Jerry Cotton. Tony Curtis said of him, "He was one of the kindest and most generous men I have ever known." Mamie Van Doren gave a rather more earthy assessment when she said, "Nader was more than beefcake. He was the whole dessert trolley."

George Nader was born George Garfield Nader, Jr., in Los Angeles, CA on October 19, 1921. He was the only child of George Garfield Nader, an oil company executive and Alice Scott, an educator. One of his mother's ancestors was mayor of St. Ives, Cornwall, England. His mother's family emigrated from England to Kansas where she was born November 3, 1891. His father, who was Lebanese and Irish, was born in Chicago on October 8, 1892 and moved to Los Angeles where he met and married Alice Scott.

Nader, Jr., went to school in Glendale where his interest in theater began for he built his own puppet theater. By the time that he reached high school, he had decided that he would like to become a producer-director. He began as a member of the school stage crew and eventually became stage manager. He graduated from Glendale High School, CA and entered Occidental College, CA. After entering college he transferred his interest from backstage work to acting. By the time he graduated with a B.A. degree he had become president of the dramatic club.

In 1943 he left college and was drafted into the U.S. Navy where he served mainly in the Pacific area as a communications officer until the Autumn of 1946. He was honorably discharged as a Lt. J.g. He enrolled at the Pasadena Playhouse where he studied for four years graduating with a Master's degree in Theatre Arts. During this time he appeared in 25 plays there as well as two more at a theater in Santa Barbara.

He was seen in the west coast premiere of Tennessee Williams' play *The Glass Menagerie* by actress Jeanne Crain who took a liking to him and brought him to the attention of director Jean Negulesco. Negulesco was directing her at the time in the film *Take Care of My Little Girl* (1951) at 20th Century–Fox. Negulesco gave him a very small part in the film which marked his screen debut. This was not the first of his films to be released. Years later he did costar with Jeanne Crain in *The Second Greatest Sex* (1955).

He slowly worked his way up from bit parts. His career was enhanced by the fact that he was willing to work overseas. Over the next few years he flew more than 30,000 miles. He went to Bombay, India to play the male lead opposite Ursula Thiess in *Monsoon* (1952). Then he went to Stockholm, Sweden where he costarred with Swedish star Anita Bjork in *Memory of Love* (1952). There was also a stay in Munich, Germany when he costarred opposite Anne Baxter in *Carnival Story* (1954). This was a backstage circus story which marked the costarring of two of the screen's most physically attractive stars. It was also a voyeur's paradise for those who liked looking at Baxter in a leotard!

George Nader (right) on location in London for the film *Nowhere to Go* (1958). He starred in the television series *Ellery Queen*.

He starred in the sci-fi film *Robot Monster* (1953) which was shot in 3-D on a negligible budget of $16,000 in four days. This has frequently been listed as one of the worst films of all time. The title figure was played by George Barrows in an ape suit with a diving bell on his head. When it was first released, audiences were more inclined to laugh than show fear. Nevertheless it is reckoned to have grossed over a million dollars. Universal signed Nader to a contract and announced that they had great plans for him. For them he appeared in the key role of the cop who takes a paternal interest in young offender Tony Curtis in *Six Bridges to Cross* (1955). For this Nader received a Golden Globe award as "the most promising newcomer of 1954." He starred opposite Jeanne Crain in *The Second Greatest Sex* (1955), a musical western based on Lysistrata with the women going on a sex strike until their cowboy lovers become more domesticated and less violent. In *Lady Godiva* (1955) he was rather more unsuitably cast as a Saxon nobleman in the eleventh century whose wife (Maureen O' Hara) made the infamous nude ride through the streets of Canterbury in Merrie Olde England. He was one of an ensemble cast headed by Jeff Chandler in the World War II naval yarn *Away All Boats* (1956). Possibly because of the elements drawn from his wartime experiences, this was Nader's personal favorite of his Universal films. His final film at Universal was *The Female Animal* (1958) in which he played a hunk who is lusted after by both a fading beauty (Hedy Lamarr) and her daughter (Jane Powell).

During the fifties scandal magazines notably *Confidential* sold millions of copies by revealing revelations about such previously taboo subjects as homosexuality and which male players inclinations veered towards making love with partners of the same sex. The public were generally kept blissfully unaware of such antics because of a plethora of photographs showing virile male stars out on arranged dates with nubile starlets courtesy of the studio publicity machine. The studio was even supposed to have spread a rumor that Nader had impregnated two waitresses. According to Hollywood folklore, Nader's studio Universal deliberately outed him in order to safeguard Rock Hudson, their much bigger investment, from having his reputation permanently destroyed if it became public knowledge that he was a homosexual.

Nevertheless Nader did a great deal of television work. Loretta Young signed him as her leading man in her television series for one drama only, but so many enthusiastic letters were received from fans that it was decided that he should star in six more stories in the long running anthology series *The Loretta Young Show*. Between September 26, 1958 and February 20, 1959 he starred in 20 live, hour length episodes as Ellery Queen in *The Further Adventures of Ellery Queen* on NBC. Producer Albert McCleery stated at the outset that they could only use four of the original *Ellery Queen* novels, but in fact six were adapted for the series. The remaining fourteen were adapted from novels by a wide variety of other writers. Les Tremayne costarred as his father Inspector Richard Queen who frequently involved his son in his more difficult cases.

Ellery Queen was a celebrated literary sleuth originally created by cousins Frederic Dannay and Manfred B. Lee in 1929. The character featured in a series of novels; a long running radio series; a live television network half hour series; and a filmed syndicated half hour television series. This was the first time that the character had featured in an hour length series and in color, although the fact that it was live could be regarded as a retrograde step. Nader's involvement in the series came about when he was approached by producer Albert McCleery in the parking lot at NBC studios in Burbank who asked him if he would like to play Ellery Queen in a live show which he was producing that fall. After Nader readily agreed, he went on to enjoy the distinction of being the only actor in the history of American television to ever star in 20 live consecutive episodes of an hour long weekly drama series. He did these episodes in California. His involvement with the series ended when he refused to move to New York to finish the series. Nader was replaced by Lee Philips, while Tremayne's character was dropped altogether. What on the face of it could have been an egregious error on Nader's part in career terms turned out to be a bagatelle. Immediately afterwards he was signed by Sir Michael Balcon to star as the handsome, charming but totally unscrupulous cad in *Nowhere to Go* (1958) in England opposite newcomer Maggie Smith. This was a compelling but downbeat thriller directed by the talented but tragic Seth Holt. In it Nader gave the best performance of his career and it remained his personal favorite of his own films. He was the star of two other television series. *The Man and the Challenge,* originally shown on NBC between September 1959 and September 1960, was a half hour series in which he played a space doctor. In the syndicated series *Shannon* first aired in 1961, he played an insurance investigator.

During the sixties he moved to West Germany where he starred in eleven movies for Constantin Films of Munich. Eight of the eleven comprised the *Jerry Cotton* series. He played the leading character, an FBI agent based in New York. Although these films were little seen outside their country of origin, they were enormously popular with German audiences and later became staples of West German television.

His worst acting experience came with the film *End Station of the Damned* which he shot in Ceylon (Sri Lanka) in 1968, an Italian-German coproduction. As he recalled, "They wrote the script as they went along and changed directors mid-film. It was hot and humid with no air conditioning and temperatures sometimes reached 125 degrees on the set. Added to this was a subplot of Byzantine intrigue no self-respecting soap opera would touch. It reached the point where I frankly feared for my life, as did my native chauffeur, who urged me to get the hell out of there at the first chance I had. As soon as I finished my last scene, telling nobody and with his help, I climbed on a plane at 4 am the next morning and fled to my villa in Rome and safety!"

His last film role was Eddie Romero's fantasy about a lost civilization *Beyond Atlantis* (1973) lensed in the Philippines. He guested on several television series, but was forced into retirement when a car accident caused an eye injury and left him unable to stand the bright glare of arc lights. From this he developed glaucoma. Instead he turned to writing. He wrote the science fiction novel *Chrome* which was published by Putnam in 1978. This was acclaimed in particular for its sensitive handling of a homosexual romance between two robots. By 1998 it was still in print in its fifth paperback edition. He also wrote two other novels which may yet be published posthumously. He was an active supporter of AMFAR (Elizabeth Taylor's AIDS research program). In addition he contributed to ASF, a private charitable fund which operated hospices in the Orange County area of California.

He lived for many years with Mark Miller previously Rock Hudson's secretary. Both of them were close friends of Hudson's. When Hudson died of AIDS in 1985, he left them most of his entire $27,000,000 estate in his will. This was contested by Hudson's former lover, Marc Christian, who after litigation was awarded $5,500,000. Nader spent his final years living quietly and comfortably with Miller in Palm Springs. While he seldom sought the limelight during his last years, he emerged in April 2000 to attend a *Jerry Cotton* retrospective in West Germany.

Nader died at the Motion Picture Country Home and Hospital in Woodland Hills, California on February 4, 2002 aged 80 of pneumonia. He was survived by Mark Miller and three cousins. He was cremated following a private service and his ashes were scattered at sea.

FILMOGRAPHY

1950: *Rustlers on Horseback, The Prowler.*
1951: *Take Care of My Little Girl, Two Tickets to Broadway, Overland Telegraph, Down Among the Sheltering Palms* (released 1953).
1952: *Phone Call From a Stranger, Monsoon.*
1953: *Sins of Jezebel, Miss Robin Crusoe, Memory of Love.*
1954: *Robot Monster, Carnival Story, Four Guns to the Border.*
1955: *Six Bridges to Cross, The Second Greatest Sex, Lady Godiva* (a.k.a. *Lady Godiva of Coventry*).
1956: *Away All Boats, Congo Crossing, The Unguarded Moment, Four Girls in Town.*
1957: *Man Afraid, Joe Butterfly, Flood Tide.*
1958: *Appointment with a Shadow, The Female Animal, Nowhere to Go.*
1962: *The Secret Mark of d'Artagnan.*
1963: *A Walk by the Sea* (also directed), *Zigzag.*
1964: *The Great Space Adventure, Alarm on 83rd Street.*
1965: *The Human Duplicators, Die Rechnung—eiskalt serviert, Der Morderclub von Brooklyn, Schusse aus dem Geigenkasten* (a.k.a. *Tread Softly*), *Mordnacht in Manhattan, Um null Uhr schnappt die Falle zu.*
1966: *Operation Hurricane.*
1967: *House of a Thousand Dolls, The Million Eyes of Sumuru.*
1968: *End Station of the Damned, Der Tod im roten Jaguar, Dynamit in gruner Seide.*
1969: *Todeschusse am Broadway.*
1973: *Beyond Atlantis.*
1974: *Nakia* (TV).

TELEVISION SERIES

1958–1959: *The Further Adventures of Ellery Queen* as Ellery Queen.
1959–1960: *The Man and the Challenge* as Dr. Glenn Barton.
1961: *Shannon* as Joe Shannon.

SOURCES

Correspondence between Nader and the author.
The Daily Telegraph. Obituary, February 9, 2002.
Martland, John. *The Stage*. Obituary, March 28, 2002.
Mizrahi, Robin. "Hudson's Beefcake Lover Was His Rock to the End." *National Enquirer.* March 12, 2002.
Nevins, Francis M. Jr. "Ellery Queen on the Small Screen." *The Golden Years of Radio and TV.* No. 1. Winter 1983.
Picture Show. "Life Story." January 1, 1955.
Quinlan, David. *Film Stars*. 5th ed. London: Batsford, 2000.
Vallance, Tom. *The Independent.* Obituary, February 8, 2002.

J. CARROL NAISH

Out of a swirling mist came a short, stocky figure, neat and dapper with a Homburg hat on his broad head, bow tie and ebony stick. A legend proclaimed, *The New Adventures of Charlie Chan* starring J. Carrol Naish. Naish was once called, "Hollywood's one man U.N." His swarthy complexion and dark hair made him a natural for Latin characters. He had notable successes on screen playing many different ethnic types, but in typical Hollywood tradition, he never played a character of his own genuine ancestry which was Irish.

Joseph Patrick Carrol Naish was born in New York City on January 21, 1897, the son of Patrick Sarsfield Naish and Catherine Moran. He was one of seven children. He could trace his ancestry back to thirteenth century Ireland and was the great great grandson of John Naish, Attorney General and later Lord Chancellor of Ireland. Educated at St. Cecilia's Academy, New York, as a boy soprano he sang in many school productions.

Naish left school at fourteen and was briefly engaged as part of a Gus Edwards' kid troupe. Then he worked as a song plugger in Tin Pan Alley. When America entered World War I, Naish enlisted in the U.S. flying service and trained as a pilot. He was sent overseas where he accumulated over 200 hours as a bomber pilot. When the war ended, he decided to remain in Europe. Joining a pianist and guitarist, the trio became part of a touring company toplined by Elsie Janis which was entertaining American troops abroad. He was seen performing by French musical comedy star Gaby Deslys who engaged him to appear in the musical comedy *Frou Fro* in Paris.

For the next few years Naish toured Europe as a variety entertainer visiting Germany, Russia, Spain and Italy. As a result he became fluent in several languages and developed a talent as a mimic and expert dialectician. In 1926 he returned to America and journeyed to Hollywood where he had a number of jobs including working in movies as an extra. A role in a stock company production of *The Pleasure of Honesty* brought him to the attention of actress Florence Reed who engaged him to play the Japanese Prince in a tour of *The Shanghai Gesture* in 1928.

At the end of the play's run, Naish made New York his home, appearing in several Broadway plays. While appearing in *Scotland Yard* in 1929, he learned that producer William Fox was looking for actors with stage experience to appear in motion pictures. Expressing interest, Naish was tested successfully and made his motion picture debut as a gangster in *Cheer Up and Smile* (1930). He was sent to Hollywood where he received acclaim playing Loretta Young's father Sun Yat Ming who was killed by the title figure (Edward G. Robinson) in *The Hatchet Man* (1932). During the 1930s Naish acquired a reputation for playing shady underworld types. He was noted for the homework which he undertook before playing a character. When cast as a gangster in *King of Alcatraz* (1938) he journeyed to New York where he attended the trial of James J. Hines in order to study the racketeers who gave evidence. He explained, "I believe in being real— literally real. That is why I am here."

Naish worked steadily in movies for the next quarter of a century. Although occasionally he toplined in a "B" picture, he found his greatest achievements were as a character actor. As he expressed it, "You get much greater inner satisfaction playing a character part—each new role is a challenge." Naish was fortunate because at that time he was in great demand as a character actor by most of the leading studios. He was proactive in that he aggressively campaigned for roles that interested him and turned down offers of long-term contracts. As he explained it," I like to go after roles and when you're under contract, you've got to do what they want you to do."

In the course of his distinguished career he was twice nominated for a Best Supporting Actor Oscar, but failed to win on both occasions. The first time was as the Italian captive Giuseppe in *Sahara* (1943) which starred Humphrey Bogart. The other occasion was as a Mexican peasant in *A Medal for Benny* (1945). These two roles are reputed to have been his favorite film parts along with *Black Hand* (1950) an atmospheric film dealing with the Mafia during the early years of the century in which he played a heroic Italian detective.

Serial fans recall him as the mad Japanese scientist Dr. Daka in the serial *The Batman* (1943). At the other end of the spectrum he worked for top directors like Jean Renoir in *The Southerner* (1945) in which he played a Southern farmer and John Ford in *The Fugitive* (1947) as a treacherous police informer and *Rio Grande* (1950) as a high ranking army officer. He played Indian Chief Sitting Bull in two films which could not have been more different namely the musical *Annie Get Your Gun* (1950) and a tragic Western appropriately called *Sitting Bull* (1954).

His most successful long running role however was in the field of radio with *Life With Luigi*, a comedy series beginning on CBS in 1948 in which he played the title character Luigi Basco, a sunny natured Italian immigrant. The radio series lasted until March 1953. It made a somewhat uneasy transition to live television via the CBS network where it lasted only a few months running from September to December 1952. For its single season, it nevertheless finished a top twenty hit in the ratings.

Naish returned to Broadway for the first time in 25 years in September 1955 to appear in a major role in two one act plays which comprised *A View from the Bridge* by Arthur Miller. His personal notices were generally excellent, but nevertheless he left the play on December 31, 1955 and returned to Hollywood to appear in some more films. The play closed on February 4, 1956.

He then starred in a syndicated black and white crime series primarily filmed in England called *The New Adventures of Charlie Chan*. He played the title role of the famous Chinese detective inspector from Honolulu in 39 fast moving episodes. A few episodes were shot in America and location shooting on the rest was done all over Europe. The character was originally created by Earl Derr Biggers in a series of novels commencing with *The House Without a Key* in 1925. The television series was popular with viewers and the mysteries hold up quite well. Naish however received rare negative reviews of his work in this series. Despite being television's

J. Carrol Naish in *The New Adventures of Charlie Chan*.

first Chan, he was not creating the role from scratch. He followed in the footsteps of such cinema Charlie Chans as Warner Oland and Sidney Toler who had the resources of a major studio, 20th Century–Fox, to enhance the quality of their work. Their Fox movies looked considerably better than the television version. The cinema Charlie Chans had only begun to decline when Toler and later Roland Winters had essayed the role for the lowly Monogram studios. The television version represented an improvement over these.

Naish also found the series physically exhausting. The main problem was his make-up which was created and applied by expert Colin Garde. It took a long time to apply each morning. Garde hovered on the set all the time to ensure that the heat from the studio did not melt it. Naish had to wear many disguises some of which, as when he played an old Chinese in the episode called "Circle of Fear," meant that he could not eat a proper lunch during a whole week's shooting. On his break he went up to his dressing-room for a glass of milk which he sipped through a straw. As he complained, "It's rugged. It's real tough. I have to put these eyelids on each time. Have to act carefully or my real eyelids show. It's a real challenge in other ways too. Must learn 15 pages every day; never a day off." This was because Chan in one guise or other appeared in nearly every scene. The actor's disposition was not helped by the fact that he was widely believed to be experiencing personal problems at the time caused by his wife's excessive drinking.

His costar in the series was James Hong who played Number One Son Barry Chan. The series was a production of Television Programs of America. The executive producer was Leon Fromkess and the producers were Sidney Marshall and Rudolph Flothow.

Naish had one other regular role in a series namely that of a Red Indian in the ABC comedy *Guestward Ho!* Ill health brought about his semi-retirement for the last decade of his life although he continued to appear on television until 1970. His once illustrious film career fell away to almost nothing and ended in ignominy with a low budget horror called *Dracula Vs. Frankenstein* (1970). He played the role in a wheel chair which fuelled speculation inaccurately that he was confined to one in real life.

During his halcyon years he resided in the Beverly Hills. He died in a La Jolla, California hospital on January 24, 1973 aged 76 of emphysema. He is buried at Calvary Cemetery, Los Angeles. He was survived by his widow Gladys Heaney, a former actress whom he met when they were both in the road company of *The Shanghai Gesture* and married on February 10, 1928. They had one daughter Carol Elaine who appeared in small roles with her father on the *Life With Luigi* series and later married Jack R. Sheridan.

Filmography

1930: *Cheer Up and Smile, Good Intentions, Scotland Yard, Double Crossroads.*
1931: *Tonight or Never, Homicide Squad, Gun Smoke, Kick In, Ladies of the Big House, The Royal Bed.*
1932: *The Mouthpiece, Week-End Marriage, The Conquerors, The Kid from Spain, Big City Blues, Two Seconds, Tiger Shark, Washington Merry-Go-Round, The Hatchet Man, Cabin in the Cotton, Beast of the City, It's Tough to be Famous, The Famous Ferguson Case, Crooner, No Living Witness.*
1933: *The Mystery Squadron* (serial), *The Devil's in Love, Elmer the Great, Arizona to Broadway, The Whirlwind, Notorious but Nice, Captured, Frisco Jenny, Ann Vickers, Central Airport, The Mad Game, The World Gone Mad, The Past of Mary Holmes, The Avenger, Silent Men, No Other Woman, The Big Chance, The Infernal Machine, The Last Trail.*
1934: *Murder in Trinidad, What's Your Racket?, The Hell Cat, Return of the Terror, British Agent, The Defense Rests, Marie Galante, Upper World, One Is Guilty, Sleepers East, Bachelor of Arts, Girl in Danger, Hell in the Heavens.*
1935: *Behind Green Lights, The President Vanishes, Black Fury, Under the Pampas Moon, Little Big Shot, The Crusades, The Lives of a Bengal Lancer, Captain Blood, Confidential, Front Page Woman, Special Agent.*
1936: *We Who Are About To Die, Two in the Dark, The Return of Jimmy Valentine, Robin Hood of El Dorado, Absolute Quiet, Ramona, The Charge of the Light Brigade, Special Investigator, Exclusive Story, The Leathernecks Have Landed, Moonlight Murder, Charlie Chan at the Circus, Anthony Adverse, Crack-Up.*
1937: *Border Cafe, Think Fast Mr. Moto, Sea Racketeers, Thunder Trail, Daughter of Shanghai, Song of the City, Hideaway, Bulldog Drummond Comes Back, Night Club Scandal.*
1938: *Hunted Men, Tip-Off Girls, Bulldog Drummond in Africa, Illegal Traffic, King of Alcatraz, Her Jungle Love, Prison Farm, Persons in Hiding.*
1939: *Undercover Doctor, Beau Geste, Hotel Imperial, King of Chinatown, Island of Lost Men.*
1940: *Golden Gloves, Typhoon, Down Argentine Way, A Night at Earl Carroll's, Queen of the Mob.*
1941: *Blood and Sand, That Night in Rio, Forced Landing, The Corsican Brothers, Mr. Dynamite, Accent on Love, Birth of the Blues.*
1942: *Jackass Mail, A Gentleman at Heart, Tales of Manhattan, Dr. Renault's Secret, Dr. Broadway, The Pied Piper, The Man in the Trunk, Sunday Punch.*
1943: *Batman* (serial), *Harrigan's Kid, Sahara, Calling Dr. Death, Good Morning Judge, Behind the Rising Sun, Gung Ho!.*
1944: *Waterfront, The Monster Maker, Two-Man Submarine, Nabonga, Enter Arsene Lupin, The Whistler, Voice in the Wind, Dragon Seed, House of Frankenstein, Mark of the Whistler, Jungle Woman.*
1945: *Strange Confession, The Southerner, A Medal for Benny, Getting Gertie's Garter, House of Frankenstein.*
1946: *Humoresque, Bad Bascomb, The Beast With Five Fingers.*
1947: *The Fugitive, Carnival in Costa Rica, Road to Rio.*
1948: *Joan of Arc, The Kissing Bandit.*
1949: *That Midnight Kiss, Canadian Pacific.*
1950: *Rio Grande, The Toast of New Orleans,*

Annie Get Your Gun, Black Hand, Please Believe Me.
1951: *Across the Wide Missouri, Mark of the Renegade, Bannerline.*
1952: *Clash by Night, Woman of the North Country, Denver and Rio Grande, Ride the Man Down.*
1953: *Beneath the 12-Mile Reef, Fighter Attack.*
1954: *Saskatchewan, Sitting Bull.*
1955: *New York Confidential, Violent Saturday, Hit the Deck, The Last Command, Rage at Dawn, Desert Sands.*
1956: *Yaqui Drums, Rebel in Town.*
1957: *The Young Don't Cry, This Could Be the Night.*
1961: *Force of Impulse.*
1964: *The Hanged Man* (TV).
1970: *Cutter's Trail* (TV), *Dracula Vs. Frankenstein.*

TELEVISION SERIES

1952: *Life With Luigi* as Luigi Basco.
(UK 1957–1958): *The New Adventures of Charlie Chan* as Charlie Chan.
(USA 1957).
1960–1961: *Guestward Ho!* as Hawkeye.

SOURCES

Cowan, Margaret. "Charlie Chan Comes to Britain." *TV Times*. September 13, 1957.
Current Biography. New York: H. Wilson, 1957.
Daily Telegraph. Obituary, January 1973.
Donnelly, Paul. *Fade to Black*. London: Omnibus, 2000.
McClure, Arthur E., and Ken D. Jones. *Heroes, Heavies and Sagebrush*. South Brunswick, NJ: Barnes, 1972.
Picture Show Annual. London: Amalgamated, 1934, 1939 and 1954.
Quinlan, David. *Illustrated Directory of Film Character Actors*. 2nd ed. London: Batsford, 1995.
Twomey, Alfred E., and Arthur F. McClure. *The Versatiles*. South Brunswick, NJ: Barnes, 1969.
Vazzana, Eugene. *Silent Film Necrology*. Jefferson, NC: McFarland, 1995.
Weaver, Tom. *It Came from Weaver Five*. Jefferson, NC: McFarland, 1996.
Winchester, Clarence. *The World Film Encyclopedia*. London: Amalgamated, 1933.
_____. *Screen Encyclopedia*. London: Winchester, 1948.

RUSSELL NAPIER

Russell Gordon Napier was born in Perth, Western Australia on November 28, 1910. He was a direct descendant of Captain Cargill who founded the settlement in Otago, New Zealand in 1848 and was the great grandson of the designer of the first Napier car. Educated in New Zealand, he obtained a Bachelor of Laws degree at Otago University. Initially he became a barrister and solicitor of the Supreme Court of New Zealand. Abandoning the law, he emigrated to England in 1935 to take up a stage career and remained.

He played in *Murder in the Cathedral* in the West End and on tour in England and America. Subsequently he appeared in Hull, Coventry and Worthing repertory companies until the outbreak of World War II. Then he served in the British army as a captain from 1940 until 1945. Upon his demobilization he returned to the West End stage and started radio work in 1946. He made his screen debut in *End of the River* (1947). Active on television from the late 1940s, he went on to make dozens of appearances. He played English, American, Australian and New Zealand parts, but no British dialects on radio and television. He also acted as narrator in many broadcasts.

The famous criminologist Edgar Lustgarten (1907–1978) introduced the series *Scotland Yard* which consisted of 39 half hour, black and white episodes based on real cases from the files of Scotland Yard. This was an anthology series, but certain of the police officers appeared on several occasions. Inspector Duggan (Russell Napier) was the closest to a regular character. The series was a hit in England where it was shown in 1955 under the title *Case Histories of Scotland Yard* and in America where it ran under the title of *Scotland Yard*. The series was produced by Jack Greenwood for Anglo Amalgamated Films. Napier continued to appear in short new films featuring this character which served as second features in the cinema until 1962. In all he appeared as Duggan sixteen times. In the late 1950s when there was a reawakening of interest in Australian lensed films with British financing, he found himself cast in character roles in them.

Off screen Napier was a keen cricketer who played as a member of the Stage Cricket Club and the London New Zealand Cricket Club.

Napier died at his home in Surbiton, Surrey,

Russell Napier, who starred in *Scotland Yard*.

England on August 19, 1974 aged 63 of a cerebral hemorrhage and the accompanying hypertension, survived by his widow, Lois Mary Caird Napier and two children.

FILMOGRAPHY

1947: *The End of the River.*
1951: *Green Grow the Rushes, Blind Man's Bluff, Death of an Angel.*
1952: *Stolen Face.*
1953: *Black Orchid, The Saint's Return* (a.k.a. *The Saint's Girl Friday*).
1954: *Conflict of Wings* (a.k.a. *Fuss Over Feathers*), *Companions in Crime, The Stranger Came Home* (a.k.a. *The Unholy Four*), *The Brain Machine, The Case of the Little Red Monkey, Terror Street* (a.k.a. *36 Hours*).
1955: *A Time to Kill, Out of the Clouds, The Blue Peter.*
1956: *The Narrowing Circle, The Man in the Road, Guilty?, The Last Man To Hang?, A Town Like Alice.*
1957: *The Shiralee, Robbery Under Arms.*
1958: *Tread Softly Stranger, A Night To Remember, Son of Robin Hood.*
1959: *The Witness, Hell is a City, The Angry Silence.*
1960: *Sink the Bismarck!*
1961: *The Mark, Francis of Assisi, Barabbas.*
1962: *Mix Me a Person, HMS Defiant* (a.k.a. *Damn the Defiant!*).
1963: *Man in the Middle.*
1966: *It!* (a.k.a. *Return of the Golem*).
1967: *The Blood Beast Terror.*
1968: *Nobody Runs Forever* (a.k.a. *The High Commissioner*), *Twisted Nerve.*
1974: *The Black Windmill.*

TELEVISION SERIES

UK 1955: *Case Histories of Scotland Yard* as Insp. Duggan.
USA 1957–1958: *Scotland Yard* as Insp. Duggan.

SOURCES

Andrews, Cyrus. *Radio and Television Who's Who.* 1st ed. London: Vox Mundi, 1950.
_____. *Radio and Television Who's Who.* 3rd ed. London: George Young, 1954.
Death Certificate. August 21, 1974.
Quinlan, David. *Illustrated Directory of Film Character Actors.* 2nd ed. London: Batsford, 1995.
Tibballs, Geoff. *TV Detectives.* London: Boxtree, 1992.

BARRY NELSON

Barry Nelson had two distinct phases of his career. During the forties he was a star at MGM in the days when that studio bragged it had more stars than were in heaven. His star did not twinkle there quite so brightly as some of the other luminaries. In later years he proved to be one of America's most durable and dependable theater stars. In the interim he starred in three television series. Since one was historic, another was a comedy and the third was a thriller, he was certainly not typecast. He might have become a major television icon if one of his single television efforts had run to a series because he was the first actor to play James Bond.

Barry Nelson was born Robert Haakon Nielson in Oakland, CA on April 16, 1920. His parents were Tryge Nielson and Lisbet (Betsy) Christophsen. They were Norwegian. He was educated at public schools in Oakland and graduated with a BA degree from the University of California at Berkeley. He financed his college education by assisting in the production of weekly radio programs. He directed amateur plays for women's clubs. He appeared as a dozen different characters in a pageant "Cavalcade of the Golden West" at the San Francisco Exhibition in 1939.

His professional acting career began with a small but enterprising deception. His college graduation was fast approaching and he had decided that he would like to be a professional actor. So he sent letters purporting to be from the theater to Hollywood studio talent scouts praising his own performance in the title role of the college production of *Macbeth* and left tickets in their names at the box office. The ploy worked beyond his wildest dreams. He was signed by MGM, the most prestigious studio in Hollywood, to a seven year contract in 1941. His initial salary was $300. He made his screen debut in *Shadow of the Thin Man* (1941), one of the series which starred William Powell and Myrna Loy. Of his debut he recalled, "I was cast as the juvenile lead, but I had never played anyone under 50 before. At Berkeley we did Chekhov, Strindberg and Shakespeare." He made several films at MGM. One, *A Yank on the Burma Road* (1942), is believed to have been the first Hollywood movie to mention the Japanese attack on Pearl Harbor.

Between 1943 and 1946 he served in the Special Services Unit of the U.S. Army Air Force. While in the services he played Bobby Grills in the Moss Hart's morale boosting show, *Winged Victory* which opened at the 44th Street Theater, Broadway on November 20, 1943, billed as Corporal Barry Nelson. He repeated the role in the film version in 1944. After the war he finished his contract with MGM from whom he parted company on good terms. Of his post-war films for them one of the most interesting was *The Beginning or the End?* (1947) in which he played Col. Paul Tibbets, Jr., the pilot who dropped the A Bomb on Japan. In a later film at MGM *Above and Beyond* (1953) Robert Taylor played the same role.

Moss Hart remembered him from *Winged Victory* and cast him in the lead of playwright Peter Sloane in *Light Up the Sky* at the Royale Theater, New York on November 18, 1948 which ran for 214 performances. He starred in a number of other Broadway hits, one of the earliest being as Donald Gresham in *The Moon is Blue* at the Henry Miller Theater from March 1951 onwards. He stayed with this for three years and simultaneously entered television. He made his television debut in "My Old Man's Badge," an episode of the CBS anthology series *Suspense* in

Barry Nelson, who starred in *The Hunter*.

1950. He was the star of three television series. His first television series was a filmed CBS summer replacement series called *The Hunter* which was a half hour, black and white series originally aired between July and September 1952. Nelson played Bart Adams, a wealthy young businessman, whose entrepreneurial skills and interests not only took him all over the world, but also involved him in hazardous situations involving international intrigue. Adams was in reality a United States undercover agent whose nickname was *The Hunter*. He proved to be a master of disguise, donning a fresh one for each episode. He most frequently rescued people who had been kidnapped by Communists or blocked Communist plans for world domination. He identified himself to friends in the European network of operatives by whistling *Frere Jacques* and ending with a wolf whistle. There were additional episodes of this series shown in syndication after the network run. Some of these episodes found their way onto another television summer replacement schedule, but this time on NBC between July and December 1954. There were also some new episodes filmed and aired on NBC in 1954, but Keith Larsen replaced Nelson as Bart Adams. In the normal scheme of show business matters, they were not mutually interchangeable actors. Nelson was unable to reprise the role because he was starring in the CBS situation comedy *My Favorite Husband* at the time.

My Favorite Husband was a live situation comedy shown on CBS between September 1953 and December 1955. He played George Cooper, a successful bank executive with an opulent suburban home and a beautiful if slightly daffy wife, Liz, who was initially played by Joan Caulfield and later by Vanessa Brown. Episodes centered around their social status and relationships with their rather snobbish neighbors. Nelson was on vacation in Jamaica after his grueling stint of 103 episodes of this series when CBS called him to play Jimmy Bond in a live, hour long, prime time version of "Casino Royale" an episode of the anthology series *Climax*. It was due to be screened in eight days. It was to be done at the CBS Television City in Hollywood on a budget of $25,000. Bond was a crew-cut American agent who drank Scotch and gambled heavily. Peter Lorre was to play the villain Le Chiffre and Linda Christian was the enigmatic heroine. It was originally aired on October 21, 1954. Nelson recalled, "It was something of a disaster. It needed rewriting, more time in rehearsal and a bigger budget. It was done in haste, the exotic flavor of the story was totally lost and they just dismantled the character. It had become almost unplayable." CBS had an option for the next half dozen Bond books, but foolishly let the option lapse.

Hudson's Bay was his third series which was syndicated in 1958 and shot in Canada. Nelson played an eighteenth century explorer who originally discovered and exploited the title area. The series ran into marketing and distribution problems which caused it to flounder. It is an obscure series which is frequently omitted from the star's credits. Even Nelson recalled it as, "a strange series of which the most memorable thing was that I had to learn to ride a horse." His television career as a guest star continued until the late eighties.

Between 1956 and 1958 he starred as Will Stockdale in *No Time for Sergeants* at Her Majesty's Theater, London. He had Sir Herbert Beerbohm Tree's original suite at the theater; garnered the best reviews of his career; and found the whole experience delightful. He resumed his Broadway career with one of his most long-running hits as Bob McKellaway in *Mary Mary* at the Helen Hayes Theater in 1961 which he repeated in the film version in 1963. He played Joe Grady as well as directing the two character play *The Only Game in Town* (1968). Later hits included as Det. McLeod in *The Detective Story* in 1973; as Reg in *The Norman Conquests* in 1975; as Dan Connors in *The Act* in 1977 for which he received a Tony nomination; and as Julian Marsh in *42nd Street* both at the Majestic Theater, NY in 1981 and on tour between 1983 and 1986. In the early nineties he toured fifty American cities in the comedy *Lend Me a Tenor*.

He made comparatively few films after the MGM years. He averaged to make a film only occasionally. Asked about this, he replied, "There were two reasons for this. I made a film whenever there wasn't a decent play to do and there wasn't one every season. I also tried to keep all the balls in the air at the same time." Of the later films the most talked about was *The Shining* (1980) directed by Stanley Kubrick. Nelson played Stuart Ullman, the landlord who originally employed Jack Nicholson. Nelson was hired for this role after Kubrick spotted him in a television show.

Barry Nelson married actress Teresa Celi in 1951, but they were later divorced. He later wed Nancy Hoy who is also his manager. His hobbies are reading, listening to music, play going, art collecting and he is an indefatigable traveler. He resides very comfortably in New York since acting has left him very well off.

FILMOGRAPHY

1941: *Shadow of the Thin Man, Dr. Kildare's Victory, Johnny Eager.*
1942: *A Yank on the Burma Road, Rio Rita, Eyes in the Night, The Affairs of Martha, Stand By For Action.*
1943: *The Human Comedy, Bataan, A Guy Named Joe.*
1944: *Winged Victory.*
1947: *Undercover Maisie, The Beginning or the End?*
1948: *Tenth Avenue Angel, Command Decision* (voice only).
1951: *The Man With My Face.*
1956: *The First Traveling Saleslady.*
1963: *Mary Mary.*
1967: *The Borgia Stick* (TV).
1969: *Seven in Darkness* (TV).
1970: *Airport.*
1972: *Pete 'n' Tillie, Climb an Angry Mountain* (TV).
1980: *Island Claws* (a.k.a. *Night of the Claw*), *The Shining.*

TELEVISION SERIES

1952: *The Hunter* as Bart Adams.
1953–1955: *My Favorite Husband* as George Cooper.
1958–1959: *Hudson's Bay* as Pierre Radisson.

MINISERIES

1977: *Washington: Behind Closed Doors.*

SOURCES

Collura, Joe. "Barry Nelson: The Good Soldier." *Films of the Golden Age.* No. 37 Summer 2004.
Conversation with Barry Nelson in 1993.
Erickson, Hal. *Syndicated Television: The First Forty Years, 1947–1987.* Jefferson, NC: McFarland, 1989.
Goldberg, Lee. "Barry Nelson, the First James Bond." Undated article, 1990s.
Herbert, Ian. *Who's Who in the Theatre.* 16th ed. London: Pitman, 1977.
Inman, David. *The TV Encyclopedia.* New York: Perigee, 1991.
Miller, Don. *B Movies.* New York: Curtis, 1973.
Picture Show Annual. London: Amalgamated, 1943.
Purgavie, Dermot. "Jimmy Bond, Very Secret Agent, Shaky Not Stirred." *You.* 1992.
Ward, Jack. *The Supporting Actors of Television, 1959–1983.* Cleveland, OK: Lakeshore West, 1996.
Winchester, Clarence. *Screen Encyclopedia.* London: Winchester, 1948.
Wise, James E., and Paul W. Wilderson III. *Stars in Khaki.* Annapolis, MD: Naval Institute, 2000.

PAUL NEWLAN

Paul Newlan was born in Plattsmouth, Nebraska on June 29, 1903. He was raised in Kansas City, Missouri and educated in Missouri. His nickname was "Tiny." He broke into show business by joining the Garden Theater in Kansas City. Instead of pursuing this, he opted to become a professional basketball and football player. Returning to show business, whilst appearing in stock in Missouri, he was spotted and offered a contract at Paramount studios. Many of his roles were so small in films that he went uncredited.

He played Captain Grey, Lee Marvin's boss and friend, in the crime series *M Squad*. One unusual feature of this series was that the male crooks that this twosome pursued had molls who were scarcely ladies of refinement. When their boyfriends or husbands were cornered, these molls started physically battering the police. Ballinger usually tackled the men, while it was up to Grey to subdue the women. His huge build meant that Newlan could play a formidable villain just as well in other crime series. He died at Studio City, California on November 23, 1973 aged 70 of congestive heart failure.

FILMOGRAPHY

1935: *Millions in the Air.*
1936: *Too Many Parents, Forgotten Faces, The Accusing Finger, Arizona Mahoney.*
1937: *The Plainsman, Man of the People, Murder Goes to College, Swing High Swing Low, Mountain Music, The Last Train from Madrid, Big City, My Dear Miss Aldrich, Carnival Queen, Prescription for Romance, Wells Fargo.*
1938: *The Big Broadcast of 1938, Cocoanut Grove, You and Me, If I Were King, Say It in French.*
1939: *Disbarred, I'm from Missouri, Broadway Serenade, The Lady's from Kentucky, The Gracie Allen Murder Case, The Hunchback of Notre Dame, Fast and Furious, Rulers of the Sea, Another Thin Man, Balalaika.*
1940: *The Gay Vagabond, The Ghost Breakers, Those Were the Days, The Great McGinty, Rangers of Fortune, North West Mounted Police.*
1941: *Hold That Ghost, Life Begins for Andy Hardy, Honky Tonk, Sea Raiders, A Date with the Falcon, Sullivan's Travels, Down in San Diego.*
1942: *Down Rio Grande Way, Devil's Trail, Jackass Mail, You Can't Escape Forever, Star Spangled Rhythm.*
1943: *Hit Parade of 1943, Du Barry Was a Lady, Crazy House, True to Life, The Phantom* (serial).
1944: *The Adventures of Mark Twain, Girl Rush, I'm From Arkansas, Lost in a Harem.*
1945: *The Man Who Walked Alone, The Last Installment, Within These Walls, The Shanghai Cobra.*
1946: *The Harvey Girls, Road to Utopia, Two Sisters from Boston, Don Ricardo Returns.*
1947: *Bells of San Fernando, Monsieur Verdoux, A Likely Story, High Barbaree, Dragnet, Secret Life of Walter Mitty, The Unfinished Dance, Copacabana, Road to Rio.*
1948: *Fury at Furnace Creek, A Southern Yankee, Force of Evil.*
1949: *The Fountainhead, Miss Grant Takes Richmond, The Inspector General.*

1950: *Wabash Avenue, Colt .45, Bright Leaf, Never a Dull Moment.*
1951: *Sugarfoot, The Lemon Drop Kid, David and Bathsheba, Callaway Went Thataway, My Favorite Spy.*
1952: *The Treasure of Lost Canyon, Rancho Notorious, Something to Live For, The Captive City, Lost in Alaska, Against All Flags, Abbott and Costello Meet Captain Kidd.*
1953: *The Lawless Breed, Sangaree, Abbott and Costello Go to Mars, Prisoners of the Casbah, The Great Adventures of Captain Kidd* (serial).
1954: *Casanova's Big Night, Drums of Tahiti, River of No Return, Demetrius and the Gladiators, Naked Alibi.*
1955: *Pirates of Tripoli, Jupiter's Darling, We're No Angels, To Catch a Thief, You're Never Too Young.*
1956: *The Court Jester, Davy Crockett and the River Pirates, The Rack.*
1957: *Trooper Hook, Badlands of Montana, The Lonely Man, The Tijuana Story.*
1958: *The Buccaneer.*
1961: *Pocketful of Miracles.*
1964: *The Americanization of Emily.*
1965: *The Slender Thread.*
1970: *There Was a Crooked Man.*

TELEVISION SERIES

1957–1960: *M Squad* as Captain Grey.
1964: *Twelve O'Clock High* as General Pritchard.

SOURCES

Brooks, Tim. *The Complete Directory to Prime Time TV Stars, 1946–Present.* New York: Ballantine, 1987.

Truitt, Evelyn Mack. *Who Was Who on the Screen.* Illustrated ed. New York: Bowker, 1984.

Twomey, Alfred, and Arthur F. McClure. *The Versatiles.* South Brunswick, NJ: Barnes, 1969.

JANE NIGH

Jane Nigh was born Bonnie Lenora Nigh in Los Angeles on February 25, 1925. She acted in plays in high school, but had no intention of becoming a professional actress. While working in the offices of an aircraft plant during World War II she was spotted by a talent scout from 20th Century–Fox who eventually signed her to a contract. She made her screen debut in *Something for the Boys* (1944). She was a very active player during the forties and early fifties, both at her home studio and on loan outs. She appeared with Bill Williams in four films of which *Blue Blood* (1951) was her personal favorite of all her movies.

She was the fourth and possibly the most vivacious actress to play the role of hot shot reporter Lorelei Kilbourne in the newspaper drama series *Big Town* which starred Pat McVey as Steve Wilson. She only played the role for a single season from 1952 to 1953, leaving when she became pregnant in real life. Her film career never recovered, but she remained an active television actress until c1960. She appeared in many regional theater productions in California. Afterwards she resided in Costa Mesa, California where she ran a successful jewelry business until 1985.

She was a popular date of the forties and her engagements provided considerable fodder for the fan magazines of the period. She was married and divorced four times. Her first husband was Victor Cutler, a male model, whom she both married and divorced in 1946. Her second husband was James Baker, a naval officer turned rancher, with whom she had a son and a daughter. They were wed between 1952 and 1962. Her third and fourth marriages were both to Norman Davidson, a businessman. With him she had a daughter named Julia who was born in 1964, but who became addicted to drink and drugs. Her

Jane Nigh, who costarred in *Big Town*.

daughter was killed in a car crash in 1985. In 1986 she suffered a stroke, but rallied sufficiently to become a committee member of her local "Stroke Busters' Association." In 1988 she moved to Bakersfield, California to be close to her second husband and other daughter.

Jane Nigh died in Bakersfield, California on October 5, 1993 after another stroke aged 68. She was survived by a sister, two children and two grandchildren.

Filmography

1944: *Something for the Boys, Laura.*
1945: *State Fair, House of Dracula.*
1946: *Whistle Stop, Dragonwyck.*
1947: *Unconquered.*
1948: *Leather Gloves, Sitting Pretty, Blue Grass of Kentucky, Give My Regards to Broadway, Cry of the City.*
1949: *Red Hot and Blue, Captain Carey U.S.A., Zamba, Fighting Man of the Plains.*
1950: *Border Treasure, Rio Grande Patrol, Operation Haylift, Motor Patrol, County Fair.*
1951: *Blue Blood, Disc Jockey.*
1952: *Fort Osage, Rodeo.*
1956: *Hold That Hypnotist.*

Television Series

1952–1953: *Big Town* as Lorelei Kilbourne.

Sources

Lamparski, Richard. *Whatever Became Of?* 11th Series. New York: Crown, 1989.
Quinlan, David. *Film Stars.* 5th ed. London: Batsford, 2000.
Ragan, David. *Who's Who in Hollywood.* 2nd ed. New York: Facts on File, 1992.
Turner, Steve, and Edgar M. Wyatt. *Saddle Gals.* Madison, NC: Empire, 1995.
Variety. Obituary, October 1993.

Lloyd Nolan

Lloyd Nolan was a reliable actor who never quite climbed the top rung of film stardom. He was an actor who was heralded for a fine body of film work rather than for a few good parts. He alternated villains and tough heroes throughout the thirties and forties. He found himself in two crime and mystery television series of the fifties, neither of which ranked amongst his more distinguished work. He was rather better served by the *Michael Shayne* film series of thrillers which he shot in the early forties. He was however a strong survivor in show business who kept active right to the end.

Lloyd Benedict Nolan was born in San Francisco, CA on August 11, 1902. He was the son of James Charles Nolan, a shoe manufacturer from Ireland and Margaret Elizabeth Shea from California. He graduated from Santa Clara Prep. School and studied English at Stanford University where he was very active in the drama club. He flunked his first year exams so he dropped out of college. Instead he shipped out on a freighter intending to travel the world. The ship caught fire in New York harbor and he had to be sent the ticket fare home.

In 1924 he appeared on the Keith-Albee vaudeville circuit in a sketch called *The Radio Robot*. In 1927 he trained for a year at the Pasadena Playhouse where he appeared in 28 productions supporting himself on money he inherited from his father. He joined a touring company of *The Front Page* which closed in New England. The next three seasons he spent at the Cape Playhouse in Dennis, Massachusetts as a stage hand. He was one of the players in *The Cape Cod Follies* which transferred to Broadway, opening at the Bijou Theater on September 18, 1929 and running for 80 performances. His earliest success came when he played Emil in *Reunion in Vienna* which starred Alfred Lunt and Lynn Fontanne. It opened at the Martin Beck Theatre on November 16, 1931, ran for 264 performances and then went on tour. The play which really made his name was *One Sunday Afternoon* which opened at the Little Theater, New York in February 1933 and ran for 322 performances. He was originally cast in a lesser role, but convinced the producers to let him play the lead of Biff Grimes.

Two subsequent shows *Ragged Army* and *Gentlewoman,* both in 1934, were flops, but he was spotted in one of them by a talent agent from Paramount who arranged to have him tested and signed to a contract. He relocated to California where he made his screen debut in *Stolen Harmony* (1935) as the lead heavy. He became a prolific film actor appearing in many movies mostly at Paramount and Columbia during the thirties. His break came when Chester Morris rejected the role of the heavy in *The Texas Rangers* (1936) which Nolan inherited.

Paramount had little interest in building him into a star so he left them. Twentieth Century–Fox wanted a new film detective series to replace *Mr. Moto*. They decided to film *Michael*

Shayne Private Detective (1940) as a single experiment with Nolan in the lead. It was derived from a series of dime novels by Brett Halliday, but only the first was based on one of his books. When the film turned out to be a box office success, they signed Nolan to a contract. He shot six sequels, but refused to do any more for fear of being typecast. Halliday was not enamored of his characterization.

His personal favorite of his films was *The Man Who Wouldn't Talk* (1940). He was the kindly Irish cop McShane in *A Tree Grows in Brooklyn* (1945). He played the senior FBI agent Insp. George Briggs investigating the case in the place which became known as *The House on 92nd Street* (1945). Nolan was so convincing in the part that he reprised the role in *The Street With No Name* (1948). While under contract to Fox, he shot other movies on loan-out notably at MGM and Warner Bros.

When the film offers began to dry up, he returned to the stage. He played the lead of Oliver Erwenter in the National Touring Company of *The Silver Whistle* in 1950 for twelve weeks. He then signed to star as Samuel Rilling in *Courtin' Time* which he played in tryouts in Boston and Philadelphia during April and May 1951, but had to drop out because of a throat infection. He made his television debut in an episode of *Theater Hour* called "The Barker" in 1950. In August 1951 William Gargan relinquished his television role of *Martin Kane Private Eye* to Nolan who played the role for a season until May 22, 1952 when he was replaced by Lee Tracy. Nolan gave the character a harder edge and did not enjoy the same good relationship with the police as his predecessor.

The play *The Caine Mutiny Court Martial* was produced by Paul Gregory and directed by Charles Laughton. It starred Nolan as Lt. Commander Philip Queeg and started on the West Coast in October 1953, playing in 67 cities before opening on Broadway at the Plymouth Theater in January 1954. His critical notices were the best of his career and he won the Donaldson Award, the New York Critics Award as the Best Actor in 1954. He toured with the show in 1955. On November 19, 1955 on *Four Star Jubilee* he played the role in a television production for which he won an Emmy Award. On June 13, 1956 he opened at the Hippodrome Theater in London, England to a box office smash and glowing critical notices. He also directed the production with an English cast which ran for 182 performances. While in England he appeared in the film *Abandon Ship!* (1957).

Upon his return to Hollywood, he continued to appear sporadically in films usually giving fine performances where he was highly billed as part of an ensemble cast. He starred in a second television series *Special Agent 7* originally aired in 1958. This was a syndicated series of 26 half hour, black and white episodes in which he played an agent for the Inland Revenue Service. This series was not a success when originally shown, has not been revived since and was consigned to the junkyard of television. It lays claim to being the most worthless program in this genre to star an actor of his caliber. His final Broadway appearance was as Johnny Condell in *One More River* which opened at the Ambassador Theater, New York on March 18, 1960, but closed after only three performances. During the sixties he was a guest on many of the top television series. His most high profile television job however was as crusty Dr. Morton Chegley in the three season sitcom *Julia* starring Diahann Carroll. His role only involved him shooting one day a week, but brought him considerable popular recognition.

While appearing in a minor role in the play *Sweet Stranger* in October 1930 he met actress Mary Mell Efird whom he married on May 23, 1933. With her he had two children who were Melinda Joyce who was born in 1941 and Jay Benedict who was born in 1943. In 1972 he revealed that his son Jay had suffered from autism. It was originally a little known and understood illness that Nolan and his wife had to live with from the time he was doing *Caine*. Later he and his wife acknowledged defeat in their battle against the illness and placed their child in a special school where their son choked to death in 1969. He later established the Jay Nolan Autistic Center in Saugus. He also served as the Honorary Chairman of the National Society for Autistic Children.

He wrote one act plays which were not staged; had a fine baritone voice which was virtually never used in films; and spoke fluent French and Spanish. His hobbies were listed as golf and archaeology and his politics were Republican. His final film was *Hannah and Her Sisters* (1986) directed by Woody Allen and released posthumously. His last television appearance was the "Murder in the Afternoon" episode of *Murder She Wrote* which originally aired on October 13, 1985. Nolan was seriously ill when it was shot and his memory so fogged that he could no

Lloyd Nolan, who starred in *Martin Kane Private Eye* and *S.A. 7*.

longer remember his lines. To her credit Angela Lansbury coaxed him through his scenes and the episode turned out fine.

Nolan had become ill with lung cancer and had battled the disease at Century City Hospital. He was released to his home in Brentwood, Los Angeles two weeks before he died on September 27, 1985 aged 83 of respiratory arrest. After his first wife died in January 1981, he was inactive for a year. He remarried Virginia Florey (née Dabney), widow of director Robert Florey, and was survived by his widow, daughter and two grandchildren. He was cremated at Grandview Crematory in Glendale and his ashes are located at Westwood Village Memorial Park, Los Angeles.

Filmography

1935: *Stolen Harmony, Atlantic Adventure, One-Way Ticket, She Couldn't Take It, G-Men.*
1936: *You May Be Next, Lady of Secrets, Counterfeit, 15 Maiden Lane, Big Brown Eyes, The Devil's Squadron, The Texas Rangers.*
1937: *Exclusive, Interns Can't Take Money, Wells Fargo, King of Gamblers, Ebb Tide, Every Day's a Holiday.*
1938: *Hunted Men, Dangerous to Know, Tip-Off Girls, King of Alcatraz, Prison Farm.*
1939: *Undercover Doctor, St. Louis Blues, The Magnificent Fraud, Ambush.*
1940: *Johnny Apollo, The Man I Married, The Man Who Wouldn't Talk, The Golden Fleecing, Charter Pilot, The House Across the Bay, Gangs of Chicago, Pier 13, Behind the News, Michael Shayne Private Detective.*
1941: *Dressed to Kill* (MS), *Sleepers West* (MS), *Blues in the Night, Blue White and Perfect* (MS), *Steel Against the Sky, Mr. Dynamite, Buy Me That Town.*
1942: *Just Off Broadway* (MS), *It Happened in Flatbush, Time to Kill* (MS), *Apache Trail, Manila Calling, The Man Who Wouldn't Die* (MS).
1943: *Bataan, Guadalcanal Diary.*
1945: *A Tree Grows in Brooklyn, The House on 92nd Street, Circumstantial Evidence, Captain Eddie.*
1946: *Two Smart People, Lady in the Lake, Somewhere in the Night.*
1947: *Wild Harvest.*
1948: *The Street with No Name, Green Grass of Wyoming.*
1949: *The Sun Comes Up, Bad Boy, Easy Living.*
1951: *The Lemon Drop Kid.*
1953: *Island in the Sky, Crazylegs.*
1956: *Santiago, The Last Hunt, Towards the Unknown.*
1957: *Abandon Ship!* (a.k.a. *Seven Waves Away*), *Peyton Place, A Hatful of Rain.*
1960: *Girl of the Night, Portrait in Black.*
1961: *Susan Slade.*
1962: *We Joined the Navy!*
1963: *The Girl Hunters, Sergeant Ryker* (TV).
1964: *Circus World* (a.k.a. *The Magnificent Showman*).
1965: *Never Too Late.*
1966: *An American Dream* (a.k.a. *See You In Hell Darling*).
1967: *The Double Man, Wings of Fire* (TV).
1968: *Ice Station Zebra.*
1969: *Airport.*
1972: *My Boys Are Good Boys.*
1973: *Isn't It Shocking?* (TV).
1974: *The Abduction of St. Anne* (TV), *Earthquake.*
1976: *The November Plan, Flight to Holocaust* (TV).
1977: *The Mask of Alexander Cross* (TV), *Fire!* (TV), *The Private Files of J. Edgar Hoover.*
1979: *Valentine* (TV).
1980: *Galyon.*

1982: *Prince Jack, It Came Upon the Midnight Clear* (TV).
1986: *Hannah and Her Sisters.*
Note: Entries in the *Michael Shayne* series are denoted MS in the filmography.

TELEVISION SERIES
1951–1952: *Martin Kane Private Investigator* as Martin Kane.
1958: *Special Agent 7* as Agent Philip Conroy.
1968–1971: *Julia* as Dr. Morton Chegley.

SOURCES
Death Certificate.
Inman, David. *The TV Encyclopedia*. New York: Perigee, 1991.
McClure, Arthur F., and Ken D. Jones. *Star Quality*. South Brunswick, NJ: Barnes, 1974.
Parish, James Robert. *The Unofficial Murder She Wrote Casebook*. New York: Kensington Books, 1997.
_____, and William T. Leonard. *Hollywood Players: The Thirties*. Carlstadt, NJ: Rainbow, 1977.
Picture Show Annual. London: Amalgamated, 1939, 1940, 1941 and 1948.
Quinlan, David. *Film Stars*. 5th ed. London: Batsford, 2000.
Schlossheimer, Michael. *Gunmen and Gangsters*. Jefferson, NC: McFarland, 2002.
Tuska, Jon. *The Detective in Hollywood*. New York: Doubleday, 1978.
Variety. "Lloyd Nolan Dies at 83; Rose Above Most of His Roles." October 1, 1985.
Ward, Jack. *Television Guest Stars*. Jefferson, NC: McFarland, 1993.
Who's Who in the Theatre. 10th and 13th eds. London: Pitman, 1947 and 1961.
Who's Who on Television. London: Independent Television, 1970.
Winchester, Clarence. *Screen Encyclopedia*. London: Winchester, 1948.

GENE O'DONNELL

Gene O'Donnell was born in New York on February 28, 1911. Commencing his career as a radio announcer in New York and Boston, he relocated to Hollywood where he had the distinction of appearing in *The Ape* (1940) which starred Boris Karloff and *The Devil Bat* (1941) which starred Bela Lugosi.

After serving in the army during World War II, he was active in New York pursuing his career in radio broadcasting, but also in a new medium called television. He played the title role in *Barney Blake, Police Reporter* which the NBC network claimed was the first ever fictional crime series. It was a half hour, live series shot at RCA's studios in New York and shown in 1948. Each week Blake and his secretary Jennifer Allen (Judy Parrish) investigated a crime, interviewed suspects and apprehended the culprit. It was a few more years before the format caught on. The sponsor, American Tobacco Company, cancelled the series after only thirteen weeks.

During the fifties O'Donnell returned to Hollywood where he appeared in character roles in a few films and made appearances on some of the better known series of the period including *Perry Mason*.

O'Donnell died in Woodland Hills, California on November 22, 1992 aged 81 of lung cancer. He was survived by his wife Dolores.

FILMOGRAPHY
1940: *Laughing at Danger, I'm Nobody's Sweetheart Now, The Ape, Queen of the Yukon.*
1941: *The Devil Bat, You're Out Of Luck, Let's Go Collegiate, Borrowed Hero, Father Steps Out, Keep 'em Flying, Paris Calling.*
1942: *So's Your Aunt Emma!, Freckles Comes*

Judy Parrish (left), Gene O'Donnell and Joan Arliss (right, guest) on the set of *Barney Blake, Police Reporter*.

Home, Police Bullets, Saboteur, Meet the Mob, Miracle Kid, One Thrilling Night, You're Telling Me.
1943: *North Star, Never a Dull Moment, Corvette K-225.*
1956: *The Great American Pastime.*
1957: *The Girl in Black Stockings, Bop Girl Goes Calypso, Hell Bound, Three Brave Men.*
1960: *Pretty Boy Floyd.*
1963: *Take Her She's Mine.*
1965: *Dear Brigitte.*
1968: *Planet of the Apes.*
1970: *The Lawyer.*

Television Series

1948: *Barney Blake, Police Reporter* as Barney Blake.

Sources

Tibballs, Geoff. *TV Detectives*. London: Boxtree, 1992.
Variety. Obituary, November 1992.

KEVIN O'MORRISON

Kevin O'Morrison was born in St. Louis, Missouri on May 25, 1916. He was the son of Sean E. O'Morrison and Dori Elizabeth Adams. His father was a farmer while his mother was a saleswoman. Between 1927 and 1930 he was educated at Illinois Military School. He was privately tutored for a university degree. He started his career in little theaters in St. Louis. He made his Broadway debut as a spear carrier in *Julius Caesar* at the Mercury Theater in 1938. During World War II he served as a corporal in the United States air force attached to the Special Services Unit. In this capacity he played Ed in *Winged Victory* both in New York and on tour.

He made his screen debut in *Dear Ruth* (1947) as Sgt. Chuck Vincent. He studied acting, directing and playwriting with Robert Lewis and Harold Clurman at the American Theater Wing in New York. Between 1947 and 1949 he used the name Kenny O'Morrison. He made his television debut in the title role of the crime series *Charlie Wild Private Detective*. This series had its genesis in the highly popular radio series *The Adventures of Sam Spade* created by Dashiell Hammett. When Hammett was blacklisted as a Communist by the House UnAmerican Activities Committee the radio series was switched to *Charlie Wild Private Detective* where it continued to be a success. The series came to television between December 22, 1950 and June 19, 1952. In that time it was shown live on three networks namely CBS, ABC and DuMont. The sponsor was Wildroot Hair Oil which is where the title character's name came from. The line producers of the series were Carlo De Angelo and Herbert Brodkin. There were 78 half hour episodes. The character as played by O'Morrison was a rough, tough New York private eye who was fond of giving suspects a knuckle sandwich as a means of obtaining information. He was ably assisted by his secretary Effie Perrine (Cloris Leachman). When the series ended its network run on CBS for the first time on June 27, 1951, O'Morrison left the series, he was replaced by John McQuade.

O'Morrison went on to make appearances in several of the anthology series of the fifties. He occasionally appeared on Broadway and in films and has been a stage manager. Since 1966 however his main occupation has been as a playwright with a penchant for rewriting his own plays so that they evolve into other plays. During the early seventies he spent two years in England studying European theater. He has also been writer-in-residence at over 30 American colleges and universities. One of his plays *A Party for Lovers* won an NRT National Play Award in 1981.

He married Linda Soma, a playwright's agent, on April 30, 1966.

Filmography

1947: *Dear Ruth.*
1948: *Saigon.*
1949: *Too Late for Tears, The Threat, The Set-Up.*
1950: *Never Fear, The Golden Gloves Story.*
1958: *The Mugger.*
1973: *The Friends of Eddie Coyle.*
1984: *The Concealed Enemies* (TV).
1988: *Funny Farm.*
1993: *Sleepless in Seattle.*
1994: *Lightning Jack.*

Television Series

1950–1951: *Charlie Wild, Private Detective* as Charlie Wild.

Miniseries

1989: *Lonesome Dove.*

Sources

Tibballs, Geoff. *TV Detectives*. London: Boxtree, 1992.

Contemporary Theatre, Film and Television. Vol. 1. Detroit: Gale Research, 1984.

PATRICK O'NEAL

Patrick O'Neal was born in Ocala, Florida on September 26, 1927. He was the son of Coke Wisdom O'Neal and Martha Hearn. His father was a fruit grower. He had one brother named Michael. He was educated at Ocala High School, Riverside Military Academy and graduated with a B.A. Degree from the University of Florida. He made his professional stage debut as Marchbanks in *Candida* at a Florida theater in 1944. Between 1952 and 1953 he served in the U.S. Air Force for which he wrote and directed films. He trained for the stage at the Actors Studio and the Neighborhood Playhouse in New York. He made his Broadway debut as Arthur Turner in *Oh Men! Oh Women!* at Henry Miller's Theater in 1954.

He made his television debut in 1952 and appeared on anthology series. He first had a regular television role in the CBS daytime soap *Portia Faces Life* which ran from April 1954 to July 1955. He costarred with Hazel Court in the British lensed television series *Dick and the Duchess*. This 26 episode, half hour, black and white television series was shown in the United Kingdom between May 21, 1959 and July 8, 1960. It aired on CBS in America between September 28, 1957 and May 16, 1958. It was produced by Sheldon Reynolds who originally made his name and a fortune with the television series *Foreign Intrigue*. *Dick and the Duchess* was a hybrid series which was partly sitcom and partly crime. Patrick O'Neal played Dick Starrett, a successful American insurance investigator based in London. He was married to Jane (Hazel Court) who was not only beautiful, but also an aristocrat with a title. The comedy derived from his attempts to ingratiate himself with her rather stuffy family, while the drama came from his investigations. His wife somehow frequently became involved in his cases. His partner Peter Jamison was played by Richard Wattis. His Scotland Yard contact was Inspector Stark played by Michael Shepley. The series was a big hit on both sides of the Atlantic. The interesting effect was that it springboarded Hazel Court to a highly successful American career, but did virtually nothing for Patrick O'Neal. Of her costar, Hazel Court had this to say, "Patrick O'Neal was a pleasant man. He was however a method actor and was trying to imitate James Dean. This is not the easiest kind of actor to work with."

He had a regular role on an NBC daytime soap *Today Is Ours* which was shown between June and September 1958. *Diagnosis Unknown* was a CBS summer replacement series shown between July and September 1960 in which he played a pathologist turned sleuth. This was his sole starring series on American television, but not a success. He was much better served by his stage work. He played defrocked Reverend T. Lawrence Shannon in the play *Shannon* initially in Italy in 1959, but later on Broadway under the revised title *Night of the Iguana* in 1961. He played the lead of Sebastian Dangerfield in the controversial play *The Ginger Man*, an off-Broadway production in 1963. The roles of Shannon and Dangerfield were reportedly his personal favorites.

He made his screen debut in *The Mad Magician* (1954). There was an attempt to turn him into a film star in the late sixties, but his rather cruel appearance and personality were better suited to playing villains. His best remembered film role was in *Chamber of Horrors* (1966). This was originally intended as a pilot for a would be television series *House of Wax* in which Cesare Danova and Wilfred Hyde White were cast as turn of the century Baltimore wax works owners turned inves-

Patrick O'Neal, who starred in *Dick and the Duchess*.

tigators. They were outshone by O'Neal as the maniac Jason Cravatte who chops off his manacled hand to avoid capture. Thereafter he fits the stump with a variety of devices with which to slaughter his victims. This pilot was deemed too violent for television showing, so extra scenes were added. It was then released theatrically by Warner Bros. instead where it made a mint of money. O'Neal would have been extremely well suited to playing a villain in a James Bond film, but somehow the opportunity never came his way. He also directed on television and occasionally film, but he never seemed to harbor too many ambitions in this direction.

He had regular roles in two other television series. In a single season CBS series *Kaz* he played Samuel Bennett, senior partner in a prestigious law firm which employed former convict turned lawyer detective Kaz (Ron Liebman). This series aired between September 1978 and August 1979. *Emerald Point NAS* was a single season CBS nighttime soap shown between September 1983 and March 1984 set against the background of a fictitious naval air station. O'Neal played an unscrupulous business magnate Harlan Adams during 1983, but was replaced midseason by Robert Vaughn.

O'Neal, his wife and brother owned a few Manhattan restaurants that were noted for hiring aspiring thespians as waiters. One of these was called "The Ginger Man" after the play in which he appeared in 1963. He and actor Carroll O'Connor also owned and operated another restaurant in Beverly Hills.

O'Neal's final film was *Under Siege* (1992) which was one of Steven Seagal's best efforts. O'Neal played the ship's captain whose birthday party provided the starting point for the action. He married Cynthia Baxter in 1956. With her he had two sons. O'Neal died in a Manhattan hospital on September 9, 1994 aged 66 of respiratory failure complicated by cancer and surprisingly tuberculosis. He was survived by his wife, brother and sons.

Filmography

1954: *The Mad Magician, The Black Shield of Falworth.*
1960: *From the Terrace, A Matter of Morals.*
1963: *The Cardinal.*
1965: *King Rat, In Harm's Way.*
1966: *Matchless, A Fine Madness, Alvarez Kelly, Chamber of Commerce, A Big Hand for the Little Lady* (a.k.a. *Big Deal at Dodge City*).
1967: *Assignment to Kill.*
1968: *Companions in Nightmare* (TV), *Where Were You When the Lights Went Out? The Secret Life of an American Wife.*
1969: *Castle Keep, Stiletto, The Kremlin Letter.*
1970: *El Condor.*
1971: *Corky* (a.k.a. *Lookin' Good*).
1972: *Cool Million* (a.k.a. *Mask of Marcella*) (TV).
1973: *Silent Night Bloody Night, The Way We Were.*
1974: *The Stepford Wives.*
1975: *Crossfire* (TV).
1976: *The Killer Who Wouldn't Die* (TV), *Twin Detectives* (TV).
1977: *The Deadliest Season* (TV), *Sharon Portrait of a Mistress* (TV), *The Last Hurrah* (TV).
1978: *To Kill a Cop* (TV), *Like Mom Like Me* (TV).
1980: *Make Me an Offer* (TV), *Studio Murders* (TV).
1984: *Spraggue* (TV).
1985: *The Stuff.*
1986: *The Return of Perry Mason* (TV).
1987: *Like Father Like Son.*
1988: *Maigret* (TV).
1989: *New York Stories.*
1990: *Q & A, Alice.*
1992: *The Diary of the Hurdy Gurdy Man, For the Boys, Under Siege.*

As Director Only:

1970: *Circle Back.*

Television Series

1954–1955: *Portia Faces Life* (a.k.a. *The Inner Flame*) as Karl Manning.
USA (1957–1958): *Dick and the Duchess* as Dick Starrett.
UK (1959–1960)
1958: *Today Is Ours* as Glen Turner.
1960: *Diagnosis Unknown* as Dr. Daniel Coffee.
1978–1979: *Kaz* as Samuel Bennett.
1983: *Emerald Point NAS* as Harlan Adams.

Miniseries

1976: *The Moneychangers.*

Sources

Cameron, Ian, and Elisabeth Cameron. *The Heavies.* London: Studio Vista, 1967.
Conversation with Hazel Court in 2004.
Copeland, Mary Ann. *Soap Opera History.* Lincolnwood, IL: Mallard, 1991.

Herbert, Ian. *Who's Who in the Theatre.* 16th ed. London: Pitman, 1977.
Inman, David. *The TV Encyclopedia.* New York: Perigee, 1991.
Lentz, Harris M. III. *Obituaries in the Performing Arts, 1994.* Jefferson, NC: McFarland, 1995.
Picture Show Annual. London: Amalgamated, 1956.
Quinlan, David. *Illustrated Directory of Film Character Actors.* 2nd ed. London: Batsford, 1995.
Rogers, Dave. *The ITV Encyclopedia of Adventure.* London: Boxtree, 1988.
Variety. Obituary, Sept. 19, 1994.
Ward, Jack. *Television Guest Stars.* Jefferson, NC: McFarland, 1993.

JACK ORRISON

Jack Orrison was born in Colorado on October 12, 1909. In the crime show *The Plainclothesman* he played the part of Sgt. Brady, who was the assistant to the title character (Ken Lynch) throughout the duration of the series. Orrison died in Los Angeles on June 3, 1986 aged 76.

Filmography
1956: *Somebody Up There Likes Me.*
1958: *Wolf Larsen, I Married a Monster from Outer Space.*
1959: *Never Steal Anything Small, Al Capone.*
1961: *Wild in the Country, The Second Time Around.*
1962: *Madison Avenue.*
1963: *Move Over Darling.*
1964: *I'd Rather Be Rich.*

Television Series
1949–1950: *Captain Video and His Video Rangers* as Commissioner of Public Safety Bell.
1949–1954: *The Plainclothesman* as Sergeant Brady.

Source
Brooks, Tim. *The Complete Directory to Prime Time TV Stars, 1946–Present.* New York: Ballantine, 1987.

FRANK ORTH

Frank Orth was born in Philadelphia on February 21, 1880. He began his career in vaudeville in 1897. Between 1928 and 1931 he appeared in the first sound foreign language shorts for Warner Bros. In the *Boston Blackie* television series he played Inspector Ferraday. He was rather on the short side to be a convincing policeman. After a throat operation he retired in 1959. He died in Los Angeles on March 17, 1962 aged 82. He was married to actress Ann Codee (1890–1961) for fifty years. She had been his partner in his vaudeville act.

Filmography
1935: *Unwelcome Stranger, The Pay-Off.*
1936: *Two Against the World, Hot Money, Polo Joe.*
1937: *Land Beyond the Law, Fly-Away Baby, Ever Since Eve, Marry the Girl, Talent Scout, San Quentin, The Devil's Saddle Legion, Prairie Thunder, The Footloose Heiress, Submarine D-I.*
1938: *The Patient in Room 18, Torchy Blaine in Panama, Little Miss Thoroughbred, Mr. Champ, Young Dr. Kildare, Nancy Drew Detective, Comet Over Broadway.*
1939: *Burn 'Em Up O'Connor, Idiot's Delight, Fast and Loose, Nancy Drew Reporter, Society Lawyer, Within the Law, Broadway Serenade, Calling Dr. Kildare, Tell No Tales, Young Mr. Lincoln, Stanley and Livingstone, Nancy Drew and the Hidden Staircase, Thunder Afloat, Dust Be My Destiny, Fast and Furious, At the Circus, Secret of Dr. Kildare.*
1940: *His Girl Friday, Dr. Kildare's Strange Case,*

Frank Orth, who costarred in *Boston Blackie*.

'Til We Meet Again, Brother Orchid, The Dr. Takes a Wife, Gold Rush Maisie, Pier 13, Boom Town, Dr. Kildare Goes Home, Pier 13, Florian, Gallant Sons, Father Is a Prince, Mexican Spitfire Out West, Dr. Kildare's Crisis, You the People, Michael Shayne Private Detective, La Conga Nights.

1941: *Let's Make Music, Come Live with Me, Road Show, The Strawberry Blonde, Ride on Vaquero, The People Vs Dr. Kildare, The Great American Broadcast, Broadway Limited, Sergeant York, Kisses for Breakfast, Dr. Kildare's Wedding Day, Navy Blues, I Wake Up Screaming, Skylark, Unholy Partners.*

1942: *They Died with Their Boots On, Blue White and Perfect, Right to the Heart, Dr. Kildare's Victory, Roxie Hart, To the Shores of Tripoli, Rings on Her Fingers, My Gal Sal, Henry and Dizzie, The Magnificent Dope, Little Tokyo USA, Footlight Serenade, Tales of Manhattan, Orchestra Wives, Springtime in the Rockies, Dr. Gillespie's New Assistant.*

1943: *Over My Dead Body, Hello Frisco Hello, Coney Island, Sweet Rosie O'Grady, The Ox-Bow Incident, The Meanest Man in the World.*

1944: *Buffalo Bill, Summer Storm, Roger Touhy Gangster, Wilson, The Impatient Years, Tall in the Saddle, Storm Over Lisbon, Carolina Blues, Greenwich Village.*

1945: *Pillow to Post, I Was a Criminal, Wonder Man, Nob Hill, Tell It to a Star, She Went to the Races, The Lost Weekend, The Dolly Sisters, Doll Face.*

1946: *Colonel Effingham's Raid, The Hoodlum Saint, Blondie's Lucky Day, Murder in the Music Hall, The Bride Wore Boots, The Well-Groomed Bride, The Strange Love of Martha Ivers, It's Great to Be Young, Wake Up and Dream, The Show-Off.*

1947: *Born to Speed, Lady in the Lake, The Guilt of Janet Ames, Mother Wore Tights, Heartaches, Gas House Kids in Hollywood, It Had to Be You.*

1948: *The Big Clock, Fury at Furnace Creek, The Girl from Manhattan, Blondie's Secret, So This Is New York.*

1949: *Family Honeymoon, Make Believe Ballroom, Red Light, Bride for Sale.*

1950: *The Great Rupert, Cheaper by the Dozen, Father of the Bride, The Petty Girl.*

1951: *Double Dynamite.*

1952: *Something to Live For.*

1953: *Houdini, Here Come the Girls.*

1955: *Not as a Stranger.*

Television Series

1951–1953: *Boston Blackie* as Inspector Ferraday.
1956: *The Brothers* as Captain Sam Box.

Sources

Brooks, Tim. *The Complete Directory to Prime Time TV Stars, 1946–Present.* New York: Ballantine, 1987.

Truitt, Evelyn Mack. *Who Was Who on Screen.* New York: Bowker, 1984.

Twomey, Alfred E., and Arthur F. McClure. *The Versatiles.* South Brunswick, NJ: Barnes, 1969.

LUCIANA PALUZZI

Luciana Paluzzi was born in Rome, Italy on June 11, 1937. After leaving Rome, she lived for some years in Milan. At the age of sixteen her original ambition was to be a naval engineer and she spent two years studying the subject at the Scientific Academy in Milan. Then she went on a visit to Rome with her mother. There she met a friend of her father who was in films. He invited her to return to Rome for a role in a film a month later. When she returned, the movie had been postponed. "I traveled between Milan and Rome five times in all," she recalled. "And each time I was told that the film was not ready to go into production." At last she was seen by director Jean Negulesco who gave her the role of Rossano Brazzi's sister in *Three Coins in the Fountain* (1954). The original film was never made. She worked in European films for six years.

A 20th Century–Fox producer, Herbert B. Swope Jr., spotted her in a European lensed screen test which she shot with Stephen Boyd in 1957. Technically the test was Boyd's, but Swope was so impressed with Paluzzi that he made a mental note that he would like to use her in a later film. When the *Five Fingers* series became a reality and a foreign actress was needed for the female lead, Swope remembered her, had the test found, showed it to Martin Manulis, production chief for the series, and arranged for her to be flown to Hollywood.

Her leading men were David Hedison and Paul Burke. Since she played Simone Genet, a high fashion model, her gowns were designed by award winning clothes designer Charles Le Maire. The story lines were international with different episodes set in many different foreign

Left to right: David Hedison, Luciana Paluzzi and Cesare Danova (guest) in *Five Fingers*.

locales, all courtesy of the Fox backlot. As the actress said at the time, "How nice if we could go on location and really visit all those places." This was a short-lived series which only lasted on the NBC network for sixteen episodes between October 1959 and January 1960. Two of the episodes were not shown by the network, but were released theatrically as second features in Europe. At the time of shooting the series she lived high in the Hollywood hills off Laurel Canyon and her home narrowly avoided being incinerated by one of the worst forest fires of the period.

Two weeks after arriving in Hollywood she met Brett Halsey, a 20th Century–Fox contract player. They became engaged two weeks later and married in January 1960. By this marriage she had a son before divorcing in 1962. She played roles in other Hollywood films before returning to Italy. While there director Terence Young, who had directed her in one of her earlier films, arranged for her to audition for the role of Domino in the James Bond film *Thunderball* (1965). Her audition was unsuccessful because the producers preferred to cast a less well known actress, Claudine Auger, in the leading role. Young however fought to cast her in the secondary but memorable part of the vicious Spectre killer, Fiona Volpe.

At the end of the film Young and Paluzzi remained good friends. When the actress remarried in 1980 to Michael Soloman, director of a public relations company, Young hastily left the set of a movie he was directing in Europe and flew to America to give the bride away at the wedding ceremony. One of her final acting assignments was an episode of *Hawaii Five-0* entitled "My Friend, the Enemy" originally aired in 1978 in which she gave an excellent performance as Liana Labella, a spirited Italian paparazza.

Paluzzi retired from acting after her second marriage and established herself as a successful executive in the Italian television industry. Later she confessed to working harder in this capacity than in her days as an actress. David Hedison said of her, "She was wonderful! Today she lives in the Beverly Hills and I still see her and her husband often."

Filmography

1954: *Three Coins in the Fountain, My Seven Little Sins.*
1956: *The Lebanese Mission, Please Mr. Balzac, Adriana Lecouvreur.*
1957: *Guaglione, Labors of Hercules.*
1958: *No Time to Die* (a.k.a. *Tank Force*), *Sea Fury.*
1959: *Journey to the Lost City, My Wife's Enemy, Carlton-Brown of the F.O.*
1961: *Return to Peyton Place.*
1962: *Vice and Virtue, The Reluctant Saint.*
1964: *Muscle Beach Party, To Trap a Spy.*
1965: *Thunderball, Let's Talk About Men.*
1966: *One Eyed Soldiers.*
1967: *Chuka, The Venetian Affair.*
1968: *Now You See It, Now You Don't* (TV), *No Roses for OSS 117, A Black Veil for Lisa, A Thousand and One Nights.*
1969: *99 Women, Captain Nemo and the Underwater City, The Green Slime.*
1970: *Powderkeg* (TV), *El Hombre que vino del odio.*
1971: *Man of Legend, Cometogether.*
1972: *Colpo grosso, grossissimo ... anzi probabile, Two Faces of Terror, Estratto dagli archivi segreti della polizia di una capitale europea, Black Gunn.*
1973: *La Polizia sta a guardare, Medusa, Mean Mother, The Italian Connection.*
1974: *The Amazons, La Sbandata, The Klansman.*

1975: *The Manhunt, The Maniac Responsible.*
1976: *The Secrets of a Sensuous Nurse, Nick the Sting.*
1978: *The Greek Tycoon, Il Commissario Verrazzano.*

TELEVISION SERIES
1959–1960: *Five Fingers* as Simone Genet.

SOURCES
Picture Show. March 22, 1958.
Picture Show Annual. London: Amalgamated, 1960.
Remenih, Maurice. *TV-Radio Mirror.* January 1960.
Rhodes, Karen. *Booking Hawaii Five-O.* Jefferson, NC: McFarland, 1997.
Rye, Graham. *The James Bond Girls.* London: Boxtree, 1995.

JERRY PARIS

Jerry Paris was born William Gerald Paris in San Francisco on July 25, 1925. He graduated from New York University and UCLA before serving in the navy during World War II. After being discharged from the navy, he joined the Actor's Studio in 1946. Commencing his career on stage both in New York and on tour, he turned to films in 1949 with unbilled bits. Slowly he progressed to secondary supporting roles by the mid-1950s. Often cast as the best friend of the hero, he did not find the one role in a classic movie which would have brought him stardom.

In the original two hour television movie *The Untouchables*, later called *The Scarface Mob*, the role of Martin Flaherty was played by Bill Williams. When it became a series, the role of Flaherty was taken over by Jerry Paris. The original intention was that Eliot Ness (Robert Stack) would only be the star of 11 of the first season's 28 shows. Flaherty would be the lead in the rest. When they came to do the first of the shows, "The George 'Bugs Moran' Story," in which Paris would assume the main role, the producers realized early that Paris' bland personality would not work alone. Ness had to front the series. Stack then made a wise decision in October 1959 to star in all of the shows. His decision reduced the Flaherty character to very much of a subordinate role. According to different sources either Jerry Paris asked to be released from his contract or Quinn Martin, who did not like the Flaherty character, made the decision to drop him. His character was transferred to another office. Paris left the series half way through the first season in December 1959 and was replaced by Anthony George as Cam Allison.

The irony was that Paris then found himself cast in another crime series *Michael Shayne* starring Richard Denning as the hero's reporter friend, Tim Rourke, which was exactly the kind of role he had been fighting to escape from. Next he joined the cast at the start of the long running sitcom *The Dick Van Dyke Show* playing Jerry Helper, the zany next-door-neighbor and dentist friend of the Petries (Dick Van Dyke and Mary Tyler Moore).

After a great deal of persuasion on Paris' part, producer Carl Reiner allowed him his first chance to direct on the show. By the middle sixties he was a regular director and in recognition of his efforts he won the Emmy Award for Outstanding Directorial Achievement in Comedy during the 1963–1964 season for *The Dick Van Dyke Show*. He was nominated again in 1965–1966. Between 1968 and 1971 he helmed six motion pictures. During the early seventies he returned to television both as producer and director, helming episodes of such sitcoms as *Happy Days* for which he received two more Emmy award nominations for Outstanding Directing in a Comedy Series in 1977–1978 and 1980–1981.

Jerry Paris, who costarred in *The Untouchables*.

To prove that he had not entirely abandoned acting in some of the episodes of the series he directed, he had small uncredited roles. He moved back into feature films and helmed his last *Police Academy 3* in the same year that he died.

He died in Los Angeles on March 31, 1986 aged 60 of complications from a brain tumor. He had been hospitalized since March 18 and had twice undergone surgery to relieve bleeding and pressure. His wife Ruth predeceased him, but he was survived by two sons, including actor Andrew Paris; a daughter; and two sisters. Although he exuded amiability on screen, indications are that in real life a lot of steel lay behind that facade.

Filmography

As Actor Only:

1949: *Sword in the Desert, Battleground, My Foolish Heart.*
1950: *Woman in Hiding, D.O.A., The Reformer and the Redhead, Outrage, Cyrano de Bergerac, The Flying Missile.*
1951: *Call Me Mister, Bright Victory.*
1952: *Submarine Command, Monkey Business, Bonzo Goes to College.*
1953: *The Glass Wall, Saber Jet, Flight to Tangier, The Wild One.*
1954: *Drive a Crooked Road, Prisoner of War, The Caine Mutiny, About Mrs. Leslie.*
1955: *Unchained, Marty, Not as a Stranger, The Naked Street, The View from Pompey's Head, Good Morning Miss Dove, Hell's Horizon.*
1956: *Never Say Goodbye, D-Day the Sixth of June, I've Lived Before.*
1957: *Zero Hour!*
1958: *The Female Animal, The Lady Takes a Flyer, Sing Boy Sing, The Naked and the Dead, Man on the Prowl.*
1959: *No Name on the Bullet, Career.*
1961: *The Great Imposter.*
1967: *Don't Raise the Bridge, Lower the River.*
1968: *Never a Dull Moment.*
1970: *But I Don't Want to Get Married!* (TV).
1972: *Evil Roy Slade* (TV), *Every Man Needs One* (TV).
1980: *Leo and Loree.*

Television Series

1957: *Those Whiting Girls* as Artie.
1959: *Steve Canyon* as Major Willie Williston.
1959: *The Untouchables* as Agent Martin Flaherty.
1960–1961: *Michael Shayne* as Tim Rourke.
1961–1966: *The Dick Van Dyke Show* as Jerry Helper.

Sources

Inman, David. *The TV Encyclopedia.* New York: Perigee, 1991.
Robertson, Ed. "The Untouchables." *Television Chronicles.* No. 7. October 1996.
Vahimagi, Tise. *The Untouchables.* London: British Film Institute, 1998.
Variety. "Jerry Paris Film TV Actor/Helmer Dies in California." April 1986.
Willis, John. *Screen World.* Vol. 38. London: Frederick Muller, 1987.

Judy Parrish

Judy Parrish first appeared on Broadway in *Dance Night* in 1938 and was a fairly frequent Broadway performer between 1938 and 1950. By far her biggest success there was *Kiss and Tell* which ran between March 1943 and June 1945. She had regular roles on two live television series of the late forties. In *Barney Blake Police Reporter* generally regarded as the first crime series, she played Jennifer Allen, the secretary and girlfriend of the title hero played by Gene O'Donnell. She continued to appear on television in anthology series until 1955. She also used the name Judith Parrish.

Television Series

1948: *Barney Blake Police Reporter* as Jennifer Allen.
1948–1949: *The Growing Paynes* as Mrs. Payne.

Source

Brooks, Tim. *The Complete Directory to Prime Time TV Stars, 1946–Present.* New York: Ballantine, 1987.

Lee Philips

Lee Philips was born in New York City on January 10, 1927. Initially he served in the navy and then went to college intending to be a writer. After joining the drama club, he changed his mind and decided to become an actor instead. He made his television debut in the "Hold Back the Night" episode of the anthology series *Studio One* in 1952. He appeared on the Broadway stage as George Preisser in *Middle of the Night* which starred Edward G. Robinson. He reprised his role in the film version in 1958. Philips was spotted by a scout from 20th Century–Fox who signed him to a contract. His most famous film role was Michael Rossi, the schoolteacher and love interest of Constance MacKenzie (Lana Turner), in the film version of *Peyton Place* (1957). Although this film was a tremendous commercial success, there was a general feeling that the part of Rossi, which was effectively the male lead, was weakly cast.

Philips was dropped by Fox after only two films and briefly worked for Columbia. When George Nader and Les Tremayne refused to accompany the production of the television series *The Further Adventures of Ellery Queen* to New York, Philips was available and assumed the lead of Ellery Queen. There was no actor playing his father because the role had been dropped. Production of the series switched from live to videotape and the episodes were in color. They were all based on original scripts and the producer was Albert McCleery. Philips appeared in twelve episodes before the series was discontinued. His episodes were shown on NBC between February 27, 1959 and June 5, 1959.

Philips only made a handful of other film appearances. He was more familiar as a television actor, continuing to make regular appearances until 1966. By this time he had abandoned acting to become a prolific director of television series episodes; miniseries; and moves for television. His first credit as a director was an episode of *The Donna Reed Show* in 1958. His career extended well into the nineties, his last recorded credits being episodes of *Diagnosis: Murder*. Perhaps not too surprisingly his strong suit as a director was reckoned to be his handling of actors rather than his mastery of camera technique.

On one of the earliest television shows in which he appeared, he met an attractive producer's assistant. He married her soon afterwards and had a daughter Caitlin Meg who was born in 1957. In private life his hobby was reading poetry. Lee Philips died at his home in Brentwood, California on March 3, 1999 aged 72 of complications from Parkinson's Disease.

Filmography

As Actor Only:

1957: *Peyton Place*.
1958: *The Hunters*.
1959: *Middle of the Night*.

Lee Philips, who starred in *Ellery Queen*.

1960: *Tess of the Storm Country*.
1963: *Psychomania* (a.k.a. *Black Autumn, Violent Midnight*).

Television Series

1959: *The Further Adventures of Ellery Queen* as Ellery Queen.

Sources

Lentz, Harris M. III. *Obituaries in the Performing Arts, 1999*. Jefferson, NC: McFarland, 2000.
Nevins, Francis Jr. "Ellery Queen on the Small Screen." *The Golden Years of TV and Radio*. No. 1. Winter 1983.
Picture Show Annual. London: Amalgamated, 1959.
TV Star Annual. No. 7. 1959.
Ward, Jack. *The Supporting Players of Television, 1959–1983*. Cleveland, OK: Lakeshore West, 1996.
Who's Who in Hollywood. New York: Dell, 1961.
Wicking, Christopher, and Vahimagi, Tise. *The American Vein*. London: Talisman Books, 1979.

Barney Phillips

Barney Phillips was born Bernard Phillips in St. Louis, MO. on October 20, 1913. He was seen in the Broadway show *Meet the People* between

December 1940 and May 1941. He was however better known on radio notably as a member of the cast on *Gunsmoke*. In particular he was a great favorite of Jack Webb. When Barton Yarborough died in 1951, Phillips briefly assumed the role as Det. Sgt. Ed Jacobs, Joe Friday's sidekick, in the television series *Dragnet*. He played the role for ten episodes before being replaced. Although he was well liked by Webb, the reason generally given for his replacement was that facially he bore too much of a resemblance to Webb who wanted a character who looked different from Joe Friday. Nevertheless Webb continued to utilize Phillips in various supporting roles throughout the series run. Phillips remained a prolific television supporting actor frequently in series produced by Quinn Martin. He also appeared in several films notably the thrillers produced and directed by Andrew L. Stone.

Phillips died in Los Angeles on August 17, 1982 aged 68 after a brief illness. He was survived by his wife, Marie DeForest, a former actress and dancer.

Filmography

1937: *Black Aces*.
1949: *The Judge*.
1952: *My Six Convicts, Has Anybody Seen My Gal?, Ruby Gentry, Eight Iron Men*.
1953: *Down Among the Sheltering Palms, The Glass Wall, The 49th Man, A Blueprint for Murder, All American*.
1955: *The Night Holds Terror, The Naked Street, The Square Jungle*.
1956: *Behind the High Wall, Julie*.
1957: *The True Story of Jesse James, I Was a Teenage Werewolf, Drango*.
1958: *Cry Terror!, Gang War, Kathy O,' The Decks Ran Red*.
1960: *The Threat*.
1964: *Della* (TV).
1966: *The Sand Pebbles*.
1970: *Run Simon Run* (TV).
1971: *Longstreet* (TV), *A Death of Innocence* (TV).
1973: *Beg Borrow or Steal* (TV), *This Is a Hijack, Shirts/Skins* (TV).
1975: *Mobile Two* (TV).
1976: *Brinks: The Great Robbery* (TV), *Law of the Land* (TV), *No Deposit No Return*.
1977: *The Amazing Howard Hughes* (TV), *Beyond Reason*.
1981: *The Girl, the Gold Watch & Dynamite* (TV).
1982: *O'Hara's Wife*.

Television Series

1952: *Dragnet* as Det. Sgt. Ed Jacobs.
1960: *Johnny Midnight* as Lt. Geller.
1964–1967: *Twelve O'Clock High* as Major "Doc" Kaiser.
1967–1968: *Felony Squad* as Captain Franks.
1977–1978: *The Betty White Show* as Fletcher Huff.

Sources

Brooks, Tim. *The Complete Directory to Prime Time TV Stars, 1946–Present*. New York: Ballantine, 1987.
Inman, David. *The TV Encyclopedia*. New York: Perigee, 1991.
Ward, Jack. *Television Guest Stars*. Jefferson, NC: McFarland, 1993.
Willis, John. *Screen World*. Vol. 34. New York: Crown, 1983.

Eric Pohlmann

Eric Pohlmann was born Erich Pollak in Vienna, Austria on July 18, 1913. He studied for the stage at the Max Reinhardt School. He acquired early experience as an entertainer at the Reiss Bar and the Raimund Theater in Vienna. While working in Czechoslovakia on stage, he met actress Liselotte Goettinger (1904–1968). They became engaged. She fled from the Nazis to London in 1938, while he followed her in 1939. They wed in May 1939 and subsequently had two sons named Michael who was born in 1942 and Stephen who was born in 1945. During their early years in England, they had many jobs including butler and cook to the Duke of Bedford. During the war Pohlmann broadcast for the BBC. European Service. He later appeared frequently on the West End stage.

He made his screen debut in 1948 and went on to amass a huge number of film and television credits. If there was a requirement for an actor to play the proprietor of a sleazy Soho gambling den or strip joint or an oily postwar black marketeer, the likelihood was that Pohlman would play the role. His foreign accent and splendid diction allowed him to play virtually any nationality except English or American. His most famous acting job was one involving only his voice. He was Ernst Stavro Blofeld in two of the *James Bond* series. Most of his parts were villainous. A notable exception were the four foreign located but studio bound episodes of the television series *Colonel March of Scotland Yard* in which he played Inspector Goron, the associate and friend of Colonel March (Boris Karloff).

Pohlmann resumed his German speaking career in 1965 and went on to appear on stage in both Germany and Austria. Sometimes he appeared in straight dramas, but he also had a good singing voice and sang in musicals. His final film was *Tales from the Vienna Woods* (1979) directed by Maximilian Schell which was shown at the London Film Festival. Pohlmann died of a heart attack at Bad Reichenhall, Bavaria, Germany on July 25, 1979 aged 66 during final rehearsals for his second appearance at the Salzburg Festival where he was playing the fat cousin in the traditional *Everyman*. He had remarried in 1976 and was survived by his widow and two sons.

FILMOGRAPHY

1948: *Portrait from Life.*
1949: *Traveler's Joy, Children of Chance, The Third Man.*
1950: *Highly Dangerous, Chance of a Lifetime, Cairo Road, Blackout, State Secret.*
1951: *There Is Another Sun* (a.k.a. *The Wall of Death*), *Hell Is Sent Out, The Clouded Yellow, The Long Dark Hall.*
1952: *The Woman's Angle, Moulin Rouge, His Excellency, Emergency Call, Penny Princess, Monsoon, Venetian Bird, The Gambler and the Lady.*
1953: *They Who Dare, The Man Who Watched the Trains Go By, The Beggar's Opera, Mogambo, Blood Orange, 36 Hours* (a.k.a. *Terror Street*),
1954: *Rob Roy, the Highland Rogue, The Flame and the Flesh, Monsieur Repois* (a.k.a. *Knave of Hearts*), *The Belles of St. Trinian's, Forbidden Cargo.*
1955: *Break in the Circle, The Glass Cage, A Prize of Gold, The Constant Husband, Gentlemen Marry Brunettes, The Adventures of Quentin Durward.*
1956: *House of Secrets, The Gelignite Gang* (a.k.a. *The Dynamiters*), *Lust for Life, Reach for the Sky, High Terrace, Anastasia, Zarak.*
1957: *Not Wanted on Voyage, The Counterfeit Plan, Let's Be Happy, Fire Down Below, Interpol* (a.k.a. *Pickup Alley*), *Across the Bridge, Barnacle Bill* (a.k.a. *All at Sea*).
1958: *Three Cornered Men, Mark of the Phoenix, Life Is a Circus, Former Up the Creek, A Tale of Two Cities, I Accuse!, The Duke Wore Jeans, The Man Inside, Nor the Moon by Night* (a.k.a. *Elephant Gun*).

Eric Pohlmann, who costarred in *Colonel March of Scotland Yard*.

1959: *Alive and Kicking, John Paul Jones, The House of the Seven Hawks, Upstairs and Downstairs.*
1960: *Snowball, Sands of the Desert, No Kidding, The Man Who Couldn't Walk, Expresso Bongo, Surprise Package.*
1961: *Visa to Canton* (a.k.a. *Passport to China*), *Carry on Regardless, The Devil's Agent, The Kitchen, The Singer Not the Song.*
1962: *Village of Daughters, Mrs. Gibbons' Boys, The Puzzle of the Red Orchid.*
1963: *The Sicilians, Shadow of Fear, Follow the Boys, 55 Days at Peking, Cairo, From Russia With Love* (voice only), *Dr. Syn Alias the Scarecrow.*
1964: *Carry on Spying, Hot Enough for June, Night Train to Paris.*
1965: *Where the Spies Are, Joey Boy, Those Magnificent Men in Their Flying Machines, Thunderball* (voice).
1967: *The Mini-Affair* (a.k.a. *The Mini-Mob*), *The Scorpio Affair* (TV), *Heisses Pflaster Koln.*
1968: *Inspector Clouseau.*
1970: *Foreign Exchange* (TV).
1971: *The Horsemen.*
1973: *Tiffany Jones.*

1975: *The Mimosa Wants to Blossom Too, The Return of the Pink Panther.*
1976: *Tea for Three.*
1979: *Ashanti, Tales from the Vienna Woods.*

TELEVISION SERIES

1956–1957: *Colonel March of Scotland Yard* as Inspector Goron.

SOURCES

Noble, Peter. *British Film and Television Yearbook, 1959/1960.* 9th ed. London: BA, 1960.
Picture Show's Who's Who on Screen. London: Amalgamated, 1956.
Quinlan, David. *Illustrated Directory of Film Character Actors.* 2nd ed. London: Batsford, 1995.
RadioTellyScope. Issue 28. "Colonel March of Scotland Yard." May/June 2005.

PONCIE PONCE

Poncie Ponce was born Ponciano Ponce in Maui, Hawaii on April 10, 1933. His mother was Maria Tabac. He was one of five brothers and had two sisters. Educated at high school in Honokaa, Hawaii, he then attended Hawaii Vocational School to learn the welding trade. Instead he was drafted into the armed forces in 1953 and spent two years in Germany. While abroad he practiced singing and playing the ukulele and doing impressions in front of the troops and in Munich nightclubs. Upon his return to Hawaii, he entered a talent contest on a Honolulu television station which he won easily. This led to other broadcasts on Hawaiian radio and television stations. After this he headed for Hollywood where he worked as a welder for a large engineering company for two years. He made a few appearances on a local Los Angeles television show called *Rocket to Stardom.*

This landed him a job as a busboy and entertainer at Ben Blue's nitery in Santa Monica when he was spotted by a producer, Artie Silver, who recommended him to Warner Bros. William T. Orr, the executive in charge of television production and the son-in-law of Jack Warner, caught his act. The following day Ponce received a call from Warner Bros. inviting him for an interview. At first he thought it was a gag and had to be convinced otherwise. When he attended the appointment at the studio, he was given an audition for the part of a native Hawaiian in a new private eye show. At the audition he improvised a lot and passed the screen test with flying colors largely because his own personality fitted the character perfectly. He was quickly signed to a contract and remained with Warners for five years.

He was cast in the role for which he is most famous as Kim in *Hawaiian Eye* which was shown on the ABC network between October 1959 and September 1963. Kim ran a one man taxi service which was frequently used by the private eyes Tracy Steele (Anthony Eisley) and Tom Lopaka (Robert Conrad). On other occasions he loyally supported the eyes by trailing suspects. At times when he could not be of service, he had a huge number of relations all over the islands on whom he could call to give assistance. Kim provided the comic relief in the series and frequently played his ukulele. He sometimes accompanied singer Cricket Blake (Connie Stevens). His trademarks were his straw hat and his musical instrument. The regular cast operated out of the poolside office at the Hawaiian Village Hotel.

While the series was in production, he made numerous personal appearances promoting the show and was a spontaneous and enthusiastic guest on chat shows. When the series ended, he remained active in show business

Left to right: **Anthony Eisley, Connie Stevens, Robert Conrad and Poncie Ponce** in *Hawaiian Eye.*

notably as a commercial spokesperson on American television for cars and a flying company. On Mexican television he was a commercial spokesperson for Bacardi Rum. He was also hired by Satori to market their whiskey to the Japanese. He has had a nightclub act for decades in which he sings Hawaiian songs; performs in shows for senior citizens; and has entertained on many cruise ships. He has also provided voices for characters in animated series. He and one of his daughters run "Poncie's Place," a fast food restaurant, not far from where he lives. His recreations are fishing and attending the racetrack.

He lives with his Chinese wife at their home in Van Nuys, California which is decorated throughout with a Hawaiian motif. He has three daughters who have danced in his nightclub act with him.

Filmography
1961: *Portrait of a Mobster.*
1968: *Speedway.*
1977: *The World's Greatest Lover.*

Television Series
1959–1963: *Hawaiian Eye* as Kazuo Kim.

Sources
Inman, David. *The TV Encyclopedia*. New York: Perigee, 1991.
Lamparski, Richard. *Whatever Became Of?* 9th Series. New York: Crown, 1985.
Woolley, Lynn, Robert W. Malsbury, and Robert G. Strange Jr. *Warner Bros. Television*. Jefferson, NC: McFarland, 1985.

Mel Prestidge

Mel Prestidge was born on July 3, 1912. He played the affable Det. Lt. Danny Quon, the Hawaiian police contact of Tracy Steele (Anthony Eisley) and Tom Lopaka (Robert Conrad), in the television series *Hawaiian Eye*. This was by far his most famous role. Perhaps the most curious omission from his credits is that he did not appear in the later television crime series *Hawaii Five-0*. Prestidge reportedly died in Texas on January 7, 1994 aged 81.

Filmography
1958: *Ghost of the China Sea, Hong Kong Confidential.*
1978: *Rescue from Gilligan's Island* (TV).

Television Series
1959–1963: *Hawaiian Eye* as Det. Lt. Danny Quon.

Source
Brooks, Tim. *The Complete Directory to Prime Time TV Stars*. New York: Ballantine, 1987.

Robert Preston

Robert Preston's personality radiated energy and ebullience. The role which allowed him the greatest latitude was in the stage version of *The Music Man* as Professor Harold Hill. He was not a notably subtle actor and there was always something of a flim flam artist about him. He came across in real life as an ambitious achiever. He started out as a B picture hero and then played villains in more prestigious films, growing a moustache to make himself look older. In later years his toupee became lusher and darker and he was criticized for giving the same hearty characterization regardless of the demands of the part. He had a particular distaste for series television. During the early fifties he briefly spelled for another vacationing actor in a crime series, but it was an experience he preferred to forget.

Robert Preston was born Robert Preston Meservey in Newton Highlands, Massachusetts on June 8, 1918 the son of Frank W. Meservey and his wife Ruth Rea. He had one younger brother Frank Jr. His father was a clothier, while his mother was a sales assistant in a record shop. He was only two years old when the family moved to Los Angeles. His mother who had a strong interest in music forced him to learn to play musical instruments as a child. He was educated at public schools and at Lincoln High School, Los Angeles. It was while attending this school that the drama teacher aroused his interest in the theater.

At the age of fifteen he left school to join a Shakespearean company headed by Patia Power, mother of actor Tyrone Power. She cast him in the title role in the play *Julius Caesar* in 1936 which marked his professional debut. He later confessed that he was scared to death all the time he played this role that his voice was going to break. Preston eventually left the company in San Diego and hitchhiked back to Los Angeles where for a time he had a job parking cars at Santa Anita Race Track. There in 1936 he met some students from the Pasadena Community Playhouse who persuaded him to attend an audition for a role. He took their advice and won the part. For the next two years he attended the Playhouse Theater School where he played forty two different parts.

He owed his screen debut to his mother. She was connected to the firm for which Bing Crosby made gramophone records. She spoke to Everett, Bing's brother, one day who talked about Preston to various people at Paramount. It was not the usual producer, director or talent scout who made the find, but a lawyer from the Paramount legal department. He was so impressed with Preston's performance in *Idiot's Delight* at the Playhouse in 1938 that he talked with great enthusiasm about it to a Paramount producer who decided to send for him and offered him a screen test. He was given a lengthy scene as Killer Mears in *The Last Mile* to enact before the cameras. When the test was seen by studio executives, Preston was immediately signed to a contract at $100 a week. At their insistence he dropped his real surname and used his first two names instead.

He made his screen debut in *King of Alcatraz* (1938) and appeared in two other minor but good B pictures. His career then received a major boost when he was chosen by Cecil B. DeMille to play Dick Allan, "the other man," in the Western railroad epic *Union Pacific* (1939) which starred Joel McCrea and Barbara Stanwyck. This ranked as one of the director's best films. Preston and Stanwyck only appeared together in one other film *The Lady Gambles* (1949), but she remained his favorite leading lady. *Union Pacific* was a big hit and won Preston good notices. He appeared in a major role in two other DeMille epics which were *North West Mounted Police* (1940) and *Reap the Wild Wind* (1942). Both were amongst Preston's biggest successes, but he despised DeMille as a bully and a sadist. Years later Preston was offered good roles in DeMille's *Unconquered* (1947) and *The Greatest Show on Earth* (1952), but his dislike of DeMille was so great that he refused to work for him again and turned them down.

He joined *18 Actors*, a theatrical group of movie stars and their wives who kept their hand in by appearing in stage plays before a live audience. He gave an excellent account of himself in *Beau Geste* (1939), William Wellman's epic foreign legion adventure in which he played Digby Geste, younger brother of Beau (Gary Cooper) and John (Ray Milland). Gary Cooper was his favorite actor. He costarred with Dorothy Lamour in a couple of her films which were *Typhoon* (1940) and *Moon over Burma* (1940). *This Gun For Hire* (1942) had him topbilled as a cop, but the classic film was stolen by Alan Ladd and Veronica Lake, turning them into top stars. This was the first of three appearances opposite Ladd. He was part of an all star cast in Paramount's war movie *Wake Island* (1942) which dealt with the real life story of one of the greatest American defeats of the early war years. He and William Bendix played brawling marine buddies.

His final film before enlisting in 1942 was *Night Plane from Chungking* (1943). For three years he was with the Army Air Force beginning as a G.I. physical fitness instructor in Florida, but subsequently being promoted until he worked his way up to the rank of Captain in Combat Intelligence in the Ninth Air Force, 555th Bombardment Squadron, serving in England, France and Belgium. During this time he planned mission routes and briefed and debriefed combat air crews. He also appeared in Joshua Logan's *Flying Soldiers Show*. He was discharged in 1945 and returned to Hollywood to finish his Paramount contract.

Paramount loaned him to independent producer Benedict Bogeaus to play Joan Bennett's cowardly husband in the triangle drama *The Macomber Affair* (1947) with Gregory Peck completing the triangle. It derived from a short story by Ernest Hemingway. Preston's performance netted him more critical acclaim than most of his other work. He supported Alan Ladd in two highly successful films. These were *Wild Harvest* (1947) which also costarred Dorothy Lamour and *Whispering Smith* (1949). The latter was his last under his Paramount contract. Paramount were reluctant to see him go, but he was not on their "A" list of stars and he became disenchanted with the kind of roles he was being offered. Louella Parsons, the famed gossip columnist, took up his petition in the newspapers and the studio dropped him shortly afterwards.

From then onwards he freelanced at a salary of $3,500 a week. He was said to be an accomplished boxer and swimmer and made a hobby of being a rancher. He made films for different studios and shot three which were released by Eagle Lion. "I felt I'd gone as far as I could in Hollywood," he said. The most significant film which he made during this period was a British thriller *Cloudburst* (1951), not for its content, but for what it led to. While working on this film in London, he noticed that after shooting the British actors would go off to perform in theaters.

On the way back to California, he stopped off in New York where he laid the basis for what amounted to a new career on Broadway.

He heard that Jose Ferrer was searching for a replacement as Oscar Jaffe in *Twentieth Century* at the Fulton Theater in 1951. Preston landed the role which was only for the final two weeks, but the critics gave him good notices, business was brisk and it allowed him to make his Broadway debut. He made his television debut in the "Blockade" episode of the anthology series *Pulitzer Prize Playhouse* in 1951. He took over from Ralph Bellamy while the latter was on summer vacation in the crime series *Man Against Crime* between June 29 and August 3, 1951. He played Mike Barnett's brother Pat newly arrived from Ireland and there was a transitional episode to introduce him. Although it was only six weeks, it was sufficient to warn him of the inherent pitfalls in doing series television. While he made frequent television appearances particularly during the fifties in anthology series, he refused to play the lead in any series because he was afraid of being typecast. He did however play a doctor for a month in 1952 on episodes of the dramatized documentary series *Anywhere USA*. This was produced by the Health Information Foundation, dealt with health issues and he probably did it because he believed in it.

He moved to live in Rye, New York and later a small estate in Greenwich, Connecticut. During the fifties he became a durable Broadway leading man. He played Joe Ferguson, a favorite role of his, in a popular revival of *The Male Animal* at the City Center Theater in April 1952 and then the Music Box Theater in May 1952. Over the next five years he appeared in a further six plays on Broadway to good reviews and respectable business. He only shot one film during this period, *The Last Frontier* (1955), which was probably the least acclaimed Western directed by Anthony Mann.

He was appearing in a road show version of *Boy Meets Girl* in Philadelphia when producer Kermit Bloomgarden came backstage and asked him if he would like to try out for the lead in *The Music Man*. Although he had never sung a note nor danced in public, he diligently practiced both as he was desperate to win the part of Harold Hill in *The Music Man* by Meredith Willson. The coveted role was his and he opened at the Majestic Theater, New York on December 19, 1957 to the best notices of his career and smash box office. He played Professor Harold Hill, the con-

Robert Preston, who starred in *Man Against Crime*.

man posing as a music teacher, who is reformed by his love for a shy small town librarian. He appeared in the show for two years and two months through 1,375 performances and won a Tony Award for his efforts as Best Actor in 1957. This show was the one which really made him a box office stage star and enabled him to take control of his career. It was also his favorite stage role.

He was flooded with film offers, but accepted one from Warner Bros. for a three picture deal because it gave him plenty of money; freedom of choice over roles; and he had heard on the grapevine that they were intending to buy the movie rights to *The Music Man*. In the event they did, but it was uncertain for a while if he was going to recreate his role on film. More bankable film stars were considered and allegedly the part was actually offered to Cary Grant who sent a memorable response to Warners, "Not only will I not play it, but if Preston doesn't do it, I won't even come to see the picture." Preston's performance in the film was a revelation to anyone who had not seen him on stage, but rather surprisingly he did not receive an Oscar nomination. His personal favorite of the three films which he shot at Warners was *The Dark at the Top of the Stairs* (1960).

He rejected two film roles during this period. The first was as Senator Van Ackerman in

Advise and Consent (1962) because the shooting schedule conflicted with *How the West Was Won* (1962) which he preferred to do. George Grizzard replaced him. The second was the lead in *The Third Secret* (1964) which Stephen Boyd later did instead. He appeared in the film musical of *Mame* (1974) opposite Lucille Ball, but the off-screen animosity between the two players who detested each other was more arresting than the film. Several films followed, but it was not until he played the part of Toddy, the ageing homosexual, opposite Julie Andrews in *Victor/Victoria* (1983) that he received an Oscar nomination as Best Actor, but he did not win. His final film role was as an intergalactic recruiting agent in *The Last Starfighter* (1984).

The Chisholms was a CBS miniseries originally shown in March and April 1979. It was a sufficient hit for CBS to decide to bring it back as a series in January 1980. Preston starred as poor but honest Virginia farmer Hadley Chisholm during the 1840s who lost his land in a legal dispute. He decided to lead his large family to a better life in California. The miniseries chronicled the hardships of the journey from Virginia to Fort Laramie, Wyoming. When it returned as a series in 1980, the Chisholms were part of an organized wagon train from Fort Laramie to California. A little oddly Hadley Chisholm died en route shortly before the demise of the series on March 15, 1980. Preston appeared in a number of movies for television of which *Rehearsal for Murder* (1982), *Finnegan Begin Again* (1985) and *Outrage!* (1986) were all well received.

He continued to perform on stage during the sixties and seventies with mixed results. His most successful role was as Michael in *I Do, I Do* which opened at the 46th Theater, New York in November 1966. For this he won a second Tony Award as Best Actor in 1968. His final Broadway musical was the role of Mack Sennett in *Mack and Mabel* which opened at the Majestic Theater on October 6, 1974. Much was expected of this production, but even Preston's customary enthusiasm could not save it from failure. His final Broadway appearance came when he succeeded George C. Scott part way through the run of *Sly Fox* at the Broadhurst Theater in May 1977. Once again he played a con artist, Foxwell J. Sly. In an interview in 1984 he said, "It's been a long career and the odd thing is that people keep doing retrospectives as though it were over. Isn't it odd that you have to keep proving you're alive?"

It was while he was appearing in the play *Night Over Taos* at the Pasadena Playhouse that he met actress Catherine Craig (nee Kay Feltus in Bloomington, Indiana on January 18, 1918). They appeared in several shows at the Playhouse together. They were both signed by Paramount. While they never appeared in any films together, he did play opposite her in her screen test. They married in Las Vegas on November 9, 1940. She soon gave up her career, aside from an occasional appearance, to be a full time wife, but they had no children. On the subject of his wife and marriage Preston once said, "She used to be an actress and a good one. She submerged her career to her marriage. In marriage someone has to be a giver and someone, a taker. I am a taker who married a giver."

Preston died on March 21, 1987 aged 68 of lung cancer in Santa Barbara, California. At that time he was living in Montecito, California. He had been ill for some months, but kept it a secret from many of his friends who expressed surprise at the news of his death. According to a publicity release Preston, who had been a heavy smoker, kept his illness a secret because he hated any fuss. He was survived by his widow and his father. In a statement issued from Camp David, President Reagan said, "He was a friend who will be missed." Preston was cremated and his ashes were scattered over the Pacific Ocean.

Filmography

1938: *King of Alcatraz, Illegal Traffic.*
1939: *Disbarred, Union Pacific, Beau Geste.*
1940: *North West Mounted Police, Typhoon, Moon over Burma.*
1941: *The Lady from Cheyenne, New York Town, The Night of January 16th, Parachute Battalion.*
1942: *Reap the Wild Wind, Pacific Blackout, Star Spangled Rhythm* (cameo), *This Gun For Hire, Wake Island.*
1943: *Night Plane from Chungking.*
1947: *The Macomber Affair, Wild Harvest, Variety Girl* (cameo).
1948: *Blood on the Moon, The Big City.*
1949: *Whispering Smith, The Lady Gambles, Tulsa.*
1950: *The Sundowners.*
1951: *My Outlaw Brother, When I Grow Up, Cloudburst, Best of the Badmen.*
1952: *Face to Face* (*The Bride Comes to Yellow Sky* episode).
1955: *The Last Frontier.*
1960: *The Dark at the Top of the Stairs.*
1962: *The Music Man, How the West Was Won.*

1963: *Island of Love, All the Way Home.*
1972: *Junior Bonner, Child's Play.*
1974: *Mame.*
1975: *My Father's House* (TV).
1977: *Semi-Tough.*
1981: *SOB.*
1982: *Victor/Victoria, Rehearsal for Murder* (TV).
1983: *September Gun* (TV).
1984: *Finnegan Begin Again* (TV), *The Last Starfighter.*
1986: *Outrage!* (TV).

TELEVISION SERIES

1951: *Man Against Crime* as Pat Barnett.
1952: *Anywhere USA* as The Doctor.
1980: *The Chisholms* as Hadley Chisholm.

MINISERIES

1979: *The Chisholms.*

SOURCES

The Annual Obituary, 1987. Chicago: St. James, 1988.
Donnelly, Paul. *Fade to Black.* London: Omnibus, 2000.
Herbert, Ian. *Who's Who in the Theatre.* 16th ed. London: Pitman, 1977.
Inman, David. *The TV Encyclopedia.* New York: Perigee, 1991.
Parish, James Robert, and Lennard DeCarl. *Hollywood Players: The Forties.* New Rochelle, NY: Arlington, 1976.
Picture Show Annual. London: Amalgamated, 1940, 1942, 1943 and 1947.
Picture Show. "Life Story." July 30, 1949.
Quinlan, David. *Film Stars.* 5th ed. London: Batsford, 2000.
Ragan, David. *Movie Stars of the '40s.* Englewood Cliffs, NJ: Prentice-Hall, 1985.
_____. *Who's Who in Hollywood.* New York: Facts on File, 1992.
Taylor, Frank. "Preston the Music Man Dies." *Daily Telegraph.* March 23, 1987.
Variety. "Robert Preston, B'way Music Man, Longtime Film Star, Dies at 68." March 25, 1987.
Winchester, Clarence. *Screen Encyclopedia.* London: Winchester, 1948.
Wise, James E. Jr., and Paul W. Wilderson III. *Stars in Khaki.* Annapolis, MD: Naval Institute, 1990.

ANNE PRÉVILLE

In the second format of the syndicated international intrigue television series, *Foreign Intrigue,* James Daly played Michael Powers, a foreign correspondent working for Associated News. His rival and romantic interest was Patricia Bennett, a reporter for Consolidated Press, played by Anne Préville. Both sought to outwit each other to obtain the scoop on a story. This appears to have been her only recorded credit.

TELEVISION SERIES

1953–1954: *Foreign Intrigue* as Patricia Bennett.

SOURCE

Erickson, Hal. *Syndicated Television: The First Forty Years, 1947–1987.* Jefferson, NC: McFarland, 1989.

WILLIAM PRINCE

William LeRoy Prince was born in Nichols, New York on January 26, 1913 the son of Gorman Prince and Myrtle Osborne. His father was a salesman, while his mother was a nurse. He had one sister. None of his family had any connection with the theater. He attended Cornell University between 1930 and 1934, but dropped out in his senior year to join a Federal Theater tour of *The Taming of the Shrew.* Acting jobs in summer stock gave him a meager foothold in the profession. During the winter months, he worked as a statistical clerk for NBC charting the popularity of radio stars. From this he obtained a job as a radio announcer.

He made his New York debut at the Manhattan Opera House on January 7, 1937 doing a walk-on in *The Eternal Road.* Later that year he was engaged by actor-producer Maurice Evans, remaining with his company for three years doing minor roles in Shakespearean productions. Prince penned a letter to Eva Le Gallienne pleading for a chance to audition. He successfully passed this and was assigned the role of Richard in Eugene O'Neill's *Ah Wilderness* which opened at the Guild Theater in October 1941 to considerable acclaim. His career received its biggest boost when he played Private Quizz West in Maxwell Anderson's *The Eve of St. Mark* which opened at the Cort Theater in October 1942.

He was seen by a scout from Warner Bros.

William Prince, who starred in *The Mask* and *Justice*.

who signed him to a contract. He moved from New York to Hollywood where he made his screen debut in *Destination Tokyo* (1943). He remained under contract with Warners until 1946. Although that studio gave him some chances and a publicity build-up, he proved to be a rather colorless leading man. At Columbia he played Barry Storm in the contemporary sequences of the bizarre but fascinating western *Lust for Gold* (1949). His best remembered film part was as the handsome but vapid Christian in *Cyrano de Bergerac* (1950) which starred Jose Ferrer in the title role.

After the expiry of his Warner's contract he re-emerged on the stage playing David Rice in *Judy O' Connor* in Connecticut and Boston in 1946. Between 1947 and 1951 he appeared in various Broadway plays. He made his television debut in "Arsenic and Old Lace" on *Studio One* in 1949. During the fifties he was a frequent player in various anthology series such as *Armstrong Circle Theater* and *Philco Playhouse*.

Prince was the star of two crime and mystery series of the fifties. The first of these was *The Mask*. It depicted the cases of two brothers who were legal partners in the firm of Guilfoyle and Guilfoyle. Walter was played by Gary Merrill and Peter was played by William Prince. The series was called *The Mask* because of the way in which these attorneys unmasked the villains. The program was originally shown live and later kinescoped. It was notable as the first hour length mystery series to feature regular characters. This made it expensive to produce and as it was unable to find a sponsor, it was axed after four months. An ABC production of fifteen black and white episodes, it was originally aired on the ABC network between January 10 and May 16, 1954.

The television series *Justice* dramatized early case files of the National Legal Aid Society. These were stories either civil or criminal in nature about people who could not afford an attorney. Initially it was an anthology series, but gradually two regular Legal Aid attorneys began to appear regularly. Jason Tyler was played by Gary Merrill, while Richard Adams was played by Dane Clark. When the latter left, Prince substituted for him in the same role. Prince appeared in an earlier episode, but his tenure was during the third season between October 2, 1955 and March 25, 1956. This live, half hour, black and white series of 88 episodes was shown on NBC between April 8, 1954 and March 25, 1956. This highly regarded series was produced by David Susskind.

Unlike many actors at this time Prince did not disdain from doing soap operas and had regular roles in five. He was best known for playing the father of the title character in *Young Dr. Malone* which was shown during the daytime on NBC between 1958 and 1963. He appeared on four soaps in regular roles over a fourteen year period. When he returned to films and guest shots on prime time television, it was as a character actor in 1971. By this time he was a far more authoritative player than he had been in his youth. He frequently played suave, ruthless big businessmen or villains and seemed to have inherited the nefarious mantle once worn by George Macready. Unfortunately the caliber of scripts which Prince sometimes appeared in did not match the standard of his acting such as Blakelock in *The Gauntlet* (1977). He remained in constant demand for film and television roles into the nineties. His theatrical career continued simultaneously well into the eighties.

Prince married Dorothy Huass on October 27, 1934 but they divorced in 1964. With her he had two sons and two daughters. Secondly, he wed actress Augusta Dabney, with whom he sometimes appeared, in 1964. She was the former wife of actor Kevin McCarthy.

Prince died at Phelps Memorial Hospital, Tarrytown, NY on October 8, 1996 aged 83. He was survived by his widow, all four children, his sister and three grandchildren.

FILMOGRAPHY

1943: *Destination Tokyo.*
1944: *Hollywood Canteen, The Very Thought of You.*
1945: *Pillow to Post, Objective Burma!.*
1946: *Shadow of a Woman, Cinderella Jones.*
1947: *Dead Reckoning, Carnegie Hall.*
1949: *Lust for Gold.*
1950: *Cyrano de Bergerac.*
1956: *Secret of Treasure Mountain, Vagabond King.*
1958: *Macabre.*
1971: *Sacco e Vanzetti.*
1972: *The Heartbreak Kid.*
1973: *Key West* (TV), *Blade.*
1974: *Night Games* (TV), *The Missiles of October* (TV).
1975: *The Stepford Wives.*
1976: *Family Plot, Network, Sybil* (TV).
1977: *Johnny We Hardly Knew Ye* (TV), *Rollercoaster, The Gauntlet, Fire Sale.*
1978: *The Cat From Outer Space.*
1979: *The Jericho Mile* (TV), *The Promise.*
1980: *Make Me an Offer* (TV), *City in Fear* (TV), *Gideon's Trumpet* (TV), *Bronco Billy, A Time For Miracles* (TV).
1981: *A Matter of Life and Death* (TV).
1982: *Love and Money, The Soldier, Moonlight* (TV), *Kiss Me Goodbye.*
1983: *Murder One, Dancer 0* (TV), *Found Money* (a.k.a. *My Secret Angel*) (TV).
1984: *Concealed Enemies* (TV).
1985: *Spies Like Us, Movers and Shakers, Fever Pitch.*
1986: *Perry Mason: The Case of the Notorious Nun* (TV).
1987: *Assassination, Nuts.*
1988: *Vice Versa, Shakedown* (a.k.a. *Blue Jeans Cop*).
1989: *Second Sight, Spontaneous Combustion.*
1990: *Steel and Lace.*
1991: *The Taking of Beverly Hills.*
1993: *The Portrait* (TV).
1994: *The Paper.*

TELEVISION SERIES

1954: *The Mask* as Peter Guilfoyle.
1955–1956: *Justice* as Richard Adams.
1958–1963: *Young Dr. Malone* as Dr. Jerry Malone.
1964–1965: *Another World* as Ken Baxter.
1968–1969: *The Edge of Night* as Senator Benjamin "Ben" Travis.
1970–1971: *A World Apart* as Russell Barry.
1978: *The American Girls* as Jason Cook.
1986: *Search for Tomorrow* as Judge Jeremiah Henderson.
1986: *Dallas* as Alex Garrett.

MINISERIES

1976: *Captains and the Kings.*
1977: *The Rhinemann Exchange, Aspen* (a.k.a. *The Innocent and the Damned*).
1984: *George Washington.*
1989: *War and Remembrance.*

SOURCES

Herbert, Ian. *Who's Who in the Theatre.* 16th ed. London: Pitman, 1977.
Lentz, Harris M. III. *Obituaries in the Performing Arts, 1996.* Jefferson, NC: McFarland, 1997.
Macall, Martin. *Preview of 1946.* London: Hollywood, 1946.
Picture Show Annual. London: Amalgamated, 1947.
Tibballs, Geoff. *TV Detectives.* London: Boxtree, 1992.
Variety. Obituary, October 21–27, 1994.
Ward, Jack. *Television Guest Stars.* Jefferson, NC: McFarland, 1993.

DENVER PYLE

Denver Dell Pyle was born in Bethune, Colorado, on May 11, 1920, the son of a homesteader. He was named after the capital of the state in which he was born. He had one older brother named Willie, who became the animator Willis Pyle, and an older sister named Skippy. He attended school in Bethune and later in Boulder, Colorado. As a child he did odd jobs. He attended the University of Colorado for two years before dropping out to pursue a career as a drummer in a dance band. When he decided that he did not wish to do this either, he drifted around eventually landing in the oil fields of Texas and Oklahoma. He had been working in a refinery for about eighteen months when on impulse he decided to head for Hollywood to look up his brother and sister who were working there.

His stay was short-lived because he returned

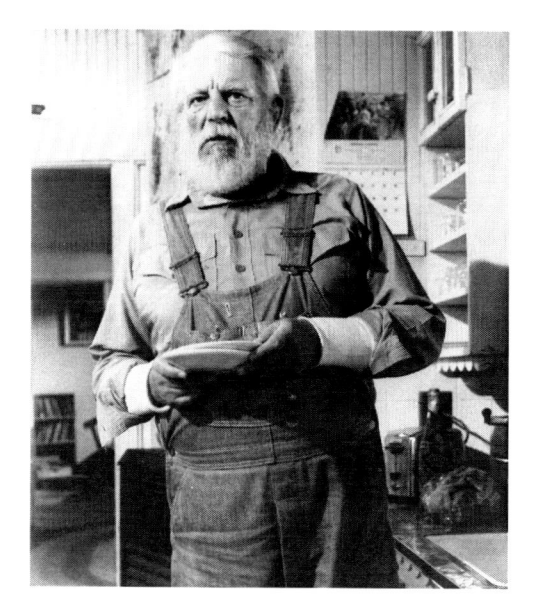

Denver Pyle, who costarred in *Code 3*.

to Boulder, obtained some more education and then went back to Hollywood in 1940 where his sister helped him to obtain a job as a page boy at NBC. When World War II broke out, he worked at Lockheed by night. Later he joined the Merchant Marines and through this served in the navy during the war. Wounded in action off Guadalcanal, he was discharged from the navy in 1942 as medically unfit. After this he married Marilee and went back to work at Lockheed as a riveter. An actor friend of his wife suggested that he try out for a play. He landed the part and did so well with it that he studied acting with various drama teachers notably Maria Ouspenskaya.

She suggested that he join the American Repertory Theater as an actor and set builder. He was involved in much little theater activity for six years. To supplement his meager earnings he worked as a waiter and as a hearing aid and insurance salesman. While appearing in *Ring Around Elizabeth* at the Glendale Center Theater, he was seen by Henry Levin who cast him in two films, *The Guilt of Janet Ames* (1947) and *The Man from Colorado* (1948).

Although he became established as a character actor, it was only in the mid–1950s that he was able to derive all his income from acting and quit his various other jobs. He made his television debut in an episode of *The Cisco Kid* in 1951. He had several regular or semi-regular roles on television. In the crime series *Code 3* he played Sgt. Murchison, deputy to Assistant Sheriff Barnett (Richard Travis). He appeared in numerous episodes of various television series in an enormous variety of different roles. Unlike many actors he was very fond of working in the television medium, although he considered that his best opportunity came in the film *Bonnie and Clyde* (1967) of which he said, "I played the Texas Ranger Frank Hamer like a B western sheriff." In later years his most familiar role was as Uncle Jesse in the television series *The Dukes of Hazzard*. After the series was over he kept busy working at his California business and on his Texas ranch. He also organized an annual charity fishing tournament to benefit the Special Olympics.

Diagnosed with lung cancer in September 1996, he underwent chemotherapy, but died of the disease on December 25, 1997 aged 77. By his first wife, whom he divorced in 1966, he had two sons. He married his second wife Tippi in 1982. Less than two weeks before his death he attended the unveiling of his star on the Hollywood Walk of Fame. He is buried at Forreston Cemetery, Forreston, Ellis County, Texas.

Filmography

1947: *The Guilt of Janet Ames, Devil Ship, Where the North Begins.*
1948: *The Man from Colorado, Train to Alcatraz, Marshal of Amarillo.*
1949: *Captain China, Hellfire, Flame of Youth, Streets of San Francisco, Too Late for Tears, Red Canyon.*
1950: *Dynamite Pass, Federal Agent at Large, The Flying Saucer, Singing Guns, Customs Agent, The Old Frontier, Jet Pilot* (released 1957).
1951: *Rough Riders of Durango, Million Dollar Pursuit, Hills of Utah.*
1952: *Oklahoma Annie, Desert Passage, The Lusty Men, Fargo, The Man from the Black Hills, The Maverick.*
1953: *Gunsmoke, Texas Bad Man, Vigilante Terror, Canyon Ambush, Rebel City, Topeka, Goldtown Ghost Raiders, A Perilous Journey.*
1954: *The Boy from Oklahoma, Drum Beat, Ride Clear of Diablo, Johnny Guitar, The Forty Niners.*
1955: *To Hell and Back, Rage at Dawn, Run for Cover, Ten Wanted Men, Top Gun.*
1956: *Please Murder Me, I Killed Wild Bill Hickok, The Naked Hills, 7th Cavalry, Yaqui Drums.*
1957: *The Lonely Man, Gun Duel in Durango, Destination 60,000, Domino Kid.*
1958: *The Left Handed Gun, Fort Massacre, The Party Crashers, China Doll, A Good Day for a Hanging.*

1959: *The Horse Soldiers, King of the Wild Stallions, Cast a Long Shadow.*
1960: *The Alamo, Home from the Hill.*
1962: *Bearheart, Geronimo, The Man Who Shot Liberty Valance.*
1963: *Mail Order Bride.*
1964: *Cheyenne Autumn.*
1965: *The Rounders, Mara of the Wilderness, Shenandoah, The Great Race.*
1966: *Gunpoint, Incident at Phantom Hill.*
1967: *Welcome to Hard Times, Bonnie and Clyde.*
1968: *Bandolero! 5 Card Stud.*
1971: *Something Big.*
1972: *Who Fears the Devil* (a.k.a. *Legend of Hillbilly John*).
1973: *Hitched!, Cahill United States Marshal.*
1974: *Sidekicks* (TV), *Murder or Mercy* (TV), *Escape to Witch Mountain.*
1975: *Winterhawk, Death Amongst Friends* (TV).
1976: *Buffalo Bill and the Indians or Sitting Bull's History Lesson, Hawmps, Welcome to LA, Guardian of the Wilderness, The Adventures of Frontier Fremont* (a.k.a. *Spirit of the Wild*).
1978: *Return from Witch Mountain.*
1981: *Legend of the Wild.*
1986: *Return to Mayberry* (TV).
1987: *Discovery Bay, Delta Fever* (a.k.a. *Summer Fever*).
1994: *Maverick, Father and Scout* (TV).
1997: *Dukes of Hazzard: Reunion!* (TV).

Television Series

1955–1956: *The Life and Legend of Wyatt Earp* as Ben Thompson.
1957: *Code 3* as Sgt. Murchison.
1965–1966: *Tammy* as Grandpa Tarleton.
1968–1970: *The Doris Day Show* as Buck Webb.
1977–1978: *The Life and Times of Grizzly Adams* as Mad Jack.
1979–1985: *The Dukes of Hazzard* as Uncle Jesse Duke.

Sources

Agence France Presse Release. Obituary, December 29, 1997.
Daily Telegraph. Obituary, January 26, 1998.
Eleventh Annual Golden Boot Award. Program, August 21, 1993.
Goldrup, Tom, and Jim Goldrup. *Feature Players: The Stories Behind the Faces*. Vol. I. Published privately, 1986.
Hayward, Anthony. *The Independent*. Obituary, December 26, 1997.
Inman, David. *The TV Encyclopedia*. New York: Perigee, 1991.
Lentz, Harris M. III. *Obituaries in the Performing Arts, 1997*. Jefferson, NC: McFarland, 1998.
McClure Arthur F., and Ken D. Jones. *Heroes, Heavies and Sagebrush*. South Brunswick, NJ: Barnes, 1972.
Quinlan, David. *The Illustrated Directory of Film Character Actors*. 2nd ed. London: Batsford, 1995.
Tibballs, Geoff. *TV Detectives*. London: Boxtree, 1992.
Towle, Patricia. "Dukes of Hazzard Star in Cancer Battle." *National Enquirer*. February 4, 1997.
Ward, Jack. *Television Guest Stars*. Jefferson, NC: McFarland, 1993.
____. *The Supporting Players of Television, 1959–1983*. Cleveland, OK: Lakeshore West, 1996.

LOUIS QUINN

Louis Quinn was born Louis Quinn Frackt in Chicago, Illinois on March 23, 1915. He was the youngest of seven children. He moved to Los Angeles in 1928 where he was educated. He began as a nightclub comedian and radio writer. He spent years writing drama and comedy scripts for radio. He hosted several radio shows in the forties most notably at the Copacabana Lounge in New York and the Crossroads Lounge in Chicago where "Quinn's Corner" was a spot for visiting celebrities.

When he gravitated to Los Angeles permanently in the late fifties he was active on radio. He was discovered when a journalist went to a town in California where Quinn was hosting a local radio show. The story the journalist originally went to cover did not materialize. Instead he turned on the radio, heard Quinn's patter and wrote a story on him instead. This story was read by an executive at Warner Bros. who in turn signed Quinn to a contract.

He played Roscoe, the racetrack tipster, on *77 Sunset Strip*. He was a valuable source of information to Stuart Bailey (Efrem Zimbalist, Jr.) and Jeff Spencer (Roger Smith). He also supplied much of the humor in the series. His trademarks were his natty clothes, straw hats and cigars. Quinn wrote much of the dialogue for his own character and the jive talk for "Kookie" (Edd Byrnes). Actor Will Hutchins recalled being on a cross country promotional coach tour for

Warner Bros. during the late fifties in which Quinn acted as host and kept all the celebrity passengers in stitches.

Once the series ended it might have been supposed that his career as a character actor would have really taken off, but his appearances amounted to a handful of low budget films and some guest shots on television. Some sources indicate that he continued to write scripts which were produced, but if so none of them can be traced. Most of his income in later years derived from being a public relations executive.

Quinn died in Los Angeles on September 15, 1988 after a brief bout with cancer at the age of 73. Quinn was married twice. His second wife was actress, singer and comedienne Christine Nelson (1928–1988) with whom he had a daughter. They sometimes appeared together, but were later divorced. She predeceased her former husband by one month. He was survived by his daughter, brother and four sisters. Actor Jesse White said of him, "He was the funniest guy I ever knew. Much funnier in real life than he ever was on screen. He was also my closest pal. When he died, I never got over it."

Filmography

1958: *Too Much Too Soon.*
1959: *Al Capone, The Trap.*
1960: *Ocean's Eleven, The Crowded Sky.*
1961: *Dondi.*
1962: *Gypsy.*
1964: *Las Vegas Hillbillies, Birds Do It.*
1971: *Welcome to the Club.*
1972: *Unholy Rollers.*
1973: *Superchick.*
1976: *All the President's Men.*
1977: *Raid on Entebbe* (TV).

Television Series

1958–1963: *77 Sunset Strip* as Roscoe.

Sources

Daily Telegraph. Death Notice. September 1988.
Inman, David. *The TV Encyclopedia.* New York: Perigee, 1991.
Interview with Jesse White in 1996.
Variety. Obituary, September 1988.
_____. Christine Nelson Obituary. August 1988.
Woolley, Lynn, Robert W. Malsbury, and Robert G. Strange. *Warner Bros. Television.* Jefferson, NC: McFarland, 1983.

George Raft

George Raft specialized in playing tough guys in thrillers during the thirties and forties. When occasion demanded he could be very sinister indeed. He once reckoned that he had been killed, wounded or sent to prison in 85% of the films in which he appeared. He died in many different ways on screen including drowning in *Souls at Sea*; being buried under tons of ice in *Spawn of the North*; and being shot to death in *Each Dawn I Die* and *Rogue Cop.*

There were many actors who were technically more accomplished than Raft, but Raft remains indelibly in the memory long after most of them have been forgotten. He was a trend setter rather than a trend fol-

Left to right: Efrem Zimbalist Jr., Edd Byrnes, Roger Smith, Richard Long and Louis Quinn in *77 Sunset Strip.*

lower and whatever he tried to accomplish on screen, he did with tremendous élan. He was one of the most successful exponents of personality acting in the history of the cinema. Hardly surprising that Edward G. Robinson once dismissed him as a showman rather than an actor. One particularly enjoyable feature of many of Raft's films were the dancing interludes. He would have been suitable for some contemporary films and at least if he had played Captain Corelli in *Captain Corelli's Mandolin*, he could have danced the tango with Penelope Cruz, unlike Nicolas Cage, who could only stand on the sidelines and watch.

Inevitably there are the comparisons with Humphrey Bogart where Raft comes off a very poor second. Raft was a self educated ex-vaudevillian from a poor family who was mainly interested in sports and who relied a lot on the judgment of agents when it came to selecting scripts. Many of them had no better judgment than his. Raft was also a stylized performer. If he made one mistake in the middle years of his career, it was that he forsook villainy altogether. He was always much more convincing as a gangster than as a good guy. Despite his image as a roughneck, Bogart came from a well-to-do family who were in the social register. He was a literate man. His years in stock meant that he was both versatile and had a nose for a good script. Some say that Bogart climbed to fame on Raft's rejected scripts. This is only partially true. If Raft had accepted scripts like *High Sierra*, the end result would still have been the same. It would have taken him longer, but Bogart would still have been an enormous success. It is impossible for instance to imagine Raft playing leading roles in *The African Queen* or *The Caine Mutiny*. Bogart found his soul mate both on and off screen in the form of Lauren Bacall. Although he was very attractive to female audiences and had many fine leading ladies onscreen, Raft had no equivalent of Lauren Bacall.

In one respect Raft's television career was unique. He originally came to television when his film career was at a low ebb with a series called *I'm the Law*. Aside from this series, he did virtually no other acting on television. He made very frequent appearances on the small screen, but these were usually of the chat show or game show variety. There were many other actors who were contemporaries of Raft whose film careers had hit the skids, but they sustained their careers by guesting on many of the most prestigious shows of the period. Raft did not. He would have

George Raft, who starred in *I'm the Law*.

been an asset to the guest line-up of many of the leading crime shows e.g. *The Untouchables*, but his name was conspicuously absent from all of them.

Raft's links with the underworld are another source of speculation. He was never a top mobster, but equally he knew and was involved with many of the leading racketeers of his day. He did favors for them and they reciprocated by keeping him alive to die of natural causes. Whenever he was interviewed on the subject, Raft always proclaimed his ignorance of their activities. Whether he was as naive as he appeared is open to question. Certainly this insider knowledge gave his screen performances a great deal of authenticity. He was also fortunate that he had a voice which matched his looks.

Raft was a tough guy with a sentimental streak. In *Lucky Nick Cain* there is a scene where Enzo Staiola (best remembered as the little boy in *Bicycle Thieves*) has to tell Raft that his girlfriend Coleen Gray has been arrested. Raft was so moved at the child's acting that tears came to his eyes. As he expressed it, "I've got a soft side, in spite of all my tough roles. I can easily be moved to tears." Other members of the film unit who witnessed this incident confirmed that it was true.

George Raft was born George Ranft in the

notorious Hell's Kitchen district of New York on September 27, 1895 the eldest son of Conrad Ranft and Eva Glockner. His father was a German who died in 1929, while his mother was Italian who died in 1937. He had four brothers and a younger sister. Three of his brothers were killed in World War I and the remaining one was killed while working construction on a skyscraper. His sister died young of tuberculosis. It was an extremely tough environment and he joined the most fearsome of the street gangs during childhood. His education he obtained at P.S. 169 and later St. Catherine's elementary school, but he spent little time there. As a child he was entranced by Broadway, the nickelodeons and baseball which remained a lifelong passion.

After a fight with his father he refused to return to school and instead became a dropout, sleeping in all manner of strange places mainly pool halls and working at all manner of jobs until World War I. In 1914 he joined a semi-professional baseball team, but soon realized that he was not going to make the grade as a full time player. This was also when he first began using the surname Raft, although he only legally changed it in 1935. He also turned professional boxer and had 17 bouts, but he was even less successful at this than baseball. After one particularly vicious beating in the ring, he quit.

He frequented dance-halls where he began to learn the art of dancing. He had no formal training, but imitated others. He became a fast Charleston dancer and secured a few engagements as a specialty dancer. He earned extra money by winning dance contests. While at one club he encountered Rudolph Valentino who suggested Raft join him at another where they were both paid to dance with women which made him a taxi-dancer. There are unconfirmed reports that Raft was a gigolo receiving money not only for his dancing, but also for sexual favors, an allegation which Raft vehemently denied all his life. His resemblance to Valentino meant that after Valentino's success, he found himself in demand at various New York theaters as a substitute for the star. When Valentino died, there were those who wanted Raft to become a second Valentino, but Raft found the notion ghoulish and fortunately decided to continue with a career founded on his own individuality.

He made the acquaintance of an agent who eventually partnered him with vaudevillian dancer Eve Shirley on a tour of New England states and later with Lily Field. Afterwards he joined a group of vaudevillians who toured small towns for two and a half years. This was where Raft honed his dancing skills.

He was one third of a touring act called Pislo, Douglas and Raft. Through the influence of his father, he obtained a job as a dancer at a Coney Island club. Although this did not last long, he was befriended by a piano player at another club where he also secured employment for a while. The name of the piano player was Jimmy Durante. Durante was subsequently bankrolled probably by the mob in a Manhattan club called the Club Durant which gave him the chance to employ Raft full time. Later Raft went to work at the El Fey nightclub fronted by the legendary hostess Texas Guinan where he danced and did some minor bootlegging on the side. In 1925 he won a role in a Broadway show *The City Chap* where he had a specialty number. When he met hoofer Elsie Pilcer, he decided to accept her offer to tour Europe as part of a dancing act in 1926. While in London he met the Prince of Wales whom he taught to dance the Charleston. Upon his return to New York he was featured in another Broadway revue entitled *Padlocks of 1927* which starred Texas Guinan. Bandleader Ben Bernie gave Raft a career boost by recommending him for a booking at the famed Palace Theatre. Raft also managed prizefighter Maxie Rosenbloom in his early days.

When Texas Guinan received an offer from Warner Bros. to go to Hollywood to appear in a film called *Queen of the Nightclubs* (1929) loosely based on her life, it was decided that Raft should accompany her as her bodyguard and have a number in the film which marked his screen debut. After completion of the movie, he returned to New York where the stock market crashed and the nightlife for a while became dire. Raft decided in favor of a career in the movies so he relocated to Hollywood where he struggled for quite some time. Director-screenwriter Rowland Brown encountered him at the Brown Derby and told him that he would be suitable for a small role as a hood/bodyguard in *Quick Millions* (1931).

There were rumors floating around that Raft was acting as an advance man for the mob. The police brought him in on suspicion of robbing the home of actress and sometime girlfriend Molly O'Day which Raft denied. He was on the point of being exiled from the state, but he had a contract at Fox for a movie called *Hush Money* (1931) as a gangster threatening Joan Bennett.

Winfield Sheehan, then Fox head of production, convinced the police that Raft was intent on a career as an actor and managed to save him. Samuel Goldwyn chose him to play a gangster in an Eddie Cantor vehicle *Palmy Days* (1931). James Cagney, who had known Raft from his New York days and liked him, recommended him to Warner Bros. for an unbilled bit as a dancer whom he slugs in *Taxi!* (1932). Raft went to the fights one night which he spent in the company of Howard Hawks who cast Raft in the career making part of the loyal henchman Guido Rinaldo in *Scarface* (1932) with Paul Muni in the title role. Raft's lack of acting experience was concealed in the film by his habit of flipping a coin, a mannerism which he borrowed from one of his New York mob acquaintances. When the film was released, it was a sensational success and propelled Raft far up the Hollywood ladder. When the film was showing in Chicago, Raft was summoned to see Al Capone upon whose life the film was allegedly based. By all accounts Capone liked the movie and Raft.

There were a number of studios wanting to put Raft under contract. He inked an exclusive deal with Paramount where he was reported to be the highest paid actor in Hollywood for a brief period in 1933. His first feature for them was *Dancers in the Dark* (1932). Although Paramount signed Raft for tough guy roles, he was at his most animated during his early years there and appeared in his widest diversity of parts during the thirties. He had casting approval and one of his early films *Night After Night* (1932) marked the screen debut of the legendary Mae West. Of this experience Raft ruefully recalled, "She stole everything but the cameras." Years later his penultimate film was the dire *Sextette* (1978) which also starred Mae West. He died two days after she did. He was loaned out to Darryl F. Zanuck's newly formed Twentieth Century Corporation for *The Bowery* (1933) opposite Wallace Beery, Fay Wray and Jackie Cooper. This was a rowdy, highly enjoyable depiction of life at the turn of the century in that area of New York and was an enormous commercial success. It was also notable for Beery and Raft playing characters with names "Chuck" Connors and Steve Brodie which later belonged to post-war actors.

Of his early Paramount films *Bolero* (1934) a dancing film with Carole Lombard was a big hit and reputedly Raft's personal favorite of his own films. A weak follow-up with Lombard *Rumba* (1935) was however a flop. During his later years at Paramount Raft became increasingly difficult over scripts and his appearances became fewer. He turned down the unsympathetic role of Powdah in *Souls at Sea* (1937). Anthony Quinn and Lloyd Nolan stood by to replace him when Raft was suspended. Instead Paramount relented and Raft played the role once the part was more sympathetically written. It was a long shoot, but a big hit and Raft's salary rose to $4,500 per week. *Spawn of the North* (1938) was an exciting saga of the Alaska Salmon Fishing industry which also did very well at the box office. During the late thirties Raft acquired a reputation of appearing in films with actors who were much more highly regarded than he, but somehow more than holding his own against them. Notable examples included Gary Cooper in *Souls at Sea* (1937), Henry Fonda in *Spawn of the North* (1938) and James Cagney in *Each Dawn I Die* (1939).

Disagreements over scripts and salary brought about an extremely acrimonious split from Paramount and it was thought that he would not work for them again. James Cagney and director William Keighley went after Raft to costar with Cagney in the exciting *Each Dawn I Die* (1939) at Warner Bros. which reestablished his reputation and contains one of his best performances as "Hood" Stacy. On the strength of this success he signed with Warners at a salary of $5,000 per week. He was at his best in *They Drive By Night* (1940), a searing trucking melodrama, in which he and Humphrey Bogart played brothers. The following year he and Edward G. Robinson teamed in *Manpower* (1941) where he and Robinson played power linesmen. This film was also notable for the off screen, on set brawl which took place between Robinson and Raft for the affections of their costar Marlene Dietrich. She was fonder of Raft.

Temperament intervened again and Raft began to turn down scripts by the yard. *High Sierra* (1941) which he rejected became a major success for Bogart. He turned down *The Maltese Falcon* (1941) because it had been filmed twice before and flopped and he could not entrust himself to fledgling director, John Huston. Much to Huston's relief, Bogart inherited the role and the film went on to be a major success. Contrary to virtually all published accounts Raft actively campaigned to win the role of Rick Blaine in *Casablanca*, but was denied the role by producer, Hal Wallis. There was an exchange of memos in April 1942 which began when Jack Warner sent one to Wallis informing him that Raft was after the part and asking Wallis's opinion. The reply from Wallis to Jack Warner dated April 13, 1942 read in part, "I have thought over very carefully the matter of George Raft in *Casablanca* ... and feel that he should not be in the picture." Ironically Raft's last film at Warner's was *Background to Danger* (1943) one of several films designed to cash in on the success of that classic.

The most familiar version of how Raft came to leave Warner Bros. is that recalled by Jack Warner. Allegedly Warner telephoned Raft, invited him to a meeting and offered to settle the matter for $10,000. Owing to a misunderstanding Raft thought that he should pay Warner that amount of money instead of the other way round so he wrote out a check and gave it to Warner. Warner practically ran with it to the bank and cashed it. Other stars have indicated however that they bought themselves out of contracts with Warner Bros., so Warner's version of what happened may not be quite accurate. Raft made a terse comment on that studio when he said, "At the studio Jack Warner made the place seem like Alcatraz."

Afterwards while Raft was not exactly deluged with offers, his agent Charles Feldman negotiated successfully for a number of one off or pact deals which kept Raft's career going during the remainder of the forties. Raft did however find himself working for such mildly eccentric independent producers as Benedict Bogeaus whose product lacked the polish and production values which Raft was used to. Most of these independent films were released through United Artists. Raft shot four films at RKO Radio of which the first ranked amongst his best. He played the title role of *Johnny Angel* (1945) an eerie, deep sea mystery which the studio had little faith in, but which turned out to be a box office bonanza. It was the first of six films directed by Edwin L. Marin. Raft set up his own production company Star Films in partnership with producer Sam Bischoff to make three films. In the event only two were ever made namely *Intrigue* (1947) and *Outpost in Morocco* (1949). The latter was a desert mystery and one of Raft's most underrated films costarring him with Marie Windsor, his best post war leading lady. This was director Robert Florey's personal favorite of his own films and opened to brisk business. Raft's personal fortunes took a downturn in 1947 when he was declared bankrupt and his finances were rocky from then onwards. That same year gangster acquaintance Bugsy Siegel was shot to death, but Raft was never charged and there was no proof that he had anything to do with it.

With the climate of the industry changing, Raft was forced to find work abroad notably playing the title role of the charming gambler in the thriller *Lucky Nick Cain* (1951). He was also paid a retainer by racketeer Frank Costello to coach him prior to giving testimony before the Kefauver Rackets Committee. Since there were no further film offers forthcoming, it was at a low point in his career that Raft turned to television with a syndicated series called *I'm the Law*. This consisted of 26 half hour, black and white episodes in which Raft played Det. Lt. George Kirby of the NYPD. It was a Cosman Production and was bankrolled by Lou Costello, the comedian. His brother Pat was the executive producer. The series was used at least once to advertise an Abbott and Costello movie. In one of the better episodes in which domestic violence camouflaged a plot to kill a woman's husband for the insurance, there was a scene set in a cinema. The audience is shown roaring with laughter at the antics of Abbott and Costello's latest feature *Jack and the Beanstalk* (1952).

Raft started work at eight in the morning and quit at six in the evening and found the pace grueling. In common with many stars from the golden era of movies, he was not used to the frenetic pace of television. His agents, Charles Feldman and Jules Levy, wanted to buy three of the half hour episodes, edit them into a feature film and pay Raft $125,000 for the privilege, but he refused. They went ahead and did it anyway. The title of the feature was *Crime Squad* which played briefly in Europe and overseas. Raft was supposed to receive a salary of $90,000 for the series, but after expenses he wound up with virtually nothing. The series sat on the shelf for a while and was eventually shown in 1953 where it was a modest success. Two years later it was reissued under the title *The George Raft Casebook*, but again Raft was cut out of the profits. Of this experience Raft said, "I thought it was a lousy series."

The talent involved was professional enough on both sides of the camera. The scripts however contained great gaps in logic and key action scenes took place off screen. Some of the stories incorporated clever ideas, but made insufficient use of them. One particularly unconvincing aspect of the series was the frequency with which Raft deliberately went into situations alone which he knew were potentially fatal instead of requesting back-up. One of the better elements of the series were the location shots of New York which were shown over the closing credits.

He went to England where he fulfilled a six week tour of the British Isles. Whilst there he was approached by producer Bernard Luber to star in three quickie features which were subsequently released by Lippert. In 1953 he was the subject of a Friars Club roast which Jack Warner, Dore Schary of MGM and Darryl F. Zanuck of 20th Century–Fox all attended. In the midst of the ribbing Raft made an emotional appeal for a job. Warner remained flint hearted, but Schary found Raft a role as gangster Dan Beaumonte in *Rogue Cop* (1954) which brought him his best notices in years. Zanuck cast him as a police detective investigating a theatrical murder in the all star *Black Widow* (1954). Raft also joined Edward G. Robinson for a poor thriller *A Bullet For Joey* (1955), but both their careers were in decline by that stage and there were no reported rifts on the set.

As a foretaste of what he was to suffer in future years producer Mike Todd invited Raft to play a cameo in his all star *Around the World in 80 Days* (1956). Initially Raft was reluctant to play such a small role, but when he found out that his old pals Marlene Dietrich, Frank Sinatra and Red Skelton were involved, he agreed to play a bouncer in the Bowery sequence. He did not face the cameras again for three years. Instead he became a talent scout for the Flamingo Hotel in Las Vegas. This experience qualified him to become entertainment director of the Capri Hotel in Havana which he did for a stint in the spring of 1958. He then returned to Hollywood where he appeared in his last good film role that of "Spats" Columbo in Billy Wilder's classic *Some Like It Hot* (1959). Originally he was hired for a week's work, but because Marilyn Monroe failed to show up so much of the time, Wilder shot extra scenes with him to fill in the time. Raft's only display of temperament was when he blew up on the last day. When Wilder gently asked him what the problem was, Raft admitted that he so enjoyed shooting the film that he did not want to see it end. His film roles thereafter were mainly confined to cameos.

Rather reluctantly he left for Havana to resume his duties at the Capri Hotel over Christmas 1958 and New Year 1959. This activity came to an abrupt end when Fidel Castro's forces overran the country and overthrew the corrupt Batista regime. Castro took control of the country's gambling casinos and closed them down. Raft was captured during the revolution, but after a tense period allowed to fly back to the United States. He did not receive any financial compensation for his lost earnings. He sold the film rights to his life story for $5,000 to Allied Artists. It was released under the title *The George Raft Story* (1961) in America and as *Spin of a Coin* in Europe, but it was not a success. Ray Danton played Raft, but Raft would have preferred Tony Curtis.

In 1960 a professed fan and businessman approached Raft with the idea of setting up a consumer discount store chain called Consumer Marts of America (CMA) with Raft to act in a public relations capacity. The first store opened in Chicago followed by a dozen others over the next two years. Raft was paid expenses, modest fees for his name and stock options. Subsequently he was made a vice president of the company which gave him financial responsibility without any authority or further remuneration. In 1964 he was told by the corporate accountant that the company had gone into liquidation with the most serious financial consequences for Raft. In the proceedings that followed, he lost most of his assets including his Beverly Hills home. In 1965 on the evening of his seventieth birthday, he was indicted on six counts of income tax evasion. After pleas of leniency from some of his old show business pals and a hearing, Raft pleaded guilty to one count and was given a suspended sentence and a small fine.

Afterwards he went to France at the behest of actor Jean Gabin to appear second billed in a gangster film *Rififi in Panama* (1966) which set a new low in artistic standards for both actors, but it was nevertheless well received. Afterwards he flew to London to front George Raft's Colony Sporting Club, a swank gaming establishment in Berkeley Square, Mayfair. Former costars such as Alice Faye and William Holden came to see him there and he attended various public relations events. He did radio and television work and there was even talk of a new film using the club as a background. He was to spend nine months of each year there for an indeterminate period of time with a three month vacation for the baseball season back in the States. He owned ten shares in the club, was paid a modest salary with the use of a Rolls Royce and a flat in Bilton Towers, Cumberland Place. The rest of the shares were owned by a syndicate which reputedly had links to organized crime. On February 25, 1967 while on his first vacation in the States, the British Home Secretary Roy Jenkins barred him from re-entering the country for his alleged associations. Raft made appeals, but to no avail. Several other share holders in the club were barred at the same time. The legal hassle is probably what prevented him from appearing in cameos in such films as *Madigan's Millions* and *Don't Make Waves*. He was pursued by creditors, forced to sell his possessions and move into a heavily mortgaged apartment in Century City, Los Angeles. The Colony Club closed its doors for the last time in 1969.

He remained heavily in debt to the IRS. and survived on a small pension from the Screen Actors' Guild and social security payments. He had a hand in organizing various nostalgia events and earned some money from commercials, his most successful being one for Alka Seltzer. In the seventies he was appointed goodwill ambassador for the Riviera Hotel in Las Vegas, but operated out of the Los Angeles office. His health began to fail. In 1972 he underwent a hernia operation and in 1980 came down with pneumonia. He suffered very badly during his last years from emphysema and was in and out of hospital for the six months before he died. He eventually died in the New Los Angeles Hospital on November 24, 1980 aged 85 from leukemia. At the time of his death he was virtually penniless. A hospital spokesman Dr. Ruxford Kennamer said, "George had been in no pain. He simply went to sleep." He had been in the hospital for about a week before he died. He is buried in the Courts of Remembrance, Sanctuary of Light at Forest Lawn Cemetery, Hollywood Hills in a crypt inscribed simply: George Raft 1895–1980. It was Pete Hamill in *The New York Post* who wrote the best epitaph for Raft when he penned, "I ... wish that someone would give him a long coat and machine gun, a pair of spats and a blonde, and let him flip a silver dollar in the air, before shooting it out with the cops. George Raft, of all people, should be allowed to go out in style."

Raft allegedly married for the first time in the teens to a much older unnamed woman who bore him a son who eventually made him a grandfather. This has never been verified. His second marriage took place in Pennsylvania in 1923 to Grayce Mulrooney variously described as a secretary or welfare worker. They were together for only a short period, but since she was a Catholic she refused to divorce him until she died in 1969. Since they were however legally separated, she was also given 10% of his earnings for life. His most important relationship was with Virginia Pine who had a daughter Joan. They lived together in a house in Coldwater Canyon and were one of the subjects of a famous *Photoplay* magazine article "Hollywood's Unmarried Husbands and Wives." Their relationship ended in 1939 partly because Raft could not obtain a divorce and partly because he became enamored of Norma Shearer, MGM star and widow of Irving Thalberg, who already had two children Irving and Katherine. She had a considerable influence on his life and there was talk of them appearing in at least two films together at MGM which did not materialize. Their relationship fizzled in 1941 for similar reasons. His last serious relationship was with Betty Grable which broke up and she later married bandleader Harry James.

Filmography

1929: *Queen of the Nightclubs, Side Street, Gold Diggers of Broadway.*
1931: *Quick Millions, Hush Money, Goldie, Palmy Days.*
1932: *Taxi!, Winner Take All, Night World, Scarface, Love Is a Racket, Dancers in the Dark, Madame Racketeer, Night After Night, If I Had a Million, Under-cover Man.*
1933: *Pick-up, The Midnight Club, The Bowery.*
1934: *Bolero, All of Me, The Trumpet Blows, Limehouse Blues* (a.k.a. *East End Chant*).
1935: *Rumba, Stolen Harmony, The Glass Key, Every Night at Eight.*
She Couldn't Take It.
1936: *It Had to Happen, Yours for the Asking.*
1937: *Souls at Sea.*
1938: *You and Me, Spawn of the North.*
1939: *The Lady's From Kentucky, I Stole a Million, Each Dawn I Die, Invisible Stripes.*
1940: *They Drive By Night* (a.k.a. *The Road to Frisco*), *The House Across the Bay.*
1941: *Manpower.*
1942: *Broadway.*
1943: *Stage Door Canteen* (cameo), *Background to Danger.*
1944: *Follow the Boys.*
1945: *Nob Hill, Johnny Angel.*
1946: *Nocturne, Whistle Stop, Mr. Ace.*
1947: *Intrigue, Christmas Eve.*
1948: *Race Street.*
1949: *Let's Go to Paris* (cameo), *Johnny Allegro* (a.k.a. *Hounded*), *A Dangerous Profession, Outpost in Morocco, Red Light.*

1951: *Lucky Nick Cain* (a.k.a. *I'll Get You For This*).
1952: *Escape Route* (a.k.a. *I'll Get You*), *Loan Shark*.
1953: *The Man From Cairo* (a.k.a. *Adventures in Algeria* and *Secrets of the Casbah*).
1954: *Rogue Cop, Black Widow*.
1955: *A Bullet for Joey*.
1956: *Around the Word in 80 Days* (cameo).
1959: *Jet Over the Atlantic, Some Like It Hot*.
1960: *Ocean's Eleven* (cameo).
1961: *The Ladies Man* (cameo).
1962: *Two Guys Abroad*.
1964: *For Those Who Think Young, The Patsy* (cameo).
1966: *Rififi in Panama* (a.k.a. *The Upper Hand*).
1967: *Casino Royale* (cameo).
1968: *Five Golden Dragons* (cameo), *Skidoo*.
1969: *Make Love Not War* (a.k.a. *The Great Sex War*) (cameo).
1970: *Deadhead Miles*.
1972: *Hammersmith is Out*.
1978: *Sextette*.
1979: *The Man With Bogart's Face* (a.k.a. *Sam Marlow Private Eye*).

TELEVISION SERIES

1952–1953: *I'm the Law* (a.k.a. *The George Raft Casebook*) as Det. Lt. George Kirby.

SOURCES

The Annual Obituary. Chicago: St. James, 1980.
Beck, H. *Inside Hollywood: Intimate Story of United Artists*. Parts II and III. Glasgow, Scotland: McKenzie, 1947.
Behlmer, Rudy. *Inside Warner Bros. (1935–1951)*. New York: Simon & Schuster, 1985.
Blumenfeld, Simon. "Gang Show." *The Stage*. August 5, 1999.
Brodie, Ian. *Daily Telegraph*. Obituary, November 25, 1980.
Bury, Lee. "Mr. Unlucky." *Daily Express*. September 7, 1978.
Daily Express. "George Raft Banned from Britain." February 24, 1967.
Daily Express. Obituary, November 25, 1980.
Films and Filming. "You've Got to Be Tough with Hollywood." 1962.
Freedland, Michael. *The Warner Bros*. London: Harrap, 1983.
The Guardian. "George Raft Banned Again." 1974.
Hamill, Pete. "The Last Caper." *New York Post*. March 4, 1967.

Kohler, Renate. *Radio Times*. October 24, 1974.
Lamparski, Richard *Whatever Became Of?* 3rd and 8th Series. New York: Crown, 1970 and 1982.
Liverpool Daily Post. Obituary, November 25, 1980.
Liverpool Echo. Obituary, November 25, 1980.
Mooring, W.H. "Tough Guy Raft." *Picturegoer*. July 23, 1949.
Parish, James Robert, and Whitney, Steven. *The George Raft File*. New York: Drake, 1973.
Picture Show. "Life Story." October 7, 1939.
Picture Show Annual. London: Amalgamated, 1934, 1936, 1938, 1941, 1949, 1952 and 1954.
Richards, Brad. "Old Black Snake: The Coiled Menace of George Raft." *Films of the Golden Age*. No. 38. Fall 2004.
Russell, Frederick. "Hollywood's Dancing Gangster." *Film Pictorial*. May 19, 1934.
Sunday Express. "George Raft Feels Like Communist or Spy." February 25, 1967.
Variety. Obituary, November 26, 1980.
Wall, Michael. "An Early Decision About Mr. Raft." *The Guardian*. February 23, 1967.
Wall, Michael. "Mr. Raft Not Allowed to Land in Britain." *The Guardian*. February 24, 1967.
Williams, Michael. "A Movie Tough Guy." *Radio Times*. 1967.
Winchester, Clarence. *Screen Encyclopedia*. London: Winchester, 1948.
Woman. Biography. 1960s.
Yablonsky, Lewis. *George Raft*. London: W.H. Allen, 1975.

RON RANDELL

A signal in Morse code is flashed, superimposed over the *OSS* title. From this emerges a large document envelope with the words "Top Secret" and that week's episode title prefaced by the word "Operation" embossed across the cover. Simultaneously an announcer's voice exclaims, "Stories straight from the annals of one of America's most effective wartime intelligence services ... the OSS!" This was the opening of the television series *OSS*.

The star of this series was Ron Randell who was born in Australia, but became something of an international celebrity during the 1950s. He was an early star of both BBC and independent television in England. During this decade it would have been difficult for any viewer not to know who he was as he zoomed from one country to another active in television, film and on stage. Such is the transitory nature of television that after 1963 no regular television or important film roles came his way. In later years Rod Taylor and Mel Gibson had the kind of careers which no doubt Randell would have liked. In 1955 he said rather prophetically, "Public tastes change fast. Nobody lasts two years in any regular television program." History of course has proved him wrong with many long running hits, but it was to be true as far as his television career and that of many of his contemporaries was concerned.

Ronald Egan Randell was born in Broken Hill, New South Wales, Australia on October 8, 1918, the son of Ernest B. Randell and his wife Louisa Maria Castello. He had one brother named Norman. He was educated at St. Mary's College, Sydney. He was active on radio for the Australian Broadcasting Commission both acting and writing plays from 1933 onwards. At the age of 18 he was interviewed by at least one big company with a view to becoming an employee. They discussed contracts, salary and retirement plans. As he recalled, "I was out of that door so fast they thought the three minute mile was a possibility."

He intended to become a professional stage actor, but World War II intervened and he was conscripted. In 1943 the Australian Army discharged him as medically unfit so he booked passage for the Mayo Clinic in Rochester, USA. In 1943 this was no pleasure cruise because the Japanese had a submarine blockade round Sydney. This was so effective that the month he left 57 ships and boats were sunk. Nevertheless he reached America safely, went to the clinic and was cured.

Deciding to pursue his ambition to be an actor in America, he journeyed to Hollywood where he made a test for Alfred Hitchcock at 20th Century–Fox for *Lifeboat*. As he recalled, "Mr. Hitchcock forgot to tell me it was the part of a cockney. I played it as an American. I didn't get the part." The only role he played in Hollywood first time around was as a marine in *The Story of Dr. Wassell* (1944).

Since no doors opened for him in America and he did not consider himself to be movie material, he decided to return to the stage in Australia. For six months he waited for a boat to Australia. During that time he worked from 10am to 3pm as a dishwasher in a café, then dashing across town to take up duties as a soda jerk from 3pm to midnight. Back in Australia he joined the Minerva Theater Group, making his first appearance in Sydney in 1943 when he played Sgt. Mulraney in *While the Sun Shines*. Between 1943 and 1946 he appeared in 18 plays in Sydney, Melbourne and Adelaide.

Columbia Studios were searching for an actor to play the title role in the life story of Sir Charles Kingsford-Smith, the Australian airman who was lost in 1935 while attempting to break the air record. The producers had contacted David Niven and others without success. Randell was given the star role largely on the strength of a strong facial similarity to the airman.

On the basis of his performance in the film *Smithy* (1946), Columbia brought him to Hollywood under contract. He recalled, "Those were the good days. A weekly check is a good thing to have around." He appeared in the title role in a couple of *Bulldog Drummond* films and one *Lone Wolf* film before Hollywood hit a production slump. Of this period he explained, "I was more of a tourist than an actor. I've been to every national park in the country. Eventually Columbia and I parted company. It wasn't so much losing film parts that hurt for I hadn't had many. It was the money. It was really like losing an inheritance which I'd had for years from some kind uncle."

He took advantage of the situation to make his Broadway debut in a double bill at the Coronet Theater in October 1949 when he played Frank Hunter in *The Browning Version* and Jack Wakefield in *Harlequinade*. At the National in New York in April 1952 he played Rev. James Morell in a revival of *Candida*. He went to London where he shot some television films before resolving to give up movies and television altogether. He stayed around long enough to make his London debut as Chester Ames in *Sweet Peril* at the St. James Theater in December 1952. He returned to Hollywood for a prestigious assignment playing Cole Porter in the film *Kiss Me Kate* (1953) for MGM.

Back in England his unwillingness to have anything to do with television resulted in a job which was to make him famous. He was persuaded by the BBC to fill in as Master of Ceremonies at the test runs for contestants on the panel game *What's My Line?* Although it was muted at the time, he did not think the BBC was serious about making him the regular M.C. He became rather bored with the idea and was flippant in his attitude to the BBC off screen which he carried over into the program. His style, wit and in particular the kiss which he blew to the ladies led to him being signed as permanent M.C. even though he privately admitted that he probably knew less about the rules than any of the contestants. As he recalled, "It must have been my innocent fresh approach that created such a stir that the resultant publicity made me well known virtually overnight in the British Isles. Owing to my good fortune in hitting the show when it was at its peak, I was swept along on its success." As a result of this, he became known for a while as "Scandal Randell" or "Romeo Randell."

This led him straight back to the movies. He was cast by Romulus Films in *I Am A Camera* (1955). This springboarded him back to Hollywood as costar of *Desert Sands* (1955). From the Yuma, Arizona location of this film he was called back to London for the narration of a suspense anthology television series called *The Vise* to be shown in America. The characters in this filmed drama series were caught in the vise of fate because of traits in their own personalities which landed them in serious trouble frequently with tragic consequences. There were 65 half hour, black and white episodes originally shown on the ABC network between October 1954 and December 1955. The same time slot and title were later used for the *Mark Saber* series which starred Donald Gray. Several episodes of the Randell narrated series were stitched together to make feature films (of little artistic merit) which were released in England. Simultaneously an independent television company began talking about a two year contract with option renewals every 13 weeks to act as compere for a Saturday evening variety show called *On the Town*.

At the time he said, "Two years is one heck of a long time. Anything lasting more than three months horrifies me. I loathe being tied down, get bored at the idea of long runs. Essentially I am an actor, not a compere. In my acting career I haven't had to worry about long runs. I toured for a year in *Candida*. By the end of that time, speaking almost the same words, playing the same part, doing the same actions, I needed a small snort of brandy at the thought of going on again next night" Despite his qualms he did sign that two year contract.

While recording *On the Town* he decided that he wanted to learn to speak fluent French. He elected to do this by moving to France so he bought a home in the French countryside in a small village near Dieppe and flew to London weekly for his Saturday shows. He already had

Ron Randell and his wife Laya Raki at the London premiere of the film *Mutiny on the Bounty* in November 1962. Randell starred in the television series *OSS*.

another home in Hollywood. He was no stranger to distances because it was estimated that in one year (1955) alone, he had traveled over 90,000 miles.

Far more to Randell's liking than being a compere was his role as ace American spy Major Frank Hawthorne in the series *OSS*. OSS stood for the Office of Strategic Services which was involved in spying and counter espionage by highly trained men in the service of their country in the tense atmosphere of World War II. Until the OSS was created, America had no official counter-espionage organization. It was superseded by the CIA in America and MI5 is its modern equivalent in England. The stories in the series were based on the actual case histories taken from official archives. Hawthorne received his assignments from the Chief (Lionel Murton). Randell was chosen for the part according to producer Jules Buck, "Because he is a tough character, who is gentle and humorous as well."

Although interiors for the series were shot at National Studios in Elstree, England with various European locations being used for exteriors, it was primarily intended for the American market. Jules Buck explained the reason for the series being shot in Europe, "We are right here in the actual locations. Many of the scenes are shot in the actual places where the events took place. It makes it more authentic." Randell drove to the studio from his small mews home each day in a flashy, pink convertible. There he labored from dawn to dusk on the series. It lasted for 26, half hour, black and white episodes. There was also plenty of American talent involved. One such person was Paul Dudley. Although he had lived in England for three years, he was an American writer who wrote most of the scripts. He was the sole person authorized to read the official files and only then after a strict security check had been carried out on him. Several directors were involved in shooting different episodes, but the best known of them was Robert Siodmak. The famous commander General "Wild Bill" Donovan was in charge of the original OSS. One of the executive producers of the series was former Colonel William Elisen, Donovan's real life aide during the war.

When his stint on *OSS* finished, Randell packed his bags and went to New York where between October 1958 and January 1960 he played Ben Jeffcoat in *The World of Suzie Wong* at the Broadhurst Theater. This was by far the biggest Broadway hit he appeared in. He wrote at least one play and a song which was a hit in Australia. He made sporadic appearances on both American and British television as a guest star throughout the sixties and into the early seventies. Between 1961 and 1966 he was active again in motion pictures. Although he and his wife attended many premieres where they networked, the big movie roles eluded him. Later stage work predominated and he was seen in many theatrical productions in England, America and Australia. During the seventies and early eighties he was a fairly frequent Broadway performer. Later he was a member of Tony Randall's American National Theater Company. It was with them that he made his final Broadway appearance in a revival of *The School for Scandal* in 1995.

In 1955 Randell said on the topic of marriage, "Twice I've tried marriage and twice it's flopped. But I learned something from these two failures. Learned enough to figure out how to make a marriage stick. So I'm not scared out of a third attempt." He became engaged to the glamorous, blonde, Swedish actress Hildy Christian in 1955 and it was expected that he would be marrying her as soon as American divorce laws made it possible. He was a Roman Catholic. It was she who originally talked him into buying a house in Hollywood. Instead he married the exotic, brunette actress Laya Raki, after a two year on-off relationship, in July 1957 at a Chelsea registry office before flying off to Hollywood for a proper church ceremony in December 1957. She was born Brunhilde Joerns in New Zealand on July 27, 1927 of a German-French father and a Dutch-Javanese mother. She was active in foreign films during the fifties. She appeared with Randell in the "Operation Sweet Talk" episode of *OSS*, but is best remembered for playing the mysterious bar manager Halima in the long running British financed, Moroccan lensed series *Crane*, which starred Patrick Allen, during the sixties.

For many years the Randells were living in an apartment in Beverly Hills, California. Ron Randell died on June 11, 2005 aged 86 of complications from a stroke at a care facility in Los Angeles. He was survived by his wife, Laya Raki.

Filmography

1944: *The Story of Dr. Wassell.*
1946: *Smithy* (a.k.a. US as *Pacific Adventure* and UK as *Southern Cross*), *A Son Is Born.*
1947: *It Had to be You, Bulldog Drummond at Bay, Bulldog Drummond Strikes Back.*
1948: *The Sign of the Ram, The Mating of Millie, The Loves of Carmen.*
1949: *Omoo Omoo the Shark God, The Lone Wolf and His Lady, Make Believe Ballroom.*
1950: *Counterspy Meets Scotland Yard, Tyrant of the Sea.*
1951: *China Corsair, Lorna Doone.*
1952: *The Brigand, Captive Women.*
1953: *The Girl on the Pier, Mississippi Gambler, Kiss Me Kate.*
1954: *The Yellow Robe, One Just Man, Three Cornered Fate.*
1955: *The Diamond Expert, Triple Blackmail, I am A Camera, Desert Sands.*
1956: *Bermuda Affair, Beyond Mombasa, The Hostage, Count of Twelve, The She-Creature, Quincannon Frontier Scout.*
1957: *The Story of Esther Costello, Morning Call* (a.k.a. *The Strange Case of Dr. Manning*), *The Girl in Black Stockings, Davy.*
1958: *Most Dangerous Man Alive* (released 1961).
1961: *King of Kings, The Phony American.*
1962: *Come Fly With Me, The Longest Day, Gold For the Caesars.*

1963: *Follow the Boys.*
1966: *Legend of a Gunfighter, Savage Pampas.*
1971: *The Seven Minutes.*
1983: *Exposed.*

Television Series
1954–1955: *The Vise* Host/Narrator.
1957–1958: *OSS* as Major Frank Hawthorne.
1977: *Lovers and Friends* (a.k.a. *For Richer, For Poorer*) as Richard Cushing.

Sources
Andrews, Cyrus. *Radio and Television Who's Who.* 3rd ed. London: George Young, 1954.
Cowen, Margaret. *TV Mirror.* "OSS Is My Big Chance." September 14, 1957.
____. "OSS Preview." *TV Times.* August 16, 1957.
Herbert, Ian. *Who's Who in the Theatre.* London: Pitman, 1977.
Linden, Eric. "Don't Fence Me In." *TV Times.* November 18, 1955.
McFarlane, Brian. *The Encyclopedia of British Film.* London: Methuen and BFI, 2003.
Picture Show Annual. London: Amalgamated, 1949, 1950 and 1956.
Rainer, Burt. "I'm Not Romeo Randell." *Picturegoer.* March 9, 1957.
Randell, Ron. "The Long Way Round." *The Film Show Annual.* London: Robinson, 1956.
Stuart, John. *An Encyclopedia of Australian Film.* New South Wales: Reed, 1984.
TV Star Annual. No. 7. 1959
TV Times. February 3, 1956.
TV Times. January 24, 1958.
Variety. Obituary, June 17, 2005.
Winchester, Clarence. *Screen Encyclopedia.* London: Winchester, 1948.

WILLIAM (BILLY) REDFIELD

William Redfield was born in New York City on January 26, 1927. He was the son of Henry Crittendon Redfield and his wife Mareta Alice George. He was educated at New York Preparatory School. As a child and youth actor he used the name Billy. He made his Broadway debut at the Booth Theater, New York in October 1936 as Roscoe Horn in *Swing Your Lady.* For the next four decades he was principally a Broadway actor appearing in many productions. He scored a notable success at the Lyceum in November 1941 as Haskell Cummings in *Junior Miss* which he played in for nearly two years.

He made his screen debut in *Back Door to Heaven* (1939), but it was to be another fifteen years before he filmed again. He played in a popular radio show for two years. He made his first television appearance in an experimental version of *Treasure Island* (1939) as Jim Hawkins and went on to make over 1,000 appearances in that medium. He starred in the title role in the television series *Jimmy Hughes, Rookie Cop.* In the first episode he played a young Korean war veteran back from the front who learns that his policeman father has been murdered. So he joined the force and avenged his death. Afterwards he investigated and solved a variety of other crimes. His steely superior was Inspector Ferguson (Rusty Lane), while his sister Betty (Wendy Drew) looked after him. This short-lived series was a DuMont production and the eight half hour, black and white episodes were shown between May 8 and July 3, 1953 on the DuMont network. In the last few episodes of the series he was replaced by Conrad Janis.

Redfield reappeared in films as an adult in *Conquest of Space* (1955). He went on to play supporting roles in a number of other movies. By far his best remembered role was as Harding in *One Flew Over the Cuckoo's Nest* (1975). He was also a writer. His best known book *Letters from an Actor* published in 1966 recounted the Sir John Gielgud Broadway production of *Hamlet* in 1964, in which he played Guildenstern. Redfield contributed a monthly column to a theatrical magazine.

William Redfield died prematurely in New York on August 17, 1976 aged 49 of a respiratory ailment complicated by leukemia. He was survived by Betsy Meade, his second wife, together with a son and daughter by a previous marriage. His son Adam was briefly an actor.

Filmography
1939: *Back Door to Heaven.*
1955: *Conquest of Space.*
1956: *The Proud and the Profane.*
1958: *I Married a Woman, All Woman.*
1961: *The Connection.*
1965: *Morituri* (a.k.a. *The Saboteur Code Name Morituri*).
1966: *Fantastic Voyage, Duel at Diablo.*
1967: *Companions in Nightmare* (TV).
1971: *A New Leaf, Such Good Friends, Pigeons.*

1972: *The Hot Rock.*
1974: *For Pete's Sake, Death Wish.*
1975: *Fear on Trial* (TV), *One Flew Over the Cuckoo's Nest.*
1977: *Mr. Billion.*

TELEVISION SERIES

1953: *Jimmy Hughes, Rookie Cop* as Jimmy Hughes.
1954: *The Marriage* as Bobby Logan.
1958: *As the World Turns* as Dr. Tim Cole.

SOURCES

Dye, David. *Child and Youth Actors.* Jefferson, NC: McFarland, 1988.
Lance, Steven. *Written Out of Television.* Lanham, MD: Madison, 1996.
Picture Show Annual. London: Amalgamated, 1957.
Tibballs, Geoff. *TV Detectives.* London: Boxtree, 1992.
Who's Who in the Theatre. 16th ed. London: Pitman, 1977.

BRIAN REECE

Brian Reece was born in Noctorum near Birkenhead, Wirral, England on July 24, 1913. He was the son of Henry Reece who ran a successful catering business and dairy and Mary Aiken who was a local singer. He had one sister. He was educated at Somerville Preparatory School and Oakham Public School at Rutland. He was active in school plays, but was no scholar. Consequently he decided to go on the stage.

He joined the Liverpool Repertory Company in 1931 where he made his debut as the blacksmith in *Strife*. Next he appeared with various repertory companies. His early career was curtailed when he suffered a serious attack of peritonitis following a routine appendix operation. Part of the cure was to breathe plenty of fresh air so he quit professional show business for three years to be a poultry farmer.

Acting remained his first love however. With the money he made from this activity he was able to move to London where he made his debut in *The Amazing Dr. Clitterhouse* in 1938. At the outbreak of war he was drafted. He started out as a gunner, but was commissioned as an officer in the Royal Artillery in 1941. While serving overseas in 1943 he served with ENSA, the entertainment unit, and broadcast a number of times from North Africa, Sicily and Algiers.

After being honorably discharged in 1946 he found the going difficult for a while. In 1947 he began playing in the musical operetta *Bless the Bride* for 886 performances as Hon. Thomas Trout. This was a massive hit. The same year he first broadcast as the upper class British police constable, Archibald Berkeley-Willoughby, better known as P.C. 49, in the radio series *The Adventures of P.C. 49* which made him a household name in England where it lasted for six years. He later repeated this role in the film *A Case for P.C. 49* (1951) which duplicated the success of the original.

In 1951 he took *The Brian Reece Show* to Korea, excerpts from which were shown on television. In 1952 he went to the Far East again and during this trip broadcast from Hong Kong, Singapore and Korea. In May 1953 he took the lead of Richard in a highly successful run of *The Seven Year Itch* at the Aldwych Theater. For this part he had to have a crew cut and lose the moustache which had been the trademark of P.C. 49.

In the television series *The New Adventures of Martin Kane* which was shot at Elstree Studios in England, he played Superintendent Page, the Scotland Yard police contact of American private eye Martin Kane (William Gargan). Reece enjoyed playing the role because it was absolutely straight and a change from the comedy parts he usually played. He regarded the move from playing P.C. 49 to Supt. Page as a promotion. Of the role he said, "Mostly I'm stuck in my office in Scotland Yard. I'm on the phone like a spider in the middle of its web. So I've invented a lot of 'business' to vary those telephone scenes— drinking tea, trying golf shoes, picking up the wrong phone. Watch out for them to see how far my invention can go."

Although William Gargan and Brian Reece were two very different types of men, off screen they became great buddies. On the final day of shooting Reece was not on call. Nevertheless he attended the grand farewell party with Gargan and the crew. A good time was had by all enlivened by song and story routines from the repertoire of Reece and Gargan.

During the halcyon years of his career Reece lived at Richmond in Surrey. His chain of success in television, film and stage continued until November 1961 when he broke a leg. Diagnosed with brittle bone disease, his condition worsened until he died in a London hospital on April 12,

Brian Reece, who costarred in *The New Adventures of Martin Kane*.

1962 aged 48. He is buried at Landican Cemetery in his native Wirral.

He married Iris McMaster at Neston Parish Church on June 3, 1940. She was a non-professional and the daughter of his partner in the poultry farm. With her he had three children who were Michael, Christopher and Susan.

FILMOGRAPHY

1954: *Fast and Loose, Orders Are Orders.*
1955: *Geordie* (a.k.a. *Wee Geordie*).
1957: *Carry On Admiral* (a.k.a. *The Ship Was Loaded*).
1961: *Watch It, Sailor.*

TELEVISION SERIES

1957–1958: *The New Adventures of Martin Kane* as Supt. Page.

SOURCES

Andrews, Cyrus. *Radio and Television Who's Who.* 3rd ed. London: George Young, 1954.
Cowan, Margaret. "Promotion Comes to PC 49." *TV Times.* September 6, 1957.
London, Peter. "Kane's in the Can." *TV Mirror.* October 5, 1957.
Noble, Peter. *British Television and Film Yearbook 1959/1960.* 9th ed. London: British and American, 1959.
McFarlane, Brian. *The Encyclopedia of British Film.* London: BFI/Methuen, 2003.
Smout, Michael. *Mersey Stars: An A–Z of Entertainers.* Wilmslow, Cheshire: Sigma Leisure, 2000.
TV Mirror. "The Story of Brian Reece." July 21, 1956.
Who's Who in the Theatre. 13th ed. London: Pitman, 1961.

MARSHALL REED

Marshall Jewel Reed was born in Englewood, Colorado on May 28, 1917. He was the son of Walter George Reed and Ruth Dustin. He commenced his acting career by appearing in children's theater at the age of ten. At high school he managed two drama groups of his own. After graduating he held various odd jobs such as horse trainer, meter reader, bookkeeper and mail clerk.

He began his professional career with the prestigious Elitch Gardens Summer Stock Theater in Denver where he built scenery and made costumes. At length he acted in some of the plays there. Next he started writing, producing and acting for a variety of theater groups in Denver. After this he toured the West Coast with his own stock company and acted in summer stock in New York and Los Angeles.

He originally came to Hollywood in 1942 working nights at Lockheed to support his family while he tried to break into pictures during the day. He made his screen debut in *Silver Spurs* (1943). He served in the navy during the latter stages of World War II and then returned to Hollywood where he resumed his movie career. He became very active as a villain in westerns particularly at Monogram. His sole starring role was in the fifteen chapter Columbia serial *Riding with Buffalo Bill* (1954). He played handsome heavies in several early television westerns. His one regular television role however was perhaps surprisingly as Inspector Fred Asher in the crime series *The Lineup* for five seasons. He enjoyed playing this role largely because of the San Francisco locations. After this series ended his roles declined both qualitatively and quantitatively.

Off screen he was on the Board of Directors of the Masquers Club. He was also head of Marshall Reed Enterprises, his own film equipment

Marshall Reed, who costarred in *The Lineup*.

rental company. He redesigned the Paramount ranch for the feature film *Shame Shame On the Bixby Boys* (1978) in which he had a bit role. He produced and directed television documentaries for charitable organizations on behalf of crippled children and retarded adults.

Reed died of a massive hemorrhage following a brain tumor at Tarzana Medical Center on April 15, 1980 aged 62. Reed who had a turbulent private life was survived by his fifth wife, Carlyn Miller, and a daughter by an earlier marriage.

Filmography

1943: *Silver Spurs, Black Hills Express, Death Valley Manhunt, Headin' for God's Country, A Guy Named Joe, Bordertown Gunfighters, The Canterville Ghost, Wagon Tracks West, Web of Danger, The Texas Kid.*

1944: *My Buddy, Tucson Raiders, Range Law, Law Men, Mojave Firebrand, Partners of the Trail, Haunted Harbor* (serial)*, Zorro's Black Whip* (serial)*, Gangsters of the Frontier, Ghost Guns, Marshal of Reno, Headin' for Trouble, Song of Nevada, The Laramie Trail, Law of the Valley.*

1945: *The Tiger Woman* (serial)*, Marshal of Laredo, Bandits of the Badlands, Colorado Pioneers, Gun Smoke.*

1946: *Drifting Along, The Haunted Mine, Shadows of the Range, Gentleman from Texas, In Old Sacramento, West of the Alamo, The Scarlet Horseman* (serial).

1947: *Riders of the South, Trailing Danger, Angel and the Badman, West of Dodge City, Land of the Lawless, The Fighting Vigilantes, Song of the Wasteland, Prairie Express, Stage to Mesa City, Cheyenne Takes Over, Song of the Saddle, On the Old Spanish Trail, Homesteaders of Paradise Valley, Wyoming.*

1948: *Sundown Riders, Dangers of the Canadian Mounted* (serial)*, Federal Agents vs. Underworld Incorporated* (serial)*, The Hawk of Powder River, The Bold Frontiersman, Song of the Drifter, Tornado Range, The Gallant Legion, Trigger Man, Dead Man's Gold, Hidden Danger, Back Trail, The Fighting Ranger, The Rangers Ride, Renegades of Sonora, Mark of the Lash, Check Your Gun, The Denver Kid, Partners of the Sunset, Courtin' Trouble, Overland Trails.*

1949: *James Brothers of Missouri* (serial)*, The Invisible Monster* (serial)*, Ghost of Zorro* (serial)*, Cowboy and the Prizefighter, Scene of the Crime, Crosswinds, Stampede, Gun Runner, Law of the West, Frontier Marshal, Navajo Trail Raiders, Square Dance Jubilee, West of El Dorado, Western Renegades, Brand of Fear, Roaring Westward, Riders of the Dusk, The Dalton Gang, Range Rogues.*

1950: *Over the Border, Rustlers on Horseback, I Was a Shoplifter, Radar Secret Service, The Savage Horder, Rider from Tucson, Six Gun Mesa, Cherokee Uprising, Silver Raiders, Outlaw Gold, Law of the Panhandle, Texas Dynamo, Rock Island Trail, California Passage, Covered Wagon Raid.*

1951: *Sailor Beware, Oh! Susanna, Gunplay, Hurricane Island, Purple Heart Diary, Nevada Badmen, Abilene Trail, Montana Desperado, Mysterious Island* (serial)*, The Longhorn, Canyon Raiders, Texas Lawmen, The Whistling Hills, Lawless Cowboys, Stagecoach Driver, Wanted Dead or Alive, Pirates of the High Seas* (serial)*, Night Riders of Montana, Oklahoma Justice.*

1952: *Sound Off, The Lusty Men, The Rough Tough West, Thundering Caravans, Laramie Mountains, Kansas Territory, Canyon Ambush, Night Raiders, Montana Incident, Texas City.*

1953: *Ride the Man Down, Weekend Father, Arena, Cow Country, Down the River.*

1954: *Jubilee Trail, Rose Marie, Gunfighters of the Northwest* (serial)*, Riding with Buffalo Bill* (serial).

1955: *New York Confidential.*
1957: *The Night the World Exploded.*
1958: *The Lineup.*
1962: *The Wild Westerners, Third of a Man.*
1964: *Madman of Mandoras* (a.k.a. *They Saved Hitler's Brain*), *Fate Is the Hunter.*
1965: *The Hallelujah Trail.*
1967: *The Long Ride Home* (a.k.a. *A Time for Killing*).
1969: *Support Your Local Sheriff.*
1971: *Lawman, The Hard Ride, Lovin' Man Jesus* (a.k.a. *The Day the Lord Got Busted*).
1972: *'Til Death.*
1977: *Shame Shame on the Bixby Boys.*

TELEVISION SERIES

1954–1959: *The Lineup* as Inspector Fred Asher.

SOURCES

Goldrup, Tom, and Jim Goldrup. *Feature Players: The Stories Behind the Faces.* Vol. 1. Published privately, 1986.

Holland, Ted. *B Western Actors Encyclopedia.* Jefferson, NC: McFarland, 1989.

Magers, Boyd. *Western Clippings.* No. 60, July/August 2004.

McClure, Arthur F., and Ken D. Jones. *Heroes, Heavies and Sagebrush.* South Brunswick, NJ: Barnes, 1972.

MICHAEL RENNIE

A tall man wearing a light mackintosh is crossing a square to the strains of zither music. He stands for a moment at a dark corner, smiles enigmatically and then vanishes. The actor was Michael Rennie, the series was *The Third Man* and the role was that of Harry Lime.

Rennie was a tall, aristocratic looking leading man who enjoyed success in British films of the forties, Hollywood movies of the fifties and converted them into television success especially as the hero of the series *The Third Man*. To this program he brought wit, style and distinctive élan. He frequently played wealthy, worldly upper bracket types. He regarded his major competition in later years as James Mason and George Sanders. Whilst he ran a poor third in terms of cinema success, Rennie scored a massive hit in television which neither of the other two managed. About television he once said, "I've discovered that over exposure on television does you no harm at all." Directors as varied as Larry Cohen and Byron Haskin were in awe of his professionalism. Cameron Mitchell warmly recalled playing golf with him. L. Q. Jones said, "What a nice man! I only ever worked with him once, but he became a good friend!" Costar Jonathan Harris remembered him for his infectious sense of humor.

Rennie was born Eric Alexander Rennie in Bradford, Yorkshire on August 25, 1909, the son of James Rennie and Edith Dobbie. His ancestry was Scottish and Jewish. His father was a well known Northern mill owner. His mother remarried on the death of her husband and became Mrs. A. Norman White. He had one sister who was apparently as tall and slim as he was. The family lived at one time at Conygham Hall, Knaresborough, Yorkshire. He was well educated at Oatlands School, Harrogate and Leys College, Cambridge.

Finishing school at eighteen, he went to work in his stepfather's mill, sorting wool for £2 a week. After four years he became manager of a spinning shed. Bored and soaked with lanolin from the greasy wool, Rennie tried unsuccessfully to obtain an introduction from a theater owning uncle to stage directors. Instead he ended up sweeping floors in the uncle's rope factory at Wakefield.

Four years later he decided he would not like the business even if he owned it. One day he arose from his desk, put on his hat and decided to hitchhike to London. There he tried all sorts of jobs including selling cars before he met a couple of men in a pub one night who told him they were extras at the film studios. Within a couple of weeks he enrolled at a Charing Cross Road Agency which specialized in supplying extras to the studios and shortly afterwards he arrived at Gaumont-British studios in Shepherd's Bush to make his first film appearance. He subsequently appeared in a dozen films without his face being shown on screen when the movies were finally released.

One day he asked the casting director if he could be given a couple of lines in the next production at Shepherd's Bush or a job as a stand-in. He remembered Rennie a couple of months later and sent for him to become a stand-in for Hollywood star Robert Young in *Secret Agent* (1936). He was also given a few speaking lines in this film. The casting director named Harold Huth, who later became a film director, took a liking to Rennie and persuaded Gaumont-British to give him a year's contract. Amongst others he had two lines in *Gangway* (1937) and four lines in *The Di-*

vorce of Lady X (1938). After a while he realized that he would need more experience if he were to make any headway in the film world. He was advised to try to obtain the necessary experience in repertory. Back in Wakefield once more, he managed to talk himself into a job as leading man in a small repertory company there. His stage debut was made as Professor Higgins in *Pygmalion*. Next came a period with York and later Windsor Repertory Companies and then he decided he would have another try at screen work. He appeared in a few films including a whole scene with John Mills in *The Big Blockade* (1941).

Between 1941 and 1944 he served in the R.A.F. Two years of his service were spent at Georgia in America as an instructor. After he was honorably discharged in June 1944, the turning point came when he played Margaret Lockwood's leading man in *I'll Be Your Sweetheart* (1945). His best remembered British film was *The Wicked Lady* (1945), a Gainsborough historical romance based on the novel by Magdalen King Hall which was Britain's top grossing film of 1946. In it he played Kit Locksby, deeply in love with Lady Barbara Skelton (Margaret Lockwood) who is secretly a seventeenth century highwaywoman.

It could not be said that his career advanced rapidly thereafter. He was unfortunate enough to star in two of England's more notorious flops namely *Idol of Paris* (1948) and *Uneasy Terms* (1948). Fortunately he attracted American attention as the Norman king in *The Black Rose* (1950) which starred Tyrone Power. The part involved only four days work. His performance in that led Ben Lyon, 20th Century–Fox's London scout, to send Darryl F. Zanuck a show reel from a subsequently successful portmanteau film Rennie was making called *Trio* with Jean Simmons. Zanuck ordered an all out test of him and optioned him for *The 13th Letter* (1951) filmed in Quebec, Canada, an unsuccessful version of an earlier and better French film, *Le Corbeau*. Around this time Rennie said, "Oh yes, I was a star all right! Or at least that's what my agent kept telling me! I regret having to leave British films and make my career in Hollywood, but the fact remains that we are only making a few films every year in British studios and I was going months and months without getting any jobs."

With the signing of his contract with Fox in 1950, he entered upon the halcyon years of his film career. His second Hollywood film *The Day the Earth Stood Still* (1951) became a classic and is his best remembered Hollywood film. This science fiction movie was based on Harry Bate's story "Farewell to the Master" first published in Astounding Magazine in October 1940. The leading role was originally offered to Claude Rains who was unable to accept it because the shooting clashed with his stage triumph of *Darkness at Noon*. This turned out to be very fortunate for Rennie.

He played Klaatu, a visitor from another planet who along with a nine foot tall robot Gort is sent to Earth to warn people that an alien planetary federation disapprove of Earth's atom bomb experiments and they must either desist or be blown up. Their spacecraft lands on the front lawn of the White House where Klaatu hopes to see the President and secure interplanetary peace. While waiting for an appointment he takes a room in a boarding house run by a widow (Patricia Neal) and her son (Billy Gray) with the intention of getting to know earthlings better.

Klaatu is shot and killed after being denounced as a fake, but a vengeful Gort reactivates him. The Earth stands still when Klaatu demonstrates his awesome power by shutting off nearly all of Earth's electricity. It is Neal who saves the day when she speaks the unforgettable phrase, "Gord! Klaatu barada nikto" which prevents Gort from destroying Earth after Klaatu's death. The last scene where Gort carries the deceased Klaatu back into the spaceship is amongst the most memorable in fifties cinema. The film was skillfully directed by Robert Wise with an effective score by Bernard Herrman.

In *Five Fingers* (1953) based upon the true story of foreign intrigue "Operation Cicero" by L.C. Moyzisch which starred James Mason, Rennie played a foreign office investigator. He played the Apostle Peter in *The Robe* (1953) and its more entertaining sequel *Demetrius and the Gladiators* (1954). He had another religious role as Father Junipero Serra in *Seven Cities of Gold* (1955). He was Tyrone Power's commanding officer in *King of the Khyber Rifles* (1953) and Count Bernadotte in *Desiree* (1954). He was seldom the star of most of the films he appeared in, but two exceptions were *Les Miserables* (1952) as Jean Valjean and the minor but suspenseful thriller *Dangerous Crossing* (1953). In *Soldier of Fortune* (1955) he supported Clark Gable and Susan Hayward as a Hong Kong police officer.

He appeared in *The Rains of Ranchipur* (1955) which was based on the bestselling novel "The Rains Came" by Louis Bromfield, previously filmed in 1939 with Tyrone Power and Myrna Loy. In this version Richard Burton played the Indian doctor Safti who is seduced by married Lady Edwina Esketh (Lana Turner), before realizing his duty is to his people and his country when a monsoon and earthquake strike. This film was shot on location in Pakistan in color which captured the spectacular special effects. Rennie was fifth billed as Lord Esketh. His character is softened from both the novel and the original film where he was played by Nigel Bruce as a boorish lout. In the remake directed by Jean Negulesco, Esketh is more of an irresponsible playboy.

A little known facet of these years was that he became narrator in residence at Fox where his distinctive speaking voice was heard in such movies as *The Desert Fox* (1951), *Pony Soldier* (1952), *Titanic* (1953) and *Prince Valiant* (1954). His family experienced a dreadful personal tragedy in May 1954 when his wife's mother was found strangled in her London flat apparently by an intruder.

His final film under the original Fox contract was *Island in the Sun* (1957). Allegedly during the shooting of this film he had a torrid affair with costar Dorothy Dandridge. He had been so cooperative that when his contract expired, Fox wanted him to sign another one with them, but he declined. He still wanted to be a top line star rather than playing second or third banana which is how Fox regarded him. As a freelance he appeared in *Omar Khayyam* (1957) as the villain and in England *Battle of the VI* (1958). Disney's *Third Man on the Mountain* (1959) told the story of a mountain boy's (James MacArthur) dream of scaling a previously unclimbed peak. He was aided by an English mountaineer (Rennie). It was beautifully shot in color in Switzerland. The title was deliberately changed to coincide with Rennie's television success, but in fact the film had nothing to do with his series. Rennie said of this film, "The story isn't worth five minutes of anybody's time, although the mountaineering scenes are wonderful." In spite of this the ploy did not work and the film did not do particularly well commercially.

Rennie had appeared on television as early as 1948 in England when he starred in a version of *Morning Departure*, a sea drama. Increasingly during the late fifties he began to be very active on television, seven out of eight of his first appearances being episodes of the anthology series *Climax*. In 1959 he was approached by the BBC

Michael Rennie, who starred in *The Third Man*.

to star in an Anglo-American television series *The Third Man* as the suave international business tycoon Harry Lime. It was based loosely on the 1949 film of the same name directed by Carol Reed and scripted by Graham Greene and the later radio series. Orson Welles had interpreted the original Harry Lime as a ruthless racketeer who had faked his own death in postwar Vienna in order to continue his black marketeering without disturbance. As played by Rennie, Harry Lime had become a legitimate businessman with offices in most countries of the Western world who now aids people, primarily beautiful women in distress. In the first episode Rennie spoke with a pronounced American accent, but from then onwards he adopted the Midatlantic accent which by common consent he was an absolute master of. His accent he based on that of Alistair Cooke of BBC's *Letter from America* fame.

James Mason was offered the role of Harry Lime ahead of Rennie, but rejected it because he still had a flourishing film career. Rennie said of him, "I somehow think he wouldn't have been right. Harry Lime needs to be played with a light touch." Shooting started at the Fox studios in California in December 1958 on the first twenty episodes which had American scriptwriters and crew. These completed, in June 1959 Rennie went to Shepperton Studios in England to shoot nineteen more with British casts and crew. The first English episode "The Best Policy" had Lime describing an incident after the war which made him abandon his life of crime. Rennie worked on the first 39 half hour episodes for eleven months in 1959 without a break. At the end of this time he was absolutely exhausted. The reason he worked so hard was because his own production company was involved in the making of the program and a hefty chunk of the profits went to Rennie. As he said, "I wouldn't have done it for a straight salary." The series was shown on BBC television from October 2, 1959 to August 19, 1960. The show was seen in syndication in the United States from September 1960 onwards.

The second season started in November 1961 with twenty episodes being shot at Desilu Studios in California. One episode *IOU* even supposedly explained how Lime cheated death at the end of the original film. The final nineteen episodes were filmed at Associated British Studios in Elstree from July 1962 onwards. They were shown on BBC television from July 2, 1962 sporadically until the final episode aired on August 27, 1965. Four episodes were never actually shown in the United Kingdom. Repeats were still being run by the BBC in the late eighties.

The series boasted stark black and white photography, a slick production, witty scripts and one throwback to the original film namely the zither music of Anton Karas. Post-war austerity in Europe was well captured in the early episodes whereas some of the later episodes were much lighter in tone. Rennie was helped immensely by the waspish characterization of Jonathan Harris as his Man Friday, Bradford Webster. The role was specifically created for Harris by the producers since the character did not exist in the original film. Although no party was held for Rennie and Harris to be introduced, they hit if off very well from the moment they first met on the set. So great was their camaraderie that they continued to meet for lunch every month for years afterwards. The series was a tremendous worldwide success from the outset and reckoned to have been one of the biggest hits in the history of syndicated television.

As a result of being in the series he found that his box office potential was boosted, so that four star roles were offered to him. One of his very few errors of judgment was rejecting the lead in *Village of the Damned* (1960) which was subsequently played by George Sanders. Rennie said, "I told the producers—'It will give the customers hysterics. It will have them rolling in the aisles with laughter.' And it's supposed to be a thriller." In fact this eerie film turned out to be a sleeper, both an artistic and commercial success.

One film which he wisely accepted was *The Lost World* (1960). An expedition led by Professor Challenger (Claude Rains) journeys to a remote region of the Amazon where he believes prehistoric life still exists. The monsters and plateau exceed his wildest dreams. Toplined Rennie starred as Lord John Roxton who ostensibly goes along for the adventure, but has a secret motive for being one of the party. This version of the classic Sir Arthur Conan Doyle story has been updated, but remains true to the spirit of the original novel. A highlight of the film are the excellent special effects with actual lizards being photographed and enlarged to represent huge, frightening prehistoric monsters. An Irwin Allen production released through 20th Century–Fox, the film was virtually reprised in 1964 as the "Turn Back The Clock" episode of *Voyage to the Bottom of the Sea*.

Rather than accept any of the other film offers, he was very pleased when he was approached to appear in a comedy on Broadway called *Mary Mary* by Jean Kerr opposite Barry Nelson and Barbara Bel Geddes. When he read the script, he very rapidly signed the contract. The play opened in March 1961 to packed houses and excellent notices. Rennie reprised his role in the film version of *Mary Mary* (1963), but it did not enjoy the same success. This play was his first theatrical appearance in America. In his last years however he did much dinner theater organized by Ben Pearson, an agent who specialized in this.

Rennie was one of several star names in Warner Bros.' commercially successful version of the Arthur Hailey bestseller *Hotel* (1967). Set in the plush St. Gregory Hotel in New Orleans, Rennie and Merle Oberon played the Duke and Duchess of Lambourne who are guilty of failing to report a hit and run homicide. Their car is damaged and they hire shady house detective Dupere (Richard Conte) to dispose of it for them. He is caught and the Duke decides to turn himself in. Unfortunately a cable snaps in the lift which sends it hurtling down the shaft killing the Duke.

Rennie was not however the first choice for the role. The original selection made by Jack Warner was Wilfred Hyde-White. Merle Oberon objected. Although she liked Hyde-White personally, she refused to accept that the Duchess would be married to a man whom she had no physical attraction towards. She believed that Rennie, whom she had worked with before in *Desiree*, would be a much more suitable choice. She and Jack Warner locked horns and it was virtually only the eve of shooting that Warner relented and Rennie was substituted.

None of the other pilots which Rennie shot ever made it to the series stage, but he was a stalwart guest star on American television throughout the sixties with multiple appearances on anthology shows; science fiction shows such as *Time Tunnel*, *The Invaders* and *Lost In Space*; westerns such as *Bonanza*; and crime series such as *The FBI*. He turned up on *Batman* playing the Sandman. In *The Man From Uncle* episode "The Thrush Roulette Affair" he played Thrush agent Barnaby Partridge who falls to his death down an elevator shaft, similar to his fate in *Hotel*.

His last good film role was in *The Power* (1967) which was derided at the time of its release, but which has since acquired minor cult status. Rennie turned out to be the title character of the mysterious Adam Hart, alias Arthur Nordland, a mad scientist intending world domination, who with his super brain can kill merely by focusing his will on an individual. Producer George Pal went on record as saying that with his appearance Rennie was totally convincing in the part and that he was the best actor of all those who had ever worked for him.

None of Rennie's plans to produce films ever came to fruition. One of his main interests in real life was watching bullfighting and he had long wanted to film the life of Manolete with himself in the leading role of the famous bullfighter. About an American television production of the late fifties, he said derisively, "Terrible. Wrongly cast. Badly produced. And it's spoiled the market for the subject. I wanted to film that biography!" Even more depressing were his appearances in a number of low budget films mainly shot on the Continent in which he gave indifferent performances. With the very low number of feature films being shot in Hollywood during the sixties, he probably felt he had to make these films to keep his name before the public eye. His other hobbies were listed as playing the clarinet and saxophone; tinkering with cars; and he was an excellent golfer with a handicap of four. He lived in Geneva, Switzerland.

Rennie died in Harrogate, Yorkshire, England on June 10, 1971 aged 61 while visiting his mother. No inquest was carried out as a police spokesman said that his death was a natural one from heart failure. He had suffered increasingly from emphysema during his final years. He originally married Joan Phyllis England in 1938, but divorced in 1945. He then married former Windmill theater glamour girl Margaret McGrath on October 1, 1946, but they divorced in 1960, the same year he became a US citizen. He was survived by his mother and a son David who was born in March 1953. Although details of his will were never made public, it is believed that income derived from residuals of *The Third Man* meant that financially he had never needed to work again. He lies buried at Harlow Hill Cemetery in Harrogate, Yorkshire.

Filmography

1936: *Secret Agent, Conquest of the Air, The Man Who Could Work Miracles, Gypsy.*
1937: *Gangway, The Squeaker* (a.k.a. *Murder on Diamond Row*), *Bank Holiday.*
1938: *The Divorce of Lady X.*
1939: *This Man in Paris.*
1941: *The Patient Vanishes* (a.k.a. *This Man is Dangerous*), *Turned Out Nice Again, Pimpernel Smith, Dangerous Moonlight, Ships With Wings, The Tower of Terror, The Big Blockade.*
1945: *I'll Be Your Sweetheart, The Wicked Lady, Caesar and Cleopatra.*
1947: *The Root of All Evil, White Cradle Inn* (a.k.a. *High Fury*).
1948: *Idol of Paris, Uneasy Terms.*
1949: *Miss Pilgrim's Progress, The Golden Madonna.*
1950: *Trio (Sanatorium* sequence*), The Body Said No!, The Black Rose.*
1951: *The House in the Square* (a.k.a. *I'll Never Forget You*), *The 13th Letter, The Day the Earth Stood Still.*
1952: *Phone Call From A Stranger, Five Fingers, Les Miserables.*
1953: *Single Handed* (a.k.a. *Sailor of the King*), *The Robe, King of the Khyber Rifles, Dangerous Crossing.*
1954: *Demetrius and the Gladiators, Princess of the Nile, Desiree.*
1955: *Mambo, Soldier of Fortune, Seven Cities of Gold, The Rains of Ranchipur.*
1956: *Teenage Rebel.*
1957: *Island in the Sun, Omar Khayyam.*
1958: *Battle of the VI.*
1959: *Third Man on the Mountain.*
1960: *The Lost World.*
1963: *Mary Mary.*

1966: *Ride Beyond Vengeance, Cyborg 2087*.
1967: *Hotel, The Power, Hondo and the Apaches* (TV), *The Young the Evil and the Savage, Death on the Run*.
1968: *Subterfuge, Desert Tanks* (a.k.a. *The Battle of El Alamein*), *The Devil's Brigade, Scaccio Internazionale*.
1969: *Operation Terror* (a.k.a. *Assignment Terror* and *Dracula Vs. Frankenstein*).
1970: *Goldseekers*.
1971: *The Last Generation*.

Television Series

USA 1960–1963: *The Third Man* as Harry Lime.
UK 1959–1965

Sources

Aaker, Everett. *TV Scene*. Issue 1. February 1989.
The Fan's Own Film Annual. London: Axtell, 1956.
Higham, Charles, and Roy Moseley. *Merle*. London: New English Library, 1983.
Noble, Peter. *Picture Parade*. London: Burke, 1952.
Picture Show. "Life Story." May 7, 1955.
Picture Show Annual. London: Amalgamated, 1943, 1947, 1952 and 1955.
Pixley, Andrew. *TV Zone*. No. 160. February 2003.
Rainer, Bart. "Pity Poor Rennie—So Overworked." *Picturegoer*. January 9, 1960
Sephton, Ken. *Movie Memories*. No. 36. Autumn 1999.
Stoddart, Sarah. "The Yes Man Says No!" *Picturegoer*. March 9, 1957.
Van Neste, Dan. "Michael Rennie Inspired Light." *Classic Images*. No. 252. June 1996
Ward, Jack. *Television Guest Stars*. Jefferson, NC: McFarland, 1993.
Weaver, Tom. *It Came from Weaver Five*. Jefferson, NC: McFarland, 1996.
Whatton, Barry. *The Stage*. August 28, 2003.
Winchester, Clarence. *Screen Encyclopedia*. London: Winchester, 1948.

STAFFORD REPP

Stafford Alois Repp was born in San Francisco, California on April 26, 1918. His nickname was Staff. He graduated from Lowe High School in San Francisco. During World War II he served in the Army Air Corps. His big break occurred

Stafford Repp, who costarred in *The Thin Man*.

when he was hired to create sound effects during the early days of television. He had a semi-regular role in the first season of *The Thin Man* when he played Lt. Ralph Raines. He was a prolific television performer, but all of his other work was overshadowed when he played Chief O'Hara in the camp television series *Batman*. He was not the first choice for the role, but the producers were very happy with their selection. His real life brother was a police officer. The brogue Repp spoke with during the series was false. He assumed it for the part.

When the series went off the air, he continued to be a jobbing actor mainly on television. His film work was very limited and included one notorious pornographic film, *Linda Lovelace for President* (1975). Most of his money however was derived from his partnership in a chain of car washes which turned out to be extremely lucrative. His final television appearance was believed to be an episode of *M*A*S*H* which aired in March 1975. On November 5, 1974 he suffered a fatal heart attack while at Hollywood Park racing track and was pronounced dead at Inglewood hospital aged 56. After his death his sister, a television writer, established the Stafford Repp Memorial Scholarship for alumni of his alma mater, Lowe High School, in San Francisco. Repp was survived by his wife and five children.

FILMOGRAPHY

1954: *Shield for Murder, Down Three Dark Streets, Black Tuesday.*
1955: *Unchained, Big House U.S.A., Not as a Stranger, Man with the Gun.*
1956: *The Killer Is Loose, The Steel Jungle, The Price of Fear, The Harder They Fall, Star in the Dust, Canyon River, The Cruel Tower, The Boss.*
1957: *Plunder Road, The Green-Eyed Blonde.*
1958: *The Brothers Karamazov, Hot Spell, I Want to Live!*
1959: *The Crimson Kimono.*
1961: *The Explosive Generation.*
1964: *A Tiger Walks.*
1965: *A Very Special Favor.*
1966: *Batman.*
1972: *Cycle Psycho.*
1975: *The Other Side of the Wind, Linda Lovelace for President.*

TELEVISION SERIES

1957–1958: *The Thin Man* as Det. Lt. Ralph Raines.
1963–1964: *The New Phil Silvers Show* as Brink.
1966–1968: *Batman* as Chief O'Hara.

SOURCES

Eisner, Joel. *The Official Batman Batbook.* London: Titan, 1987.
Inman, David. *The TV Encyclopedia.* New York: Perigee, 1991.
Ward, Burt. *Boy Wonder: My Life in Tights.* Los Angeles: Logical Figments, 1995.
West, Adam, with Jeff Rovin. *Back to the Batcave.* London: Titan, 1994.
Willis, John. *Screen World.* Vol. 26. London: Frederick Muller, 1975.

ADDISON RICHARDS

This actor was born Addison Whitaker Richards Jr. in Zanesville, Ohio on October 20, 1887. He graduated with a BA degree from Washington State University and did postgraduate work at Pomona College. He began his acting career in *The Pilgrimage Play* in 1926. In 1931 he became associate director of the Pasadena Playhouse and acted there as well. He made his screen debut in 1933 and went on to amass dozens of credits as a freelance character actor. At MGM he played Polly Benedict's (Ann Rutherford) father in the *Andy Hardy* film series.

Addison Richards, who starred in *Pentagon Confidential* and costarred in *Grand Jury.*

Amongst the television series in which he appeared was *Pentagon U.S.A.*, a summer replacement series shown on CBS between August and October 1953. It was derived from the files of the Criminal Investigation Division of the U.S. Army. The series started out as *Pentagon Confidential*, but by the time of the second telecast, the title had been altered to *Pentagon U.S.A.* Richards played the army officer who was shown deploying investigators to work on that week's case and giving them the background. His office was located in the Pentagon, Washington which gave the series its title. Although this half hour series was shown live for ten weeks, it attracted little attention. He also had a recurring role as Fullerton, the head of the Grand Jury, in the television series *Grand Jury* which starred Lyle Bettger.

The 76-year-old actor died in Los Angeles on March 22, 1964 after a heart attack. He was married to Patricia Richards and had a daughter, Ann. He is buried at Oak Park Cemetery, Claremont, LA County, California.

FILMOGRAPHY

1933: *Lone Cowboy, Riot Squad.*
1934: *Let's Be Ritzy, The Love Captive, The Case Of The Howling Dog, Beyond The Law, Our Daily Bread, Gentlemen Are Born, Babbitt, The*

St. Louis Kid, British Agent, 365 Nights In Hollywood, The Girl From Missouri, A Lost Lady.
1935: *Black Fury, Only Eight Hours, G-Men, Home On The Range, The Eagle's Brood, The Frisco Kid, A Dog Of Flanders, Sweet Music, Society Doctor, Here Comes The Band, The White Cockatoo, Front Page Woman, Little Big Shot, Dinky, Alias Mary Dow, The Crusades, Freckles, Ceiling Zero, The Petrified Forest.*
1936: *Bullets Or Ballots, Sutter's Gold, Public Enemy's Wife, Trailin' West, Road Gang, Song Of The Saddle, The Law In Her Hands, Jail Break, Anthony Adverse, The Case Of The Velvet Claws, Hot Money, China Clipper, Smart Blonde, God's Country And The Woman, Man Hunt, Colleen, The Walking Dead, The Black Legion, Draegerman Courage.*
1937: *Ready Willing And Able, Her Husband's Secretary, White Bondage, Dance Charlie Dance, The Singing Marine, Love Is On The Air, The Barrier, Wine Women And Horses, Empty Holsters.*
1938: *Flight Into Fame, Alcatraz Island, The Black Doll, The Last Express, Accidents Will Happen, Valley Of The Giants, Boys Town, Prison Nurse, The Devil's Party, Gateway.*
1939: *Whispering Enemies, They Made Her A Spy, Twelve Crowded Hours, Off The Record, Inside Information, Burn 'Em Up O'Connor, Andy Hardy Gets Spring Fever, They All Come Out, Thunder Afloat, Geronimo, Espionage Agent, Nick Carter Master Detective, Bad Lands, Exile Express, The Gracie Allen Murder Case, I Was A Convict, Tell No Tales, When Tomorrow Comes, The Mystery Of The White Room.*
1940: *Santa Fe Trail, Andy Hardy Meets Debutante, Boom Town, Northwest Passage, The Man From Dakota, The Man From Montreal, The Lone Wolf Strikes, Edison The Man, Charlie Chan In Panama, South To Karanga, Wyoming, Gangs Of Chicago, The Girl From Havana, My Little Chickadee, Arizona, Flight Command, Moon Over Burma, Black Diamonds, Cherokee Strip, Slightly Honorable, Public Deb No. 1, Island Of Doomed Men, Give Us Wings, Flight Angels, My Little Chickadee.*
1941: *Ball Of Fire, Dive Bomber, Western Pacific, Tall Dark And Handsome, Back In The Saddle, Sheriff Of Tombstone, The Great Lie, Men Of Boys Town, Mutiny In The Arctic, International Squadron, Texas, Her First Beau, Badlands Of Dakota, Andy Hardy's Private Secretary, I Wanted Wings, Strawberry Blonde, The Trial Of Mary Dugan, Design For Scandal, Sealed Lips, Our Wife, They Died With Their Boots On, Western Union.*
1942: *My Favorite Blonde, The Lady Has Plans, Cowboy Serenade, Pacific Rendezvous, A-Haunting We Will Go, Secrets Of A Coed, Man With Two Lives, Secret Agent For Japan, The Pride Of The Yankees, Seven Day's Leave, Men Of Texas, Top Sergeant, Secret Enemies, Flying Tigers, War Dogs, A Close Call For Ellery Queen, Friendly Enemies, The Mystery Of Marie Roget, Pride Of The Army, Ship Ahoy!, Ridin' Down The Canyon, Underground Agent, War Dogs.*
1943: *Destroyer, Headin' For God's Country, Corvette K-225, Where Are Your Children?, The Mystery Of The 13th Guest, Mystery Broadcast, The Deerslayer, Air Force, A Guy Named Joe, Always A Bridesmaid, Smart Guy, The Mad Ghoul, Salute To The Marines, Hit Parade of 1943.*
1944: *Raiders Of Ghost City* (serial), *The Fighting Seabees, Follow The Boys, Three Men In White, Moon Over Las Vegas, Roger Touhy Gangster, A Night Of Adventure, Marriage Is A Private Affair, Since You Went Away, The Mummy's Curse, The Sullivans, Are These Our Parents?, Barbary Coast Gent, Three Little Sisters, Border Town Trail, Grissly's Millions.*
1945: *The Master Key* (serial), *Duffy's Tavern, The Royal Mounted Rides Again* (serial), *Lady On A Train, The Chicago Kid, God Is My Co-Pilot, Betrayal From The East, Rough Tough And Ready, Bells Of Rosarita, Come Out Fighting, I'll Remember April, Black Market Babies, Danger Signal, The Shanghai Cobra, Men In Her Diary, Strange Confession, The Adventures Of Rusty, Spellbound, Bewitched, Leave Her To Heaven, Divorce, The Tiger Woman.*
1946: *Secrets Of A Sorority Girl, Angel On My Shoulder, The Criminal Court, The Hoodlum Saint, Step By Step, Renegades, Don't Gamble With Strangers, The Mummy's Curse, Anna And The King Of Siam, Love Laughs At Andy Hardy, Dragonwyck, Courage Of Lassie.*
1947: *The Millerson Case, Monsieur Verdoux, Call Northside 777, Reaching From Heaven.*
1948: *Lulu Belle, The Saxon Charm, A Southern Yankee.*
1949: *The Rustlers, Henry The Rainmaker, Mighty Joe Young.*
1950: *Davy Crockett Indian Scout.*
1955: *Illegal, High Society, Fort Yuma.*
1956: *Walk The Proud Land, Reprisal!, Everything But The Truth, When Gangland Strikes, Fury At Gunsight Pass, The Ten Commandments, The Broken Star, The Fastest Gun Alive.*
1957: *Last Of The Badmen, Gunsight Ridge.*
1958: *The Saga Of Hemp Brown.*

1959: *The Oregon Trail.*
1960: *All The Fine Young Cannibals, The Dark At The Top Of The Stairs.*
1961: *The Gambler Wore A Gun, Frontier Uprising, The Flight That Disappeared.*
1962: *Saintly Sinners.*
1963: *The Raiders.*
1964: *For Those Who Think Young.*

TELEVISION SERIES

1953: *Pentagon USA* as The Colonel.
1958–1959: *Cimarron City* as Martin Kingsley.
1959: *Grand Jury* as Fullerton.
1959–1960: *Fibber McGee And Molly* as Doc Gamble.
1963: *Ben Jerrod* as John Abbott.

SOURCES

Brooks, Tim. *The Complete Directory to Prime Time TV Stars, 1946–Present.* New York: Ballantine Books, 1987.
Parish, James Robert. *Hollywood Character Actors.* New Rochelle, NY: Arlington, 1978.
Quinlan, David. *Illustrated History of Film Character Actors.* 2nd ed. London: Batsford, 1995.
Twomey, Alfred E., and Arthur F. McClure. *The Versatiles.* South Brunswick, NJ: Barnes, 1969.

GRANT RICHARDS

Grant Richards was born in New York on December 21, 1911. He was educated at William and Mary College and the University of Miami. His Broadway debut was in *Halfway to Hell* in 1934. On the strength of this he moved to Hollywood where he made his screen debut as Bob Claiborne, a heavy, in the western *Hopalong Cassidy Returns* (1936). He was initially under contract to Paramount, but his career soon declined to poverty row. The best remembered of his films was *Night of Mystery* (1937) in which he played Philo Vance. This was a "B" picture remake of *The Greene Murder Case* (1929) which had starred William Powell. Richards was considered to be one of the weakest actors to have played the role. During the thirties he was also on the radio in the popular series *Gangbusters*. With his career in the doldrums he returned to New York where in 1940 and 1942 he appeared in a couple of flop Broadway plays.

Richards served during World War II as a private with the air corps attached to the entertainment division. While still in the services, he appeared on Broadway in the musical drama *Winged Victory* by Moss Hart between November 1943 and May 1944. His career for the next decade largely remains a mystery. He did not appear on Broadway nor do records indicate that he did much live television or make any films. For the first season of the live NBC summer replacement series *Door with No Name* he played secret agent Doug Carter, whose boss John Randolph (Mel Ruick) gave him assignments which took him all over the world. Richards may have been prevented from returning to this series because he had landed himself another berth with a regular role as Warren Nash in the soap opera *Love of Life*. He then played Peter Davis in a second short-lived soap opera, *Follow Your Heart.*

He then dropped out of sight again, but surfaced in Hollywood in 1957 where he began to make television guest appearances at a rapid rate. He also appeared in some very low budget films. Rather intriguingly all the movies were directed by the same director, Edward L. Cahn. Richards's busy life came to an end on July 4, 1963 when he was killed in an automobile accident in Los Angeles aged 51. In a bizarre coincidence both Richards and his former wife, the beautiful sometime actress Joan Valerie (1914–1983), were killed

Raymond Burr (left) and Grant Richrds in *Perry Mason*. Richards costarred in *The Door with No Name.*

in separate road crashes. Richards and Valerie appeared together in the film *Just Off Broadway* (1942). Richards was apparently survived by a son.

Filmography

1936: *Hopalong Cassidy Returns.*
1937: *Night of Mystery, On Such a Night.*
1938: *My Old Kentucky Home, Under the Big Top, Love on Toast.*
1939: *Risky Business, Inside Information.*
1940: *Isle of Destiny.*
1942: *Just Off Broadway.*
1959: *Inside the Mafia, Guns Girls and Gangsters, The Four Skulls of Jonathan Drake.*
1960: *Oklahoma Territory, Twelve Hours to Kill, Music Box Kid.*
1961: *You Have to Run Fast, Secret of Deep Harbor.*

Television Series

1951: *Door with No Name* as Doug Carter.
1952–1953: *Love of Life* as Warren Nash.
1953–1954: *Follow Your Heart* as Peter Davis.

Sources

Brooks, Tim. *The Complete Directory to Prime Time TV Stars, 1946–Present.* New York: Ballantine, 1987.
Hyatt, Wesley. *Short-Lived Television Series, 1948–1978.* Jefferson, NC: McFarland, 2003.
Parish, James Robert. *The Great Movie Series.* South Brunswick, NJ: Barnes, 1971.

EDWIN RICHFIELD

Edwin Ronald Richfield was born in London, England on September 11, 1921. His twin careers as a writer and an actor ran concurrently since he was a schoolboy at Andover in Hampshire. He read "The Monkey's Paw" by W.W. Jacobs which made such an impact on him that he decided to dramatize it. The play was staged for the benefit of the school, an event he so enjoyed that he decided to become an actor. After leaving school he worked with various concert parties as an impersonator. As he later recalled, "My family eventually dragged me out of that, but it was wonderful experience."

After this he seemed to be destined for a career in the civil service. The war intervened and in 1940 he found himself in the Royal Air Force where he served as a wireless operator. During the war he had time to reflect on his career. When he was demobilized in 1946, he went into repertory. He stayed nine months touring northern towns before going to London, confident that he knew it all.

This turned out not to be the case and he was literally down to his last pound when he landed an understudy role in the West End. Years of bit parts followed. At this stage his writing talent surfaced again because he supplemented his meager earnings by writing songs and comedy dialogue for revues. He made his screen debut in 1950. His luck finally changed and he went on to make dozens of film and television appearances. His best remembered film role was as a beggar in *Ben Hur* (1959). Two of his scripts were filmed during the sixties.

His ability as a mimic came in useful for he was asked to play an incredible variety of character parts. He made his mark in the television series *The Buccaneers* as a pirate. He played Insp. Mornay, the colleague and comrade of Insp. Duval (Charles Korvin), in the highly successful crime series *Interpol Calling*. He was best known however for his portrayal of Steve Gardiner who combined sleuthing with being a theatrical agent in the television serial *The Odd Man*. Gardiner and his wife Mary (Sarah Lawson) were running a business and trying to hold their crumbling marriage together. Their paths crossed on several occasions with that of South, a mute assassin, and they found themselves involved in a series of exciting adventures. Richfield was originally set to play a lesser role in the series, but he persuaded director Derek Bennett to cast him in the title role. *The Odd Man* consisted of three separate series of eight episodes. He was slightly unfortunate in that the character who really caught on with the public was Chief Insp. Rose (William Mervyn) who went on to appear in a couple of spin-off series of his own. Creator Edward Boyd described Richfield as, "An East End Bogart."

Richfield did star in the BBC serial *199 Park Lane* which dealt with the idle rich in a block of luxury flats, but it was such a complete failure that it ended after only a short run in 1965. The BBC serial *Eastenders* which made its debut in 1982 used the reverse format in that it deals primarily with lowlifes in the East End. This has proven to be the biggest success in the BBC's serial history. Richfield was an active television guest star frequently in villainous roles throughout the sixties. In the late seventies he became a stalwart of the Royal Shakespeare Company, appearing in several classical plays. His most notable stage success was as the South African jailer Warrant Officer Snyman in *The Jail Diaries of Albie Sachs.*

He was married to the beautiful and stylish actress Jan Holden in 1953. She was born in Southport, England in 1931 and they met when they appeared together in a play in Blackpool. With her he had a son Simon who was born in 1957 and twin daughters Belinda and Arabella who were born in 1960. They were the fourth generation twins on their mother's side. At this time they lived in a large house in Hampstead, London. His closest friends in show business were Martin Benson and Michael Gough. Jan Holden hit the television jackpot when she played Harriet Carr, the personnel officer in *Harpers West One,* a drama series based round a London department store. Richfield's career notably flourished when they were married, but the competitiveness of the industry drove them apart and they were divorced in 1973. In 1999 one of his twin daughters died of a brain tumor. Jan Holden died in 2005. He was later married and divorced from Gaynor Stuart.

During the last years of his life he resided at The Old Mill, Penybont, Oswestry, Shropshire where he continued as an actor-writer. It has to be said that he appeared in little of note during his last years. He died on August 2, 1990 at the Royal Shrewsbury Hospital, Shrewsbury, Shropshire aged 68 of lung cancer.

Charles Korvin (left) and Edwin Richfield in *Interpol Calling.*

Filmography

1950: *Ha'penny Breeze.*
1953: *The Blue Parrot, Park Plaza 605 (a.k.a. Norman Conquest), Flannelfoot.*
1954: *The Blue Peter (a.k.a. Navy Heroes), The Black Rider, What Every Woman Wants, Conflict of Wings (a.k.a. Fuss Over Feathers), Mask of Dust (a.k.a. Race for Life).*
1956: *The Hide-Out, The Brain Machine, X the Unknown, Find the Lady.*
1957: *Quatermass II (a.k.a. Enemy from Space), The Big Chance, Account Rendered, The Adventures of Hal 5.*
1958: *Up the Creek, Life Is a Circus, Innocent Meeting, No Trees in the Street.*
1959: *Tommy the Toreador, Model for Murder, Inn for Trouble, Ben Hur.*
1960: *Sword of Sherwood Forest.*
1961: *The Boy Who Stole a Million.*
1962: *Village of Daughters.*
1963: *The Break, Just for Fun.*
1965: *The Face of Fu Manchu, Secret of Blood Island.*
1967: *Quatermass and the Pit.*
1983: *Champions.*

Television Series

1955–1956: *The Buccaneers* as Crewman Armando.
1959–1960: *Interpol Calling* as Insp. Mornay.
1962–1963: *The Odd Man* as Steve Gardiner.
1965: *199 Park Lane.*

Sources

Bayne, Charles. "Jan Holden's Twin Career." *TV Times.* September 4, 1961.
Daily Telegraph. Obituary, August 1990.
Death Certificate.
Finch, Brian. "Man Behind the Odd Man." *TV Times.* May 1962.
_____. "Odd Man Counts His Blessings." *TV Times.* May 20, 1962.

Ewan Roberts

Ewan Roberts was born in Edinburgh, Scotland on April 29, 1914 the son of Frederick James Simpson Hutchison and his wife Nora

McEwan. He was educated at Melville College, Edinburgh Institution and Peebles High School. In spite of being color blind, he started out as a tweed designer in a woolen mill. He left the mill in 1934 after answering an advertisement in a theatrical magazine for "Heavy young actor—drama—variety—shares."

He made his first appearance on the stage at the Lyceum, Edinburgh in September 1935 as Lord Hastings in *The Scarlet Pimpernel* with the Jevan Brandon-Thomas company. Between 1936 and 1940 he acquired vast experience with repertory companies at Colwyn Bay, Warrington, Gourock, Hoylake and Jesmond, Newcastle-upon-Tyne. Between 1941 and 1946 he served with the Royal Navy Volunteer Reserve.

He joined the Old Vic Company, at the New Theater for the 1946–1947 season, appearing in all the plays and understudying Sir Ralph Richardson as Inspector Goole in *An Inspector Calls* in which he also appeared. During 1947–1948 he toured the Middle East as Richard Halton in *On Approval*. In 1949 he was engaged with the Tennant Players in various roles. His biggest early success in the commercial theater was as the manservant Menzies in *Castle in the Air* at the Adelphi Theater, London in December 1949. He repeated his role in the film version. He went on to make numerous appearances in the West End of London of which the best remembered was at the Phoenix Theater from September 1957 onwards when he played Mackintosh in *Roar Like a Dove*. He went on to appear in every one of more than a thousand performances of the play and subsequently toured in it.

He made his screen debut in *Dulcimer Street* (1948) and went on to play supporting roles in several films. He also worked as dialogue director in some films. He made his television debut in 1953 when he played Inspector Ames. Ames was a regular police officer who frequently referred cases to Colonel March (Boris Karloff), the head of the Department of Queer Complaints in the television series *Colonel March of Scotland Yard*. One of his greatest assets as an actor, namely his resonant Scottish accent, almost proved to be his undoing because he was advised to tone it down after the start of the series. As he explained it, "The series had been sold to America and they might have found me difficult to follow. You'll notice my accent more in some later episodes as they weren't shown in the order they were originally shot." The relationship between March and Ames was a bantering one with an undercurrent of good humor. One characteristic of Ames was that he had an amazing memory for the case histories of criminals which frequently irritated and confounded Colonel March. The episodes bear the production date of 1954. The series was syndicated in America and shown in England during 1956 and 1957 where it proved to be a considerable success. A decade later Roberts had a semi-regular role as Morton, Earl of Lenox, in the highly successful swashbuckling series *Sir Francis Drake*.

Roberts usually played authority figures such as judges, doctors and police officers who were not easily dominated. Once asked his favorite part, he replied, "The one I'm playing." His hobbies were listed as gardening, farming, cooking and collecting silver. He sometimes helped to sell silver for a friend who had a shop in the vaults under Chancery Lane in London. A journalist who once expressed surprise that he found time for farming was told, "Oh, that's a fantasy hobby. I've always wanted to own a farm." Roberts lived in a second floor apartment. Once when queried on where his garden was, he proudly exhibited a single hyacinth in a pot!

In fact Roberts never did buy the farm because he remained consistently employed as a stage actor until he died on January 10, 1983 in London aged 68. He was married to the literary agent Margery Vosper who died in 1981 and was survived by his son John, who was born in 1950, together with a daughter.

Filmography

1948: *Dulcimer Street* (a.k.a. *London Belongs to Me*).
1950: *Shadow of the Eagle*.
1951: *The Man in the White Suit*.
1952: *Castle in the Air, The Crimson Pirate, Derby Day, Mandy, Angels One Five*.
1953: *The Titfield Thunderbolt, The Heart of the Matter*.
1954: *River Beat*.
1955: *The Ladykillers, Port of Escape*.
1957: *Let's Be Happy* (a.k.a. *King's Rhapsody*), *High Tide at Noon, Curse of the Demon* (a.k.a. *Night of the Demon*).
1961: *What a Whopper!*
1962: *Day of the Triffids*.
1963: *The Traitors, Five to One, The Three Lives of Thomasina, The Partner*.
1968: *Hostile Witness, Mayerling*.
1970: *Country Dance*.

1972: *Baffled!* (TV), *Adolf Hitler—My Part in His Downfall.*
1973: *The Internecine Project.*

TELEVISION SERIES

1956–1957: *Colonel March of Scotland Yard* as Inspector Ames.
1961–1962: *Sir Francis Drake* as Morton, Earl of Lenox.

SOURCES

The Daily Telegraph. Obituary, January 1983.
Herbert, Ian. *Who's Who in the Theatre.* 16th ed. London: Pitman, 1977.
Palmer, Scott. *British Film Actors' Credits, 1985–1987.* London: St. James, 1988.
Scott, Esme. "His Scots Is for Home Use Only." *TV Times.* April 27, 1956.
The Stage. Obituary, January 1983.

LYNNE ROBERTS

Lynne Roberts was born Theda May Roberts in El Paso, Texas on November 22, 1922. She was the daughter of Hobart K. Roberts, an automobile executive and May Dell Holland. By all accounts Holland was a typically aggressive stage mother. Roberts had one brother John who was born in 1920. She was only a few days old when she left Texas with her parents and went to Hollywood. She was enrolled in Lawlor's Professional School in Hollywood where she learned singing, dancing and drama. With her brother she formed an act which toured vaudeville. The Christian name of her stage name Lynn (minus the e) Roberts was derived from a character whom she played on radio.

She made her screen debut in *Bulldog Edition* (1936) at Republic. Between 1938 and 1939 she was under contract to Republic. Herbert J. Yates, head honcho at Republic, so admired the musical combination of Rodgers and Hart that he wanted his own team. So he insisted that Lynn Roberts change her name to Mary Hart. After that he paired her with Roy Rogers in seven features billed as Rogers and Hart. She also appeared in a couple of serials. Her contract was terminated when she requested an increase in salary to meet medical bills for her sick father. When this was refused, she left the studio to freelance.

She disliked her stage name and as a freelance she took the opportunity of dropping it and reverting back to her original screen name with an added e, namely Lynne Roberts. Between 1940 and 1943 she was under contract to 20th Century–Fox where she appeared in mysteries, westerns and dramas. Possibly the best of these was *Quiet Please Murder* (1942) playing a librarian helping to solve a mystery set in a library which pitted her against Nazi agents in America.

Her studio biography stated that she stood 5'3" tall with auburn hair and blue eyes. She again found a berth at Republic where she was under contract between 1944 and 1948. She was leading lady to Roy Rogers again in one western. She also starred with Gene Autry in three westerns at Republic and later another at Columbia.

As a freelance once again she costarred with Don Haggerty in the early television crime series *The Cases of Eddie Drake* in 1949. Haggerty played the hardboiled private eye who feels the need to explain himself to a psychiatrist, Dr. Karen Grayle, originally played by Patricia Morison. When Morison left, she was replaced by Lynne Roberts as another psychiatrist, Dr. Joan Wright, who was researching into the criminal mind. The series was shelved after only nine episodes had been shown. The balance were first broadcast when the series went into syndication in 1952. Four episodes of the Haggerty-Roberts combination were edited together to make two second features *Murder Ad-Lib* and *Pattern for Murder* which were released theatrically in England in the early fifties. She was active on television until 1953 when she largely retired at the request of her then husband. Her last appearance was believed to be an episode of *The Life and Legend of Wyatt Earp* in 1955.

Roberts had a messy private life. She married William Englebert, Jr., an airline company executive, in January 1941. With him she had a son, William Englebert III, born in April 1942. She divorced her first husband in December 1944. In December 1944 she married Louis John Gardella, a production assistant at Republic studios who later worked for Hughes Aircraft Company. She was divorced from her second husband in January 1952. In June 1953 she married Hyman Samuels, a brassiere manufacturing executive. With him she had a daughter, Peri Margaret, born in 1955. She divorced her third husband in November 1961. Her fourth husband was professional wrestler Don Sebastian whom she wed in 1971. She was legally separated from him at the time of her death.

Lynne Roberts, who costarred in *The Cases of Eddie Drake*.

On December 16, 1977 she fell in the bathroom of her home in Sherman Oaks, California and lapsed into a coma after striking her head. She died at Los Angeles USC Medical Center of respiratory failure following an intercranial hemorrhage on April 1, 1978 aged 55 survived by her son, daughter and brother. She was buried alongside her mother at Forest Lawn Memorial Park on April 4, 1978.

Filmography

As Lynn Roberts:

1936: *Bulldog Edition.*
1937: *Circus Girl, Stella Dallas, Dangerous Holiday.*
1938: *Mama Runs Wild, Call the Mesquiteers, The Hollywood Stadium Mystery, The Higgins Family, The Lone Ranger* (serial), *Billy the Kid Returns.*

As Mary Hart:

1938: *Come on Rangers, Shine on Harvest Moon, Dick Tracy Returns* (serial), *Heart of the Rockies.*
1939: *Rough Riders' Round-up, Should Husbands Work?, Frontier Pony Express, Southward Ho!, In Old Caliente, The Stadium Murders, The Mysterious Miss X, My Wife's Relatives.*

As Lynn Roberts:

1940: *Everything's on Ice, Street of Memories, High School, Star Dust, The Bride Wore Crutches.*
1941: *Romance of the Rio Grande, Ride on Vaquero!, The Bride Wore Crutches, A Yank in the RAF, Riders of the Purple Sage, Last of the Duanes, Moon over Miami, Sun Valley Serenade.*
1942: *Young America, Dr. Renault's Secret, The Man in the Trunk, Quiet Please Murder.*
1943: *Three Sisters of the Moors.*

As Lynne Roberts:

1944: *The Ghost That Walks Alone, Port of 40 Thieves, My Buddy, The Big Bonanza.*
1945: *The Chicago Kid, Behind City Lights, The Phantom Speaks, Girls of the Big House.*
1946: *The Magnificent Rogue, The Inner Circle, Sioux City Sue.*
1947: *The Pilgrim Lady, That's My Gal, Robin Hood of Texas, Saddle Pals, Winter Wonderland.*
1948: *Lightnin' in the Forest, The Timber Trail, Eyes of Texas, Madonna of the Desert, Secret Service Investigator, Sons of Adventure.*
1949: *Trouble Preferred, A Dangerous Profession.*
1950: *Dynamite Pass, Call of the Klondike, The Blazing Sun, The Great Plane Robbery, Hunt the Man Down.*
1952: *Because of You, The Blazing Forest.*
1953: *Port Sinister.*

Television Series

1949: *The Cases of Eddie Drake* as Dr. Joan Wright.

Sources

Holland, Ted. *B Western Actors Encyclopedia.* Jefferson, NC: McFarland, 1989.
Picture Show Annual. London: Amalgamated, 1942.
Picture Show's Who's Who on Screen. London: Amalgamated, 1956.
Quinlan, David. *Film Stars.* 5th ed. London: Batsford, 2000.
Roberts, Barrie. *Classic Images.* Vol. 290. August 1999.
Starkey, Eleanore. *Western Clippings: Western Ladies.* No. 3. November 1997.
Turner, Steve, and Edgar M. Wyatt. *Saddle Gals.* Madison, NC: Empire, 1995.

Cesar Romero

If television viewers had been given the name of Cesar Romero in the sixties, they would chorus, "The Joker!" They knew him best as the fiendish arch villain from the camp television series *Batman*. It was however thought that when he began, a different fate awaited him. As he recalled, "When I started in motion pictures, they said I was going to be the next Valentino." With his greasy black hair, dazzling display of teeth and swarthy complexion, he was ideally cast as Latin lovers and gigolos. Since he had a Latin name, he was given this label. He later explained, "My background is Cuban, but I'm from New York City. I'm a Latin from Manhattan."

At a time when most heroes were true blue Americans, this meant that he was seldom the star of a film and usually did not win the girl at the end. For a man of his height, he was an amazingly agile and nimble dancer. In the career longevity stakes he came out a winner. Physically he remained handsome into old age and the quality of his work did not diminish. His career does represent something of a triumph of style over substance, but on the topic of his numerous films he reflected, "Believe me I take every job that's offered to me whether it's the Cisco Kid or a comic in a musical. I put all I know into each part and relax whenever I get the chance." He was much more popular particularly with women than his film track record suggests. In October 1942 there was a special Fox screening in San Francisco to which a galaxy of stars was transported by train. They were all outshone by Romero who, although a featured player, proved to be the idol of the crowds.

His nickname was "Butch." He was once asked how he came by it to which he replied, "It was at a party when George Murphy went round the table giving us all the most inappropriate nicknames he could think of. Mine stuck!" He was a favorite escort of many of the top female players in Hollywood such as Joan Crawford and the dyke lesbian actress Margaret Lindsay who fondly regarded him as her best dancing partner. Some have expressed regret that he did not write his memoirs since he was an integral part of the Hollywood social scene for decades and one of the few who genuinely knew where all the skeletons were buried.

Cesar Julio Romero, Jr., was born in New York City on February 15, 1907 the son of Cesar Julio Romero and Maria Mantilla Marti. His parents were Cuban immigrants. His grandfather was José Marti, the liberator of Cuba, who led the Cubans in their nineteenth century revolt against Spain. His father was an importer-exporter of sugar refining machinery to Cuba who died in 1951. His mother was a sometime concert singer who died in 1962. He had a brother and two sisters. He was from a very affluent family. He received a sound education at Sandford School, Redding Ridge, Connecticut; Riverdale Country School, New Jersey; and between 1923 and 1926 at Collegiate School, New York. He spoke fluent Spanish. When the Cuban sugar market collapsed in the twenties, his father lost his livelihood. He had to go out to work to support his family. He was initially employed as a courier at the First National Bank in Manhattan, but soon decided that this was not for him. Instead he formed a nightclub act with heiress Liz Higgins between 1926 and 1929. It was sufficiently successful for the duo to be hired for a revue called *Lady Do* at the Liberty Theater, New York in 1927 which lasted for 56 performances.

A burst appendix ended his career as a hoofer. Instead he switched to the stage. The stock market crash of 1929 wiped out the family fortune and the New York stage scene went quiet for a while. Briefly he worked in a New York department store, but soon left when he landed a part in *The Street Singer* which opened on September 17, 1929 and ran for 191 performances. He was seen by a producer who was seeking a replacement for Tullio Carminati in the hit Broadway comedy *Strictly Dishonorable*. Romero signed to play Count di Ruvo in the national touring company in which he enjoyed considerable success between 1930 and 1931. On the strength of this he segued into lead roles in a few more plays between 1931 and 1934. By long chalks his biggest success was as the jealous chauffeur Ricci in *Dinner at Eight* which opened at the Music Box Theater in 1932 and which he played more than 300 times both on Broadway and on the road. His only known relationship with a woman was with Marion Harris (1905–1944), an experienced musical comedy actress and cabaret entertainer, who originally persuaded him to grow his trademark moustache. When he refused to accompany her to Paris, their relationship ended, but he did not seem particularly upset by this.

He made an inauspicious screen debut in a low budget, independent film *The Shadow Laughs* (1933) as Tony Rico which he preferred to forget. While appearing in the play *All Points West* in 1934, he was screen tested by MGM. He relocated to Hollywood permanently in April 1934, where he landed the role of the gigolo Chris Jorgensen in *The Thin Man* (1934). He did not succeed in impressing the hierarchy at MGM so they dropped him after a year. Universal then had him under contract between 1934 and 1937, but he spent most of his time there shooting movies on loan to 20th Century–Fox. Two films released through United Artists did a lot to establish his reputation. He was the evil Mir Jaffir in *Clive of India* (1935) and Andre De Pons who fell in love with the cardinal's ward in *Cardinal Richelieu* (1935). These roles proved that he could convincingly play characters of vastly different nationalities.

He thought that it would be a good career move to be the leading man to Marlene Dietrich in *The Devil is a Woman* (1935). Although the film was visually stunning and Dietrich was fascinating, the film was a commercial failure. Romero hated working for director Josef von Sternberg whom he considered a sadist. He was much better served by another leading lady, Shirley Temple, in *Wee Willie Winkie* (1937) as Koda Khan. This led to a seven year contract at 20th Century–Fox which was later renewed for a further seven years. Studio head Darryl F. Zanuck liked him and made sure that he was kept regularly employed by the studio in a variety of interesting roles. Romero was very much a part of the Hollywood social scene during the period and he moved in very high circles in the film capital. He was on the A list for parties mainly because of his dancing skills.

His breakthrough came when he played a supporting role in *The Return of the Cisco Kid* (1939) which starred Warner Baxter as the charming and dashing bandit created by O. Henry. When Baxter was deemed too old to play the lead any longer, Romero assumed the role which he went on to play in six films. Although the films were commercially very successful, his mincing interpretation was deemed offensive to South Americans who lobbied Washington. Pressure was exerted on Fox to change the style of series, but rather than capitulate they dropped the Cisco Kid. It was later resurrected at Monogram. Instead Fox cast Romero in a number of pleasant escapist musicals starring such personalities as Alice Faye and Betty Grable which did much to further the South American good neighbor policy which was thought essential at the time. Romero brought his entire family to Hollywood where they all lived in a sprawling French Colonial house which he bought in Brentwood.

His tenure at Fox was interrupted by World War II. He enlisted in the Coast Guard at Long Beach, California in October 1942. He spent most of his time in the service aboard a Coast Guard manned transport attack ship, the USS Cavalier. He did not seek a commission, but nevertheless reached the rank of chief boatswain's mate. He was initially in the Hawaiian islands; took part in the invasion of Saipan; and the invasion of the Philippines. After leaving the ship Romero was sent on public relations tours which boosted morale between 1944 and 1945. When he returned home, he discovered so many of his relations were now living in his house that he settled into an apartment over the garage. After being honorably discharged in 1946, the studio decided to send him and his very good friend, Tyrone Power, on a goodwill tour of South America which turned out to be a big success. Romero returned to the screen as the swashbuckling Spanish conquistador Hernan Cortés in *Captain from Castile* (1947) which starred Tyrone Power. This was Romero's personal favorite of his own films, is generally regarded as his best role and was a huge commercial success.

Unfortunately most of his remaining films at Fox were disappointing and his contract was terminated in 1950. An indication of his declining stature was the fact that *Love That Brute* (1950) was a remake of *Tall, Dark and Handsome* (1941). In the original film he had played the hero. In the remake he had the supporting role of a gangster. He went through rather a rocky period after this and was down to his last several thousand dollars. He phoned his agent and instructed him that he would accept any film role; would open supermarkets; and would even do television. He was also a model for Petrocelli suits. He came to England to star with David Niven in a musical *Happy Go Lovely* (1950). He returned twice more for a couple of B movies. In *Scotland Yard Inspector* (1952) he played the title role of an American cop on loan to Scotland Yard. In *Street of Shadows* (1953) he played a slot machine owner and sometime racketeer who is framed for a murder he did not commit. For some reason, presumably to do with the low budget, the producers of this film gave the hero a Morris Minor to drive around in. Romero, who was one of the taller and more strapping actors, found obvious difficulty climbing in and out of this small vehicle! One of his more prestigious films followed as Marquis Henri de Labordere in *Vera Cruz* (1954).

He made his television debut in *The Jack*

Carter Show Gravediggers of 1950: A Musical Extravaganza. He guest starred on many of the most prestigious series of the time. He starred in the international intrigue series *Passport to Danger*. Each episode of this series began with an announcer saying, "One of the vital functions of the US Government is to maintain diplomatic relations with other countries. In every friendly and civilized nation in the world there is an American embassy or legation ... the most reliable and confidential means of communication is the courier service. Armed only with his passport like a global postman, he delivers the top secret dispatches of our government." There is then a cut to Romero with a dispatch briefcase being handcuffed to his wrist. He is next shown at passport control. He is asked his name, Steven McQuinn, and his profession which is diplomatic courier. The passport controller then stamps his passport with that week's destination. Stock footage of a plane in flight follows with Romero introducing the episode.

Scripts of *Passport to Danger* were solidly written and well developed with plenty of exciting action scenes. It was one of the better syndicated series of the period. Romero made a handsome and dashing hero and for once he was centre stage in the proceedings. Good looking women abounded and Romero was perpetually trying to help either a damsel or a friend in distress. The resolutions were usually pat but satisfying. There were 39 half hour, black and white episodes of this series originally shown between 1954 and 1956. Rabco was the production company and the show was filmed using the facilities of the Hal Roach Studios in Hollywood. The creator of the series was Robert C. Dennis.

Romero had a travel series of his own called *Cesar's World* which was particularly nebulous. His characterization as the Joker in the sixties television series *Batman* which numbered twenty appearances revived his career. He played the same role in the feature film *Batman* (1966). He thoroughly enjoyed playing this role, but he refused to shave his trademark moustache, so it was covered over with makeup. Adam West, who played Batman, admired him for the enormous energy he brought to the part. Romero's income as a result of this series was higher than for a

Cesar Romero, who starred in *Passport to Danger*.

number of years. Unfortunately he chose to plough most of these earnings into a chain of eight men's clothing stores and a restaurant called *Cappucino* which he opened during a temporary lull in his career in 1972. He proved to be a hopeless businessman and these ventures cost him thousands of dollars.

To recoup some of his losses he returned full time to show business in 1976. He made appearances in some Disney films which enhanced his reputation, but most of his later films were of poor quality. He was very active on the dinner theater circuit during the seventies in plays which were generally well received. He continued to appear on television and celebrated his eightieth birthday on the set of the prime time soap *Falcon Crest* in which he played Jane Wyman's husband, Peter Stavros. He later played Sophia's boyfriend on the successful sitcom *The Golden Girls* during the nineties.

His sister Maria, with whom he had shared a house for two decades, died on March 24, 1991 aged 85. He himself suffered a minor stroke in 1992 and later from diabetes and arthritis. Romero eventually died on January 1, 1994 aged 86 at 9:10 pm at St. John's Hospital and Health Center in Santa Monica, California. The immediate cause of death was respiratory arrest and pulmonary embolus due to a blood clot in his right leg after being hospitalized about ten days earlier with severe bronchitis and pneumonia. He was survived by a brother, three nieces, a nephew and three great nephews. He was cremated and then his ashes were buried in the Sanctuary of Dreams at Inglewood Memorial Park, Inglewood, California.

Romero never married. As he explained, "My home was an ideal bachelor establishment. I turned it into a family set-up. First, I had my parents move in. Then I got my two sisters to join us. One of them has two kids who came along as well. How could I get married when I had so many responsibilities?" All of this was designed to camouflage one of Hollywood's best known secrets namely that Romero was a rampant homosexual despite the numerous women who swooned over him.

Filmography

1933: *The Shadow Laughs.*
1934: *The Thin Man, Cheating Cheaters, British Agent.*
1935: *The Good Fairy, Strange Wives, Clive of India, Cardinal Richelieu, Hold' Em Yale, The Devil Is a Woman, Diamond Jim, Metropolitan, Rendezvous, Show Them No Mercy.*
1936: *Love Before Breakfast, Nobody's Fool, Public Enemy's Wife, 15 Maiden Lane.*
1937: *She's Dangerous, Armored Car, Wee Willie Winkie, Dangerously Yours.*
1938: *Happy Landing, My Lucky Star, Always Goodbye, Five of a Kind.*
1939: *Wife Husband and Friend, The Little Princess, Return of the Cisco Kid, Charlie Chan at Treasure Island, Frontier Marshal.*
1940: *Viva Cisco Kid* (CK), *Lucky Cisco Kid* (CK), *He Married His Wife, The Cisco Kid and the Lady* (CK), *The Gay Caballero* (CK).
1941: *Tall Dark and Handsome, Romance of the Rio Grande* (CK), *Ride on Vaquero!* (CK), *The Great American Broadcast, Dance Hall, Week-End in Havana.*
1942: *A Gentleman at Heart, Tales of Manhattan, Orchestra Wives, Springtime in the Rockies.*
1943: *Coney Island, Wintertime.*
1947: *Captain from Castile, Carnival in Costa Rica.*
1948: *Deep Waters, That Lady in Ermine, Julia Misbehaves.*
1949: *The Beautiful Blonde from Bashful Bend.*
1950: *Love that Brute, Once a Thief, Happy Go Lovely.*
1951: *FBI Girl, The Lost Continent.*
1952: *Scotland Yard Inspector* (a.k.a. *Lady in the Fog*), *The Jungle.*
1953: *Street of Shadows* (a.k.a. *Shadow Man*), *Prisoners of the Casbah.*
1954: *Vera Cruz, The Sword of Grenada.*
1955: *The Americano, The Racers.*
1956: *Around the World in 80 Days* (cameo), *The Leather Saint.*
1957: *The Story of Mankind* (cameo).
1958: *Villa!*
1959: *My Private Secretaries.*
1960: *Ocean's 11, Pepe* (cameo).
1961: *7 Women from Hell.*
1962: *If a Man Answers, We Shall Return, The Castilian.*
1963: *Donovan's Reef.*
1964: *A House Is Not a Home.*
1965: *Two on a Guillotine, Sergeant Deadhead, Marriage on the Rocks, Broken Saber* (TV).
1966: *Batman.*
1967: *Madigan's Millions.*
1968: *Hot Millions, Crooks and Coronets* (a.k.a. *Sophie's Place*).
1969: *How to Make It* (a.k.a. *Target Harry*), *Skidoo, The Midas Run, A Talent For Loving, Latitude Zero, Don't Push I'll Charge When I'm Ready* (TV).
1970: *The Computer Wore Tennis Shoes.*
1971: *Soul Soldier.*
1972: *Now You See Him Now You Don't, The Proud and the Damned, The Specter of Edgar Allan Poe.*
1973: *Timber Tramp.*
1974: *The Strongest Man in the World.*
1975: *Won Ton Ton the Dog Who Saved Hollywood* (cameo).
1977: *Kino the Padre on Horseback* (a.k.a. *Mission to Glory*).
1979: *Monster.*
1983: *Vultures in Paradise* (a.k.a. *Flesh and Bullets*).
1984: *Lust in the Dust.*
1988: *Judgment Day, Mortuary Academy.*
1990: *Simple Justice.*

Note: Films in which Cesar Romero played the Cisco Kid are denoted CK in the filmography.

Television Series

1953–1954: *Your Chevrolet Showroom* Host.
1954–1956: *Passport to Danger* as Steve McQuinn.
1968: *Cesar's World* Host.
1966–1968: *Batman* as The Joker.
1985–1987: *Falcon Crest* as Peter Stavros.

Sources

Corneau, Ernest N. *The Hall of Fame of Western Film Stars*. North Quincy, MA.: Christopher, 1969.
Daily Mail. "Latin Lover's Talent Went Beyond a Joke Role." January 1994.
Daily Telegraph. Obituary, January 1994.
Death Certificate.
Donnelly, Paul. *Fade to Black*. London: Omnibus, 2000.
Finch, Christopher, and Linda Rosenkrantz. *Gone Hollywood*. London: Weidenfeld and Nicholson, 1980.
Hadleigh, Boze. *Hollywood Gays*. New York: Barricade, 1986.
Inman, David. *The TV Encyclopedia*. New York: Perigee, 1991.
Liverpool Echo. "Veteran Star Dies." January 1994.
Lentz, Harris M. III. *Obituaries in the Performing Arts, 1994* Jefferson, NC.: McFarland, 1995.
McClure, Arthur F., and Ken D. Jones. *Star Quality*. South Brunswick, NJ: A.S. Barnes, 1974.
Natale, Richard. *Variety*. Obituary, January 1994.
Parish, James Robert, and William T. Leonard. *Hollywood Players: The Thirties*. Carlstadt, New Jersey: Rainbow, 1977.
Picture Show Annual. London: Amalgamated, 1937, 1939, 1941, 1942, 1943, 1949.
Quinlan, David. *Film Stars*. 5th ed. London: Batsford, 2000.
Reyes, Luis, and Peter Rubie. *Hispanics in Hollywood: A Celebration of 100 Years in Film and Television*. Hollywood: Lone Eagle, 2000.
Skinner, John Walter. *Who's Who on the Screen*. Worthing, England: Madeleine, 1983.
Wallace, Leonard, and Alan Warwick. "The Strange Fascination of Butch." *Picturegoer*. July 22, 1950.
Ward, Jack. *Television Guest Stars*. Jefferson, NC: McFarland, 1993.
Weissberg, Brad. "Joyful Cesar Romero Died Planning for the Future at 86." *National Enquirer*. January 1994.
Winchester, Clarence. *Screen Encyclopedia*. London: Winchester, 1948.
Wise, James E., and Anne Collier Rehill. *Stars in Blue*. Annapolis, MD: Naval Institute, 1997.

Anthony Ross

Anthony Ross was born in New York City on February 23, 1909. A graduate of Brown University, he did post graduate studies at the Sorbonne, Paris and the University of Nancy in France. He made his New York stage debut at the Waldorf Theater on November 3, 1932 as Cossack in *Whistling in the Dark*. He appeared in many plays on the New York stage until 1942.

He then served three years with the forces during World War II during which time he was attached to the entertainment unit. While in the services he appeared in the revue *This is the Army*. During the war he also appeared in Moss Hart's morale boosting play *Winged Victory* as Ross and was set to repeat his role in the 20th Century-Fox screen version when, for undisclosed reasons, his part was recast.

After being honorably discharged, he reappeared on stage at the Playhouse, New York in March 1945 when he originated the role of The Gentleman Caller in Tennessee Williams' *The Glass Menagerie* in which he played until August 1946. He scored a notable stage success playing Arthur Dodd, a character based on Harold Ross editor of the New Yorker, in *Season in the Sun* which opened at the Cort in September 1950. It marked the directorial debut of Burgess Meredith. Ross had to leave the play on health grounds.

He made his motion picture debut in *Kiss of Death* (1947) as Williams. Thereafter he interspersed films with stage roles. His best remembered film role was as Phil Cook, the mercenary producer, in *The Country Girl* (1954). He added an extra string to his bow when he played the part of Det. Lt. Richard Hale in a television crime series *The Telltale Clue* (1954). Hale was the head of criminology of the Metropolitan Homicide Squad in a large unnamed metropolis. He examined crimes in considerable detail with a view to discovering the one piece of evidence which would reveal the villain. Forensic science and his keen mind both played a part in this process. Despite ingenious stories this series lasted for only 13 live, black and white, half hour episodes on the CBS network. It was a summer

Anthony Ross (left) and Robert Taylor in the film *Rogue Cop* (1954).

replacement series seen between July and September 1954.

Ross was appearing as Dr. Gerald Lyman in *Bus Stop* at the Music Box Theatre, New York from March 1955 onwards. A few hours after performing there on October 26, 1955 he collapsed and died of a heart attack aged 46.

Filmography

1947: *Kiss of Death, Boomerang!*
1949: *The Window.*
1950: *The Skipper Surprised His Wife, Perfect Strangers, Between Midnight and Dawn, The Gunfighter, The Flying Missile, The Vicious Years.*
1951: *On Dangerous Ground.*
1953: *Taxi, Girls in the Night.*
1954: *Rogue Cop, The Country Girl.*

Television Series

1954: *The Telltale Clue* as Det. Lt. Richard Hale.

Sources

Jones, Ken D., Arthur F. McClure, and Alfred E. Twomey. *Character People* Secaucus, NJ: Citadel, 1979.

Meredith, Burgess. *So Far So Good*. Boston: Little, Brown, 1994.

Parker, John. *Who's Who in the Theatre*. 12th ed. London: Pitman, 1957.

Gena Rowlands

When Gena Rowlands began her career, she was not enthused about film or television. As she recalled, "I just wanted to do stage work, but then my husband John got interested in film. He intrigued us all into following him. He was kind of like the Pied Piper." Her husband was John Cassavetes. Although she became famous in his films, she seemed to have had no difficulty maintaining her own identity. Making movies became the family business. They produced their own movies with their own money. When they ran out of money, they would stop the cameras, obtain a gig in the mainstream and wait until they could afford to continue. It might have been supposed that when her husband died, she would have been so linked to him that her career would have sputtered to a stop. Instead she became one of the busiest actresses of her generation during the nineties and into this century.

Gena Rowlands was born Virginia Cathryn Rowlands in Cambria, Wisconsin on June 19, 1930. Her parents were Edwin Merwin Rowlands, a banker and state senator and Mary Allen Neal, an artist. As a child she moved to Virginia where much later she won a scholarship to the Jarvis Repertory Company in Washington D.C. She attended the University of Wisconsin in 1947 and the American Academy of Dramatic Arts. Between 1951 and 1953 she performed in stock. She made her Broadway debut understudying the Girl in *The Seven Year Itch* later playing the role in the national touring company in 1953. She was chosen by Joshua Logan to play the role of Betty Price in the highly successful Broadway play *Middle of the Night* at the American National Theater and Academy (ANTA) during 1956 and 1957.

She did a lot of live television on the popular anthology series of the fifties when the industry was based in New York. Between 1954 and 1955 she starred in *Top Secret USA,* an obscure syndicated series produced by Revue consisting of 26 half hour, black and white episodes. Paul Stewart played Professor Brand and Gena Rowlands played his assistant, Powell. Both worked for the Office of Scientific Information. It was a series which was shown at the height of the Communist scare of the fifties, but is hardly remembered today.

In September 1953 she met John Cassavetes at acting school and they married in New York on March 19, 1954. With him she had three children who are a son Nicholas who was born in 1959; a daughter Alexandra, nicknamed "Xan," who was born in 1965; and another daughter Zoe who was born in 1970.

She made her screen debut in *The High Cost of Loving* (1958). When she and her husband relocated to Hollywood, she was seen in guest shots in a number of filmed television series between the late fifties and the middle seventies. She earned plaudits for her sensitive playing of Teddy Carella, the deaf mute wife of Detective Steve Carella (Robert Lansing) in the *87th Precinct* television series derived from the novels by Ed McBain during 1961 and 1962.

She appeared in films which her husband directed beginning with Sophie Widdicombe in *A Child Is Waiting* (1963). In the process she earned a reputation as an actress who emoted close to the edge. Her husband's films increasingly began to resemble tedious, overlong filmed drama workshops. Nevertheless she received two Best Actress Oscar nominations for *A Woman Under the Influence* (1974) and *Gloria* (1980). In the latter she played the title role of a feisty, streetwise, former mistress of a gang lord who goes on the run with a child while trying to escape the wrath of the mob. This was the most commercially orientated of Cassavetes films.

After her husband's death in 1989, she was largely absent for a couple of years. During this time by her own admission she suffered from depression. She resumed her career playing Holly Hunter's mother, Marilyn Bella, in *Once Around* (1991). She played Georgia King, the mother of Julia Roberts, in *Something to Talk About* (1995). When her son Nick made his directorial debut in *Unhook the Stars* (1995) she played the leading role of Mildred Hawks, who suffers a mid-life crisis when her children have left home. Nick Cassavetes tended to stick much more closely to the script than his father and the role she played was much quieter. Of this experience she said, "I would have choked Nick, held him by the throat, if he had considered anyone else for the role of Mildred."

Some of her television roles have been particularly well received. In 1985 she received an Emmy nomination as Outstanding Lead Actress in a Television Series or Special for *An Early Frost*. She received an Emmy Award for Best Performance by an Actress in a Miniseries or Motion

Gena Rowlands in the film *Gloria* (1980). She costarred in the TV series *Top Secret USA* and later *87th Precinct*.

Picture Made for Television for *The Betty Ford Story* (1987) and *Face of a Stranger* (1991). She received an Emmy award nomination for Best Performance by an Actress in a Miniseries or Motion Picture Made for Television for *The Color of Love: Jacey's Story* (2000). She was nominated for an Emmy award as Outstanding Lead Actress in a Miniseries or Movie for *Wild Iris* (2001). She won an Emmy award for Outstanding Supporting Actress in a Miniseries or Movie for *Hysterical Blindness* (2002). She won a Daytime Emmy award for Outstanding Performer in a Children/Youth/Family Special for *The Incredible Mrs. Ritchie* (2003).

At last report she was continuing to reside in the same house in Los Angeles which she lived in with her late husband.

Filmography

1958: *The High Cost of Loving*.
1962: *Lonely Are the Brave, The Spiral Road*.
1963: *A Child Is Waiting*.
1967: *Tony Rome*.
1968: *Faces*.
1969: *Machine Gun McCain*.
1971: *Minnie and Moskowitz*.
1974: *A Woman Under the Influence*.
1976: *Two Minute Warning*.

1977: *Opening Night.*
1978: *A Question of Love* (TV), *The Brinks Job.*
1979: *Strangers: The Story of a Mother and Daughter* (TV).
1980: *Gloria.*
1982: *Tempest.*
1983: *Thursday's Child* (TV).
1984: *Love Streams.*
1985: *An Early Frost* (TV).
1987: *Light of Day, The Betty Ford Story* (TV).
1988: *Another Woman.*
1990: *Montana* (TV).
1991: *Once Around, Night on Earth, Face of a Stranger* (TV), *Ted and Venus.*
1992: *Crazy in Love.*
1993: *Silent Cries* (TV).
1994: *Parallel Lives* (TV).
1995: *Something to Talk About* (a.k.a. *Grace under Pressure*), *The Neon Bible.*
1996: *Unhook the Stars.*
1997: *She's So Lovely.*
1998: *Best Friends for Life* (TV), *Paulie, Hope Floats, The Mighty, Grace and Glorie* (TV), *Playing by Heart.*
1999: *The Weekend.*
2000: *The Color of Love: Jacey's Story* (TV).
2001: *Wild Iris* (TV).
2002: *Hysterical Blindness* (TV), *Charms for the Easy Life* (TV).
2003: *The Incredible Mrs. Ritchie* (TV).
2004: *The Notebook, Taking Lives.*
2005: *The Skeleton Key.*
2006: *Paris je t'aime.*

TELEVISION SERIES

1954–1955: *Top Secret USA* as Powell.
1961–1962: *87th Precinct* as Teddy Carella.
1967: *Peyton Place* as Adrienne Van Leyden.

SOURCES

Blondinka, Anne. "Histoire de Couples Gena Rowlands and John Cassavetes." *Femme Actuelle.* No. 932. August 11, 2002.
Erickson, Hal. *Syndicated Television: The First Forty Years, 1947–1987.* Jefferson, NC: McFarland, 1989.
Inman, David. *The TV Encyclopedia.* New York: Perigee, 1991.
McNab, Geoffrey. "Mother Courage." *The Independent.* July 3, 1997.
Picture Show Annual. London: Amalgamated, 1960.
Quinlan, David. *Film Stars.* 5th ed. London: Batsford, 2000.
Tulard, Jean. *Dictionnaire Du Cinéma Les Acteurs.* 7th ed. Paris: Robert Laffont, 2004.
Ward, Jack. *Television Guest Stars.* Jefferson, NC: McFarland, 1993.

MEL RUICK

Mel Ruick was born in Boise, Idaho on July 8, 1898. He was primarily a stage and radio actor and bandleader. He played the leading role of John Randolph, a spymaster, in the early television series *Door with No Name.* This was a summer replacement series of only eight half hour, black and white episodes shown on the NBC network in July and August 1951. The title referred to the door to John Randolph's office. Randolph was head of a top secret government agency which sent operatives, primarily Doug Carter (Grant Richards), all over the world to track down enemies of the USA. When the series returned the following year, the title had changed to *Doorway to Danger.* John Randolph was still there, but played by another actor, Roland Winters. Carter had however disappeared. Ruick moved on to play a medical man in another television series *City Hospital.* He later had a regular role on a short-lived daytime soap opera.

Ruick died in Los Angeles County on December 24, 1972 aged 74. He was married and divorced from actress Laurene Tuttle (1906–1986). They were the parents of actress Barbara Ruick (1930–1974).

FILMOGRAPHY

1935: *The Gilded Lily.*
1936: *The President's Mystery, The Milky Way.*
1937: *Torture Money, Navy Blues, Saratoga.*
1940: *Kitty Foyle.*
1941: *Whistling in the Dark, Two Latins from Manhattan, Moon over Miami, Sun Valley Serenade, Remember the Day.*
1942: *There's One Born Every Minute, Rings on Her Fingers, The Lady Has Plans, Holiday Inn, Bombay Clipper, Junior G-Men of the Air* (serial), *Man from Headquarters.*
1947: *Kiss of Death.*
1953: *Taxi.*
1965: *The Human Duplicators.*

TELEVISION SERIES

1951: *Door with No Name* as John Randolph.
1952–1953: *City Hospital* as Dr. Barton Crane.
1954–1955: *First Love* as Paul Kennedy.

SOURCES

Brooks, Tim. *The Complete Directory to Prime Time Network and Cable TV Shows.* 8th ed. New York: Ballantine, 1999.

Copeland, Mary Ann. *Soap Opera History.* Lincolnwood, IL: Mallard, 1991.

HOWARD ST. JOHN

Howard St. John was born in Chicago, Illinois on October 9, 1905. He was the son of Sidney St. John and his wife, Maud O'Connor. He was educated at St. Ignatius School, St. Boniface College, Winnipeg and the University of Alabama. He made his first stage appearance at the Punch and Judy Theater in 1925 when he succeeded Warren William as Keith Reddington in *Nocturne.* He dropped out of the stage and pursued a career on Wall Street between 1927 and 1932.

He returned to the stage in May 1932 when he played the role of Murdock at the Playhouse Theater in *Bulls, Bears and Asses.* Over the next thirty years he was a very active stage actor until his final appearance in 1962 at the Helen Hayes Theater when he played Oscar Nelson in *Mary Mary* for a year. He made his screen debut in 1949 and his first television appearance in 1944. In the television crime series *The Investigator* he played the role of retired newspaperman Lloyd Prior who with his swinging bachelor son Jeff (Lonny Chapman) solved various crimes. This was a live, summer replacement series shown between June and September 1958 on NBC and generally regarded as one of the weakest of the genre ever shown on television.

St. John died of a heart attack at his home in Manhattan on March 13, 1974 aged 68. He was married to Lois Bolton who survived him.

FILMOGRAPHY

1949: *The Undercover Man, Shockproof.*
1950: *The Men, Born Yesterday, Mister 880, David Harding Counterspy, Customs Agent, Counterspy Meets Scotland Yard, 711 Ocean Drive.*
1951: *Strangers on a Train, Saturday's Hero, Goodbye My Fancy, The Big Night, The Sun Sets at Dawn, Starlift, Close to My Heart.*
1952: *Stop You're Killing Me.*
1954: *Three Coins in the Fountain.*
1955: *The Tender Trap, Illegal, I Died a Thousand Times.*
1956: *World in My Corner.*

Howard St. John, who costarred in *The Investigator.*

1959: *Li'l Abner.*
1961: *Sanctuary, Cry for Happy, One Two Three, Lover Come Back, Lafayette.*
1962: *Madison Avenue.*
1964: *Fate Is the Hunter, Strait-Jacket, Sex and the Single Girl, Strange Bedfellows, Quick Before It Melts.*
1966: *Matchless.*
1967: *Banning.*
1969: *Don't Drink the Water.*

TELEVISION SERIES

1951–1952: *Fairmeadows U.S.A* as John Olcott.
1958: *The Investigator* as Lloyd Prior.
1965–1966: *Hank* as Dr. Lewis Royal.

SOURCES

Jones, Ken D., Arthur F. McClure, and Alfred E. Twomey. *Character People.* Secaucus, NJ: Citadel, 1979

Variety. Obituary, 1974.

Who's Who in the Theatre. 15th ed. London: Pitman, 1972.

GEORGE SANDERS

"I hate interviews because I do not get paid for them. I hate to give autographs and never do.

I am always rude to people. I am not a sweet person. I am a disagreeable person. I am a hateful person. I like to be hateful." So spoke George Sanders who elevated snobbery to a fine art. He was probably the most successful Hollywood player of the cad or bounder. His cultured voice and sleek charm, mixed with a hint of menace, made him an in-demand supporting actor for over thirty years. His name in a cast list frequently counted for more than a nominal lead. He was not a particularly successful television actor, although he did a lot of it particularly after his financial woes dictated the need for quick cash. He seemed to have boundless self confidence, yet throughout his life, he was dogged by self doubt. Off screen he tended to be aloof and not socialize much, yet at other times he was witty and gregarious. As an actor his colleagues have testified that he was a consummate professional with a flawless technique. Of the type of character who made his name, Sanders said in later years, "I really don't mind being typecast as a cad. I'm quite used to it now. I suppose it did upset me to begin with—but that was many years ago."

At MGM his unusual looks enabled him to play a couple of romantic leads. On the strength of these Louis B. Mayer invited him to lunch with a view to discussing a contract at MGM and promoting him as a romantic leading man. Sanders declined the invitation giving an explanation much later in life, "Professionally speaking, the mortality rate amongst stars is extremely high, whereas a good character actor is almost indestructible."

George Sanders was born in St. Petersburg, Russia on July 3, 1906. He was the son of Henry Sanders and Margaret Kolbe. His father was allegedly English, although he was more likely an illegitimate child of a Russian aristocrat (probably Prince Von Oldenburg), and his profession was assistant director of a rope factory. His mother was a Russian socialite whose family had money. His mother and father were married in 1903. He had one brother who was Thomas Charles Sanders, later the actor Tom Conway, who was born in St. Petersburg on September 15, 1904. He had a sister named Margaret who was born in St. Petersburg on October 27, 1912.

Sanders had a very happy childhood in Russia under the Czar until the outbreak of World War I. His family had relatives in England. He and his brother left Russia and went to England. They were later joined by their mother and sister. His father fled Russia during the revolution. Most of his assets were lost and he did not do much business in England thereafter. George Sanders and his brother were educated at Dunhurst, a preparatory school in Hampshire, for two years and then went to Bedales School at Petersfield in 1917. There they were unsettled and sought refuge in amateur dramatics. Finally they went to Brighton College, a second rate public school. George Sanders was there between 1919 and 1923 where he proved to be good academically and at sports. His family's reduced circumstances meant that he was perpetually short of funds and left him with psychological scars which haunted him all of his life.

In 1923 he enrolled at Manchester Technical Institute to study textiles. For twelve months he worked at the Manchester Textiles Company at which he had little flair and subsequently lost his job. In 1926 he became a salesman for the British and American Tobacco Company in South America. Based in Argentina, he spent four happy years there where he became a fluent Spanish speaker. He was good at the job, but fired for a social blunder involving his boss. He then ventured to Chile where he was employed by another tobacco company in a similar capacity. His tenure in South America ended abruptly when he was jailed after being challenged to a duel over a woman. He won the duel, but was arrested and thrown out of South America. He returned to England in December 1929.

After a period of unemployment, he was employed for a short time by LINTAS, the advertising branch of the manufacturers Lever Brothers. Another employee was Greer Garson who persuaded him to join her amateur dramatics group. An uncle who escaped from St. Petersburg paid for him to have singing lessons. He was heard singing at a party by a producer who offered him a job in a revue called *Ballyhoo* in 1932 as a singer and piano player. His inexperience showed and he was fired. He then joined the B.B.C for a year which he spent acting in radio plays. Simultaneously he did some nightclub work in London.

His first major West End production was *Conversation Piece* in which he had two parts and went with it to New York in 1934 where it flopped. He had the male lead in *Further Outlook* which opened on October 29, 1935. He received good reviews, but after it closed he did not appear on stage again for thirty years. He continued radio acting with the BBC. He made his screen debut as one of three gods in the opening scene of *The Man Who Could Work Miracles* (1936).

In 1936 he signed a long term contract with British and Dominion Studio, but when it burned down, its assets were acquired by 20th Century–Fox. Fox's head honcho Darryl F. Zanuck was shooting *Lloyds of London* (1936) and in desperate need of refined British actors to bolster the production. Sanders was sent to Hollywood where he was tested for and won the role of the haughty villain Lord Everett Stacy. His reviews were uniformly good. It was also the first film in which his character was an adversary of Tyrone Power who became a good friend. Sanders was costarring with Power in *Solomon and Sheba* in Spain in 1958 when Power died of a heart attack on location. Sanders delivered the eulogy at his funeral.

Sanders signed a contract with Fox who used him in several of their films. They wanted to give him a star promotion, but they soon found out that Sanders was arrogant and unconcerned about playing the Hollywood social game. He detested Zanuck and was not slow to speak his mind. To punish him Fox loaned him to RKO Radio to play the title role in *The Saint* series based on the character created by Leslie Charteris. The series proved profitable, but ended because of a dispute between RKO and Charteris who was dissatisfied with the onscreen exploits of his hero. Almost immediately Sanders swapped this character for the interchangeable one of Gay Lawrence, "The Falcon" in the first four films of the series shot at RKO. Charteris sued RKO and won an out of court settlement. Sanders' final film in this series was *The Falcon's Brother* (1942) in which his character is killed off and replaced by his brother, Tom Lawrence. Sanders arranged for his real life brother, now calling himself Tom Conway, to replace him in the series. Surprisingly he made a greater success of it than his brother, George. They only appeared together in one other film, *Death of a Scoundrel* (1956), in which Sanders starred and Conway had a bit.

George Sanders made a tremendous impact in two films directed by Alfred Hitchcock. He played the odious blackmailing cousin Jack Favell in *Rebecca* (1940) and heroic reporter Scott ffolliott in *Foreign Correspondent* (1940). He made a number of films in which he played Nazis or Germans. The film however which was probably his best starring role was *The Moon and Sixpence* (1942) for United Artists. It was directed by Albert Lewin. It did much to establish Sanders' onscreen character as a cynical cad, disdainful of both women and materialism. In this film derived from the 1919 novel by Somerset Maugham, he played Charles Strickland. The character was loosely based on Paul Gaugin. Strickland was an apparently successful businessman who left his work and family behind to go to the South Seas where he lives in poverty to paint before dying of leprosy. His paintings become very valuable after his death. It was one of Sanders' personal favorites of his films. Herbert Marshall played Maugham himself, under the name of Geoffrey Wolfe, a role which he repeated in *The Razors Edge* (1946).

Sanders did next to nothing to raise money for British war relief which did not endear him to the British colony in Hollywood. Although he was in near perfect health, he did not serve in the armed forces during World War II because of an alleged back injury. One of his most impressive roles was as Lord Henry Wootton in the masterly *The Picture of Dorian Gray* (1944) directed by Albert Lewin from the novel by Oscar Wilde. Of all the leading ladies he worked with, he admitted that he liked Lucille Ball the most. They costarred in the English set thriller *Lured* (1947).

He married Susan Larson (real name Elsie Poole), a 25 year old American former waitress turned budding actress at Hollywood Methodist Church on October 27, 1940. They originally met on the Fox lot. She left him on December 10, 1946 and they divorced in Los Angeles on January 27, 1947. He found the divorce extremely painful, even though he had treated her like a doormat. He underwent analysis and did not do much work in 1947 which explains the dearth of film releases in 1948. He met Hungarian socialite Zsa Zsa Gabor at a party in April 1947. They eloped and wed in Las Vegas on April 1, 1949. It was an extremely volatile union not helped by the fact that Zsa Zsa Gabor decided she wanted a film career of her own. They divorced in Los Angeles on April 2, 1954, although they remained close. They appeared in one film together, *Death of a Scoundrel* (1956), made after they divorced.

He won a Best Supporting Actor Oscar as waspish theater critic Addison DeWitt in *All About Eve* (1950). He had a fine baritone singing voice, but it was only used once on screen in one of his best films *Call Me Madam* (1953) based on the Irving Berlin show. The star was Ethel Merman with Sanders playing Cosmo Constantine. On Broadway he signed a contract to replace Ezio Pinza in the musical *South Pacific*, but developed a mysterious ailment, in reality galloping stage fright, and was released from contract without ever having sung a note.

George Sanders Mystery Theater was a summer replacement series shown on NBC between June 22, 1957 and September 14, 1957. It consisted of 13 filmed half hour, black and white episodes produced by Screen Gems. It was an anthology series hosted and narrated by Sanders in his usual witty way. He starred in a few of the segments. The cast list was usually third division and the stories were frequently of the person in jeopardy type. This series was some of the stars least well remembered work.

Sanders desired all his working life to be a business tycoon, but his financial acumen was zilch. He created Husan Limited in California in 1956 to finance, develop and market inventions. He appointed himself Managing Director, formed a partnership, rented a small factory and hired workers. The business failed disastrously and he lost all of his own money and that of the investors. The sheriff seized both his house and car and his personal bank accounts were frozen. He fled the country and eventually ended up in Lausanne, Switzerland where good salaries from movies and tax avoidance schemes temporarily propped up his ailing finances.

He wed thirdly Benita Hume at the British consulate in Madrid on February 10, 1959. She was born in 1906, was a former actress and the widow of Ronald Colman. This marriage was by far his most successful and they were a very happy combination. In 1960 his autobiography *Memoirs of a Professional Cad*, a witty but superficial book, was published.

With his attorney and business manager Thomas Roe, he created a company called Roturman S.A. Through Roe he met a rogue Englishman Denis Loraine. They persuaded Sanders to form a subsidiary company called CADCO. In turn CADCO invested heavily in a company created by Loraine called Royal Victoria Sausages Limited. This involved pig breeding in England which would lead to the making of delicious sausages according to a recipe. Sanders money was used to open a factory in Sussex. The venture almost immediately ran into difficulties and showed losses in the Annual Report of 1961–1962 of £130,000.

There was then an attempt by Loraine to recoup their losses. He persuaded the Board of Trade to subsidize the company with funds from the Glenrothes Development Company. The condition was that the sausage company would have to operate from a factory in the depressed Glenrothes area of Scotland. As neither Roe nor Loraine professed to have funds beyond their company salaries, it was left up to Sanders alone to sign the notes. CADCO was required to match the subsidy and guarantee a loan of £300,000 from the Royal Bank of Scotland. There was also £100,000 illegally channeled from Scotland to Italy for an Italian venture involving fruit and vegetables. Sanders allegedly suggested this expansion, although he later vehemently denied it.

Inefficiency, lack of management control, hopeless financial planning and cash flow problems combined to cause CADCO to collapse in September 1964. The Bank of Scotland demanded that Sanders honor his personal guarantee. Sanders fled from the British Isles to California where he bought a small house in Brentwood. He obtained a guest shot on *The Rogues* in 1964 after which his television career was off and running. He also continued to make feature films throughout the sixties. Nevertheless on October 27, 1966 he filed for bankruptcy listing assets of $57,657 (approx. £20,000) and liabilities of $933,258 (approx. £332,000). He said in the bankruptcy petition that he had signed bank guarantees of $1,250,000 (approx. £447,000).

He claimed to have been the victim of an international swindle, but the investigation into CADCO by the Board of Trade concluded that he was far from as naive as he appeared. No criminal charges were however brought against him. Roe and Loraine were later arrested in Switzerland and America respectively for counterfeiting. Sanders definitely was not involved in this. Sanders said, "I am perfectly prepared to be called a fool, but I am not a rogue. As I have learned to my cost, I am as much a fool in business as I expect the Board of Trade and the Bank of Scotland would be on stage." The Board of Trade report stated, "Sanders is materially responsible for the launching of this disastrous venture." One aspect supporting his culpability was that as early as July 1963, Sanders' wife Benita Hume refused to channel any more of her own money into CADCO. She later said, "Frankly I just didn't have any more money to play around with." Sanders said in conclusion, "I am totally financially ruined. I have lost £167,000, my wife has lost £47,000 and another £300,000 is still outstanding in guarantees. I have no choice but to go bankrupt. I find it hard to believe I would have conspired to make myself bankrupt."

There was no shortage of film roles during the sixties during which he shot movies in quick succession in a variety of different locations around the world. In some he played the lead, while in others he was a supporting player. He costarred with a number of British television comedians who made some bumbling attempts to become cinema stars.

In late 1966 he received an offer to play the lead in a Broadway bound musical called simply *Sherry!* It was derived from the celebrated comedy play *The Man Who Came to Dinner* by George S. Kaufman and Moss Hart. Sanders played the waspish critic Sheridan Whiteside. Sanders played Whiteside in the Boston tryouts only and was lambasted by the critics. He was forced to relinquish the part when Benita Hume became seriously ill with cancer and subsequently died at Weems Farm, Kent, England on November 1, 1967. The musical did go to Broadway where it soon folded.

In 1969 he suffered a stroke followed by a series of smaller stokes. He did make progress towards a recovery, but was forced to turn down a number of film roles because his health simply was not up to it. His illness rendered him unable to play the piano which was his chief form of relaxation. He was living in Majorca where he devised a television series with a light work load to star himself to be shot in England. It was later abandoned when a tax levy made it uneconomic.

After Benita Hume's death he lived off and on with divorced Mexican actress Lorraine Chanel, whom he met while playing a drug dealer in the vile *The Candy Man* (1969) in Mexico. She was a good influence on his life, but they nevertheless parted company. The only film amongst his later ones to find wide public acceptance was one in which he did not actually appear. He voiced Shere-Khan, the tiger, in the Walt Disney cartoon *The Jungle Book* (1967). *The Kremlin Letter* (1970) was his last big budget film, but he was embarrassed to be playing "The Warlock," a transvestite agent. His last batch of films were low budget British efforts of very little merit. He did talk of retirement, but his agent did not want him to retire since he was one actor whom his agent had no difficulty finding work for. His standard fee for a film in the sixties was $50,000. His fourth marriage was to Magda Gabor, sister of Zsa Zsa, on December 4, 1970 in Indio, California. Regretting his impetuosity almost immediately, he walked out on the marriage which was annulled in mid–January 1971.

George Sanders, who hosted *George Sanders Mystery Theater.*

While shooting a film in London in 1970, he stayed with writer Helga Moray. She later lived with him at times between 1970 and 1972, but was not a good influence on his life. She liked to drink and encouraged him to do so, despite his illness. She also persuaded him to sell his beloved home in Majorca which left him without roots. He suffered from serious depression exacerbated by his excessive drinking and dependency on pills. Afterwards he lived in hotels and with Helga Moray in her London flat.

In 1972, seriously ill by this time, he went to visit his sister in England. He planned to share a small country estate with her, but also wanted to buy a villa near Barcelona to spend the winters. On April 23, 1972 he checked into a hotel at a seaside resort in Castelldefels, ten miles south of Barcelona. He went to bed the night of April 24 and asked to be woken early. When he did not respond to a morning call, the manager went to investigate. A civil guard spokesman said the hotel manager found the 65 year old actor's nude body sprawled on the floor of his room at lunch time. Five empty barbiturate containers were nearby. He had taken a fatal overdose of the drug Nembutal washed down with vodka. He left behind a note which read, "Dear World I am leaving because I am bored. I feel I have lived long enough. I am leaving you with your worries in this sweet cesspool. Good luck!" He left another note in which he stated he had enough money to pay for a funeral. He had about $9,000 in cash and checks in his hotel room. His body was cremated on May 4, 1972 and his ashes were scattered over the English Channel.

Filmography

1936: *The Man Who Could Work Miracles, Strange Cargo, Dishonor Bright, Find the Lady, The Outsider* (released 1939), *Things to Come, Lloyds of London.*
1937: *Love Is News, Slave Ship, Lancer Spy, The Lady Escapes.*
1938: *International Settlement, Four Men and a Prayer.*
1939: *Mr. Moto's Last Warning, The Saint Strikes Back, Confessions of a Nazi Spy, The Saint in London, Nurse Edith Cavell, Allegheny Uprising, So This Is London.*
1940: *Green Hell, The Saint's Double Trouble, The House of the Seven Gables, Rebecca, The Saint Takes Over, Foreign Correspondent, Bitter Sweet, The Son of Monte Cristo.*
1941: *The Saint in Palm Springs, Rage in Heaven, Man Hunt, The Gay Falcon, Sundown, A Date with the Falcon.*
1942: *Son of Fury, The Falcon Takes Over, Her Cardboard Lover, Tales of Manhattan, The Moon and Sixpence, The Falcon's Brother, The Black Swan, Quiet Please Murder.*
1943: *This Land is Mine, They Came to Blow Up America, Appointment in Berlin, Paris After Dark.*
1944: *The Lodger, Action in Arabia, Summer Storm.*
1945: *Hangover Square, The Picture of Dorian Gray, The Strange Affair of Uncle Harry.*
1946: *A Scandal in Paris, The Strange Woman.*
1947: *The Private Affairs of Bel Ami, The Ghost and Mrs. Muir, Lured* (a.k.a. *Personal Column*), *Forever Amber.*
1949: *The Fan, Samson and Delilah.*
1950: *All About Eve, Blackjack* (a.k.a. *Captain Blackjack*).
1951: *I Can Get It for You Wholesale, The Light Touch.*
1952: *Ivanhoe, Assignment—Paris!*
1953: *Call Me Madam.*
1954: *Witness to Murder, King Richard and the Crusaders, Journey to Italy* (a.k.a. *The Lonely Woman, Voyage to Italy, The Strangers*).
1955: *Moonfleet, The Scarlet Coat, The King's Thief, Jupiter's Darling.*
1956: *Never Say Goodbye, While the City Sleeps, That Certain Feeling, Death of a Scoundrel.*
1957: *The Seventh Sin.*
1958: *The Whole Truth, From the Earth to the Moon.*
1959: *That Kind of Woman, Solomon and Sheba, A Touch of Larceny.*
1960: *The Last Voyage, Bluebeard's Ten Honeymoons, Village of the Damned, Trouble in the Sky* (a.k.a. *Cone of Silence*).
1961: *The Rebel* (a.k.a. *Call Me Genius*), *Five Golden Hours.*
1962: *Operation Snatch, In Search of the Castaways.*
1963: *Cairo, The Cracksman, Ecco* (narrated only).
1964: *Dark Purpose, A Shot in the Dark, The Golden Head.*
1965: *The Amorous Adventures of Moll Flanders.*
1966: *The Quiller Memorandum, Trunk to Cairo.*
1967: *Warning Shot, Good Times, The Jungle Book* (voice only), *One Step to Hell* (a.k.a. *King of Africa*).
1968: *The Best House in London.*
1969: *The Candy Man, The Body Stealers.*
1970: *The Kremlin Letter, Rio 70.*
1971: *Endless Night, Doomwatch.*
1972: *Psychomania* (a.k.a. *The Death Wheelers*), *Night of the Assassin.*

Television Series

1957: *George Sanders Mystery Theatre* Host and narrator.

Sources

Barry, John. "Was George Sanders of CADCO Guilty?" *Sunday Times.* 1967.
Blumenfeld, Simon. "By George!" *The Stage.* May 21, 1998.
Daily Mail. August 17, 2002.
Daily Telegraph. "George Sanders Dead." April 26, 1972.
Daily Telegraph. Obituary, April 26, 1972.
Daily Telegraph. "Suicide Note Found by Film Actor's Body." April 26, 1972.
Donnelly, Paul. *Fade to Black.* London: Omnibus, 2000.
Houseman, Victoria. *Made in Heaven: Unscrambling the Marriages and Children of Hollywood Stars.* Chicago: Bonus, 1991.
Mank, Gregory William. *The Hollywood Hissables.* Metuchen, NJ: Scarecrow, 1989.
Parish, James Robert. *The Hollywood Death Book.* 1st ed. Las Vegas: Pioneer, 1991.

Perry, Jeb H. *Screen Gems: A History of Columbia Pictures Television, 1948–1983*. Metuchen, NJ: Scarecrow, 1991.
Picture Show Annual. London: Amalgamated, 1939, 1940, 1941, 1943, 1947, 1952 and 1956.
Quinlan, David. *Film Stars*. 5th ed. London: Batsford, 2000.
Reuter and British United Press Release. "Mr. Sanders Files for Bankruptcy." October 28, 1966.
Richards, Jeffrey. "The Last of the Classic Cads." *Sunday Telegraph*. November 1991.
Sanders, George. *Memoirs of a Professional Cad*. New York: Avon, 1960.
TV Times. "West End." November 18, 1962.
Vanderbeets, Richard. *George Sanders: An Exhausted Life*. London: Robson, 1990.
Winchester, Clarence. *Screen Encyclopedia*. London: Winchester, 1948.

GLORIA SAUNDERS

Gloria Saunders was born in Columbia, South Carolina on September 29, 1927. Her best remembered film role was as WAC Operator Sparky in the exciting thriller *O.S.S.* (1946). She was the radio operator who flirted with a spy via the wireless until he is found and killed by the Nazis.

On television she had semi-regular roles in two series in both of which she played Orientals. In *Mysteries of Chinatown* Marvin Miller played Dr. Yat Fu who owned a curio shop in San Francisco, but was also an amateur detective. Saunders played his niece Ah Toy who sometimes assisted him in his cases. Later in *Terry and the Pirates*, which derived from a comic strip, she played a villainess, "Dragon Lady." Her career came to a stop during the late fifties. She married twice and had a child.

Gloria Saunders died prematurely on June 4, 1980 aged 52.

FILMOGRAPHY

1945: *Out of This World*.
1946: *O.S.S.*
1951: *Cry Danger, Crazy over Horses, Northwest Territory*.
1952: *Red Snow, Captive Women* (a.k.a. *3,000 A.D.*).
1953: *The Robe, Prisoners of the Casbah*.

Gloria Saunders, who costarred in *Mysteries of Chinatown*.

TELEVISION SERIES

1949–1950: *Mysteries of Chinatown* as Ah Toy.
1952: *Terry and the Pirates* as Lai Choi San, "Dragon Lady."

SOURCES

Erickson, Hal. *Syndicated Television: The First Forty Years, 1947–1987*. Jefferson, NC: McFarland, 1989.
Tibballs, Geoff. *TV Detectives*. London: Boxtree, 1980.

NICHOLAS SAUNDERS

Nicholas Saunders was born Nikita Soussanin in Kiev, Russia on June 2, 1914 the son of Nicholas Soussanin (1889–1975) and Suzanne Stormier. His father was an actor in Russia and later in Hollywood. He graduated from Hollywood High School and trained for the stage with various Russian teachers. He became an actor, writer, dialect coach and stage manager. He made his Broadway debut in *Lady in the Dark* in 1943. He became a very busy stage actor in Broadway plays, off Broadway plays and on tour in a career which lasted for nearly fifty years.

He made his television debut in 1947. In the

crime series *Martin Kane Private Eye* he played Det. Sgt. Ross for two seasons. He had the recurring role of Captain Barker in *The Phil Silvers Show*. On radio he was a Russian language announcer for the Voice of America and Radio Liberty. He married Gedda Petry an actress on October 22, 1938 and has a daughter named Lanna who became an actress and a son named Theodore who became a jazz pianist. At last report he was continuing to reside in New York.

Filmography

1964: *Fail Safe*.
1971: *Bananas*.
1976: *The Next Man*.
1978: *Paradise Alley*.
1981: *Arthur*.
1983: *Daniel*.

Television Series

1950–1952: *Martin Kane Private Eye* as Det. Sgt. Ross.
1955–1959: *The Phil Silvers Show* as Captain Barker.

Sources

Brooks, Tim. *The Complete Directory to Prime Time TV Stars, 1946–Present*. New York: Ballantine, 1987.
Contemporary Theatre, Film and Television. Vols. 1 and 6. Detroit: Gale Research, 1984 and 1989.
Ragan, David. *Who's Who in Hollywood*. New York: Facts on File, 1991.

Simon Scott

Simon Scott was born Daniel Dale Simon in Monterey Park, California on September 21, 1920. He joined the Peninsula Players, a summer stock company in Fishcreek, Wisconsin in 1940 as an actor and stagehand. He returned there periodically to perform. During World War II he served with the U.S. Coast Guard. Afterwards he went to New York and toured with the Margaret Webster Shakespeare Company.

He began making film and television appearances during the 1950s. In the early episodes of the crime series *Markham*, Roy Markham (Ray Milland) had a leg man who traveled with him and made most of the arrangements. This man was called John Riggs and was played by Simon Scott. Within a couple of months of the series beginning, Riggs was gone and Markham made all his own plans. Scott became a prolific supporting player on television where he usually played authority figures. His best remembered television role was as General Arnold Slocum, the hospital administrator, in the television series *Trapper John M.D.* which he played in for six years.

When the series went off the air, Scott retired. Shortly afterwards he was diagnosed with Alzheimer's disease. After 1988 he resided at the John Douglas French Center for Alzheimer's disease. He died at Los Alamitos, California on December 11, 1991 aged 71 of the disease. He was survived by his brother and sister.

Filmography

1954: *The Raid, Black Tuesday*.
1956: *I've Lived Before, Accused of Murder*.
1957: *Battle Hymn, Man of a Thousand Faces*.
1959: *No Name on the Bullet, Compulsion*.
1961: *The Honeymoon Machine*.
1962: *Moon Pilot, The Couch*.
1963: *The Ugly American*.
1964: *Father Goose*.
1965: *Strange Bedfellows*.
1966: *Dead Heat on a Merry-Go-Round*.
1968: *In Enemy Country*.
1971: *Cold Turkey*.
1972: *Welcome Home Johnny Bristol* (TV), *The Man*.
1974: *The Disappearance of Flight 412* (TV).
1975: *Barbary Coast* (TV), *The Hindenburg*.
1977: *Tail Gunner Joe* (TV), *Twilight's Last Gleaming*.
1979: *Return of the Mod Squad* (TV).

Television Series

1959: *Markham* as John Riggs.
1963: *General Hospital* as Fred Fleming.
1965–1966: *McHale's Navy* as General Bronson.
1979–1985: *Trapper John M.D.* as General Arnold Slocum.

Miniseries

1976: *Once an Eagle*.

Sources

Brooks, Tim. *The Complete Directory to Prime Time TV Stars, 1946–Present*. New York: Ballantine, 1987.
Variety. Obituary, December 23, 1991.
Ward, Jack. *Television Guest Stars*. Jefferson, NC: McFarland, 1993.

SYDNA SCOTT

Sydna Scott was born Sydna Scott Mac-Fetridge either in Chicago or Evanston, Illinois on June 12, 1914. Between 1944 and 1950 she was primarily a stage actress appearing in several plays. She also made over 1,000 radio broadcasts. She married actor Jerome Thor. She and her husband starred in the first format of the early television series *Foreign Intrigue*. Thor played Robert Cannon, a European correspondent for an American wire service, whose assignments took him into danger all over Europe although Stockholm was his base of operations. Scott played his rival, reporter Helen Davis.

Sydna Scott died in a Los Angeles hospital on June 23, 1996 aged 82 of cancer.

FILMOGRAPHY

1964: *Circus World*.
1965: *Crack in the World*.
1966: *Scalplock* (TV).
1975: *Mr. Sycamore*.
1983: *10 to Midnight*.
1985: *Avenging Angel*.
1988: *Scrooged, Messenger of Death*.

TELEVISION SERIES

1951–1953: *Foreign Intrigue* as Helen Davis.

SOURCES

Erickson, Hal. *Syndicated Television: The First Forty Years, 1947–1987*. Jefferson, NC: McFarland, 1989.
Lentz, Harris M. III. *Obituaries in the Performing Arts, 1996*. Jefferson, NC: McFarland, 1997.

BRUCE SETON

Actors come from all walks of life, but Bruce Seton was unusual in one respect. He was virtually the only star of a crime or mystery series during the 1950s who in real life inherited a title. He became the 11th Baronet of Abercorn, a title which was created in 1663. His most memorable contribution to show business was playing the role of Robert Fabian in the BBC television series *Fabian of the Yard*.

Bruce Lovat Seton was born in Simla, India on May 29, 1909, the son of Sir Bruce Gordon Seton (1868–1932), the 9th Baronet of Abercorn, C.B., and his wife Ellen Mary Armstrong who died in 1960. His father was a serving soldier. He was educated at Edinburgh Academy and Sandhurst. Beginning his career as a soldier, he was commissioned in the Black Watch, but resigned in 1932. Switching to show business, he became a dancer in the Drury Lane Theater chorus. As part of a specialty dance act with Betty Astell, he broke into films initially in musicals, but later as the hero of straight dramas.

During the Second World War he rejoined the Army, retiring as a major in the Cameronians (Scottish Rifles). He was awarded the U.S. Medal of Freedom in 1945. In post-war films however he was relegated to supporting roles. Anthony Beauchamp was once well known as one of the leading Society photographers in Britain and the USA and as a husband of Sarah Churchill, the drunken daughter of Winston. Beauchamp committed suicide in 1958. He became a television producer with a series called *Fabian of the Yard*, based on the real life adventures of Inspector Robert Fabian, the famous Scotland Yard detective. John Larkin also produced some episodes. On the strength of his radio characterization of Flint in *Flint of the Flying Squad*, Seton was cast in the lead.

Left to right: **Alfred Travers (director), Anthony Beauchamp (producer), Kieron Moore (guest), Pascale Petit (guest) and Bruce Seton on location in *Fabian of the Yard*.**

There were 39 half hour, black and white episodes shot at Carlton Hill studios and on location. Investigating major crimes, Fabian was an advocate of forensic science and modern methods as an aid to capturing criminals. He was courteous with a clipped delivery. The real Fabian made brief appearances in the series to provide either an introduction or an epilogue. The series was shown on CBS in America under the titles of *Patrol Car* and *Fabian of Scotland Yard*. Seton was earning £100 a week during the time when the series was being made. Episodes of the series were later edited into two feature films called *Fabian of the Yard* and *Handcuffs London*. It was a Trinity Production Limited and the special theme music was by Eric Spear. After the highly successful show ended, Seton found he had become deeply identified in the public mind with the Fabian character and producers were reluctant to cast him in other roles.

In 1962 he had one of his lungs removed and was also declared bankrupt. He became the eleventh baronet of his line in 1963, succeeding his brother, Sir Alexander Hay Seton (1904–1963). He never used his hereditary title in show business and there was little money attached to it. In 1963 he was granted his discharge from bankruptcy and devoted himself to new enterprises such as writing a serial for a boys' magazine and organizing entertainments for RAF men. His hobbies were listed as playing the bagpipes and composing pipe music.

Seton died at his home in London, England on September 27, 1969 aged 60 of lung cancer. He married the Russian born actress Tamara Desni in 1937 whom he divorced in 1940. In 1940 he wed actress Antoinette Cellier who survived him and with whom he had a daughter. His widow died in January 1981 aged 67. The title passed to his cousin Christopher Bruce Seton.

Filmography

1935: *Blue Smoke, Flame in the Heather, The Shadow of Mike Emerald, Sweeney Todd the Demon Barber of Fleet Street, The Vandergilt Diamond Mystery.*
1936: *Melody of My Heart, Wedding Group, Jack of All Trades, The Man Who Changed His Mind, Annie Laurie, The End of the Road, Cafe Colette, Love from a Stranger.*
1937: *Racing Romance, Song of the Road, Fifty Shilling Boxer, Father Steps Out, The Green Cockatoo.*
1938: *If I Were Boss, Weddings are Wonderful, You're the Doctor, Miracles Do Happen.*
1939: *Old Mother Riley Joins Up, The Middle Watch, Lucky To Me.*
1946: *The Curse of the Wraydons.*
1948: *The Story of Shirley Yorke, Scott of the Antarctic, Look Before You Love, Whisky Galore!, Bonnie Prince Charlie, Bond Street.*
1949: *The Blue Lamp.*
1950: *Portrait of Clare, Paul Temple's Triumph, Take Me to Paris, Blackmailed, Seven Days to Noon.*
1951: *White Corridors, High Treason, Worm's Eye View.*
1952: *The Second Mrs. Tanqueray, Emergency Call, Rough Shoot.*
1953: *The Cruel Sea.*
1954: *Doctor in the House, Eight O'Clock Walk, Delayed Action, Fabian of the Yard.*
1955: *Man of the Moment, Handcuffs London.*
1956: *Breakaway, West of Suez.*
1957: *There's Always a Thursday, Morning Call, The Crooked Sky, Zoo Baby, Undercover Girl.*
1958: *Violent Moment, Hidden Homicide.*
1959: *Make Mine A Million, John Paul Jones, Life in Danger, Strictly Confidential, Operation Cupid, Trouble With Eve.*
1960: *The League of Gentlemen, Carry On Constable, Just Joe, Greyfriars Bobby.*
1961: *The Frightened City, Gorgo, Freedom to Die, The Valiant.*
1962: *Ambush in Leopard Street, Dead Man's Evidence, The Prince and the Pauper, The Pot Carriers.*
1963: *Dr. Syn Alias the Scarecrow.*
1965: *The Legend of Young Dick Turpin.*

Television Series

1954–1956: *Fabian of the Yard* as Inspector Robert Fabian.
1956: Shown in the USA as *Patrol Car* and *Fabian of Scotland Yard.*

Sources

Daily Telegraph. Obituary, Sept. 28, 1969.
Picture Show Annual. London: Amalgamated, 1939.
Quinlan, David. *Illustrated Directory of Film Character Actors.* 2nd ed. London: Batsford, 1995.
Speed, F. Maurice. *Film Review, 1953–1954.* London: MacDonald, 1953.
Truitt, Evelyn Mack. *Who Was Who on Screen.* 2nd ed. New York: Bowker, 1984.
Vahimagi, Tise. *British Television: BFI Illustrated Guide.* Oxford: Oxford University Press, 1994.

Who Was Who, 1961–1970 London: Adam and Charles Black, 1972.

MICHAEL SHEPLEY

Michael Shepley was born Arthur Michael Shepley-Smith at Plymouth, Devon on September 29 (St. Michael's Day), 1907. His parents were Stancliffe Shepley-Smith and Edith Mary Horn. His father was a clergyman who lived to be 85, while his mother lived to be in her nineties. He was educated at Westminster School where the twin passions of his life, cricket and acting, took hold. He was captain of the school cricket team. He reckoned he owed his acting career to his prowess at cricket together with the friends he made through it.

His acting career began at Oriel College, Oxford where he was reading history. He was about to take his degree when an old school chum, Jevan Brandon Thomas, offered him the role of Charley Wyckham in *Charley's Aunt*. Shepley and Thomas had been members of the same cricket team at Westminster School and Thomas's father, Brandon Thomas, had written the original play. At the age of twenty when Shepley should have been studying for his exams, he made his professional stage debut at the Grand Theater, Hull on July 24, 1927 in *Charley's Aunt* subsequently touring Canada in it for four months.

Back in England he made his West End debut at Wyndham's Theater on July 4, 1928 as Clerk of the Court in *Justice* by John Galsworthy. He appeared in other plays by Galsworthy notably *Exiled* at Wyndham's in June 1929 in which the playwright wrote the part of the Journalist especially for him. Shepley went to New York where he made his Broadway debut in *The Middle Watch* at the Times Square Theater on October 15, 1929 as Commander Baddeley. His theatrical career continued uninterrupted until 1940 except for a period of eighteen months in 1934–1935 when he temporarily abandoned the stage to concentrate on films.

From 1940 to 1941 he served in the Police Reserve, but then returned to the theater. By 1945 he had become one of the top supporting actors on the West End stage. His success continued unabated after World War II. A big post war hit was *Lady Windermere's Fan* as Lord Augustus Lorton at the Haymarket from August 1945 in which he played for over a year. His theatrical

Michael Shepley, who costarred in *Dick and the Duchess*.

career however probably reached its peak when he appeared at the Vaudeville from August 1947 to 1949 as Beecham, the butler, in *The Chiltern Hundreds* which ran to over 600 performances.

He made a reputation for himself in films and on television. He acted in some of the first B.B.C. television plays broadcast from Alexandra Palace in London. With Heather Thatcher he acted in *Family Affairs*, the first family television serial made in England. The type of role in which he appeared most frequently was as an amiable bumbler or best friend of the hero. Sometimes he was effectively cast in more serious roles. Unlike most actors he was never unemployed. For many years he lived in Chiswick, London.

Perhaps surprisingly he played quite a number of police officers both on stage and screen. One of these was the hybrid comedy crime television series *Dick and the Duchess* in which he played Det. Insp. Stark, the police contact of insurance investigator Dick Starrett (Patrick O'Neal) and his wife Jane (Hazel Court). Court recently recalled of Shepley, "He was a very pleasant man to work with."

Shepley's virtually unbroken chain of success continued in films, television and particularly the stage until he returned to England after a tour of Australia in *The Amorous Prawn* in 1961 when he became seriously ill. An inveterate pipe smoker, he died at the Royal Marsden Hospital, Chelsea, London on September 28, 1961 of bronchopneumonia and cancer of the larynx, one day before his 54th birthday. He was married to Patricia Stock, daughter of legendary beauty and model Eva Carrington "The Gibson Girl," who was his closest surviving relative.

Filmography

1931: *Black Coffee.*
1933: *A Shot in the Dark.*
1934: *Are You a Mason?, Bella Donna, Tangled Evidence, Lord Edgware Dies, The Green Pack, Open All Night.*
1935: *Lazybones, Vintage Wine, The Rocks of Valpré* (a.k.a. *High Treason*), *The Ace of Spades, Squibs, Jubilee Window, Private Secretary, The Triumph of Sherlock Holmes, That's My Uncle.*
1936: *Dishonor Bright, In the Soup.*
1937: *Beauty and the Barge.*
1938: *Crackerjack* (a.k.a. *The Man With a Hundred Faces*), *Housemaster, It's in the Air* (a.k.a. *George Takes the Air*).
1939: *Goodbye Mr. Chips.*
1940: *Contraband* (a.k.a. *Blackout*).
1941: *Quiet Wedding.*
1942: *The Great Mr. Handel, Women Aren't Angels.*
1943: *The Demi-Paradise* (a.k.a. *Adventure for Two*).
1944: *Henry V.*
1945: *A Place of One's Own, I Live in Grosvenor Square* (a.k.a. *A Yank in London*).
1947: *Mine Own Executioner, Nicholas Nickleby.*
1949: *Helter Skelter, Maytime in Mayfair, Elizabeth of Ladymead.*
1951: *Mr. Denning Drives North, Secret People.*
1952: *Home at Seven* (a.k.a. *Murder on Monday*).
1953: *You Know What Sailors Are.*
1954: *Trouble in the Glen, Happy Ever After* (a.k.a. *Tonight's the Night*), *Out of the Clouds.*
1955: *Where There's a Will, An Alligator Named Daisy, Doctor at Sea.*
1956: *My Teenage Daughter* (a.k.a. *Teenage Bad Girl*), *Dry Rot, The Passionate Stranger.*
1957: *Not Wanted on Voyage.*
1958: *Gideon's Day* (a.k.a. *Gideon of Scotland Yard*).
1960: *Just Joe.*
1961: *Don't Bother to Knock* (a.k.a. *Why Bother to Knock?*), *Double Bunk.*

Television Series

US (1957–1958): *Dick and the Duchess* as Detective Inspector Stark.
UK (1959–1960)

Sources

Bartley, C.L. "Michael Shepley: The Friendly Actor." *TV Times*. May 25, 1956.
Death Certificate.
McFarlane, Brian. *The Encyclopedia of British Film*. London: BFI Methuen, 2003.
Noble, Peter. *The British Film Yearbook, 1947–1948*. London: Skelton Robinson British Yearbooks, 1948.
Picturegoer. "British Film and TV Who's Who Part 9." November 21, 1953.
Quinlan, David. *Illustrated Directory of Character Actors*. 2nd ed. London: Batsford, 1995.
Tibballs, Geoff. *TV Detectives*. London: Boxtree, 1992.
Who's Who in the Theatre. 13th ed. London: Pitman, 1961.

Louis Sirgo

Louis Sirgo was born in Louisiana on February 27, 1924. He was a real life serving police officer with the rank of Captain. He was cast as Det. Lt. John Conroy, the crime busting partner of Det. Lt. Vic Beaujac (Stacy Harris) in the series *N.O.P.D.* and the two feature film spin-offs. He obtained special leave of absence from his regular duties to undertake this role which was intended to establish Louisiana and New Orleans as a desirable place for film and television production.

Once the series was over Sirgo resumed his police duties. A popular and diligent officer, he eventually attained the rank of Deputy Police Superintendent, but was tragically shot down and killed at the head of his men while trying to apprehend a terrorist sniper in New Orleans on January 7, 1973 aged 48. He was survived by his widow, Joyce, and two daughters.

Filmography

1958: *New Orleans After Dark.*
1962: *Four for the Morgue.*

Television Series

1956: *N.O.P.D.* (a.k.a. *New Orleans Police Department*) as Det. Lt. John Conroy.

Sources

Martin, Len D. *The Allied Artists Check List.* Jefferson, NC: McFarland, 1993.
Tibballs, Geoff. *TV Detectives.* London: Boxtree, 1993.

EVERETT SLOANE

"As a business proposition radio is sound and occasionally satisfying. The theater is ego satisfying, but otherwise unreliable; the movies are a lump of money." So spoke Everett Sloane in 1944. He was once described as a "diminutive dynamo with a voice that can squeak or boom." It would have been interesting to know his verdict on television, a medium in which he spent a great deal of time during the last decade of his career. Temperamentally off screen he found it difficult to relax and was intellectually and artistically impatient.

Everett H. Sloane was born in New York City on October 1, 1909 the son of Nathaniel I. Sloane who came from New York and Rose Gerstein who was born in Boston. When he was seven his first role was as Puck in a school production of *A Midsummer Night's Dream*. He was stage struck as a child and persuaded his father to take him to the theater every Saturday afternoon. He was educated at Public School 46 in Manhattan and Townsend Harris Hall High School in New York. He enrolled at the University of Pennsylvania in Philadelphia, but dropped out in 1927 to join a stock company at the Hedgerow Theater in Moylan, Pennsylvania. He made his first appearance in New York in an off Broadway play in 1928.

Despite good reviews, he failed to secure other roles so he became a stockbroker's runner on Wall Street at a salary of $17 a week. His salary rose to $140 a week when he was promoted to partner's assistant within twelve months. As with so many others a serious downturn in his fortunes came with the stock market crash in 1929 which reduced his salary by 50%. To help him survive a script writer friend arranged for him to be hired as the hero's assistant in a radio show at $20 a broadcast. Other engagements followed at such a rapid rate that he was able to quit his job on Wall Street.

Throughout the thirties he was heard on a variety of radio shows usually at least once a night mainly of the soap opera or crime variety. He made his Broadway bow as Rosetti in *Boy Meets Girl* which opened at the Cort Theater, New York on November 27, 1935 and lasted for 669 performances. He made other Broadway appearances and toured during the thirties. He joined the *Mercury Theater of the Air* in 1938, a radio series devised and presented by Orson Welles. As such Sloane was a member of the original cast of the broadcast of *War of the Worlds*. This panicked America because it was so realistic that many listeners thought Martians were genuinely landing on Earth.

Since he was a member of the Mercury Players, he went to Hollywood where he made his screen debut as Bernstein, the general manager of Charles Foster Kane's (Orson Welles) publishing empire in *Citizen Kane* (1941). He followed this up with a memorable supporting role as Kopeikin in *Journey into Fear* (1942), a tense thriller which described itself as "A Mercury Theater Production," but was directed by Norman Foster. By the time these films were being shown, Sloane was back on Broadway and radio.

Between 1942 and 1948 he appeared in Broadway plays enjoying his greatest success as Sergeant Leonard Booth in *A Bell for Adano* which opened at the Cort Theater on December 6, 1944 and lasted for 304 performances. He later directed a couple of stage productions. Simultaneously he was making numerous radio broadcasts. He once estimated that in his first fifteen years on radio, he appeared in an average of 20 programs a week, playing 15,000 different parts including Winston Churchill and Adolf Hitler. He played Hitler over 100 times which was more than any other actor. In a good season, he earned $50,000 from radio.

He relocated to Hollywood in the late forties where he played Arthur Bannister, the world's greatest criminal lawyer and crippled husband of Rita Hayworth, in the film noir *The Lady from Shanghai* (1948). This was another of Orson Welles' productions with a classic shoot-out in a hall of mirrors. Sloane's personal favorite of his screen roles was allegedly Mario Belli in *Prince of Foxes* (1949) again with Orson Welles. Until 1952 Sloane played in several movies in diverse characterizations which earned him good notices. Of these his role as Albert Mendoza, the head of a murder for payment organization, in *The Enforcer* (1951) was outstanding.

During the fifties Sloane entered television which gave him plenty of opportunities. He made his television debut in the "Vincent Van

Everett Sloane, who hosted *Official Detective*.

Gogh" episode of *Philco TV Playhouse* in 1950. During the years 1953 and 1954 he made only a few television appearances and no films. He was however active on radio as Captain Frank Kennelly on the radio program *21st Precinct*, a role which he relinquished in October 1955. Of his many television roles, the best remembered was as Walter Ramsey, the business tycoon driven solely by his desire for profits, in *Patterns*. This was written by Rod Serling and originally shown on *Kraft Television Theater* on NBC on January 12, 1955. It earned Sloane glowing notices and recognition came in an Emmy award nomination as "Best Actor—Single Performance" in 1955. He repeated the role in the film version in 1956. He directed and wrote occasional scripts for television and supplied the voice of many cartoon characters.

Official Detective was a Desilu/NTA series of 39 episodes which was syndicated in 1957. It derived from a radio series which dramatized true stories from the files of *Official Detective* magazine. The television series was a slow starter in the ratings which gradually gathered momentum as a result of a highly successful promotional campaign with Sloane at the forefront. He served as host, narrator and occasional star of the series.

The series covered a wide range of subjects and featured several different law enforcement agencies in varied places. It was vetted for accuracy by the magazine researchers and diverse technical advisers were present on the set to ensure authenticity.

Sloane's final two film roles were in Jerry Lewis comedies, a genre which Sloane was not normally associated with, but in which he acquitted himself well. Apparently despondent over his encroaching blindness, Sloane committed suicide at his Brentwood, California home by taking an overdose of sleeping pills on August 6, 1965 aged 55. His final television appearance was in the "In the Bag" episode of *Honey West* on November 5, 1965 which was aired posthumously. He was survived by his widow Luba Herman, whom he wed in 1933, a son named Nathaniel and a daughter named Erika. He is buried at Rosedale Memorial Park, Los Angeles.

FILMOGRAPHY

1941: *Citizen Kane*.
1942: *Journey into Fear*.
1943: *We Accuse* (narrator only).
1948: *The Lady from Shanghai*.
1949: *Prince of Foxes, Jigsaw*.
1950: *The Man*.
1951: *Sirocco, The Sellout, The Prince Who Was a Thief, The Enforcer* (a.k.a. *Murder Inc.*), *The Desert Fox, The Blue Veil, Bird of Paradise*.
1952: *Way of a Gaucho*.
1955: *The Big Knife*.
1956: *Somebody Up There Likes Me, Patterns, Lust for Life*.
1958: *Marjorie Morningstar, The Gun Runners*.
1960: *Home from the Hill*.
1961: *By Love Possessed*.
1962: *Brushfire!*
1963: *The Man from the Diner's Club*.
1964: *Ready for the People* (TV), *Hercules and the Princess of Troy, The Patsy, The Disorderly Orderly*.

TELEVISION SERIES

1957: *Official Detective* Host and narrator.

SOURCES

Anger, Kenneth. *Hollywood Babylon II*. London: Arrow, 1986.
Current Biography. New York: H. Wilson, 1957.
DeLong, Thomas A. *Radio Stars*. Jefferson, NC: McFarland, 1996.
Erickson, Hal. *Syndicated Television: The First*

Forty Years, 1947–1987. Jefferson, NC: McFarland, 1989.
Inman, David. *The TV Encyclopedia.* New York: Perigee, 1991.
The International Dictionary of Films and Filmmakers: Actors and Actresses. Vol. III. Chicago: St. James, 1986.
Parish, James Robert. *Hollywood Character Actors.* New Rochelle, NY: Arlington House, 1978.
Quinlan, David. *Illustrated Directory of Film Character Actors.* 2nd ed. London: Batsford, 1995.
Roberts, John. "Everett Sloane—Multi-Media Actor." *Classic Images.* Vol. 321. March 2002.
Speed, F. Maurice. *Film Review, 1966–1968.* London: W.H. Allen, 1967.
Tibballs, Geoff. *TV Detectives.* London: Boxtree, 1992.
Twomey, Alfred E., and Arthur F. McClure. *The Versatiles.* South Brunswick, 1969.
Variety. Obituary, August 18, 1965.
Ward, Jack. *Television Guest Stars.* Jefferson, NC: McFarland, 1993.

ARCHIE SMITH

Archie Smith was born in Richmond, Virginia May 10, 1918. He taught at Penn State before going to Broadway where he made his debut in *The Madwoman of Chaillot* in December 1948 which ran until January 1950. In the early crime series *Crime Photographer*, which lasted a year, he played the reporter Jack Lipman who wrote the copy to go with the exciting photographs that "Flash" Casey (Darren McGavin) took. Smith's final Broadway appearance was in *The Andersonville Trial* which lasted between December 1959 and June 1960. During the 1970s he was a member of Seattle Repertory Company and in 1983 joined the Denver Center Theater Company with whom he appeared in many productions. He died at his home in Denver, Colorado on June 8, 2004 aged 86 of Parkinson's disease. He was married to actress Kay Doubleday (1936–1995), with whom he had two children.

FILMOGRAPHY

1965: *Across the River, The Slender Thread.*
1986: *Manhunt for Claude Dallas* (TV).
1987: *Prison for Children* (TV).
1991: *Conagher* (TV).
1992: *Perry Mason: The Case of the Fatal Framing* (TV).
1995: *Things to Do in Denver When You're Dead.*
1997: *Asteroid* (TV).
1998: *Strangeland.*

TELEVISION SERIES

1951–1952: *Crime Photographer* as Jack Lipman.

SOURCES

Lentz, Harris M. III. *Obituaries in the Performing Arts, 2004.* Jefferson, NC: McFarland, 2005.
Tibballs, Geoff. *TV Detectives.* London: Boxtree, 1992.

ROGER SMITH

Roger Smith was an actor who was made and broken by television. On the big screen his charisma did not come across well. On the small screen however he was most impressive. In an episode of *Wagon Train* in 1958 he played a young doctor who was having a confrontation with actor Charles Bickford. Bickford was an older, much more experienced actor who in theory should have buried Smith. Instead Smith held his own in the scenes they shared. He enjoyed great success as the private investigator Jeff Spencer in *77 Sunset Strip.* Once this series was over, his own star dimmed rapidly. Relative to his ability, he probably had the least successful post series career of any Warner Bros. television contract player. He was not the luckiest of actors physically being both accident prone and later plagued by ill health. Indeed by this time he would probably be a distant memory except for his high profile wife, Ann-Margret. He also had a considerable musical talent which was used very well from time to time on *77 Sunset Strip.* As Efrem Zimbalist once expressed it, "He was never the greatest singer in the world, but I'd like you to produce a better guitar player than Roger."

Roger Smith was born in the South Gate area of Los Angeles on December 18, 1932, the son of Dallas and Leone Smith. His father was a clothing manufacturer. By 1938 he was taking singing, tap dancing and elocution lessons. At seven he became one of the Meglin Kiddies and was soon appearing in shows which raised money for war bonds. In 1945 he moved with his family to Nogales, Arizona, a small town on the Mexican border. He was the only American child in a Mexican neighborhood and as such was frequently involved in fistfights. While being educated at Nogales high school, he appeared in every play being staged there and became president of the school's acting club. He was the star linebacker on the high school football team. Between 1950 and 1954 while attending the University of Arizona, in Tucson, on a football athletic scholarship, he won several talent competitions as a singer and guitarist. He and his pal Travis Edmonson won the university's talent show on the strength of which they appeared on television in *Amateur Hour* hosted by Ted Mack.

During two and a half years active service in the Naval Reserve, he continued to sing and strum at various functions. While stationed in Hawaii, he met James Cagney in 1955 who was shooting *Mr. Roberts* there. Although he once upbraided Smith for watching *Citizen Kane* on television on a fine day instead of being outside enjoying the fresh air, Cagney became a lifelong friend who persuaded Smith he might have a career as an actor. Once his naval stint was over in March 1955 he relocated to Hollywood determined to become a professional actor. He gave himself a limited amount of time to succeed. His deadline was virtually up when a talent scout from Warners gave him a chance to read. The result was sufficiently good for him to be put in a drama class. A girl in the class had an audition at Columbia. She asked him to read the scene at the audition with her. The fate of the girl is unknown, but the studio signed him. On July 28, 1956 he wed the beautiful former model turned movie star, Victoria Shaw. "She proposed to me!" he recalled. "I was afraid to ask her—she was a star and I was a nobody."

Victoria Shaw was born Jeanette Elphick in Sydney, Australia on May 25, 1935. She made her screen debut in her native country in the film *The Phantom Stockman* (1953) under her real name. She emigrated to America where she became a star at Columbia Pictures under the name of Victoria Shaw. Smith met her at an acting class. They were assigned a beach scene together so he suggested that they rehearse on the beach. She agreed, but somehow they ended up at Disneyland. At the time of their wedding she was shooting her best remembered film role in *The Eddy Duchin Story* (1956) as Chiquita. Together they had three children: a daughter Tracey who was born in July 3, 1957, a son Jordan who was born in October 4, 1958 and another daughter Dallas who was born on December 23, 1961.

He made his screen debut in *No Time to be Young* (1957) and made two other films for the studio before being dropped. He also played a small recurring role in the television sitcom *Father Knows Best* which was produced by the Columbia television subsidiary Screen Gems. After a few months fruitless quest, he managed to re-establish contact with James Cagney who became his mentor. Cagney recommended Smith to Universal to play the role of Lon Chaney, Jr., in the biopic *Man of a Thousand Faces* (1957) with Cagney playing Lon Chaney, Sr. On the strength of his performance in this, Warner Bros. signed Smith to a contract. In 1958 he was asked by director Morton Da Costa to play the older Patrick Dennis in *Auntie Mame* (1958) with Rosalind Russell in the title role. In 1959 Cagney persuaded Warner Bros. to loan Smith to Universal to costar with him in *Never Steal Anything Small*.

Warner Bros. was looking for a personable young actor to play the role of Jeff Spencer, the partner of Stuart Bailey (Efrem Zimbalist, Jr.) in the hour length, private eye series *77 Sunset Strip*. When Roy Huggins created *Maverick*, he discovered that it was impossible for one actor to carry the burden of shooting an hour length show each week, so he introduced another leading character. Warners remembered this when they came to shoot *77 Sunset Strip* and they created the character of Jeff Spencer which meant the leads could alternate each week. Jeff Spencer came from a Midwest farming family. He worked his way through college and law school and then joined the FBI as an undercover agent. After two years of working on one case, the FBI could obtain a conviction only by using Spencer's testimony in open court. Spencer's value as an undercover agent was therefore nullified. The FBI offered him a desk job, but this was not to his liking. Instead he went to the West Coast, met Stuart Bailey and became his partner. Smith had some genuine misgivings about accepting the role because he felt that he looked more like the "All-American Boy" and not at all like a typical private eye. When he found out that the majority of real life plainclothes detectives were aged between 23 and 28 and did not look like investigators, his confidence grew.

At first Smith proved to be much less popular than either of his costars Efrem Zimbalist, Jr., and Edd Byrnes and was in danger of being dropped until he loosened up whereupon fan mail deluged in. Although there were three stars in the series, they were an extremely harmonious combination of personalities. It once reached a point when Zimbalist and Smith were unable to shoot a scene together without breaking into laughter. An indication of Smith's popularity was that when he made a promotional tour by bus to thirty United States cities in 1959, he was mobbed everywhere he went. In 1959 he tripped over a flowerpot and fell while carrying a hi-fi set. He had to have an operation to alleviate a blood clot on his brain. The operation was a success. He had a little trouble with some words when he became tired, but it was the only after-effect and disappeared after a few weeks.

He was scathing about the quality of some episodes of *77 Sunset Strip* so he wrote seven scripts himself. The best remembered was "The Silent Caper" originally aired on June 3, 1960 which involved a stripper named Jingle Bells who is kidnapped by gangsters in order to prevent her testifying before a crime commission. What made this episode highly unusual was that it does not have one line of spoken dialogue. He scripted and appeared with his wife in "The Down Under Caper," originally aired on January 5, 1962, which was set in her native Australia. The studio verdict about the scripts which he wrote was that they were generally no worse, no better than most of the other writers' scripts. He also cut a couple of records during his tenure at the studio, but they were not particularly profitable. He appeared with immense success in the series for five seasons until 1963 when he and all the other regulars were dropped, with the exception of Zimbalist, who carried on alone for a further season until the demise of the series. The final episode with Jeff Spencer at the forefront was called "The Left Field Caper" involving a Little League Baseball team which originally aired on April 26, 1963.

Producers did not exactly rush to his door with offers of work. He toured in the play *Sunday in New York* and did a nightclub act singing and playing guitar in Milwaukee and later San Francisco. His film career reached its lowest ebb when he played a minor role of a detective in *For Those Who Think Young* (1964) in which he was even billed beneath George Raft! To all intents and purposes he was unemployed for twelve months when James Cagney came to his professional rescue by persuading Warner Bros. to cast him in the title role in the situation comedy *Mr. Roberts* following the book by Thomas Heggen, the play by Heggen and Joshua Logan and the film. Both play and film were great successes and starred Henry Fonda. The television series starring Smith lasted for only one season of 30 episodes.

Another sometime Warner Bros. contract player Will Hutchins believes that Smith seri-

Roger Smith, who starred in *77 Sunset Strip*.

ously overestimated the cachet which *77 Sunset Strip* would bring him when it came to playing other roles. Life on the domestic front was scarcely any more serene. In 1964 he split from Victoria Shaw and their divorce became final in 1965. In 1973 he obtained sole custody of their children. She married and divorced again, dividing the rest of her life between America and Australia before eventually dying prematurely aged 53 in Sydney on August 17, 1988 after an asthma attack.

In 1961 in the company of another Warner player, Peter Brown, he met Ann-Margret for the first time. Sparks did not ignite, but they certainly did when he encountered her again in 1964. There are those who believe that Ann-Margret caused the original rift in his first marriage, but in truth the split with Victoria Shaw occurred before he met Ann-Margret again. He became engaged to Ann-Margret in a horse drawn carriage in Central Park, New York in 1966 and married her on May 8, 1967 at the Riviera Hotel in Las Vegas.

Professionally his career remained in the doldrums. He was cast in a large role in the Otto Preminger film *Hurry Sundown* (1967), but was replaced prior to production starting by John Philip Law with no public explanation being given. In 1968 he played his final acting role to date when he was cast as down at heel gumshoe Richard Rogue in a television pilot *Rogue's Gallery* produced by A.C. Lyles. This was a sad echo of his former glory and was not picked up as a series. At that time Ann-Margret's career was also in a slump, so Smith decided to take over and manage her which he did with considerable skill and enthusiasm. He wrote the screenplay of *C.C. And Company* (1970) which starred his wife.

His hobbies were listed as skin diving, riding and shooting marlin with a bow and arrow. He shared a fascination with his wife for fast motorbikes which at times has been a perilous adventure. He also knew how to fly which was fortunate when on September 9, 1972 his wife was badly injured when she fell from a platform while performing in her act at the Sahara Hotel in Las Vegas. He seized a plane and was able to fly her to a plastic surgeon. In 1980 he was diagnosed as suffering from myasthenia gravis, a wasting disease of the muscles. He and his wife have remained a very attached couple and he has occasionally been seen at public events with her in recent years when his disease has been in remission. They reside in Beverly Hills.

Filmography

1957: *No Time to be Young, Operation Mad Ball, Man of a Thousand Faces*.
1958: *Crash Landing, Auntie Mame*.
1959: *Never Steal Anything Small*.
1964: *For Those Who Think Young*.
1968: *Seven Men and One Brain* (a.k.a. *Criminal Affair, Criminal Symphony*), *Rogue's Gallery*.

Television Series

1957–1958: *Father Knows Best* as Doyle Hobbs.
1958–1963: *77 Sunset Strip* as Jeff Spencer.
1965–1966: *Mr. Roberts* as Lt. Douglas Roberts.

Sources

Ann-Margret, with Todd Gold. *Ann-Margret: My Story*. London: Orion, 1995.
ATV Television Star Book. London: Purnell, 1961, 1962 and 1963.
Goff, Madison L. "I Hate My Husband's Co-stars." *TV and Movie Screen*. November, 1959.
Griffith, David. "The 77 Sunset Strip Story." *TV Times*. October 30, 1960.
Laing, Nora. "The Eyes of 77 Sunset Strip." *TV Times*. September 4, 1959.
Peer, Robert. "Roger Smith Answers 50 Intimate Questions." *Movie Life*. November 1959.
Stewart, John. *An Encyclopedia of Australian Film*. New South Wales: Reed, 1984.
Stoddard, Sylvia. *Television Chronicles*. No. 12. January 1998.
Woolley, Lynn, Robert W. Malsbury, and Robert G. Strange, Jr. *Warner Bros. Television*. Jefferson, NC: McFarland, 1985.

Arthur Space

Arthur Space was born in New Brunswick, New Jersey on October 12, 1908. His parents were Charles Augustus Space and Isabelle Barrett. He was educated at grammar and high schools in New Brunswick where he was very sporting. In high school he became interested in drama. In his senior year in high school he was chosen to play male parts in the plays staged by the New Jersey College for Women. Between 1927 and 1935 he appeared in many of their plays. The night he graduated from high school, he boarded a tramp steamer as a member of the crew, sailing to South America. Upon his return he held various early jobs including working on a Pennsylvania railroad construction gang before joining a drama workshop group.

At the age of 26 he was playing leading man parts in the East Orange Stock Company. He did summer stock and became a fixture on the subway circuit in and around New York. Later out of work, he was a beachcomber in New Jersey for a couple of years prior to going to Hollywood where he arrived with very little money and one decent suit. In 1939 Space had worked for director Sylvan S. Simon in a play in New York. Simon helped him to break into films in 1941. Simon considered him his talisman and gave him parts in other productions he directed.

Space made his first television appearance in experimental television in New York in 1935. He went on to appear in over 150 films and made 350 television appearances. During the second season of the television series *Crusader* he had a semi-regular role as Walter Cronan, who sometimes hired Matt Anders (Brian Keith). It was however a role in the anthology series *Medic* in 1955 which gave him greater visibility and led to more important roles. In his spare time Space worked with the Spotlighters, a group of industry professionals, dedicated to aid the Youth Foundation in every possible manner.

Space died at his Hollywood home on January 13, 1983 aged 74 of cancer. He married Mollie Campbell in 1936 and had two daughters. He was survived by both his daughters.

FILMOGRAPHY

1941: *The Bugle Sounds, Riot Squad.*
1942: *Rio Rita, Tortilla Flat, Grand Central Murder, Enemy Agents Meet Ellery Queen, Tish, Random Harvest, Quiet Please Murder, Tennessee Johnson* (a.k.a. *The Man on America's Conscience), Reunion in France, Andy Hardy's Double Life.*
1943: *They Came to Blow Up America, This Is the Army, Salute to the Marines, The Man from Down Under, Swing Shift Maisie, The Dancing Masters, A Guy Named Joe, The Heavenly Body, Whistling in Brooklyn.*
1944: *Ladies Courageous, The Ghost That Walks Alone, Rationing, Wing and a Prayer, Wilson, Marriage Is a Private Affair, The Big Noise, Strange Affair, The Mark of the Whistler, Thirty Seconds Over Tokyo, Dark Shadows, Music for Millions, Gentle Annie.*
1945: *This Man's Navy, The Woman in the Window, Leave It to Blondie, The Clock, Son of Lassie, Twice Blessed, The Hidden Eye, Our Vines Have Tender Grapes, Abbott and Costello in Hollywood, The Crimson Canary.*
1946: *Bad Bascomb, The Man Who Dared, Boys' Ranch, Black Beauty, The Mysterious Mr. Valentine, Courage of Lassie, Gentleman Joe Palooka, Child of Divorce, Home in Oklahoma, The Cockeyed Miracle, The Secret of the Whistler, Magnificent Doll, That Brennan Girl, Lost City of the Jungle* (serial), *The Great Morgan.*
1947: *Mr. District Attorney, The Guilt of Janet Ames, The Red House, Millie's Daughter, Heartaches, The Rustlers of Devil's Canyon, The Crimson Key, The Invisible Wall, Her Husband's Affairs, Big Town After Dark.*
1948: *I Love Trouble, Homecoming, The Fuller Brush Man, Silver River, A Southern Yankee, Tap Roots, Walk a Crooked Mile, The Return of October, Joan of Arc, Fighter Squadron, The Paleface.*
1949: *Shockproof, The Lone Wolf and His Lady, El Paso, Mr. Belvedere Goes to College, Sorrowful Jones, Lust for Gold, House of Strangers, Any Number Can Play, Miss Grant Takes Richmond, Chicago Deadline, Mary Ryan Detective.*
1950: *Father Is a Bachelor, The Good Humor Man, The Vanishing Westerner, Federal Man, The Happy Years, The Fuller Brush Girl, The Killer That Stalked New York.*
1951: *Tomahawk, Night Riders of Montana, Three Guys Named Mike, Up Front, Her First Romance, Government Agents vs. Phantom Legion* (serial), *Utah Wagon Train, The Barefoot Mailman.*
1952: *Jet Job, Red Ball Express, Sound Off, African Treasure, Jumping Jacks, Here Come the Marines, Sudden Fear, Fargo, Feudin' Fools, Rainbow 'Round My Shoulder, Because of You.*
1953: *Battle Circus, Confidentially Connie, Canadian Mounties vs. Atomic Invaders* (serial), *So This Is Love* (a.k.a. *The Grace Moore Story), Clipped Wings, The Man from the Alamo, Last of the Pony Riders, Back to God's Country, The Eddie Cantor Story.*
1954: *Yankee Pasha, Ring of Fear, A Star Is Born, Target Earth, Drum Beat, The Silver Chalice.*
1955: *Panther Girl of the Congo* (serial), *Rage at Dawn, Eternal Sea, Foxfire, A Man Alone, The Spoilers.*
1956: *The Killer Is Loose, Away All Boats.*
1957: *The Spirit of St. Louis, 20 Million Miles to Earth.*
1958: *Twilight for the Gods.*
1959: *Day of the Outlaw, A Summer Place.*
1960: *Gunfighters of Abilene.*
1964: *Taggart.*
1968: *The Shakiest Gun in the West.*
1971: *Shoot Out, Bedknobs and Broomsticks.*
1972: *Terror House* (a.k.a. *Terror on the Menu).*
1973: *Frasier the Sensuous Lion.*
1974: *Herbie Rides Again, The Bat People.*
1975: *The Strongest Man in the World.*
1976: *The Lindbergh Kidnapping Case* (TV).
1977: *Mansion of the Doomed* (a.k.a. *Massacre Mansion).*
1978: *The Swarm.*
1979: *Hot Rod* (TV), *Patient in the Dark.*
1980: *On the Nickel.*

TELEVISION SERIES

1954–1964: *Lassie* as Doc. Weaver.
1956: *Crusader* as Walter Cronan.
1960–1962: *National Velvet* as Herbert Brown.

SOURCES

Goldrup, Tom, and Jim Goldrup. *Feature Film Players: The Stories Behind the Faces.* Vol. 1. Published privately, 1986.
Jones, Ken D., Arthur F. McClure, and Alfred E. Twomey. *Character People.* Secaucus, NJ: Citadel, 1979.
Ward, Jack. *The Supporting Players of Television, 1959–1983.* Cleveland, OK: Lakeshore West, 1996.

Willis, John. *Screen World*. Vol. 35. London: Frederick Muller, 1984.

ROBERT STACK

Robert Stack suffered as an actor for a while because his thesping took second place to his sporting achievements. His career was also hampered by the attitudes of studio heads who regarded him as a dilettante in show business. Since he came from a wealthy family, he must therefore be pursuing acting as a hobby rather than as a career. He was forced to play juvenile leads long after he was too old. Parts of substance were a long time coming, but perseverance won the day in the end. His most successful television series was *The Untouchables* in which he played Eliot Ness. Here he was dubbed "The Great Stoneface" because his restrained intensity and conservative attire sharply contrasted with the flamboyant bad guys and made him the epitome of television cool. This was no accident. As he once explained, "I structured Ness as a counterpuncher."

He has had his fair share of narrow escapes and health problems. As he recalled, "Three times I nearly died: in a 120 miles an hour boat smash, in a motorcycle crash and once when a film stunt went wrong. George Kennedy, a sweet guy, gave me a two handed hit and nearly broke my neck." He once described series television in this way, "Doing a television series is like making love to a gorilla: you don't stop when you want to, you stop when she lets go."

Robert Charles Stack was born in Los Angeles, California on January 13, 1919, the son of James Langford Stack who was a self made millionaire businessman and advertising giant who died in 1929 and leading socialite Elizabeth Modini Wood. He had one elder brother James L. Stack, Jr. A fifth generation Californian, he was the descendant of one of the state's first families. In 1849 his great grandfather was one of the first five families to settle in Los Angeles which was then a tiny pueblo. The same ancestor opened the second theater there. His grandmother Marina Perrini was a renowned opera singer and his grandfather Carlos Modini was also a singer.

His father and mother divorced when he was only a year old. He went to live in Europe with his mother when he was three years old, while his brother remained with his father. At the age of six when he returned to the United States, he spoke fluent French and Italian, but no English while his older brother could not speak to him without an interpreter. His parents remarried in 1928 and engaged a tutor for him so that by the time he was due to enter school, he could speak English as though he had never left America. He first attended a private school, the Carl Curtis School in Hollywood. He also spent an unhappy year at the Beverly School for Boys before being enrolled in Los Angeles High School.

From an early age he was exposed to music and learned to play the clarinet and saxophone. Although it was a skill which he seldom employed in his films, Stack could also sing. Between 1937 and 1938 he attended the University of Southern California where he took a great interest in sports. While still at high school he teamed with his brother to race in the international outdoor motor championship at Venice, Italy and later won many trophies with his racing hydroplane, Thunderbird. At the age of 16, he came second in the all–American skeet shooting championship and subsequently many trophies came his way. Another sport which he excelled at was polo and while at college he was on the varsity team. He ultimately had to give up this sport on doctors' orders because he had broken his wrist three times while playing.

It was while he was at college that he became interested in dramatics. So in 1938 he decided to enroll in drama and singing classes at the El Capitan College of the Theater which was run by Henry Duffy. As he later recalled, "My singing classes had been going badly and my tutor told me to go down to Universal and listen to Deanna Durbin. I did, and while I was standing off to one side of the set, Joe Pasternak came over and offered me a role in the film." Pasternak was searching for a handsome, young Prince Charming actor to give Deanna Durbin her first onscreen kiss in *First Love* (1939). Stack fitted the bill and was chosen for the part of Ted Drake. He did not find it a particularly enjoyable experience since make-up artist Jack Pierce altered his appearance, Durbin was aloof and he played his main love scene to a blackboard. In spite of this his reviews were acceptable, teenage girls gushed over him and he became a star.

On the strength of this he signed a standard seven year pact with Universal starting at $150 per week. Universal loaned him to MGM to play Otto von Rohn in *The Mortal Storm* (1940). His participation in this harrowing movie attack on the Nazis ensured his place, along with the rest of the cast, on Hitler's "Death List" if Germany won the war. He was then reteamed with Deanna Durbin in *Nice Girl?* (1941). Another highlight of his early career was playing Lt. Sobinski opposite the legendary Carole Lombard in the classic comedy *To Be or Not to Be* (1942) directed by Ernst Lubitsch for United Artists.

When America entered World War II, Stack tried to enlist in the Navy Air Corps, but was rejected. Instead he was allowed to enlist in the navy as a gunnery officer. He commenced as an ensign and when he was discharged after three and a half years, he was a lieutenant. While in the services, he received an offer to star opposite Judy Holliday in an unspecified film for Liberty Pictures. This was an ambitious independent outfit fronted by three top directors (Frank Capra, William Wyler and George Stevens), but Stack and James Stewart were the only actors under contract. The film to be directed by George Stevens did not come to pass. When Stack was honorably discharged, he returned to Hollywood to find himself as socially popular as ever, but "resting" as far as film acting opportunities were concerned.

He hoped to appear in more meaty roles, but an early post war role was as Stephen Andrews, Elizabeth Taylor's romantic interest, in *A Date with Judy* (1948). With relatively few film offers forthcoming, he misguidedly accepted an offer to appear in a Broadway bound stage revival of a dodo of a play *The Girl of the Golden West*. This opened at the Westport Country Playhouse in Westport, Connecticut in 1949 and did go briefly to New York. His co-stars were June Havoc and Murvyn Vye. Since Vye was a heavy imbiber who was incapable of remembering his lines, it turned out to be an embarrassment not the launching pad to a successful career on the Great White Way which Stack had hoped.

For John Wayne's company Batjac he played Chuck Regan, that rarity an American matador, in *The Bullfighter and the Lady* (1951) directed by Budd Boetticher which was shot on location in Mexico. It is generally regarded as one of both the star and director's best films. Stack became fascinated in the subject and, after the film was shot, he had the opportunity to practice his skills briefly on a real bull. When his next film *My Outlaw Brother* (1951), in which he played a dual role, proved to be a flop, he temporarily found himself unemployed. In the interval that followed, at the suggestion of his agent, he shot the pilot to a projected television series called *The Phantom Pirate*, an experience so dismal that he bought up the only prints and buried them.

He did however star in *Bwana Devil* (1952), a poor African adventure film shot at the Paramount ranch instead of the Dark Continent. It was notable as the first 3-D film and made its producer Arch Oboler a fortune. It scared audiences because lions seemed to leap out of the screen into their lap and spears appeared to be thrown directly at them. Of his released films the actor regarded his career low point as *The Iron Glove* (1954) a quickie swashbuckler produced by Sam Katzman for Columbia. Stack also tested for the role of "Curly" in the film version of *Oklahoma*, but not surprisingly lost out to Gordon MacRae.

He finally landed a good role as Sullivan, the airline captain, who temporarily goes berserk when his commercial airliner develops a serious fault in the film version of the Ernest K. Gann bestseller *The High and the Mighty* (1954). The rights to the novel were bought by John Wayne's Batjac company and Stack actively campaigned to win the role. It was directed by William Wellman for Warner Bros. release and was an enormous commercial success. While shooting the film Stack caught a cold which developed into pneumonia, resulting in a stay in hospital.

Darryl F. Zanuck, head of 20th Century-Fox, saw *The High and the Mighty* and offered him a contract which he eagerly signed. Almost immediately he landed the role of Steve Kenner, an Army sergeant, masquerading as gangster Eddie Spannier in Sam Fuller's exciting crime film *House of Bamboo* (1955) lensed in Japan which was a reworking of the studio's earlier *The Street With No Name* (1948). He appeared in another good film at the studio *Good Morning, Miss Dove* (1955), but then Zanuck left Fox to become an independent producer. Stack did not appeal to the incoming faction. After he rejected a couple of terrible scripts, he found himself on suspension. As a result of appearing with John Wayne, he had a one picture a year option with Wayne's company. In the event *The High and the Mighty* was their only film together. By some complicated political maneuvering which involved Wayne and the option, Stack found himself in the odd position of being unable to work for his home studio, but able to accept offers from rival studios.

The one which turned out to be his biggest career break up to that time came from Universal where director Douglas Sirk showed enormous faith in him by casting him as Kyle Hadley, a tortured dipsomaniac Texas oil baron in *Written on the Wind* (1956). This gave him the chance to play a more complex character than ever before and he rose to the challenge. His performance was rewarded with a Best Supporting Actor Oscar nomination much to the consternation of the executives at Fox. Buddy Adler, the studio head, summoned him and told him that he was back in favor. He again found himself falling from grace when he signed a contract to star in *The Sun Also Rises*, but was nixed for the lead by Ava Gardner. Apparently she bore him a grudge because he had rejected her sexual advances some years before after shooting *The Bullfighter and the Lady*. Gardner had a well known fetish about matadors and bulls. Tyrone Power replaced him. Studio politics prevented Stack from winning the Oscar for *Written on the Wind*. His costars were Rock Hudson, Lauren Bacall and Dorothy Malone. Three of the same costars (Hudson, Malone and Stack) reteamed much less successfully for *Tarnished Angels* (1957). Stack and Bacall starred together again in the lachrymose *The Gift of Love* (1958).

Robert Stack and Dorothy Malone played husband and wife in *The Last Voyage* (1960), an exciting disaster film made even more realistic by the fact that producer-director Andrew L. Stone insisted on a real ocean liner being sunk on camera. Stone rented the ship, the Ile de France, from a Japanese salvage company. Although Stone had a contract to allow him to sink the liner, the Japanese company had no intention of honoring the bargain. They wanted not only to collect their fees from Stone, but also to salvage certain valuable parts of the ship which would be impossible if she were flooded. They used a variety of threats and delaying tactics before the ship was sunk and the film was eventually finished.

The ambition of Eliot Ness from an early age was to be a detective. After graduating from the University of Chicago, he found work as an agent for a credit company before obtaining employment with the Prohibition Bureau of the U.S. Department of Justice. The city during the late twenties was run by the syndicate headed by Al Capone. This incensed Ness who was invited to a meeting of the "Secret Six," a special committee formed by the Chicago Chamber of Commerce, who were devoted to combating organized crime. He outlined his plan to form an elite group of agents who were incorruptible, had no Mob connections and whose past was beyond reproach. This was given formal sanction by the United States District Attorney who named Ness their leader. Ness initially appointed ten men to the task. In the television version of the story, Ness had only seven. After his men refused a bribe from the Mob, Ness called a press conference where his corps were dubbed "The Untouchables." After a two year battle Capone was finally charged with income tax evasion in October 1931 and was sentenced to eleven years in Atlanta prison in May 1932. He was later moved to Alcatraz where he died in 1947. "The Untouchables" were disbanded in 1932. In 1955 Ness began writing his bestselling memoirs *The Untouchables* with veteran reporter Oscar Fraley which were published in 1957 shortly after Ness died of a heart attack on May 16, 1957 at age 54.

In early 1959 Desi Arnaz announced that his company Desilu Productions (jointly owned by Desi himself and his spouse Lucille Ball) had bought all the rights to *The Untouchables* and was adapting these memoirs for a two hour thriller to be shown on consecutive weeks on the CBS anthology television series *The Desilu/Westinghouse Playhouse*. Simultaneously an alternative version was being prepared which would be shown theatrically in Europe under the title *The Scarface Mob*. It was shot on a budget of $600,000. Quinn Martin was the producer, Phil Karlson directed and the script was written by Paul Monash.

The initial choice for the lead of Ness was Van Heflin, but he rejected it. The next choice was Van Johnson, but very shortly before shooting was to start he demanded more money. This appeared to be a misunderstanding. Johnson thought he was going to be paid $10,000 per hour whereas Desilu had set $10,000 as his total fee. Arnaz and Martin then turned to Robert Stack whom they had some difficulty locating. There was no question at this time of this single thriller evolving into a television series. They eventually found Stack at Chasen's restaurant, signed him at 2 am and fitted him for costumes on the Sunday before the four week shoot was to commence on Monday March 16, 1959.

He still regarded himself as pre-eminently a motion picture star so he was about to pass on the role, but his silver tongued agent Bill Shiffrin persuaded him to change his mind. He based his characterization on three real life people namely Audie Murphy, stuntman Carey Loftin, and his navy roommate Buck Mazza. They were three brave men, but they never bragged about it. Amongst those cast as "The Untouchables" were Bill Williams as Martin Flaherty and Abel Fernandez as William Youngfellow. Neville Brand played Al Capone with Bruce Gordon as his first lieutenant Frank "The Enforcer" Nitti. The narration supplied by Walter Winchell was considered to be another inspiration. Television insiders however were rather shocked at the choice of Winchell. One of America's best known factual commentators during the thirties, he had become a gossip monger of the worst sort by the fifties. It was Winchell who accused Lucille Ball of being a Communist during the height of the witch hunts in 1953. Despite this, Winchell was used in two Desilu series, but the announcer and Desilu made strange bedfellows. Wilbur Hatch wrote the music for the original *Desilu Playhouse* production. The first half of *The Untouchables* was aired on April 22, 1959 and was a smash hit. The other half aired a week later on April 29, 1959 and did even better in the ratings.

Such was the response to the show that CBS began to consider turning it into a weekly series. Stack initially declined, but changed his mind when Arnaz offered him a big salary together with a percentage of the profits. He became President of both Langford Productions and St. Pierre Productions in 1959. He sold Langford, a dummy corporation derived from his father's middle name, to Desilu for 25% of the show which in effect made him a co-producer. It was a non-exclusive deal which he signed which enabled him to take time off to shoot *The Last Voyage* for MGM in Japan for two months from May to July 1959. He and Abel Fernandez were the only two of the original "Untouchables" who reprised their roles in the subsequent series. The predominantly film actors in the original production refused to do a television series, so other less discriminating actors were substituted. Jerry Paris took over from Bill Williams as Martin Flaherty. Nick Georgiade played Enrico Rossi, a witness to a gangland execution whom Ness protects and later recruits as shown in the first episode of the series "The Empty Chair." About half way through the first season, Paris left the series. Anthony George in the role of Cam Allison replaced him. Allison was killed off in "The Frank Nitti Story" which was the final episode of the first season. In turn Paul Picerni took over as Lee Hobson. He continued for the remaining three seasons. Quinn Martin was the executive producer during the first season, while Jerry Thorpe replaced him in the second. Alan Armer was executive producer during the third season.

ABC outbid CBS for the rights to the series which premiered on October 15, 1959. The cases had the substance of truth, but were mainly fictional. In particular Ness was shown apprehending a number of criminals whose cases in reality he had nothing to do with. Director Walter Grauman succinctly summed up the series when he said, "The show is dramatic fiction with documentary authenticity." The series was constantly reviled by Italian-American groups who regarded it as being an attack on them. This view was basically nonsense. There were several gangsters with Italian names in the series because the real life gangsters whom Ness apprehended were Italians in many cases. Equally however many of the Italian characters shown in the episodes were upright responsible citizens. A constant presence was Italian Enrico Rossi as one of "The Untouchables." The series picked up steam after a slow start and became an immense success. It was compulsive viewing in millions of households. In terms of ratings the series came in at number 43 during its first season. Its most successful season was 1960–1961 when it zoomed to eighth equal, but it was back to number 41 by the end of the third. Motion picture writers who normally disdained television contributed scripts for it. Gifted actors from the New York theater scene and distinguished Jewish actors moonlighted in it between more serious gigs. This continued for three seasons until the cost of hiring these people became prohibitive.

To obtain the authentic look for the series such as the vintage automobiles made the costs high. The cost of each episode was $110,000 even with black and white photography which made it one of the most expensive shows on television at the time. Night sequences were genuinely shot at night which gave the series an eerie atmosphere, but caused the costs to soar. Each episode initially aimed to be shot in five days, but some spilled over into six or even seven. To compensate two episodes were shot simultaneously. The episodes were mainly shot at the Desilu Studios at Forty Acres with some shooting being done at Gower Studios. Both crew and cast worked extremely long hours which made stress levels high and contributed to one fatality when Wilbur Bradley, the series leading cameraman, died of a heart attack. Stack rose at about 6:30 AM to start shooting around 8 AM.

At the end of the first season *The Untouch-*

Robert Stack in *The Untouchables*.

ables received six Emmy award nominations, including Best Dramatic Show, of which it won four. Stack won one for Outstanding Performance by an Actor in a Series 1959–1960 presented to him on June 20, 1960. He brought an intensity to the part which was rare in television in those days and made him a consistently interesting and powerful character. Although he always kept himself in check, his rare, unpredictable flashes of temper made him a hero to remember. Elizabeth Ness, the crimebuster's widow, personally endorsed Stack's interpretation of her husband's character. Somebody once said to Stack, "You really think you're Eliot Ness." The actor replied, "No, I don't think I'm Ness, but I sure as hell know I'm not Al Capone."

The series was much criticized for its violence which now seems relatively tame. Much more was hinted at than was ever shown. Much of the horror was not shown graphically, but clever direction depicted it by revealing the faces and body language of characters reacting to it. To depict the era without violence would have been a total distortion of the truth. In essence a certain amount of violence was what made the series successful. *The Untouchables* was the subject of three Congressional investigations. In particular the level of violence upset Congress although the series was a morally uplifting one with good always triumphing over evil.

The level of violence together with the campaign by the Italian-American community which included a boycott of the cigarette manufactured by the sponsors eventually led a to a showdown with the network and the studio. From this meeting in March 1961 a pact was made whereby no hoodlums were allowed to have Italian names; Italian named characters were always to be shown in a positive light; and Enrico Rossi was to be featured more prominently in episodes. Since other minority ethnic groups were to be involved in organized crime, their names were to be used instead. This caused such an outcry that by the time of the series demise, the only politically correct names which could be used were innocuous English ones. In spite of these criticisms the series remained consistently popular for three seasons.

The fourth season episodes were executive produced by Leonard Freeman and Alvin Cooperman. They tried to downscale the violence in favor of characterization which produced boredom. Ness was shown as losing some cases and as a victim in others. On the more positive front they brought in a second unit to shoot fresh footage all over Los Angeles. The original orchestrations for the series were composed by Nelson Riddle. These were complemented by jazz specialist Pete Rugolo in the final season. A few of the later episodes were back door pilots to prospective television series, but none made the grade in their own right. Tampering with the basic formula proved to be a mistake in audience terms. Freeman and Cooperman departed midway through the fourth season to be replaced by the returning Alan Armer who stayed with it to the finish.

Despite the fact that ratings had declined, it was still doing well compared to other ABC series so the network wanted to continue for a fifth season. Stack however was unable to continue because the grueling pace over so many years had caused a hemorrhage in his vocal cords as well as physical exhaustion. Stack was at a disadvantage in this respect compared to his Warner counterparts who had double leads in series for this very reason. While he was not in every scene, he was in every episode. No one could substitute for him and it took a toll on his health. The series ended after four seasons and 118 episodes with "A Taste of Pineapple" a particularly distasteful and unlikely episode. In 1962 Desilu reedited the two part episodes "The Unhired Assassin" and "The Big Train" and released them theatrically across the country as *The Guns of Zangara* and *Alcatraz Express* respectively.

There was a successful film version of *The Untouchables* (1987) and a syndicated television series revival *The Untouchables* in 1993–1994 which did nothing to tarnish the reputation of the original and suffered much the same faults as most action series of the nineties. Stack himself reprised the role in a 1991 telemovie *The Return of Eliot Ness* which was shown on CBS. Although he rejected several drafts of the script before he agreed to do it, it made most viewers long nostalgically for the magic of the originals.

At the height of the war, he made a perilous trip to Vietnam to boost the morale of the troops. Stack's next venture into series television was *The Name of the Game*. Each of the three stars of the series Stack, Tony Franciosa and Gene Barry appeared in rotation in their own self-contained episodes of ninety minutes duration. One of the others would appear in a show where another star had the lead to give continuity. The link between them was Harold Publications, a Los Angeles based publishing empire created and owned by Glenn Howard (Barry). Stack played Dan Farrell, senior editor of "Crime" magazine. Farrell was a former FBI agent turned newspaperman who had entered journalism as a means of exposing organized crime. This three season series for Universal television ran on the NBC network between September 1968 and September 1971.

Stack signed a motion picture–television deal with Universal prior to shooting this series. Prior to *The Untouchables* his fee for a film was about $90,000. The series raised his feature film asking price to $120,000. It was supposed to be a one picture a year deal and indeed he did shoot a film for them called *Story of a Woman* (1969) which was shot on location in Europe, but went over budget. When it flopped, Universal found all sorts of excuses to dodge the commitment. Stack had a choice of three scripts, but if he passed on them, Universal had fulfilled their part of the bargain and did not have to pay him. Stack rejected two worthless scripts, but agreed to do a tacky reworking of *Tobruk* (1966) which was now called *Raid on Rommel* (1971). Believing that Stack would reject this too, the same script had been offered to and accepted by Richard Burton. The position became very ugly, but Stack backed down when the studio agreed to pay him his entire salary as if he had done the movie.

His next television series was called *Most Wanted* (1976–1977) which was a Quinn Martin production for the ABC network. It had originally started out as a script where a female police psychiatrist investigates a crime about a group of nuns who have been raped. The script was recycled without much change except that Stack was now in the lead! It was originally supposed to premiere in the 10 pm slot on Thursdays. Instead it was abruptly switched to 10 pm on Saturdays opposite the phenomenally successful CBS series *The Carol Burnett Show*. When NBC began showing movies in this timeslot, Burnett's audience remained loyal. While the movies with box office names were shown on NBC, Burnett won the night. When movies were shown on NBC which lacked star power, audiences switched to *Most Wanted* in droves. This knocked Burnett off her pedestal and gave ABC victory. There were only twenty episodes of this series made which were shown between October 1976 and April 1977. Stack starred as Captain Linc Evers, leader of the "most wanted" unit which was an elite task force of the LAPD who devoted their efforts to capturing criminals on the mayor's "most wanted" list. As Stack ruefully explained, "We reached number seven in the ratings by the end of the season. The show was cancelled the day after we gave our victory party. It's never happened before to a show at number seven."

According to one unconfirmed report the executive producer of the series, Quinn Martin, found himself in a meeting with the ABC network head. In the course of the meeting there was an argument during which Martin slammed down an ashtray on a desk with such force that it rebounded and hit the network head squarely in the chest. Shortly afterwards all Martin's programs were cancelled including *Most Wanted* and his pilots were not picked up. Of this experience Stack went on to say, "I always like to do 60 episodes if I can. That means that I then own 25 % of the show and have an annuity for life." In 1980 his memoirs *Straight Shooting* were published. Stack's next series *Strike Force* which was shown on the ABC network between November 1981 and September 1982 had almost exactly the same premise as *Most Wanted*. Unfortunately the results were no more successful this time around. Stack played Captain Frank Murphy, head of a special unit within the LAPD which tackled only the toughest cases.

On the big screen he played General Stilwell in *1941* (1979) which was one of the few films to be directed by Steven Spielberg to flop. It did however give Stack a rare opportunity to play comedy. He was one of a number of players who spoofed himself in *Airplane!* (1980) as Kramer, a stuffy air traffic controller, but he was offered no more comedy roles.

In 1996 he sued three former business managers whom he claimed looted his accounts at several banks to the tune of over $400,000. Stack scored another television success when he became host of the public service documentary series *Unsolved Mysteries* for NBC. The series started life in January 1987 when Raymond Burr hosted a special which examined four real life mysteries. This achieved such high ratings that six more specials were produced during 1987 and 1988, two hosted by Karl Malden and the other four by Robert Stack. In September 1988 a regular series began hosted by Stack. It investigated unsolved crimes, reunited long lost relatives, sought heirs to unclaimed fortunes and examined legends and psychic phenomena. One failing which it did not suffer from was lack of suitable material. The series was cancelled by NBC in September 1997, but was exhumed by CBS for two short runs in 1998 and 1999. In the final season Virginia Madsen cohosted with Stack.

He explained the success of the series, "The people who produce this show spend good money to make the dramatic re-enactments very real and they honestly care about the victims. Also its about extraordinary things happening to ordinary people." It was not however his favorite job. The reason for this was that *Unsolved Mysteries* was not acting. It was a lonely life in which he filmed his segments away from the dramatized re-enactments and could not relate to the other performers which he believed was the essence of acting. So he accepted other assignments as well, fitting them in when he could. The series received an Emmy award nomination as "Outstanding Informational Series" in 1995.

Robert Stack died on May 14, 2003 aged 84. His wife found him slumped in his Los Angeles home at 5 pm. The actor had undergone radiation treatment for prostate cancer in October 2002. His wife said, "He had a bout with a tumor, but that was gone. It wasn't that, it was his heart. He was too weak. He couldn't have lived through a by-pass."

On January 23, 1956 in Beverly Hills he married former cover girl and actress Rosemarie Bowe who was born in 1932. They had two children a daughter Elizabeth Langford who was born in 1957 and a son Charles Robert who was born on May 22, 1958. Both his wife and children were with him in the house at the time when he died. He is buried at Westwood Memorial Park, Los Angeles County, California.

Although he was deceased, his voice already recorded was heard posthumously in the play *The Little Shop of Horrors* from August 2003 onwards. His widow's comment was, "At last, he's doing Broadway." After his death TV critic Marc Berman said of him, "He was one of the unsung heroes of early television. He was as influential as Red Skelton, Jackie Gleason and Robert Young. He was just a more subtle actor who never drew attention to himself."

FILMOGRAPHY

1939: *First Love*.
1940: *A Little Bit of Heaven, The Mortal Storm, When the Daltons Rode*.
1941: *Nice Girl?, Badlands of Dakota*.
1942: *To Be or Not to Be, Men of Texas, Eagle Squadron*.
1948: *A Date With Judy, Miss Tatlock's Millions, Fighter Squadron*.
1950: *Mr. Music*.
1951: *The Bullfighter and the Lady, My Outlaw Brother*.
1952: *Bwana Devil*.
1953: *War Paint, Saber Jet, Conquest of Cochise*.
1954: *The High and the Mighty, The Iron Glove*.
1955: *House of Bamboo, Good Morning Miss Dove*.
1956: *Great Day in the Morning, Written on the Wind*.
1957: *The Tarnished Angels*.
1958: *The Gift of Love*.
1959: *John Paul Jones, The Scarface Mob* (TU:TV).
1960: *The Last Voyage*.
1962: *The Guns of Zangara* (TU:TV), *Alcatraz Express* (TU:TV).
1963: *The Caretakers* (a.k.a. *Borderlines*).
1966: *Is Paris Burning?, Action Man* (a.k.a. *Leather and Nylon*).
1967: *The Corrupt Ones* (a.k.a. *The Peking Medallion*).
1969: *The Story of a Woman*.
1974: *The Strange and Deadly Occurrence* (TV).
1975: *Adventures of the Queen* (TV).
1976: *Murder on Flight 502* (TV), *Most Wanted* (TV).
1978: *A Second Wind* (a.k.a. *Check-Up*).
1979: *1941, Undercover with KKK* (TV: Narrator only).
1980: *Airplane!*
1983: *Uncommon Valor*.

1985: *Midas Valley* (TV).
1986: *Transformers The Movie* (voice only), *Big Trouble*.
1987: *Perry Mason: The Case of the Sinister Spirit* (TV).
1988: *Plain Clothes, Dangerous Curves, Caddyshack II*.
1990: *Joe Versus the Volcano*.
1991: *The Return of Eliot Ness* (TV).
1996: *Beavis and Butthead Do America* (voice only).
1998: *BASEketball*.
1999: *Mumford, Sealed With a Kiss* (TV) (a.k.a. *First Comes Love*), *Totally Irresponsible*.
2000: *H.U.D.* (TV).
2001: *Killer Bud*.

Note A film denoted "TU:TV" is a feature film derived from a double part episode of *The Untouchables*.

TELEVISION SERIES

1959–1963: *The Untouchables* as Eliot Ness.
1968–1971: *The Name of the Game* as Dan Farrell.
1976–1977: *Most Wanted* as Captain Linc Evers.
1981–1982: *Strike Force* as Captain Frank Murphy.
1987: *Falcon Crest* as Roland Saunders.
1988–1999: *Unsolved Mysteries* Host/Narrator.
1992: *Final Appeal From the Files of Unsolved Mysteries*.

MINISERIES

1984: *George Washington*.
1985: *Hollywood Wives*.

SOURCES

Benson, Jim. "The Return of Eliot Ness." *Variety*. December 1991.
Daily Mail. May 21, 2003.
Daily Mail. Obituary, May 16, 2003.
Daily Telegraph. Obituary, May 16, 2003
Davidson, Bill. "Is Flashing the Great Stone Face Such a Crime?" *TV Guide*. August 26, 1989.
Davis, Victor. "Untouchable by Time." *Daily Express*. September 11, 1978.
_____. "Why Vintage TV Cop Eliot Ness Is Making a Cautious Comeback. Old Warrior Returns to the Mean Streets." *The Mail on Sunday*. December 3, 1989.
Etter, Jonathan. *Quinn Martin, Producer*. Jefferson, NC: McFarland, 2004.
Gaskin, Margaret. *TV Times*. "Crimewatch" 1990.
Hayward, Anthony. *The Independent*. Obituary, May 19, 2003.
Lentz, Harris M. III. *Obituaries in the Performing Arts, 2003*. Jefferson, NC: McFarland, 2004.
Modern Screen. May and July 1982.
National Enquirer. "I Was Ripped Off for Half a Million Bucks." 1996.
Picture Show. "Life Story." September 8, 1956.
Robertson, Ed. *Television Chronicles*. No. 7. October 1996.
Skinner, John Walter. *Who's Who on the Screen*. Worthing: Madeleine, 1983.
Smith, Bob, Robin Mizrahi, and Pete Trujillo. "Robert Stack's Brave Fight for Life." *National Enquirer*. November 19, 2002.
Stack, Robert, and Mark Evans. *Straight Shooting*. New York: MacMillan, 1980.
Vahimagi, Tise. *The Untouchables*. London, England: BFI, 1998.

LYNN STALMASTER

Lynn Stalmaster was the son of a Nebraska Supreme Court Judge. He started in high school as a radio actor and also acted in the theater. As a child he suffered from asthma and was consequently very shy. The family moved from Omaha, Nebraska to Beverly Hills. He discovered that he came out of his shell whenever he could play another character which was a form of self expression. He was educated at UCLA and upon graduation a friend who was working as an assistant to Lew Wasserman persuaded the agency MCA to sign him as an actor. He appeared in a couple of films and some television shows before deciding that he lacked the discipline to become a great actor and that his talents were better behind the camera.

Eventually he was working as an assistant to two television producers who asked him to do the casting for their television shows which is how his career as a casting director started. He broke into casting for films when the office of director Robert Wise asked him to do the casting of the film *I Want to Live!* (1958) which starred Susan Hayward. From there he went on to amass over 400 credits as a casting director. Occasionally he played a small role himself such as the semi-regular but uncredited role of the photographer "Rush" in the newspaper series *Big Town*. He has continued in his career as a leading casting director until the present day.

FILMOGRAPHY

(As Actor)

1951: *Flying Leathernecks, The Steel Helmet.*

TELEVISION SERIES

1954–1955: *Big Town* as Rush.

SOURCE

The Hollywood Reporter. "Lynn Stalmaster, Casting Director." January 8, 2004.

VIRGINIA STEFAN

Virginia Stefan was born in Buffalo, New York in 1925. She was raised in Buffalo. This television actress is best remembered for playing Eva Philbrick, wife of Herbert Philbrick (Richard Carlson), in the television series *I Led 3 Lives*. At the time she expressed surprise that many viewers took the series so seriously that they wrote in to the producers to report suspected Communists in their own neighborhoods. She did not appear in every episode, but the scenes between her and her spouse were well written and played. They were quite convincing as a husband and wife. She was particularly good at expressing the anxiety of someone living under the constant strain of being discovered and eliminated by the Communist party. Stefan appeared in other television series such as *Richard Diamond Private Detective*. Her last credits date from the early sixties.

In real life Stefan was her married name for she was wed to television and radio ad agency head, Bud Stefan. She divorced him, but then attracted some attention when she remarried him in 1963. Virginia Stefan died prematurely in New York City on May 5, 1964 aged 38 of a heart attack, survived by her husband, mother and brother.

TELEVISION SERIES

1953–1956: *I Led 3 Lives* as Eva Philbrick.

SOURCES

Brooks, Tim, and Earle Marsh. *The Complete Directory to Prime Time Network and Cable TV Shows, 1946–Present*. 8th ed. New York: Ballantine, 2003. .

Variety. Obituary, May 1964.

CONNIE STEVENS

One of the most popular characters in the crime series *Hawaiian Eye* was Cricket Blake, alias actress Connie Stevens. She worked for the private eyes in the series and was a close and loyal pal of theirs. Tracy Steele (Anthony Eisley) called her "lover," but on his part it was a platonic relationship. There are indications however that in the series she regarded it as something more serious. In the episode "Three Tickets to Lani" she stated that she intended to become Tracy Steele's wife. In the episode "Dime a Dozen" when a rich socialite (Joanna Barnes) made a play for Steele, Cricket became very jealous. She has been referred to as "a female Kookie," a reference to Warner Bros.' other successful crime series, *77 Sunset Strip.*

With her musical ability, Connie Stevens proved to be more versatile than many of her Warner Bros. contemporaries. Whilst never a major movie player on the Hollywood "A" list, she proved to be a durable second rank star. There are not many avenues of show business which she has not explored and her outside activities have kept her name in the limelight. Of all the Warner Bros.' actresses of the period who starred in series, she had maintained the highest profile. She was once described as, "a woman for all seasons."

Connie Stevens was born Concetta Rosalie Ann Ingolia in Brooklyn, New York on August 8, 1938. She was the daughter of Peter Ingolia and Eleanor McGinley. Using the name Teddy Stevens, her father was a professional nightclub musician. She is of mixed Italian, Irish and Cherokee origins. She was the second of five children. After her parents divorced, her mother married again and had another family. The child actor John Megna (1952–1995) was her half brother. Up to the age of five, she only spoke Italian. After the divorce of her parents she was sent to boarding school. She had a very unhappy childhood.

She moved to Los Angeles with her father when she was fifteen years old. There she attended Sacred Heart Academy in Los Angeles and Hollywood Professional School. Her first professional experience was a bit role in the stage musical *Finian's Rainbow* produced by the Hollywood Repertory Theater. Her musical career began at the age of sixteen when she sang in a group called *The Three Debs*. In 1957 she appeared in a bakery commercial which brought her to the attention of film producers who soon cast her in teen problem movies. She made her screen debut in *Young and Dangerous* (1957). Her first television appearance was in the "Misfire" episode of *Sugarfoot* in 1957. This was a Warners' series and they signed her to a seven year deal incorporating records, television and films. Her studio biography indicated that she stood 5'2" tall, weighed 110 lbs. and had strawberry blonde hair with blue eyes. Her hobbies were listed as dancing, riding, ice skating and listening to jazz records. She did not like rising in the morning and did not eat breakfast.

She found her perfect big screen soul mate in hunky Troy Donahue and they were teamed by Warners in a few features in the early sixties which proved very profitable. Although they made a handsome couple, they were not particularly enamored of one another in real life. Like many of her contemporaries she fought for better roles at Warner Bros. When these were not forthcoming, she rebelled and was suspended. When she came back, possibly at a bigger salary, it was to the same kind of material.

Her most famous television role was as Cricket Blake in the series *Hawaiian Eye*. She so impressed executives at Warner Bros. that she was assigned the role before any scripts had been written. Cricket Blake had three jobs. She worked as a singer, a photographer, and at the detective agency run by Tracy Steele (Anthony Eisley) and Tom Lopaka (Robert Conrad). A small part of each episode was given over to a song sung by Cricket in the nightclub attached to the hotel. The character was loosely based on a girl named Cricket with similar occupations whom a Warners script editor had met in Hawaii while doing background research for the series. The series was a great success and made her a household name. During the final season Troy Donahue came on board to play the hotel social director Phil Barton, although he and Connie Stevens did not generate too many sparks together. Their final appearance together was an episode of *Fantasy Island* in 1981.

One of Cricket's most notable characteristics was the crazy straw hats which she wore. Connie Stevens went shopping for the straw hats herself in places as diverse as Hawaii, San Francisco, Los Angeles and New York. Even the most expensive cost less than $10. If she could not find

Left to right: Anthony Eisley, Connie Stevens and Robert Conrad in *Hawaiian Eye*.

what she wanted she asked the studio wardrobe department to make hats to her own designs. Of these she said, "They can look like a button or an elephant's ear. So long as they are what the well dressed and chic Hawaiian beachcomber would wear."

She went to work at 5 am and only returned at 6 pm. She admitted she slept most of Saturdays. Even so, the combination of shooting the series, feature films, cutting records and making personal appearances made for a hectic life which caused her to suffer nervous exhaustion. To recover she dropped out of the series during the final season and was temporarily replaced by Sunny Day (Tina Cole). She returned to the series for a few episodes before it ended. The episode "Blow Low, Blow Blue" is notable for both Cricket and Sunny Day appearing. *Hawaiian Eye* was shown on the ABC network from October 7, 1959 to September 10, 1963.

Stevens recorded as a solo artist on the Warner Bros. label almost as soon as it was formed. Between 1958 and 1962 she cut four albums for them. Her single *Sixteen Reasons* reached the top of the charts in 1961. She and Edd "Kookie" Byrnes sang a duet *Kookie Kookie Lend Me Your Comb* which proved to be a big hit in 1960.

Her next television series was *Wendy and Me*, a one season sitcom shown on ABC between September 14, 1964 and September 6, 1965 which paired her with the legendary comedian George Burns where the setting was a Southern California apartment house. She was later the star of *Starting from Scratch* (1988–1989), a syndicated comedy series in which she played the hyperactive ex-wife of a veterinarian and mother of his children. She spent a great deal of time in his home looking after their kids despite the divorce.

Her best remembered television movie was *The Sex Symbol* (1974) a thinly veiled biopic of Marilyn Monroe with Connie Stevens in the title role. As shot the movie contained some very raunchy scenes and barbed political references. It came under so much fire from various factions even before its ABC network showing that it was heavily edited for television. The cuts in length and content made it too bland to offend anyone although in its theatrical showings overseas, her nude scenes were restored.

She made her Broadway debut in *The Star Spangled Girl* in 1967 for which she received a Theater World Award. She has been a headliner in Atlantic City, Las Vegas and many other top concert venues both in America and worldwide. She has performed in front of U.S. Presidents and soldiers in Vietnam. She accompanied Bob Hope on tours in 1969 and to the Persian Gulf in 1987. She has made multiple appearances on *Fantasy Island, The Love Boat* and *Murder She Wrote*. Appropriately she played Pamela Anderson's mother on *Baywatch*.

She has been an astute property speculator from her earliest days in Hollywood. In 1960 she sold her first Hollywood home and made enough profit to buy two houses. One she shared with her father while the other she let. In 1974 she bought a 27 room mansion on a two and a half acre estate in the Holmby Hills area of Los Angeles formerly owned by Sonja Henie. On the estate she designed and had built two adjoining town houses for her daughters. She owns a house in Puerto Vallarta, Mexico; a Manhattan apartment; a house in Palm Springs; and a 55 acre family retreat in Wyoming. One recent report indicated that she owned as many as seventeen houses.

Since the 1990s she has been extremely successful in business as CEO and President of *Forever Spring*. This is a popular cosmetic skin care product range which developed from a six step skin care regimen used by the actress for years. She is the driving force behind *Project Windfeather* which has awarded full college scholarships to Native American youths; delivered surplus goods to Indian reservations nationwide; and provided summer camps for native American children who have never left a reservation.

She is very active in the charitable organization *Dignity* which has aided the mentally and physically handicapped to become working members of the community. The Connie Stevens Center for Independent Living in Wyoming, named in her honor, is a facility to house and educate these people. She has appeared in many television commercials, some of them affiliated with public service announcements against drunk driving. She has produced and cowritten a video series on modern parenting called *The Birth of a Parent*.

She married firstly actor James Stacy in 1963 in a Catholic church ceremony in Sherman Oaks, California attended by 700 guests. They were divorced in 1966. She married secondly performer Eddie Fisher in 1967, but they were divorced in 1969. With him she had two daughters who are Joely born in 1967 and Tricia Leigh born in 1968. She raised them as a single parent. In 1996 she and her daughters recorded an album *Tradition ... A Family at Christmas* which was released through her own recording company, Shane.

Life has not always been smooth for her even in more recent times. In November 1994 she flew to Vietnam with a camera crew to shoot a television documentary on US women who served in the war. When the crew accidentally filmed Vietnamese military bases in the background, the authorities arrested and detained her for five days as a suspected spy. Her cameras were confiscated, but she was allowed to leave and managed to escape with the film. The resulting documentary called *A Healing* was eventually released in 1997 to critical acclaim.

On December 7 1994 back in Los Angeles she became seriously ill and was rushed to Cedars-Sinai Medical Center in the middle of the night. Her suffering was only relieved on December 11 when she had her gallbladder removed. She was further hit with the news that her former husband, James Stacy, was in deep trouble. He had been battling personal demons since losing his left arm and left leg in a motorcycle accident in 1973. He pleaded guilty in November 1994 to trying to molest the eleven year old daughter of a friend in Los Angeles. Facing a long jail sentence he fled to Hawaii where he made an unsuccessful bid to commit suicide by jumping off a cliff. With his former wife's aid, he returned to Los Angeles where he served a jail sentence. She is also believed to have witnessed the Twin Towers disaster from her Manhattan apartment.

Connie Stevens tours for eight weeks of

each year, as frequently as possible in the company of her daughters. She has been the recipient of several humanitarian awards and a Parent of the Year award. She has been very active in Republican politics and is a Roman Catholic.

Filmography

1957: *Young and Dangerous, Eighteen and Anxious.*
1958: *Dragstrip Riot* (a.k.a. *The Reckless Age*), *The Party Crashers, Rock-a-Bye Baby.*
1960: *Alakazam the Great* (a.k.a. *The Enchanted Monkey*) (voice only).
1961: *Susan Slade, Parrish.*
1963: *Palm Springs Weekend.*
1965: *Two on a Guillotine, Never Too Late.*
1966: *Way ... Way Out.*
1969: *Mister Jerico* (TV).
1971: *The Grissom Gang, The Last Generation.*
1972: *Call Her Mom* (TV), *Playmates* (TV), *Every Man Needs One* (TV).
1974: *The Sex Symbol* (TV).
1976: *Scorchy.*
1978: *Sergeant Pepper's Lonely Hearts Club Band* (cameo).
1979: *Love's Savage Fury* (TV).
1980: *Murder Can Hurt You!*
1981: *Side Show* (TV).
1982: *Grease 2.*
1987: *Back to the Beach, Tapeheads.*
1988: *Bring Me the Head of Dobie Gillis* (TV).
1996: *James Dean—Race with Destiny, Love Is All There Is.*
2001: *Returning Mickey Stern 2.*

As Director:

1997: *A Healing Vietnam 1995—Dedicated to the Women Who Served.*

Television Series

1959–1963: *Hawaiian Eye* as Cricket Blake.
1964–1965: *Wendy and Me* as Wendy Conway.
1971: *Kraft Music Hall Presents The Des O'Connor Show* as herself.
1988–1989: *Starting from Scratch* as Helen Shepherd DeAngelo.
2002: *Titus* as Juanita Titus.

Miniseries

1980: *Scruples.*

Sources

Chapman, Ray. "Straw-hat Blonde." *TV Times.* December 11, 1960.

Dunn, Angela Fox. "Connie Stevens Ensuring Her Children Will Never Have to Struggle as She Did." *Hello.* October 1994.
Holston, Kim. *Starlet.* Jefferson, NC: McFarland, 1988.
Inman, David. *The TV Encyclopedia.* New York: Perigee, 1991.
National Enquirer. July 29, 1997.
_____. "Hollywood Zoneheads." June 20, 2000.
Press Release.*Connie Stevens.* March 4, 1996.
Quinlan, David. *Film Stars.* 5th ed. London: Batsford, 2000.
Towle, Patricia, and Andy Soloman. "Connie Stevens Rushed Into Surgery After Five Days in Vietnam Jail." *National Enquirer.* December 1995.
Woolley, Lynn, Robert W. Marsbury, and Robert G. Strange Jr. *Warner Bros. Television.* Jefferson, NC: McFarland, 1985.

Craig Stevens

Craig Stevens helped to herald a new breed of television detective heroes as the title character in *Peter Gunn* memorable for its film noir style, deadpan humor and jazzy score. He played small roles in many films of the forties and fifties. Some of his film assignments almost seemed beneath his dignity. He was such a handsome, personable actor that it is difficult to understand the reason why stardom proved so elusive for so long. Had it not been for television it might have remained forever out of his reach. He was married to Alexis Smith, an actress of equal stature, which dictated several switches of balance throughout their lives whenever one or other of their careers was flourishing.

Craig Stevens was born Gail Shikles, Jr., in Liberty, Missouri on July 8, 1918, the son of Gail Shikles, Sr., and Marie Hughes, both of whom came from Missouri. His father was a local teacher. He was studying at the University of Kansas on the strength of a basketball scholarship with the intention of becoming a dentist. As he later recalled, "My shyness took me into acting in the first place." He was so self conscious that he was unable to say a word when he stood up in class. His father insisted he take a course in public speaking. His speech teacher doubled as the drama coach. Stevens was persuaded to try out for a role in a school play. Initially he was not keen, but after his first role, his ambition changed. More than twelve college plays followed.

After he was discovered in a university play by a Hollywood talent scout, it seemed that screen fame would not be far away. He was enrolled at the Paramount Studios' drama school where he studied for six months. At the end of that time the principal advised him to obtain some legitimate stage experience. So he returned to Kansas City and worked with a local stock company. Afterwards he enrolled at the Pasadena Playhouse in California and then toured the Pacific coast with a traveling stock company. He made his screen debut as a senate reporter in *Mr. Smith Goes to Washington* (1939).

He was signed by Warner Bros. in 1941 on the strength of a resemblance to Cary Grant. His first film for them was a minor role in *Affectionately Yours* (1941). One of the early films in which he appeared was *Dive Bomber* (1941). He only had a small part, but it was where he first noticed the female lead Alexis Smith, even though they did not have any scenes together. It was not until they played leads in a later film *Steel Against the Sky* (1941) that they met again and started going together. Three years later on June 18, 1944, as soon as he returned from the Air Force, they married at the Church of the Recessional, Forest Lawn, Glendale, California.

The hazard that wrecked so many Hollywood marriages loomed. Her career went ahead in leaps and bounds, while his was interrupted by three years away at the war. When he returned, he was nearly forgotten while she was close to top stardom. He appeared briefly in uniform in the films *This Is the Army* (1943) and *Hollywood Canteen* (1944). He was ambitious and sought decent roles, but the studio gave him lesser parts in some medium budget pictures before dropping him from their roster of contract players. His final role for them was in the short *Melodies of Memory Lane* (1948) in which he starred as composer Stephen Foster. He said, "I thought I was finished."

As a freelance he had the brief but important role of a murder suspect who is accidentally killed by cop Dana Andrews in the excellent film noir *Where the Sidewalk Ends* (1950). Possibly the nadir of his film career was reached when he supported the Bowery Boys in *Blues Busters* (1950). He played straight man to Abbott and Costello in *Abbott and Costello Meet Dr. Jekyll and Mr. Hyde* (1953) and was seen in the early scenes of *The French Line* (1954) as the boyfriend of heiress Jane Russell. He played the loyal henchman of a town tyrant in Budd Boetticher's *Buchanan Rides Alone* (1958). When its hero Randolph Scott rides out of the town's corpse ridden streets at the film's climax, it is the basically decent Stevens who is left to run the town.

On stage in Los Angeles he appeared in a 26 week engagement in the title role in *Mr. Roberts* in 1955 which he regarded as the acme of his stage career. He and his wife toured in the national company of the musical *Plain and Fancy* in 1956. He appeared in anthology television series such as *Four Star Playhouse* and did song and dance routines in *The Dinah Shore Show*. His agents were negotiating for him to appear in the national company of *Bells are Ringing* when Blake Edwards chose him to play the hero in *Peter Gunn* which premiered on the NBC network on September 22, 1958 and was a smash hit. It was a Spartan production which was an independent production company consisting of Blake Edwards and Don Sharpe. They shot a pilot called "The Kill." They sold it to Bristol-Myers, the first sponsor who saw it, who owned the Monday night 9 PM slot. Edwards wrote many of the scripts which were shot like a mini film noir. He supervised post production and hired Henry Mancini, with whom he had worked before, to compose the theme music.

Peter Gunn was a suave, smooth talking, aggressive private investigator with a crew cut. He always looked very neat and clean in contrast to the lowlife denizens of the tawdry surroundings in which he found himself. Edwards chose his hair style and clothes. In each episode he would be presented with a mystery by a client which he would have to solve in the allotted half hour time span. Frequently he was involved in a fist fight. While he had a work address which was a plush apartment at 351, Ellis Park Road, Los Angeles, his free time was spent at a jazz night club called "Mother's" where his girlfriend Edie Hart (Lola Albright) was the resident vocalist. The formidable "Mother" was played by Hope Emerson during the first season, but was replaced in the later seasons by Minerva Urecal. Herschel Bernardi was his police contact and friend, Lt. Jacoby.

In 1958–1959 *Peter Gunn* received an Emmy nomination as Best Dramatic Series—Less Than One Hour. In the 1958–1959 season it was rated No. 16 in the highest rated programs. In the 1960–1961 season it slipped to No. 29. The violence was underlined by original jazz themes composed by the inimitable Henry Mancini which established a pattern to be copied by several other series such as *Johnny Staccato*. Mancini's music proved to be so popular that RCA issued two best selling albums with music from the series. *Peter Gunn* was shown on the NBC network between 1958 and 1960 before switching networks to ABC between 1960 and 1961. The series was not widely shown in England until years later because it was considered excessively violent, although its success was replicated virtually everywhere that it was shown. The series ended after 114 episodes, the final original episode being shown on June 26, 1961 with reruns until September 25, 1961. Stevens recalled, "I worked on the series for almost four years. It did a lot for me. It was one of the most successful television series ever produced in the States, but I realized that if I stayed on as Peter Gunn much longer, I would become typed in the part." Blake Edwards film commitments had become so great that he took it off the air, but the series was never cancelled.

Stevens then journeyed to Europe to play the globetrotting photographer journalist Michael Strait in *Man of the World* (1962), an ATV series where he shot 20 episodes with Tracy Reed as his Girl Friday, Maggie. He had a keen interest in clothes. His wardrobe was said to contain about fifty suits and sixteen casual outfits. Around the studios at Shepperton where *Man of the World* was shot, he became identified with his liking for Norfolk style corduroy jackets and sports trousers. He was glad to escape the rut of typecasting adding, "Another reason was that I very much wanted to work in England. Alexis made a picture in England several years ago and she adores the place." One throwback to *Peter Gunn* was the theme music of this series was also written by Henry Mancini. The series was a considerable success particularly in Europe, but it ended in something of a debacle. Scheduled shooting of the final six episodes coincided with the notorious actors' strike in 1962 when Actors' Equity went head to head with ATV for four months. Although the strike was resolved, other commitments prevented Stevens from shooting the remaining scripts.

At the Shubert Theater on October 3, 1963 he made his Broadway debut in the musical *Here's Love* with Janis Paige. The book, music and lyrics were by Meredith Willson from the source "Miracle on 34th Street." It became a moderate success more because of its subject matter than its intrinsic merit. The book was considered superficial, while the score was unmemorable. Stevens had a good baritone voice which was

Craig Stevens in *Peter Gunn*.

never used in movies, but he did not seem particularly at home with his comedy solo "She Hadda Go Back." He continued in the show until July 25, 1964. He then returned to television with *Mr. Broadway* in which he played a press agent Mike Bell whose zeal to protect the public image of his clients involved him in perilous situations usually with overtones of comedy. Although it had an interesting premise, it lasted only half a season of 13 episodes in 1964. The producers of *Mr. Broadway* bought him out of his *Here's Love* contract for $30,000.

In 1967 Blake Edwards coscripted and directed *Gunn* which was a feature film derived from the television series with Stevens in his original role. The feature which was not widely seen did not duplicate the success of its pedigree, being deemed overly violent. The sleazy milieu of the film was the wrong one for Stevens and was too repellent for most tastes. Color was also a mistake because it looked too garish as compared to the original black and white noir look of the original. Neither Lola Albright nor Herschel Bernardi were available to reprise their original roles for different reasons which upset Craig Stevens. Edwards also gave Stevens his last major film role in a film *SOB.* (1981) notable as the film in which Julie Andrews flashed her bare breasts to the disgust of all who preferred her more wholesome image.

In 1973 he toured as Henry Higgins in *My Fair Lady* and in 1975 toured in a one man show *Nash at Nine* in which he played Ogden Nash. He avoided television for about five years after the *Mr. Broadway* failure. He began to guest star in series again in the late sixties and in 1975 he had the regular role of Walter Carlson in *The Invisible Man* series which starred David McCallum. In retrospect it is a pity that an excellent pilot which he shot called *The Cabot Connection* (1977) did not make it to a series. His final television appearance was as a guest star on a *Marcus Welby M.D.* television special in 1988.

Stevens and his wife divided their time between homes in New York and California. She preferred the East Coast, while he preferred the West Coast. They appeared together in the films *Affectionately Yours, Dive Bomber, Steel Against the Sky, The Doughgirls* and finally the European lensed *The Trout* (1982). They frequently performed on stage together notably in a touring version of *Forty Carats* and the national company of *Cactus Flower*. Although Smith retired in 1959, she made a triumphant Broadway debut in 1971 winning a Tony for her performance in *Follies*. She was born in Penticton, Canada on June 8, 1921 and died in Los Angeles on June 9, 1993. The greatest regret of his life was that they did not have any children together.

After her death he formed a close relationship with Frances Bergen, mother of actress Candice and widow of ventriloquist Edgar. He died at 1:55 am at Cedars-Sinai Medical Center in Los Angeles on May 10, 2000 aged 81 of pneumonia following a three month battle with cancer. There were no funeral services at his request. The Neptune Society arranged for his body to be cremated and his ashes scattered at sea off the coast of Los Angeles County. His hobbies were listed as playing tennis and golf, building furniture, painting and sculpture. His estate amounted to approximately $2 million.

Filmography

1939: *Mr. Smith Goes to Washington.*
1941: *Affectionately Yours, Law of the Tropics, Dive Bomber, Steel Against the Sky.*
1942: *Secret Enemies, Now Voyager, Spy Ship, The Hidden Hand.*
1943: *This Is the Army.*
1944: *Hollywood Canteen, The Doughgirls, Since You Went Away.*
1945: *God Is My Co-Pilot, Roughly Speaking, Too Young to Know.*
1946: *Humoresque, The Man I Love.*
1947: *That Way with Women, Love and Learn.*
1949: *The Lady Takes a Sailor, Night Unto Night.*
1950: *Where the Sidewalk Ends, Blues Busters.*
1951: *The Lady From Texas, Drums in the Deep South, Katie Did It.*
1952: *Phone Call From a Stranger.*
1953: *Murder Without Tears, Abbott and Costello Meet Dr. Jekyll and Mr. Hyde.*
1954: *The French Line.*
1955: *Duel on the Mississippi.*
1957: *The Deadly Mantis.*
1958: *Buchanan Rides Alone.*
1967: *Gunn.*
1968: *The Limbo Line.*
1970: *McCloud: Who Killed Miss USA?* (a.k.a. *Portrait of a Dead Girl*) (TV).
1972: *The Snoop Sisters* (a.k.a. *The Female Instinct*) (TV).
1974: *The Killer Bees* (TV), *The Elevator* (TV).
1977: *The Love Boat II* (TV).
1978: *Secrets of Three Hungry Wives* (TV).
1981: *SOB.*
1982: *The Trout.*
1986: *Condor* (TV).
1988: *Marcus Welby MD: A Family Affair* (TV).

Television Series

1958–1961: *Peter Gunn* as Peter Gunn.
1962: *Man of the World* as Michael Strait.
1964: *Mr. Broadway* as Mike Bell.
1975–1976: *The Invisible Man* as Walter Carlson.
1981: *Dallas* as Craig Stewart.

Miniseries

1976: *Rich Man Poor Man Book I* as Asher Berg.

Sources

Daily Telegraph. Obituary, May 18, 2000.
Death Certificate.
Ferguson, Ken, and Sylvia Ferguson. *ATV Television Show Book.* London: Purnell, 1963.
_____. *Television Stars.* London: Purnell, 1966.
Inman, David. *The TV Encyclopedia.* New York: Perigee, 1991.
Johnson, Patricia. "This Is What Makes a Man of the World." *TV Times.* November 3, 1962.
Meyers, Rick. *Murder on the Air.* New York: Mysterious, 1989.

National Enquirer. "Death of TV's Peter Gunn Ends a Lifetime of Love." June 6, 2000.

Parish, James Robert, and Lennard DeCarl. *Hollywood Players: The Forties.* New Rochelle, NY: Arlington, 1976.

Quinlan, David. *Film Stars.* 5th ed. London: Batsford, 2000.

TV Star Annual. No. 7. 1959.

Vallance, Tom. *The Independent.* Obituary, May 15, 2000.

Ward, Jack. *Television Guest Stars.* Jefferson, NC: McFarland, 1993.

Who's Who in Show Biz. London: Purnell, 1963.

JULIE STEVENS

Julie Stevens was born in St. Louis, Missouri on November 23, 1916. She made an abortive attempt to enter films during 1939–1940 when she was under contract to Warners. Later on television she became the third actress to play Lorelei Kilbourne in the newspaper drama series *Big Town* which starred Pat McVey as Steve Wilson. As with others she only lasted a season. Never a particularly comfortable film or television player, she was a stalwart of national radio initially in Chicago and later in New York. She played the title character in the soap opera *The Romance of Helen Trent* for sixteen years between 1944 and 1960. In retirement she continued to be active in local radio in Massachusetts and did community theater on Cape Cod.

Stevens died in Wellfleet, Massachusetts on August 26, 1984 aged 67.

FILMOGRAPHY

1939: *Private Detective.*
1940: *Honeymoon Deferred, Castle on the Hudson, Tear Gas Squad, Murder in the Air.*

TELEVISION SERIES

1951–1952: *Big Town* as Lorelei Kilbourne.

Note: She was not the actress of the same name, born in Prestwich, England in 1936, best known for playing Venus Smith in the television series *The Avengers.*

SOURCES

Brooks, Tim. *The Complete Directory to Prime Time TV Stars, 1946–Present.* New York: Ballantine, 1987.

DeLong, Thomas A. *Radio Stars.* Jefferson, NC: McFarland, 1996.

MARK STEVENS

Mark Stevens was an enigma. Although he overcame numerous obstacles to become a star, his career somehow lost its way. He was a dependable leading man whose career peaked at 20th Century–Fox. When he was under contract there during the forties, he specialized in tough thrillers and Technicolor musicals. It was said that from the beginning of any film, his concentration on his work was total and he only relaxed completely between pictures. Once cast adrift his career declined, but he extended it by turning director. He became a well known television name by starring in two mystery series *Big Town* and *Martin Kane.* In his television career he made a strong attempt to emulate the success of Jack Webb, but in Stevens' case it did not work. He acquired a bad reputation in Hollywood which possibly also harmed his career.

Mark Stevens was born Mark Richard Stevens in Cleveland, Ohio on December 13, 1915. His father was an American flyer. He was only a few months old when his parents divorced. When he was three his mother brought him to England to live with her parents, Captain and Mrs. William Morrison, in Folkestone, Kent. Three years later, both his grandmother and grandfather having died, he and his mother returned to Cleveland to live for a year. After this they went to live in Montreal with his mother's sister where he received his education from private tutors and at various schools. He was a rebellious child and expelled from virtually every school he ever attended. From the age of seven when he saw his first stage show, he determined that he would be an actor. Although it was a stage show he had seen, the screen was the object of his ambition.

When he was twelve, his mother married again. His stepfather, James Cooke, was vice-president of the Railway and Engineering Supply Company in Montreal. At the age of about fourteen, he jumped off a diving board, missed his timing and hit the end of the board as he came down. It was a painful injury which flared up years later and necessitated him having operations, one of which laid him up for months. This injury also contributed to his prickly nature in Hollywood.

When he reached the age of sixteen, he decided that it was time he did something about his career. His mother and stepfather were not at all keen on him becoming an actor, so to save

Mark Stevens, who starred in *Big Town* and *Martin Kane*.

them embarrassment he adopted the name of Stephen Richards and sought an audition with the Corona Barn players in Montreal and was promptly engaged. Next he became juvenile lead with the Atterbury Players, a Montreal stock company where he played in a number of melodramas. He also did some radio work and fulfilled night club engagements. During the time he was struggling for success in acting he had many disappointments and there were many occasions when he was near starvation.

His parents were well-to-do, but because of their disapproval of his choice of a career, he accepted help from them only on a few occasions. At their insistence he even went into his father's business for a time and was shifted from department to department in a vain attempt to find some aspect of the business in which he might find an interest. His love of acting refused to die and he continued to show up for his performances at the local stock company at 8 pm, finish at 11:30 pm, go to a nightclub where he had a job as a singer and M.C., return home at 3 am and then be on time at his stepfather's business the next morning.

Eventually he felt that he could not stand business life any longer so he set off for Chicago en route for Hollywood. Luck was not with him for a nearly fatal attack of ptomaine poisoning took him home again. Once more he tried to fall in with the wishes of his family and follow a career other than the stage. He turned his art studies to account by taking a job as a commercial artists' apprentice with an engineering company. Despite his efforts, he could not help being bored and this at last led to him being fired. Many a job he had after that. Meanwhile he still satisfied his longing for acting by playing in stock companies at night.

One day he set off for Chicago again, this time with the purpose of enlisting in the Air Force, but he was turned down for every branch of the service because of the back injury suffered in the diving accident. He returned to Canada and again worked at odd jobs. Then he obtained some engagements with the Montreal Repertory Theater and this fired his theatrical ambition anew. On the pretext of visiting friends he went to New York in 1938, but he was not successful in obtaining a stage engagement. Although he tried every employment agency in town, he could not obtain any other type of job either. He endured months of near starvation and slept rough, but at last he had to put his pride in his pocket and write his stepfather to wire him the money to return home.

After several more jobs it occurred to him that he might be able to reach the screen via radio. He managed to wangle a job on the technical side and later became an announcer and wrote, directed and starred in dramas. He was narrator of a program called *Canada Carries On* which depicted Canada's part in the war effort. He saved money from his radio jobs and then decided to tackle Hollywood. He was active in radio for a spell in Akron, Ohio. He arrived in Hollywood in June 1943 with $500 in savings in his pocket, but made the mistake of spending his money recklessly by taking a suite at an expensive hotel and visiting swanky nightclubs. Soon he was penniless. He pawned his clothes, took an inexpensive room at Long Beach and started on a round of the studios with no luck at all. Soon he was sleeping on the beach.

Then through a friend's introduction he met an actor's agent, Nat Goldstone, who arranged for him to try the film studios again. This time he was more successful. Twentieth Century–Fox, Warner Bros. and MGM all agreed to give him a screen test. The Fox test was unavoidably postponed. To reach Warner Bros.' studio, he had to travel twelve miles. He had no money so he tried unsuccessfully to hitchhike passing cars, but finally had to walk there. He arrived late and was extremely tired, but he passed his screen test and won a contract at $100 a week. He made several appearances for them under the name of Stephen Richards, a reversal of his real name, but once he realized that Warners were not going to promote him as star material, he wanted to quit. He had a good role as Errol Flynn's co-pilot in *Objective Burma* (1945), but in England this film was greeted with a public outcry and withdrawn from release after only a few days at Warners Theater in Leicester Square, London. The reason was because it claimed that the Americans won Burma single-handedly with no contribution from the British. Most of Stevens' part in *God is My Co-Pilot* (1945) ended up on the cutting room floor. He was given only one speech to deliver in another film *Pride of the Marines* (1945). Then he found out that he had been given what amounted to a bit part in another film. He refused to show up on the set, thereby achieving his goal namely cancellation of his contract.

That same day 20th Century–Fox signed him up to a long term contract without even bothering to test him. He was cast by them fourth billed in *Within These Walls* (1946), a modest but intriguing prison film. For this studio he reverted back to his real name. Then he was borrowed by RKO Radio to costar with Joan Fontaine in *From This Day Forward* (1946). After this he was fourth billed, but the focal point as a private eye, in *The Dark Corner* (1946), a mystery thriller which really put him over. Fox were so pleased that they gave him a new contract.

A bit player on the set of *Objective Burma* introduced him to Annelle Hayes, an attractive college student from Texas, who had been brought to Warner Bros. for a screen test. He proposed on a roller coaster in Ocean Park and in March 1945 he married her. For five months they were unable to find anywhere to live in Hollywood because of the number of people who wanted to live there. The bride had to go on living at the studio club while he stayed with friends. They eventually found a small apartment overlooking Pickfair, Mary Pickford's home. His main hobby was painting seascapes and landscapes in oils and he enjoyed some success selling them. His back injury prevented him from playing sports so he contented himself with going for long walks. He and his wife nearly split up in 1947 when he became romantically involved with Hedy Lamarr who wanted to use him in two of her independent films. In the event he appeared in neither. Eventually he and his wife reconciled. He and his wife had two children, a son Mark Richard born in 1946 and a daughter Arrelle, but divorced in 1962. In 1964 his ex-wife sued him for failing to maintain alimony and child support payments.

Onscreen he had the role of Olivia de Havilland's husband in the prestigious *The Snake Pit* (1948). He starred as an FBI agent in another excellent thriller *The Street With No Name* (1948) with Richard Widmark. Of the Technicolor musicals in which he appeared *I Wonder Who's Kissing Her Now* (1947) opposite June Haver in which he played old time tunesmith Joe Howard was the best. Oddly, although he had a fine singing voice, his singing was dubbed.

When he parted company with Fox, he started freelancing from a position of strength. He turned director where he revealed a talent for handling suspense, but his own productions like *Timetable* (1955) were somewhat undermined by budgetary limitations. He also produced as well as starred in four of his films. He appeared in some Westerns both in films and on television, but it was not a genre to which he was ideally suited.

He made his first television appearance in 1951 in an episode of the syndicated anthology series *Story Theater*. He was an active performer mainly in anthology series throughout the fifties. In 1953 he assumed the lead in *Martin Kane* for the final season of that series and insisted the title be changed from *Martin Kane Private Eye* to *Martin Kane*. Kane was a smooth talking private investigator with a ready wit and a reasonable relationship with the police who during his season were represented by Lt. Grey (King Calder). Stevens was the fourth and last actor to play the role in the television series which was shown on the NBC network. He made changes to the scripts of *Martin Kane*, eliminated his pipe smoking in favor of cigarettes and insisted the character be called Martin not Marty. He tried to eliminate clichés and unnecessary fights.

When the newspaper drama series *Big Town* switched networks from CBS to NBC in 1954, Patrick McVey was dropped and Stevens was hired instead to play the role of Steve Wilson. For the second season he formed Mark Stevens Television Productions in 1955 and bought all rights to the series. Not only did he become his own producer, but he also directed and scripted some segments as well. He instantly promoted his own character from being a reporter to the editor. He tried to introduce more realistic stories drawn from real newspaper files. His characterization was a great deal more intense and serious than the more light-hearted one which McVey had played. He also had a different star reporter and girlfriend each season. The first was Lorelei Kilbourne (Trudy Wroe) while the second was Diane Walker (Doe Avedon). The Stevens episodes were later syndicated as *Headline* and *Byline Steve Wilson*. He plainly had delusions that he was going to become a powerful television entrepreneur such as Jack Webb or William Boyd, but the series was axed after he had played the role for two seasons. Stevens bitched that it had fallen victim to network politics. The time slot which the network had allocated for it did not justify increased production costs, but they refused to change the time slot because Stevens rather than the network owned the show.

By the late 1950s he had become disillusioned and semi-retired from acting in 1956 to concentrate on running a music publishing business, Mark Stevens Music Inc., which was similar to a business which Jack Webb pursued. He had also invested in various other outside business interests such as a uranium mine. Stevens remained active in show business. He directed and was a guest star on television, but he was never as powerful again. He also announced grand plans to buy land where he intended to erect his own studio. This did not come to fruition.

Instead in 1958 he abruptly left Hollywood and went into exile in Majorca for fifteen years where he operated a bar and restaurant. The reason for this became obvious when in 1962 he filed a voluntary bankruptcy petition in American federal court listing debts of nearly $500,000 while his assets totaled only $500. When living in Spain, he wrote a few novels which did not find much popular success. Presumably his back problem must eventually have cleared up because at least one source indicates that he was a tennis coach as well. His final American film was *Fate is the Hunter* (1964) in which he was very effective in his scenes as a former airline pilot who has descended via booze to the gutter. This film indicated a possible future as a character actor which in the event failed to materialize. Whilst in Spain he directed movies. He starred in four films in Europe which were an unfortunate coda to his film career. He also made appearances in small roles in a few dire Spanish movies which were never seen outside their country of origin. In 1974 he returned to Hollywood, but in spite of his grafting for the next decade, the only roles he could find were six guest shots on television, the last of which seems to have been an episode of *Scarecrow and Mrs. King* originally telecast in 1987. He was not at all pleased to discover that a porno actor Marc Stevens was using a similar name.

Mark Stevens returned to Spain where he died in obscurity at Majores of cancer on September 15, 1994 aged 78 survived by his two children. There were no newspaper obituaries of him ever published, but he does have a star on Hollywood's Walk of Fame located at Hollywood Boulevard.

Filmography

1943: *Destination Tokyo, Background to Danger, Northern Pursuit.*
1944: *Passage to Marseilles, The Doughgirls, Hollywood Canteen.*
1945: *Objective Burma, Pride of the Marines, Rhapsody in Blue, God is My Co-Pilot.*
1946: *Within These Walls, From This Day Forward, The Dark Corner.*
1947: *I Wonder Who's Kissing Her Now?*
1948: *The Snake Pit, The Street With No Name.*
1949: *Will James' Sand, Oh You Beautiful Doll!, Dancing in the Dark.*
1950: *Please Believe Me, Between Midnight and Dawn.*
1951: *Target Unknown, Katie Did It, Reunion in Reno, Little Egypt.*
1952: *Jack Slade, The Lost Hours* (a.k.a. *The Big Frame*).
1953: *Mutiny, Torpedo Alley.*
1954: *Cry Vengeance* (also directed).
1955: *Timetable* (also directed).
1957: *Gunsight Ridge, Gun Fever* (also directed).
1958: *Gunsmoke in Tucson.*
1960: *September Storm.*
1963: *Escape from Hell Island* (also directed).
1964: *Fate is the Hunter.*
1965: *Frozen Alive.*
1966: *Sunscorched* (also directed), *Go with God Gringo.*
1969: *Espana otra vez.*
1970: *La Lola dicen que no vive sola.*
1971: *Es usted mi padre?*
1972: *La Furia del Hombre Lobo* (a.k.a. *The Fury of the Wolfman, The Wolfman Never Sleeps*).

TELEVISION SERIES

1953–1954: *Martin Kane* as Martin Kane.
1954–1956: *Big Town* as Steve Wilson.

SOURCES

Henry, Martyn. *Film Collector*. No. 56. Fall 1977.
Inman, David. *The TV Encyclopedia*. New York: Perigee, 1991.
Ingram, Frances. "Man of Many Talents." *Classic Images*. No. 332. February 2003.
Lentz, Harris M. III. *Obituaries in the Performing Arts, 1994*. Jefferson, NC: McFarland, 1996.
Picture Show Annual. London: Amalgamated, 1947, 1948, 1950, 1952, 1953 and 1956.
Picture Show. "Life Story." Vol. 50, No. 1297. September 9, 1946.
Quinlan, David. *Film Stars*. 5th ed. London: Batsford, 2000.
Rovin, Jeff. *The Great American Television Series*. South Brunswick, NJ: Barnes, 1977.
Stannage, Robert. *Film Favourites*. London: Film Book Club, 1946.
Winchester, Clarence. *Screen Encyclopedia*. London: Winchester, 1948.

PAUL STEWART

Paul Stewart was born Paul Sternberg in New York City on March 13, 1908. He was the son of Maurice D. Sternberg and Nathalie Caroline Nathanson. He was educated at Columbia University between 1927 and 1928 and at Brooklyn Law School from 1928 to 1930. To fund his studies he worked part time at the law firm of Dun and Bradstreet and at the Allied Board of Trade. From 1930 onwards he pursued a career as an actor and director. He toured with a road company, but returned to New York in 1931. During a quiet spell he obtained casual employment as an apartment rental agent while seeking acting opportunities.

He made his Broadway debut as a newspaperman in *Two Seconds* and made other appearances on Broadway and in summer stock. He moved into radio and in total went on to make nearly 5,000 broadcasts. Between 1935 and 1939 he was part of Orson Welles' Mercury Theater Group working on *The March of Time* radio series. He acted as producer of Mercury Theater of the Air including the notorious *War of the Worlds* broadcast in 1938 which panicked America. Between 1938 and 1941 he became a director of daytime radio serials for CBS and NBC. Orson Welles brought him to Hollywood to make his screen debut in *Citizen Kane* (1941) in the role of Raymond, Kane's oily valet. He appeared in a few more features before producing *News from America* radio show for the Office of War Information between 1944 and 1945. Then he worked in a producing, directing, writing capacity for David O. Selznick and later Dore Schary.

In the late forties he resumed his acting career and notched up several fine characterizations mainly as gangsters, but also playing agents and business managers. From 1950 onwards he also appeared on television. *Top Secret U.S.A.* was an obscure syndicated series of 26 half hour, black and white episodes produced by Revue, Universal's television wing in 1954. Paul Stewart and Gena Rowlands starred as operatives of the Bureau of Science Information in a series which mingled science fiction with international intrigue. Stewart directed at least one episode of this.

In 1956 he announced that he intended to continue his career primarily as a director. He then went on to helm multiple episodes of mainly crime orientated television series which were done in an anonymously professional manner. Plans to direct feature films did not work out. In spite of his resolve to devote himself almost totally to this craft, he still found himself accepting acting roles in film and television. He served as host and narrator of the syndicated series *Deadline*, a newspaper anthology series. It dramatized events in the lives of newspaper reporters. It was produced by Flamingo Films and Pyramid Productions in 1959. There were 39 half hour, black and white episodes. Stewart starred in 13 of these and helmed several segments of this series. Although newspaper stories are not necessarily violent, this series aimed for quick profits by emphasizing the action content and therefore most of the episodes were crime orientated.

In 1974 while on location in Mexico shooting *Bite the Bullet*, Stewart suffered a heart attack, but recovered and resumed his career. He went on directing and acting into the 1980s. He died in a Los Angeles hospital on February 17, 1986 aged 77. He had been in hospital since the previous November when he had suffered a heart attack. He wed vocalist Peg LaCentra (1910–1996) in 1939 who survived him.

Stewart was one of the founders of the American Federation of Television and Radio Actors (A.F.T.R.A.). He was very active in union

Paul Stewart, who hosted *Deadline* **and starred in** *Top Secret U.S.A.*

affairs both in A.F.T.R.A and the Screen Actors Guild (S.A.G.).

Filmography

1941: *Citizen Kane.*
1942: *Johnny Eager.*
1943: *Mr. Lucky, Government Girl.*
1948: *Berlin Express* (narrated only).
1949: *Champion, Illegal Entry, Easy Living, Twelve O'Clock High, The Window.*
1950: *Edge of Doom, Walk Softly Stranger.*
1951: *Appointment with Danger.*
1952: *Deadline U.S.A., Carbine Williams, We're Not Married, Loan Shark.*
1953: *The Bad and the Beautiful, The Juggler, The Joe Louis Story.*
1954: *Deep in My Heart, Prisoner of War.*
1955: *Kiss Me Deadly, The Cobweb, Chicago Syndicate.*
1956: *Hell on Frisco Bay, The Wild Party.*
1957: *Top Secret Affair.*
1958: *King Creole.*
1959: *Flor de mayo* (a.k.a. *Beyond All Limits*).
1963: *A Child Is Waiting.*
1965: *The Greatest Story Ever Told.*
1967: *In Cold Blood.*
1969: *How to Commit Marriage.*
1970: *Carter's Army* (TV).
1971: *City Beneath the Sea* (a.k.a. *One Hour to Doomsday*) (TV).
1972: *Fabulous Trinity.*
1973: *F For Fake.*
1975: *Day of the Locust, Murph the Surf* (a.k.a. *Live a Little Steal a Lot, You Can't Steal Love*), *Bite the Bullet.*
1976: *W.C. Fields and Me.*
1977: *Opening Night.*
1978: *Revenge of the Pink Panther, The Nativity* (TV).
1981: *S.O.B., Nobody's Perfekt.*
1982: *Tempest.*
1983: *Emergency Room* (TV).
1985: *Seduced* (TV).

Television Series

1954: *Top Secret U.S.A.* as Professor Brand.
1959: *Deadline* Host and narrator.
1966–1967: *The Man Who Never Was* as Paul Grant.

Miniseries

1978: *The Dain Curse.*

Sources

Annual Obituary. Chicago: St. James, 1987.
DeLong, Thomas. *Radio Stars.* Jefferson, NC: McFarland, 1996.
Erickson, Hal. *Syndicated Television: The First Forty Years, 1947–1987.* Jefferson, NC: McFarland, 1989.
Inman, David. *The TV Encyclopedia.* New York: Perigee, 1991.
Parish, James Robert. *Hollywood Character Actors.* New Rochelle, NY: Arlington, 1978.
Quinlan, David. *Illustrated Directory of Film Character Actors.* 2nd ed. London: Batsford, 1996.
Twomey, Alfred E., and Arthur F. McClure. *The Versatiles.* South Brunswick, NJ: Barnes, 1969.
Variety. Obituary, February 1986.
Ward, Jack. *Television Guest Stars.* Jefferson, NC: McFarland, 1993.
Wicking, Christopher, and Tise Vahimagi. *The American Vein.* London: Talisman, 1979.
Willis, John. *Screen World.* Vol. 28. London: Frederick Muller, 1987.

Harold J. Stone

Harold J. Stone was born Harold Hockstein in Manhattan, New York on March 3, 1913. He was an only child. His father, Jacob Hockstein, was a well known Yiddish actor, stage manager and theater owner. The "J" in Harold's stage name stood for Jacob. His original ambition was to become a doctor. He enrolled in premedical studies at New York University, graduating with a B.A. Degree. Then he went on to do two years at the University of Buffalo Medical School. When his father died in 1931 and the Depression hit, he was forced to quit because there was no more money.

After doing various odd jobs, he decided to seek an acting career so he joined a co-operative theater in New Jersey in 1936, but this soon folded. Then he acquired some experience in stock and on radio. In 1939 he was hired through a relative to be a company security officer in a revue at the World's Fair. He devised himself a well received sketch in that. He made his Broadway debut in *The World We Make* as a Polish father in 1940. This play was followed by *Morning Star* for which he received a Theater World Award as one of the Ten Best Character Performances of 1939–1940. He did some successful plays after that for which he received glowing notices.

He originally went to Hollywood to shoot *Cloak and Dagger* (1946), but director Fritz Lang refused to use him because he had no movie experience. He stayed nine months, but could not land a part so back he went to New York to marry his first wife. A chance meeting with a couple of producer acquaintances led to him being hired as a stage manager for nine months in a touring company. After that he returned to New York where he did more stage work and eventually live television. Even then he found the going tough. To earn money to pay his debts for his daughter's birth, he did a stint as a cab driver.

Eventually in the early fifties he became frenetically busy doing live television and the play *Stalag 17* both in London and on Broadway. He was spotted doing a live television show by a talent agent from Columbia pictures. Columbia tested him and cast him as a sympathetic Jewish sports editor in the boxing film *The Harder They Fall* (1956) which was notable as Humphrey Bogart's last movie. Stone's personal favorite of his own films was another boxing film he made in the same year *Somebody Up There Likes Me* as Nick Barbella. For Alfred Hitchcock he played police officer Lt. Bowers in *The Wrong Man* (1956). Exteriors were shot in New York in a bitterly cold March and for various reasons it was an extremely difficult shoot. Interior scenes were shot in California which went better. Stone's

Harold J. Stone, who costarred in *Grand Jury*.

efforts were rewarded with Hitchcock's total approval. After this Stone did some summer stock and returned to New York.

He went to Hollywood to shoot *Slander* (1956) and moved there permanently initially renting, but later buying property in Brentwood. He appeared in several feature films and guested in many television series. He played regular roles in five television series, but oddly only one, *Grand Jury*, was a drama. The rest were all comedies.

Grand Jury was a well made, exciting series shot by National Telefilm Associates for Desilu which dramatized stories about investigations into the Mob. In keeping with this theme, the action was fast and furious. Most episodes ended with a fistfight. The series was at its best in showing how ordinary people were threatened by organized crime. There were 39 black and white, half hour episodes of this syndicated series originally shown between 1959 and 1960. Lyle Bettger and Harold J. Stone were the leading investigators, both of whom looked at home in this milieu.

Although Stone was based in California, he found himself commuting to New York for guest roles in series such as *The Defenders*. For one of these episodes of *The Nurses* he received an Emmy award nomination for Outstanding Single Performance by an Actor in a Leading Role during 1963–1964. He amassed a vast number of television credits. Although he was once one of the most ubiquitous character actors, the title of his last feature film *Hardly Working* (1981), summed up the state of his acting career during the last two decades.

Stone married firstly to Joan in 1946. His first wife died in 1961. With her he had a son named Michael who was born in 1949 and a daughter named Jennifer who was born in 1952. He remarried in 1962 to Miriam. With his second wife he had another son named Robert. They legally separated in 1964, but never divorced.

He died at the Motion Picture Country Home and Hospital, Woodland Hills, California on November 18, 2005 aged 92. He was survived by his 3 children and 4 grandchildren. He is buried at Mount Sinai Memorial Park, Los Angeles.

Filmography

1956: *The Harder They Fall, Somebody Up There Likes Me, The Wrong Man, Slander.*
1957: *House of Numbers, The Garment Jungle, Man Afraid, The Invisible Boy.*
1959: *These Thousand Hills, Stampede at Bitter Creek* (TV).
1960: *Spartacus.*
1962: *The Chapman Report.*
1963: *Showdown, "X"—The Man With the X-Ray Eyes.*
1965: *Girl Happy, The Greatest Story Ever Told.*
1967: *The St. Valentine's Day Massacre, The Big Mouth.*
1969: *Olsen Gang in a Fix.*
1970: *Breakout* (TV), *Which Way to the Front?*
1971: *The Seven Minutes.*
1972: *Pickup on 101.*
1975: *The Legend of Valentino* (TV), *The Wild McCulloughs, Mitchell, The Werewolf of Woodstock* (TV).
1981: *Hardly Working.*

Television Series

1949: *The Hartmans* as the handyman.
1952: *The Goldbergs* as Jake Goldberg.
1959–1960: *Grand Jury* as John Kennedy.
1969–1970: *My World and Welcome to It* as Hamilton Greeley.
1972–1973: *Bridget Loves Bernie* as Sam Steinberg.

Sources

Erickson, Hal. *Syndicated Television: The First Forty Years, 1947–1987.* Jefferson, NC: McFarland, 1989.
Goldrup, Tom, and Jim Goldrup. *Feature Players Stories: Behind the Faces.* Vol. 2. Published privately, 1992.
Hayward, Anthony. *The Independent* Obituary, December 5, 2005.
Inman, David. *The TV Encyclopedia.* New York: Perigee, 1991.
Lance, Steven. *Written Out of Television.* Lanham, MD: Madison, 1996.
Nelson, Valerie J. *L.A. Times* Obituary, November 19, 2005.
Nielsen, Ray. "Harold Stone: The Wrong Man." *Classic Images.* No. 220. October 1993.
Picture Show Annual. London: Amalgamated, 1958.
Quinlan, David. *Illustrated Directory of Film Character Actors.* 2nd ed. London: Batsford, 1995.
Variety Obituary, November 21, 2005.
Ward, Jack. *Television Guest Stars.* Jefferson, NC: McFarland, 1993.

Suzanne Storrs

Suzanne Storrs was born in Salt Lake City, Utah in 1934. Her sole regular role in a crime television series was as Janet Halloran, the wife of Det. Jim Halloran (James Franciscus), during the first season of *The Naked City*. When Franciscus opted to leave the series before it resumed in an hour length format, her part became redundant and the character was dropped. Between 1958 and 1961 Storrs appeared in episodes of other television series. Her final television appearance was the last episode of the western television series *Sugarfoot* which starred Will Hutchins. She understudied a role in the Broadway play *The Rehearsal* in 1963 before dropping out of sight.

Television Series

1958–1959: *The Naked City* as Janet Halloran.

Sources

Brooks, Tim. *The Complete Directory to Prime Time TV Stars, 1946–Present.* New York: Ballantine, 1987.
Tibballs, Geoff. *TV Detectives.* London: Boxtree, 1992.

Ludwig Stossel

Ludwig Stossel was born in Lockenhaus, Austria on February 12, 1883 and received his early formal education in Graz, Austria. He was trained at the Academy of Dramatic Art in Vienna and began working in the profession at the age of seventeen. Until 1938 he worked as an actor in Germany and Austria under many leading directors. He was imprisoned by the Nazis after they invaded Austria, but managed to escape initially to England. Then in 1940 he fled to America where he appeared in films and later on television for the next thirty years. At first he received money from a charity, the European Film Fund. He appeared in three of the finest films ever made. In *Pride of the Yankees* (1942) he played Pop Gehrig, the father of baseball player Lou Gehrig (Gary Cooper). In *Casablanca* (1942) he played Mr. Leuchtag, Carl's (S.Z. Sakall) friend who is emigrating to America. In *Call Me Madam* (1953) he played the Grand Duke.

In the short-lived television series *Casablanca* he played the headwaiter Ludwig, basically the same role S.Z. Sakall played in the original film. In the television crime series *Man with a Camera* he had a semi-regular role as Anton Kovac, whose photographer son Mike (Charles Bronson) sometimes sought his advice. During the 1960s Stossel was chosen by the Italian Swiss Colony wine makers to be their commercial spokesperson. Clad in an Alpine hat and leather trousers his motto was that he was "That Little Old Winemaker, Me!," in a series of commercials that spanned a decade. This was very lucrative and gave him a greater degree of economic security than most of his contemporaries who had fled from the Nazis.

Stossel died in Beverly Hills, CA on January 29, 1973 aged 89 survived by his wife, Eleanore.

Filmography

1927: *Herkules Maier.*
1929: *Gunstling von Schonbrunn* (a.k.a. *Favorite of Schonbrunn*), *Moblierte Zimmer, Katharina Knie.*
1930: *Skandal um Eva, Bockbierfest.*
1931: *Die Privatsekretarin, In Wien hab' ich einmal ein Madel geliebt, Opernredoute* (a.k.a. *Opera Ball*), *Die Koffer des Herrn O.F., Man braucht kein Geld, Hilfe! Uberfall, Elisabeth von Osterreich.*
1932: *Die Grafin von Monte-Christo, Der Rebell, Strich durch die Rechnung* (a.k.a. *Spoiling the Game, The Upset Plan*).
1933: *Hande aus dem Dunkel, Das Testament of Dr. Mabuse* (a.k.a. *The Crimes of Dr. Mabuse*), *Heimkehr ins Gluck, Rund um eine Million, Johannisnacht.*
1934: *Eine Nacht in Venedig* (a.k.a. *A Night in Venice*), *Nordpol—Ahoi!*
1937: *Pfarrer von Kirchfeld* (a.k.a. *The Pastor from Kirchfeld*).
1940: *Return to Yesterday, Dead Man's Shoes, Four Sons, The Man I Married, Dance Girl Dance, The Flying Squad, Jennie.*
1941: *Back Street, Man Hunt, Underground, Great Guns, Marry the Boss's Daughter, Down in San Diego.*
1942: *All Through the Night, Woman of the Year, King's Row, I Married an Angel, The Pride of the Yankees, Iceland, Who Done It?, Casablanca, Pittsburgh, The Great Impersonation, Tennessee Johnson* (a.k.a. *The Man on America's Conscience*).
1943: *They Came to Blow Up America, Hitler's Madman, Action in the North Atlantic, Hers to Hold, Above Suspicion, The Strange Death of Adolf Hitler.*
1944: *Bluebeard, The Climax, Lake Placid Serenade.*
1945: *Dillinger, Her Highness and the Bellboy, Yolanda and the Thief, House of Dracula.*
1946: *Girl on the Spot, Miss Susie Slagle's, Cloak and Dagger, Temptation.*
1947: *The Beginning or the End?, This Time for Keeps, Song of Love, Escape Me Never.*
1948: *A Song Is Born.*
1949: *The Great Sinner.*
1951: *As Young as You Feel, Corky of Gasoline Alley, Too Young to Kiss.*
1952: *The Merry Widow, Somebody Loves Me, No Time for Flowers.*
1953: *Call Me Madam, White Goddess, The Sun Shines Bright.*
1954: *Geraldine, Deep in My Heart.*
1958: *Me and the Colonel, From the Earth to the Moon.*
1959: *The Blue Angel.*
1960: *G.I. Blues.*

Television Series

1955–1956: *Casablanca* as Ludwig.
1958–1960: *Man with a Camera* as Anton Kovac.

Sources

Harmetz, Aljean. *Round Up the Usual Suspects.* London: Weidenfeld and Nicholson, 1993.
Inman, David. *The TV Encyclopedia.* New York: Perigee, 1991.
Twomey, Alfred E., and Arthur F. McClure. *The Versatiles.* New York: Barnes, 1969.
Willis, John. *Screen World.* Vol. 25. London: Muller, 1974.

Randy Stuart (left) and Alan Hale, Jr., in *Biff Baker U.S.A.*

RANDY STUART

Randy Stuart was born Elizabeth Shaubell in Iola, Kansas, on October 12, 1924. She started out at the age of three with her parents in their touring company. She had every kind of show business experience in vaudeville, stock, radio and television. After her parents settled in California, she went to college where her appearance in a play was seen by a talent scout. She did a test scene from *The Women* which was filmed. The test was seen by Hal B. Wallis who wanted to place her under contract, but had no suitable project for her. He allowed her to keep the test however which came to the attention of 20th Century–Fox who signed her to a contract in 1947.

She made her screen debut in *The Foxes of Harrow* (1947) as Rex Harrison's mother, in the prologue scene in which his character, Stephen Fox, is born. She was seen in supporting roles in some major Fox features dating from the late 1940s. Her studio biography indicated that she had blue eyes, blonde hair and stood 5'4½" tall. By far her best known film role was at Universal when she played Louise Carey, the wife of *The Incredible Shrinking Man* (1957) which starred Grant Williams in the title role.

She made her television debut in 1952. Her first regular series role was in *This Is the Life*, the religious series produced by the Lutheran Church which depicted a Christian family's attempts to deal with the problems of everyday life. The family was called the Fishers, and Stuart played the eldest daughter. She was seen in a rather more mature role in *Biff Baker USA* which was shown on CBS between November 1952 and March 1953. Biff Baker (Alan Hale Jr.) traveled the world in search of merchandise for his import business, but usually met trouble along the way. Stuart played his capable wife and partner, Louise. There was a certain amount of banter in their relationship, but she always accompanied her husband on his travels, so there was a lot of love and loyalty too. When Biff Baker was kidnapped in one episode, she refused to be left behind and joined the search to find him. Her character was very well integrated into the series. She found shooting it was physically very demanding however. She and Hale were well cast as a husband and wife combination. Possibly because Biff Baker was a man who worked for a living, the series emerged as far less dated than the rich, snobbish husband and wife sleuths who lounged around solving crimes as a hobby.

For a single season she brought romance into the life of Wyatt Earp when she played the owner and operator of the Birdcage Saloon in the famous television western series. She was very active at Warner Bros. in the late 1950s and early 1960s notably in *Bourbon Street Beat* where she had the occasional role as a female private eye. She semi-retired in 1964. In the revival of the *Dragnet* series in the late sixties, she had the recurring role of the wife of Officer Bill Gannon (Harry Morgan). Her last recorded appearance was an episode of *Police Woman* in 1976 in which she had a single scene as a judge.

Off screen in 1964 she was involved in Project Prayer, a movement dedicated to allowing voluntary prayer in public schools. In the same year she was active in the unsuccessful Goldwater presidential campaign. She was a founder of a Celebrity Speakers Bureau and wrote speeches for Ronald Reagan when he ran for Governor of California.

Although she had been married with children, Randy Stuart lived the last part of her life as a virtual recluse in Bakersfield, California, where she wanted neither publicity nor correspondence. She died there on July 20, 1996 at age 71 of lung cancer.

Filmography

1947: *The Foxes of Harrow*.
1948: *Sitting Pretty, The Street with No Name, Apartment for Peggy*.
1949: *I Was a Male War Bride, The Fan, Whirlpool, Dancing in the Dark*.
1950: *All About Eve, Stella*.
1951: *I Can Get It for You Wholesale*.

1952: *Room for One More.*
1956: *Star in the Dust.*
1957: *The Incredible Shrinking Man.*
1958: *The Man from God's Country.*

TELEVISION SERIES

1952–1953: *Biff Baker USA* as Louise Baker.
1952–1956: *This Is the Life* as Emily Fisher.
1959–1960: *The Life and Legend of Wyatt Earp* as Nellie Cashman.

SOURCES

Lentz, Harris M. III. *Obituaries in the Performing Arts, 1996.* Jefferson, NC: McFarland, 1997.
Magers, Boyd. "Empty Saddles." *Western Clippings.* Sept./Oct. 1996.
Picture Show Annual. London: Amalgamated, 1951.
Ward, Jack. *The Supporting Players of Television, 1959–1983.* Cleveland, OK: Lakeshore West, 1996.
Weaver, Tom. *Science Fiction and Fantasy Film Flashbacks.* Jefferson, NC: McFarland, 1998.

BARRY SULLIVAN

Barry Sullivan was often called upon to support some of the greatest actresses of the silver screen in their post-war films. Unlike some of his weak pre-war equivalents, Sullivan had a fairly strong presence which made itself felt so that fireworks were guaranteed. Possibly this reached its zenith in *Forty Guns* (1957) in which Barbara Stanwyck was held captive. Sullivan wounded her deliberately and then shot dead her would be captor without blinking an eye. His height and mellifluous voice were decided assets in his career. He was one of only a small number of actors who moved between large and small screens without ever becoming either typecast or passé.

In real life Sullivan was rather a tense and sensitive individual who sought solace in drink. He was far too professional to drink when working and it did not affect his career. Veteran independent producer Sid Pink used him as the star of *Pyro* (1964), an offbeat but very commercially successful film shot in Spain. He considered Sullivan one of the most talented actors who ever worked for him. When sober he was an erudite and charming man. Pink recalled however that bleak moods would descend upon the actor who would go on benders which made him prone to fits of violent rage and gutter language.

Patrick Francis Barry Sullivan was born in New York City on August 29, 1912, the son of Cornelius Daniel Sullivan. His father was a real estate operator of Irish origin. He was the third of five sons all of whom followed different careers. His early ambition was to become a lawyer and with this career in mind, he studied at both New York University and Temple University in Philadelphia. He dropped his first two Christian names at an early age. At college he played both football and baseball.

While at Temple University, he was chosen as the male lead in a college production of *Holiday*. The leading lady was an extremely tall girl and it was necessary for her to play opposite a leading man who was taller than she. The football team was assembled and the tallest man told to step out. At nearly six feet three, this was Sullivan. His appearance in that and other college plays made him realize that he would rather be an actor than a lawyer.

Once his college days were over he spent several seasons in summer stock. He gained valuable experience, but made little money. In order to supplement his income he did all kinds of other jobs. There were stints ushering in a theater, buying knickknacks for a chain of department stores and even washing cars. He made his professional stage debut in 1936 in the part of Bing Edwards in *Brother Rat.* At that time Eddie Bracken was in the cast and they shared digs together. He made his first Broadway appearance in *I Want a Policeman* which opened in January 1936. His first four Broadway plays were all flops. Sullivan played with Alfred Lunt and Lynn Fontanne in *Idiot's Delight* (1938); with Ina Claire and Henry Daniell in *Yankee Fable* (1938); the romantic lead in *The Man Who Came to Dinner* (1939) which was by far his biggest hit; with Fay Wray in *Mr. Big* (1941) which opened and closed in a week; with Jane Cowl in *Ring Around Elizabeth* (1941) which had a similar fate; and Diana Barrymore's brother in *The Land is Bright* (1941).

In April 1942 he was appearing on Broadway in *Johnny Two By Four* when he received the offer of a Paramount contract. He did not arrive on the West Coast to begin the contract until the end of June where his first assignment was a patriotic short *We Refuse to Die.* He made his proper screen debut in *The Woman of the Town* (1943) which starred Claire Trevor. Part of his expenses at Temple University had been paid for by working at the university diner. That experience stood him in good stead when he briefly returned to New York in December 1942 where he washed

Barry Sullivan, who starred in *Harbormaster* and *The Man Called X*.

dishes with Raymond Massey at the famed Stage Door Canteen.

Of the first batch of films which he made *And Now Tomorrow* (1944) stood out. His character was engaged to his factory owner boss (Loretta Young). Alan Ladd played a dedicated doctor in an effort to prove that he could play a quieter, more introspective and romantic part. While the film was a commercial success, it was not the kind of film Ladd's fans expected and he seldom tried this kind of role again. Off screen however Ladd helped Sullivan by taking him to view the rushes and pointing out the flaws in his performance. Since Sullivan was a stage trained actor, he tended to play too broadly. He felt much happier about cinema acting after Ladd's one to one master class.

Paramount loaned Sullivan to the King Brothers for two features both costarring him with ice skater turned movie star Belita whom he thought was a flake, but a delightful person. The first was *Suspense* (1946) released by Monogram notable as the only ice skating film noir. The second was *The Gangster* (1947) released through Allied Artists. Sullivan had the title role in this arty crime drama which was probably more enjoyable for the players than the audience. It was allegedly his personal favorite of his own films. He played the disgruntled husband Tom Buchanan in *The Great Gatsby* (1949) which starred Alan Ladd in the title role of this version of the F. Scott Fitzgerald novel. As a freelance actor Sullivan appeared in *Payment on Demand* (1950) at RKO, a melodrama in which he played a corporation attorney who wanted to end his marriage to ruthless Bette Davis.

In 1949 he made the switch from Paramount to MGM where he remained in steady employment. One of his strongest studies in villainy was *Cause for Alarm* (1951) shot in an early television style format. He played the insanely jealous husband of Loretta Young who frames her on a murder charge. One of his most prestigious films was *The Bad and the Beautiful* (1952) in which he played an ambitious Hollywood director who wants to shoot Lana Turner's next movie. He appeared in other films with Turner, one of which *Another Time, Another Place* (1958) marked his first trip to Europe. One of his best films at MGM was *Cry of the Hunted* (1953) a chase thriller which benefited from taut direction and a witty script.

He was the leading man to Claudette Colbert in *Texas Lady* (1955) at RKO, one of her last movies. He appeared opposite Barbara Stanwyck on three occasions. The first of these was *Jeopardy* (1953) in which he played her husband. The couple and their son are vacationing in Mexico when he accidentally finds himself trapped under a rotting jetty with the tide coming in. The only help which Stanwyck can find is from an escaped convict (Ralph Meeker) in this taut John Sturges directed thriller. He appeared with Stanwyck in two westerns *The Maverick Queen* (1956) and *Forty Guns* (1957). The latter, directed by Sam Fuller, was ridiculed when first released, but has since acquired a cult status. He played the husband of Joan Crawford in *Queen Bee* (1955).

He made his television debut in an episode of *Ford Theater* in 1953. In 1954 he made a triumphant return to Broadway to play the defense attorney in *The Caine Mutiny Court-Martial* adapted by Herman Wouk from his bestselling novel. He and Lloyd Nolan later repeated their roles in a prestigious television version shown on *Four Star Jubilee* on CBS in 1955. His final Broadway appearance in *Too Late the Phalarope* was a flop in 1956. Sullivan turned to television increasingly in later years and was the star of four series. The first of these was *The Man Called X*. This derived from an enormously popular wartime radio series which starred Herbert Marshall. In the television version Sullivan played secret agent Ken Thurston whose missions involved him traveling all over the world to rescue beautiful maidens in distress and kidnapped scientists from behind the Iron Curtain. The stories came from genuine government files, the studio backlot provided the locations and the technical adviser was a former U.S. Naval Intelligence officer. This syndicated series from ZIV lasted for 39 half hour, black and white episodes which were originally shown during 1955 and 1956.

He then went on to shoot *Harbormaster* which consisted of 26 half hour, black and white episodes produced by United Artists originally aired during 1957 and 1958. This was a hybrid series part crime and part adventure. Scott Island was a small, secluded island off the New England coast. He played Captain David Scott whose ancestors had settled in this place during the previous century. Scott's job was to take care of all matters relating to shipping and anchorage on the island, but he was also a police officer. His assistant harbormaster was the able bodied Jeff Kittridge (Paul Burke). The main eating house on the Island was the Dolphin Restaurant run by Ann Morrison (Nina Wilcox) who wanted to become romantically involved with Scott. Captain Dan (Mike Keene), Professor Wheeler (Murray Matheson) and the young boy Danny (Evan Elliott) were also involved in the stories. Thirteen episodes of this series were originally screened on the CBS network between September and December 1957. The series switched networks to ABC where a further thirteen episodes were screened between January and June 1958 under the title of *Adventures at Scott Island*.

His third series was a western *The Tall Man* and the most highly regarded of the four. It lasted for two seasons and a total of 78 half hour, black and white episodes produced by Revue and shown on NBC between September 1960 and September 1962. Sullivan played Deputy Sheriff Pat Garrett, nicknamed "The Tall Man," while Clu Gulager played Billy the Kid. The series was a heavily fictionalized account of the friendship and conflict between the two. Eventually this led to a real life showdown in which Billy the Kid was killed by one of Garrett's men, although this was not shown in the series. Sullivan's final television series was another western series *The Road West* which was shown on NBC between September 1966 and August 1967. Sullivan played Benjamin Pride, a widower who took his family from Springfield, Ohio to Kansas shortly after the end of the Civil War. Stories derived from problems which members of the family encountered once they arrived there. There were 26 hour length, color episodes in this series produced by Universal. A two hour film was edited from the footage and later shown theatrically under the title *This Savage Land*.

He was one of two actors who substituted for Raymond Burr on *Perry Mason* when the actor was indisposed for the second time. Sullivan reluctantly did "The Case of the Thermal Thief" which aired in January 1965. His best remembered television appearance however was in the television pilot of the *Night Gallery* (1969) series in which he played a fugitive war criminal. This was a three story supernatural anthology which served as Steven Spielberg's television directing debut. The spin-off anthology series which featured Rod Serling as host was in a similar vein to his previous series *The Twilight Zone*. Sullivan featured in the pilot episodes of a number of other series. He also appeared in *Savage* (1973) which was Spielberg's final television film to date. Although he continued to make film appearances, Sullivan frequently had too little screen time to make his considerable presence felt. One of his final film roles provided an exception. This was *Earthquake* (1974) in which he played the jealous head of the seismological institute who refused to accept the dire warnings of his younger assistant. He spent a lot of time during the last years of his career railing against the new Hollywood and the untalented trendies who ran it. Nevertheless he went on working and his outbursts did not affect his career in the slightest.

Sullivan continued acting until 1980 when he retired because of ill-health. His last television appearance was an episode of *Vegas* which originally aired in 1980. House decorating, watching football and baseball were listed amongst his recreations, but playing golf was his favorite hobby. He died at his Sherman Oaks, California home on June 6, 1994 aged 81 of a long standing respiratory ailment. He was cremated and his ashes given to his family.

He was married and divorced three times. His first was Marie Brown, a stage actress, whom he married in 1937 and divorced in 1957. Secondly, he married Swedish actress and former Miss Stockholm of 1952, Gita Hall who was born in 1929 (with whom he appeared in the film *Wolf Larsen*) secretly on July 25, 1958. This only became public knowledge when he divorced her in September 1959. They later remarried, but divorced again on April 10, 1961. As he expressed it,

"I hate the publicity because of my kids." He married Egyptian actress Desiree Sumara aged 23 in 1963, but divorced her in 1965. She testified at the divorce hearing that he showed her no physical affection. She further stated that he alternated mood swings, going for hours without speaking to her and then having violent temper tantrums. He had three children who were a son John Cornelius born in 1941; an actress daughter Jenny who was born in December 1946; and another daughter, Patsy, born in 1957 (by Gita Hall) who married singer-songwriter Jimmy Webb. The existence of his third child was only revealed when he filed for divorce from Hall for the first time and it emerged that Patsy had been born while he was still married to his first wife. Sullivan was survived by all three offspring together with a number of grandchildren.

His daughter Jenny wrote the play *J for J* after she found a packet of unmailed letters in 1995 written by her father decades earlier to her brother, Johnny, who was born mentally retarded. The play premiered in 2001 with John Ritter playing Johnny and Jenny playing herself. Eventually Jenny was left to care for her brother. She is currently artistic director of the Rubicon Theater in Ventura, California.

Filmography

1943: *The Woman of the Town, High Explosive.*
1944: *Lady in the Dark, And Now Tomorrow, Rainbow Island.*
1945: *Getting Gertie's Garter, Duffy's Tavern* (cameo).
1946: *Two Years Before the Mast, Suspense.*
1947: *Framed, The Gangster.*
1948: *Smart Woman, Bad Men of Tombstone.*
1949: *The Great Gatsby, Any Number Can Play, Tension.*
1950: *Payment on Demand, Nancy Goes to Rio, A Life of Her Own, The Outriders, Grounds for Marriage.*
1951: *Three Guys Named Mike, Inside Straight, No Questions Asked, The Unknown Man, Cause for Alarm.*
1952: *Skirts Ahoy!, The Bad and the Beautiful.*
1953: *Jeopardy, Cry of the Hunted, China Venture.*
1954: *Playgirl, The Miami Story, Loophole, Her 12 Men.*
1955: *Strategic Air Command, Queen Bee, Texas Lady.*
1956: *The Maverick Queen, Julie.*
1957: *The Way to the Gold, Dragoon Wells Massacre, Forty Guns.*
1958: *Wolf Larsen, Another Time Another Place.*
1960: *Seven Ways to Sundown, The Purple Gang.*
1962: *The Light in the Piazza.*
1963: *A Gathering of Eagles.*
1964: *Pyro* (a.k.a. *Wheel of Fire*), *Stage to Thunder Rock, My Blood Runs Cold, Man in the Middle.*
1965: *Harlow* (Electronovision version), *The Demon Planet* (a.k.a. *Planet of the Vampires*).
1966: *Intimacy, An American Dream* (a.k.a. *See You in Hell Darling*), *The Poppy is Also a Flower* (a.k.a. *Danger Grows Wild*).
1967: *Shark!* (released 1970).
1968: *This Savage Land* (TV), *How to Steal the World, Buckskin, The Silent Treatment.*
1969: *Night Gallery* (TV), *The Immortal* (TV), *Tell Them Willie Boy is Here, It Takes All Kinds.*
1970: *Goldseekers, The House on Greenapple Road* (TV).
1971: *Yuma* (TV), *Cannon* (TV).
1972: *The Candidate* (voice only), *Kung Fu* (TV).
1973: *Savage* (a.k.a. *Watch Dog*) (TV), *Letters from Three Lovers* (TV), *The Magician* (TV), *Pat Garrett and Billy the Kid.*
1974: *Earthquake, Hurricane* (TV).
1975: *The Human Factor, Take a Hard Ride.*
1976: *Survival, Collision Course* (TV), *Napoli Violenta* (a.k.a. *Death Dealers*).
1977: *Oh God!*
1978: *No Room to Run, Caravans.*
1979: *Casino* (TV).

Television Series

1955–1956: *The Man Called X* as Ken Thurston.
1957–1958: *Harbormaster* (a.k.a. *Adventures at Scott Island*) as Captain David Scott.
1960–1962: *The Tall Man* as Dep. Sheriff Pat Garrett.
1966–1967: *The Road West* as Benjamin Pride.

Miniseries

1976: *Once an Eagle, Rich Man Poor Man Book II.*
1978: *The Bastards, The Immigrants.*
1979: *Backstairs at the White House.*

Sources

Daily Mail. "Gatsby Star Dead at 81." June 14, 1994.
Daily Telegraph. Obituary, June 14, 1994.
The Independent. Obituary, June 11, 1994.
Inman, David. *The TV Encyclopedia.* New York: Perigee, 1991.
Lance, Steven. *Written Out of Television.* Lanham, MD: Madison, 1996.

Lentz, Harris M. III. *Obituaries in the Performing Arts, 1994*. Jefferson, NC: McFarland, 1996.
McClelland, Doug. *Forties Film Talk*. Jefferson, NC: McFarland, 1992.
Picturegoer. "Close Up." August 7, 1943.
Picture Show. "Life Story." June 14, 1958.
Picture Show Annual. London: Amalgamated, 1947, 1950, 1952 and 1955.
Pink, Sidney. *So You Want to Make Movies*. Sarasota, FL: Pineapple, 1989.
Skinner, John Walter. *Who's Who on the Screen*. Worthing, England: Madeleine, 1983.
Sullivan, Barry. *The Eighth Hollywood Album*. London: Sampson Low, 1953.
TV Star Annual. No. 7. 1959.
Variety. Obituary, June 20, 1994.
Ward, Jack. *Television Guest Stars*. Jefferson, NC: McFarland, 1993.
Who's Who in Hollywood. No. 16. New York: Dell, 1961.

Frank Sully

Frank Sully was born Frank Sullivan in St. Louis, Missouri on June 17, 1908. He was educated at St. Teresa's College. Originally he was in vaudeville and on stage in the road company of *Girl Crazy*. He gravitated to Hollywood where he made his screen debut in 1934. . He went on to appear in over 100 films. He had a recurring role in the *Boston Blackie* film series starring Chester Morris in which he played Det. Sgt. Matthews. He had another recurring role in the *Joe Palooka* film series starring Joe Kirkwood, Jr., in which he played Looie. In the television series *The Files of Jeffrey Jones* after Vince Barnett was fired, Sully took over as the sympathetic bartender to whom private eye Jones (Don Haggerty) unburdened himself. Sully died at the Motion Picture Country Home and Hospital, Woodland Hills, California on December 17, 1975 aged 67 survived by a daughter.

Filmography

1934: *Murder at the Vanities, Caravan.*
1935: *Alibi Ike, Fighting Youth, Mary Burns Fugitive.*
1936: *Follow the Fleet, Small Town Girl, Gentle Julia, I Married a Doctor, Fury, Poppy, Rhythm on the Range, Theodora Goes Wild.*
1937: *Black Legion, Criminals of the Air, They Gave Him a Gun, Captains Courageous, Riding on Air, High Wide and Handsome, Life Begins at College, Live Love and Learn, Daughter of Shanghai, Radio Patrol.*
1938: *White Banners, Test Pilot, The Crowd Roars, Hold That Co-ed, Youth Takes a Fling, His Exciting Night, Thanks for Everything, Newsboys' Home*
1939: *The Great Man Votes, Society Lawyer, Sorority House, Some Like It Hot, Another Thin Man, The Night of Nights.*
1940: *The Fighting 69th, Castle on the Hudson, The Grapes of Wrath, Lillian Russell, Escape to Glory, I Can't Give You Anything But Love Baby, The Doctor Takes a Wife, Cross-Country Romance, The Return of Frank James, Young People, He Stayed for Breakfast, Yesterday's Heroes, City for Conquest, Street of Memories, Dr. Kildare's Crisis.*
1941: *Golden Hoofs, Nice Girl?, A Girl a Guy and a Gob, Double Date, The Flame of New Orleans, She Knew All the Answers, Mountain Moonlight, Let's Go Collegiate, You'll Never Get Rich, You're in the Army Now, The Body Disappears, Private Nurse.*
1942: *All Through the Night, Sleepytime Gal, To the Shores of Tripoli, Rings on Her Fingers, True to the Army, Two Yanks in Trinidad, Inside the Law, Yankee Doodle Dandy, Parachute Nurse, The Talk of the Town, A Man's World, My Sister Eileen, Lucky Legs, The Daring Young Man, The Boogie Man Will Get You, Laugh Your Blues Away.*
1943: *One Dangerous Night, Power of the Press, They Got Me Covered, The More the Merrier, Murder in Times Square, Redhead from Manhattan, It's a Great Life, Two Senoritas from Chicago, Good Luck Mr. Yates, Thousands Cheer, Dangerous Blondes, There's Something About a Soldier.*
1944: *The Ghost That Walks Alone, Two Girls and a Sailor, Secret Command.*
1945: *Boston Blackie Booked on Suspicion, Boston Blackie's Rendezvous, Along Came Jones, I Love a Bandleader, Calling All Fighters, Out of the Depths.*
1946: *One Way to Love, A Close Call for Boston Blackie, The Gentleman Misbehaves, Throw a Saddle on a Star, Talk About a Lady, The Phantom Thief, Renegades, Dangerous Business, It's Great to Be Young, Crime Doctor's Man Hunt, Boston Blackie and the Law.*
1947: *South of the Chisholm Trail, Wild Harvest.*
1948: *Trapped by Boston Blackie, Blondie's Reward, Let's Live a Little, Gun Smugglers.*
1949: *Boston Blackie's Chinese Venture, Joe Palooka*

in the *Counterpunch, Trapped, Tell It to the Judge, Bodyhold.*
1950: *Joe Palooka Meets Humphrey, Blondie's Hero, Killer Shark, The Good Humor Man, Square Dance Katy, Beauty on Parade, The Reformer and the Redhead, Joe Palooka in Humphrey Takes a Chance, Rookie Fireman, Watch the Birdie.*
1951: *Prairie Roundup, The Red Badge of Courage, Father's Little Dividend, Rich Young and Pretty, The People Against O'Hara, Let's Make It Legal, Man in the Saddle, I Want You.*
1952: *Night Stage to Galveston, Mutiny, With a Song in My Heart, The Sniper, The Girl in White, No Room for the Groom.*
1953: *Man in the Dark, Take Me to Town, Northern Patrol, Bad for Each Other.*
1954: *The Battle of Rogue River, Silver Lode, The Law vs. Billy the Kid.*
1955: *The Man from Bitter Ridge, Jungle Moon Men, The Naked Street, The Tender Trap, Last of the Desperadoes, The Spoilers.*
1956: *The Houston Story, Frontier Gambler, You Can't Run Away from It, Friendly Persuasion, The Desperadoes Are In Town.*
1957: *Pal Joey, Rockabilly Baby, The Buckskin Lady.*
1958: *Man from God's Country, The Last Hurrah.*
1959: *The Gunfight at Dodge City.*
1962: *Gypsy.*
1963: *Bye Bye Birdie.*
1965: *Zebra in the Kitchen.*
1968: *Funny Girl.*

Television Series

1952: *The Files of Jeffrey Jones* as the Bartender.
1962–1965: *The Virginian* as Danny.

Sources

Douglas, Warren. *The Light's Getting Yellow.* Published privately, 2000.
Willis, John. *Screen World.* Vol. 27. London; Frederick Muller, 1976.

Lyle Talbot

Lyle Talbot was born Lysle Henderson in Pittsburgh, Pennsylvania on February 8, 1902. He was the son of Edward Henderson, a Scotsman and Florence Talbot. His mother died when he was young and he was raised in Nebraska by his maternal grandmother. She adopted him and changed his surname to the family one of Talbot. He began in show business in 1919 as an amateur magician and toured with a traveling hypnotist. From there he joined a touring company and then a resident stock company in Sioux Falls, South Dakota for two years. Eventually he had his own stock company in Memphis, Tennessee for a few years. When the theaters were closing down in the early thirties, Talbot gravitated to Hollywood where his stage experience proved an invaluable asset for a career as an actor in talking pictures.

He did a test at Warners who signed him to a seven year contract and changed the spelling of his Christian name to Lyle. He was one of the founder members of the Screen Actors Guild. He preferred the parts he played on loan outs to other studios rather than the gangster roles which he was assigned at his home studio. Finally after six years they agreed to release him from contract. After that he freelanced for the remainder of his career. Later in the international intrigue television series *Dangerous Assignment* he played the Commissioner who gives Brian Donlevy his assignments in some episodes. In the sitcom *The Adventures of Ozzie and Harriet* he played Joe Rudolph. He played Paul Fonda in *The Bob Cummings Show*. He appeared in an episode of the new *Alfred Hitchcock Presents* in 1986. He continued to appear on stage both in straight plays and musicals in dinner theaters and touring companies until the nineties. The longest run he ever had in a play was *Separate Rooms* which ran for two years on Broadway from 1939 to 1940.

He married firstly Marjorie Cramer in 1937. Secondly he married Tommye Adams in 1942. Thirdly he married Kevin McClure in 1946. All three of these marriages ended in divorce. In 1949 he married Margaret Carol Epple with whom he had two sons and two daughters. His sons were Stephen who was born in 1949 and David who was born in 1952. His daughters were Cynthia who was born in 1953 and Margaret who was born in 1955. His wife died in 1991. He lived in Studio City for forty years and then sold the house and moved to San Francisco to be near his sons. He died at his San Francisco home on March 3, 1996 aged 94 of natural causes survived by his children.

Filmography

1932: *The Purchase Price, Big City Blues, Three on a Match, Miss Pinkerton, Stranger in Town, Klondike, Love Is a Racket, No More Orchids, Unholy Love, The Thirteenth Guest, 20,000 Years in Sing Sing.*

1933: *Ladies They Talk About, 42nd Street, College Coach, The Life of Jimmy Dolan, Parachute Jumper, A Shriek in the Night, Girl Missing, Mary Stevens MD, She Had to Say Yes, Havana Widows.*

1934: *The Dragon Murder Case, Mandalay, A Lost Lady, Fog Over Frisco, One Night of Love, Registered Nurse, Return of the Terror, Murder in the Clouds, Heat Lightning.*

1935: *While the Patient Slept, Party Wire, Page Miss Glory, Chinatown Squad, The Case of the Lucky Legs, Red Hot Tires, Oil for the Lamps of China, It Happened in New York, Broadway Hostess, Our Little Girl.*

1936: *Murder by an Aristocrat, Trapped by Television, The Law in Her Hands, Mind Your Own Business, The Singing Kid, Boulder Dam, Go West Young Man.*

1937: *Second Honeymoon, Three Legionnaires, The Affairs of Cappy Ricks, Westbound Limited, What Price Vengeance?*

1938: *Get-a-Way, I Stand Accused, Change of Heart, Call of the Yukon, One Wild Night, The Arkansas Traveler.*

1939: *They Asked for It, Forged Passport, Second Fiddle, Torture Ship.*

1940: *A Miracle on Main Street, Parole Fixer, He Married His Wife.*

1941: *A Night for Crime.*

1942: *They Raid by Night, She's in the Army, Mexican Spitfire's Elephant.*

1943: *Man of Courage.*

1944: *One Body Too Many, Dixie Jamboree, Are These Our Parents?, Up in Arms, The Falcon Out West, Mystery of the River Boat* (serial), *Gambler's Choice, Sensations of 1945.*

1945: *Trail to Gunsight.*

1946: *Murder Is My Business, Strange Impersonation, Gun Town, Song of Arizona, Chick Carter Detective* (serial), *Shep Comes Home.*

1947: *Danger Street, The Vigilante* (serial).

1948: *Appointment with Murder, Joe Palooka in Winner Take All, Quick on the Trigger, The Vicious Circle, Parole Inc., The Devil's Cargo, Highway 13, Thunder in the Pines.*

1949: *Wild Weed, Sky Dragon, Fighting Fools, Mississippi Rhythm, Batman and Robin* (serial), *Joe Palooka in the Big Fight, The Mutineers, Ringside.*

1950: *Border Rangers, Atom Man Vs Superman* (serial), *Cherokee Uprising, Everybody's Dancing, Revenue Agent, Lucky Losers, Federal Man, Tall Timber, The Jackpot, Champagne for Caesar, Triple Trouble.*

1951: *Abilene Trail, The Man from Sonora, Jungle Manhunt, Lawless Cowboys, Purple Heart Diary, Colorado Ambush, Oklahoma Justice, Fury of the Congo, Fingerprints Don't Lie, Texas Lawman, Hurricane Island, Gold Raiders, Varieties on Parade, Blue Blood.*

1952: *The Old West, Sea Tiger, With a Song in My Heart, Son of Geronimo* (serial), *Kansas Territory, Montana Incident, Outlaw Women, Desperadoes' Outpost, The Daltons' Women, Feudin' Fools, African Treasure, Texas City, Untamed Women, Wyoming Roundup, Mesa of Lost Women* (voice only).

1953: *Down Among the Sheltering Palms, White Lightnin,' Trail Blazers, Tumbleweed, Star of Texas.*

1954: *Tobor the Great, Captain Kidd and the Slave Girl, The Desperado, The Hidden Face, Jail Bait, There's No Business Like Show business, Two Guns and a Badge, The Steel Cage, Trader Tom of the China Seas* (serial), *Gunfighters of the Northwest* (serial).

1955: *Jail Busters, Sudden Danger.*

1956: *Calling Homicide, The Great Man, Plan 9 from Outer Space.*

1958: *Hot Angel, The Notorious Mr. Monks, High School Confidential.*

1959: *City of Fear.*

1960: *Sunrise at Campobello.*

Lyle Talbot, who costarred in *Dangerous Assignment.*

Television Series

1952: *Dangerous Assignment* as the Commissioner.
1956–1966: *The Adventures of Ozzie and Harriet* as Joe Rudolph.
1955–1959: *The Bob Cummings Show* as Paul Fonda.

Sources

Brooks, Tim. *The Complete Directory to Prime Time Television Stars, 1946–Present*. New York: Ballantine, 1987.
Goldrup, Jim, and Tom Goldrup. *Feature Players: Stories Behind the Faces*. Vol. 2. Published privately, 1992.
Lentz, Harris M. III. *Obituaries in the Performing Arts, 1996* Jefferson, NC: McFarland, 1997.
McClure, Arthur F., and Ken D. Jones. *Star Quality*. Cranbury, NJ: Barnes, 1974.
Quinlan, David. *The Illustrated Directory of Film Character Actors*. 2nd ed. London: Batsford, 1995.

Nita Talbot, who costarred in *Man Against Crime* and *The Thin Man*.

NITA TALBOT

Nita Talbot was born Anita Sokol in New York City on August 8, 1930. She trained at the Irvine School of the Theater. She made her screen debut in 1949 and first appeared on television in 1951. She made her Broadway debut at the Booth Theater in the short-lived comedy *Never Say Never* which opened and closed in November 1951. She appeared in two other comedies on Broadway during the fifties. She made appearances on many of the leading television anthology series during that decade and had a recurring role in a daytime soap opera. She also had a recurring role as Gloria in the crime series *Man Against Crime* which starred Ralph Bellamy. In total she appeared in about ten episodes between 1952 and 1954.

During the second season of *The Thin Man* she had a semi-regular role as Beatrice Dane. Nick Charles (Peter Lawford) was formerly a police officer. Even when he retired from this after marrying Nora (Phyllis Kirk), he maintained contact with some of the crooks whom he had known in his past. One of them was the highly attractive confidence trickster Beatrice Dane, alias Blondie Collins, who proved useful in helping him to crack cases when he played at being an amateur detective. Nora Charles particularly disliked her. Asked her opinion of Ralph Bellamy and Peter Lawford she replied, "I adored both Ralph Bellamy and Peter Lawford."

Nita Talbot continued to have a successful career mainly on television into the nineties. Her last Broadway appearance dated from 1969. A highlight of her television career was when she received an Emmy award nomination for Outstanding Performance by an Actress in a Supporting Role in a Comedy for an appearance in *Hogan's Heroes* during the 1967–1968 season. Her favorite role was as Marya, the Russian spy, in that series and all the regular actors in *Hogan's Heroes* were her favorite leading men.

She was married to Don Gordon and Tom Geas. By Tom Geas she has a daughter, Nicole and she has a granddaughter, Olivia. For recreation she likes to bake, sew and knit.

Filmography

1949: *It's a Great Feeling*.
1950: *Caged, Montana, Bright Leaf, This Side of the Law*.
1951: *On Dangerous Ground*.
1956: *Bundle of Joy*.
1957: *This Could Be the Night*.
1958: *I Married a Woman, Once Upon a Horse*.
1962: *Who's Got the Action?*
1965: *Girl Happy, A Very Special Favor, That Funny Feeling*.

1967: *The Cool Ones.*
1970: *The Movie Murderer* (TV).
1971: *They Call It Murder* (TV).
1972: *Buck and the Preacher.*
1973: *What Are Best Friends For?* (TV), *The Manchu Eagle Murder Caper Mystery.*
1974: *The Rockford Files* (TV).
1975: *Day of the Locust.*
1977: *Sex and the Married Woman* (TV).
1979: *The Sweet Creek County War, Double Take.*
1980: *Serial, Turnover Smith* (TV), *Island Claws* (a.k.a. *Night of the Claws*).
1982: *Night Shift, Frightmare, The Concrete Jungle.*
1983: *The Other Woman* (TV), *Chained Heat.*
1985: *Fraternity Vacation, Movers and Shakers.*
1986: *The Check Is in the Mail.*
1989: *Jake Spanner Private Eye* (TV).
1990: *Puppet Master II, Diggin' Up Business.*
1992: *Amityville 1992: It's About Time.*

TELEVISION SERIES

1952–1954: *Man Against Crime* as Gloria.
1954–1955: *Search for Tomorrow* as Rose Peterson.
1956: *Joe and Mabel* as Mabel Spooner.
1958–1959: *The Thin Man* as Beatrice Dane.
1960: *Hot Off the Wire* (a.k.a. *The Jim Backus Show*) as Dora.
1973: *Here We Go Again* as Judy Evans.
1979: *Supertrain* as Rose Casey.
1981–1982: *General Hospital* as Delfina.
1988–1989: *Starting from Scratch* as Rose.

SOURCES

Correspondence between Nita Talbot and the author.
Picture Show Annual. London: Amalgamated, 1959.
Ward, Jack. *Television Guest Stars.* Jefferson, NC: McFarland, 1993.

WILLIAM TALMAN

William Whitney Talman, Jr., was born on February 4, 1915 in Detroit, Michigan. He was the first son of William Talman, Sr., and Ada Barber. He had a younger brother named Tom. He came from an affluent family. His father was vice-president of a company which manufactured industrial heat measuring recording machines and yachts. He was sent to Public School in a limousine each day which meant that he had to fight his way in and out.

He was better at athletics than his studies. He attended Cranbrook School in Michigan and Dartmouth College where he started a drama club. He left Dartmouth in his sophomore year after an accident. A freshman gave him the loan of a car so that he could visit a girlfriend at another college. A bus forced the car off the road and it hit a tree. A boy who was with them was killed and it later turned out that the car was stolen. Talman was asked to resign from Dartmouth which he did. Although he was invited back the following year, he never returned.

After this he became an evangelist; worked in a district attorney's office; was a tennis pro; and an M.C. in nightclubs. None of these occupations suited him and a friend suggested that he try Broadway. He made his Broadway debut in *Of Mice and Men.* He was appearing in *Spring Again* in January 1942 when he was drafted. He entered the service as a private and saw 30 months of active service in the Pacific where he won a commission as a major. During the war his duties included managing a school which trained soldiers to mount shows. He also trained boxing and baseball teams. After the war he returned to Broadway where he appeared in more plays.

In 1949 he moved to Hollywood where he made his screen debut in *I Married a Communist* (1949). He was under contract to RKO Radio and made a number of other movies usually cast as a villain. His best remembered film role was as Emmett Myers in the film noir *The Hitch-Hiker.* He also coscripted a couple of feature films. He attended an audition for the *Perry Mason* series. He became world famous as the district attorney Hamilton Burger who lost every case to Perry Mason. "Talman is really a wonder. He actually looks as if he expects to win a case," Erle Stanley Gardner enthused.

In 1960 Talman was one of several people arrested at a wild Hollywood party after a raid by police. Not only were drugs discovered in the house, but everyone there including Talman was nude. Talman claimed that he was innocent and had only dropped in on the party for a drink. On March 17, 1960 he was fired by CBS before his case came to trial on the grounds that he had violated the morals clause in his contract. In a court hearing held in June 1960, Talman was acquitted. Nevertheless he was unofficially blacklisted by Hollywood producers. Richard Boone helped him through this rough period by hiring him for supporting roles in a couple of episodes of *Have Gun Will Travel.* In the meantime the entire cast

Left to right: William Talman and Raymond Burr in *Perry Mason.*

of *Perry Mason* gave him their support. In particular Raymond Burr fought vigorously to have him reinstated with the network. CBS was flooded with letters from the public insisting that Talman was innocent. Finally in December 1960 CBS relented and allowed Talman to return. At this time his annual salary for the series was said to be $65,000.

He married firstly actress Lynne Carter in 1942. She sued him for divorce in November, 1951 citing extreme cruelty. She claimed that he had been abusive to her in front of her friends. The divorce was granted in September 1952 with custody of the couple's three year old daughter, Lynda, and 24% of his income going to Carter. He married secondly actress Barbara Read in 1953. With her he had two children who were Barbie and Billy. They were divorced in September 1959. Barbara Read committed suicide in December 1963 by closing up her house and then turning on gas jets. She left a note behind in which she blamed ill health for her action. He married Margaret Larkin in 1962. With her he had two children who were Tim and Susan. He also adopted her two children, Steve and Debbie, from a previous marriage.

After the series ended in 1966, he went on a six week tour of Vietnam to entertain the troops. Upon his return home he was diagnosed with lung cancer. A heavy smoker for most of his life, he was annoyed by a newspaper article he read about actors being afraid to make anti-smoking broadcasts for fear of losing opportunities to make lucrative tobacco commercials. Instead he offered to make a short film for the American Cancer Society some of which was shown in 1968 and 1969 as a television anti-smoking commercial. He was the first actor to ever make such a commercial. When the commercial was being made Talman was terminally ill and in a great deal of pain.

Talman died of cardiac arrest owing to complications from lung cancer at West Valley Community Hospital in Encino, California on August 30, 1968 aged 53. He is buried at Forest Lawn, Hollywood Hills.

Filmography

1949: *I Married a Communist* (a.k.a. *The Woman on Pier 13*), *Red Hot and Blue, The Kid from Texas.*
1950: *Armored Car Robbery.*
1951: *The Racket.*
1952: *One Minute to Zero.*
1953: *The Hitch-Hiker, City That Never Sleeps.*
1955: *Big House USA, Smoke Signal, Crashout.*
1956: *The Man Is Armed, Two Gun Lady, Uranium Boom.*
1957: *The Persuader, Hell on Devil's Island.*
1967: *The Ballad of Josie.*

Television Series

1957–1966: *Perry Mason* as Hamilton Burger.

Sources

Associated Press. Release. 1960.
Brooks, Tim. *The Complete Directory to Prime Time TV Stars, 1946–Present.* New York: Ballantine, 1987.
Inman, David. *The TV Encyclopedia.* New York: Perigee, 1991.
Jones, Ken D., Arthur F. McClure, and Alfred E. Twomey. *Character People.* Secaucus, NJ: Citadel, 1979.

Kelleher, Brian, and Diana Merrill. *The Perry Mason TV Showbook.* New York: St. Martin's, 1987.

Quinlan, David. *Illustrated Directory of Film Character Actors.* 2nd ed. London: Batsford, 1995.

GORDON TANNER

Gordon Tanner was born in Toronto, Canada on July 17, 1918. In the television series *Saber of London* he played Larry Nelson, the assistant of one armed detective Mark Saber (Donald Gray). Tanner died on August 3, 1983 aged 65.

FILMOGRAPHY

1949: *Golden Arrow* (a.k.a. *Gay Adventure*).
1951: *Talk of a Million* (a.k.a. *You Can't Beat the Irish*).
1956: *House of Secrets* (a.k.a. *Triple Deception*).
1957: *Fire Down Below, Time Lock, Campbell's Kingdom.*
1958: *A Woman of Mystery, On the Run, Carry on Sergeant, Sheriff of Fractured Jaw.*
1959: *Floods of Fear.*
1961: *The Green Helmet.*

Gordon Tanner, who costarred in *Saber of London*.

1964: *Dr. Strangelove or How I Learned to Stop Worrying and Love the Bomb.*
1965: *The Return of Mr. Moto, Where the Spies Are.*
1967: *The Vulture.*
1974: *Caravan to Vaccares.*
1975: *Eskimo Nell.*

TELEVISION SERIES
1958: *Saber of London* as Larry Nelson.

SOURCE
Tibballs, Geoff. *TV Detectives.* London: Boxtree, 1992.

COLIN TAPLEY

Colin Tapley was born in Dunedin, New Zealand on May 7, 1909. He was educated at Christ's College, Christchurch, New Zealand. In 1930 he ventured to England where he joined the Royal Air Force and participated in Admiral Byrd's expedition. An unspecified accident put paid to that career. He worked his passage home. In 1933 he entered Paramount's Search for Beauty competition and was chosen as the male New Zealand winner, one of 30 winners internationally. He journeyed to Hollywood where he made his screen debut in *Search for Beauty* (1934). On the strength of this he was given a stock contract by Paramount. In Hollywood he shared an apartment with actor friend Eldred Tidbury (who later became known as Donald Gray). Their paths would cross again professionally. Tidbury was another winner of the Search for Beauty competition, but he had won the grand prize of $1,000.

Allegedly Tapley was rejected by Mae West as her leading man in *Belle of the Nineties* (1934) because of his too ripe, upper bracket, English accent. This virtually sealed his fate because he never became a top star. Instead he played many supporting roles in films mainly at his home studio. A personal favorite of his was the classic saga of the British empire, *Lives of a Bengal Lancer* (1935), in which he played Lt. Barrett, an army spy who disguised himself as an Indian. His worst acting experience came with *Booloo* (1938) in which he played Captain Robert Rogers who tried to trap a white tiger in the Malayan jungle. He disliked this part because he was the only male member of the cast who trekked to the actual jungle to shoot some exterior scenes. While

Left to right: Alan Wheatley, unidentified player, unidentified player, Colin Tapley, Dennis O'Keefe in the film *The Diamond*. Colin Tapley costarred in the television series *Mark Saber*.

there the rain deluged down, the monkeys screamed unceasingly and he contracted dysentery.

When war broke out he was unable to go to England, so instead he went to Ottawa, Canada where he enlisted in the Royal Canadian Air Force along with fellow actor, Robert Coote. Since Tapley had previous experience as a flyer, he was offered the job of flying instructor which he did for a couple of years. Then he was transferred to the Royal Air Force in England where he served as an air force controller. One particularly hair-raising experience occurred when he was forced to bail out of an aircraft which was on fire. He survived and on account of this was awarded membership of the Caterpillar club. This was a piece of jewelry given by a parachute manufacturer to anyone who had jumped from a stricken plane and landed safely by parachute.

After his honorable discharge he left his wife and children in England while he returned to New Zealand for the first time since 1933. He did not intend to re-establish himself as an actor. Instead he made an abortive attempt to start a launch service at Wanaka, but ran into financial and other difficulties. So he went back to Hollywood where he did manage to appear briefly in the epic *Samson and Delilah* (1949) for his old studio. This film was directed by Cecil B. De Mille for whom he had worked before. Although De Mille was autocratic, Tapley could tolerate him. Nevertheless his enthusiasm for Hollywood had gone and he did not like the political climate. So he packed his bags and returned with his family to England. He was kept steadily employed throughout the 1950s usually acting as authority figures. He made something of a career playing police inspectors of which his Inspector Davis in the exciting British thriller *Cloudburst* (1951) was particularly good.

He had kept in touch with Donald Gray who was instrumental in having him cast as Inspector Chester, the police contact of one armed private eye Mark Saber, in the television series

Mark Saber. The format of the series was later somewhat revamped and the show re-emerged as *Saber of London*. Tapley however played exactly the same role, but for some reason the character was now known as Inspector Parker. Once the series ended, Tapley was able to find other film and television parts. His last film appearance dated from 1969, but he continued to act sporadically until 1983.

For many years he maintained an apartment in the very fashionable Knightsbridge area of London, but also had a country cottage in the Cotswolds. He died at his home in Coates, Gloucestershire on December 1, 1995 aged 86 and his funeral was held in Gloucester. He was survived by his wife, son and a step daughter.

Filmography

1934: *Search for Beauty, Double Door, Limehouse Blues, Come on Marines!, Murder at the Vanities, The Pursuit of Happiness.*
1935: *The Black Room, Becky Sharp, The Crusades, Lives of a Bengal Lancer, The Last Outpost, Peter Ibbetson, My Marriage, Without Regret.*
1936: *Early to Bed, The Return of Sophie Lang, Too Many Parents, The Preview Murder Mystery, The Sky Parade, Till We Meet Again, Thank You Jeeves.*
1937: *Wild Money, The Crime Nobody Saw, Hotel Haywire, King of Gamblers, Night of Mystery, Bulldog Drummond Escapes, Maid of Salem, Souls at Sea.*
1938: *Booloo, If I Were King, Storm Over Bengal.*
1939: *The Light That Failed.*
1940: *Women in War.*
1941: *Arizona.*
1949: *Samson and Delilah.*
1951: *Cloudburst.*
1952: *Angels One Five, Wings of Danger* (a.k.a. *Dead on Course*), *Wide Boy.*
1953: *Strange Stories, The Steel Key, Noose for a Lady, Three Steps to the Gallows* (a.k.a. *White Fire* released 1955).
1954: *The Diamond* (a.k.a. *Diamond Wizard*).
1955: *The Dam Busters, Little Red Monkey* (a.k.a. *The Case of the Little Red Monkey*).
1956: *Barbados Quest* (a.k.a. *Murder on Approval*).
1957: *Stranger in Town.*
1958: *The Safecracker, Rogue's Yarn, Blood of the Vampire, High Jump.*
1959: *Innocent Meeting, Man Accused, An Honorable Murder, Night Train for Inverness.*
1960: *Compelled.*
1961: *So Evil So Young, Strongroom, In the Doghouse.*
1962: *Emergency, The Lamp in Assassin Mews, Gang War, Paranoiac.*
1963: *Shadow of Fear.*
1969: *Fraulein Doktor.*

Television Series

US (1955–1957): *Mark Saber* as Det. Insp. Chester.
UK (1957–1959)
US (1957–1960): *Saber of London* as Det. Insp. Parker.
UK (1959–1961)

Sources

Interview with Tapley in 1993.
McFarlane, Brian. *The Encyclopedia of British Film*. London: BFI Methuen, 2003.
Picture Show Annual. London: Amalgamated, 1936 and 1942.
Picture Show's Who's Who on Screen. London: Amalgamated, 1956.
Quinlan, David. *Illustrated Directory of Film Character Actors*. 2nd ed. London: Batsford, 1995.
Tibballs, Geoff. *TV Detectives*. London: Boxtree, 1992.

Kent Taylor

Kent Taylor once worked with director W.S. Van Dyke in *I Take This Woman* (1940). He had a big scene in a nightclub with Hedy Lamarr where there were lots of extras. He had to ask her for a dance, trip the light fantastic round the floor, remember his lines, avoid colliding with the extras and dance to no music. Music would have interfered with the dialogue so it was dubbed in later. It was a complicated shot with no coverage or other angles. Van Dyke did not do much rehearsing either. So Taylor was presented with his greatest challenge. He had to do that complicated maneuver plus get Miss Lamarr back to her table at the proper time with no rehearsal. He accomplished it in one take.

Kent Taylor's trademark was his pencil thin moustache. Occasionally he shaved it off to play a character role as in *Payment on Demand*. He looked as if he was born to wear a tuxedo. He played leads in so many minor films that he was once dubbed "King Of The Bs." During the 1950s he starred in a couple of television series,

Kent Taylor, who starred in *Boston Blackie*.

one of which was a crime series called *Boston Blackie*.

Kent Taylor was born Louis William John Henry Von Weiss on May 11, 1906 on a ranch outside Nashua, Iowa. He was raised on a farm and educated at a local high school where he first performed in plays, sang in the glee club and as a teenager played sax in a dance band. Upon leaving school at the age of sixteen, he worked as a window dresser and as a navvy, carrying cement for a concrete mixing machine. At the Darrah Institute Of Technology in Chicago, he studied engineering for two years. The acting bug bit, so he joined a touring repertory company.

When his father retired from farming, the family relocated to California at the heart of the Depression in 1931. Kent Taylor supported himself for a while as a salesman for the canvas business which his father had started in their new state. While applying for work as an extra at Paramount Studios, he was noticed by a casting director who was so impressed with his physique and appearance that he cast him as a dress extra. Shortly afterwards the same casting director asked him to appear in a screen test opposite Claire Dodd. Despite the fact that there was no pay, Taylor readily agreed. So well did he photograph that studio executives signed him to a long term contract with Paramount. His most frequent on screen partner was Evelyn Venable with whom he appeared in several films.

He spent seven years under contract at Paramount, two at Universal and two at 20th Century–Fox. During World War II he entertained troops in North Africa. Although he was almost continuously employed, he did not rise to top stardom. He accepted every role assigned to him, never complaining about the quality of the scripts nor the size of his roles. He was an extremely self effacing person who sought to overcome his shyness by drinking. Alcohol had the effect of dampening his ambition. Although he quit drinking in the early 1950s, one detrimental long-term effect was that he gradually lost the faculty for remembering his lines.

Boston Blackie was the creation of Jack Boyle in a series of short stories in Cosmopolitan magazine from 1910 onwards. These stories were collected in a book in 1918. The film *Boston Blackie's Little Pal* appeared in 1919. The best known Boston Blackie was Chester Morris who appeared in a series of 14 films for Columbia between 1941 and 1949. When Morris refused to appear in the television series, Taylor took over. Originally he was a gentleman safecracker, but by the time Taylor came to play him in a syndicated television series, he had become an ex-thief turned private eye. He lived in Los Angeles and was assisted by his girlfriend Mary Wesley (Lois Collier). He had frequent brushes with the law represented by Inspector Faraday (Frank Orth). Episodes were frequently quite light hearted in tone, but it was regarded as an adult series and played late at night. Ziv the producer secured the television rights from Boyle's widow and rented studio space at Eagle Lion to shoot the program. Stabbings were kept to a minimum because the producer hated knives. Up to three episodes were shot simultaneously. The series which ran for fifty eight half hour episodes from 1951–1953 was very successful. Each segment cost $21,000 to produce which was expensive in those days. The first twenty six episodes were shot in black and white, while the last thirty two were shot in color.

His other television series which was also for Ziv was *Rough Riders* (1958–1959) in which he played a veteran union officer in the Civil War. At its end three soldiers who had intended to travel West in search of a new life joined forces for mutual companionship and protection on the journey. En route they encountered Indians, bandits and other assorted cut-throats. This series which was broadcast on the ABC network lasted for 39 episodes.

After the series ended, Taylor returned to irregular work in feature films. He appeared in "B" pictures produced by such characters as Maury Dexter and Al Adamson. Taylor's final appearance was a telemovie called *The Phantom Of Hollywood* (1974) in which ironically he played one of a couple of buyers of a once famous studio. For recreation in real life he was a keen golfer and he also enjoyed riding.

In the 1980s Kent Taylor underwent several heart operations. He had been under care by a nurse at his North Hollywood home before being hospitalized for the last time on April 9, 1987. He died in his sleep at the Motion Picture Country Home And Hospital in Woodland Hills, California on April 11, 1987 aged 80. He was survived by his widow Augusta Kulek (whom he wed in 1932) and his three children: Kay, Judy and Bill. He lies buried at Westwood Village Memorial Park in Los Angeles.

Filmography

1931: *Road To Reno*.
1932: *Dancers in the Dark, Forgotten Commandments, Two Kinds of Women, Husband's Holiday, The Devil and the Deep, Merrily We Go To Hell, The Sign of the Cross, Make Me a Star, If I Had a Million, Sinners in the Sun, Blonde Venus*.
1933: *Mysterious Rider, A Lady's Profession, The Story of Temple Drake, Sunset Pass, I'm No Angel, White Woman, Cradle Song, Under the Tonto Rim*.
1934: *Death Takes a Holiday, Many Happy Returns, David Harum, Double Door, Mrs. Wiggs of the Cabbage Patch, Limehouse Blues*.
1935: *The County Chairman, College Scandal, Smart Girl, Without Regret, Two-Fisted, My Marriage*.
1936: *The Sky Parade, Florida Special, Ramona, The Accusing Finger*.
1937: *When Love Is Young, Wings over Honolulu, The Lady Fights Back, A Girl with Ideas, Prescription for Romance, Love in a Bungalow*.
1938: *The Jury's Secret, The Last Express*.
1939: *Four Girls in White, Pirates of the Skies, The Gracie Allen Murder Case, Five Came Back, Three Sons, Escape to Paradise, I Take This Woman*.
1940: *Sued for Libel, Two Girls on Broadway, The Girl in 313, Men Against the Sky, I'm Still Alive, The Girls from Avenue A*.
1941: *Washington Melodrama, Repent at Leisure*.
1942: *Mississippi Gambler, Tombstone The Town Too Tough To Die, Army Surgeon, Half Way to Shanghai, Frisco Lil, Gang Busters* (serial).
1943: *Bombers' Moon*.
1944: *Roger Touhy Gangster, Alaska*.
1945: *The Daltons Ride Again*.
1946: *Smooth as Silk, Young Widow, Tangier, Deadline for Murder, Dangerous Millions*.
1947: *Second Chance, The Crimson Key*.
1948: *Half Past Midnight*.
1950: *Federal Agent at Large, Western Pacific Agent, Trial Without Jury*.
1951: *Payment on Demand*.
1954: *Playgirl, Track the Man Down*.
1955: *Secret Venture, Ghost Town, The Phantom from 10,000 Leagues*.
1956: *Slightly Scarlet, Frontier Gambler*.
1957: *The Iron Sheriff*.
1958: *Fort Bowie, Gang War*.
1960: *Walk Tall*.
1961: *The Purple Hills*.
1962: *The Broken Land, The Firebrand*.
1963: *The Day Mars Invaded Earth, Harbor Lights, Law of the Lawless, The Crawling Hand*.
1968: *Brides of Blood*.
1970: *Hell's Bloody Devils* (a.k.a. *The Fakers, Smashing the Crime Syndicate*), *Satan's Sadists*.
1971: *The Mighty Gorga*.
1974: *Girls for Rent, The Phantom of Hollywood* (TV).

Television Series

1951–1953: *Boston Blackie* as Boston Blackie.
1958–1959: *Rough Riders* as Captain Jim Flagg.

Sources

Erickson, Hal. *Syndicated Television: The First Forty Years, 1947–1987*. Jefferson, NC: McFarland, 1989.
Imber, Larry. "Forgotten Man." *Films of the Golden Age*. No. 5. Summer 1996.
Inman, David. *The TV Encyclopedia*. New York: Perigee, 1991.
Lamparski, Richard. *Whatever Became Of?* 7th Series. New York: Bantam, 1977.
Picture Show Annual. London: Amalgamated, 1936 and 1941.
Pringle, David. *Imaginary People*. London: Grafton, 1987.
Tibballs, Geoff. *TV Detectives*. London: Boxtree, 1992.

Robert Taylor

It would be easy to dismiss Robert Taylor as a handsome leading man, but he worked diligently at his craft and eventually won considerable acclaim for his acting ability. Initially he was a smooth leading man with an unlined face, but as he grew older his visage acquired much more character so that some of his later roles were amongst his most interesting. He was much admired in his own time by costars and technical personnel whom he worked with for his professionalism and pleasant, down-to-earth attitude. As the years have rolled by since his death, his reputation has become somewhat tarnished by memories of his appearance in front of the House UnAmerican Activities Committee. This seems somewhat short-sighted in that while Taylor was a Republican and conservative, John Wayne was much more right wing and extreme in his attitudes. Wayne's legend however has continued to grow. Taylor sought to emulate Wayne by being the towering star of his later films where he left the romancing to younger players, but he did not succeed to the same degree. When his film career faltered, he turned to television as the star of a crime series which ranked amongst the best on television.

Robert Taylor was born Spangler Arlington Brugh in Filley, Nebraska on August 5, 1911, the son of Spangler Andrew Brugh and his wife Ruth Stanhope. His father was of Pennsylvania-Dutch origin, while his mother was of Scottish-English descent. He was an only child. His father was a former grain merchant turned doctor. When he was seven, the family moved to Beatrice, Nebraska where he lived for the next few years of his life. His mother was a dominant, neurotic woman who developed a heart condition early on which she used as an excuse to impose her will on her family.

As a child he studied the cello, but later he became a good athlete at track and tennis and an excellent public speaker. In 1929 he graduated from high school with the intention of becoming a doctor. His mother however wanted him to continue his study of the cello. Initially he enrolled at Doane College which was located nearby, but he was responsive to the tuition of Professor E. Gray, a music teacher at the college. When Gray was transferred to Pomona College in Claremont, California, he followed his teacher there. At this college he drifted into student dramatics. In his senior year he was seen in a play *Journey's End* in which he played Captain Stanhope by Ben Piazza, an MGM scout. Piazza was so impressed that he offered to sign him, but Taylor was reluctant to agree because he wanted to graduate. After graduation as a Bachelor of Liberal Arts, Taylor enrolled in the Neely Dixon Dramatic School in Hollywood.

His father died in October 1933, but did not leave his family well provided for. His mother moved to Hollywood where she lived with her son and sought to dominate every facet of his life. He was tested by Samuel Goldwyn, but nothing came of it. A little later he was noticed by Oliver Tinsdell, an MGM drama coach who arranged to have him tested by MGM and in February 1934 he was awarded a seven year contract commencing at $35 a week. At the suggestion of Ida Koverman, Louis B. Mayer's personal assistant, his name was changed to Robert Taylor.

He started out by being loaned to Fox Films to play the juvenile lead in *Handy Andy* (1934) which starred Will Rogers. He was awe struck working with Rogers on his first film, but the star was kind and encouraging to him. Next he was loaned to Universal to play Frank Morgan's son in *There's Always Tomorrow* (1934). At his home lot he played a fleeting role in *A Wicked Woman* (1934) and appeared in *Buried Loot* (1934), the first of the *Crime Does Not Pay* series of shorts. He continued to appear at MGM in either small roles or low budget films, but he was kept on contract as his fan mail continued to grow.

Universal were searching for an attractive young actor who could bring conviction to the part of a playboy turned doctor in *Magnificent Obsession* (1935), the film version of the novel by Lloyd C. Douglas. Irene Dunne, the top-lined player, and director John M. Stahl were reviewing excerpts from Taylor's MGM movies and agreed that he would be right for the role. The film was a tremendous success, fan mail deluged in and MGM who until then had shown little faith in him, realized they had a new star on their hands. The movies which he made afterwards were increasingly prestigious. While shooting *His Brother's Wife* (1936), he met Barbara Stanwyck, a talented but dominant actress, who set about transforming his life and passing on her extensive knowledge of film acting and show business. They costarred together in *This is My Affair* (1937) which was a historical, political thriller, but which many took to be a comment on their relationship at the time. They eventually eloped to San Diego where they wed on May 13, 1939 and honeymooned in Bucks County, Pennsylvania. In their declining years, long after their divorce, they appeared together in a modest thriller *The Night Walker* (1965).

He appeared in *The Gorgeous Hussy* (1936) which starred Joan Crawford and *Camille* (1937) which starred Greta Garbo. In the latter he played Armand, Camille's younger lover which made him a hot property. In 1936 he was placed fourth in the top ten box office stars. In 1937 he was placed third and in 1938 he was in sixth place. When he tried to obtain a raise from MGM commensurate with his increasing popularity, Louis B. Mayer turned on the waterworks and gave Taylor the "You're like a son to me" routine. Afterwards when his agent asked him if he had obtained the raise, he replied, "No, but I gained a father!" MGM did however honor his request for a more macho image by casting him in a better range of film, one of which was *A Yank at Oxford* (1938). This was the first MGM British production, in which he starred as Lee Sheridan, the American athlete who attends the English University and is initially snubbed for his brashness, but comes through in the end. This was the first of his two appearances opposite Vivien Leigh.

Left to right: Mark Goddard, Robert Taylor and Tige Andrews in *The Detectives*.

The second was *Waterloo Bridge* (1940) in which she played a ballet dancer who falls in love with serviceman Taylor, but who in his absence turns to prostitution. This leads her to break off their engagement and to her ultimate suicide. Told in flashback from the perspective of an older man, it was derived from the play by Robert E. Sherwood and Taylor was much acclaimed for his sensitive handling of his role. The film was an enormous commercial success and remained his personal favorite of his own films.

His indoor hobby was cooking and he had a collection of cookbooks. While shooting *Flight Command* (1940), Taylor had become interested in flying which led to him taking this up as a hobby. He soon obtained his wings and piloted his own plane much to his wife's and mother's consternation. He played a gangster *Johnny Eager* (1942) opposite Lana Turner which was the kind of film he liked and proved popular. In May 1943 he signed a new twenty year contract with MGM at $4,000 a week. His final film before joining the armed forces was *Song of Russia* (1944) in which he played an American musical conductor who has a romance with a Russian pianist (Susan Peters) against a background of classical music. This was to have unfortunate repercussions some years later when he was called upon to testify before the House UnAmerican Activities Committee. He did not want to shoot the film, but was persuaded to do so by Mayer and the State Department. Taylor was a staunch anti–Communist all his life and with the backing of a major studio behind him, his career was never in jeopardy.

As a licensed civilian pilot when he entered the armed forces in 1943, he enlisted in the Naval Air Corps. He was commissioned as a lieutenant and asked for combat service as a pilot, but at 32 was considered too old. Instead he became a flying instructor, directed several excellent training films and was later assigned to narrate the war documentary *The Fighting Lady* (1944) which won an Academy Award for best documentary. He was honorably discharged on November 5, 1945 as a Senior Grade Lieutenant.

After the war he returned to Hollywood to resume his career where he had left off. His first post war film was called *Undercurrent* (1946) which paired him with Katharine Hepburn. It did reasonably well commercially, but he was woefully miscast as a psycho and only the brisk direction of George Cukor saved it. As with Clark Gable, Taylor's career was extremely slow starting again after World War II and the two men sought solace in hunting together which proved to be some consolation in their lives.

Taylor did work constantly from 1949 onwards. MGM still had enormous faith in him, but it proved to be a couple of years before the good times returned. He shot *Quo Vadis?* (1951) in Italy which was a massive Roman spectacle derived from the novel by Henry Sienkiewicz in which he played Marcus Vinicius. It was directed by Mervyn LeRoy who had also helmed *Waterloo Bridge*. His costar was Deborah Kerr and the critics agreed that the period costumes and the genre of film agreed with him. The public so heavily endorsed the film that it grossed $12 million and was the fourth most successful movie in cinema history up to that time.

This opened up whole new avenues of film roles for him. His track record during the fifties was one of the best of any star actor. MGM gave him their best scripts in virtually every genre whether westerns, war films, swashbucklers and thrillers and Taylor consistently gave of his best. Not all of these films were commercially successful, but they all had solid production values and as a body of work, he could be very proud of them. Possibly his best postwar performance was contained in *Above and Beyond* (1953) in which he played Colonel Paul Tibbets, the pilot assigned to drop the atomic bomb on Nagasaki. His costar was Eleanor Parker in the first of their three films together. She was by common agreement his best postwar leading lady.

Domestically he fared less well when in 1950 word reached Barbara Stanwyck that he was having a romantic relationship with an Italian starlet, Lia De Leo, while shooting *Quo Vadis?* Stanwyck filed suit for divorce on December 16, 1950. They were divorced in a three minute hearing on February 21, 1951. She was given the house worth $100,000 together with all the furnishings and fittings and 15% of his earnings as alimony until he died. He remarried in Jackson Lake, Wyoming aboard a boat at the foot of Grand Teton Mountain on May 24, 1954 to the German model turned film actress Ursula Thiess. She was divorced from German film director George Thiess with whom she had two children, Manuela and Michael. Subsequently she had two children with Taylor who were Terry born on June 18, 1955 and Tessa born on August 16, 1959.

Taylor completed his MGM contract with *Party Girl* (1958) in which he played a crippled lawyer and then formed his own company called Robert Taylor Productions with an asking price of $200,000 plus a percentage of the gross. There was an option for two more films at MGM which they subsequently exercised. Generally however there were not too many takers for his services. He complained that producers were ignoring him, but he rejected scripts that required him to romance actresses who were decades younger than himself. This is a little surprising since actors of similar age or only slightly younger continued to play romantic roles for many years without any such qualms.

Taylor bought a ranch in Mandeville Canyon in 1959 where his neighbor was Dick Powell, the star turned television mogul, who had his own production company called Four Star Television. He prevailed upon Taylor to try television with a format he was ideally suited to. Starting on October 10, 1959 he starred in a half hour series called *The Detectives Starring Robert Taylor*. He played a widowed Police Captain Matt Holbrook who leads a team of four diverse detectives. Initially they were Lt. John Russo (Tige Andrews) of burglary; Lt. James Conway (Lee Farr) of homicide; and Lt. Otto Lindstrom (Russell Thorson) of bunko.

For many years Taylor turned a blind eye towards television. His first appearance on television came when he agreed to take part in "The Scene Stealer" episode of MGM's *The Thin Man*. He found the pace so rushed and the experience so painful that he vowed never again to make another television appearance. He explained, "I know it used to be fashionable for movie people to say derogatory things about television. I was guilty myself. I admit it. I liked the idea of *The Detectives*, but I didn't know how the public would take to it. The attitude of many big stars to TV has changed over the years. I guess mine had to too! I decided to play the part and I'm pleased to say the series has proved to be very successful."

His salary was $150,000 for the first season and he owned 50% of the series which was sponsored by Proctor and Gamble. The budget was $50,000 an episode. At the time Taylor did not even own a television set, but he mellowed and bought one soon after the series started. The first season on the ABC network consisted of 33 half hour, black and white episodes. After the first season Lee Farr left to be replaced by Sgt. Chris Ballard (Mark Goddard). The second season on the ABC network consisted of 34 half hour, black and white episodes. After the second season Russell Thorson left to be replaced by Sgt. Steve Nelson (Adam West). For the third and final season the title was changed to *Robert Taylor's The Detectives*. It consisted of 30, hour length, black and white episodes shown on the NBC network. He was paid a salary of $300,000 plus 40% ownership of the series. The only hint of a romantic relationship for Holbrook in the series was when Taylor's wife Ursula Thiess showed up occasionally playing police reporter Lisa Bonay. The series was eventually cancelled after the third season, but the reason was not poor ratings. The final original episode was aired on May 18, 1962, while repeats were aired until September 21, 1962.

Almost immediately afterwards Taylor signed to shoot another television series with Robert Loggia in which they both played representatives of the United States Department of Health, Education and Welfare. After about half a dozen episodes were made, the series ended in controversy and was never aired. He then returned to the declining feature film market where he found the pickings were lean and the quality of his films poor. His career did however improve once again in 1966 when Ronald Reagan left the entertainment industry to run for Governor of California. At the time Reagan was hosting a syndicated but successful series called *Death Valley Days*. He relinquished the job to Taylor who served as host and occasional star. He continued in this capacity until he died which allowed him to maintain a decent standing within the industry.

Although possessed of a fine physique, he had survived throughout much of his career on a diet of black coffee and a sixty a day cigarette habit. He became ill with lung cancer and had his right lung removed on October 8, 1968. He was then in hospital seven times over a period of nine months until he eventually died at 10:30 am on June 8, 1969 at St. John's Hospital, Santa Monica at the age of 57. During his final hours Ursula Thiess was at this bedside. Before he was readmitted he said he thought that he was recovering after giving up smoking and shedding 30 lb. He was buried at Forest Lawn Memorial Park, Glendale, California. His will left 50% of his estate to his widow and two children and 50% to his senile mother who was living in a nursing home. Although his ranch was worth over a million dollars, the amount of cash which he left was virtually zero.

Taylor once said about himself, "I was a punk kid from Nebraska who had an awful lot of the world's good things dumped in his lap." Possibly however the most accurate tribute came in the eulogy delivered by Ronald Reagan who said of him, "He respected his profession and he was a superb master of it."

FILMOGRAPHY

1934: *Handy Andy, There's Always Tomorrow, A Wicked Woman*.
1935: *Society Doctor, Times Square Lady, West Point of the Air, Murder in the Fleet, Broadway Melody of 1936, Magnificent Obsession*.
1936: *Small Town Girl, Private Number, His Brother's Wife, The Gorgeous Hussy*.
1937: *Camille, Personal Property, This is My Affair, Broadway Melody of 1938*.
1938: *A Yank at Oxford, Three Comrades, The Crowd Roars*.
1939: *Stand Up and Fight, Lucky Night, Lady of the Tropics, Remember?*
1940: *Flight Command, Waterloo Bridge, Escape*.
1941: *Billy the Kid, When Ladies Meet*.
1942: *Johnny Eager, Her Cardboard Lover*.
1943: *Stand By For Action, Bataan, The Youngest Profession* (cameo).
1944: *Song of Russia*.
1946: *Undercurrent*.
1947: *High Wall*.
1949: *The Bribe*.
1950: *Ambush, The Conspirator, The Devil's Doorway*.
1951: *Quo Vadis?, Westward the Women*.
1952: *Ivanhoe*.
1953: *Above and Beyond, I Love Melvin* (cameo), *Ride Vaquero!, All the Brothers Were Valiant*.
1954: *Knights of the Round Table, Valley of the Kings, Rogue Cop*.
1955: *Many Rivers to Cross, Quentin Durward*.
1956: *The Last Hunt, D-Day the Sixth of June, The Power and the Prize*.
1957: *Tip on a Dead Jockey*.
1958: *Saddle the Wind, The Law and Jake Wade, Party Girl*.

1959: *The Hangman, The House of the Seven Hawks.*
1960: *The Killers of Kilimanjaro.*
1963: *The Miracle of the White Stallions, Cattle King.*
1964: *A House is Not a Home.*
1965: *The Night Walker.*
1966: *Johnny Tiger.*
1967: *Savage Pampas, Return of the Gunfighter* (TV), *Hondo and the Apaches* (TV).
1968: *The Glass Sphinx, Where Angels Go—Trouble Follows, The Day the Hotline Got Hot.*

Note: Some sources credit Taylor with a final film credit *Devil May Care* with Lex Barker, but this film has never received a public showing and doubts have been expressed as to whether it was ever filmed.

Television Series

1959–1961: *The Detectives starring Robert Taylor* as Capt. Matt Holbrook.
1961–1962: *Robert Taylor's The Detectives* as Capt. Matt Holbrook.
1966–1968: *Death Valley Days*—Host and occasional star.

Sources

Associated Press. Obituary, June 1969.
Daily Express. Obituary, June 1969.
Death Certificate.
Ferguson, Ken. *Television Show Book.* London: Purnell, 1965.
Parish, James Robert, and Ronald L. Bowers. *The MGM Stock Company: The Golden Era.* London: Ian Allen, 1973.
Picture Show Annual. London: Amalgamated, 1940 and 1949.
Quirk, Laurence J. *The Films of Robert Taylor.* Secaucus, NJ: Citadel, 1975.
Wayne, Jane Ellen. *Robert Taylor.* London: Robson, 1987.
Winchester, Clarence. *Screen Encyclopedia.* London: Winchester, 1948.
Wise, James E., and Anne Collier Rehill. *Stars in Blue.* Annapolis, MD: Naval Institute, 1997.

Frank Thomas

Frank Thomas was born in St. Joseph, Missouri on July 13, 1889. His acting career commenced at the Van Dyke Stock Company in St. Joseph. He toured the United States in various plays before appearing on Broadway during the teens. He married actress Mona Bruns (1899–2000), who later became well known in soap operas. Their son, Frankie, who was born in New York on April 9, 1921 and who died at Sherman Oaks, CA on May 11, 2006 aged 85, also became a well known actor who was most famous for playing the title role in *Tom Corbett, Space Cadet.* In 1934 Frank Thomas made his screen debut in *Wednesday's Child* using the name of Tom Franklin. In 1935 father and son appeared on Broadway in *Remember the Day.* Following this Frank Thomas was signed with RKO.

Between 1935 and 1937 he appeared in numerous films for this studio. From 1938 to 1943 he was a busy freelance character actor. In 1943 he and his family returned to New York where he was in *Chicken Every Sunday* on Broadway in 1944. He was very active on radio and in early television. He appeared as the father in the CBS situation comedy *Wesley* in which he costarred with his wife. In the crime series *Martin Kane Private Eye* he played Captain Burke who was the friend and police contact of Martin Kane (William Gargan). During the fifties he played the editor in the soap opera *Love of Life.* In the early seventies he and his wife costarred in *The Cycle,* an experimental short, shown at the Cannes Film Festival.

Frank Thomas died in Tujunga, California on November 25, 1989 aged 100 of cardiac arrest. He was survived by his wife and son. He and his wife may be unique in the annals of show business in that they were possibly the only moderately famous married couple who both lived to be centenarians.

Filmography

1934: *Wednesday's Child.*
1936: *The Last Outlaw, M'Liss, The Ex–Mrs. Bradford, Don't Turn 'em Loose, Wanted! Jane Turner, Without Orders, Racing Lady, Mummy's Boys, Grand Jury, Criminal Lawyer, The Big Game.*
1937: *We're on the Jury, Don't Tell the Wife, China Passage, The Man Who Found Himself, The Outcasts of Poker Flat, You Can't Beat Love, Breakfast for Two, You Can't Buy Luck, They Wanted to Marry, The Soldier and the Lady, Meet the Missus, High Flyers, Forty Naughty Girls, Danger Patrol, The Big Shot, Behind the Headlines.*
1938: *Bringing Up Baby, Maid's Night Out, Blind Alibi, Vivacious Lady, The Wrong Way Out, This Marriage Business, Strange Faces, Smashing the Rackets, The Renegade Ranger, Quick Money, Night Spot, Mr. Doodle Kicks Off, A Man to Re-*

member, *Law of the Underworld, Joy of Living, Go Chase Yourself, Everybody's Doing It, Crime Ring, Crashing Hollywood.*
1939: *Burn 'em Up O'Connor, Idiot's Delight, The Rookie Cop, They All Came Out, Bachelor Mother, They Made Her a Spy, Society Lawyer, Secret Service of the Air, The Mysterious Miss X, The Man from Dakota, Grand Jury Secrets, Geronimo, Disbarred, Death of a Champion, $1000 a Touchdown, The Story of Alexander Graham Bell, Rose of Washington Square.*
1940: *Scandal Sheet, Chad Hanna, Shooting High, Saga of Death Valley, Queen of the Mob, Maryland, Brigham Young—Frontiersman, Lillian Russell.*
1941: *Wyoming Wildcat, A Shot in the Dark, Sucker List, Wild Bill Hickok Rides, Three Sons o' Guns, Sierra Sue, Obliging Young Lady, The Monster and the Girl, Life with Henry, Arkansas Judge, Among the Living.*
1942: *Reap the Wild Wind, Dangerously They Live, The Talk of the Town, The Great Man's Lady, Sunset Serenade, Sunset on the Desert, The Postman Didn't Ring, Mountain Rhythm, Apache Trail, A Desperate Chance for Ellery Queen, Eyes in the Night, Henry Aldrich Editor.*
1943: *Hello Frisco Hello, No Place for a Lady.*
1950: *The Sleeping City.*

TELEVISION SERIES

1949: *Wesley* as Mr. Eggleston.
1949–1950: *The Black Robe* as the Judge.
1951–1952: *Martin Kane Private Eye* as Captain Burke.
1950s: *Love of Life* as the Editor.
1965–1966: *Paradise Bay* as Judge Grayson.

SOURCES

Brooks, Tim. *The Complete Directory to Prime Time TV Stars, 1946–Present.* New York: Ballantine, 1987.
Copeland, Mary Ann. *Soap Opera History.* Lincolnwood, IL: Mallard, 1991.
Twomey, Alfred E., and Arthur F. McClure. *The Versatiles* South Brunswick, NJ: Barnes, 1969.
Variety. Obituary, December 1989.

JEROME THOR

Jerome Thor was born in Brooklyn, New York on January 5, 1915. He trained for the stage at the Neighborhood Playhouse. His early career was spent as a Broadway actor, appearing in such productions as *The Marriage Proposal* and *Golden Boy*. He appeared on television as a guest star in early anthology series developed from radio shows such as *Suspense*.

Thor played the lead during the first two seasons of the filmed syndicated series *Foreign Intrigue* which was launched in 1951. It was produced in Europe by entrepreneur and member of the international jet set, Sheldon Reynolds. Thor played Robert Cannon who was a foreign correspondent working for the Amalgamated News Service based in Stockholm. Thor virtually created the stereotype of the trench coat wearing investigative reporter. One of his original overcoats is on display in the Smithsonian Institute in Washington D.C. His real life wife Sydna Scott costarred as Helen Davis who was a friendly rival reporter working for another agency. Thor starred in 78 episodes of this series which was very popular largely because it was shot on location and offered views of glamorous foreign places to millions of viewers who in those days were scarcely likely to see such places for themselves. The only disappointment was that the series was shot in black and white. There was a political theme to many of the early stories which frequently involved chasing fugitive Nazis across Europe. The supporting casts were usually European players whose names meant very little or society chums of producer Reynolds. The series was later reissued under the title *Dateline Europe*. Foreign In-

Jerome Thor, who starred in *Foreign Intrigue*.

trigue received three Emmy nominations as Best Mystery, Action or Adventure Program in 1952, 1953 and 1954, but failed to win on any occasion.

In 1953 the series was revamped. Thor and Scott were replaced by James Daly and Anne Préville. Thor received little distinction as an actor in later years, being seen in occasional films or television episodes in small roles until the late eighties. His film career ended on a dismally low note. His final film was *Kinjite: Forbidden Subjects* (1989) in which he was credited as a pervert.

Thor died in Westwood, California on August 12, 1993 aged 78 of cardiac arrest. He was survived by his widow whom he wed in 1946.

Filmography

1959: *Riot in Juvenile Prison.*
1963: *55 Days at Peking.*
1964: *The Fall of the Roman Empire.*
1965: *House of Black Death.*
1971: *O'Hara United States Treasury: Operation Cobra* (TV).
1972: *Incident on a Dark Street* (TV).
1974: *Mr. Sycamore.*
1976: *The Great Houdini* (TV), *Stalk the Wild Child* (TV).
1977: *The Amazing Howard Hughes* (TV), *Murder in Peyton Place* (TV).
1979: *Love and Bullets.*
1983: *10 to Midnight.*
1986: *Murphy's Law.*
1988: *Messenger of Death.*
1989: *Kinjite: Forbidden Subjects.*

Television Series

1951–1953: *Foreign Intrigue* (a.k.a. *Dateline Europe*) as Robert Cannon.

Sources

Erickson, Hal. *Syndicated Television: The First Forty Years, 1947–1987.* Jefferson, NC: McFarland, 1989.
Lance, Steven. *Written Out of Television.* Lanham, MD: Madison, 1996.
Variety. Obituary, August 1993.

June Thorburn

June Thorburn was born in Kashmir, India on June 7, 1931 the daughter of an army colonel. She received her early education in India and besides doing very well in class, she also excelled in sports. When she was only five years old, she began to ski. By the age of twelve she was junior ladies skiing champion of India.

With the end of the war in 1945, she finished her education in England. Her future career was decided when she took up amateur theatricals with an army company. In 1949 she was invited to join Aldershot Repertory Company. She remained there for nearly a year and then made her West End, London debut in *Life With Father*. Further repertory work followed in Eastbourne and Margate and she also obtained early experience of television work. A period of repertory in Southampton was followed by a very successful appearance at the Garrick Theater, London in *Red Letter Day* with Hugh Williams.

Given a film test, she made her screen debut in *The Pickwick Papers* (1952) as Arabella. Next she appeared opposite Jack Hawkins as Doris Ferraby in the classic war film *The Cruel Sea* (1952). The Rank Organization realized that she had good screen possibilities so they placed her under contract. Of the films she made for them a comedy *Touch and Go* (1955) as Peggy Fletcher was where she made her first big impact on audiences. This film also starred Jack Hawkins. Although Rank were good at providing her with publicity, she despised the marshmallow roles which she became typed in by them.

In September 1952 she married Aldon Richard Bryse-Harvey and had a daughter Heather who was born in 1953. Her first marriage ended in divorce in 1957. She thus became a single parent long before it was fashionable. Of this experience she said, "I'll feel sorry for the man, if I ever marry again. He will have to peel off a whole skin of bitterness before discovering the real me. I was always known for my honesty and frankness. And I always looked for the best in others. With the break-up of my marriage I became more suspicious, more guarded — more cynical if you like. Lonely? Of course I'm lonely. But I feel it's better to be alone and emotionally safe than involved."

It was said that she carried on working at a rate of knots to support her daughter and a large flat in Hampstead, London where they lived. As an actress she had to fight hard to show producers that she was not just a pretty face. In the last half of 1959 she worked on eight television episodes and three television plays. She also costarred in the film *The 3 Worlds of Gulliver* (1960). Of this film experience she recalled, "I must confess that I liked it better than my part in *tom thumb* (1958) for MGM, although that was great fun to work on. And I needed the money they paid me at M.G.M.—£1,700 for seventeen days' work."

Among the television episodes which she appeared in was an episode of *The Four Just Men* which starred Jack Hawkins. Later on in the same series she played the semi-regular role of Vicky, the personal assistant to New York lawyer Jeff Ryder (Richard Conte). In this role she appeared in four episodes. For this she had to assume an American accent. "It's extraordinary how I got the part," she enthused. "I was in a Continental train coming back from a skiing holiday in Austria. I was walking down the corridor when I heard two men talking about show business. They knew me." One of them was Basil Appleby, casting director of *The Four Just Men*. "Can you speak American?" he asked her. "I haven't yet, but I'll try," she replied. She made a tape recording of her voice using an American accent which was so convincing that she won the part.

Afterwards the producer of the television series *Tales of the Vikings* rang her and said, "I hear you're a pretty offbeat girl. Well this character I have in mind jumps from the mast of a ship and stabs three men. That's the start. Then you can take it from there." She did and won the role. Afterwards she played the spirited heroine of a few swashbuckling films. Another television play in which she appeared was *Lord Arthur Savile's Crime* (1960) from the play by Constance Cox in which she costarred with Terry-Thomas. They had worked together before in the film *tom thumb* in which she played the fairy queen. It was said around this time that when not working she liked to go to auctions and pick up pieces of furniture.

She continued to appear in films and on television until 1964. Then she remarried to Morton Smith-Petersen and had another daughter. She quit show business because the amount of time she had spent working had ruined her first marriage and she was determined that her second marriage would not go the same way as her first.

At age 36, June Thorburn was returning to England after a vacation in Spain aboard an Iberia Airlines Caravelle airliner from Malaga bound for London. On November 4, 1967 it descended too low and flew into the southern slope of Black Down Hill at Fernhurst, Sussex, England killing all 37 people on board. The cause of the crash was never determined. The actress was survived by her second husband and two daughters. Her death was doubly tragic because she was pregnant at the time. In her will she left £9,024.

June Thorburn, who costarred in *The Four Just Men*.

Filmography

1952: *The Pickwick Papers, The Cruel Sea.*
1953: *The Triangle.*
1954: *Fast and Loose, Delayed Action, Orders Are Orders, Children Galore, The Death of Michael Turbin.*
1955: *The Hornet's Nest, Touch and Go* (a.k.a. *The Light Touch*).
1956: *True as a Turtle.*
1958: *Rooney, tom thumb.*
1959: *Broth of a Boy.*
1960: *The Price of Silence, The 3 Worlds of Gulliver, Escort for Hire.*
1961: *Fury at Smuggler's Bay, Don't Bother to Knock, Transatlantic, The Spanish Sword.*
1962: *Design for Loving.*
1963: *The Scarlet Blade, Master Spy.*

Television Series

1959–1960: *The Four Just Men* as Vicky.

Sources

Cowan, Margaret. "Four Just Men—Three Smart Girls." *TV Times.* May 15, 1960.
Daily Mail Yearbook. 69th ed. London: Associated Newspapers, 1969.

McFarlane, Brian. *The Encyclopedia of British Film.* London: BFI/Methuen, 2003.
Noble, Peter. *The British Film and Television Yearbook 1962/63.* 12th ed. London: BA, 1963.
Picture Show. "Life Story." April 26, 1958.
Picture Show Annual. London: Amalgamated, 1960.
Quinlan, David. *Illustrated Directory of Film Stars.* 5th ed. London: Batsford, 2000.
Rainer, Burt. "June Thorburn Faces Up to Life." *Picturegoer.* January 2, 1960.
TV Times. "Lord Arthur Savile's Crime." January 3, 1960.
Willis, John. *Screen World.* Vol. 19. New York: Muller, 1968.

RUSSELL THORSON

Russell Thorson was born in Wisconsin on October 14, 1906. He was based mainly in New York and Chicago. He broadcast in numerous radio shows. He acted in both the radio and television versions of the soap opera *One Man's Family.* On television he played a veteran detective in the crime series *The Detectives Starring Robert Taylor.* He later appeared in bit parts in numerous television shows and films usually playing professional types. He died in Van Nuys, California on July 6, 1982 aged 75 of cancer, survived by his widow and three stepchildren.

Russell Thorson, who costarred in *The Detectives*.

FILMOGRAPHY

1949: *Easy Living.*
1951: *Double Dynamite.*
1954: *Dangerous Mission.*
1956: *Please Murder Me, Hot Rod Girl.*
1957: *Zero Hour, Undersea Girl, Half Human, Destination 60,000.*
1958: *Tarawa Beachhead, I Want to Live!, Gun Fever, Good Day for a Hanging.*
1960: *Gunfighters of Abilene.*
1963: *It Happened at the World's Fair.*
1964: *36 Hours.*
1965: *Two on a Guillotine, My Blood Runs Cold.*
1967: *Hang 'em High, A Covenant with Death.*
1968: *Hawaii Five-O* (TV).
1969: *The Stalking Moon, The Learning Tree.*
1970: *Night Slaves* (TV), *Incident in San Francisco* (TV).
1972: *The Screaming Woman* (TV).
1973: *The Blue Knight* (TV), *Walking Tall.*
1974: *Manhunter* (TV).
1975: *Guilty or Innocent: The Sam Sheppard Murder Case* (TV).

TELEVISION SERIES

1949–1955: *One Man's Family* as Paul Barbour.
1959–1961: *The Detectives Starring Robert Taylor* as Det. Lt. Otto Lindstrom.
1962–1963: *The Virginian* as Sheriff Stan Evans.

SOURCES

Brooks, Tim. *The Complete Directory to Prime Time TV Stars, 1946–Present.* New York: Ballantine, 1987.
Variety. Obituary, August 11, 1982.
Ward, Jack. *The Supporting Players of Television.* Cleveland, OK: Lakeshore West, 1996.

REGIS TOOMEY

John Regis Toomey was born in Pittsburgh, PA on August 13, 1898. He was the son of Francis and Marie Toomey. His parents were Irish Americans. He had two sisters who were Othelia and Sarah and one brother named Ord. He was educated at Peabody High School and the University of Pittsburgh. Prior to attending college, his first job was as an assistant property boy, but this was unsatisfactory because he wanted to act. His original intention was to become a lawyer, but the lure of show business proved to be too strong. At the University he belonged to "Cap and Gown" which was the amateur theatrical society where for two years he had the lead in the annual play. During the annual summer vacations he joined a summer stock company for three years in succession.

After graduating in 1922 he went to Los Angeles where his parents were now living, but initially his life did not go well. Despite his education he was reduced to laboring in a road gang consisting entirely of Mexicans in Los Angeles. When he was recommended by his college to a steel manufacturing company who asked them for some recent graduates for their sales department, he took the job. On vacation in New York, his urge to be a professional actor surfaced. He wandered into a theater where *Rose Marie* was being rehearsed and was engaged as understudy to star Dennis King and appeared in the chorus as well. Following this came his London engagement for two seasons in *Little Nellie Kelly* as the juvenile lead. While there in 1925 he met and married Kathryn Scott, an English musical comedy actress. She died in 1981.

He returned to Los Angeles to introduce his wife to his family. While there he was offered a leading role in a show *Hit the Deck* which was to be produced at a Los Angeles theater. After finishing this, he was proposed for the role of Danny McGann in the film *Alibi* (1929) by the director's then wife, actress Jewel Carmen (1897–1984) who had met him socially. The director Roland West (1885–1952) disagreed, but since his wife had brought Toomey to his attention, he agreed to test him. In fact he tested him for the role of Tommy Glennon which was subsequently played by Pat O'Malley. When he saw the results of the test, West changed his mind and agreed with his wife and cast Toomey in the role of Danny McGann. This was the first all talking gangster melodrama and received a Best Film Oscar nomination.

Although he was one of the first stage players to enter films with the advent of talkies, Toomey's career rapidly declined in stature. Nevertheless he went on to appear in over 150 films and was a welcome addition to any cast list no matter how small the role. Aside from being

Mary Carlisle and Regis Toomey in the film *One Frightened Night* (1935). Toomey costarred in the television series *Richard Diamond Private Detective*.

under contract to Paramount in the early thirties and a Warners contract for a couple of years in the early forties, he remained a freelance actor throughout his film career. He was not noted for any one particular part, more for the sheer volume of his work. In 1941 he created a movie record by kissing co-star Jane Wyman for three minutes and eight seconds in *You're in the Army Now*. Her then husband, Ronald Reagan, did not mind and became a lifelong friend of Toomey. On September 22, 1991 Reagan and Nancy Davis visited him at the Motion Picture and Television Country Home and Hospital in Woodland Hills where Toomey had resided for some time.

From 1950 onwards he was a very familiar television face. He was a regular in five series. On *Richard Diamond, Private Detective* he played Diamond's (David Janssen) initial police contact Det. Lt. McGough. His best remembered television stint was as Det. Sgt. Les Hart, the assistant of police chief Amos Burke (Gene Barry) in *Burke's Law*. His final television appearance was believed to be an episode of *It's a Living* in 1982. In real life Toomey was a leader of Los Angeles community's civic and charitable organizations.

He died at the Motion Picture Country Home and Hospital in Woodland Hills, California on October 12, 1991 aged 93 of natural causes survived by his brother.

FILMOGRAPHY

1929: *Alibi, The Wheel of Life, Illusion, Rich People*.

1930: *Street of Chance, Framed, Crazy That Way, The Light of Western Stars, Shadow of the Law, Good Intentions, A Man from Wyoming.*

1931: *Other Men's Women, Scandal Sheet, Finn and Hattie, The Finger Points, Kick In, Murder by the Clock, Graft, 24 Hours, Touchdown.*

1932: *Under Eighteen, Shopworn, The Midnight Patrol, The Crowd Roars, They Never Come Back, A Strange Adventure* (a.k.a. *The Wayne Murder Case*), *The Penal Code.*

1933: *State Trooper, Soldiers of the Storm, Laughing at Life, She Had to Say Yes, Big Time or Bust.*

1934: *What's Your Racket?, Picture Brides, Murder on the Blackboard, She Had to Choose, Redhead.*

1935: *Shadow of Doubt, Red Morning, Great God Gold, G Men, One Frightened Night, Manhattan Moon, Shadows of the Orient, Reckless Roads, Skull and Crown.*

1936: *Bulldog Edition, Bars of Hate.*

1937: *Midnight Taxi, Big City* (a.k.a. *Skyscraper Wilderness*), *Back in Circulation, Submarine D-I.*

1938: *The Invisible Menace, Blind Alibi, Hunted Men, Illegal Traffic, His Exciting Night.*

1939: *The Phantom Creeps* (a.k.a. *The Shadow Creeps*) (serial), *The Mysterious Miss X, Smashing the Spy Ring, Pirates of the Skies, Wings of the Navy, Society Smugglers, Street of Missing Men, Union Pacific, Confessions of a Nazi Spy, Trapped in the Sky, Indianapolis Speedway, Hidden Power, Thunder Afloat.*

1940: *His Girl Friday, Northwest Passage, 'Til We Meet Again, North West Mounted Police, March on Marines, Arizona.*

1941: *The Lone Wolf Takes a Chance, A Shot in the Dark, Reaching for the Sun, Meet John Doe, The Devil and Miss Jones, The Nurse's Secret, Dive Bomber, Law of the Tropics, New York Town, You're in the Army Now, They Died With Their Boots On.*

1942: *Bullet Scars, I Was Framed, The Forest Rangers, Tennessee Johnson* (a.k.a. *The Man on America's Conscience*).

1943: *Adventures of the Flying Cadets* (serial), *Destroyer, Jack London, Tornado* (narrator only).

1944: *Phantom Lady, Follow the Boys, Song of the Open Road, Raiders of Ghost City* (serial), *The Doughgirls, Dark Mountain, When the Lights Go On Again, Murder in the Blue Room.*

1945: *Betrayal from the East, Strange Illusion* (a.k.a. *Out of the Night*), *Spellbound, Follow That Woman.*

1946: *Mysterious Intruder, The Big Sleep, Her Sister's Secret, Sister Kenny, Child of Divorce, The Big Fix.*

1947: *The Thirteenth Hour, The Guilty, High Tide, Magic Town, The Bishop's Wife.*

1948: *Reaching From Heaven, I Wouldn't Be in Your Shoes, Raw Deal, Station West, The Boy with Green Hair.*

1949: *Mighty Joe Young, Come to the Stable, The Devil's Henchman, Beyond the Forest.*

1950: *Dynamite Pass, Undercover Girl.*

1951: *Frenchie, Tomahawk, Cry Danger, Mrs. O'Malley and Mr. Malone, Navy Bound, Show Boat, The Tall Target, The People Against O'Hara.*

1952: *Never Wave at a WAC, My Six Convicts, The Battle at Apache Pass, Just for You, My Pal Gus.*

1953: *It Happens Every Thursday, Son of Belle Starr, Island in the Sky, Take the High Ground, The Nebraskan*

1954: *Drums Across the River, The High and the Mighty, The Human Jungle.*

1955: *Guys and Dolls, Top Gun.*

1956: *Great Day in the Morning, Three for Jamie Dawn, Dakota Incident.*

1957: *Curfew Breakers.*

1958: *Sing Boy Sing, Joy Ride.*

1959: *Warlock.*

1960: *Guns of the Timberland.*

1961: *The Last Sunset, King of the Roaring 20s—The Story of Arnold Rothstein, Voyage to the Bottom of the Sea, The Errand Boy.*

1964: *Man's Favorite Sport.*

1966: *The Night of the Grizzly.*

1967: *Gunn.*

1969: *Change of Habit, The Out-of-Towners.*

1970: *Cover Me Babe.*

1972: *The Carey Treatment.*

1974: *The Phantom of Hollywood* (TV), *God Bless Dr. Shagetz.*

1976: *Won Ton Ton the Dog Who Saved Hollywood.*

1979: *C.H.O.M.P.S*

Note: *God Bless Dr. Shagetz* was never finished, but footage of it was incorporated into another horror film *Evil Town* released in 1987.

Television Series

1954–1955: *The Mickey Rooney Show* (a.k.a. *Hey Mulligan!*) as Joe Mulligan.

1957–1958: *Richard Diamond Private Detective* as Det. Lt. McGough.

1961–1962: *Shannon* as Bill Cochran.

1963–1965: *Burke's Law* as Det. Sgt. Les Hart.

1966–1969: *Petticoat Junction* as Dr. Burton Stuart.

Sources

The Annual Obituary. Chicago: St. James, 1991.
Bermingham, Cedric Oswald. *Stars of the Screen*. 2nd ed. London: Herbert Joseph, 1932.
_____. *Stars of the Screen*. 3rd ed. London: Herbert Joseph, 1933.
Brooks, Tim. *The Complete Directory to Prime Time TV Stars*. New York: Ballantine, 1987.
Donnelly, Paul. *Fade to Black*. London: Omnibus, 2000.
Inman, David. *The TV Encyclopedia*. New York: Perigee, 1991.
Parish, James Robert. *Hollywood Character Actors*. New Rochelle, NY: Arlington, 1978.
The Picturegoer's Who's Who and Encyclopedia. 1st ed. London: Odham's Press, 1933.
Picture Show Annual. 1931. London: Amalgamated, 1931.
Picture Show Annual. 1933. London: Amalgamated, 1933.
Quinlan, David. *Illustrated Directory of Film Character Actors*. 2nd ed. London: Batsford, 1995.
Ragan, David. *Who's Who in Hollywood*. 2nd ed. New York: Facts on File, 1992.
Reed, Langford, and Hetty Spiers. *Who's Who in Filmland*. 3rd ed. London: Chapman and Hall, 1931.
Ross, J.S. *Stars of the Screen*. 4th ed. London: Herbert Joseph, 1934.
Twomey, Alfred, and Arthur F. McClure. *The Versatiles*. South Brunswick, NJ: Barnes, 1969.
Variety. Obituary, October 1991.
Ward, Jack. *The Supporting Players of Television, 1959–1983*. Cleveland, OK: Lakeshore West, 1996.
Winchester, Clarence. *The World Film Encyclopedia*. London: Amalgamated, 1933.

LEE TRACY

Lee Tracy was the actor who placed his career in jeopardy in the course of a single day. It was Sunday, November 19, 1933. He was in Mexico to shoot an MGM film called *Viva Villa*, a biopic of the legendary Pancho Villa played by Wallace Beery. There were numerous protests before the incident because it was claimed that the movie was defamatory about Mexico. Tracy was asleep in the afternoon, after a heavy night's imbibing, in his room on the seventh floor of a luxury hotel in Mexico City. Two costars, one of whom was Irving Pichel, came to his room and woke him up to enquire about tickets to a bullfight. Drinking again and clad only in a blanket, Tracy wandered on to the balcony of the room. The balcony overlooked a busy street in the city. A brass band was playing in celebration of an historic event, while the crack Chapultepec Military Academy troops were passing by. Tracy allegedly let the blanket slip and began hurling insults at the crowd and soldiers.

He was arrested the following day. After two hours at the police station, his release was effected by the American consulate. He was later rearrested and the studio was fined 2,000 pesos. Some accounts state that he fled by plane to Juarez where he walked across the International Bridge to freedom. Others state that he fled the country by plane to El Paso, Texas. From there he took the train back to Los Angeles where he claimed that it was all a misunderstanding. Howard Hawks was replaced at his own request as director by Jack Conway and the film was shot in Hollywood. Stuart Erwin replaced Tracy. Since it was a troubled shoot from its initial stages, there was a general feeling that Tracy was used as a scapegoat.

On screen Tracy's best performances generally came in films where he played hot shot reporters or shyster lawyers who spat out dialogue like machine gun bullets and seldom repented on their unscrupulous actions. Off screen Tracy liked to live life on his own terms, hated contracts, but liked deep sea fishing and baseball games.

William Lee Tracy was born in Atlanta, Georgia on April 14, 1898 the son of William Lindsay Tracy and Rachel Lee Griffith. His father was a general superintendent of motive power for a railroad company, while his mother was a sometime school teacher. The nature of his father's job meant that the family lived in many places. He was educated at Western Military Academy in Alton, Illinois and Union College, Schenectady, New York from where he graduated in 1918.

His original show business ambition was to be a magician. While at college he attended a couple of performances of a play and went backstage to complement the star who offered him a position with the company. World War I prevented him from making the most of this opportunity. He was commissioned as a Second Lieutenant with the Army Information Branch. His brief military tenure was spent at Fort Lee, VA. After his discharge he became a railroad em-

Lee Tracy, who starred in *The Amazing Mr. Malone*, *Martin Kane Private Eye* and *New York Confidential*.

ployee. He studied electrical engineering and worked as an electrician.

On a whim he quit this to go on the stage in 1919. He acquired experience in vaudeville and stock. His first Broadway appearance was as Joe in *The Show Off* which opened at the Playhouse Theater, New York on February 5, 1924. He became a star as Roy Lane in the play *Broadway* which opened at the Broadhurst Theater on September 16, 1926 and ran for 603 performances. Another major stage success was *The Front Page* which opened at the Times Square Theater on August 14, 1928. Tracy played the role of Hildy Johnson, the motor-mouth reporter, in the classic play by Charles MacArthur and Ben Hecht.

On the strength of this success, he was signed to a Fox contract, making his screen debut in *Big Time* (1929). He appeared in only three films for them before being loaned to independent studio Tiffany for *She Got What She Wanted* (1930). A personality clash with director James Cruze caused him to walk off the set. His contract with Fox was terminated shortly afterwards. Disillusioned with Hollywood, he returned to New York where he appeared in a couple of other stage productions.

His rapid fire delivery and abrasive personality made him a natural for Warner Bros. who signed him to a contract in 1932. He shot four films for them. The most commercially successful of these was the classic horror film *Doctor X* (1932) in which he played the reporter who exposes the villain as an apparent cripple who can create synthetic flesh. By way of contrast he was hilarious as a gossip columnist in *Blessed Event* (1932), a characterization based on Walter Winchell. He was then offered a contract by Harry Cohn at Columbia if he would refrain from drinking. Tracy's response was that his mother had begged him to sign the pledge on her deathbed which he refused to do because he did not have the strength of character. Since he scarcely considered Cohn more saintly than his mother, he would have to decline. Cohn accepted this logic so Tracy signed the contract and eventually made the movies.

RKO Radio signed him for *The Half Naked Truth* (1932), but during production the studio instigated a lawsuit claiming that his absence from the set had resulted in costly delays. Tracy's doctor responded by giving evidence that his patient had suffered a nervous breakdown. The studio replied that his imbibing had more to do with it. The case was eventually settled out of court and he completed the film. Despite his wild reputation, MGM were still keen to have him under contract and signed him in 1933 at $2,000 a week for a five year contract. His career as a top flight screen star seemed made. Of the five films which he shot at MGM, the most prestigious was the all star *Dinner At Eight* (1933).

After the Mexican incident MGM cancelled his contract on November 22, 1933. Despite his behavior the public seemed to be almost universally on his side and sent sacks of mail to MGM and the papers in his defense. It might have been supposed that he would have been blacklisted, but studios such as Paramount and Universal still hired him for features. At Universal he was particularly unfortunate to be in *Sutter's Gold* (1936) with Edward Arnold. This was a notorious flop and was Tracy's last prestigious film until his final one. In October 1935 he opened at the Plymouth Theater, Boston in the play *Bright Eyes* and took it to Broadway where it folded after only seven performances.

He enjoyed more luck in the London, England production of *Idiot's Delight* which opened at the Apollo Theater on August 30, 1938. He succeeded Raymond Massey as Harry Van.

While there Tracy made his television debut in an experimental television production in London in 1938. Between 1936 and 1940 he was under contract to RKO Radio for whom he shot seven B pictures. At the Guild Theater, New York he briefly appeared in *Every Man For Himself* which opened in December 1940, but closed after only three performances. At the start of World War II he reenlisted in the army where he served as a captain, C.M.P. in the Allied Military Government.

After the war he shot three films for poverty row studios and returned to the stage. On April 4, 1949 he opened in *The Traitor* as the Chief Intelligence Officer, Captain Gallagher. In September 1950 he made his American television debut reprising his role in *The Traitor*. Since he was no longer in demand for film roles, he was free to concentrate on television. He was the star of three crime and mystery series. *The Amazing Mr. Malone* starred him as streetwise criminal attorney John J. Malone. It derived from a series of novels by Craig Rice which had served as the basis for a few films and a long running radio series since 1947. The character was considerably improved from the printed page by the time he came to television. Tracy played him as a wisecracking charmer with a fondness for liquor and the ladies. Nevertheless the series survived for only 13 half hour, black and white episodes shown live on the ABC network between September 24, 1951 and March 10, 1952 where it alternated with *Mr. District Attorney*.

His second television series was *Martin Kane Private Eye* in which he became the third actor to play the private detective following William Gargan and Lloyd Nolan. His stint was shown on the NBC network between September 1952 and June 1953. His third television series *New York Confidential* was a syndicated one produced by TPA and lasting for 39 half hour, black and white, filmed episodes. It was first shown in 1958. It became a success because of a saturation publicity campaign using Tracy as a front man for personal appearances and taped television advertisements prior to the start of the series. Tracy in a ripe piece of typecasting played a cynical newspaperman. It derived from a bestselling book by Jack Lait and Lee Mortimer.

In the spring of 1955 he went to Australia to play Captain Queeg in *The Caine Mutiny Court-Martial*. His last great stage role was as ex–President Arthur Hockstader in *The Best Man* by Gore Vidal which opened at the Morosco Theater on March 31, 1960. For this he received a Tony nomination, but lost to Melvyn Douglas who was appearing in the same play. When the play became a film in 1964, Tracy repeated his role and received a Best Supporting Actor Oscar nomination. On October 7, 1965 he opened in *Minor Miracle* which closed after only two performances. It was his last Broadway role. His final television appearance was an episode of *Ben Casey* in 1965.

In mid–1968 he underwent surgery for cancer of the liver and was recovering at his home in Pacific Palisades, CA. On October 16 he suffered a relapse and reentered St. John's Hospital in Santa Monica where he died on October 18, 1968 aged 70. He was buried beside his parents in Shavertown, Pennsylvania. Despite his drinking habits, he had sound financial ability. He had invested his earnings wisely mainly in California real estate and amassed a fortune of between two and three million dollars.

He and fellow dipsomaniac actress Isabel Jewell were an item for a few years on the Hollywood scene, but never married. Instead he eloped to Yuma, Arizona with socialite divorcee Mrs. Helen Thomas Wyse on July 19, 1938. He left the income from his investments in trust to his wife for life and then to be divided amongst various charities. The irony was that the institutions he left his money to were dedicated to the very principles he had spent his life rebelling against.

FILMOGRAPHY

1929: *Big Time*.
1930: *Born Reckless, Liliom, She Got What She Wanted, On the Level*.
1932: *The Strange Love of Molly Louvain, Love Is a Racket, Doctor X, Blessed Event, Washington Merry-Go-Round, The Night Mayor, The Half-Naked Truth*.
1933: *Clear All Wires, Private Jones, The Nuisance, Dinner at Eight, Turn Back the Clock, Bombshell, Advice to the Lovelorn*.
1934: *I'll Tell the World, You Belong to Me, The Lemon Drop Kid*.
1935: *Carnival, Two Fisted*.
1936: *Sutter's Gold, Wanted—Jane Turner*.
1937: *Criminal Lawyer, Behind the Headlines*.
1938: *Crashing Hollywood*.
1939: *Fixer Dugan, The Spellbinder*.
1940: *Millionaires in Prison*.
1942: *The Payoff*.
1943: *Power of the Press*.

1945: *Betrayal from the East, I'll Tell the World.*
1947: *High Tide.*
1964: *The Best Man.*

Note: *I'll Tell the World* (1945) was a remake of the 1934 film with the same title. Tracy played the lead in both versions.

TELEVISION SERIES

1951–1952: *The Amazing Mr. Malone* as John J. Malone.
1952–1953: *Martin Kane Private Eye* as Martin Kane.
1958: *New York Confidential* as Lee Cochran.

SOURCES

Hamann, G.D. *Hollywood Scandal in the '30s.* Hollywood: Filming Today, 1999.
Inman, David. *The TV Encyclopedia.* New York: Perigee, 1991.
McClure, Arthur, and Ken D. Jones. *Star Quality.* South Brunswick, NJ: Barnes, 1974.
Parish, James Robert, and William T. Leonard. *Hollywood Players: The Thirties.* Carlstadt, NJ: Rainbow, 1977.
Picturegoer's Who's Who and Encyclopedia. London: Odham's, 1933.
Picture Show Annual. London: Amalgamated, 1931, 1934, 1935 and 1936.
Quinlan, David. *Film Stars.* 5th ed. London: Batsford, 2000.
Who's Who in the Theatre. 13th ed. London: Pitman, 1962.
Winchester, Clarence. *The World Film Encyclopedia.* London: Amalgamated, 1933.

RICHARD TRAVIS

Richard Travis was born William B. Justice, Jr., in Carlsbad, New Mexico on April 17, 1913. He was the son of William B. Justice, Sr., who was born in Illinois and his wife Ella O. Spain who was born in Arizona. His ancestry was English. He was raised in Paragould, Arkansas where he attended high school. He left school at the age of eighteen.

He was doing publicity and art poster work for the Majestic Theater there before going to Hollywood. While in Hollywood he became a radio announcer and sportscaster and wrote and published an entertainment tabloid called "Cinemag." Simultaneously he was trying to break into movies. He was a good rider and did extra work primarily in Westerns before Warners cast him in a propaganda short entitled *Here Comes the Cavalry* (1941).

Bette Davis saw him in this and was so impressed that she strongly recommended him to Warners for a leading role of Bert Jefferson in *The Man Who Came To Dinner* (1941). He was under contract to Warner Bros. until drafted in 1943. He served in the U.S. Army until he was honorably discharged in 1945. He then set about picking up the threads of his acting career, but was confined to leading roles in "B" pictures for small, independent outfits like Film Classics and Lippert.

Travis was active in television from the early 1950s onwards. Eventually he managed to land the starring role in a series of his own called *Code 3*. This program concerned the Code 3 cases of Assistant Sheriff Barnett (Travis) of the Los Angeles County Sheriff's Department which were those involving murder, grand theft and kidnapping. Eugene W. Biscialuz, the real sheriff of Los Angeles at the time, made fleeting appearances presumably to underline its authenticity since it was based on actual case files. His assistants were played by Fred Wynn and Denver Pyle.

This series was produced by Hal Roach and amounted to 39 half hour, black and white episodes. Travis was the kind of handsome, personable leading man who could have attained real stardom in television if he had been attached to

Richard Travis, who starred in *Code 3*.

the right series. *Code 3* was originally intended to rival *Highway Patrol* and to be shown on the ABC network, but in the event was syndicated instead, where it proved to be too close a carbon copy to win wide public acceptance.

Travis was little seen after this series turned out not to be the success he envisaged. During a post-war lull in his career he had begun to dabble in California real estate. Later he reverted back to his real name where, as head of his own business, he became one of the most affluent realtors in Southern California.

Previously in good health, he was found dead at his lavish Pacific Palisades home where he lived alone at 1:30 PM on July 11, 1989 aged 76 of arteriosclerotic cardiovascular disease. A childless widower, he was survived by his brother Jack T. Justice of Ventura, California. He was buried at St. Michael Angel's churchyard in the Cotswolds, Worcestershire, England.

Filmography

1940: *King of the Royal Mounted* (serial).
1941: *The Green Hornet Strikes Again* (serial), *West of the Rockies, Riders of Death Valley* (serial), *International Squadron, Navy Blues, Dive Bomber, The Bride Came C.O.D., The Man Who Came to Dinner.*
1942: *The Postman Didn't Ring, Busses Roar, The Big Shot, Escape from Crime.*
1943: *Truck Busters, Spy Train, Mission to Moscow.*
1944: *The Last Ride.*
1947: *Undercover Maisie, Backlash, Big Town After Dark, Jewels of Brandenburg.*
1948: *Waterfront at Midnight, Speed to Spare, Out of the Storm, The Babe Ruth Story.*
1949: *Alaska Patrol, Sky Liner.*
1950: *Operation Haylift, One Too Many* (a.k.a. *The Important Story of Alcoholism and Mixed-Up Women), Motor Patrol, Lonely Hearts Bandits.*
1951: *Passage West, Mask of the Dragon, Roaring City, Pier 23, Danger Zone, Fingerprints Don't Lie.*
1953: *Mesa of Lost Women.*
1955: *The Girl in the Red Velvet Swing, City of Shadows, An Annapolis Story.*
1956: *Blonde Bait.*
1959: *Missile to the Moon.*
1966: *Cyborg 2087.*

Television Series

1956–1957: *Code 3* as Assistant Sheriff George Barnett.

Sources

Death Certificate.
Erickson, Hal. *Syndicated Television: The First Forty Years, 1947–1987.* Jefferson, NC: McFarland, 1989.
Picture Show Annual. London: Amalgamated, 1943.
Tibballs, Geoff. *TV Detectives.* London: Boxtree, 1992.

Les Tremayne

"Radio was the one medium that made the actor a home-owning, tax paying, family-raising, stay-in-one-place person. With regular hours and good working conditions, he became an honest citizen (in the eyes of the community for the first time)." So spoke Les Tremayne, who was one of America's foremost radio performers for decades. His career also embraced television and films. Ann Robinson, the female lead in the movie *The War of the Worlds* (1953), recalled being "absolutely thrilled" to work with him as she had grown up listening to one of his radio shows *The First Nighter*. She added, "Here was one of my favorite idols, Les Tremayne, and a voice you'll never forget as long as you live, a magnificent voice."

During the 1940s his speaking voice was chosen as one of the three most instantly recognizable in the United States. Bing Crosby and President Franklin D. Roosevelt were the other two. Tremayne once reckoned that in a 60 year career he had worked on over 30,000 radio broadcasts at a rate of 45 per week during the thirties.

Les Tremayne was born in Balham, South London on April 16, 1913. He had his first professional job at the age of three when he appeared in a silent film with his mother, actress Dolly Tremayne. In 1917 the family moved to Chicago where he learned to hide his British accent after being beaten by bullies. After a year in high school, he was forced to quit by his father in 1927 and go to work. Encouraged by his mother to try show business, he acted in little theaters, danced in vaudeville and worked as an amusement park barker before landing his first radio job in *Fu Manchu* in 1930.

His silken voice made him an excellent choice for romantic parts. Don Ameche was the original romantic lead in the radio series *The First Nighter* between 1930 and 1936. *The First Nighter*

Les Tremayne, who starred in *Ellery Queen*.

was a weekly radio drama anthology in which the title figure was a toff who introduced each half hour, two act play from amongst the audience of theatergoers in "The Little Theatre just off Times Square." The irony was that the show was not broadcast from New York, but from Chicago. As the theater quieted down, the host would purr, "The house lights have dimmed and the curtain is about to go up on tonight's production." When Ameche left to accept a Hollywood contract, Tremayne requested to audition as his replacement and won the coveted lead. To simulate the proper atmosphere, Tremayne wore a top hat, white tie and tails and carried a cane in front of the live audience. Although he became a hugely successful radio actor, he received no offers from Hollywood.

In 1943 he quit the show and went to Hollywood in an abortive attempt to gatecrash movies. Instead he became a radio player in New York notably starring as Nick Charles in the crime series *The Thin Man*. He fronted other shows and hosted a breakfast-time talk show which aired six days a week.

In 1949 he made his Broadway debut in *The Detective Story* by Sidney Kingsley, a somewhat overrated melodrama set in the shabby detective squad room of a police precinct in New York. Tremayne received glowing reviews as an abortionist's lawyer and stayed with the show for its entire 18 month run. As a direct result of this he was invited to go to Hollywood.

He went on to appear in over 25 films of which his best remembered role was as one of the stars with third billing as Major General Mann in George Pal's *The War of the Worlds* (1953). He played the officer in charge of the futile military campaign to rid California of invading Martians. His explanation of the creature's invasion plans is considered by sci-fi fans to be a masterpiece of exposition. Another of his most famous film roles was in *North by Northwest* (1959) in which he played the auctioneer who gradually becomes more confused and bewildered by the bizarre behavior of Cary Grant, who is deliberately trying to disrupt the auction and be arrested in order to escape assassins.

His first television roles were as early as 1939 on the Zenith experimental channel in Chicago. He later moved into television where he landed a leading role in the soap opera *One Man's Family* (1950). He appeared as a regular in two other soaps much later namely *One Life to Live* and *General Hospital*. In the crime series *The Further Adventures of Ellery Queen* he played Inspector Richard Queen, the police officer father of sleuth Ellery Queen (George Nader) for the first twenty episodes. The series went out live from Hollywood. When the producer decided to change the location of the series to New York, both Nader and Tremayne declined to go with it. The character of Inspector Queen was eliminated from the series, leaving the next Ellery (Lee Philips) to go it alone.

Throughout his long career Tremayne's voice was featured in numerous commercials, voice-overs and documentaries. One particular highlight of this facet of his career was that he supplied the voice of a radio newsreader in the James Bond film *Goldfinger* (1964). In the mid–1980s he cohosted and coproduced *Please Stand By*, a history of radio, an accredited college course of 30 half hour programs. He was a founder member of both the radio union A.F.T.R.A. (then called A.F.R.A.) in 1937 and Pacific Pioneer Broadcasters in 1966. In 1995 he was elected to the Radio Hall of Fame.

Tremayne died at St. John's Health Center, Santa Monica, California of heart failure on December 19, 2003 aged 90. He was married and divorced from actresses Lenore Kingston (1913–1993) and Alice Reinheart (1910–1993). He was survived by his widow, Joan, whom he wed in

1980 together with a brother, Charles Henning. A celebration of his life and career was held at Westwood Village Memorial Park, Los Angeles on January 7, 2004.

FILMOGRAPHY

1951: *The Racket, The Blue Veil.*
1952: *It Grows on Trees, Francis Goes to West Point.*
1953: *I Love Melvin, The War of the Worlds, Dream Wife.*
1954: *Susan Slept Here.*
1955: *A Man Called Peter.*
1956: *The Lieutenant Wore Skirts, Forbidden Planet* (narrator only), *Rodan* (narrator only), *Everything But the Truth, The Unguarded Moment.*
1957: *The Monolith Monsters, The Wings of Eagles* (narrator only).
1958: *The Perfect Furlough.*
1959: *North by Northwest, Say One for Me, The Monster of Piedras Blancas, The Angry Red Planet.*
1960: *The Gallant Hours, The Story of Ruth.*
1962: *Shoot Out at Big Sag, King Kong vs. Godzilla, The Slime People.*
1964: *Goldfinger* (voice only), *MGM's Big Parade of Comedy* (narrator only).
1966: *The Fortune Cookie* (a.k.a. *Meet Whiplash Willie*).
1967: *Creature of Destruction.*
1970: *Strawberries Need Rain.*
1974: *Snakes* (a.k.a. *Fangs* and *Holy Wednesday*).

TELEVISION SERIES

1949–1950: *One Man's Family* as Bill Herbert.
1958–1959: *The Further Adventures of Ellery Queen* as Inspector Richard Queen.
1974–1977: *Shazam!* as the Voice of Mentor.
1987: *One Life to Live* as Victor Lord.
1988: *General Hospital* as Edward Quartermaine.

SOURCES

DeLong, Thomas A. *Radio Stars.* Jefferson, NC: McFarland, 1996.
Lamparski, Richard. *Whatever Became Of?* 5th Series. New York: Crown, 1974.
Lentz, Harris M. III. *Obituaries in the Performing Arts, 2003.* Jefferson, NC: McFarland, 2004.
Nevins, Francis Jr. "Ellery Queen on the Small Screen." *The Golden Years of Radio and TV.* Winter 1983.
Vallance, Tom. *The Independent.* Obituary, December 24, 2003.
Ward, Jack. *The Supporting Players of Television, 1959–1983.* Cleveland, OK.: Lakeshore West, 1996.

TOM TULLY

Tom Tully was born in Durango, Colorado on August 21, 1896. Originally he intended to have a career in the navy. When he failed his entrance exam to the Naval Academy, he enlisted as an ordinary sailor. After his discharge he became a reporter on the Denver Post. Desire for a higher salary sent him to New York where he entered radio. Over 3,000 broadcasts followed. He became a stage actor and made his Broadway debut in *Call Me Ziggy* in 1937, but suffered a few flops. Finally he scored a notable success in *The Time of Your Life* during 1939 to 1940. A few other short-lived Broadway plays followed, but the unpredictability of the theater made him want to enter the movies where he saw more future. He briefly appeared in the movie *Carefree* (1938), but did not film again until he gravitated to Hollywood to play Shirley Temple's father in *I'll Be Seeing You* (1944). He went on to make numerous other films. He received an Oscar nomination as Best Supporting Actor for playing Captain De Vriess in *The Caine Mutiny* (1954). His last film role was a memorable one as a crooked gun dealer in *Charley Varrick* (1973).

He made his television debut in "The Death Chase" episode of *Personal Appearance Theater* (1952). For five seasons he played tough cop Inspector Matt Grebb on the CBS series *The Lineup* in which he appeared between October 1, 1954 and September 1959. Much of the series was shot on location in San Francisco with the full co-operation of the San Francisco police department. There were 183 half hour, black and white episodes produced by Desilu. For the final season the series became an hour in length. Grebb was dropped from the series after the fifth season, but Tully must have remained on reasonable terms with the producers because he showed up again for a single episode of the final season which was called "Prelude to Violence" originally aired in November 1959. During this period Tully lived in some style in a two storey, Spanish style house deep in the Hollywood hills. He was a prolific television series guest star during the sixties. He had a recurring role as the father of Rob Petrie in *The Dick Van Dyke Show.* He later had a regular role in the *Shane* television series.

While in Vietnam with Bob Hope enter-

Tom Tully, who starred in *The Lineup*.

taining the troops, he became infected by a filarial worm, similar to the worm which causes elephantiasis. After his return to America, his condition was diagnosed as serious enough to warrant an operation. After a blood clot in a major vein in his leg cut off circulation, his leg had to be amputated close to the hip in 1970. The amputation was performed in a hospital in Laguna Beach close to where he was then living in San Juan Capistrano. Complications from this surgery led to his condition deteriorating and he later suffered from pleuritis, deafness and serious debilitation which ultimately led to his death in Newport Beach, CA on April 27, 1982 aged 85. He was married three times. His second wife was Frances McHugh whom he wed in 1938. She died in 1953. He subsequently wed Ida Johnson in 1954. He was survived by his widow together with a stepdaughter Nina who was born in 1938.

Filmography

1938: *Carefree*.
1943: *Mission to Moscow, Northern Pursuit, Destination Tokyo*.
1944: *Secret Command, The Town Went Wild, I'll Be Seeing You*.
1945: *The Unseen, Kiss and Tell, Adventure*.
1946: *The Virginian, Lady in the Lake, 'Til the End of Time*.
1947: *Intrigue, Killer McCoy, Scudda Hoo! Scudda Hay!*
1948: *June Bride, Blood on the Moon, Rachel and the Stranger*.
1949: *The Lady Takes a Sailor, A Kiss for Corliss, Illegal Entry*.
1950: *Where the Sidewalk Ends, Branded, Tomahawk*.
1951: *The Lady and the Bandit, Texas Carnival, Love Is Better than Ever, Return of the Texan*.
1952: *Lure of the Wilderness, Ruby Gentry, The Turning Point*.
1953: *Trouble Along the Way, Sea of Lost Ships, The Moon Is Blue, The Jazz Singer*.
1954: *Arrow in the Dust, The Caine Mutiny*.
1955: *Love Me or Leave Me, Soldier of Fortune*.
1956: *Behind the High Wall*.
1958: *Ten North Frederick*.
1960: *The Wackiest Ship in the Army*.
1964: *The Carpetbaggers*.
1965: *McHale's Navy Joins the Air Force*.
1968: *Coogan's Bluff*.
1969: *Any Second Now* (TV).
1973: *Charley Varrick, Hijack!* (TV).
1980: *In the Child's Best Interest* (a.k.a. *A Child's Cry*) (TV).
1981: *Madame X* (TV).

Television Series

1954–1959: *The Lineup* as Inspector Matt Grebb.
1966: *Shane* as Tom Starett.

Sources

Inman, David. *The TV Encyclopedia*. New York: Perigee, 1991.
Neville, Olga. "Men Behind the Big Beat." *TV Mirror*. October 4, 1958.
Parish, James Robert. *Hollywood Character Actors*. New Rochelle, NY: Arlington, 1978.
Quinlan, David. *Illustrated Directory of Film Character Actors*. 2nd ed. London: Batsford, 1995.
Tibballs, Geoff. *TV Detectives*. London: Boxtree, 1992.
Twomey, Alfred E., and Arthur F. McClure. *The Versatiles*. South Brunswick, NJ: Barnes, 1969.
Ward, Jack. *The Supporting Players of Television, 1959–1983*. Cleveland, OK: Lakeshore West, 1996.

Tim Turner

Tim Turner was born John Freeman-Turner in Bexley, Kent on September 7, 1924. He was the son of Charles Freeman-Turner who worked for the admiralty. He entered the entertainment industry in 1951. He made an unusual contribution to the British television series *The Invisible Man*. This was based on an idea by H.G. Wells, but suggested and developed for television by Larry White. The introduction to the program proclaimed, "A man who can investigate crimes without being seen. A man who can go where no ordinary man could hope to enter. A man searching for the answer to his invisibility—The Invisible Man." The series was a hybrid one mixing elements of science fiction, crime and international intrigue. Peter Brady was an industrial research scientist conducting experiments into optical density. He discovered how to make matter invisible. In the laboratory however a test backfired when an accident showered him with chemical particles which rendered him invisible without being able to return to his previous form.

In the first episode of the series "Secret Experiment" he was trapped and imprisoned by the British Government who saw him as a threat to society. In prison he convinced the authorities that he was a decent, law abiding citizen who had been the victim of a tragic accident. He was released on condition that he undertook hazardous missions for the British Government who found his invisibility very useful. He also chose to use his unique powers to benefit others. The rest of the series was spent in trying to find a formula which would render him visible again. Simultaneously he undertook assignments for the government and solved emergency situations which occurred. He was assisted by his attractive sister Diane (Dee) (Lisa Daniely). His small niece Sally (Deborah Watling) was also a regular. The tragedy was that by the time the series ended, Brady was no closer to finding the antidote to his condition. He had however put quite a number of crooks behind bars.

In the episodes Brady appeared smothered in bandages, wearing an overcoat or laboratory coat, complete with dark glasses and a hat. He could make himself invisible within seconds by discarding the glasses, hat and coat and unwrapping the bandages. The question which audiences asked at the time was as to the identity of the actor playing Peter Brady. This was never satisfactorily explained. Producer Ralph Smart (1908–2001) was rather evasive on the subject. "It would shatter the illusion," he said, "But I can tell you this much. Peter Brady's voice belongs to actor Tim Turner."

The series was accomplished with considerable technical skill for its time. It was the creating of these special effects which was probably the most interesting aspect of the series. One problem was that of creating the illusion of a car driving along a highway with nobody at the wheel. One way of filming this was to have a hidden stuntman, who lay full length on the floor of the car with the nearside door slightly ajar so that he could see where he was going. He held the bottom of the steering wheel with one hand and used the other hand to operate the foot controls. Alternatively the driver could be integrated into the upholstery with a false seat dropped over him. Small holes were bored in the false seat for him to look through. Similarly when the script called for Brady to take a drink, the glass was suspended from two thin wires which were not noticed by the camera. Wires were also used when Brady was called upon to pick up an object from the table or smoke a cigarette.

This series was an Official Films Production for Independent Television Company (ITC) Limited. It was shot at National Studios, Elstree. There were 26 half hour, black and white episodes originally aired in the United Kingdom between June 18, 1959 and October 22, 1961 and shown in America on CBS-TV between November 4, 1958 and September 22, 1960. Some sources insist that Tim Turner only played the character for the first 13 of the 26 episodes. He definitely did play the character however because in one episode "Man in Disguise," Turner played a double role both as Brady and as Nick, a character impersonating Brady. Turner apparently asked for a pay rise, but when this was refused he quit the series in disgust. The actor who played the role during the last 13 episodes had a different build from Turner.

Turner did stage work, made appearances in other television series and appeared in several prestigious British films of the fifties. He was also well known as the host and commentator of the Rank documentary short film series *Look at Life*. He married stage, film and television actress Patricia Plunkett on October 27, 1951. She was born in London on December 17, 1926. At one time they lived in Dulwich Village, South London. They both quit show business in the early sixties. She died at St. Stephens Hospital, Chelsea, London on October 13, 1974 aged 47 of Bronchopnumonia due to cerebral infarction after accidentally choking on a piece of meat. At that time Patricia Turner was a resident of Lancing, Worthing, Sussex. Her occupation was listed as antique dealer. Her husband was still listed as Tim Turner, but it is understood that he was no longer living with her at the time. His subsequent occupation was unknown and he has been posted as one of the missing players of the screen.

Filmography

1952: *Moulin Rouge, The Gift Horse, Hindle Wakes, Top Secret* (a.k.a. *Mr. Potts Goes to Moscow*).
1953: *The Red Beret* (a.k.a. *Paratrooper*).
1954: *The Night of the Full Moon, Mask of Dust* (a.k.a. *Race for Life*), *Companions in Crime*.
1955: *The Dam Busters, Police Dog*.
1956: *A Town Like Alice*.
1958: *A Night to Remember, Grip of the Strangler, Nowhere to Go, Dunkirk*.
1959: *Operation Amsterdam*.
1960: *Jackpot, Not a Hope in Hell*.

Television Series

1958–1960 (USA): *The Invisible Man* as Peter Brady.
1959–1961 (UK)

Sources

Commercial Television Year Book and Directory. 6th ed. London: Business, 1961.
Death Certificate, Patricia Ruth Turner. October 19, 1974.
Dowland, Peter. *ATV Show Book*. London: Adprint, 1958.
Leader, David. *ATV Television Show Book*. London: Adprint, 1959.
Marriage Certificate, Tim Turner and Patricia Plunkett.
Noble, Peter. *The British Film and Television Yearbook*. London: British and American Press, 1959 and 1967.
Palmer, Scott. *British Actors' Film Credits, 1895–1987*. London: St. James, 1988.
Rogers, Dave. *The ITV Encyclopedia of Adventure*. London: Boxtree, 1988.
_____, and S. J. Gilles. *The Rogers & Gilles Guide to ITC*. 1st ed. England: S.J.G. Communications Services, 1997.

Beverly Tyler

Beverly Tyler was born Beverly Jean Saul in Scranton, Pennsylvania on July 5, 1928. Her father was an executive with a typewriter company, while her mother was a secretary. She was educated at Scranton High School and was a soloist in the church choir. She had music and singing lessons from childhood and sang on radio. On her first trip to New York in 1942 to escape a blustery November wind, she and her mother presented themselves at the Manhattan offices of MGM without an appointment and asked for an audition. In spite of her limited experience she had such a beautiful voice that she was signed to a contract. Producer Joe Pasternak, ever searching for another Deanna Durbin, flew from Hollywood to New York to direct her screen test personally. Almost before she realized what was happening, she was on her way to Hollywood with her parents.

In the four years that followed she was given intensive training for her future career. Being of school age she had to attend ordinary educational classes, but she was also taught dancing, diction, dramatics and given singing lessons to improve her voice. She appeared in two films during her training. During World War II she had some experience in entertaining for she participated in U.S.O tours of military bases and hospitals and served at the celebrated Hollywood Canteen. Her first important role was in *The Green Years* (1946) in which she and Tom Drake acquitted themselves very well as the young romantic leads. This was her personal favorite of her own films. These two stars appeared again together in a drama about the A bomb *The Beginning or the End?* (1947).

She did appear briefly on Broadway in a musical *Firebrand of Florence* (1945) in which she sang. She was also a guest soloist with at least one orchestra and later sang on television shows. With the exception of the early credit *Best Foot Forward* (1943), none of the films she shot at MGM were musicals. She did test for leads in musicals, but lost out to other actresses. Allegedly she came across as rather too sophisticated for some of the more innocent roles which were going at MGM at the time. Her studio biography indicated that she had auburn hair, green eyes and stood 5'3½" tall.

After her tenure at MGM ended, she freelanced quite successfully during the fifties notably at Universal and Columbia. She became the fifth actress to play the role of hot shot reporter Lorelei Kilbourne in the newspaper drama television series *Big Town* which starred Pat McVey at Steve Wilson. As with all the others she only lasted a single season in the role. During her film

Beverly Tyler, who costarred in *Big Town*.

and television years she kept in trim by swimming, dancing and practicing ballet steps. Her hobbies were listed as playing the piano and collecting records.

In 1962 she married Jim Jordan, Jr., a comedy writer–director, son of Jim Jordan, Sr. and Marion Jordan, professional entertainers known as Fibber McGee and Molly. With him she has a son. In 1972 she moved with her husband to a ranch house on the outskirts of Reno, Nevada where they were active in real estate development. Her acting in later years was confined to emoting in plays at Reno's Little Theater. She died in hospital at Reno, Nevada on November 23, 2005 aged 78 of a pulmonary embolism. She was survived by her son and 3 half-sisters.

Filmography

1943: *The Youngest Profession, Best Foot Forward.*
1946: *The Green Years.*
1947: *The Beginning or the End?, My Brother Talks to Horses.*
1950: *The Palomino, The Fireball.*
1952: *The Cimarron Kid, The Battle at Apache Pass.*
1957: *Voodoo Island, Chicago Confidential.*
1958: *Toughest Gun in Tombstone, Hong Kong Confidential.*

Television Series

1953–1954: *Big Town* as Lorelei Kilbourne.

Sources

Dye, David. *Child and Youth Actors.* Jefferson, NC: McFarland, 1988.
Lamparski, Richard. *Whatever Became Of?* 11th Series. New York: Crown, 1989.
Picture Show. "Life Story." January 17, 1959.
Picture Show Annual. London: Amalgamated, 1948.
Variety. Obituary December 6, 2005.

Minerva Urecal

Minerva Urecal was born in Eureka, California on September 22, 1894. Her stage surname was an anagram of the town and state in which she was born. She began making films in 1933 after radio experience. She appeared in numerous films in small roles where she was regarded as a bargain basement Marjorie Main.

Television added to her stature as an actress. She finally landed top billing playing the formidable title character in the Canadian lensed television series *The Adventures of Tugboat Annie.* This was a syndicated series of 39 episodes originally shot in 1956, but only shown in America from March 1958 onwards. The character, created by Norman Reilly Raine, featured in a number of stories in The Saturday Evening Post. In the classic comedy film *Tugboat Annie* (1933), the character was played by Marie Dressler, a hard act to follow.

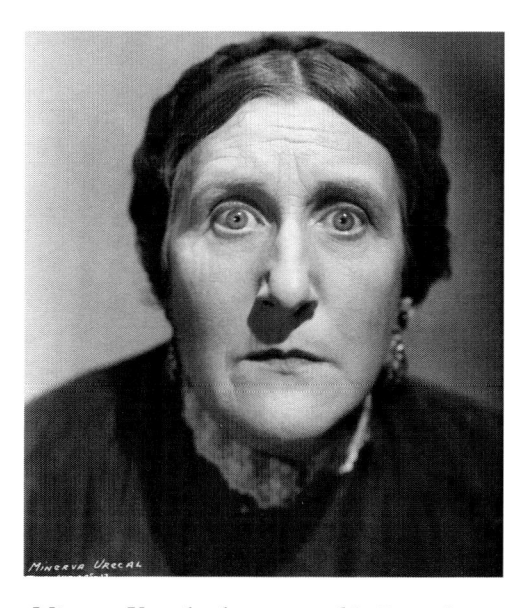

Minerva Urecal, who costarred in *Peter Gunn*.

When Hope Emerson quit playing the nightclub owner "Mother" in the crime series *Peter Gunn*, Minerva Urecal succeeded her in the role for the final two seasons. She did not play the part in such an accomplished manner as her predecessor. Therefore the role of "Mother" was gradually diminished, but the screen time devoted to Edie Hart (Lola Albright) and Det. Lt. Jacoby (Herschel Bernardi) was correspondingly increased. Neither players nor viewers objected to this.

Minerva Urecal died in Glendale, California on February 26, 1966 aged 71 of a heart attack. She was cremated and her ashes are contained in an urn in Hollywood Forever Cemetery, Los Angeles County, California. She was survived by her husband, Max Holtzer.

Filmography

1933: *Meet the Baron.*
1934: *Sadie McKee, Student Tour, Straight Is the Way, You Can't Buy Everything.*
1935: *Biography of a Bachelor Girl, Bonnie Scotland, The Man on the Flying Trapeze, Here Comes the Band.*
1936: *Fury, God's Country and the Woman, Bulldog Edition, Love on a Bet, The Three Godfathers* (a.k.a. *Miracle in the Sand*).
1937: *Behind the Mike, Ever Since Eve, Exiled in Shanghai, The Go Getter, Her Husband's Secretary, Life Begins with Love, Love in a Bungalow, Mountain Justice, Oh Doctor!, Charlie Chan at the Olympics, Live Love and Learn, Portia on Trial, She Loved a Fireman.*
1938: *Air Devils, Dramatic School, City Streets, The Devil's Party, Frontier Scout, In Old Chicago, Lady in the Morgue, Prison Nurse, Start Cheering, Thanks for Everything, Wives Under Suspicion.*
1939: *Dancing Co-Ed, Destry Rides Again, Golden Boy, Four Girls in White, Little Accident, No Place to Go, Second Fiddle, Sabotage, Should Husbands Work?, She Married a Cop, S.O.S. Tidal Wave, Unexpected Father, Missing Evidence, You Can't Cheat an Honest Man.*
1940: *Boys of the City* (a.k.a. *The Ghost Creeps*), *No No Nanette, The Sagebrush Family Trails West, Wildcat Bus, You Can't Fool Your Wife, San Francisco Docks.*
1941: *Accent on Love, Arkansas Judge, Billy the Kid, Bowery Blitzkrieg, The Cowboy and the Blonde, Dressed to Kill, Lady for a Night, A Man Betrayed, Marry the Boss's Daughter, Man at Large, Golden Hoofs, Moon Over Her Shoulder, Murder Among Friends, Murder by Invitation, Never Give a Sucker an Even Break, Sailors on Leave, Six Lessons from Madame La Zonga, Skylark, The Trial of Mary Dugan, They Died With Their Boots On, The Wild Man of Borneo.*
1942: *The Corpse Vanishes, Beyond the Blue Horizon, Almost Married, The Daring Young Man, Henry and Dizzy, In Old California, My Favorite Blonde, Henry Aldrich Editor, The Living Ghost, Man in the Trunk, Quiet Please Murder, The Powers Girl, Riding Through Nevada, Sons of the Pioneers, Sweater Girl, That Other Woman, A Tragedy at Midnight.*
1943: *The Ape Man, Dangerous Blondes, Ghosts on the Loose, Hit the Ice, Keep 'em Slugging, Kid Dynamite, Klondike Kate, My Kingdom for a Cook, So This Is Washington, The Song of Bernadette, Shadow of a Doubt, White Savage, Wagon Tracks West, Here Comes Elmer, A Stranger in Town, Dixie Dugan, Dangerous Blondes.*
1944: *And Now Tomorrow, Block Busters, The Bridge of San Luis Rey, The Doughgirls, County Fair, Crazy Knights* (a.k.a. *Ghost Crazy*), *Irish Eyes Are Smiling, It Happened Tomorrow, Louisiana Hayride, Kismet, Mr. Skeffington, Moonlight and Cactus, Music in Manhattan, Man from Frisco, Mark of the Whistler, One Mysterious Night, When Strangers Marry* (a.k.a. *Betrayed*).
1945: *A Bell for Adano, The Bells of St. Mary's, Crime Doctor's Manhunt, George White's Scandals, The Kid Sister, A Medal for Benny, Mr. Muggs Rides Again, Out of This World, Sensation Hunters, State Fair, Who's Guilty?* (serial), *Men in Her Diary, Wanderer of the Wasteland, Colonel Effingham's Raid, Salty O'Rourke.*
1946: *The Bride Wore Boots, California, The Dark Corner, Little Miss Big, No Leave No Love, Rainbow Over Texas, Sensation Hunters, Sioux City Sue, The Trap, Swell Guy, The Virginian, Wake Up and Dream, Without Reservations, The Well-Groomed Bride.*
1947: *Blaze of Noon, Apache Rose, Bowery Buckaroos, Cynthia, The Lost Moment, Saddle Pals, The Secret Life of Walter Mitty, Ladies' Man, The Devil Thumbs a Ride, Undercover Maisie, Heartaches.*
1948: *April Showers, Carson City Raiders, Family Honeymoon, Fury at Furnace Creek, Good Sam, Marshal of Amarillo, The Night Has a Thousand Eyes, The Noose Hangs High, Joan of Arc, Secret Service Investigator, Sitting Pretty, Sundown at Santa Fe, The Snake Pit, The Strange Mrs. Crane.*

1949: *Big Jack, Holiday in Havana, The Loveable Cheat, Master Minds, Outcasts of the Trail, Down to the Sea in Ships, Scene of the Crime, Song of Surrender, Take One False Step, The Traveling Saleswoman, Side Street.*
1950: *The Arizona Cowboy, Harvey, The Jackpot, Mister 880, Quicksand, My Blue Heaven, The Milkman.*
1951: *The Great Caruso, Mask of the Avenger, Stop That Cab, Texans Never Cry, Dear Brat, The Raging Tide.*
1952: *Aaron Crick from Punkin Creek, Harem Girl, Gobs and Gals, Fearless Fagan, Lost in Alaska, Anything Can Happen, Oklahoma Annie.*
1953: *By the Light of the Silvery Moon, Niagara, She's Back on Broadway, The Woman They Almost Lynched.*
1955: *A Man Alone, Double Jeopardy, Martin, Sudden Danger.*
1956: *Miracle in the Rain, Crashing Las Vegas, Death of a Scoundrel.*
1957: *Footsteps in the Night.*
1960: *The Adventures of Huckleberry Finn.*
1962: *Mr. Hobbs Takes a Vacation.*
1964: *The 7 Faces of Dr. Lao.*
1965: *That Funny Feeling.*

TELEVISION SERIES

1952–1953: *The RCA Victor Show* as Mrs. Pratt.
1953–1954: *The Ray Milland Show* as Dean Josephine Bradley.
1956: *The Adventures of Tugboat Annie* as Tugboat Annie Brennan.
1959–1961: *Peter Gunn* as "Mother."

SOURCES

Erickson, Hal. *Syndicated Television: The First Forty Years, 1947–1987.* Jefferson, NC: McFarland, 1988.
Lance, Steven. *Written Out of Television.* Lanham, MD: Madison, 1996.
Quinlan, David. *Illustrated Directory of Film Character Actors.* 2nd ed. London: Batsford, 1996.
Willis, John. *Screen World.* Vol. 18. London: Frederick Muller, 1967.

VICKI VOLA

Vicki Vola was born in Denver, Colorado on August 27, 1916. She made her radio debut in her native city before moving briefly to Hollywood and then permanently to New York where she was very active on radio. Her best known radio role was as Miss Miller, secretary to the title character, in the series *Mr. District Attorney* which lasted for over twelve years. Jay Jostyn had the title role in the show. When it transferred to television, the leads moved with it. The television version looked like a photographed radio play and only had a brief run on ABC between October 1951 and June 1952.

Vola, who was a divorcee, continued to reside in Manhattan until she died on July 21, 1985 aged 68.

TELEVISION SERIES

1951–1952: *Mr. District Attorney* as Miss Miller.
1970: *Love Is a Many Splendored Thing* as Mrs. Johnson.

SOURCES

Brooks, Tim. *The Complete Directory to Prime Time TV Stars, 1946–Present.* New York: Ballantine Books, 1987.
DeLong, Thomas A. *Radio Stars.* Jefferson, NC: McFarland, 1996.
Lamparski, Richard. *Whatever Became Of?* 6th Series. New York: Bantam, 1976.

SKIP WARD

Skip Ward was born in Cleveland, Ohio on September 12, 1932. He served in the air force before coming to Hollywood to commence his movie career in 1958. He frequently used the name James Ward. He had the regular role of Officer Pete Larkin in the crime series *The Lineup* during its final season. When he was appearing in the film *Night of the Iguana* (1964) he was described as a young actor experiencing his first big break.

The other acting breaks did not come his way and instead he turned producer in the early seventies notably as associate producer of the television series *The Dukes of Hazzard.* He returned to acting briefly during the early nineties. He died at the Motion Picture Country Home and Hospital in Woodland Hills, California on July 4, 2003 aged 70 after a long illness. Between 1963 and 1964 he was married and divorced from Michelle Triola who later lived with and sued Lee Marvin in the famous palimony case. Later Ward was married to Julie Payne, the daughter of John Payne and Anne Shirley, but that marriage too ended in divorce.

Deborah Watling

Deborah Watling was born in Fulmer Chase, Buckinghamshire, England on January 2, 1948. She is the daughter of Jack Watling (1923–2001) and his wife Patricia Hicks. Both of her parents were professional actors. She has one older half sister Dilys (by her mother's previous marriage); one younger sister Nicola; and one younger brother Giles. All of them entered show business, but her younger sister abandoned it in favor of the church. Her parents moved around quite a lot and consequently she attended a number of different schools, all of which she loathed. She was brought up as a Roman Catholic.

Her godfather, actor Willoughby Gray, rang up her mother and told her that producer Ralph Smart was looking for a little girl to play Sally Brady, the niece of the title character, in *The Invisible Man* television series. She attended the interview with her mother. When Smart asked her to read for him, she replied, "I don't read." Her mother remonstrated with her. She did the reading and was awarded the part. The series was originally shown in America on CBS between November 1958 and September 1960. It was aired in England between June 1959 and October 1961. It was still being shown on satellite channels into the nineties. She appeared in 16 out of the 26 episodes before returning to school.

Her original ambition however was not to be an actress, but a dentist. After failing her O levels, she quit conventional school and enrolled at a stage academy only to leave after three weeks because she considered what she was being taught unreliable. She obtained an agent and landed the part of Alice in a BBC play *The Life of Lewis Carroll* (1965). Between 1965 and 1967 she played roles in a number of television series. In 1967 she was offered the role of Victoria Waterfield, Doctor Who's assistant, in the classic BBC sci-fi series *Doctor Who*. She was in the era when Patrick Troughton played Dr. Who. Frazer Hines played Jamie, his other assistant. She was offered the role by producer Innes Lloyd who remembered her from the Radio Times cover for *The Life*

Filmography

1958: *Run Silent Run Deep, Roadracers.*
1961: *Voyage to the Bottom of the Sea.*
1963: *The Nutty Professor.*
1964: *The Night of the Iguana, Kiss Me Stupid, Kitten with a Whip.*
1965: *Red Line 7000.*
1966: *Is Paris Burning?*
1967: *Hombre, Easy Come Easy Go.*
1969: *The Mad Room.*
1970: *Myra Breckinridge.*
1973: *The Devil and LeRoy Bassett.*
1991: *Do or Die.*
1992: *Hard Hunted.*
1993: *Fit to Kill.*

Television Series

1959–1960: *The Lineup* as Officer Pete Larkin.
1961: *The Gertrude Berg Show* as Joe Caldwell.

Sources

Brooks, Tim. *The Complete Directory to Prime Time Television Stars, 1946–Present.* New York: Ballantine, 1987.

Lentz, Harris M. III. *Obituaries in the Performing Arts, 2003.* Jefferson, NC: McFarland, 2004.

Ragan, David. *Who's Who in Hollywood.* New York: Facts on File, 1992.

Zec, Donald. *Marvin: The Story of Lee Marvin.* London: NEL, 1980.

James "Skip" Ward in the film *Night of the Iguana* (1964). He costarred in the television series *The Lineup*.

of *Lewis Carroll*. She was a big success as Victoria, but the greater part of her work is missing believed lost because the BBC in a false economy move wiped these episodes off the tapes. They little realized what a goldmine they were destroying.

She was unemployed in the acting profession for eighteen months after that. During this time she opened her own boutique which she ran quite successfully. She then landed the role of Julie Robertson in the highly rated BBC soap opera *The Newcomers* which she appeared in for a couple of years until it ended. She was particularly unfortunate in terms of the amount of her television work now available for reviewing because all 430 episodes of this soap opera were also wiped by the BBC during the 1970s. She had turned the management of the boutique over to a friend who ran it into the ground which cost Deborah Watling a lot of money and convinced her that ordinary business and acting did not mix.

After this she went on to make numerous other television appearances notably a regular role in *Danger UXB*. She also appeared in the films *Take Me High* (1973) with Cliff Richard and *That'll Be the Day* (1973) with David Essex. She made her London stage debut in *A Bequest to the Nation*. During the eighties and nineties she worked extensively on the stage both touring and in the West End. She has a reputation for playing comedy particularly farce, but she is equally adept at dramatic parts. In 1995 she took a few days out from a play she was doing in the West End to reprise the role of Victoria Waterfield in the direct to video release *Downtime* which turned out to be quite successful commercially and afforded her great satisfaction.

She has directed plays at Frinton Repertory Company which is a family run concern and the last provincial repertory company in England. She has also acquired extensive experience in another English tradition namely pantomime in which she has latterly enjoyed herself playing the character parts such as Fairy Godmother.

Deborah Watling married and divorced actor Anthony Verner with whom she costarred in *The Newcomers*. She is currently married to Steven Turner, a lighting technician. She lives in Essex, England.

Filmography

1973: *Take Me High*, *That'll Be the Day*.
1995: *Downtime*.

Left: Tim Turner (?) and young Debbie Watling in *The Invisible Man*.

A grown-up Debbie Watling.

Television Series

1958–1960 (USA): *The Invisible Man* as Sally Brady.
1959–1961 (UK)
1967–1968: *Dr. Who* as Victoria Waterfield.
1969–1970: *The Newcomers* as Julie Robertson.
1979: *Danger UXB* as Norma Baker.

Miniseries

1978: *Lillie*.

Sources

Conversation with Deborah Watling in 1997.
Funny Money Theater Program Biography.
Howe, David, and Mark Stammers. *Doctor Who Companions*. London: Virgin Publishing/Doctor Who Books, 1995.
Murder by Misadventure. Theater Program Biography.
TV Times. May 30, 1958.
Vaross. Issue No. 8, Summer 1997.
Who's Who on Television. London: Independent Television, 1970.
Woodward, Ian. "Relationships: My Sister Was a Monster, but Life Was Never Dull." *Daily Mail*. August 22, 1995.

RICHARD WATTIS

Richard Wattis once said about the roles he played, "I suppose I do have an understanding of this particular sort of personality. I really don't think it's me. At least I hope not. I do find very conventional people rather boring and lifeless." With his owlish glasses and flexible lips, his character was often a flustered, supercilious authority type. Even to this day casting directors in England still refer to "a Richard Wattis type" and everyone knows exactly who is meant.

Richard Wattis was born in Wednesbury, Staffordshire, England on February 25, 1912. His parents were Cameron Tom Wattis and Margaret Janet Preston. He was educated at King Edward's School, Birmingham and Bromsgrove School, Worcestershire. He was formerly engaged in the family electrical engineering company business. He studied for the stage under J. Baxter Somerville at Croydon Repertory Theater. He made his professional debut at the Royal Theater, Brighton in September 1935 in *The Little Minister*. His first appearance on the West End stage was at the Aldwych on June 30, 1948 as Lord Seymour

Richard Wattis, who costarred in *Dick and the Duchess*.

Sandgate in *Ambassador Extraordinary*. He went on to make many other stage appearances.

He made his screen debut in an uncredited bit in *A Yank at Oxford* (1937). Although it was over a decade before he filmed again, he rapidly became one of Britain's busiest supporting actors. In many of his films he only had a couple of scenes, but nonetheless created fully rounded characters. This is particularly demonstrated in *The Inn of the Sixth Happiness* (1958) in which he played the travel agent who sold missionary Gladys Aylward (Ingrid Bergman) her ticket to China.

Television added another string to his bow. The television series *Dick and the Duchess* was a successful mixture of comedy and crime dealing with Dick Starrett (Patrick O'Neal), an American insurance investigator in London, together with his aristocratic wife Jane (Hazel Court). Wattis played the role of Peter Jamison, Starrett's boss. Court recently recalled of him, "Richard Wattis was wonderful. I loved going to work each day because I could meet and talk to him." Most of his other television work was overshadowed by his clever playing of Charles Fulbright Brown, the next door neighbor of Eric Sykes and Hattie Jacques, in the long-running British situation comedy, *Sykes*.

The fact that Wattis was almost continuously employed made him a wealthy man and enabled him to live a very comfortable life in his fashionable London pad. Wattis was unmarried and a homosexual almost to the point of being camp. During the 1950s he cruised private gay bars searching for hunks which was dangerous both from a physical standpoint together with the fact that homosexuality was against the law at that time in England. Many actresses adored him for his sparkling wit, but the notable exception was Marilyn Monroe with whom he appeared in *The Prince and the Showgirl* (1957). She was homophobic and wanted nothing to do with him. She refused to show up on the set on many days for different reasons, but Wattis kept the rest of the cast and crew in good spirits with his hilarious theatrical anecdotes.

On February 1, 1975 Richard Wattis collapsed and died aged 62 of a heart attack in a London restaurant while dining with friends.

Filmography

1937: *A Yank at Oxford.*
1949: *Marry Me!, Kind Hearts and Coronets, Helter Skelter, Stop Press Girl, The Chiltern Hundreds.*
1950: *The Happiest Days of Your Life, The Clouded Yellow, Your Witness* (a.k.a. *Eye Witness*).
1951: *Appointment with Venus* (a.k.a. *Island Rescue*), *Lady Godiva Rides Again.*
1952: *Song of Paris, The Happy Family, Mother Riley Meets the Vampire, Made in Heaven, The Importance of Being Earnest, Stolen Face, Derby Day. Penny Princess, Top Secret* (a.k.a. *Mr. Potts Goes to Moscow*), *Appointment in London.*
1953: *The Intruder, The Final Test, Background, Top of the Form, Innocents in Paris, Colonel March Investigates, Small Town Story, Blood Orange, Park Plaza 605* (a.k.a. *Norman Conquest*).
1954: *The Belles of St. Trinians, Doctor in the House, Lease of Life, Hobson's Choice, The Crowded Day, The Colditz Story.*
1955: *Escapade, As Long As They're Happy, Man of the Moment, See How They Run, The Time of His Life, I Am a Camera, A Yank in Ermine, An Alligator Named Daisy, Simon and Laura, Jumping for Joy, The Man Who Never Was.*
1956: *The Silken Affair, Around the World in 80 Days, The Man Who Knew Too Much, Eyewitness, It's a Wonderful World, The Green Man, The Iron Petticoat, A Touch of the Sun.*
1957: *The Prince and the Showgirl, The Abominable Showman, Second Fiddle, Barnacle Bill* (a.k.a. *All at Sea*), *High Flight, Blue Murder at St. Trinian's, The Little Hut.*
1958: *The Inn of the Sixth Happiness, Ten Seconds to Hell, The Captain's Table.*
1959: *The Ugly Duckling, Libel, Left Right and Centre, Your Money or Your Wife, Follow a Star, Follow That Horse!*
1961: *Very Important Person, Dentist on the Job, Nearly a Nasty Accident.*
1962: *Play It Cool, I Thank a Fool, Bon Voyage!, The Longest Day, Come Fly with Me.*
1963: *The V.I.P.s.*
1964: *Carry On Spying.*
1965: *The Amorous Adventures of Moll Flanders, The Battle of the Villa Fiorita, The Legend of Young Dick Turpin, Up Jumped a Swagman, You Must Be Joking!, Bunny Lake Is Missing, The Alphabet Murders, Operation Crossbow.*
1966: *The Liquidator, The Great St. Trinian's Train Robbery.*
1967: *Casino Royale.*
1968: *Wonderwall, Chitty Chitty Bang Bang.*
1969: *Monte Carlo or Bust* (a.k.a. *Those Daring Young Men in Their Jaunty Jalopies*).
1970: *Games That Lovers Play, Egghead's Robot.*
1971: *Tam Lin, The Troublesome Double.*
1972: *Sex and the Other Woman, That's Your Funeral, Diamonds on Wheels.*
1973: *Take Me High.*
1974: *Confessions of a Window Cleaner.*

Television Series

US (1957–1958): *Dick and the Duchess* as Peter Jamison
UK (1959–1960)
1960–1961: *Sykes* as Mr. Charles Brown.
1970–1973

Sources

Conversation with Hazel Court in 2004.
Donnelly, Paul. *Fade to Black*. London: Omnibus, 2000.
McFarlane, Brian. *The Encyclopedia of British Film*. London: BFI Methuen, 2003.
Newley, Patrick. "Heydays: Tricky Dicky." *The Stage*. September 14, 2000.
Parker, John. *Who's Who in the Theatre*. 15th ed. London: Pitman, 1972.
Quinlan, David. *The Illustrated Directory of Film Character Actors*. 2nd ed. London: Batsford, 1996.
Tibballs, Geoff. *TV Detectives*. London: Boxtree, 1992.

Who's Who on Television. London: Independent Television, 1970.

Willis, John. *Screen World*. Vol. 27. London: Frederick Muller, 1976.

JACK WEBB

Dark, grim and crew-cut, Jack Web's laconic style, deadpan face and clipped delivery lent themselves well to playing the role of Police Sergeant Joe Friday in the television series *Dragnet*. As producer, director and star Webb had a major impact on American television. He could do pretty much what he liked as he liked. As a person he was a workaholic. His real life personality inspired mixed feelings. He was once called, "The Orson Welles of Television." Costar Ben Alexander said of him, "Jack Webb is the closest thing to a genius Hollywood has seen in years." Although he had a very loyal repertory company of actors whom he used constantly over the years, other actors intensely disliked him. Actor Grant Williams claimed that virtually the only personality clash he ever had was with Webb. Of his most famous character Webb recalled, "I called him Joe Friday. Some have said I was thinking of Robinson Crusoe and his Man Friday. Or that I thought of it on a Friday. I don't really know where it came from, except that I wanted a name that had no connotations at all. He could be Jewish or Greek or English or anything. He could be all men to all people in their living room."

Jack Randolph Webb was born in Santa Monica, California on April 2, 1920, the son of Samuel Chester Webb and Margaret Smith. His father was Jewish and his mother, the daughter of a surveyor for the Santa Fe Rail Road, was Catholic. Both of his parents came from Idaho. Since his parents were separated when he was only two and he was taken to live with his mother and grandmother, Emma Smith, he remembered nothing of his father. He was raised in poverty and slime in downtown Los Angeles and suffered from asthma as a child. He showed early talent when he took a particular interest in art and drama at Belmont High School and was elected president of his senior class. After graduating in 1938 he was offered an art scholarship to the University of Southern California, but was forced to decline to support his mother and worked for four years in a men's clothing store. Simultaneously he occasionally performed in local radio broadcasts.

An interest in flying prompted him to join the Army Air Corps in 1942 where he was an aviation cadet at St. John's University in Minnesota. He wrote, directed and was master of ceremonies of two USO variety shows. After ill fated solo attempts at piloting B-26 bombers, he spent the balance of the war as a buck private behind a desk at Laughlin Field, Texas. After being granted a dependency discharge in 1945, he relocated to San Francisco where he was hired by ABC's local station KGO to announce news coverage of the United Nations conference and also worked as a disc jockey on an early morning jazz show called *The Coffee Club*. Shortly thereafter he won the lead in the ABC radio detective series *Pat Novak For Hire* which lasted 26 weeks. It was scripted by Richard L. Breen who later wrote for *Dragnet*.

After a row Breen quit the station and he and Webb returned to Los Angeles in 1947. This created an outcry from fans of *Pat Novak For Hire* so Breen created a similar show called *Johnny Modero Pier 23* which lasted on radio from April to September. Webb played the lead and introduced his staccato delivery in it. Fans still insisted on the return of *Pat Novak For Hire* so in 1949 ABC revived it for national broadcasting.

Webb began obtaining employment in motion pictures believed to be through the influence of his first wife, Julie London. Two of the best of his early roles were as Norm Butler, a paraplegic war veteran in Stanley Kramer's *The Men* and as Artie Green, William Holden's playboy friend, in *Sunset Boulevard* (1950). The role which had the greatest impact on his subsequent career was as Lee Jones, a lab technician, in *He Walked By Night* (1948). On the set of this police story which was done in the semi-documentary style he encountered LAPD Sergeant Marty Wynn who was acting as technical adviser. He gently chided Webb on the lack of realism in many Hollywood police thrillers. Webb asked him if a radio series based on police files might be possible. Webb did extensive research with the co-operation of the LAPD. As he later recalled, "I spent the nights riding in police patrol cars, researched crime-lab files by day and finally came up with *Dragnet*."

On June 3, 1949 *Dragnet* made its radio debut as a summer replacement on NBC. It won many awards and by 1951 it had become the most popular show on the air. It was during this time that Webb developed his distinctive Sgt. Friday characterization. He did the show because he was starving and to keep the wolf from the door. As Julie London recalled, "When I first got pregnant, we were broke and Jack tried to think of a show he could do for a fast thirteen weeks that would pay for the baby. He came up with *Dragnet.*" He formed his own production company called Mark VII Limited to shoot the series. The title stood for nothing. The pilot episode of *Dragnet* was shown on NBC television on December 16, 1951. It was called "The Human Bomb" and cost $38,000 to produce. The regular series began on January 3, 1952 with Webb acting as producer, director and star. An announcement preceded each show, "Ladies and gentlemen, the story you are about to see is true, only the names have been changed to protect the innocent." The program's terse, everyday dialogue, realistic plotting and incorporation of legitimate police procedure set it apart from the violent gangster and private eye dramas which were then prevalent.

A stickler for authenticity, he befriended real police detectives and studied the way they dressed, talked and acted. He had their jargon off pat. Highlights were Friday's polite, but businesslike warning, "just the facts ma'am"; "My name's Friday—I'm a cop"; "It was 3:55... We were working the day watch out of homicide"; and "Book him on a 502." These phrases passed into national folklore, but were frequently lampooned. Inevitably criminals were apprehended and each show featured an epilogue revealing what sentence was given to the miscreants with them staring guiltily at the audience. As a director Webb favored close-ups, quiet speaking, no garish make-up for the actors and liberal use of eerie background music and sound effects to create suspense. Webb tried to keep the actors natural by withholding scripts and having them read cold from cue cards. Gaps in time or the flow of narrative were bridged by Webb's first person narration. He had an exact replica of the LAPD squad room constructed on the lot. It was accurate down to the calendars and the extension numbers of the telephones. Each episode was shot on a frenzied two day shooting schedule. Webb himself worked a 14 hour day, six days a week. It was said that he spent Sundays checking out the competition. Webb had his own building on the Republic lot where *Dragnet* was shot. He used the upstairs apartment which was spacious and comfortable and furnished in early American style. He had a Filipino houseboy who ruled over this domain. It was said that he was an excellent cook who combined culinary duties with being Webb's valet.

Jack Webb, who starred in *Dragnet*.

The series was off to a tragic start when Barton Yarborough who played Friday's Mexican-American sidekick Detective Sergeant Ben Romero for the opening three episodes died of a heart attack. Webb with his drive for realism had the character die the same way. He replaced him with Barney Phillips as Sgt. Ed Jacobs, but they soon parted company. Officer Frank Smith was very briefly played by Herb Ellis and Harry Bartell. Webb replaced them rapidly with chunky, avuncular Ben Alexander which was a felicitous piece of casting. He remained with the show from 1953 to its demise the first time around in 1959. In 1956 Webb permitted a touch of romance in the series in the form of Friday's girlfriend played by Marjie Millar. Later Friday had a fiancée. She was Ann Baker played by Dorothy Abbott.

Webb was proud of the series absence of violence compared with its competitors. In the first sixty episodes only fifteen bullets were fired, there were three fights and half a dozen punches were thrown. The series dealt mostly with domestic and white collar criminals, never with organized crime, serial killers or corrupt cops. It dealt disapprovingly with student protests and teenage sex and drug abuse and its moralizing reflected

Webb's own personal and political philosophy. The original run of *Dragnet* resulted in 281 half hour, black and white episodes. Towards the end of the series Joe Friday was promoted to lieutenant and Frank Smith passed the exam and was promoted to sergeant. On March 24, 1959 Lt. Joe Friday and Sgt. Frank Smith solved their final original case, although reruns aired until August 23, 1959.

In 1955 MCA paid Webb and his Mark VII Limited partners Michael Meshekoff and Stanley Meyer $5,000,000 for the syndication rights. In syndication the series was known as *Badge 714*. In 1966 Webb sold all his interests including the rights to the name *Dragnet* to MCA for $5,000,000 in cash and an undisclosed percentage of future profits of the series. *Dragnet* won Emmy awards as "Best Mystery or Intrigue Series" in 1952, 1953 and 1954 and was nominated in 1955 as "Best Action or Adventure Series." Webb himself was nominated as "Best Actor" in 1952; twice in 1953 as "Best Male Star, Regular Series" and "Most Outstanding Personality"; in 1954 as "Best Actor Starring in a Regular Series"; and in 1956 as "Best Director—Film Series." He did not win on any of these occasions. The series won innumerable other awards including many citations from LAPD and other law enforcement groups. At the peak of its popularity in the late 1950s *Dragnet* attracted nearly forty million viewers a week. It finished twentieth in the Nielsen ratings in 1952; fourth in 1953; second in 1954; third in 1955; eighth in 1956; and eleventh in 1957.

The phenomenal success of the series enabled Webb to make his feature film debut starring and directing the full length movie version of *Dragnet* (1954) which grossed $4,750,000 in domestic rentals alone. The following year he directed and starred in *Pete Kelly's Blues* (1955) which he had done as an NBC radio series in 1951 and which he produced as a television series in 1959. The film which was set during the prohibition era heavily underlined Webb's personal interest in jazz. An aficionado of 1920s jazz, Webb owned two music leasing companies Mark VII Music and Pete Kelly's Music.

In 1957 Webb produced, directed and starred in *The D.I.* in which he played a Parris Island drill instructor Sgt. Jim Moore who whips raw recruits into fully fledged marines. His acting style in this film was shrill and inflexible. Moore has a tentative romance with Annie, a shop assistant, played by Jackie Loughery, Miss U.S.A. of 1952 and later Mrs. Jack Webb. There was also a relationship between Moore and a spoiled, deeply troubled, compulsive quitter Private Owens (Don Dubbins). Webb had spotted Dubbins playing a small role in the classic film *From Here To Eternity* (1953). The name of the character Dubbins had played was Friday.

Webb performed similar chores in the obscurely titled *-30-* (1959) which is a journalist's way of signing off. It was set entirely in the office of a large metropolitan newspaper, spanning the events of one night, intercutting the personal lives of the staff with the news stories as they develop. Told with warmth and humor, attention was hooked to the drama in the outside world solely through the reactions and emotions of the staff. Webb played the night editor, Sam Gatlin. William Conrad chewed the scenery magnificently as his second-in-command, Jim Bathgate.

Webb's final feature was *The Last Time I Saw Archie* (1961), a service comedy toplining Robert Mitchum as a real life GI. Archie Hall who was apparently always looking for a scam. Webb played his goldbricking buddy. After the film was released the real Archie sued! Under the pseudonyms of John Farr and Tex Grady, Webb wrote five novels between 1959 and 1963 and one non-fiction work. He was also a tireless worker for cerebral palsy charities.

In February 1963 Webb was named head of television production at Warner Bros. This appointment showed up his shortcomings in an executive capacity. He ruined several existing programs without creating any worthwhile new ones. It took precisely eight months for him to wreak havoc and his three year contract was abruptly terminated amidst a flurry of litigation. The case was finally settled out of court for the full amount of his contract as well as a pact to make feature films which never materialized.

He served as host and narrator of *G.E. True*, a half hour anthology series sponsored by General Electric. In 1965 he signed with Universal where he made a new series of *Dragnet* which ran to 98 color, half hours. It was shown between 1967 and 1970. Henry Morgan played Friday's new sidekick, Officer Bill Gannon. Gannon was something of a hypochondriac and self styled gourmet. His other pet interest was in marrying Friday off. Webb and Morgan had previously appeared together in the thriller films *Dark City* (1950) and *Appointment with Danger* (1951). The series was again one of the highest rated crime series on television. It finished twenty first in the

Nielsen ratings in 1967 and twentieth in 1969. There was also a telemovie *Dragnet '69* which had started out as a pilot, but was not aired until three years after it was made. It was originally held back because it was intended to release it theatrically which did not happen. Neither it nor the series explained why Friday who had been promoted to lieutenant when the original series had ended was now demoted to a sergeant again. Webb did however address this in a press release in which he explained that the rank of lieutenant would involve too much paper pushing for Friday. The demotion meant that Friday could spend more time pounding the streets. In 1987 there was a popular, affectionate, if not entirely successful artistically, spoof feature of *Dragnet* starring Dan Ackroyd. Harry Morgan had been elevated to the rank of Captain by this time.

Webb began producing other television series through Mark VII. Nearly a dozen of these rolled off the assembly line between 1968 and 1975. The most successful were *Adam 12*, a realistic portrayal of the daily rounds of two uniformed patrolmen that was sometimes shown in the LAPD training classes and *Emergency!* based on actual paramedical and fire cases. Amongst others which rapidly came and went were *The D.A.*, *O'Hara United States Treasury*, *Hec Ramsey*, *Chase*, *The Rangers* and *Mobile One*. In 1974 Webb moved to 20th Century–Fox where he produced such pilots as *Sam* a revival of the cop and partner format and *Project UFO* which became a successful NBC series. Despite his intensity, Webb became something of a back number during the late 1970s and early 1980s. He disapproved of some of television's more irreverent cop shows, but hoped to make a comeback with a new series called *The Department* which he had been working on at the time of his death.

Webb married Julie London, the sultry actress and singer, in 1947. They originally met in LA when she was fifteen and he was 21, dated for a year before he entered the service, but did not see each other again until he appeared on her doorstep when he had been discharged. With her he had two daughters Stacy born in 1950 and Lisa born in 1952. In August 1953 his wife took their two children and moved to Paris before returning to Palm Springs where she filed for a separation. The reason was because Webb was so driven that he was seldom home. Following an amicable divorce in 1954 she received a settlement of $800,000 and an annual income of $18,000. Webb's two daughters were to share a $50,000 trust fund at maturity. She and her subsequent husband Bobby Troup, who had been her musical arranger, appeared together in a later Webb series *Emergency!* His daughter Stacy, a widow aged 46, was killed after her car broadsided a police cruiser at 9:30 pm when she was driving in an alcohol induced state. She died at Desert Hospital, Palm Springs, California ironically on Friday, September 27, 1996, about an hour after being admitted. In 1955 Webb married Dorothy Towne, but they divorced in 1957. In 1958 he wed former Miss USA. of 1952, Jackie Loughery, but they divorced in 1964.

He died at his West Hollywood, Los Angeles apartment home on December 23, 1982 aged 62 of a heart attack caused by arteriosclerosis and alcoholism. His fourth wife Opal Gates (a.k.a. Wright) whom he married in 1980, was at his bedside when he died. He was buried at Forest Lawn Memorial Park, Los Angeles. He was given a memorial tribute by the LAPD., the first such service to be given for a civilian. His badge number 714 was returned to the LAPD. chief's office where it was retired from use forever.

FILMOGRAPHY

1948: *He Walked by Night*, *Hollow Triumph* (a.k.a. *The Scar*).
1950: *Halls of Montezuma*, *The Men*, *Dark City*, *Sunset Boulevard*, *You're in the Navy Now* (a.k.a. *USS. Teakettle*).
1951: *Appointment with Danger*.
1954: *Dragnet* (also directed).
1955: *Pete Kelly's Blues* (also directed).
1957: *The DI* (also directed).
1959: *-30-* (a.k.a. *Deadline Midnight*) (also directed).
1961: *The Last Time I Saw Archie* (also directed).
1969: *Dragnet* (TV) (also directed).

TELEVISION SERIES

1952–1959: *Dragnet* as Sgt. Joe Friday.
1962–1963: *G.E. True* host/narrator.
1967–1970: *Dragnet* as Sgt. Joe Friday.
1973: *Escape* narrator.

SOURCES

The Annual Obituary. 1982. Chicago: St. James, 1983.
Colville, Gary, and Patrick Lucanio. "Behind Badge 714: The Story of Jack Webb and Dragnet." *Filmfax*. Issues No. 40 and 41. August and October 1993.
Daily Telegraph. Obituary, December 24, 1982.

Death Certificate.
Ely, Suzanne. "Jack Webb's Daughter Killed in Crash with Cop Car." *National Enquirer*. October 1996.
Neville, Olga. "I'm a Tough Guy to Work With." *TV Mirror*. September 7, 1957.
Variety. Obituary, December 29, 1982.

RICHARD WEBB

John Richard Webb was born in Bloomington, Illinois on September 9, 1915, the son of John Richard Webb and Laura Gail Gunnett. He was educated at John Brown University between 1930 and 1933. His original ambition was to become a Methodist minister and he studied at Bible college, but lost his faith. Instead he served in the U.S. Army First Coast Artillery between 1936 and 1938. He became a male model with the famous John Powers Agency and commenced his acting career on stage in New York before gravitating to Hollywood. He enrolled at the Bliss Hayden Dramatic School where he played opposite Veronica Lake in a comedy. A talent scout from Paramount saw them and arranged to have them both signed to a contract. Both made their official debuts in *I Wanted Wings* (1941), although Webb appeared uncredited before that. He did not make the impact that Lake did and played small parts. He was then drafted and served in the Panama Canal Zone between 1941 and 1945, rising to the rank of major. Later he became a lieutenant colonel in the U.S. Army Reserve.

After the war he returned to Hollywood where he resumed his career appearing in several motion pictures for various studios. Despite his handsome, virile appearance he did not advance beyond supporting roles in features. The medium which really launched him as a star was television and the vehicle was *Captain Midnight*. This series originated on radio and was shown on CBS television from September 1954 to May 1956. It was later run in syndication under the title *Jet Jackson Flying Commando*. Captain Midnight, whose real name was Jim Albright, and his partner Ichabod Mudd (Sid Melton) were leaders of the Secret Squadron, a group of crime busters, who waged "the struggle against evil men everywhere." Fans, who at their peak numbered six million, sent in coupons from the drink Ovaltine to become members of the Secret Squadron. Personal appearances by Webb in the character were a guaranteed sell out and he was a tremendous draw everywhere.

After years of relative obscurity being thrust into the limelight made Webb uneasy. Already an imbiber from his Paramount days onwards, he developed a serious drinking problem. This in turn led to confrontations with the law. One such incident in 1959 occurred while Webb was boozing on an airplane flight between New Orleans and Miami. He tried to make a citizen's arrest of two insurance salesmen whom he claimed were Soviet agents. In 1960 neighbors of the actor called police because he was exhibiting violent tendencies and brandishing a loaded revolver. When police arrived at his home, they seized several assorted guns and thousands of rounds of ammunition. Webb was charged with disturbing the peace, fined $150 and placed on probation for two years. This led him to join Alcoholics Anonymous of which he remained a member for 33 years.

Webb was the star of another television series called *U.S. Border Patrol* in which he played Deputy Chief Don Jagger. This half crime and half western series derived from the actual case files of the organization and dealt with the efforts of the U.S. Border Patrol to stem the flow of drugs, illegal aliens, weapons and subversives into America. The series was shot in several different states all over the country. There were 39 half

Richard Webb, who starred in *U.S. Border Patrol*.

hour, black and white episodes shown of this successful syndicated series between 1958 and 1959. Sam Gallu Productions produced the series which was sponsored by the influential Amoco (American Oil Company). Of the two series in which he starred Webb preferred *U.S. Border Patrol* because the budgets were more generous; the quality of the acting by many of the guest stars was higher; and the fact that he visited so many different parts of America.

In total Webb appeared in 260 television episodes and at least eight stage plays. When his acting career wound down in the late 1960s, he started a new career as a writer in 1970. His books frequently dealt with the paranormal and the occult. He frequently lectured in psychic phenomenon. He also wrote a novel entitled "The Little Giant of Panamint Valley." He became a television writer/producer with *The Legend of Eli and Lottie Johl* in 1966.

In the wake of the nostalgia boom, Webb began developing a new television series derived from the original *Captain Midnight* in which he intended to play Captain Midnight's father, Colonel Midnight. The projected series did not make it to the tube, but in 1977 a recruiting film based upon the hero called *Captain Midnight Makes General* was developed and produced by the U.S. Army and the U.S. Army Reserve. In 1986 Webb donated all his memorabilia to a *Captain Midnight* display at the Smithsonian Institute's National Air and Space Museum in Washington. Webb, who was an active member of many professional and social organizations, became a favorite at many television conventions in later years.

Webb died in Van Nuys, California on June 10, 1993 aged 77 of a self inflicted gunshot wound. He had been despondent over a debilitating respiratory illness, authorities said. He married firstly Elizabeth Regina Sterns in 1942 with whom he had two daughters. They were Richelle Regina who became a homemaker and Patricia Gail who at last report was a nurse and officer in the Marine Corps. He married secondly publicist and later realtor Florence Pauline Morse in January 1949. He was survived by his widow, two daughters, four grandchildren and a great-grandson.

Filmography

1940: *Rancho Grande*.
1941: *I Wanted Wings, West Point Widow, Sullivan's Travels, Among the Living, Hold Back the Dawn*.
1942: *The Remarkable Andrew, The Lady Has Plans, This Gun For Hire, American Empire*.
1946: *OSS*.
1947: *Sweet and Low, Variety Girl, Out of the Past* (a.k.a. *Build My Gallows High*).
1948: *Night Has a Thousand Eyes, My Own True Love, Isn't It Romantic?, The Big Clock*.
1949: *Sands of Iwo Jima, A Connecticut Yankee in King Arthur's Court, Bride of Vengeance*.
1950: *The Invisible Monster* (serial).
1951: *Starlift, I Was a Communist for the FBI, Distant Drums*.
1952: *This Woman is Dangerous, Carson City, Mara Maru*.
1953: *The Nebraskan*.
1954: *Prince Valiant, The Black Dakotas, A Star is Born, Jubilee Trail, Three Hours to Kill*.
1955: *Count Three and Pray, Artists and Models*.
1957: *The Phantom Stagecoach*.
1959: *On the Beach*.
1960: *12 to the Moon*.
1963: *Attack of the Mayan Mummy*.
1965: *Town Tamer, Git!*
1966: *The Cat*.
1967: *Hillbillies in a Haunted House*.
1968: *Hell Raiders*.
1969: *The Gay Deceivers*.
1972: *Beware! The Blob*.
1974: *Never the Twain*
1975: *The Werewolf of Woodstock*.
1976: *Time Travelers* (TV).
1977: *Mulefeathers* (a.k.a. *The West is Still Wild*).

Note: Webb starred in one serial for Republic called *The Invisible Monster* which in 1966 was edited into a television feature under the title *Slaves of the Invisible Monster*.

Television Series

1954–1956: *Captain Midnight* as Captain Midnight.
1958–1959: *U.S. Border Patrol* as Deputy Chief Don Jagger.

Sources

The Annual Obituary. 1993. Chicago: St. James, 1994.
Lamparski, Richard. *Whatever Became Of?* 9th Series. New York: Crown, 1985.
Summers, Neil. *The Official TV Western Book*. Vol. 4. Vienna, WV: Old West Publishing, 1992.
Variety. Obituary, June 1993.
Ward, Jack. *The Supporting Players of Television, 1959–1983*. Cleveland, OK: Lakeshore West, 1996.

MARY K. WELLS

Mary K. Wells was born in Omaha, Nebraska on December 1, 1920. She was raised in Long Beach, California. After a fruitless attempt to break into movies in the forties, she relocated to New York. She was the second actress to play reporter Lorelei Kilbourne in the television series *Big Town* which starred Patrick McVey as Steve Wilson. She only played the role for most of the first season. Almost the whole of the rest of her career was spent in soap operas. She had regular roles in six of them. After this she switched to being a writer primarily for the ABC daytime soap opera *All My Children* for which she received two writing team Emmy awards in 1985 and 1988.

Mary K. Wells died in Manhattan on August 14, 2000 aged 79 of complications from a colon infection.

Television Series

1950–1951: *Big Town* as Lorelei Kilbourne.
1955–1956: *Love of Life* as Ellie Crown.
1956: *As the World Turns* as Louise Cole.
1956–1957: *Edge of Night* as Sgt. Helen Kilbourne.
1960–1961: *The Brighter Day* as Sandra Talbot Dennis.
1961–1970: *Edge of Night* as Louise Grimsely Capice.
1971: *The Secret Storm* as Nola Hollister.
1972–1974: *Return to Peyton Place* as Hannah Cord.

Sources

Brooks, Tim. *The Complete Directory to Prime Time TV Stars*. New York: Ballantine, 1987.
Copeland, Mary Ann. *Soap Opera History*. Lincolnswood, IL: Mallard, 1991.
Lentz, Harris M. III. *Obituaries in the Performing Arts, 2000*. Jefferson, NC: McFarland, 2001.

NINA WILCOX

Nina Wilcox was born in New York City on January 17. She appeared on Broadway in the play *Tall Story* in 1959. One of two regular roles she played on television was in *Harbormaster* which ran on both CBS and ABC. This was a one season show aired between September 1957 and June 1958. The title role was played by Barry Sullivan as Captain David Scott who acted as a one man police force and ran the harbor at Scott Island, an island off the New England Coast. He spent his off duty time at the Dolphin Restaurant run by Anna Morrison (Nina Wilcox) whose interest in him extended way beyond serving him meals. The series was too short lived for viewers to see how the relationship developed. Nina Wilcox has latterly been posted as one of the missing players of the screen.

Television Series

1957–1958: *Harbormaster* (a.k.a. *Adventures at Scott Island*) as Anna Morrison.
1981: *Jessica Novak* as Audrey Stiles.

Sources

Brooks, Tim, and Earle Marsh. *The Complete Directory to Prime Time, Network and Cable TV Shows*. 8th ed. New York: Ballantine, 2003.
Tibballs, Geoff. *TV Detectives*. London: Boxtree, 1993.

HUGH WILLIAMS

Hugh Anthony Glanmor Williams was born in Bexhill-on-Sea, Sussex, England on March 6, 1904. His nickname was Tam. He was the son of Hugh D.A. Williams and Hilda Lewis. His stepfather was playwright and teacher Mordaunt Sharp. He had a great love of travel ever since the age of seven when he went to New Zealand, Australia, China and Japan. He was educated at Haileyburg College and then went to Switzerland for a year to cram for his exams. Having decided that he would prefer to be an actor, he then insisted on going to the Royal Academy of Dramatic Art in London. While at RADA he met his first wife actress Gwynne Whitby (1903–1984) whom he married in 1925. With her he had two daughters, but the marriage was later dissolved in 1940.

He made his first stage appearance at the Hipperdrome, Margate on July 25, 1921 as Tim Bradbury in *The Charm School*. On March 7, 1922 he made his London debut at the Kingsway Theater with a walk-on part in *The Yellow Jacket*. He had his first speaking part at the same theater in June 1922 as Andres in *Spanish Lovers*. He became a member of the Liverpool Repertory Company in August 1923 and remained there for two and a half years, playing a variety of roles in nearly thirty modern plays. After this he returned to the London stage where he played a variety of parts. He recalled, "Looking back I think I was amazingly lucky. But at the time being young and foolish, I just took it all for granted."

In September 1927 he went to Australia where he toured with Dame Irene Vanburgh in several plays. Then in December 1928 he resumed his London stage career which was again interrupted when he toured Canada and the United States in *Journey's End* between September 1929 and June 1930 playing the part of Captain Stanhope. During this tour the company went to Hollywood where he stopped off long enough to make his screen debut in *Charley's Aunt* (1930). Upon his return to England in November 1930 he was once more in constant demand for the West End stage and it was not long before he commenced work for the British screen, his first film in England being *A Night in Montmartre* (1931).

His career went from strength to strength until his work in *Sorrell and Son* (1933) secured him a Hollywood contract. He recalled, "I was the most appalling failure. Everything seemed to go wrong. Even my moustache wasn't right." Nevertheless he did manage sterling performances in two classic Hollywood films. He played Steerforth in *David Copperfield* (1935) and Hindley in *Wuthering Heights* (1939). Theatrical work in London re-established his reputation and by 1939 he had become one of the leading West End actors. His final West End stage appearance before the war was as Nicholas Randolph in *Dear Octopus* at the Queen's Theatre in June 1939 in which he succeeded John Gielgud. He appeared in several British films during the thirties most notably *Bank Holiday* (1937) directed by Carol Reed. He played Geoffrey, the boyfriend of nurse Catherine Lawrence (Margaret Lockwood). He was so handsome and charming that it stretched credibility to accept that she would have preferred Stephen Howard (John Lodge).

He signed a contract with Alexander Korda and appeared in some exciting war films. Between 1939 and 1945 he served in the British army notably as part of Phantom Intelligence and took part in the invasion of Normandy. He was demobbed in 1945 and made a rather half hearted attempt to return to the London stage commencing at the Embassy in October 1945 as Jack in *Zoo in Silesia*. He was the happy possessor of a long term film contract at an excellent salary which turned out to be his undoing. Korda seldom used him, but instead loaned him out for films of which he made quite a number in the immediate post war period.

Even so between film roles he was left with quite a lot of spare time. As he later recalled, "Instead of going back on stage, I decided to live it up in the South of France. The war years had been hard. I'd got married during the war without a honeymoon so I decided to relax and enjoy myself." Money seemed no object, but by 1950 the contract was no more and the film offers had dried up. The way he remembered it was, "By 1951, I was thousands in debt to the Income Tax authorities and I was bankrupt. It took me four and a half years to clear everything, and I was deeply affected by it—both emotionally and in my way of life."

He was forced to accept whatever roles he could obtain. At the Playhouse Theater in April 1950 he played Mr. Dulcimer in a revival of *The Green Bay Tree* and was active again on the stage during the early fifties. Unhappily he did not really age into a character actor. Instead he became an old leading man, one commodity where supply always outstripped demand. He was a long-time friend of Jack Hawkins who found him bits in a couple of his films, but by the mid fifties his film career was virtually over. He tried television and played a police inspector and friend of Charlie Chan (J. Carrol Naish) in three episodes of *The New Adventures of Charlie Chan*. Much more to his liking was being the narrator Mallowby in the *Somerset Maugham Hour* anthology series in 1960. His character was generally believed to be based on Maugham himself whom Williams actually knew. In 1950 while on holiday at Cap Ferrat in the South of France, he was taken by a mutual friend to the author's villa.

Then in 1956 a whole new career opened up for him and his second wife, former actress and model Margaret Vyner (1913–1993) whom he wed in 1940. He recalled, "Out of work one long winter, we decided to write a play *Plaintiff in a Pretty Hat* which opened at the Duchess in October 1956." Williams played the Earl of Hewlyn who was harassed by a houseful of women while his wife gave birth upstairs. It was a success. They became two of the last and most successful playwrights of light drawing room comedy. Even in the fifties this genre was deemed somewhat outdated, but Williams who usually took the leading role in their plays achieved a large and loyal following in the West End. After writing four plays in as many years they scored two highly profitable hits notably *The Grass is Greener* (1958)

Hugh Williams, who costarred in *The New Adventures of Charlie Chan*.

which was filmed in 1961; one limited success which lost money but earned good critical reviews; and one outright flop. Depending on how well the play did, they were either flush of money or strapped for cash.

Their biggest hit which became the toast of London was when they collaborated on the musical comedy *Charlie Girl* which opened at the Adelphi in 1965. This earned the worst critical notices they had ever had, but it was an enormous commercial success in the West End where it ran for years. It gave both Williams and its star Dame Anna Neagle greater success and more financial stability than they had known for decades.

Hugh Williams continued to write plays and appear in them, of which there were about a dozen in all. He opened in a new play written by his wife and himself only a couple of days before he was taken seriously ill and died of throat cancer after surgery in a London hospital on December 7, 1969 aged 65. He was survived by his widow; a son Simon, born in 1946, an actor best known as Captain Bellamy in the *Upstairs Downstairs* television series; a daughter Polly (1950–2004), a former model whose second husband was the actor Nigel Havers; another son Hugo, a poet, born in 1960; and two daughters from his previous marriage. The touching letters of Hugh and Margaret Williams written to each other when they were apart during the war were later edited by their granddaughter and published in book form.

Filmography

1930: *Charley's Aunt.*
1931: *A Night in Montmartre, A Gentleman of Paris.*
1932: *In a Monastery Garden, Whiteface, Insult, Down Our Street, After Dark, Rome Express.*
1933: *Bitter Sweet, The Jewel, This Acting Business, Sorrell and Son.*
1934: *All Men are Enemies, Outcast Lady* (a.k.a. *A Woman of the World*).
1935: *Elinor Norton, David Copperfield, Let's Live Tonight, Lieutenant Daring R.N., The Last Journey, The Amateur Gentleman, Her Last Affaire.*
1936: *The Man Behind the Mask, The Happy Family, Gypsy.*
1937: *The Perfect Crime, Side Street Angel, The Dark Stairway, The Windmill, Brief Ecstasy, Bank Holiday.*
1938: *Dead Men Tell No Tales, His Lordship Goes to Press, Premiere* (a.k.a. *One Night in Paris*).
1939: *Inspector Hornleigh, Wuthering Heights, The Dark Eyes of London* (a.k.a. *The Human Monster*).
1941: *Ships With Wings.*
1942: *One of Our Aircraft is Missing, The Day Will Dawn, Talk About Jacqueline, The Secret Mission.*
1946: *A Girl in a Million.*
1947: *Take My Life, An Ideal Husband.*
1948: *The Blind Goddess, Elizabeth of Ladymead.*
1949: *Paper Orchid, The Romantic Age* (a.k.a. *Naughty Arlette*).
1952: *The Holly and the Ivy, Gift Horse* (a.k.a. *Glory at Sea*).
1953: *The Fake, Twice Upon a Time, The Intruder, Star of My Night.*
1966: *Khartoum.*
1967: *Doctor Faustus.*

Television Series

1956–1957: *The New Adventures of Charlie Chan* as Det. Insp. Carl Marlowe.
1961–1962: *Somerset Maugham Hour* as Mallowby.

SOURCES

Daily Telegraph. Margaret Williams Obituary, November 1993.
Dunn, Kate. *Always and Always.* London: John Murray, 1996.
Griffith, David. "The Two Careers of Hugh Williams." *TV Times.* November 6, 1960.
Iliff, Jay. "Family Drama That Never Ends." *Sunday Express.* March 2, 1997.
The Picturegoer's Who's Who and Encyclopedia. 1st ed. London: Amalgamated, 1933.
Picture Show. Biography, January 21, 1950.
Picture Show Annual. London: Amalgamated, 1935, 1936, 1937, 1938, 1941 and 1948.
Quinlan, David. *Film Stars.* 5th ed. London: Batsford, 2000.
Sweet, Matthew. *Shepperton Babylon.* London: Faber and Faber, 2005.
Who's Who in the Theatre. 10th, 12th, and 13th eds. London: Pitman, 1947, 1957 and 1961.
Winchester, Clarence. *Who's Who On the Screen.* London: Winchester, 1948.
_____. *The World Film Encyclopedia.* London: Amalgamated, 1933.

VAN WILLIAMS

Van Williams was born Van Zandt Jarvis Williams in Fort Worth, Texas on February 27, 1934 the son of Bernard Williams. His father was a successful businessman with oil, real estate and cattle interests. He won a football scholarship to Texas Christian University at Fort Worth. In his freshman year he married a co-ed. In 1954 his wife gave birth to twin daughters. Shortly afterwards he obtained a divorce and dropped out of college.

He headed for Honolulu. While there he taught skin diving at Henry Kaiser's Hawaiian Village Hotel and then became assistant manager of the hotel's aluminum dome theater. He also established a salvage business. Of his show business career he recalled, "A chance meeting with Mike Todd started it. He tried to convince me I had the looks and personality for show business. I tried to laugh off the idea, but Mike's vitality and personality overcame my doubts." Before taking this advice he went back to college where he completed his degree in business administration.

He has subsequently admitted that when he arrived in Hollywood in 1958 he had no acting experience whatsoever. As he recalled, "It certainly wasn't easy until I was advised to study dramatic art, have my voice trained and lose my Southern accent." Nevertheless within a short time he met an agent at a party who introduced him to casting director Robert Walker of Revue Productions. Walker brought him to the attention of the producers of *General Electric Theater.* He made his television debut in a show which starred Ronald Reagan. Following this Williams was signed to a contract with Revue. Four months later Warner Bros. bought his contract. For them he played the part of Kenny Madison, an oil rich young Texan studying at Tulane College and working for a firm of private detectives simultaneously in *Bourbon Street Beat.* The two private detectives were Rex Randolph (Richard Long) and Cal Calhoun (Andrew Duggan) who ran a private detective agency "Randolph and Calhoun Special Services" located on Bourbon Street in New Orleans next door to the Old Absinthe House. The program began on ABC on October 5, 1959. Even though the series only lasted one season, the character of Kenny Madison was very well liked by fans, especially in the two episodes in which he had the major part, and Williams had received a mountain of fan mail.

The character resurfaced this time in Miami as Ken Madison, again played by Van Williams, in *Surfside 6.* This was another slick Warners series about three private investigators who operated out of the "Surfside" houseboat at Wharf 6 moored adjacent to Miami Beach's luxury hotel, The Fontainebleau. Madison has now graduated in law and was working as a fully fledged private investigator. The other two private eyes were Sandy Winfield II (Troy Donahue) and Dave Thorne (Lee Patterson). The leads rotated, but Williams featured in more episodes than the others. The other stars of the series were Diane McBain who played Daphne Dutton, the beautiful and wealthy resident of the neighboring houseboat and Margarita Sierra who played nightclub singer Cha Cha O'Brien. *Surfside 6* ended after two seasons in 1962.

Although Williams had made his big screen debut in *Tall Story* (1960), he continued in television. *The Tycoon* was a single season sitcom shown on ABC between September 1964 and September 1965 with Walter Brennan in the title role of Walter Andrews, a cantankerous millionaire. Williams played Pat Burns, his young assistant and private airplane pilot. The other series in which Williams starred for a single season was

Van Williams, who costarred in *Bourbon Street Beat*.

The Green Hornet which ran on ABC between September 9, 1966 and July 14, 1967. *The Green Hornet* was derived from a radio series of the 1930s and 1940s. Williams played Britt Reid, a crusading newspaper editor and publisher of The Daily Sentinel, who fought crime disguised as The Green Hornet. Only District Attorney Scanlon (Walter Brooke), his secretary Lenore "Casey" Case (Wende Wagner) and Reid's martial arts expert manservant Kato (Bruce Lee) knew his real identity. The series was made by the same production team as the one which made *Batman*. Certain changes were made in bringing *The Green Hornet* to television. As well as "The Daily Sentinel" Reid owned a TV station. The villains he confronted were frequently involved in organized crime. The crime fighting gadgetry was made state of the art. This included The Green Hornet's car, the Black Beauty, and a special non-lethal gun which immobilized his enemies rather than killed them. Of this series he said, "I knew the politicking would kill the show long before it went off the air." When producer William Dozier insisted that the show should be expanded from 30 to 60 minutes to develop the characters further, ABC refused. Williams recalled, "When the network said no, it spelled the end of the show."

After this experience he decided that he no longer wished to be an actor. He did shoot other pilots, but it was nearly a decade before he played the lead in another series. This was a rather obscure NBC series called *The Westwind* in which he played Steve Andrews, an underwater photographer, who travels with his family through the Hawaiian islands. The family have adventures which increase their knowledge of the sea. *The Westwind* was the name of their yacht. The series was shown between September 1975 and September 1976. His final acting role for many years was an episode of *The Rockford Files* in 1979.

Instead he established a thriving business in Santa Monica which sells and rents two way radios and cellular phones. He also helped authorities nab illegal users of the radio frequencies Williams' clients used to conduct business. He has been involved with legislators to pass laws to prevent radio bandits. He is also a volunteer reserve deputy in the L.A. County Sheriff's Department. In addition to his regular business he owns working cattle ranches in Texas and on the North Shore of Oahu in Hawaii.

The one role which he did turn down was a regular part on the prime time soap opera *Falcon Crest*. The reason for this was because the part conflicted with the running of his business and he could not afford the time to do both. Apparently he has no regrets over this. He did however have a cameo as the director of the first episode of *The Green Hornet* in *Dragon: The Bruce Lee Story* (1993). This did not prompt a return to show business.

He remarried in 1959. With his second wife Vicki he has three daughters and is now a grandfather. At last report he was residing in Pacific Palisades. He professes to being a private person who does not miss show business. Nevertheless he has made appearances at the Hollywood Collectors Convention signing autographs and chatting with fans at the Beverly Garland Hotel in North Hollywood.

Filmography

1960: *Tall Story*.
1963: *The Caretakers*.
1966: *Batman* (voice only).
1975: *The Runaways* (TV).
1979: *The Night Rider* (TV).
1993: *Dragon: The Bruce Lee Story*.

TELEVISION SERIES

1959–1960: *Bourbon Street Beat* as Kenny Madison.
1960–1962: *Surfside 6* as Ken Madison.
1964–1965: *The Tycoon* as Pat Burns.
1966–1967: *The Green Hornet* as Britt Reid (a.k.a. The Green Hornet).
1975–1976: *The Westwind* as Steve Andrews.

MINISERIES

1978: *Centennial, How the West Was Won.*

SOURCES

Conversation with Williams in 1996.
Groves, Bill. "The Green Hornet." *The Television Chronicles*. No. 1. April 1995.
Inman, David. *The TV Encyclopedia*. New York: Perigee, 1991.
Lamparski, Richard. *Whatever Became Of?* 9th Series. New York: Crown, 1985.
Sandler, Adam. "Lost and Found." *Variety*. 1993.
TV Times. "Crime Busters from Wharf 6." 1962.
Woolley, Lynn, Robert W. Malsbury, and Robert C. Strange Jr. *Warner Bros. Television*. Jefferson, NC: McFarland, 1985.

LEWIS WILSON

Lewis Wilson was born on January 28, 1920. He was notable for being the first actor to play the role of the comic strip character, Batman, in the Columbia serial *The Batman* (1943). He was not particularly successful in the part. He never appeared in another serial and his other roles at Columbia were bits. In the early television crime series *Craig Kennedy Criminologist*, in which Donald Woods was the title character, Wilson played the decidedly secondary role of the sometimes foolhardy reporter, Walt Jameson. This was his final part of any importance before he slid into obscurity. Reputedly a bitter man, he refused to discuss his acting career in later years. He eventually died in San Francisco on August 9, 2000 aged 80. He was married to Dina Wilson with whom he had a son named Michael. After their divorce his former wife married Albert "Cubby" Broccoli, the producer of the *James Bond* film series. Michael G. Wilson, Wilson's son and Albert Broccoli's stepson, became the executive producer of the series.

Lewis Wilson as "Batman." He later costarred in *Craig Kennedy Criminologist*.

FILMOGRAPHY

1943: *The Batman* (serial), *Redhead from Manhattan, Good Luck Mr. Yates, First Comes Courage, My Kingdom for a Cook, There's Something About a Soldier.*
1944: *The Racket Man, Sailor's Holiday, Once Upon a Time.*
1951: *Wild Women.*
1954: *Naked Alibi.*

TELEVISION SERIES

1952: *Craig Kennedy Criminologist* as Walt Jameson.

SOURCES

Harmon, Jim, and Donald F. Glut. *The Great Movie Serials: Their Sound and Fury*. New York: Doubleday, 1972
Lentz, Harris M. III. *Obituaries in the Performing Arts, 2000*. Jefferson, NC: McFarland, 2001.
Weiss, Ken, and Ed Goodgold. *To Be Continued*. New York: Crown, 1972.

ROLAND WINTERS

Roland Winters was born Roland Winternitz in Boston, MA on November 22, 1904. His

Roland Winters as Charlie Chan in one of the films he shot for Monogram. He starred in the television series *Doorway to Danger*.

father Felix Winternitz was the first violinist and concert master of the Boston Symphony Orchestra. He was raised in Boston. As a restless teenager, he worked abroad for two summers on a commercial boat. At the age of sixteen, he began acting on stage in stock companies. In 1924 he landed a small role in the Broadway production of *The Firebrand*. After it closed he played in stock for several more years. He had bits in a couple of silent movies, but they led nowhere.

In 1932 he went into radio in Boston. In 1938 he gravitated to New York where he was a radio announcer, performer and sports reporter. He made his proper screen debut in *13 Rue Madeleine* (1946) which starred James Cagney. He became a friend of Cagney's and occasionally played a small role in some of his films. Following earlier actors Warner Oland and Sidney Toler, he tested for and immediately landed the role of the Asian detective Charlie Chan in a series of six truly dire films for Monogram between 1947 and 1949. The balance of his film career he spent playing military officers, medical men and business tycoons, roles in which he seemed altogether more at home. He played the father of Elvis Presley and the husband of Angela Lansbury in *Blue Hawaii* (1962).

Doorway to Danger was a summer replacement television series which was shown initially on NBC and later ABC for three years between 1951 and 1953. The title started as *Door with No Name*, but was changed to *Doorway to Danger* for the second season. Both referred to the door to John Randolph's office. Randolph was the head of a top secret federal agency, who sent operatives to all corners of the globe when the security of the USA was threatened. The actors who played Randolph changed each season. Winters inherited the role from Mel Ruick. During the second season on NBC Winters played the role between July and August 1952 for a total of eight black and white, half hour episodes. He relinquished the role in the third season to Raymond Bramley. There was one significant difference during the second season. During the first and third seasons the leading operative was Doug Carter who was also played by two different actors. During the second season Randolph had no leading operative so he was seen each week dispatching diverse agents to deal with malefactors. Of the three actors who played Randolph, Winters had the most distinguished career by far. Winters had regular roles in other television series, but they were all comedies. *Doorway to Danger* was his sole drama, a genre with which his heavy build and serious features made him seem very suited. As a television supporting actor, he was at his most prolific during the fifties and sixties although he remained active as an actor for a decade after that.

Between 1978 and 1983 he served as President of the Players Club, a theatrical organization. He died in Englewood, New Jersey on October 22, 1989 of a stroke aged 84. He was twice married, but both his wives predeceased him. His first wife was Ada Rowe whom he wed in 1930. He was survived by a brother.

FILMOGRAPHY

1946: *13 Rue Madeleine*.
1947: *The Chinese Ring* (CC).
1948: *The Golden Eye* (CC), *The Feathered Serpent* (CC), *Docks of New Orleans* (CC), *The Shanghai Chest* (CC), *The Return of October*, *Kidnapped*, *Cry of the City*.
1949: *Sky Dragon* (CC), *Once More My Darling*, *Tuna Clipper*, *A Dangerous Profession*, *Abbott and Costello Meet the Killer*, *Malaya* (a.k.a. *East of the Rising Sun*), *Captain Carey USA* (a.k.a. *After Midnight*).
1950: *Guilty of Treason*, *The West Point Story*, *Killer Shark*, *Convicted*, *Between Midnight and Dawn*, *The Underworld Story*, *To Please a Lady*, *Jet Pilot* (released 1957).

1951: *Follow the Sun, Inside Straight, Sierra Passage, Raton Pass.*
1952: *She's Working Her Way through College.*
1953: *So Big, A Lion Is in the Streets.*
1956: *Bigger Than Life.*
1957: *Top Secret Affair.*
1959: *Never Steal Anything Small, Cash McCall.*
1961: *Everything's Ducky, Blue Hawaii.*
1962: *Follow That Dream.*
1970: *Loving.*
1973: *Miracle on 34th Street* (TV).
1979: *You Can't Go Home Again* (TV).

Note: The six Monogram films in which he played Charlie Chan are noted CC in the filmography.

TELEVISION SERIES

1951–1952: *Mama* as Uncle Chris.
1952: *Doorway to Danger* as John Randolph.
1953–1956: *Meet Millie* as J.R. Boone, Sr.
1965–1966: *The Smothers Brothers Show* as Leonard J. Costello.

MINISERIES

1978: *The Dain Curse.*

SOURCES

DeLong, Thomas A. *Radio Stars*. Jefferson, NC: McFarland, 1996.
Inman, David. *The TV Encyclopedia*. New York: Perigee, 1991.
Lance, Steven. *Written Out of Television*. Lanham, MD: Madison, 1996.
Okuda, Ted. *The Monogram Checklist*. Jefferson, NC: McFarland, 1987.
Parish, James Robert. *Hollywood Character Actors*. New Brunswick, NJ: Arlington, 1978.
Quinlan, David. *Illustrated Directory of Film Character Actors*. 2nd ed. London: Batsford, 1996.
Tuska, Jon. *The Detective in Hollywood*. New York: Doubleday, 1978.
Twomey, Alfred E., and Arthur F. McClure. *The Versatiles*. South Brunswick, NJ: Barnes, 1969.
Variety. Obituary, Nov. 1, 1989.
Vazzana, Eugene Michael. *Silent Film Necrology*. Jefferson, NC: McFarland, 1995.
Willis, John. *Screen World*. Vol. 41. London: Muller, 1991.

JOHN WITTY

John Witty was born Robert John Blanchflower Featherstone Witty in Bristol, England on September 17, 1915. He was the son of a banker and stockbroker. He was educated at Clifton College, Bristol. From there he won a classical scholarship to Exeter College, Oxford from which he graduated with a Bachelor of Arts degree. From 1936 to 1937 he was President of Oxford University Dramatic Society. He was originally intended for the diplomatic service, but was diverted into an acting career. While still an undergraduate he made his first professional stage appearance with Oxford Repertory Company. He then trained for the stage at the Webber Douglas Academy of Dramatic Art.

World War II intervened in which he served as a Captain with the Royal Artillery. After being invalided out, he returned to acting in repertory at Oxford and Colwyn Bay. Next he played the juvenile lead for two years in a highly successful play *No Medals* at the Vaudeville Theater in the West End of London. In 1944 he made his screen debut in a minor role in *Champagne Charlie* which starred Tommy Trinder and Stanley Hol-

John Witty, who costarred in *Dial 999*.

loway and was possibly the most accurate depiction of the British musical hall ever captured on film. Witty began radio broadcasting for the BBC in 1944.

He first appeared on television in *The Queen's Husband* for the BBC in 1946. He went on to make over 6,000 radio and television broadcasts and over 1,000 audio visual commentaries in the United Kingdom and abroad. He also did numerous voiceovers in commercials and dubbed foreign language films into English. In the crime series *Dial 999* he played Det. Sgt. West, assistant to Mike Maguire (Robert Beatty).

Witty married firstly Genine Graham (1926–1997) former opera singer turned actress and early television personality. They appeared together in the films *Hangman's Wharf, Hell Below Zero* and *The Vault of Horror*. They also did one of the earliest shows, *Mail Call*, ever shown on British independent television. After they divorced, he married secondly Susan. He had a daughter named Sara-Jane and a son named Jonathan. Whilst he traveled a great deal, notably to Paris and Rome connected with his voice work, his most permanent home was in London.

John Witty died in Bristol, England on January 14, 1990 aged 74.

Filmography
1944: *Champagne Charlie.*
1948: *Love in Waiting, Christopher Columbus.*
1949: *Hangman's Wharf.*
1950: *Soho Conspiracy.*
1951: *Captain Horatio Hornblower RN.*
1953: *Hell Below Zero, Three's Company, Solution By Phone.*
1954: *Alive on Saturday.*
1955: *A Prize of Gold.*
1958: *Moment of Indiscretion.*
1961: *The Frightened City.*
1965: *The Curse of Simba.*
1973: *The Vault of Horror.*

Television Series
1955–1956: *Mail Call* Host and presenter.
1958–1959: *Dial 999* as Det. Sgt. West.

Sources
Andrews, Cyrus. *Radio and Television Who's Who*. 3rd Edition. London: George Young, 1954.
Laffan, Patricia. "The Wittys Invite You to Write." *TV Times*. November 11, 1955.
Noble, Peter. *The British Film and Television Yearbook, 1970*. London: British and American, 1970.
Tibballs, Geoff. *TV Detectives*. London: Boxtree, 1992.
Walker, Derek. "They're Stars Whether You Like It or Not." *Picturegoer*. September 24, 1955.
Who's Who on Television. London: Independent Television, 1980.

ANNA MAY WONG

Anna May Wong was one actress whom Hollywood did not do right by. Although she was a slacks and sweater girl in private, at public appearances she was a clotheshorse who dressed in native Chinese garb. She quite deliberately cultivated an air of mystery about herself, but her personality made her one of the most fascinating and enigmatic players of the twenties and thirties. She had the potential to be a major star, but this was denied her because of the shortsighted attitudes which prevailed in the industry at the time when her career was at its zenith. It was only when she traveled to Europe that she received the acclaim she deserved. After World War II she found roles hard to come by. During the early days of television she became the first female and the first Asian-American to be the toplined star of a legitimate crime series, *The Gallery of Madame Liu-Tsong*.

Anna May Wong was born in the Chinatown section of Los Angeles on January 3, 1905, the daughter of Sam Wong and his second wife, Lee Gon Toy. Her mother was killed as the result of a car accident in 1930. Her father died in October 1949. She was one of seven children. Her real name was Wong Liu Tsong which literally meant Frosted Yellow Willow. Her father owned and operated a laundry. Although English was the primary language in the home, they were raised according to Chinese custom.

She was educated at a mission school in Chinatown and Los Angeles High School. She was fascinated by movies from childhood. At the age of 14 in 1919 she met James Wang, who doubled as a minister and an agent between Chinese extras and the studios. Wang was struck by her potential and sent her over to Metro Pictures where he arranged to have her hired as an extra in *The Red Lantern* (1919). This film was being shot in Chinatown and she was one of the lantern bearers. At first her father was extremely displeased with her, but later relented to a certain extent when he realized that she could earn money from acting. She was an extra in a few further films.

She graduated from high school in 1921, by which time she had played her first credited role as Toy Sing in *Bits of Life* (1921) as Lon Chaney's wife. Then she was cast in the leading role in *The Toll of the Sea* (1922), the first true Technicolor film shot in Hollywood. Between movies she modeled for a furrier in Los Angeles. Her big break came when she was cast by Douglas Fairbanks, Sr., as the Mongol Slave in *The Thief of Bagdad* (1924) in which she enjoyed considerable success. She had a good role as Tiger Lily in *Peter Pan* (1924), but her career did not rush on at quite the pace that it should have done.

What prevented her from becoming a megastar was that love scenes, specifically kissing between Asians and Caucasians, were not permitted on screen in those days. A typical example of her position in the Hollywood firmament was *Mr. Wu* (1927) in which she would have been ideal in the lead female role of Nang Ping. Instead Renee Adorée played that role, while Anna May Wong was relegated to the secondary role of Nang Ping's cousin. While she worked fairly regularly, she became increasingly disenchanted with the Hollywood casting system where Caucasian actors played Asians made up in yellowface.

To escape this she learned to be proficient in French and German languages and then accepted an offer to star in *Song* (1928) in Germany in the title role as a Malayan dancer. She inked a deal to appear in other German films. From there she journeyed to England where she appeared to excellent effect as Sho-Sho, a streetwalker who becomes a cabaret artiste, in *Piccadilly* (1929). Her first talkie was *The Flame of Love* (1930) as Hai-Tang in which her own voice was used in the French, German and English versions. She appeared as herself in the all-star film revue *Elstree Calling* (1930). She made her stage debut in *The Circle of Chalk* which opened at the New Theater, London on March 14, 1929 and lasted for five weeks. Possibly because of her California accent, the critics were not kind to her, but public response was good. This was derived from a German play which was in turn an adaptation of a famous Chinese singsong of the thirteenth century. Her leading man was a very young Laurence Olivier.

She was totally accepted by London society and lived initially at Claridges Hotel and then later at an apartment in Park Lane. Guests at parties she attended included Somerset Maugham and Wellington Koo, Chinese ambassador to Great Britain. Her etiquette occasionally left a little bit to be desired as when she attended a party in honor of Alfred Lunt and Lynn Fontanne, she became so flustered at meeting the Prince of Wales that she forgot to curtsy. In 1930 she ventured to Vienna where she appeared on stage in *Springtime* to respectable notices and hot box office. Upon her return to America she made her Broadway debut in *On the Spot* by Edgar Wallace which opened at the Forrest Theater on October 29, 1930. It was a major hit and ran for 167 performances. She then went on tour with it to other cities. She signed a contract with Paramount in May 1931 and moved to Hollywood. She was almost immediately cast in *Daughter of the Dragon* (1931) in which she played Ling Moy, the daughter of the evil genius Dr. Fu Manchu (Warner Oland). This film was a commercial success. Her second film for Paramount was *Shanghai Express* (1932) which was her best remembered talkie as Hui Fei, the traveling companion of the infamous Shanghai Lil (Marlene Dietrich). Warner Oland again costarred as the evil bandit Henry Chang. In this film she was raped by Chang, but in the end stabs him to death. In real life the charming Oland was a good friend of hers.

Afterwards she went on a coast to coast vaudeville tour climaxing with an elaborate production at the Capital Theater, New York in 1933. On loan to independent company World Wide she played Mrs. Pyke in *A Study in Scarlet* (1933) which starred Reginald Owen as Sherlock Holmes. In addition to her fluency in languages her hobbies around this time were listed as horse riding, golf, tennis, playing the piano and painting. She was also an excellent cook of Chinese cuisine.

Since Paramount had no further projects for her, she journeyed to England where she made her first appearance on the London variety stage at the Holborn Empire in June 1933 and then shot three films. She played Lui Chang, a dockside café proprietress who sacrifices herself to save a young English orphan from a brutal seaman, in *Tiger Bay* (1934). Next she was Taou Yen, the Manchu Princess who marries into a nineteenth century shipping family in Bristol, in the tragic *Java Head* (1934). The film was bedeviled with censorship trouble because of her love scenes with John Loder who played her husband. This was the first time she had actually been kissed on

Anna May Wong in the film *Daughter of the Dragon* (1931). She later starred in the television series *The Gallery of Mme. Liu-Tsong*.

screen by a Caucasian. As he recalled in his memoirs *Hollywood Hussar*, "There was quite a lot of kissing in the picture and in those days interracial love scenes on the screen were frowned upon." Nevertheless for this very reason the film is reputed to be Wong's personal favorite of her own films. She then had the female lead of the slave girl Zahrat in *Chu Chin Chow* (1934) opposite John Garrick (1902–1966), a successful musical comedy derived from a long-running London stage success. Her finale dance sequence was choreographed by ballet dancer Anton Dolin. Back in Hollywood, Paramount cast her as Tu Tuan, George Raft's mistress, in the intriguing *Limehouse Blues* (1934). Afterwards she toured Europe with a successful one woman show, climaxing at the Embassy Club in London where she sang and danced to wide acclaim. In 1935 she undertook a successful tour of Scandinavia. She broadcast for the BBC notably in King George V's Jubilee Programme in 1935. She did broadcast on radio in America, but this was not her favorite medium.

In 1936 she sailed for a long planned vacation to China. Being emancipated in China during this period did not meet with universal approval, but she stayed for several months. While there she met her father's first wife. She left China because the Sino-Japanese war broke out. Back in America she wrote a series of articles for the *New York Herald Tribune* about her Chinese experiences which were published in 1937. In the summer of 1937 she appeared on stage at the Westchester County Playhouse in *Princess Turandot*. Later she inked a new non-exclusive contract with Paramount. For them she shot four exciting programmers which are still highly regarded by film buffs. One of these *Dangerous to Know* (1938) was a reworking of her stage success *On the Spot*. At Warners she appeared in *When Were You Born?* (1938) as Mei Lee Ling, a quickie involving astrology. Her biggest professional disappointment was losing the role of Olan, the first wife of Paul Muni, in *The Good Earth* (1937) at MGM which she tested for. She rejected the role of the concubine, the second wife, because it was degrading to the Chinese.

When her Paramount contract expired, there were no further Hollywood offers so she toured Australia with her highly successful one woman show. Upon her return to America she had a subordinate role as a patriotic Chinese diplomat Lois Ling in *Ellery Queen's Penthouse Mystery* (1941). Her career was in the doldrums when she graced two low budget films at PRC in 1942. Both were topical films detailing Chinese resistance to the Japanese. Potentially much more interesting was a projected biography of Madame Chiang Kai-Shek, but this was shelved indefinitely. She made her final stage appearance in summer stock in *The Willow Tree* in 1943.

She spent the war years working tirelessly for the USO and China War Relief including auctioning items which she had acquired on her visit to China.

In 1946 she bought a house in Santa Monica called Moongate and converted it into four apartments. Two she rented out, while she lived in one and her brother Richard in the other. She became a practicing Christian Scientist. She briefly returned to films in *Impact* (1949) in which she was effective in an important supporting role as Su Lin, a housekeeper.

She then turned to television with her own series, *The Gallery of Madame Liu-Tsong*. The character she played had the actresses' own real name. It was shown on the DuMont network between August 27, 1951 and November 21, 1951. Originally shot as a batch of six episodes, she played an art gallery proprietress with world wide connections who encounters crime while searching for rare art objects for her galleries. Seven more episodes were shot which dropped the gallery and broadened the scope of the series which was now called simply *Madame Liu-Tsong*. She played a Chinese exporter battling more general crimes. Described by the network as "a good girl against bad men," the series was a DuMont Production of 13 half hour, black and white episodes. The fact that it did not showcase her talents to better advantage and last longer was a considerable disappointment. It is understood that the kinescopes of all the DuMont series were dumped in one of the New York rivers during the 1970s when it was reckoned that it would cost too much to preserve them. One reputable source however has stated that at least one episode of this series has survived.

Her most acclaimed television performance was a version of "The Letter" on *Producers Showcase* in 1956 in which she played Mrs. Hammond. Between 1956 and 1961 there were seven television guest shots, the last of which was "Josephine Little: Dragon by the Tail," an episode of *The Barbara Stanwyck Theater* originally aired on January 30, 1961. In 1956 she sold Moongate and bought a smaller home in Santa Monica which she shared with her photographer brother, Richard. Her final film appearance was when she played Tani, the housekeeper, in *Portrait in Black* (1960) produced by Ross Hunter for Universal. The same producer cast her in an important role in *Flower Drum Song* (1961), but she fell ill and was replaced by Juanita Hall.

On February 3, 1961 at 3 pm she died in her sleep at her Santa Monica home after suffering a massive heart attack at age 56. Her physician Dr. Robert Skeets said that she had been in good health and had no history of heart trouble. It was however revealed that she had been ill with Laennac's Cirrhosis, a liver disease since 1950, the cause of which is alcoholism. She was cremated at the Chapel of the Pacific at Woodlawn Cemetery on February 9, 1961 and her ashes laid in an unmarked grave near her mother's coffin at Rosedale Cemetery, Los Angeles. In her will dated May 1947 she left jewelry, furs and a $25,000 legacy to her older sister Lulu, also known as Ying Wong, who had been her business manager throughout her career. The balance of her estate which amounted to about $60,000, she left to her brother Richard. Her other brothers were disinherited because she had provided for them during her lifetime. Her other sister Mary committed suicide in 1940. Anna May Wong never married.

The Anna May Wong who appeared in the films *The Savage Innocents* (1959) and *Just Joe* (1960); an episode of *Danger Man* (1960); and the British television series *Voodoo Man* (1960) is not the same actress. This actress who was born in Singapore and was much younger said, "My ambition is to meet the original Anna May Wong. If I can live up to my namesake then I have achieved something." The original died before the meeting could take place.

Filmography

1919: *The Red Lantern*.
1920: *Dinty*.
1921: *A Tale of Two Worlds, The White Mouse, Outside the Law, The First Born, Shame, Bits of Life*.
1922: *The Toll of the Sea*.
1923: *Mary of the Movies, Drifting, Thundering Dawn*.
1924: *The Thief of Bagdad, The Fortieth Door* (serial), *The Alaskan, Peter Pan*.
1925: *Forty Winks, His Supreme Moment*.
1926: *Fifth Avenue, The Silk Bouquet* (a.k.a. *The Dragon Horse*), *A Trip to Chinatown, The Desert's Toll* (a.k.a. *The Devil's Toll*).
1927: *The Chinese Parrot, Driven from Home, Mr. Wu, Old San Francisco, The Devil Dancer, Streets of Shanghai*.
1928: *Across to Singapore, The Crimson City, Chinatown Charlie, Song* (a.k.a. *Show Life* and *Wasted Love*).
1929: *The City Butterfly* (a.k.a. *The Pavement Butterfly*), *Piccadilly*.
1930: *Elstree Calling* (cameo), *Sabotage, The Flame of Love* (a.k.a. *The Road to Dishonor*) (and French and German versions).
1931: *Daughter of the Dragon*.
1932: *Shanghai Express*.
1933: *A Study in Scarlet*.
1934: *Tiger Bay, Chu Chin Chow, Java Head, Limehouse Blues* (a.k.a. *East End Chant*).
1937: *Daughter of Shanghai* (a.k.a. *Daughter of the Orient*).
1938: *Dangerous to Know, When Were You Born?*
1939: *King of Chinatown, Island of Lost Men*.
1941: *Ellery Queen's Penthouse Mystery*.
1942: *Bombs Over Burma, Lady from Chungking*.
1949: *Impact*.
1960: *Portrait in Black*.

Television Series

1951: *The Gallery of Madame Liu-Tsong* (a.k.a. *Madame Liu-Tsong*) as Madame Liu-Tsong.

SOURCES

Bourne, Stephen. "Most Exotic Villainess." *The Stage*. November 1995.
Chronicle. "Anna May Wong, Dainty Star of the Thirties, Dies." February 4, 1961.
Donnelly, Paul. *Fade to Black*. London: Omnibus, 2000.
Hodges, Graham Russell Gao. *Anna May Wong: From Laundryman's Daughter to Hollywood Legend*. New York: Palgrave Macmillan, 2005.
Inman, David. *The TV Encyclopedia*. New York: Perigee, 1991.
Leibfried, Philip, and Chei Mi Lane. *Anna May Wong: A Complete Guide to Her Film, Stage, Radio and Television Work*. Jefferson, NC: McFarland, 2003.
National Film Theatre, London program, December 1995.
Parish, James Robert, and William T. Leonard. *Hollywood Players: The Thirties*. Carlstadt, NJ: Rainbow, 1977.
The Picturegoer's Who's Who and Encyclopedia. 1st ed. London: Odhams Press, 1933.
Picture Show Annual. London: Amalgamated, 1926, 1928, 1930, 1931, 1935, 1936, 1939, 1940.
Quinlan, David. *Film Stars*. 5th ed. London: Batsford, 2000.
Ragan, David. *Movie Stars of the '30s*. Englewood Cliffs, NJ.: Prentice-Hall, 1985.
Roberts, Barrie. "Anna May Wong: Daughter of the Orient." *Classic Images*. No. 270. December 1997.
Slide, Anthony. *Silent Portraits*. New York: Vestal, 1989.
Springer, John, and Jack Hamilton. *They Had Faces Then*. Secaucus, NJ: Citadel, 1984.
Stuart, Ray. *Immortals of the Screen*. Los Angeles, CA: Sherbourne, 1985.
Tibballs, Geoff. *TV Detectives*. London: Boxtree, 1992.
TV Times. 1960.
Vazzana, Eugene. *Silent Screen Necrology*. Jefferson, NC: McFarland, 1995.
Winchester, Clarence. *The World Film Encyclopedia*. London: Amalgamated, 1933.

GEORGE WOODBRIDGE

George Woodbridge was born in Exeter, Devon on February 16, 1907. His parents were Arthur Knott Woodbridge and Jessie Ellen Beer.

George Woodbridge, who costarred in *Stryker of the Yard*.

He was educated at Exeter School where his main subject was physics. He became more interested in drama and made his first stage appearance at the Festival Theater, Cambridge in January 1928 in *Caesar and Cleopatra*. His London debut was at the New Theater in June 1928 as the Lieutenant in *Spread Eagle*. In a theatrical career which spanned thirty years he appeared in numerous plays ranging from modern productions to classics including Shakespeare. He appeared in both the West End and toured with repertory companies. As a character actor, he was seldom unemployed. His rotund build and ruddy complexion made him ideal casting for such parts as the First Gravedigger in *Hamlet*. His biggest theatrical success however was as Ben in *Love for Love* which he played in for over a year in two separate companies during 1943 and 1944.

His screen debut came in a semi-documentary propaganda film *Mein Kampf—My Crimes* (1940) dealing with Hitler's rise to power. He went on to appear in numerous films frequently cast as a farmer, publican or lower rank police officer. In later years he appeared in some Hammer horror films in different characterizations. He was appearing in experimental television programs in the late 1930s. He was featured in a

BBC play *Men of Darkness* (1948), about the French Resistance during the war, which enjoyed considerable acclaim. On television he played Det. Sgt. Hawker, the amiable assistant of the formidable Chief Inspector Robert Stryker (Clifford Evans), in the crime series *Stryker of the Yard*. In the classic BBC television serial *The Forsyte Saga* (1967) he was splendidly cast as Uncle Swithin Forsyte. In the popular BBC soap opera *The Newcomers* he had a recurring role for a while as Jacob Penrose during the late 1960s. He did the first season of a lunchtime children's television series *Inigo Pipkin* as the avuncular title character which featured both live actors and puppets. He had just begun the second season when he died suddenly in London on March 31, 1973 aged 66. His death was written into the show which was then retitled *The Pipkins*. In real life he was married to Mary Jowitt.

Filmography

1940: *Mein Kampf—My Crimes*.
1941: *The Saint Meets the Tiger, The Black Sheep of Whitehall, The Tower of Terror, The Big Blockade*.
1942: *The Day Will Dawn*.
1943: *Escape to Danger, The Life and Death of Colonel Blimp*.
1945: *A Diary for Timothy*.
1946: *Green for Danger, I See a Dark Stranger* (a.k.a. *The Adventuress*).
1947: *The October Man, Temptation Harbor, My Brother Jonathan, Blanche Fury*.
1948: *Bonnie Prince Charlie, Escape, The Queen of Spades, The Fallen Idol, The Red Shoes, The Bad Lord Byron, Silent Dust*.
1949: *Children of Chance*.
1950: *The Naked Earth* (a.k.a. *The Naked Heart*), *Double Confession, Trio, The Black Rose*.
1951: *Cloudburst*.
1952: *Isn't Life Wonderful?, The Crimson Pirate, Murder in the Cathedral*.
1953: *The Story of Gilbert and Sullivan* (a.k.a. *The Great Gilbert and Sullivan*), *The Flanagan Boy* (a.k.a. *Bad Blonde*), *The Bosun's Mate*.
1954: *The Night of the Full Moon, Mad About Men, An Inspector Calls, The Green Buddha, Conflict of Wings* (a.k.a. *Fuss over Feathers*), *For Better For Worse, Companions in Crime, Third Party Risk* (a.k.a. *The Deadly Game*).
1955: *A Yank in Ermine, Richard III, Passage Home, The Constant Husband, An Alligator Named Daisy, Lost*.
1956: *Eyewitness, Three Men in a Boat, The Passionate Stranger* (a.k.a. *A Novel Affair*), *Now and Forever*.
1957: *Day of Grace, High Flight, The Moonraker, A King in New York, The Good Companions*.
1958: *The Revenge of Frankenstein, Jack the Ripper, Dracula* (a.k.a. *The Horror of Dracula*), *A Tale of Two Cities, The Son of Robin Hood*.
1959: *The Siege of Pinchgut* (a.k.a. *Four Desperate Men*), *Breakout, The Mummy, Jack the Ripper, The Flesh and the Fiends* (a.k.a. *Mania*).
1960: *Two Way Stretch, The Brides of Dracula*.
1961: *Curse of the Werewolf, Only Two Can Play, The Piper's Tune, What a Carve Up!, Raising the Wind*.
1962: *Out of the Fog, The Iron Maiden* (a.k.a. *Swingin' Maiden*), *The Amorous Prawn*.
1963: *Nurse on Wheels, Heavens Above!, Carry on Jack, The Scarlet Blade*.
1964: *Dead End Creek*.
1965: *Dracula—Prince of Darkness*.
1966: *The Reptile*.
1967: *The Magnificent 6 and ½*.
1969: *Where's Jack?, Take a Girl Like You, David Copperfield* (TV).
1970: *All the Way Up*.
1971: *Up Pompeii*.
1972: *Along the Way, Diamonds on Wheels, Doomwatch*.

Television Series

US (1953–1955): *Stryker of the Yard* as Det. Sgt. Hawker.
UK (1961–1963): *Stryker of Scotland Yard*.
1972–1973: *Inigo Pipkin* as Inigo Pipkin.

Sources

Gaye, Freda. *Who's Who in the Theatre*. 13th ed. London: Pitman, 1961.
McFarlane, Brian. *The Encyclopedia of British Film*. London: Methuen-BFI, 2003.
Noble, Peter. *The British Film Yearbook, 1947–1948*. London: Skelton Robinson British Yearbooks, 1948.
Quinlan, David. *Illustrated Directory of Film Character Actors*. 2nd ed. London: Batsford, 1996. .
Rogers, Dave. *The ITV Encyclopedia of Adventure*. London: Boxtree, 1988.
Tibballs, Geoff. *TV Detectives*. London: Boxtree, 1992.

Donald Woods

Donald Woods was born Ralph L. Zink in Brandon, Manitoba, Canada on December 2, 1906, the son of a businessman. His brother is the actor Russ Conway. His father was ill and his doctors suggested that he should seek a warmer climate. He emigrated with his parents to California in 1913 where his father died shortly afterwards. His mother became a naturalized American and so did her sons. He was educated at Burbank High School where his original ambition was to be a writer. While in high school he wrote a one act play which had at least one role that was well written. When the play was performed, he played this role himself. He enjoyed the experience so much that he decided to change his ambition to acting.

He attended the University of California at Berkeley where he majored in drama and played football. When he married in 1927, he dropped out of college before obtaining his degree. Instead he joined a small stock company in Long Beach, California at a salary of $35 a week. For the next six years he acquired extensive experience in stock and on tour performing in classic plays. He also appeared on Broadway twice. In 1933 while appearing in a play with the prestigious Elitch Theater Company in Denver, he was spotted by an agent who subsequently arranged for him to be signed by Warner Bros. at the salary of $1,000 a week. They gave him a big build-up.

He made his screen debut as Stan Janowski, a Maine backwoods farmer, in *As the Earth Turns* (1934). Although his personal notices were good, the film was not the commercial success which the studio had envisaged. He was loaned to Fox for a couple of pictures before returning to his home lot where he had leading roles in three mysteries including the fast moving *Fog Over Frisco* (1934). Although his peers regarded him technically as a very sound actor, this film revealed his weakness as a film player namely that he was always somewhat bland. His on-screen personality lacked the dynamism of James Cagney and Pat O'Brien.

He was loaned to MGM for the small role of Charles Darnay for whom Sidney Carton (Ronald Colman) goes to the guillotine in *A Tale of Two Cities* (1935). It is a little surprising that he was cast in this film because the essence of the novel is that Carton and Darnay bore a strong facial resemblance to one another whereas Colman and Woods were not in the least bit alike. Woods had featured roles in two major productions at Warners which were *Anthony Adverse* (1936) and *The Story of Louis Pasteur* (1936).

By the late thirties he slipped into the ranks of players who proliferated in second features. Warners continued to pick up his option because they found it profitable to loan him to other studios. He made a competent Perry Mason in *The Case of the Stuttering Bishop* (1937). Some of these "B" pictures such as *Danger on the Air* (1938) opposite Nan Grey were of excellent quality. They teamed so well professionally that it led to him having a long-running part as Dr. Leslie Foster with Grey in the radio serial *Those We Love* (1938–1945). He played the long-suffering spouse of the Mexican Spitfire (Lupe Velez) in the first three entries of the film series shot at the RKO Radio Studios. He admitted in later years that he accepted many "B" pictures because he was raising a young family at the time and could not afford to turn down many assignments. He also found it fun to make most of them. His biggest professional disappointment was not landing the role of George Gipp which Ronald Reagan played in *Knute Rockne All American* (1940). From 1937 onwards he served on the Board of the Screen Actors Guild.

His first love remained the theater and in 1940 he toplined at the Guild Theater on Broadway in *Quiet Please*, but the play folded after only sixteen performances. When he returned to Hollywood he starred in his only serial the twelve chapter *Sky Raiders* (1941) at Universal. During the forties he continued to play leading roles in quickies and small parts in bigger films. A Warner Bros. two reeler in which he appeared entitled *Star in the Night* won an Oscar for best short subject. In 1949 he accompanied Constance Bennett and Charles Ruggles to Berlin where they appeared in the play *Over 21* for the forces stationed in that city. They staged the same play in Paris and Copenhagen.

During the fifties his film activity decreased, but he made many television appearances notably in live anthology shows and hosted others. His main residence at this time was at Old Greenwich, Connecticut, but he could not adjust to the climate. He was the star of the crime series *Craig Kennedy Criminologist*. Craig Kennedy was the hero of a series of novels by Arthur B. Reeve which appeared between 1912 and 1936. The character featured in half a dozen movies between 1915 and 1936. In 1951 he became the hero

Donald Woods in the film *Corregidor* (1943). He later starred in the television series *Craig Kennedy Criminologist*.

of a television series in which he was a criminologist working at Columbia University with Woods in the leading role. He was supported by Sydney Mason who played Police Inspector J.J. Burke and Lewis Wilson who played Evening Star reporter, Walter Jameson. In this well made series there was as much emphasis on gun and fist fights as there was on deductions and reasoning. The series was an early attempt to show the importance of forensic science in crime deduction which became a staple element of more recent crime series. There were 26 half hour, black and white, filmed episodes produced by the Weiss Brothers as a syndicated series. It was the first series to be shown in American army hospitals abroad. According to actress Mara Corday, who appeared in one episode "Tall, Dark and Dead," the series ended in rather a bizarre way when Woods suffered a nervous breakdown on the set and was carted off to a mental hospital on a stretcher to recuperate.

Woods was later heard on CBS radio as the host of the variety program *The Woolworth Hour* in 1955. During the fifties he toured in road show versions of popular plays. In 1959 he visited Palm Springs for the first time to do a play, fell in love with the climate and lifestyle of the place and decided to relocate there with his family. Much of his income in later years was derived from commission received for brokering successful real estate deals in the Palm Springs area. In 1960 he played the lawyer in *Two For the Seesaw* for six months in Los Angeles before touring and doing summer stock. In 1962 he received excellent notices in a short-lived play Ibsen's *Rosmersholm* off–Broadway. In 1965 he had a leading role in Dore Schary's play *One By One* which opened at the Belasco Theater, New York, but flopped. His most consistent work in television during the sixties was playing the regular role of Johnny Brent in the sitcom *Tammy* for 26 episodes. In 1970 he did summer stock and subsequently appeared in three highly successful revivals in Chicago. In the early seventies he was the guest actor in residence at the Seattle Repertory Theater. He also backed promising new plays such as *Nuts* which was originally staged in Los Angeles in 1972 and was later filmed with Barbra Streisand. One of his last recorded television appearances was an episode of *Mississippi* in 1984.

He married Josephine Van der Horck in 1927 who died in 1972. With her he had a son Conrad who became a tennis professional and oil painter and a daughter Linda who married and lived in Florida. In 1976 he married his first wife's best friend Ella Harlan in London, England who also predeceased him. Afterwards he had a close relationship with actress Marsha Hunt.

Woods died in his sleep at his home at the Las Palmas Retirement Center in Palm Springs, CA on March 5, 1998 aged 91. He was survived by both his children and five grandchildren.

Filmography

1934: *As the Earth Turns, Charlie Chan's Courage, The Merry Wives of Reno, Sweet Adeline, Fog Over Frisco, She Was a Lady.*

1935: *The Case of the Curious Bride, The Frisco Kid, Stranded, The Florentine Dagger, A Tale of Two Cities, Anna Karenina.*

1936: *Anthony Adverse, The Story of Louis Pasteur, Isle of Fury, A Son Comes Home, Road Gang, The White Angel.*

1937: *Big Town Girl, Once a Doctor, Charlie Chan on Broadway, Talent Scout, Sea Devils, The Case of the Stuttering Bishop.*

1938: *I Am the Law, The Black Doll, Romance on the Run, Danger on the Air.*

1939: *Heritage of the Desert, Beauty for the Asking, The Girl from Mexico, The Mexican Spitfire.*

1940: *Mexican Spitfire Out West, Forgotten Girls, City of Chance, Love Honor and Oh Baby!, If I Had My Way.*
1941: *Bachelor Daddy, I Was a Prisoner on Devil's Island, Sky Raiders* (serial).
1942: *The Gay Sisters, Thru Different Eyes.*
1943: *Corregidor, Hi Ya Sailor!, So's Your Uncle, Watch on the Rhine.*
1944: *The Bridge of San Luis Rey, Hollywood Canteen, The Life of Goebbels, Enemy of Women.*
1945: *God is My Co-Pilot, Wonder Man, Roughly Speaking, Voice of the Whistler.*
1946: *Night and Day, Never Say Goodbye, The Time the Place and the Girl.*
1947: *The Return of Rin Tin Tin, The Bells of San Fernando, Stepchild.*
1949: *Daughter of the West, Barbary Pirate, Scene of the Crime, Free for All.*
1950: *The Lost Volcano, Mr. Music, Johnny One-Eye.*
1951: *All That I Have.*
1953: *The Beast From 20,000 Fathoms, Born to the Saddle.*
1959: *I'll Give My Life.*
1960: *Thirteen Ghosts.*
1961: *Five Minutes to Live.*
1964: *Kissin' Cousins.*
1965: *The Satan Bug.*
1966: *Dimension 5, Moment to Moment.*
1967: *Istanbul Express* (TV), *A Time to Sing.*
1969: *True Grit.*

Television Series

1951–1952: *Craig Kennedy Criminologist* as Craig Kennedy.
1953–1954: *The Orchid Award* Host.
1955–1956: *Damon Runyon Theatre* Host.
1965–1966: *Tammy* as John Brent.

Sources

Collura, Joe. "Nice Guys Don't Always Finish Last." *Classic Images*. No. 215. May 1993.
DeLong, Thomas. *Radio Stars*. Jefferson, NC: McFarland, 1996.
Lamparski, Richard. *Whatever Became Of?* 9th Series. New York: Crown, 1985.
Lentz, Harris M. III. *Obituaries in the Performing Arts, 1998*. Jefferson, NC: McFarland, 1999.
Magers, Boyd. *Western Clippings*. No. 23 May/June 1998.
Picture Show Annual. London: Amalgamated, 1936, 1937, 1941 and 1942.
Quinlan, David. *Film Stars*. 5th ed. London: Batsford, 2000.
Tibballs, Geoff. *TV Detectives*. London: Boxtree, 1992.
Weaver, Tom. *It Came from Weaver Five*. Jefferson, NC: McFarland, 1996.

Trudy Wroe

Trudy Wroe was originally a model from 1951 onwards. Her film career was negligible, but she was the sixth and final actress to play Lorelei Kilbourne in the newspaper drama series *Big Town* which starred Mark Stevens as Steve Wilson. She only played the part for one season between 1954 and 1955. When Stevens revamped the series the following season, her character was dropped. She did commercials including an extended one for Ford motors which involved traveling on a bus up the coast of California with a group of actors. One was Don Durant whom she married on February 28, 1959. Durant was the star of the western series *Johnny Ringo* who eventually became a realtor and investment broker. With him she had a daughter Heidi born in 1962 and a son Jeff who was born in 1964. From 1959 to 1998 they lived in Encino, California. In June 1998 they moved to a new home they built in Dana Point, California. They also traveled extensively. She was widowed in 2005.

Filmography

1953: *Son of Sinbad.*
1956: *Beyond a Reasonable Doubt.*

Television Series

1954–1955: *Big Town* as Lorelei Kilbourne.

Sources

TV Guide. "Model Wives." Undated.
TV/Radio Mirror. May 1960.
TV Yearbook. #8. 1959.

Fred Wynn

Fred Wynn played the role of Lt. Bill Hollis in the crime series *Code 3*. He was one of the assistants of Assistant Sheriff Barnett (Richard Travis) of the Los Angeles Sheriff's Department as they conducted investigations into serious crimes which were homicide, grand theft and kidnapping. This appears to have been Wynn's only credit and he has latterly been posted amongst the lost players of the screen.

Television Series

1957: *Code 3* as Lt. Bill Hollis.

Source

Tibballs, Geoff. *TV Detectives*. London: Boxtree, 1992.

BARTON YARBOROUGH

Barton Yarborough was born in Goldthwaite, Texas on October 2, 1900. He ran away from home to join vaudeville and had a solid background in community theater. He was a member of Eva Le Gallienne's repertory company. During the 1920s he entered radio. In 1932 he began playing Cliff Barbour in the highly successful radio soap opera *One Man's Family* which he continued to broadcast in until his death. He entered films in 1940. By far his most famous film role was as the southern accented Doc Long in the short-lived Columbia mystery series, *I Love a Mystery*, a role which he had played on radio.

In 1949 he began playing Det. Sgt. Ben Romero in the *Dragnet* radio series opposite Jack Webb as Det. Sgt. Joe Friday. He was a close friend of Webb in real life and was a drinking and poker playing buddy of his. When the series transferred to television in December 1951, Yarborough moved with it and his future seemed assured. Unfortunately he had only shot the first two episodes, when the day after shooting the second, he fell seriously ill and died four days later in Burbank, California on December 19, 1951 at the age of 51. The official cause of death was a heart attack. In a case of art imitating life, Webb had the character in the television series expire in exactly the same way.

Yarborough married actress Vera Vague (a.k.a. Barbara Jo Allen) and with her had a daughter named Joan who was born in 1930. Sometimes he and his wife worked together on radio notably in *One Man's Family*. They also appeared together in a two reeler called *Hiss and Tell* (1946) which won an Oscar nomination as best short. By that time however they were divorced.

Filmography

1940: *Before I Hang*.
1941: *They Meet Again, Let's Go Collegiate*.
1942: *The Ghost of Frankenstein, Saboteur*.
1945: *I Love a Mystery* (DL), *Captain Tugboat Annie, Red Dragon*.
1946: *Idea Girl, The Devil's Mask* (DL), *The Unknown* (DL), *Wife Wanted*.
1947: *Kilroy Was Here*.
1948: *The Babe Ruth Story*.
1949: *Henry the Rainmaker*.

Note: Films in which Yarborough played the part of Doc Long are denoted DL in the filmography.

Television Series

1951: *Dragnet* as Det. Sgt. Ben Romero.

Sources

Brooks, Tim. *The Complete Directory to Prime Time TV Stars, 1946–Present*. New York: Ballantine, 1987.
DeLong, Thomas A. *Radio Stars*. Jefferson, NC: McFarland, 1996.
McClelland, Doug. "Vera Vague of Mirth and Men." *Films of the Golden Age*. Number 34. Fall 2003.

JOHN ZAREMBA

John Zaremba was born in Chicago, Illinois on October 22, 1908. He was a prolific television performer. He had a semi-regular role as Special Agent Jerry Dressler, the F.B.I. Contact for Herbert Philbrick (Richard Carlson), in the television series *I Led 3 Lives*. Zaremba is better remembered for playing Dr. Raymond Swain in the sci-fi series *The Time Tunnel*. He later had a recurring role in the prime time soap opera *Dallas* in which he continued to appear until his death. He died in Newport Beach, California on December 15, 1986 aged 78 of a heart attack.

Filmography

1950: *Pirates of the High Seas* (serial).
1952: *Young Man with Ideas*.
1953: *The Magnetic Monster*.
1954: *Human Desire*.
1955: *Tight Spot, Cell 2455 Death Row, 5 Against the House, Chicago Syndicate, Apache Ambush*.
1956: *Ransom!, The Houston Story, Earth vs. The Flying Saucers, He Laughed Last, The Power and the Prize, Reprisal!*
1957: *Hit and Run, The Night the World Exploded, 20 Million Miles to Earth, Zero Hour!*
1958: *Young and Wild, The Case Against Brooklyn, The Saga of Hemp Brown, Tarawa Beachhead, Frankenstein's Daughter*.

1959: *Battle of the Coral Sea, Vice Raid.*
1960: *Because They're Young, The Gallant Hours, Key Witness.*
1962: *Dangerous Charter.*
1963: *A Gathering of Eagles.*
1966: *Follow Me Boys.*
1970: *R.P.M.*
1971: *Scandalous John.*
1972: *The War Between Men and Women.*
1974: *Herbie Rides Again, Manhunter* (TV).
1975: *The Abduction of Saint Anne* (TV), *The Legend of Lizzie Borden* (TV).
1977: *The Death of Richie* (TV), *Brothers.*
1978: *Return to Fantasy Island* (TV), *The Time Machine* (TV).
1979: *The Ordeal of Patty Hearst* (TV).
1981: *The Sophisticated Gents* (TV), *Advice to the Lovelorn* (TV).

TELEVISION SERIES

1953–1956: *I Led 3 Lives* as Agent Jerry Dressler.
1966–1967: *The Time Tunnel* as Dr. Raymond Swain.
1978–1986: *Dallas* as Dr. Harlen Danvers.

SOURCES

Brooks, Tim. *The Complete Directory to Prime Time TV Stars, 1946–Present.* New York: Ballantine, 1987.
Ward, Jack. *Television Guest Stars.* Jefferson, NC: McFarland, 1993.

EFREM ZIMBALIST, JR.

Talent and hard work won Efrem Zimbalist, Jr., the lead in two of the most exciting crime series ever on television *77 Sunset Strip* and *The FBI.* Quinn Martin, executive producer of *The FBI,* summed up his success story, "Efrem has the knack of looking intellectually tough rather than just plain rough." Zimbalist's daughter Stephanie attributes his appeal to three factors, "Nobility, integrity and humility." If an individual had a problem whether legal or medical, business or romantic the characters he played were usually the ones people desired as their counselors. He also radiated sophistication and savoir-faire. One of his achievements may be unique in the annals of show business namely that he may be the only actor who has been a star of a television series or miniseries in every decade since the 1950s.

Efrem Zimbalist, Jr., was born in New York City on November 30, 1918. He is the son of Russian born Efrem Zimbalist, Sr. (1889–1985), a world famous violinist, and Rumanian born Reba Feinsohn (1884–1938), known professionally as opera singer Alma Gluck. He had a sister Maria Virginia born in 1916 and a half sister on his mother's side, Marcia Davenport (1905–1996), the best selling novelist who wrote *Valley of Decision.* He was educated at Fay School, Southborough, Massachusetts and St. Paul's Preparatory School, Concord, New Hampshire. He went to Yale University, but was thrown out twice for "high jinks and low marks."

He went to New York and became a page at the NBC radio network. He decided he wanted to be a radio star, rehearsed a number of different accents and was finally given a part. It led nowhere. He studied drama at the Neighborhood Playhouse in New York until April 2, 1941 with the intention of becoming an actor. Instead World War II intervened. He served as a First Lieutenant in the US infantry, was wounded in action and was awarded the Purple Heart. During the war he met Alfred Lunt and made friends with Joshua Logan and Garson Kanin.

Afterwards he returned to New York where he made his professional stage debut in *The Rugged Path* which starred Spencer Tracy in November 1945. He joined the prestigious American Repertory Theater which was an attempt to start an Old Vic in New York. He appeared in many distinguished plays frequently rehearsing one as he was appearing in another. He established a reputation as a successful producer when he co-produced the operas *The Medium, The Telephone* and *The Consul* at the Barrymore Theater, New York. For his efforts as a producer he won a Pulitzer Prize in 1950. He made his screen debut in *House of Strangers* (1949) which starred Edward G. Robinson.

In 1950 after the death of his first wife he dropped out of acting completely and served as assistant to his father at the Curtis Institute of Music in Philadelphia. When he felt able to face an audience again, he returned to the theater, aiming for Broadway. He recommenced his career by joining a stock company in Hammonton, New Jersey in 1954. He simultaneously appeared in a daytime soap *Concerning Miss Marlowe* in which Louise Allbritton played Margaret Marlowe a middle aged actress who recalls her love affairs.

He played suave international lawyer Jim Gavin. His outstanding performance on Broadway in the play *Fallen Angels* in 1955 secured him a Warner Bros. contract. Nothing much happened until Joshua Logan recommended him for a leading role as an Air Force Colonel who commands Karl Malden and romances his daughter Natalie Wood in *Bombers B-52*(1957).

He made six theatrical features for Warners of which *Home Before Dark* (1958) in which he starred opposite Jean Simmons was his personal favorite. After these he was offered the leading role of private investigator Stuart Bailey in *77 Sunset Strip*. He recalls, "The reason I ended up doing the series was that I had no choice—the small print in my contract stated that Warner Bros. had the right to use me in TV." The origins of *77 Sunset Strip* lay in some novellas which Roy Huggins had penned. Two of them appeared in "The Saturday Evening Post" in 1946, while another appeared in "Esquire" magazine in 1952. One of these *I Love Trouble* had been made into a film in 1948 by Columbia Pictures with Franchot Tone as the smooth private investigator, Stuart Bailey. In this film however Bailey did not operate from offices on the Sunset Strip. From another derived a screenplay "Anything for Money" which appeared in a Warner Bros. anthology *Conflict* in 1956, this being Zimbalist's first connection with the role. From a third, scripted by Marion Hargrove, derived a motion picture, *Girl on the Run* (1958), in which Stuart Bailey saved a nightclub singer who was menaced by a hired killer also served as pilot to the series. The young hair-combing killer played by Edd Byrnes quickly reformed and became a mainstay of the series as Kookie. A new official pilot "Lovely Lady, Pity Me," which was shown on the ABC network on October 19, 1958, marked the start of the series and was also a complicated ruse to ensure that Warners did not have to pay Roy Huggins any royalties. This was the first hour length private detective series.

Stuart Bailey was a suave ex–OSS officer, languages expert and Ivy League PhD. He was the son of a professor of languages at Harvard. On his return to civilian life, he did not fancy the sedate university milieu. So he pulled up his roots and went to the West Coast to open a detective agency. His partner was Jeff Spencer (Roger Smith), a former government undercover agent who had a law degree. Together they operated from *77 Sunset Strip*. Producer Howie Horwitz once explained about the origin of the show's title. "The Strip is one-and-a-half miles of Sunset Boulevard in Los Angeles. It consists of expensive shops, night clubs and restaurants. We picked it because we wanted a glamorous location for Bailey's office. We chose the number 77 merely because it is alliterative—it fits in well with Sunset Strip." At the time the real Number 77 was a model agency and the proprietor of the agency who ran it was besieged with tourists demanding to see Stuart Bailey's office. Their cases took them all over the world. They were never far from beautiful women either. At the time when he first began to do the show, Zimbalist confessed that he knew less about real life private investigators than anyone else of his acquaintance. He learned quickly because his characterization was very convincing. It became an enormously successful series. During the 1959–1960 season it was the most popular ABC network show, ranking sixth. It was ranked thirteenth during the 1960–1961 season and thirtieth during the 1961–1962 season. He received a single Emmy award nomination in 1958–1959 as Best Actor in a Leading Role (Continuing Character) in a Dramatic Series, but lost to Raymond Burr for *Perry Mason*.

The episode of *77 Sunset Strip* which showcased him to best advantage was "Reserved For Mr. Bailey" which originally aired on January 8, 1961. Stuart Bailey is lured to his office late one night, knocked unconscious and wakes up in a ghost town in the desert. He finds his name in the hotel register, a reservation and a key. A mysterious voice informs him that he is marked for death. Out in the street is a gallows with a note which reads, "Reserved For Mr. Bailey" attached to the noose. Subsequently Bailey is subjected to guns with no firing pins; a working pay phone but no change; and three wax dummies round a card table with a vacant spot for Bailey where his cards are "dead man's hand." Eventually Bailey gains the upper hand and his potential assassin is killed in a fire. This episode is unique in the series because no one appears in it except Bailey. Even the villain is only a voice (supplied by sometime actor and later director Robert Douglas) and is incinerated off screen. To his credit Zimbalist held audience interest from first to last. This is his personal favorite amongst the episodes, although he believes the real hero was Montgomery Pittman, the man who wrote and directed it.

Next door to No. 77 was Dino's, an upper class restaurant named after Dean Martin, whose

Left to right: Patrice Wymore (guest) and Efrem Zimbalist, Jr., in *77 Sunset Strip*.

jive talking car park attendant Kookie (Edd Byrnes) often featured in the cases and who had ambitions to be a private investigator. The team was completed by Roscoe (Louis Quinn), the racehorse tout and the glamorous French secretary Suzanne Fabray (Jacqueline Beer). For a single season Rex Randolph (Richard Long) was a third partner. Later when Kookie was upped to being a fully fledged private eye he was replaced as a car lot attendant by J.R. Hale (Robert Logan) who spoke in initials. The official law was represented by Det. Lt. Gilmore (Byron Keith). Although Zimbalist has a high regard for both Roger Smith and Edd Byrnes, he admits that he has seldom seen them in recent years. He adds, "Our lives, as is not uncommon in this town, are united only in being disunited!"

He threatened to leave *77 Sunset Strip* in 1962, but executives at Warner Bros. quietly but firmly talked him out of it. The show would have collapsed without him. Despite the attractive gimmicky quality of the performances by members of the supporting cast, he gave the show its strength and stability. In the final season of *77 Sunset Strip*, the format changed. "Never to Have Loved" originally aired on June 14, 1963, was the final Bailey case in the old format. Jack Webb became executive producer and brought his own distinctive style to the show, but it was a shotgun marriage and not a wedding. Webb dropped all of the original cast of the program with the exception of Bailey. He now had new offices at the century old Bradbury Building in downtown Los Angeles which ruined the whole point of the title and a wisecracking secretary Hannah (Joan Staley) to whom he dictated his cases. Webb totally misunderstood the Stuart Bailey character. Bailey was a cavalier, but not a cynic. He was a successful, respected, professional person not some down at heel gumshoe grubbing for dollars and cents by peeking through keyholes.

The final season limped along for twenty episodes of which five were a multipart story entitled "Five Steps to Murder." Bailey found himself hot on the trail of European art treasures stolen by the Nazis. He was seen on New York's East Side, strolling down the Champs Elysees in Paris and Rome's Via Venato. Jack Webb assembled a half million dollar collection of antiques to give the show authenticity. They included two 150 year old French needlepoint chairs and a couple of life sized Italian hand carved statues of musicians thought to be three centuries old. They were selected from a French antique collection bought by the studio just after the war and rated amongst the most valuable props in Hollywood. What remains most vividly in the memory however was the repartee between Bailey and the cynical Det. Lt. Butter (Richard Conte). As usual his leading lady, Diane McBain, was beautiful. She is run down and killed by a hit and run driver leaving Bailey desolate and alone at the end. It took nine writers to concoct this and the guest list was one of the longest and most impressive in television history. It was not enough however. For audiences the new *77 Sunset Strip* was a mass turnoff and the ratings declined. *77 Sunset Strip* ended after six seasons and 206 episodes in September 1964.

In between seasons of *77 Sunset Strip* Zimbalist sandwiched a few features. The main ones were based on bestselling novels which failed to ignite on screen. A typical example was *By Love Possessed* (1961) which took the cozy, shiny lid of American upper middle class life and revealed all kinds of mud and marital unhappiness below. He was cast as ambitious New England attorney, Arthur Winner, who is having a torrid affair with his impotent partner Julius Penrose's (Jason Robards) tramp of a wife Marjorie (Lana Turner). It was adapted from the novel by James Gould

Cozzens, but suffered in the transition because it attempted to make a subordinate character (Turner) the focus of the film. John Sturges the director was renowned for action films, but was in out of his depth. Jason Robards, who was particularly caustic about this movie, said the title should have been changed to *By Love Depressed*! The low box office returns from these outings gave weight to Jack Warner's contention, that once an actor had been continuously exposed on television, his name had very little box office value left.

After *77 Sunset Strip* ceased production Zimbalist asked for and obtained his contract release from Warners to concentrate on features. He scarcely broke stride before he was back in another long-running television series. He recalls, "My reasons for actually seeking a second series, in contrast to having been carried, as it were, bound and gagged to the first were the poor quality of the material I was offered in the intervening year and a half. The two films (*Harlow* and *The Reward*) were frightful, and although television was kinder to me during that period, I felt *The FBI* offered the most promise at a time when the movie kingdoms were breaking up into principalities and the principalities seemed ready to rush headlong into anarchy with scarcely a backward glance." Before accepting the role however he checked with David Janssen who was then starring in *The Fugitive,* another QM Production. Janssen strongly urged him to accept the lead. Zimbalist's career received a big boost when he was personally chosen by J. Edgar Hoover, Director of the FBI, to play Inspector Lewis Erskine in the new Quinn Martin/Warner Bros. television series *The FBI*. This institution had been popular in movies since the early sound period and many actors had been well cast as agents, but he personified the calm, professional, businesslike agent who tracked down his quarry with a maximum of efficiency and a minimum of emotion.

The format of the show became stereotyped over the years. Each episode started with a crime. Prior to the opening credits, there would be a freeze frame and the criminal's name, crime and file number would be blazed across the screen. Afterwards Lewis Erskine and his team would investigate the crime, interview the suspects, possibly go undercover and arrest the culprits. The series had surface gloss, slickness of production and a very high degree of professional competence in all areas. The cases were fictionalized versions of authentic FBI files. They ranged across the United States and involved counterfeiters, extortionists, the Mafia, Communist spies and radical bombings and terrorism during the era of Vietnam dissent.

Assistant FBI director Arthur Ward (Philip Abbott) lasted throughout all nine seasons, but Erskine's partner changed. His first assistant from 1965 to 1967 was Special Agent Jim Rhodes (Stephen Brooks). A theme in the first season was the conflict between Erskine and Rhodes who wanted to marry Erskine's daughter Barbara (Lynn Loring). Since Erskine had lost his own wife when she was gunned down by bullets intended for him, he had no desire to see his own daughter end up the same way. The matter was never resolved since Miss Loring was dropped from the cast for the second season. Zimbalist had not been too happy about this soap opera aspect of the series from the outset and his instincts proved sound when the ratings dramatically increased from the second season onwards. William Reynolds played Special Agent Tom Colby from 1967 to 1973. For the final season Shelly Novack took over as Special Agent Chris Daniels.

Before being allowed to play Erskine an exhaustive check was carried out on Zimbalist by the real FBI. They already had his fingerprints on file from the days when he served in the American forces during World War II. They also checked on whether he had any criminal convictions; was a compulsive gambler; alcoholic; income tax evader; and on his political beliefs. He emerged with a character a judge could envy. For three weeks he was a student at the FBI Academy at Quantico, Virginia where trainee G Men live like monks, while they are taught a range of skills including marksmanship and effective surveillance.

He visited Washington to be filmed driving past several famous landmarks. He met J. Edgar Hoover several times during the run of the series. Hoover emerged with a glowing opinion of the actor. He said, "Efrem has captured the esprit de corps of the FBI.... He has helped to depict the dedication of law enforcement officers to duty, integrity and law and order." The FBI found themselves deluged with letters from viewers saying that Inspector Erskine portrayed what they thought a real G Man should look and act like. Quinn Martin was even more enthusiastic. He said, "Efrem off screen is a man of quiet tastes and sober habits ... if any one man has sold this series to Hoover and the American public it is

Efrem." In addition to his salary Quinn Martin gave Zimbalist a twenty per cent ownership of the series. Zimbalist signed on initially for five years and wanted to quit after that because of the demands of the series. Quinn Martin persuaded him to continue for another five years. One incentive was increasing his ownership to twenty five per cent of the series.

The FBI, which was long the anchor of the ABC network's Sunday night lineup, lasted through nine seasons and 236 episodes. It was ranked 29th in the list of most highly rated programs during the 1966–1967 season, 22nd during the 1967–1968 season, 18th in the 1968–1969 season, 24th in the 1969–1970 season, 10th in the 1970–1971 season, 17th in the 1971–1972 season and 29th in the 1972–1973 season. It received a single Emmy award nomination during the 1968–1969 season as Outstanding Dramatic Series. Some early episodes of the series in which Erskine confronted the Mafia were edited excitingly into a clumsily titled feature film *Cosa Nostra, An Arch Enemy of the FBI* (1967) and released theatrically overseas. The series was still riding high in the ratings when it was axed which was an inexplicable network decision. ABC replaced it with *The Sonny Comedy Hour* which starred Sonny Bono. This was hardly a fair exchange especially as the substitute proved to be one of the biggest disasters the network ever had in the ratings and failed to last a season.

Once *The FBI* ceased Zimbalist was faced with the same problem all actors in long-running series have namely typecasting. The only outside work which he had been able to fit in during these years was playing Sam Hendrix, the husband of Audrey Hepburn, in the highly successful thriller *Wait Until Dark* (1967). He particularly enjoyed working with Miss Hepburn. The coming of the permissive era however had created a new breed of hero: violent, promiscuous, musclebound and inarticulate. One kind of movie which he was suited for was the disaster cycle. He played the blinded airline pilot Troy Stacy for Universal in *Airport 1975* (1974). His Jumbo Jet 747 is involved in a mid-air collision with a small plane whose pilot Scott Freeman (Dana Andrews) has suffered a fatal heart attack. One scene where Stacy is carried off the stricken plane once it has landed was never filmed because the budget had run out. Film buffs were quick to point out the coincidence of Zimbalist piloting the big plane and Andrews the little plane when the reverse had been true in *The Crowded Sky* (1960). The characterization in the scripts of these films was particularly dim and relied extensively on high caliber players to flesh them out. *Airport 1975* was a box office bonanza.

Zimbalist was absent from the screen for the next few years during which time there were reports that he had semi-retired to play golf and was contemplating running for Governor of California. Around this time he said, "I wouldn't mind returning to the TV grind, but it certainly isn't a burning ambition with me." More recently he recalled, "*The FBI* was enormously popular.... Of course Hollywood hated the show. They hated Hoover and they hated me for being in the show. I lost work because of it.... They never talk about the second black list." Quinn Martin had created a clever idea for a new series *Ladies Man* in which Zimbalist would star as an attorney who only accepted females as clients. The networks flatly refused to consider that one and it never even reached the pilot stage. One that did was a comedy *Wild About Harry* which was developed from 1976 onwards, but surfaced on NBC two years later. This was a situation comedy in which Zimbalist played a divorced architect who falls in love with a lady half his age. It met with very positive audience reaction when it was shown and Zimbalist loved the idea because he believed that it would enable his career to take off in another direction. This one was scuppered by one of the network executives who stated that the problem with it was that Zimbalist was an FBI agent and no way could an FBI agent be allowed to star in a comedy. This proved to be a particular disappointment to him.

Instead he resurfaced in a television movie *A Family Upside Down* (1978) for which he received an Emmy award nomination as Outstanding Performance by a Supporting Actor in a Comedy or Drama Special. This rekindled his ambition and over the next few years he appeared in some films for television. One of his most characteristic roles was in *Terror Out of the Sky* (1978) in which he played Dr. David Martin, Head of the National Bee Centre in New Orleans, who saves a community from a swarm of killer bees, but only at the cost of his own life. There were some particularly attractive romantic interludes in which Martin dallied with his assistant, Jeannie Devereaux (Tovah Feldshuh). This combination of science fiction and romance ranked amongst his personal favorites. The film was a sequel to *The Savage Bees* (1976) in which he did not appear. The character of Jeannie Devereaux in the earlier film was played by another actress Gretchen Corbett.

He again tried to return to series television on more familiar ground in the early 1980s with *A Family in Blue* in which he played the patriarch of a family who all have some connection with the police force, but only the pilot was shot. One ambition which he did fulfill in 1983 was when he appeared with his daughter Stephanie in "The Sting of Steele" episode of *Remington Steele*. He played a charming confidence trickster, Daniel Chalmers. They had a very memorable scene together where they gracefully danced a waltz whilst simultaneously furthering the plot. This scene was so well played that it has become part of the folklore of 1980s television. His character was so well received that he went on to play the character again in several other episodes of the series, although the final revelation that he was Remington Steele's father was very unconvincing. He had a running role in one season of the Aaron Spelling show *Hotel* (1986) as the leader of the consortium striving to acquire the hotel. He also found time to return to the stage in limited engagements of a number of classic plays.

He was a particular favorite of executives at the Family Channel who persuaded him to play Zorro's father during the first season of *Zorro* with Duncan Regehr in the title role. It was shot in Spain, but located in nineteenth century California. He found the role a welcome change. He enthused, "Zorro is almost classical in style. This production transposes you into a different mindset with its colorful costumes and sets." The location shooting was by all accounts terribly arduous and he was missing his home so he relinquished the role to Henry Darrow in the later seasons.

During the nineties his distinctive voice was as much in demand as his physical presence and he voiced such diverse characters as Alfred, the butler, in *Batman* and King Arthur in *The Legend of Prince Valiant*, both animated series. He has also read audio books. With guest shots on television he has maintained a higher profile than many of his contemporaries who have simply folded their tents and disappeared into the shadows. He also had a successful one man show *MacArthur* in which he toured.

For forty years he lived on an estate in Encino, California which was a haven for wildlife. For recreation he played tennis and golf. He has long been active in Republican politics and did public relations and civic duties in Los Angeles.

In terms of religious beliefs he is a Born Again Christian. He currently resides in Solvang, California. He has supported national charities such as Childhelp USA as a celebrity ambassador. In May 2000 he was awarded a humanitarian award, The Hands of Compassion, for his efforts. In 2003 a memoir written by him, *My Dinner of Herbs*, was published and he undertook a national tour publicizing it. In California in 2004 he appeared with daughter Stephanie on stage for the first time together in the classic play, *Night of the Iguana*, by Tennessee Williams. Interestingly he played her grandfather in the play.

He married Emily McNair in 1941, an aspiring actress whom he met at the Neighborhood Theatre. She died in 1950. He has a daughter Nancy born in 1945 who during the nineties was Program Administrator for the Virginia Slims Tennis Championships. His son Efrem III, who was born in 1948, is President and Chief Executive Officer of his own company of magazines. He has four grandchildren, all his son's children. Zimbalist married again on February 12, 1956 to Loranda Stephanie Spalding. The marriage was dissolved in December 1961. Realizing divorce was a mistake, they remarried in 1972. He has a daughter Stephanie who was born in New York on October 8, 1956. She is an actress best known for her role as Laura Holt, female private eye in the *Remington Steele* series and for a number of television movies. Although he has always declared he became an actor by process of career elimination, he is one person who did find his true vocation in life.

FILMOGRAPHY

1949: *House of Strangers*.
1957: *Bombers B-52* (a.k.a. *No Sleep Till Dawn*), *Band of Angels*.
1958: *Too Much Too Soon, The Deep Six, Home Before Dark, Violent Road, Girl on the Run* (TV).
1960: *The Crowded Sky*.
1961: *A Fever in the Blood, By Love Possessed*.
1962: *The Chapman Report*.
1965: *The Reward, Harlow* (electronovision version).
1967: *Wait Until Dark, Cosa Nostra—An Arch Enemy of the FBI* (TV).
1974: *Airport 1975*.
1975: *Who is the Black Dahlia?* (TV).
1978: *A Family Upside Down* (TV), *Terror Out of the Sky* (TV).
1979: *The Best Place To Be* (TV), *The Gathering Part II* (TV).

1981: *The Avenging*.
1983: *The Baby Sister* (TV), *Shooting Stars* (TV).
1988: *Elmira* (a.k.a. *A Place Called Elmira, The Street Corner Kids*).
1989: *The Street Corner Kids: The Sequel*.
1991: *Hot Shots*.
1998: *Cab to Canada* (TV).

TELEVISION SERIES

1954–1955: *Concerning Miss Marlowe* as Jim Gavin.
1958–1964: *77 Sunset Strip* as Stuart Bailey.
1965–1974: *The FBI* as Inspector Lewis Erskine.
1986: *Hotel* as Charles Cabot.
1989–1990: *Zorro* as Don Alejandro Sebastian de la Vega.
1999: *A Year to Remember* Host and narrator.

MINISERIES

1980: *Scruples*.
1993: *Trade Winds*.
2001: *The First Day* (a.k.a. *Dawn of Our Nation*).

SOURCES

ATV Television Showbook. London: Purnell, 1961 and 1962.
Boehme, Christina. *Films of the Golden Age*. No. 29. Summer 2002.
Correspondence between Zimbalist and the author.
Current Biography. New York: H. Wilson, 1960.
Etter, Jonathan. *Quinn Martin, Producer*. Jefferson, NC: McFarland, 2003.
Graham, John. "The Right Man for the Job." *TV Times*. August 31, 1967.
Griffiths, David. "The 77 Sunset Strip Story." *TV Times*. October 30, 1960.
Laing, Nora. "The Eyes of 77 Sunset Strip." *TV Times*. September 4, 1959.
Meyers, Ric. *Murder on the Air*. New York: Mysterious, 1989.
Photoplay. "Father's advice" 1980.
_____. "Whatever Happened to Efrem Zimbalist Jr.?" 1977.
Stoddard, Sylvia. *Television Chronicles*. No. 12. January 1998.
TV Star Annual. No. 7. 1959.
TV Times. "FBI Get Their Man." 1965.
TV Times. "Stripped of Opportunity." 1988.
TV Times. "Stuart Bailey of Five." 1964.
Variety "A Place Called Elmira." February 1994.
Variety. "Zorro" review. February 1990.
Weekend. "On the Sunny Side of the Strip." April 17–23, 1963.
Woman. Biography, 1960s.
Woolley, Lynn, Robert W. Malsbury, and Robert G. Strange Jr. *Warner Bros. Television*. Jefferson, NC: McFarland, 1985.
Yenne, Bill. *The Legend of Zorro*. Greenwich, CT: Brompton, 1991.
Zimbalist, Efrem Jr. *My Dinner of Herbs*. New York: Limelight, 2003.

APPENDIX 1: TELEVISION SERIES CATALOG

Information about television series is presented in the following order:

Title; alternative title; country of origin; original airdates; production company or producer; network or syndicated; number of episodes; black and white or color; live or filmed; length of each episode; plot synopsis; prime time series time of airing; names of players who appear in this book.

1. *The Adventures of Dr. Fu Manchu* USA 1955–1956 Television Programs of America/Studio City TV Productions, Inc. (Republic). Syndicated, 13 episodes. B/W Film, ½ hour.

Plots hatched by Oriental arch fiend in quest for world domination based on characters created by Sax Rohmer.
Glen Gordon, Lester Matthews, Clark Howat, Carla Balenda, Laurette Luez, John George.

2. *The Adventures of Ellery Queen* USA Oct. 14, 1950–Nov. 26, 1952 Norman and Irving Pincus. DuMont/ABC, 78 episodes. B/W Live, ½ hour.

Cases of famed crimewriting sleuth and his policeman father created by Frederic Dannay and Manfred B. Lee.

DuMont	9/50–12/51	Thursday	9–9:30
ABC	12/51–3/52	Sunday	7:30–8
ABC	4/52–12/52	Wednesday	9–9:30

Richard Hart, Lee Bowman, Florenz Ames.

3. *Adventures of the Falcon* USA 1955 Federal Telefilms Inc. Syndicated, 39 episodes. B/W Film, ½ hour.

Escapades of Michael Waring, international secret agent, code name "The Falcon," both in the USA and overseas.
Charles McGraw.

Adventures of McGraw see *Meet McGraw*

Adventures of Scott Island see *Harbormaster*

4. *African Patrol* GB 1957–1958 Grosse-Krasne/Kenya Productions. Syndicated, 39 episodes. B/W Film, ½ hour.

Cases of a British patrol inspector stationed in Kenya.
John Bentley

5. *The Amazing Mr. Malone* USA Sept. 24, 1951–Mar. 10, 1952 Edgar Peterson. ABC, 13 episodes. B/W Live, ½ hour.

Cases of a wisecracking, womanizing lawyer.
Monday 8–8:30
Lee Tracy.

Badge 714 see *Dragnet*

6. *Barney Blake Police Reporter* USA April 22, 1948–July 8, 1948 Wynn Wright. NBC, 13 episodes. B/W Live, ½ hour.

Crime-solving adventures of police reporter and his Girl Friday.
Thursday 9:30–10
Gene O'Donnell, Judy Parrish.

7. *Behind Closed Doors* USA Oct. 2, 1958–April 9, 1959 Screen Gems. NBC, 26 episodes. B/W Film, ½ hour.

Anthology series dramatizing case files of admiral in naval intelligence.
Thursday 9–9:30
Bruce Gordon.

8. *Biff Baker USA* USA Nov. 13, 1952–Mar. 26, 1953 Revue. CBS, 26 episodes. B/W Film, ½ hour.

Adventures encountered by husband and wife team while running an import business all over the world.

608   Appendix 1: Television Series Catalog

Thursday 9–9:30
Alan Hale, Jr., Randy Stuart.

9. *Big Town* a.k.a. *City Assignment, Heart of the City, Headline, Byline Steve Wilson* USA Oct. 5, 1950–Oct. 2, 1956 Gross Krasne/Mark Stevens Television Productions. CBS/Dum/NBC, 240 episodes. B/W 1950–1952 Live, 1952–1956 Film, ½ hour.

Headline-making stories investigated by Steve Wilson, crusading editor of *The Illustrated Press*.

Cast 1: Patrick McVey, Maggie Hayes, Mary K. Wells, Julie Stevens, Jane Nigh, Beverly Tyler.

Cast 2: Mark Stevens, Trudy Wroe, Doe Avedon, Barry Kelley, John Doucette, Lynn Stalmaster.

10. *Bold Venture* USA 1959 ZIV. Syndicated, 39 episodes. B/W Film, ½ hour.

Adventures in the Bahamas of a seafaring tough guy and his attractive ward.
Dane Clark, Joan Marshall, Bernie Gozier.

11. *Boston Blackie* USA 1951–1953 ZIV. Syndicated, 58 episodes. 26 B/W Film, 32 Color, ½ hour.

Escapades of a reformed jewel thief turned suave private investigator in Los Angeles.
Kent Taylor, Lois Collier, Frank Orth.

12. *Bourbon Street Beat* USA Oct. 5, 1959–Sept. 26, 1960 Warner Bros. ABC, 39 episodes. B/W Film, Hour.

Cases of private investigation agency located in New Orleans
Monday 8:30–9:30
Richard Long, Andrew Duggan, Arlene Howell, Van Williams.

13. *Brenner* USA June 6, 1959–Sept. 13, 1964 CBS Productions. CBS, 26 episodes. B/W Film, ½ hour.

Realistic New York–based cases centering around father and son cops and their relationship.
6/59–10/59 Saturday 9–9:30
5/64–9/64 Sunday 9:30–10
Edward Binns, James Broderick.

Byline Steve Wilson see *Big Town*

Calling Mr. Diamond see *Richard Diamond, Private Detective*

Case Histories of Scotland Yard see *Scotland Yard*

14. *The Cases of Eddie Drake* USA 1949, 1952 Lindsley Parsons. Syndicated, 26 episodes. B/W Film, ½ hour.

Cases of a private eye who dictated them to a female psychologist who is researching a book on criminal behavior.
Don Haggerty, Patricia Morison, Lynne Roberts.

15. *Charlie Wild, Private Detective* USA Dec. 22, 1950–June 19, 1952 Carl De Angelo/Herbert Brodkin. CBS/ABC/DuMont, 60 episodes. B/W Live, ½ hour.

Cases of a two-fisted New York private investigator created by Dashiell Hammett.
CBS 12/50–3/51 Friday 9–9:30
CBS 4/51–6/51 Wednesday 9–9:30
ABC 9/51–3/52 Tuesday 8–8:30
Dum 3/52–6/52 Thursday 10–10:30
Kevin O'Morrison, John McQuade, Cloris Leachman.

City Assignment see *Big Town*

16. *City Detective* USA 1953–1955 Revue. Syndicated, 65 episodes. B/W Film, ½ hour.
Cases, which take him all over the country, of a wisecracking police detective with a liking for the ladies.
Rod Cameron.

17. *Code 3* USA 1957 Hal Roach. Syndicated, 39 episodes. B/W Film, ½ hour.

Cases of an assistant sheriff in Los Angeles County investigating Code 3 crimes (murder, robbery and kidnapping).
Richard Travis, Fred Wynn, Denver Pyle.

18. *Colonel March of Scotland Yard* GB 1956–1957 Fountain Films/Panda Productions/Official Films Presentation. Syndicated, 26 episodes. B/W Film, ½ hour.

Bizarre cases investigated by the eye patch–wearing head of Scotland Yard's Department of Queer Complaints. Based on *The Department of Queer Complaints* by Carter Dickson.
Boris Karloff, Ewan Roberts, Eric Pohlmann.

19. *Coronado 9* USA 1959–1960 Revue. Syndicated, 39 episodes. B/W Film, ½ hour.

Adventures of a retired naval officer turned private investigator located on the Coronado Peninsular near San Diego.
Rod Cameron.

20. *Counterthrust* USA 1959 ABC Films. Syndicated, 13 episodes. B/W Film, ½ hour.
Secret agents battle Communist infiltration throughout the world.
Tod Andrews, Diane Jergens.

21. *The Court of Last Resort* USA Oct. 4, 1957–

April 11, 1958 Walden Productions Inc./Paisano Productions. NBC, 26 episodes. B/W Film, ½ hour.

Dramatizations of the files of a committee of crime experts who investigate cases where there is serious doubt as to the guilt of a convicted prisoner.
Friday   8–8:30
Lyle Bettger, Paul Birch.

22. *Craig Kennedy Criminologist* USA 1952 Adrian Weiss. Syndicated, 26 episodes. B/W Film, ½ hour.

Investigations of a criminologist at Columbia University.
Donald Woods, Sydney Mason, Lewis Wilson.

23. *Crime Photographer* USA Apr. 19, 1951–June 5, 1952 CBS Productions. CBS, 39 episodes. B/W Live, ½ hour.

The exploits of Flash Casey, crime photographer at the *Morning Express* newspaper in New York.
Thursday   10:30–11
   Cast 1: Richard Carlyle, John Gibson
   Cast 2: Darren McGavin, Cliff Hall, Jan. Miner, Donald McClelland, Archie Smith.

24. *Crime with Father* USA Aug. 31, 1951–Jan. 18, 1952 Wilbur Stark. ABC, 16 episodes. B/W Film, ½ hour.

Exploits of a crime-busting father and daughter duo.
Friday   9–9:30
Rusty Lane, Peggy Lobbin.

Cross Current see *Foreign Intrigue*

25. *Crusader* USA Oct. 7, 1955–Dec. 28, 1956 Revue. CBS, 52 episodes. B/W Film, ½ hour.

Adventures of a stalwart freelance writer who wages a one-man war to help oppressed people everywhere.
Friday   9–9:30
Brian Keith, Arthur Space.

26. *The D.A.'s Man* USA Jan. 3, 1959–Aug. 29, 1959 Jack Webb Mark V11/Universal. NBC, 26 episodes. B/W Film, ½ hour.

Cases of an undercover investigator for the New York City District Attorney's Office.
Saturday   10:30–11
John Compton, Ralph Manza.

27. *Dangerous Assignment* USA 1951–1952 Donlevy Development Co. Inc. Don W. Sharpe/National Broadcasting Co. Syndicated, 39 episodes. B/W Film, ½ hour.

Exploits of an undercover agent for the U.S. government all over the world who is given his assignments by "the Commissioner."
Brian Donlevy, Herb Butterfield, Lyle Talbot.

Dateline Europe see *Foreign Intrigue*

28. *Deadline* USA 1959 Pyramid Productions/Flamingo Films. Syndicated, 39 episodes. B/W Film, ½ hour.

Anthology series dramatizing events, mainly involving crime, in the lives of news reporters.
Paul Stewart.

Deadline for Action see *Wire Service*

29. *Decoy* a.k.a. *Police Woman Decoy* USA 1957 Pyramid/Official Films. Syndicated, 39 episodes. B/W Film, ½ hour.

Cases undertaken by a New York female undercover cop.
Beverly Garland.

30. *The Detectives Starring Robert Taylor* a.k.a. *Robert Taylor's Detectives* USA Oct. 16, 1959–Sept. 21, 1962 Four Star. ABC/NBC, 97 episodes. B/W Film, 67½ hour, 30 hour.

Cases of a veteran police captain who heads a team of plainclothes detectives dealing with different crimes.
ABC   10/59–9/61   Friday   10–10:30
NBC   9/61–9/62   Friday   8:30–9:30
Robert Taylor, Tige Andrews, Lee Farr, Russell Thorson.

31. *Detective's Wife* USA July 7, 1950–Sept. 29, 1950 CBS Prods. CBS, 13 episodes. B/W Live, ½ hour.

Comic take on a private eye who yearns for a quiet life and whose cases are complicated by his wife's desire to become involved.
Friday   8:30–9
Lynn Bari, Donald Curtis.

32. *Dial 999* USA 1958–1959 Towers of London/ZIV. Syndicated, 39 episodes. B/W Film, ½ hour.

Cases of a Canadian police officer seconded to the Metropolitan Police in London.
Robert Beatty, Duncan Lamont, John Witty.

33. *Dick and the Duchess* GB Sept. 28, 1957–May 16, 1958 Sheldon Reynolds. CBS, 26 episodes. B/W Film, ½ hour.

Detective comedy featuring cases of an American insurance investigator living in London

whose aristocratic wife cannot resist meddling in his business.
CBS 9/57–3/58 Saturday 8:30–9
CBS 3/58–5/58 Friday 7:30–8
Patrick O'Neal, Hazel Court, Richard Wattis, Michael Shepley.

34. *Dick Tracy* USA Sept. 11, 1950–Feb. 12, 1951 P.K. Palmer. ABC and Syndicated, 39 episodes. B/W Film, ½ hour.
26 network
13 syndicated

Exploits of lantern-jawed comic strip hero in a fictitious city against a memorably named group of villains.
ABC 9/50–10/50 Wednesday 8:30–9
ABC 10/50–12/50 Monday 8:30–9
ABC 1/51–2/51 Tues. 8–8:30
Ralph Byrd, Angela Greene, Joe Devlin, Dick Elliott.

35. *Door with No Name* a.k.a. *Doorway to Danger* USA July 6, 1951–Oct. 1, 1953 Walter Selden. NBC, ABC, 26 episodes. B/W Film, ½ hour.

Chief of a top secret government agency monitors activities of his agents designed to prevent espionage in the United States.
NBC 7/51–8/51 Friday 9–9:30
NBC 7/52–8/52 Friday 9–9:30
ABC 7/53–10/53 Thursday 8:30–9
   Cast 1951: Mel Ruick, Grant Richards.
   Cast 1952: Roland Winters.
   Cast 1953: Raymond Bramley, Stacy Harris.

Doorway to Danger see *Door with No Name*

36. *Dragnet* a.k.a. *Badge 714* USA Dec. 16, 1951–Aug. 23, 1959 Dragnet Productions. NBC, 281 episodes. B/W Film, ½ hour.

Classic series detailing the cases of a Los Angeles cop and his partner, told with documentary attention to detail.
12/51–12/55 Thursday 9–9:30
1/56–9/58 Thursday 8:30–9
9/58–6/59 Tuesday 7:30–8
7/59–9/59 Sunday 8:30–9
Jack Webb, Ben Alexander, Barton Yarborough, Barney Phillips, Herb Ellis, Harry Bartell.

Ellery Queen see *The Further Adventures of Ellery Queen*

Fabian of Scotland Yard see *Fabian of the Yard*

37. *Fabian of the Yard* a.k.a. *Patrol Car, Fabian of Scotland Yard* GB 1954–1956 Trinity Productions Limited/Anthony Beauchamp. Syndicated, 39 episodes. B/W Film, ½ hour.

Dramatizations of case histories of a leading detective of Scotland Yard.
Bruce Seton.

Federal Men in Action see *Treasury Men in Action*

38. *The Files of Jeffrey Jones* USA 1953 Lindsley Parsons. Syndicated, 39 episodes. B/W Film, ½ hour.

Cases of a sports-loving private investigator.
Don Haggerty, Tristram Coffin, Gloria Henry, Frank Sully, Vince Barnett.

39. *Five Fingers* USA Oct. 3, 1959–Jan. 9, 1960 20th Century–Fox. NBC, 16 episodes. B/W Film. Hour.

Exploits of an American counterspy who goes all over the world posing as a theatrical and club booking agent.
Saturday 9:30–10:30
David Hedison, Luciana Paluzzi, Paul Burke.

Foreign Assignment see *Foreign Intrigue*

40. *Foreign Intrigue* a.k.a. *Dateline Europe, Overseas Adventure, Cross Current, Foreign Assignment* International 1951–1955 Sheldon Reynolds. Syndicated, 156 episodes. B/W Film, ½ hour.

Format 1: Stockholm-based, trench-coated European correspondent for an American wire service exposes political subversives and spies.
Jerome Thor, Sydna Scott.

Format 2: Paris-based American correspondent for Consolidated Press battles former Nazis and other fanatics.
James Daly, Anne Préville.

Format 3: In Vienna, an American hotelier comes into conflict with assorted villains guilty of various crimes.
Gerald Mohr.

41. *The Four Just Men* GB 1959–1960 Sapphire Films/Hannah Weinstein. Syndicated, 39 episodes. B/W Film, ½ hour.

Efficient World War II fighting unit are reunited a decade later to combat world crime.
Jack Hawkins, Dan Dailey, Richard Conte, Vittorio De Sica, Andrew Keir, Honor Blackman, June Thorburn, Lisa Gastoni, Anthony Bushell.

42. *Front Page Detective* USA July 6, 1951–Nov. 13, 1953 Jerry Fairbanks Inc. DuMont and Syndicated, 39 episodes. B/W Live, ½ hour.

Incorruptible newspaper columnist with a penchant for solving homicides recounts his cases.

| 7/51–2/52 | Friday | 9:30–10 |
| 10/53–11/53 | Friday | 8–8:30 |

Edmund Lowe, Paula Drew, Frank Jenks.

43. *The Further Adventures of Ellery Queen* a.k.a. *Ellery Queen* USA Sept. 26, 1958–Aug. 1959 Albert McCleery. NBC, 32 episodes. Color Live, Hour.

| Friday | 8–9 |

Cases of famed crimewriting sleuth and his policeman father.
George Nader, Lee Philips, Les Tremayne.

44. *The Gallery of Mme Liu-Tsong* a.k.a. *Mme Liu-Tsong* USA Aug. 27, 1951–Nov. 21, 1951 DuMont Productions. DuMont, 13 episodes. B/W Film, ½ hour.

Chinese-American art gallery owner doubles as an exotic sleuth.

| 8/51–10/51 | Monday | 8:30–9 |
| 10/51–11/51 | Wednesday | 9–9:30 |

Anna May Wong.

45. *Gangbusters* USA Mar. 20, 1952–Dec. 25, 1952 NBC Productions. NBC, 21 episodes. B/W Film, ½ hour.

Action-packed anthology series which involved dramatizations of the deeds of major criminals from authentic police and FBI files.

| Thursday | 9–9:30 |

Phillips H. Lord.

The George Raft Casebook see *I'm the Law*

46. *George Sanders Mystery Theater* USA June 22, 1957–Sept. 14, 1957 Screen Gems. NBC, 13 episodes. B/W Film, ½ hour.

Anthology mystery series featuring twist endings and a suave star host.

| Saturday | 9–9:30 |

George Sanders.

47. *Grand Jury* USA 1959 Desilu. Syndicated, 39 episodes. B/W Film, ½ hour.

Case files of the Grand Jury in their fight against organized crime.
Lyle Bettger, Harold J. Stone.

48. *Harbor Command* USA 1957–1958 ZIV. Syndicated, 39 episodes. B/W Film, ½ hour.

Case files of the seagoing crime unit in a large city.
Wendell Corey.

H.G. Wells' Invisible Man see *The Invisible Man*

49. *Harbourmaster* a.k.a. *Adventures at Scott Island* USA Sept. 26, 1957–June 29, 1958 UA Productions. CBS, ABC, 26 episodes. B/W Film, ½ hour.

Escapades of a harbormaster on an island off the coast of New England who doubles as a one-man rescue and police unit.

| CBS | 9/57–12/57 | Thursday | 8–8:30 |
| ABC | 1/58–6/58 | Sunday | 8:30–9 |

Barry Sullivan, Paul Burke, Nina Wilcox, Murray Matheson, Mike Keene, Evan Elliott.

50. *Hawaiian Eye* USA Oct. 7, 1959–Sept. 10, 1963 Warner Bros. ABC, 133 episodes. B/W Film, Hour.

Cases of private investigators attached to the poolside office of the Hawaiian Village Hotel in the exotic location of Hawaii.

| 10/59–9/62 | Wednesday | 9–10 |
| 10/62–9/63 | Tuesday | 8:30–9:30 |

Anthony Eisley, Robert Conrad, Connie Stevens, Poncie Ponce, Mel Prestidge, Doug Mossman.

Headline see *Big Town*

Heart of the City see *Big Town*

51. *Highway Patrol* USA 1955–1959 ZIV. Syndicated, 156 episodes. B/W Film, ½ hour.

Classic series of the case files of the patrol chief of the fighting organization dedicated to apprehending those who violate state laws.
Broderick Crawford, William Boyett.

Hollywood Offbeat see *Steve Randall*

52. *The Hunter* USA July 3, 1952–Dec. 26, 1954 Official Films/Edward J. Montagne. CBS, NBC and Syndicated, 26 episodes. B/W Film, ½ hour.

American businessman who is also a master of disguise battles Communist agents all over the world.

CBS	7/52–	Thursday	9–9:30
CBS	7/52–9/52	Wed	9:30–10
NBC	7/54–12/54	Sunday	10:30–11

Barry Nelson, Keith Larsen.

53. *I Cover Times Square* USA Oct. 5, 1950–Jan. 11, 1951 Harold Huber Productions. ABC, 13 episodes. B/W Film, ½ hour.

Investigations of a crusading newspaperman into organized crime in New York.

| Thursday | 10–10:30 |

Harold Huber.

54. *I Led 3 Lives* USA 1953–1956 ZIV. Syndicated, 117 episodes. B/W Film, ½ hour.

Episodes derived from the real-life story of Herbert A. Philbrick, family man, Communist

Party member and counterspy for the U.S. government.
Richard Carlson, Virginia Stefan, John Zaremba, Ed Hinton, Patricia Morrow.

55. *I'm the Law* a.k.a. *The George Raft Casebook* USA 1952–1953 Cosman. Syndicated, 26 episodes. B/W Film, ½ hour.
Cases of a New York City detective as he battles vice and corruption.
George Raft.

56. *Inspector Mark Saber—Homicide Squad* a.k.a. *Mystery Theater* USA Oct. 5, 1951–June 1954 Roland Reed Productions. ABC, 78 episodes. B/W Film, ½ hour.
Adventures of a suave British detective seconded to an urban American police force.
10/51–4/52	Friday	8–8:30
4/52–6/52	Wednesday	9:30–10
10/52–6/53	Monday	8–8:30
10/53–6/54	Wednesday	7:30–8
Tom Conway, James Burke.

57. *International Detective* GB 1959–1961 Delfry Productions/Official Films (A. Edward Sutherland). Syndicated, 39 episodes. B/W Film, ½ hour.
Assignments of one operative in the William J. Burns International Detective Agency whose cases take him all over the world.
Arthur Fleming.

58. *Interpol Calling* GB 1959–1961 J. Arthur Rank/Jack Wrather. Syndicated, 39 episodes. B/W Film, ½ hour.
Cases of a police inspector attached to the International Criminal Police Organisation (Interpol).
Charles Korvin, Edwin Richfield.

59. *The Investigator* USA June 3–Sept. 2, 1958 NBC Prods. NBC, 13 episodes. B/W Live, ½ hour.
Swinging private investigator and his retired newspaperman father team up to solve cases.
Tuesday 8–8:30
Lonny Chapman, Howard St. John.

60. *The Invisible Man* a.k.a. *H.G. Wells' Invisible Man* GB Nov. 4, 1958–Sept. 22, 1960 Official Film Production for the Independent Television Prog. Co. Ltd. CBS, 26 episodes. B/W Film, ½ hour.
Chemist accidentally makes himself invisible in a laboratory. While searching for the formula to restore himself, he loans out his talents as a detective.
11/58–5/59	Tuesday	8–8:30
5/59–7/59	Thursday	7:30–8
7/60–9/60	Thursday	7:30–8
Tim Turner, Lisa Daniely, Debbie Watling.

61. *I Spy* GB 1955–1956 Guild Films. Syndicated, 39 episodes. B/W Film, ½ hour.
Series of spy stories, some of them historical, hosted by "Anton the Spymaster."
Raymond Massey.

62. *Jimmy Hughes Rookie Cop* USA May 8–July 3, 1953 DuMont Prods. DuMont, 8 episodes. B/W Film, ½ hour.
Young Korean war veteran joins the police after his father is killed, avenges his father's death and takes on tough assignments.
Friday 8:30–9
Billy Redfield, Conrad Janis, Rusty Lane, Wendy Drew.

63. *Johnny Staccato* a.k.a. *Staccato* USA Sept. 10, 1959–Mar. 24, 1960 Revue. NBC, 27 episodes. B/W Film, ½ hour.
Poorly paid jazz pianist in a Greenwich Village Club supplements income by taking on private investigations.
Thursday 8:30–9
John Cassavetes, Eduardo Ciannelli.

64. *Justice* USA April 8, 1954–Mar. 25, 1956 David Susskind. NBC, 88 episodes. B/W Live, ½ hour.
Dramatization of cases from the files of the National Legal Aid Society.
| 4/54–6/55 | Thursday | 8:30–9 |
| 10/55–3/56 | Sunday | 10:30–11 |
Dane Clark, Gary Merrill, William Prince.

65. *The Lawless Years* USA Apr. 16, 1959–Sept. 22, 1961 California National Productions/Jack Chertok. NBC, 47 episodes. B/W Film, ½ hour.
Dramatizations of the cases of Barney Ruditsky, a real-life New York cop, in the days of the "Roaring Twenties" and Prohibition.
4/59–6/59	Thursday	8–8:30
7/59–9/59	Thursday	8:30–9
10/59–3/60	Thursday	10:30–11
5/61–9/61	Friday	9–9:30
James Gregory, Robert Karnes.

66. *The Lineup* a.k.a. *San Francisco Beat* USA Oct. 1, 1954–Jan. 20, 1960 Desilu/Marjeff. CBS, 201 episodes. B/W Film, 183½ hour, 18 hour.
Documentary style dramatizations of the files of the San Francisco Police Department.

10/54–9/59 Friday 10–10:30
9/59–1/60 Wednesday 7:30–8:30
Cast 1954–1959: Warner Anderson, Tom Tully, Marshall Reed.
Cast 1959–1960: Warner Anderson, William Leslie, Rachel Ames, Tod Barton, Skip Ward.

67. *Lock Up* USA 1959–1961 ZIV. Syndicated, 78 episodes. B/W Film, ½ hour.
Case files of corporation lawyer who defends those unjustly accused of crimes.
Macdonald Carey, John Doucette, Olive Carey.

68. *The Lone Wolf* a.k.a. *Streets of Danger* USA 1954 Gross-Krasne. Syndicated, 39 episodes. B/W Film, ½ hour.
Cases of a clever former crook turned private investigator nicknamed "The Lone Wolf."
Louis Hayward.

69. *M. Squad* USA Sept. 20, 1957–Sept. 13, 1960 Latimer Prods. for Revue. NBC, 115 episodes. B/W Film, ½ hour.
Cases of a hard-nosed cop who is part of an élite group of plainclothes detectives fighting crime in Chicago.
9/57–9/59 Friday 9–9:30
9/59–1/60 Friday 9:30–10
1/60–9/60 Tuesday 10–10:30
Lee Marvin, Paul Newlan.

Mme Liu-Tsong see *The Gallery of Mme Liu-Tsong*

70. *Man Against Crime* USA Oct. 7, 1949–Aug. 19, 1956 Edward J. Montagne/Paul Nickell. CBS/NBC/DuMont, 221 Episodes. B/W Live and film, ½ hour.
Cases of two-fisted New York private investigator Mike Barnett.
CBS 10/49–3/52 Friday 8:30–9
CBS 4/52–6/52 Thursday 9–9:30
CBS 10/52–6/53 Wednesday 9:30–10
CBS 7/53–10/53 Friday 8:30–9
Dum 10/53–4/54 Sunday 10:30–11
NBC 10/53–7/54 Sunday 10:30–11
NBC 7/56–8/56 Sunday 10–10:30
Ralph Bellamy, Robert Preston, Frank Lovejoy.

71. *The Man Behind the Badge* USA 1955 Bernard Procktor/Buckeye Productions. Syndicated, 39 episodes. B/W Film, ½ hour.
Series dramatizing real-life cases of mysteries involving men or women working for different branches of law enforcement agencies.
Charles Bickford.

Appendix 1: Television Series Catalog 613

72. *The Man Called X* USA 1956 ZIV. Syndicated, 39 episodes. B/W Film, ½ hour.
Dramatizations of government files involving a secret agent whose missions take him all over the world into perilous situations.
Barry Sullivan.

73. *Man with a Camera* USA Oct. 10, 1958–Feb. 8, 1960 Lewis–Sharpe. ABC, 29 episodes. B/W Film, ½ hour.
Former war photographer turned freelance snapper accepts assignments from numerous sources which cause him to turn detective.
10/58–3/59 Friday 9–9:30
10/59–2/60 Monday 10:30–11
Charles Bronson, Ludwig Stossel, James Flavin.

74. *Manhunt* USA 1959–1961 Screen Gems. Syndicated, 78 episodes. B/W Film, ½ hour.
Veteran cop and newspaperman in San Diego tackle cases derived from the case files of the San Diego Police Department.
Victor Jory, Patrick McVey, Charles Bateman, Rian Garrick, Chuck Henderson.

75. *Mark Saber* a.k.a. *The Vise* GB Dec. 1955–June 1957 Danziger Brothers. ABC, 52 episodes. B/W Film, ½ hour.
Adventures of a one-armed private detective based in London.
Friday 9:30–10
Donald Gray, Michael Balfour, Diana Decker, Colin Tapley, Patrick Holt.

Mark Saber (1957–1960) see *Saber of London*

76. *Markham* USA May 2, 1959–Sept. 22, 1960 Revue. CBS, 60 episodes. B/W Film, ½ hour.
Cases of Roy Markham, a wealthy New York–based lawyer turned private eye.
5/59–1/60 Saturday 10:30–11
1/60–9/60 Thursday 9:30–10
Ray Milland, Simon Scott.

77. *Martin Kane Private Eye* USA Sept. 1, 1949–June 17, 1954 NBC Prods. NBC, 195 episodes. B/W Live, ½ hour.
Cases of a tough, two-fisted, wisecracking New York private eye who works closely with the police.
Thursday 10–10:30
William Gargan, Lloyd Nolan, Lee Tracy, Mark Stevens, Walter Kinsella, Fred Hillebrand, Horace McMahon, Nicholas Saunders, Walter Greaza, Frank Thomas, King Calder.

Martin Kane, Private Investigator see *The New Adventures of Martin Kane*

78. *The Mask* USA Jan. 10, 1954–May 16, 1954 ABC Prods. ABC, 15 episodes. B/W Live, Hour.

Two attorneys who are brothers and partners in a law firm tackle assorted criminal cases.

| 1/54–6/54 | Sunday | 8–9 |
| 3/54–4/54 | Tuesday/Wednesday | 8–9 |

Gary Merrill, William Prince.

79. *Meet McGraw* a.k.a. *The Adventures of McGraw* USA July 2, 1957–Apr. 1, 1958 Lewis-Sharpe. NBC, 33 episodes. B/W Film, ½ hour.

Violent loner for hire punches his way through various tough situations.

Tuesday 9–9:30

Frank Lovejoy.

80. *Mickey Spillane's Mike Hammer* USA 1957–1959 Revue. Syndicated, 78 episodes. B/W Film, ½ hour.

Violent pulp fiction private detective based in New York investigates cases with the emphasis on sex and sadism.

Darren McGavin, Bart Burns.

81. *Mr. and Mrs. North* USA Oct. 3, 1952–July 20, 1954 Bernard L. Shubert. CBS/NBC, 57 episodes. B/W Film, ½ hour.

Tales of Greenwich Village publisher and his wife who investigate various mysteries.

| CBS | 10/52–9/53 | 10–10:30 |
| NBC | 1/54–7/54 | 10:30–11 |

Richard Denning, Barbara Britton, Francis De Sales.

82. *Mr. District Attorney* USA Oct. 1, 1951–June 23, 1952 ABC Prods. ABC, 13 episodes. B/W Live, ½ hour.

Crusading district attorney solves complex cases.

Monday 8–8:30

Jay Jostyn, Vicki Vola, Len Doyle.

83. *Mr. District Attorney* USA 1954–1955 ZIV. Syndicated, 78 episodes. B/W Film, ½ hour.

Crusading district attorney solves complex crime cases.

David Brian, Jackie Loughery.

84. *Mysteries of Chinatown* USA Dec. 4, 1949–Oct. 23, 1950 ABC Prods. ABC, 35 episodes. B/W Live, ½ hour.

Investigations undertaken by Dr. Yat Fu, a herb and curio shop proprietor, in San Francisco.

12/49–5/50	Sunday	9:30–10
5/50–9/50	Sunday	9–9:30
9/50	Tuesday	8:30–9
10/50	Monday	8:30–9

Marvin Miller, Gloria Saunders.

Mystery Is My Business see *The New Adventures of Ellery Queen*

Mystery Theater see *Inspector Mark Saber—Homicide Squad*

85. *The Naked City* a.k.a. *Naked City* USA Sept. 30, 1958–Sept. 11, 1963 Screen Gems. ABC, 138 episodes. B/W Film, 39½ hour, 99 hour.

Classic gritty series of police investigations set against the backdrop of the New York City metropolis with the famous tag line, "There are eight million stories in the Naked City."

| 9/58–9/59 | Tuesday | 9:30–10 |
| 10/60–9/63 | Wednesday | 10–11 |

Cast 1958–1959: John McIntire, James Franciscus, Harry Bellaver, Horace McMahon, Suzanne Storrs.

Cast 1960–1963: Paul Burke, Horace McMahon, Harry Bellaver.

86. *The New Adventures of Charlie Chan* GB 1957–1958 Television Programs of America in association with The Independent Television Company Ltd. Syndicated, 39 episodes. B/W Film, ½ hour.

Cases of the renowned sleuth, an ex police inspector in Honolulu, currently traveling in England and Europe with his son. From the character created by Earl Derr Biggers.

J. Carrol Naish, James Hong, Rupert Davies, Hugh Williams.

87. *The New Adventures of Ellery Queen* a.k.a. *Mystery Is My Business* USA 1954 Norven Productions/ITC/TPA. Syndicated, 32 episodes. B/W Film, ½ hour.

Cases of famed crimewriting sleuth and his policeman father.

Hugh Marlowe, Florenz Ames.

88. *The New Adventures of Martin Kane* a.k.a. *Martin Kane, Private Investigator* GB 1957–1958 ZIV/Towers of London. Syndicated, 39 episodes. B/W Film, ½ hour.

Return of a wisecracking, two-fisted, American private investigator whose cases now have him relocated to London.

William Gargan, Brian Reece.

New Orleans Police Department see *N.O.P.D.*

89. *New York Confidential* USA 1958 TPA. Syndicated, 39 episodes. B/W Film, ½ hour.

Cases investigated by a two-fisted, crusading reporter in New York.

Lee Tracy.

90. *N.O.P.D.* a.k.a. *New Orleans Police Department* USA 1956 Minot Films/MPA TV. Syndicated, 39 episodes. B/W Film, ½ hour.
 Cases of two police officers based in the city of New Orleans. The cases were derived from the actual files of the New Orleans Police Department.
Stacy Harris, Louis Sirgo.

91. *Not for Hire* USA 1959 California National Productions. Syndicated, 39 episodes. B/W Film, ½ hour.
 Adult-themed investigations undertaken by a sergeant with the U.S. Army Criminal Investigations Department.
Ralph Meeker, Lizabeth Hush, Ken Drake.

92. *Official Detective* USA 1957 Desilu/NTA. Syndicated, 39 episodes. B/W Film, ½ hour.
 Dramatizations of cases from the pages of *Official Detective Magazine*.
Everett Sloane.

93. *OSS* GB Sept. 26, 1957–Mar. 17, 1958 ITC/Buckeye. ABC, 26 episodes. B/W Film, ½ hour.
 Dramatizations of the case files of the Office of Strategic Services, a forerunner of the C.I.A. and wartime equivalent of M.I.5.
9/57–1/58　　　　Thursday　　　　9:30–10
1/58–3/58　　　　Monday　　　　7:30–8
Ron Randell, Lionel Murton.

Overseas Adventure see *Foreign Intrigue*

94. *Paris Precinct* a.k.a. *World Crime Hunt* France 1953 Etoile Prods/Guild Films/MPTV. Syndicated, 26 episodes. B/W Film, ½ hour.
 Cases of two plainclothes police inspectors from the French Sûreté who combat crime on the streets of Paris.
Louis Jourdan, Claude Dauphin.

95. *Passport to Danger* USA 1954–1956 Rabco/Hal Roach/ABC films. Syndicated, 39 episodes. B/W Film, ½ hour.
 Adventures of a diplomatic courier which take him all over the world.
Cesar Romero.

Patrol Car see *Fabian of the Yard*

96. *Pentagon Confidential* a.k.a. *Pentagon USA* USA Aug. 6, 1953–Sept. 24, 1953 CBS Prods. CBS, 10 episodes. B/W Live, ½ hour.
 Dramatizations of criminal investigations files undertaken by the U.S. Army. Assignments were given out by a fictitious colonel whose office was located in the Pentagon.

Thursday　　　　　　　　　　10–10:30
Addison Richards, Edd Binns, Gene Lyons.

Pentagon USA see *Pentagon Confidential*

97. *Perry Mason* USA Sept. 21, 1957–Sept. 4, 1966 Paisano. CBS, 271 episodes. 270 B/W, 1 Color Film, Hour.
 Classic courtroom dramas surrounding the cases undertaken by defending attorney Perry Mason on behalf of his clients. Created by Erle Stanley Gardner.
9/57–9/62　　　Saturday　　　7:30–8:30
9/62–9/63　　　Thursday　　　8–9
9/63–9/64　　　Thursday　　　9–10
9/64–9/65　　　Thursday　　　8–9
9/65–9/66　　　Sunday　　　　9–10
Raymond Burr, Barbara Hale, William Hopper, William Talman, Ray Collins.

98. *Peter Gunn* USA Sept. 22, 1958–Sept. 25, 1961 Spartan (Blake Edwards). NBC/ABC, 110 episodes. B/W Film, ½ hour.
 Influential series depicting the cases of a suave, crewcut private investigator who operates out of a plush apartment and a jazz nightclub.
NBC　9/58–9/60　　Monday　　9–9:30
ABC　10/60–9/61　Monday　　10:30–11
Craig Stevens, Lola Albright, Herschel Bernardi, Hope Emerson, Minerva Urecal.

99. *Philip Marlowe* USA Oct. 6, 1959–Mar. 29, 1960 Goodman-Todson/California National Prods. ABC, 26 episodes. B/W Film, ½ hour.
 Famous hard-boiled private investigator, created by Raymond Chandler, becomes marshmallow when transferred to television.
Tuesday　　　　　　　　　　9:30–10
Philip Carey.

100. *The Plainclothesman* USA Oct. 12, 1949–Sept. 19, 1954 DuMont Prods. DuMont, 130 episodes. B/W Film, ½ hour.
 Cases of an unnamed, unseen police lieutenant in a big city which had the novelty of using subjective camera technique—i.e., the camera became the eyes of the detective.
10/49–5/50　　　Wednesday　　　9–9:30
5/50–5/51　　　Wednesday　　　9:30–10
6/51–9/54　　　Sunday　　　　9:30–10
Ken Lynch, Jack Orrison.

Police Woman Decoy see *Decoy*

101. *Public Defender* USA Mar. 11, 1954–June 23, 1955 Showcase (Hal Roach, Jr. and Carroll Case). CBS, 69 episodes. B/W Film, ½ hour.

Cases of an attorney who defends those who are poor and cannot afford to hire legal representation. Episodes were based on authentic files from public defender agencies around the country.

3/54–7/54	Thursday	10–10:30
7/54–9/54	Thursday	9–9:30
9/54–6/55	Thursday	10–10:30

Reed Hadley.

102. *Racket Squad* USA June 7, 1951–Sept. 28, 1953 Showcase (Hal Roach, Jr. and Carroll Case). CBS, 98 episodes. B/W Film, ½ hour.

Cases of a police captain who heads a unit devoted to exposing confidence tricksters. Derived from authentic police files from various parts of the country.

6/51–12/52	Thursday	10–10:30
1/53–7/53	Thursday	10:30–11
7/53–9/53	Monday	9–9:30

Reed Hadley.

103. *Richard Diamond, Private Detective* a.k.a. *Calling Mr. Diamond* USA July 1, 1957–Sept. 6, 1960 Four Star. CBS/NBC, 78 episodes. B/W Film, ½ hour.

Format 1: Former New York cop turned private investigator is assisted by old contacts on the force.

Format 2: Cases of the same private detective who has now relocated to Hollywood, complete with beautiful girlfriend, swank apartment and convertible. He is assisted by a sultry switchboard operator.

CBS	7/57–9/57	Monday	9:30–10
CBS	1/58–9/58	Thursday	8–8:30
CBS	2/59–9/59	Sunday	10–10:30
NBC	10/59–1/60	Monday	7:30–8
NBC	6/60–9/60	Tuesday	9–9:30

Cast 1: David Janssen, Regis Toomey.

Cast 2: David Janssen, Barbara Bain, Russ Conway, Mary Tyler Moore, Roxane Brooks.

Robert Taylor's Detectives see *The Detectives Starring Robert Taylor*

105. *Rocky King, Detective* a.k.a. *Rocky King, Inside Detective* USA Jan. 14, 1950–Dec. 26, 1954. DuMont Productions. DuMont, 195 episodes. B/W Live, ½ hour.

Cases of a hard-working detective on the New York homicide squad.

1/50–7/50	Saturday	8:30–9
7/50–3/51	Friday	9:30–10
3/51–12/54	Sunday	9–9:30

Roscoe Karns, Earl Hammond, Todd Karns, Grace Carney.

Rocky King, Inside Detective see *Rocky King, Detective*

SA 7 see *Special Agent 7*

106. *Saber of London* a.k.a. *Mark Saber* GB Oct. 13, 1957–May 15, 1960 Danziger Brothers. NBC, 83 episodes. B/W Film, ½ hour.

Adventures of a one-armed private detective, based in London, whose cases take him all over the world.

9/57–12/57	Friday	7:30–8
10/58–5/59	Sunday	7–7:30
10/59–5/60	Sunday	6:30–7

Donald Gray, Neil McCallum, Gordon Tanner, Robert Arden, Colin Tapley.

San Francisco Beat see *The Lineup*

107. *Scotland Yard* a.k.a. *Case Histories of Scotland Yard* GB Nov. 17, 1957–Apr. 6, 1958 Anglo Amalgamated. ABC, 39 episodes. B/W Film, ½ hour.

Anthology series featuring cases derived from the files of Scotland Yard. Hosted by noted criminologist Edgar Lustgarten.

11/57–3/58	Sunday	10–10:30
5/58–6/58	Wednesday	9:30–10
8/58–10/58	Friday	10–10:30

Russell Napier.

108. *Sea Hunt* USA 1957–1961 ZIV/Ivan Tors. Syndicated, 156 episodes. B/W Film, ½ hour.

Adventures of Mike Nelson, ex navy frogman turned underwater investigator.

Lloyd Bridges.

109. *Secret File USA* Netherlands 1954 Cinetone Productions/An Official Films Presentation. Syndicated, 26 episodes. B/W Film, ½ hour.

Army Intelligence major based in Holland tracks down Communists all over the world.

Robert Alda.

110. *77 Sunset Strip* USA Oct. 10, 1958–Sept. 9, 1964 Warner Bros. ABC, 206 episodes. B/W Film, Hour.

Cases of a firm of private investigators operating from a glamorous location in Hollywood.

10/58–10/59	Friday	9:30–10:30
10/59–9/62	Friday	9–10
9/62–9/63	Friday	9:30–10:30
9/63–2/64	Friday	7:30–8:30
4/64–9/64	Wednesday	10–11

Efrem Zimbalist, Jr., Roger Smith, Edd Byrnes, Richard Long, Louis Quinn, Jacqueline Beer, Byron Keith.

111. *Shadow of the Cloak* USA June 6, 1951–April 3, 1952 DuMont Productions. DuMont, 39 episodes. B/W Film, ½ hour.

Adventures of chief agent of International Security Intelligence battling international crime.

| 6/51–11/51 | Wednesday | 9:30–10 |
| 12/51–4/52 | Thursday | 9–9:30 |

Helmut Dantine.

112. *Sherlock Holmes* France 1954 Sheldon Reynolds. Syndicated, 39 episodes. B/W Film, ½ hour.

Mainly original cases of the celebrated sleuth created by Sir Arthur Conan Doyle.
Ronald Howard, Howard Marion-Crawford, Archie Duncan.

113. *Special Agent 7* a.k.a. *SA 7* USA 1958–1959 TPA/Revue. Syndicated, 26 episodes. B/W Film, ½ hour.

Cases investigated by an agent of attempts to defraud the Internal Revenue Service.
Lloyd Nolan.

Staccato see *Johnny Staccato*

114. *State Trooper* USA 1957–1959 Revue. Syndicated 104 episodes. B/W Film, ½ hour.

Cases of the chief investigator for the Nevada State Police derived from authentic police files.
Rod Cameron.

115. *Steve Randall* a.k.a. *Hollywood Offbeat* USA Nov. 7, 1952–Jan. 30, 1953 Marion Parsonett/Lester Lewis. DuMont, 13 episodes. B/W Film, ½ hour.

Suave disbarred lawyer turns private detective until he can succeed in being allowed to practice law again.
Friday   8–8:30
Melvyn Douglas.

116. *The Stranger* USA June 25, 1954–Feb. 11, 1955 DuMont Prods. DuMont, 34 episodes. B/W Film, ½ hour.

Anthology detective series verging on the supernatural about a nameless man who appears from nowhere, helps the victim of crime by logical deductions and then disappears without payment.
Friday   9–9:30
Robert Carroll.

Streets of Danger see *The Lone Wolf*

Stryker of Scotland Yard see *Stryker of the Yard* (aka *Stryker X of Scotland Yard*)

117. *Stryker of Scotland Yard* GB 1953 Hollywood Television Services/Republic Pictures Corporation. Syndicated, 39 episodes. B/W Film, ½ hour.

Cases of an honest and dependable Chief Inspector from Scotland Yard.
Clifford Evans, George Woodbridge.

118. *Target* USA 1957–1958 ZIV. Syndicated, 39 episodes. B/W Film, ½ hour.

Stories of crime, mystery and suspense, the common theme of which was some terrifying force in pursuit of a human target.
Adolphe Menjou.

119. *The Tell Tale Clue* USA July 8–Sept. 23, 1954 CBS Productions. CBS, 13 episodes. B/W Live, ½ hour.

Police lieutenant who is head of criminology department of a large, unnamed metropolitan city uses the latest innovations in science and technology to help solve crimes.
Thursday   10–10:30
Anthony Ross.

120. *The Thin Man* USA Sept. 20, 1957–June 26, 1959 MGM. NBC, 78 episodes. B/W Film, ½ hour.

Cases with a humorous slant of an extremely wealthy New York socialite couple who find themselves involved in mysteries.
Friday   9:30–10
Peter Lawford, Phyllis Kirk, Stafford Repp, Tol Avery, Jack Albertson, Nita Talbot, Pat Donahue.

121. *The Third Man* GB/USA 1959–1962 BBC/National Telefilm Associates of America. Syndicated, 78 episodes. B/W Film, ½ hour.

Suave, charming ex-racketeer who now runs his own import-export business becomes involved in mysteries in various parts of the world.
Michael Rennie, Jonathan Harris.

122. *This Man Dawson* USA 1959 ZIV. Syndicated, 39 episodes. B/W Film, ½ hour.

Police department official embarks on mission to rid unnamed big city of corporate and political corruption.
Keith Andes.

123. *Tightrope!* USA Sept. 8, 1959–Sept. 13, 1960 Screen Gems/Clarence Greene and Russell Rouse. CBS, 37 episodes. B/W Film, ½ hour.

Undercover agent infiltrates organized crime.
Tuesday   9–9:30
Michael Connors.

124. *Top Secret USA* USA 1954 Revue/Marion Parsonnet. Syndicated, 26 episodes. B/W Film, ½ hour.

Cases drawn from the files of the Bureau of Science Information.
Paul Stewart, Gena Rowlands.

125. *Treasury Men in Action* a.k.a. *Federal Men in Action* USA Sept. 11, 1950–Sept. 30, 1955 Pyramid Productions. ABC/NBC, 130 episodes. B/W Film, ½ hour.

Dramatizations of real-life cases from the files of the U.S. Treasury Department.

ABC	9/50–12/50	Monday	8–8:30
NBC	4/51–4/54	Thursday	8:30–9
ABC	10/54–6/55	Thursday	8:30–9
ABC	6/55–9/55	Friday	8:30–9

Walter Greaza.

126. *21 Beacon Street* USA July 2, 1959–Sept. 24, 1959 Filmways. NBC, 13 episodes. B/W Film, ½ hour.

Crack team of private investigators operating from a Boston address undertake criminal cases.
Thursday   9:30–10
Dennis Morgan, Joanna Barnes, Brian Kelly, James Maloney.

127. *The Untouchables* USA Oct. 15, 1959–Sept. 10, 1963 Desilu. ABC, 117 episodes. B/W Film, Hour.

Classic series depicting the battle of Eliot Ness and his élite band of agents against organized crime during the "Roaring Twenties."
10/59–10/61   Thursday   9:30–10:30
10/61–9/62   Thursday   10–11
9/62–9/63   Tuesday   9:30–10:30
Robert Stack, Jerry Paris, Abel Fernandez, Nick Georgiade.

128. *U.S. Border Patrol* USA 1959 CBS Films. Syndicated, 39 episodes. B/W Film, ½ hour.

Adventures of law enforcement agency battling crime on land, sea and air along 6,000 miles of United States border.
Richard Webb.

129. *The Vise* GB 1954–1955 Danziger Brothers. ABC, 65 episodes. B/W Film, ½ hour.

Anthology drama series with strong elements of mystery and suspense depicting people caught in "the vise" of fate owing to their own misdeeds.
Friday   9:30–10
Ron Randell.

The Vise (1955–1957) see *Mark Saber*

130. *Wire Service* a.k.a. *Deadline for Action* USA/GB Oct. 4, 1956–Sept. 23, 1957 Sharpe-Lewis. ABC, 39 episodes. B/W Film, Hour.

Assignments involving crime and adventure in different parts of the world of three independent roving reporters for the Trans-Globe Wire Service.
10/56–2/57   Thursday   9–10
2/57–9/57   Monday   7:30–8:30
Dane Clark, George Brent, Mercedes McCambridge.

World Crime Hunt see *Paris Precinct*

APPENDIX 2: PLAYERS TOO LATE FOR DATE RANGE

The following players were omitted because although they were regulars in the television series covered in this book, they joined these series after the closing date of December 31, 1959.

Richard Anderson, *Perry Mason* (1965–1966) as Det. Lt. Steve Drumm.

Todd Armstrong, *Manhunt* (1960–1961) as Det. Carl Spencer.

Tina Cole, *Hawaiian Eye* (1962–1963) as Sunny Day.

Robert Crawford, *Manhunt* (1960–1961) as Det. Phil Burns.

Troy Donahue, *Hawaiian Eye* (1962–1963) as Phil Barton.

Anthony George, *The Untouchables* (1960) as Cam Allison.

Mark Goddard, *The Detectives Starring Robert Taylor* (1960–1962) as Sgt. Chris Ballard.

Wesley Lau, *Perry Mason* (1961–1965) as Det. Lt. Andy Anderson.

Robert Logan, *77 Sunset Strip* (1961–1963) as J.R. Hale.

Steve London, *The Untouchables* (1960–1963) as Jack Rossman.

Nancy Malone, *Naked City* (1960–1963) as Libby.

Paul Picerni, *The Untouchables* (1960–1963) as Lee Hobson.

Joan Staley, *77 Sunset Strip* (1963–1964) as Hannah.

Michael Steffany, *Manhunt* (1960–1961) as Det. Paul Kirk.

Ursula Thiess, *The Detectives Starring Robert Taylor* (1960–1962) as Lisa Bonay.

Adam West, *The Detectives Starring Robert Taylor* (1961–1962) as Sgt. Steve Nelson.

Grant Williams, *Hawaiian Eye* (1960–1963) as Greg MacKenzie.

BIBLIOGRAPHY

Books

Alicoate, Jack. *The Film Daily Yearbook of Motion Pictures, 1957.* New York: Film Daily, 1957.

The Annual Obituary Chicago: St. James, various years.

Ann-Margret, with Todd Gold. *My Story.* London: Orion, 1994.

Beck, Marilyn. *Hollywood.* New York: Hawthorn, 1973.

Brooks, Tim. *The Complete Directory to Prime Time TV Stars.* New York: Ballantine, 1987.

_____, and Earle Marsh. *The Complete Directory to Prime Time Network and Cable TV Shows 1946–Present.* 8th ed. New York: Ballantine, 2003.

Byrnes, Edd. *Kookie No More.* New York: Barricade, 1996.

Cameron, Ian, and Elisabeth Cameron. *Broads.* London: Studio Vista, 1969.

_____, and _____. *The Heavies.* London: Studio Vista, 1967.

Collins, Max Allan, and John Javna. *The Critics' Choice: The Best of Crime and Detective TV.* New York: Harmony, 1988.

Contemporary Authors. Detroit: Gale Research, various years through 1995.

Contemporary Theatre, Film and Television: A Biographical Guide. 55 vols. Detroit: Gale Research, various years through 2004.

Current Biography Yearbook. New York: Wilson, various years through 1995.

DeLong, Thomas A. *Radio Stars: An Illustrated Dictionary of 953 Performers, 1920 through 1960.* Jefferson, NC: McFarland, 1996.

Donnelly, Paul. *Fade to Black: A Book of Movie Obituaries.* London: Omnibus, 2000.

Doyle, Billy. *The Ultimate Directory of Silent and Sound Era Performers.* Lanham, MD: Scarecrow, 1999.

Dye, David. *Child and Youth Actors Filmographies of Their Entire Careers, 1914–1985.* Jefferson, NC: McFarland, 1988.

Erickson, Hal. *Syndicated Television: The First Forty Years, 1947–1987.* Jefferson, NC: McFarland, 1989.

Essoe, Gabe. *The Book of Movie Lists.* Westport, CT: Arlington House, 1981.

_____. *The Book of TV Lists.* Westport, CT: Arlington House, 1981.

Etter, Jonathan. *Quinn Martin, Producer.* Jefferson, NC: McFarland, 2003.

Evans, Jeff. *The Penguin TV Companion.* London: Penguin, 2001.

Everson, William K. *The Detective in Film.* Secaucus, NJ: Citadel, 1972.

Fetrow, Alan G. *Feature Films, 1940–1949: A United States Filmography.* Jefferson, NC: McFarland, 1994.

_____. *Feature Films, 1950–1959: A United States Filmography.* Jefferson, NC: McFarland, 1999.

_____. *Sound Films, 1927–1939: A United States Filmography.* Jefferson, NC: McFarland, 1992.

Fireman, Judy. *TV Book: The Ultimate Television Book.* New York: Workman, 1977.

Gabor, Zsa Zsa, with Wendy Leigh. *One Lifetime Is Not Enough.* London: Headline, 1991.

Gianakos, Larry. *Television Drama Series Programming, 1947–1982.* 4 vols. Metuchen, NJ: Scarecrow, 1978–1983.

Goldberg, Lee. *Unsold Television Pilots: 1955 through 1988.* Jefferson, NC: McFarland, 1990.

Goldrup, Tom, and Jim Goldrup. *Feature Players: The Stories Behind the Faces.* 3 vols. Published privately, 1986, 1992 and 1999.

Hagen, Ray, and Laura Wagner. *Killer Tomatoes: 15 Tough Film Dames.* Jefferson, NC: McFarland, 2004.

Hardy, Phil. *Gangsters.* London: Aurum, 1998.

Hawkins, Jack. *Anything for a Quiet Life.* London: Coronet, 1975.

Hayward, Anthony, and Deborah Hayward. *TV Unforgettables.* Enfield, Middlesex: Guinness, 1993.

Hill, Ona L. *Raymond Burr: A Film, Radio and Television Biography.* Jefferson, NC: McFarland, 1994.

Houseman, Victoria. *Made in Heaven: Unscrambling

the Marriages and Children of Hollywood Stars. Chicago: Bonus, 1991.
Hyatt, Wesley. *Short-lived Television Series, 1948–1978: Thirty Years of More Than 1,000 Flops.* Jefferson, NC: McFarland, 2003.
Inman, David. *The TV Encyclopedia.* New York: Perigee, 1991.
Jarvis, Everett. *Final Curtain: Deaths of Noted Film and TV Personalities.* New York: Citadel, 1995.
Jones, Ken D., Arthur F. McClure, and Alfred E. Twomey. *Character People.* Secaucus, NJ: Citadel, 1979.
Lamparksi, Richard. *Whatever Became Of?* Series 1 to 11. New York: Crown, 1967–1989.
Lawford, Patricia Seaton, with Ted Schwarz. *Peter Lawford: Mixing with Monroe, the Kennedys, the Rat Pack and the Whole Damn Crowd.* London: Futura, 1990.
Leibfried, Philip, and Chei Mi Lane. *Anna May Wong: A Complete Guide to Her Film, Stage, Radio and Television Work.* Jefferson, NC: McFarland, 2004.
Lentz, Harris M., III. *Obituaries in the Performing Arts.* 11 vols. through 2004. Jefferson, NC: McFarland, 1994–2005.
Maltin, Leonard. *Classic Movie Guide.* New York: Plume, 2005.
_____. *Movie Guide 2005.* New York: Plume, 2004.
Martindale, David. *Television Detective Shows of the 1970s: Credits, Storylines and Episode Guides for 109 Series.* Jefferson, NC: McFarland, 1991.
Marvin, Pamela. *Lee: A Romance.* London: Faber and Faber, 1996.
Marx, Kenneth S. *Star Stats: Who's Whose in Hollywood.* Los Angeles: Price, Stern, Sloan, 1979.
Massey, Raymond. *A Hundred Different Lives.* London: Robson, 1979.
McCambridge, Mercedes. *The Quality of Mercy.* New York: Times Books, 1981.
McClelland, Doug. *Forties Film Talk: Oral Histories of Hollywood with 120 Lobby Posters.* Jefferson, NC: McFarland, 1992.
McFarlane, Brian. *The Encyclopedia of British Film.* London: Methuen/BFI, 2003.
Merrill, Gary, with John Cole. *Bette, Rita and the Rest of My Life.* New York: Berkley, 1990.
Meyers, Ric. *Murder on the Air.* New York: Mysterious, 1989.
Meyers, Richard. *TV Detectives.* San Diego, CA: Barnes, 1981.
Mitchum, John. *Them Ornery Mitchum Boys.* Pacifica, CA: Creatures at Large, 1989.
Moore, Mary Tyler. *After All.* New York: Dell, 1995.
Noble, Peter. *The British Film Yearbook 1946 and 1947–1948.* London: Skelton-Robinson British Yearbooks, 1946 and 1948.
_____. *International Film and TV Year Book 33rd Year.* London: Screen International, 1979.
O'Neil, Thomas. *The Emmys: Starwars, Showdowns and the Supreme Test of TV's Best.* New York: Penguin, 1992.
Palmer, Scott. *British Film Actors' Credits, 1895–1987.* Jefferson, NC: McFarland, 1988.
Parish, James Robert. *Hollywood Death Book.* Las Vegas, NV: Pioneer, 1992.
_____, and Don E. Stanke. *The Debonairs.* New Rochelle, NY: Arlington House, 1975.
_____, and Lennard De Carl. *Hollywood Players: The Forties.* New York: Arlington House, 1976.
_____, and Steven Whitney. *The George Raft File.* New York: Drake, 1973.
_____, and William T. Leonard. *Hollywood Players: The Thirties.* Carlstadt, NJ: Rainbow, 1977.
People Almanac. Various editions through 2004. New York: Cader, various years.
Perry, Jed H. *Screen Gems: History of Columbia Pictures Television from Cohn to Coke, 1948–1983.* Metuchen, NJ: Scarecrow, 1991.
Picture Show Annual. 32 volumes through 1960. London: Amalgamated, various years 1926–1960.
Picture Show's Who's Who on Screen. London: Amalgamated, 1956.
The Picturegoer's Who's Who and Encyclopedia of the Screen Today. London: Odham's, 1933.
Pink, Sidney. *So You Want to Make Movies: My Life as an Independent Film Producer.* Sarasota, FL: Pineapple, 1989.
Quigley, Martin, Jr. *International Motion Picture Almanac.* New York: Quigley, 1961 and 1966.
Quinlan, David. *British Sound Films: The Studio Years, 1928–1959.* London: Batsford, 1984.
_____. *Film Stars.* 5th ed. London: Batsford, 2000.
_____. *Illustrated Directory of Film Character Actors.* Second Edition. London: Batsford, 1996.
Ragan, David. *Movie Stars of the 30's.* New Jersey: Prentice-Hall, 1985.
_____. *Movie Stars of the 40's.* New Jersey: Prentice-Hall, 1985.
_____. *Who's Who in Hollywood.* 2nd ed. New York: Facts on File, 1992.
Rogers, Dave. *The ITV Encyclopedia of Adventure.* London: Boxtree, 1988.
Rout, Nancy E., Ellen Buckley, and Barney M. Rout. *The Soap Opera Book: Who's Who in Daytime Drama.* West Nyack, NJ: Todd, 1992.
Rovin, Jeff. *The Great Television Series.* South Brunswick, NJ: Barnes, 1977.
Sackett, Susan. *Prime Time Hits: Television's Most Popular Network Programs 1950–Present.* New York: Billboard, 1993.
Schlossheimer, Michael. *Gunmen and Gangsters.* Jefferson, NC: McFarland, 2002.
Shulman, Arthur, and Roger Youman. *How Sweet It Was; Television: A Pictorial Commentary.* New York: Bonanza, 1966.
Silver, Alain, and Elizabeth Ward. *Film Noir.* London: Secker and Warburg, 1980.
Skinner, John Walter. *Who's Who on the Screen.* Wor-

thington, England: Madeleine Productions, 1983.
Smout, Michael. *Mersey Stars: An A–Z of Entertainers*. Wilmslow, Cheshire: Sigma, 2000.
Stack, Robert, and Mark Evans. *Straight Shooting*. New York: Macmillan, 1980.
Stallings, Penny. *Forbidden Channels: The Truth They Hide from TV Guide*. New York: HarperPerennial, 1991.
Steen, M.F. *Celebrity Death Certificates*. Jefferson, NC: McFarland, 2003.
_____. *Celebrity Death Certificates 2*. Jefferson, NC: McFarland, 2005.
Sullivan, Steve. *Glamour Girls: The Illustrated Encyclopedia*. New York: St. Martin's Griffin, 1999.
Terrace, Vincent. *The Complete Encyclopedia of Television Programs 1947–1976*. 2 vols. South Brunswick, NJ: Barnes, 1976.
_____. *Experimental Television, Test Films, Pilots and Trial Series, 1925 through 1995: Seven Decades of Screen Almosts*. Jefferson, NC: McFarland, 1997.
_____. *Fifty Years of Television: A Guide to Series and Pilots 1937–1988*. New York: Cornwall, 1991.
Thomey, Tedd. *The Glorious Decade*. New York: Ace, 1971.
Tibballs, Geoff. *TV Detectives*. London: Boxtree, 1992.
Truitt, Evelyn Mack. *Who Was Who On Screen*. New York: Bowker, 1977 (2nd ed.) and 1984 (illus. ed.).
Tulard, Jean. *Dictionnaire du Cinéma: Les Acteurs*. 7th ed. Paris: Robert Laffont.
Tuska, Jon. *The Detective in Hollywood*. New York: Doubleday, 1978.
Twomey, Alfred E., and Arthur F. McClure. *The Versatiles*. South Brunswick, NJ: Barnes, 1969.
Vahimagi, Tise. *The Untouchables*. London: British Film Institute, 1998.
VanDerBeets, Richard. *George Sanders: An Exhausted Life*. London: Robson, 1990.
Vazzana, Eugene Michael. *Silent Film Necrology: Birth and Deaths of Over 9000 Performers, Directors, Producers and Other Filmmakers of the Silent Era, Through 1993*. Jefferson, NC: McFarland, 1995.
Ward, Jack. *The Supporting Players of Television 1959–1983*. Cleveland, OK: Lakeshore West, 1996.
_____. *Television Guest Stars*. Jefferson, NC: McFarland, 1993.
Wayne, Jane Ellen. *Robert Taylor*. London: Robson, 1987.
Weaver, John T. *Forty Years of Screen Credits 1929–1969*. Metuchen, NJ: Scarecrow, 1970.
_____. *Twenty Years of Screen Credits 1908–1928*. Metuchen, NJ: Scarecrow, 1971.
Weaver, Tom. *Interviews with B Science Fiction and Horror Movie Makers: Writers, Producers, Directors, Actors, Moguls and Makeup*. Jefferson, NC: McFarland, 1988.
Whitney, Steven. *Charles Bronson, Superstar*. New York: Dell, 1975.
Wicking, Christopher, and Tise Vahimagi. *The American Vein*. London: Talisman, 1979.
Willis, John. *Screen World*. Vols. 18–42. London: Frederick Muller, and London: Hutchinson, various years through 1991.
Winchester, Clarence. *Screen Encyclopedia*. London: Winchester, 1948.
_____. *The World Film Encyclopedia*. London: Amalgamated, 1933.
Wise, James E., Jr., and Anne Collier Rehill. *Stars in Blue: Movie Actors in America's Sea Services*. Annapolis, MD: Naval Institute Press, 1997.
_____, and _____. *Stars in the Corps: Movie Actors in the United States Marines*. Annapolis, MD: Naval Institute Press, 1999.
_____, and Paul W. Wilderson III. *Stars in Khaki: Movie Actors in the Army and Air Services*. Annapolis, MD: Naval Institute Press, 2000.
Woolley, Lynn, Robert J. Malsbury and Robert G. Strange, Jr. *Warner Brothers Television*. Jefferson, NC: McFarland, 1985.
Yablonsky, Lewis. *George Raft*. London: W.H. Allen, 1975.
Zec, Donald. *Marvin: The Story of Lee Marvin*. London: New English Library, 1979.
Zimbalist, Efrem, Jr. *My Dinner of Herbs*. New York: Limelight, 2003.

Periodicals

Classic Images
Filmfax
Films of the Golden Age
Modern Screen Who's Who in TV
Movie Memories
The National Enquirer
Picturegoer
Picture Show
The Radio Times
The Stage
TV Chronicles
TV Guide
TV Mirror
TV Star Annual
The TV Times
Variety
Western Clippings

INDEX

Numbers in *bold italics* indicate pages with photographs.

Abandon Ship! 428
Abbott, Bud 456, 520
Abbott, Dorothy 577
Abbott, Philip 603
Abbott and Costello Meet Dr. Jekyll and Mr. Hyde 303, 520
Abbott and Costello Meet the Killer, Boris Karloff 303
ABC Armchair Theatre 366
Abe Lincoln in Illinois 361
Abie's Irish Rose 65
Above and Beyond 423, 550
Accent on Youth 321
Ackroyd, Dan 579
The Act 424
Action in the North Atlantic 130, 361
Actors Studio 285
A.D. 271
Adam Had Four Sons 181
Adam Smith 311
Adam-12 63, 579
Adams, Dori Elizabeth 431
Adams, Dorothy 13
Adams, Julie 92
Adams, Nick 143
Adams, Tommye (Abigail) 538
Adamson, Al 547
Adler, Buddy 510
Adler, Luther 48
Adorée, Renee 591
Adreon, Franklin 236
Adventures at Scott Island 535, 582, 607
The Adventures of Dr. Fu Manchu 26, 231, 232, *235*, 236, 282, 346, 347, 365, 607
The Adventures of Ellery Queen 12, 61, 62, 257, 607
The Adventures of M. Hercule Poirot 283
The Adventures of McGraw 342, 607
The Adventures of Ozzie and Harriet 185, 404, 538
The Adventures of P.C. 49 464
The Adventures of Philip Marlowe 402

The Adventures of Quentin Durwood 324
The Adventures of Rin Tin Tin 214
The Adventures of Robin Hood 204, 205, 304, 324
The Adventures of Sam Spade 382, 431
Adventures of the Falcon 376, 607
The Adventures of Tom Sawyer 294
The Adventures of Tugboat Annie 569
Advise and Consent 330, 446
A.E.S. Hudson Street 349
An Affair to Remember 182
Affectionately Yours 520, 522
Africa—Texas Style 281
African Patrol 45–47, 607
The African Queen 453
Ah Wilderness 447
The Airmail Mystery 216
Airplane! 74, 514
Airplane II: The Sequel 74, 219
Airport 249
Airport 1975 604
Aitken, Mary 464
The Alaskans 205, 324, 337
Albert, Eddie 227
Albert R.N. 36
Albertson, Jack *5*, 6, 617
Albertson, Leo 5
Albertson, Mabel 5
Albright, John Paul 6
Albright, Lola 6–7, 8, 211, 520, 521, 570, 615
Albright, Marion Alba 6
Alcatraz Express 513
The Alcoa Hour 72
Alcoa Premiere 357
Alda, Alan 10
Alda, Ann 10
Alda, Robert 8–*9*, 10, 616
Alda, Robert, Jr. 10
Alda, Vincent 10
Alda and Henry 8
Aldrich, Robert 124, 384, 385
Alexander, Ben 10–*11*, 12, 34, 211, 576, 577, 610

Alfred Hitchcock Presents 158, 362, 384, 538
Alias Jesse James 155
Alias Nick Beal 397
Alibi 557
All About Eve 352, 392, 491
All I Desire 337
All My Children 582
All My Sons 353
All Points West 481
All the King's Men 159, 161, 368
All the Way Home 48
Allan, Elizabeth 259
Allan, Ted 125
Allbritton, Louise 600
Allegret, Marc 297
Allen, Adrianne 362
Allen, Barbara Jo 599
Allen, Irwin 253, 254, 270
Allen, Patrick 462
Allen, Woody 428
Aloma of the South Seas 222
Alternative Medicine 334
Altshuler, Ira *201*
Alves-Lico, Angela 110
Alves-Lico, Dorothy 110
Always Goodbye 29
Amana 249
Amateur Hour 504
The Amazing Dr. Clitterhouse 464
The Amazing Mr. Malone 296, 560, 561, 607
The Amazing Mr. X 30, 165
Ambassador Extraordinary 574
Ambrose 21
Ameche, Don 29, 563, 564
An American Romance 192
Ames, Florenz 12, 13, 62, 257, 352, 607, 614
Ames, Judith (Rachel) 13–15, 613
Ames, Michael 19
Ames, Susan 13
The Amorous Prawn 500
Amos 'n' Andy 296
And Now Tomorrow 534
And On We Go 363
And Then There Were None 266

625

Anderson, Barbara 94
Anderson, Gerry 25
Anderson, Gwen 173
Anderson, Dame Judith 226, 233, 361
Anderson, Leeta 16
Anderson, Lynda 19
Anderson, Maxwell 52, 343, 447
Anderson, Michael 16
Anderson, Pamela 518
Anderson, Richard 94, 373, 619
Anderson, Robert 50
Anderson, Sylvia 25
Anderson, Warner 14–15, 16, 613
The Andersonville Trial 193, 503
Andes, Keith 16–17, 18, 617
Andes, Mark 17
Andes, Matthew 17
Andes, William 16
Andrews, Barbara 19
Andrews, Dana 520, 604
Andrews, Gina 19
Andrews, Hazel May 390
Andrews, Henry Rowland 19
Andrews, John 19
Andrews, Julie (actress) 404, 446, 522
Andrews, Julie (Tige Andrew's daughter) 19
Andrews, Steve 19
Andrews, Tige 18–19, *549*, 550, 609
Andrews, Tod 19–20, 293, 608
Andrews, Tony 19
Androwas, George 18
Andy Hardy (film series) 309, 473
Angel, Heather 265
Angel Street 294
Angels One Five 260
The Animal Kingdom 222, 223
Ankers, Evelyn 181, 183
Ankney, Carla 221
Ankrum, Morris 150
Ann-Margret 503, 505, 506
Anna Christie 52
Annie Get Your Gun 44, 419
Annie Laurie 407
Annie McGuire 405
Anniversary Waltz 112, 353
Another Man's Poison 392
Another Thin Man 44
Another Time, Another Place 534
Another World 271, 353
Anouilh, Jean 199, 280, 303
Anthony Adverse 265, 596
Anthony and Cleopatra 233
Anything for a Quiet Life 262
Anywhere USA 445
The Ape 430
The Apple Cart 259
Appleby, Basil 555
Appointment with Crime 36

Appointment with Danger 255, 578
The Aquanauts 327
Arbuckle, Roscoe "Fatty" 387
Archer 69, 314
Ardale 280
Arden, Robert 20–*21*, 22–23, 238, 616
Are You Now and Have You Ever Been? 271
Are You Now or Have You Ever Been? 306
Arise My Love 396
Arkin, Alan 125
Arlen, Michael 152, 376
Arless, Jean 354
Arliss, Anita 226
Arliss, George 99, 226
Arliss, Jean *430*
Armchair Theatre 47
Armer, Alan 511, 512
Armstrong, Ellen Mary 497
Armstrong, Robert 99
Armstrong, Todd 295, 619
Armstrong Circle Theater 448
Arnaz, Desi 232, 510, 511
Arnold, Danny 241
Arnold, Edward 560
Arnow, Max 368
Around the World in 80 Days 344, 457
Arrest That Woman 352
Arrested Development 89
Arrowhead 313
The Arsenal Stadium Mystery 100
Arsenic and Old Lace 233, 303
Arthur, Jean 303, 391, 396
Arthur, Robert 166
As the Earth Turns 596
As the World Turns 201
As You Desire Me 197
As You Like It 333
Ashby, Hal 354
Ashby, Joan 354
Asner, Ed 227
The Asphalt Jungle 168
Asquith, Anthony 157, 280
The Assassin 283
Assault on a Queen 149
Assignment: Munich 145
Assignment: Vienna 144, 145
Astell, Betty 497
Astor, Mary 66, 361
At Mrs. Beams 360
At Sword's Point 246
At War with the Army 392
At Your Request 36
Atwater, Barry 373
Atwater, Edith 353
Aubrey, James 140
The Auctioneer 200
Auer, Mischa 21

Auger, Claudine 436
Aumont, Jean Pierre 299, 388
Auntie Mame 31, 239, 504
Autry, Gene 228, 272, 479
Autumn Crocus 258
Avedon, Doe *23*, 24, 526, 608
Avedon, Richard 23
The Avengers 58, 59, 523
Avery, Evelyn 340
Avery, Tol 24, 617
Away All Boats 416
The Awful Truth 41
Aylen, Colonel Ernest 328
Aylen, May 328
Ayres, Lew 183

Baa Baa Black Sheep 145
Babes in Arms 167
Babette Goes to War 280
Bacall, Lauren 80, 132, 355, 453, 510
Bacardi Rum 443
The Bachelor Father 395
Back Door to Heaven 463
Back Home 178
Background to Danger 456
The Bad and the Beautiful 534
Baden-Powell, Lord 46
Badge 714 578, 607
Badger, Clarence 294
Bain, Barbara 24–*25*, 26, 287, 616
Baird, John Logie 258
Baker, James 426
Baker, Stanley 212
Balcon, Sir Michael 416
Balenda, Carla 26–27, 282, 607
Balfour, Kathleen 27
Balfour, Michael *27*–28, 238, 613
Balfour, Perry 27
Balfour, Shane 27
Ball, Lucille 17, 140, 141, 181, 446, 491, 510, 511
Ball, Suzan 338
Ballyhoo 490
Balsam, Martin 227
Banacek *349*, 364
Bank Holiday 583
Banks, Joan 342
Banks, Monty 328
The Barbara Stanwyck Theater 593
Barbary Coast 191
Bardot, Brigitte 280
Bare, Richard L. 105
Barefoot in the Park 30
Bari, John 29
Bari, Lynn 28–*29*, 30–31, 164, 165, 609
Barker, Lex 139, 552
Barnes, Alice 31

Barnes, Barry K. 99
Barnes, Joanna 31–*32*, 408, 516, 618
Barnes, John Pindar 31
Barnes, Judith 31
Barnett, Luke 32
Barnett, Vince 32–34, 537, 610
Barney Blake, Police Reporter 1, *430*, 438, 607
Barney Miller 241
Baron Munchausen 251
Barrault, Jean-Louis 104
Barrett, Isabelle 506
Barrie, Barbara 227
Barrie, J.M. 29, 260, 303
Barrows, George 416
Barry, Gene 513, 557
Barrymore, Diana 533
Barrymore, Ethel 119, 226
Barrymore, John 388
Barrymore, Lionel 362
Bartell, Harry 34, 577, 610
Bartfield, Mel 354
Barton, Tod 15, 34–35, 613
Baruch, André 402
Basehart, Richard 270
Basie, Count 356
Bate, Harry 468
Bateman, Charles 35, 294, 613
Batman (cartoon series) 605
Batman (TV series) 316, 471, 472, 481, 483, 586
The Batman (serial) 419, *587*
The Battle of the River Plate 414
Battle of the V1 469
Battlestar Gallactica 254
Baur, Elizabeth 94, 203
Bautzer, Greg 106, 174
Baxley, Gary 208
Baxter, Anne 361, 415
Baxter, Cynthia 433
Baxter, Warner 181, 343, 482
Bayes, Nora 408
Baywatch 518
Beach, Annette 202
Beach Ball 107
The Beast with Five Fingers 9
Beatty, Charles Thompson 35
Beatty, Robert 35–*36*, 37–38, 324, 590, 609
Beatty, Warren 220
Beau Geste (film, 1939) 191, 192, 396, 444
Beau Geste (play) 258, 265
Beauchamp, Anthony *497*
Beautiful but Dangerous 9
Beaverbrook, Lord 37
Becket 20
Beckwith, Reginald 36
Bedlam 303
Beer, Jacqueline *39*–40, 602, 616
Beer, Jessie Ellen 594

Beery, Noah, Jr. 373
Beery, Wallace 79, 148, 164, 455, 559
The Beginning or the End? 423, 568
Behind Closed Doors 233, 234, 607
Behind That Curtain 301
Behind the Iron Mask 246
Being There 199
Bel Geddes, Barbara 470
Belita 534
A Bell for Adano 501
Bell Telephone Hour 14
Bellamy, Charles Rexford 40
Bellamy, Lynn 42, 43
Bellamy, Ralph 40–*41*, 42–44, 156, 445, 540, 613
Bellamy, Willard 42, 43
Bellaver, Bianca Vaughan 44
Bellaver, Harry *44*–45, 87, 88, 380, 614
Bellaver, Maria 44
Bellaver, Matteo 44
Belle of the Nineties 543
The Bells 301
Bells Are Ringing 520
The Bells of St. Mary's 223
Ben Casey 347, 561
Ben Hall 367
Ben Hur 260, 476
Bendix, William 444
Beneath the Planet of the Apes 241
Benet, Stephen Vincent 361
Benevides, Robert 96, 97
Benighted 197
Bennett, Constance 256, 596
Bennett, Derek 476
Bennett, Joan 265, 266, 444, 454
Benson 271
Benson, Martin 477
Bentley, John 45–*46*, 47–48, 607
Bentley, Joyce 47
Bentley, Roger 47
A Bequest to the Nation 573
Bergen, Candice 374, 522
Bergen, Edgar 333, 522
Bergen, Frances 522
Bergman, Andrew 125
Bergman, Gertrude 254
Bergman, Ingrid 61, 181, 197, 355, 397, 574
Bergner, Elizabeth 294
Berkeley Square 61
Berlin, Irving 391, 491
Berlin Express 322
Berman, Marc 514
Bernardi, Bernard 48
Bernardi, Helen *48*
Bernardi, Herschel 7, 48–49, 520, 521, 570, 615
Bernhard, Harvey 158

Bernie, Ben 454
Bernstein, Elmer 123
Best Foot Forward 568
The Best Man 199, 224, 342, 561
The Best of Everything 299
The Best of Steinbeck 19
Beswick, Martine 220
Bettger, Franklin Lyle (b. 1888) 49
Bettger, Franklin Lyle (b. 1942) 49, 51
Bettger, Lyle 49–*50*, 51, 56, 473, 529, 609, 611
Bettger, Lyle, Jr. 49, 50, 51
Bettger, Mary Rolfe 49, 50, 51
Bettger, Paula 50, 51
The Betty Ford Story 487
The Betty Hutton Show 153
The Beverly Hillbillies 334
Bey, Turhan 329
Beyond Atlantis 417
Beyond the Blue Horizon 181, 410
Beyond the Forest 69
Biano, Solly 105
Bickford, Charles 51–*53*, 54, 378, 503, 613
Bickford, Doris 53
Bickford, Loretus 52
Bickford, Rex 53
Bicycle Thieves 186, 453
Il Bidone 162
Biff Baker USA 246, 247, *532*, 607, 608
The Big Blockade 468
The Big Caper 13
The Big Clock 395
The Big Combo 148
The Big Country 53
The Big Heat 356
Big Jack 148
The Big Knife 107
The Big Parade 343
The Big Red One 357
The Big Spin Show 26
Big Time 560
Big Town 23, 195, 263, 264, 317, *382*, 383, 426, 515, 523, 524, 525, 526, 568, 569, 582, 598, 608
Big Trouble 125
Big Trouble in Little China 277
The Big Valley 338
Biggers, Earl Derr 419, 614
Bill Comes Back 294
The Bill Dana Show 253
Billie 330
Billy Budd 356
The Bing Crosby Show 227
Binns, Briget 55
Binns, Edward 54–*55*, 56, 79, 608, 615
Binns, Judy 55

Binns, Nancy 55
Birch, Don 56, 57
Birch, Jennifer 56, 57
Birch, Mike 56, 57
Birch, Paul 50, *56*–58, 609
Birds of Prey 258, 259
Bischoff, Sam 456
Biscialuz, Eugene W. 562
Bite the Bullet 527
Bits of Life 591
Bitzer, Reverend Robert 29
Bjork, Anita 415
Black Bart 341, 377
Black Beauty 181
The Black Castle 303
The Black Cat 302
The Black Dakotas 392
Black Hand 419
The Black Room 302
The Black Rose 260, 468
The Black Scorpion 182
Black Sheep Squadron 145
Black Widow (film, 1954) 457
Black Widow (film, 1987) 277
Blackman, Barbara 58
Blackman, Honor 58–*59*, 60–61, *169*, 610
Blackman, Ken 58
Blackman, Yvonne 58
Blackstone, Harry 296
Blade Runner 277, 317
Blair, Linda 369
Blake, Grey Wilson 172
Blake's 7 37, 324
Blanchard, June *266*, 267
Bless the Bride 464
Blessed Event 560
Blind Alley 41
Blind Date 199
Blomquist, Will 211
Blondie 13
Blood and Sand 29
Bloom, Claire 176
Bloomgarden, Kermit 445
Blown Away 74
Blue, Ben 442
Blue Blood 426
The Blue Gardenia 92
Blue Hawaii 588
Blues Busters 520
The Bob Cummings Show 7, 538
The Bob Mathias Story 292
Bob Vila's Home Again 286
The Bodysnatcher 303
Boetticher, Budd 509, 520
Bogarde, Dirk 100
Bogart, Grace 371
Bogart, Humphrey 37, 66, 70, 71, 80, 117, 129, 130, 132, 143, 341, 355, 361, 376, 403, 419, 453, 455, 476, 529

Bogeaus, Benedict 66, 408, 444, 456
Boghosian, Rose 268
Bogy, Anne 323
Bold Venture 131, 132, 236, 354, *355*, 608
Bolero 396, 455
Bolger, Ray 166
Bolt, Robert 311
Bolton, Lois 489
Bombers B-52 601
Bonanza 263, 471
Bond, Ward 378
Bonner, Isobel 132
Bonnie and Clyde 450
Bono, Sonny 604
The Boogie Man Will Get You 303
A Book at Bedtime 351
Boolo 543
Boomerang! 317
Boone, Richard 541
Boorman, John 357
Booth, Adrian 69
Boren, Lamar 73
Born Again 67
Born Yesterday 27, 161, 163, 171, 391
Borzage, Frank 131
Boss Lady 30
Boston Blackie (film series) 537
Boston Blackie (TV series) 136, 434, 546, 608
Boston Blackie's Little Pal 546
Botany Bay 252
Boulting, John 58
Bourbon Street Beat 202, 203, 255, 282, 283, 337, *338*, 532, 585, 586, 608
Bowe, Roemarie 514
The Bowery 455
The Bowery Boys 520
Bowman, Lee 12, 61, *62*, 63, 181, 257, 607
Bowman, Lee, Jr. 62
Boy Meets Girl 375, 445, 501
The Boy Who Cried Wolf 248
Boyd, Edward 476
Boyd, Stephen 435, 446
Boyd, William 526
Boyd Q.C. 2
Boyer, Charles 174, 297, 298, 299, 321
Boyett, John 63
Boyett, Kevin 63
Boyett, Suzy 63
Boyett, William 63, 64, 611
Boyle, Jack 546
Bracken, Eddie 533
Brackett, Charles 396
Bradley, Wilbur 511
Brady, Alice 52
Brady, William A. 196

The Brady Bunch 271
Bramley, Raymond 64, 255, 588, 610
Brand, Max 362
Brand, Neville 511
A Brand New Life 333
Brando, Marlon 314, 371, 384
Brandon, Henry 235
Brannigan 385
The Brass Ring 285
Brass Target 125
The Brat 343
The Brave Don't Cry 310
Brave Eagle 326
Brazzi, Rossano 435
Bread, Love and Dreams 186
Bread, Love and Jealousy 186
The Bread Winner 258
Breakfast at Tiffany's 404
Breakthrough 341
Breakthrough at Reykjavik 37
Breen, Richard L. 576
Breitenberger, Augustus (Gus) 104
Breitenberger, Jo-Ann 104
Breitenberger, Vincent 104
Brennan, Walter 585
Brenner 55, 78, 79, 608
Brent, Barry 66
Brent, George 64–*65*, 66–68, 105, 132, *369*, 618
Brent, Suzanne 66
Brewster, Diane 288
Brian, David 68–*69*, 70, 296, 340, 614
The Brian Keith Show 314, 315
The Brian Reece Show 464
The Bride of Frankenstein 302
Bride of the Gorilla 91
Bride of Vengeance 112, 397
Bridges, Beau 70, 74, 75
Bridges, Jeff 70, 74, 75
Bridges, Jordan 74
Bridges, Lloyd 70–*71*, 72–75, 616
Bridges, Lloyd Vernet, Sr. 70
Bridges, Lucinda (Cindy) 70, 75
Bridie, James 204
Bright Eyes 560
Bright Promise 20
Brisson, Frederick 412
Brisson, Lance 412
British Agent 223
Britton, Barbara 76–78, *182*, 185, 614
Broadway 560
Broccoli, Albert (Cubby) 587
Broderick, Helen 160
Broderick, James 55, 78, *79*, 608
Broderick, Matthew 79
Broderick, Patricia 79
Brodkin, Herbert 431

Brody, Estelle 395
Broken Arrow 413
Broken Journey 14
Bromfield, Louis 66
Bronson, Anthony Charles 82, 83
Bronson, Charles 79–*81*, 82–84, 216, 531, 613
Bronson, Jason 82
Bronson, Katrina Holden 82, 83
Bronson, Kim 83
Bronson, Paul 82, 83
Bronson, Suzanne Frances 82, 83
Bronson, Valentine 82, 83
Bronson, Zuleika Jill 82, 83
Brooke, Walter 586
Brooks, Roxane 84–85, 287, 616
Brooks, Stephen 603
Brother Rat 49, 375, 391, 533
Brown, Chamberlain 293
Brown, Clarence 252
Brown, Courtney 73
Brown, Fredric 117
Brown, Harriet 70
Brown, Joe E. 104
Brown, John 361
Brown, Johnny Mack 109
Brown, Lucile 216
Brown, Marie 535
Brown, Peter 293, 505
Brown, Rowland 454
Brown, Vanessa 424
Browne, Joan 10
Browne, Kathie 374
The Browning Version 280, 460
Bruce, Nigel 469
Brugh, Spangler Andrew 548
Bruns, Mona 552
Bryce-Harvey, Aldon Richard 554
Bryce-Harvey, Heather 554
Brynner, Yul 411
The Buccaneers 158, 476
Buchanan, Sidney 71
Buchanan Rides Alone 520
Buchinski, Charles 80, 84
Buchinsky, Charles 80, 84
Buck, Jules 461, 462
Buckskin 374
Buggy, Hugh 310
Buggy, John 310
Buggy, Maggie 310
Buggy, Michael 310
Buggy, Patrick 310
Buggy, Tom 310
A Bug's Life 254
Buick 89
The Buick Circus Hour 104
Bulldog Drummond film series 152, 460
Bulldog Edition 479
A Bullet for Joey 457

The Bullfighter and the Lady 509, 510
Bulls, Balls, Bicycles and actors 53
Bulls, Bears and Asses 489
Bunchinsky, Walter 80
Bunny, May Summerville 328
Buried Loot 548
Burke, Brian 89
Burke, Dina 89
Burke, James 85–86, 152, 612
Burke, Martin 86
Burke, Marty 86
Burke, Paul 45, *86*–89, 220, 269, 380, 435, 535, 610, 611, 614
Burke, Paula 89
Burke, Santa 86
Burke's Law 557
Burlesque 167
Burlesque USA 10
Burnett, Carol 513
Burnett, Don 327
Burns, Bart 89, 90, 614
Burns, George 517
Burns, Ray 218
Burns, Robert 408
Burns, Sherman 218
Burns, William J. 218, 612
Burr, Aaron 90
Burr, Geraldine 90, 96, 97
Burr, James Edmond 90
Burr, Michael Evan 96
Burr, Minerva 97
Burr, Raymond 2, 90–*93*, 94–99, 137, 140, 165, 248, *249*, 250, *278*, 348, *475*, 514, 535, *542*, 601, 615
Burr, William Johnston, Sr. 90, 96
Burton, Richard 22, 37, 213, 299, 469, 513
Bus Stop 382, 486
Bush, Andrea 320
Bush, Kathryn 320
Bush, Warren 320
Bushell, Anthony 99, *100*–101, 148, 169, 186, 261, 610
Bushell, Charles 99
Buswell, Phyllis Eileen 257
Butterfield, Herb 101–102, 192, 609
Butters, Frank P. 375
Butterworth, Peter 177
Buttons, Red 319
Bwana Devil 77, 509
By Love Possessed 602, 603
Byline Steve Wilson 526, 608
Byrd, Carroll 103
Byrd, Ralph *102*–104, 189, 240, 610
Byrd, Admiral Richard E. 102, 543
Byrne, Mary 104

Byrnes, Edd 104–*105*, 106–108, 451, *452*, 504, 601, 602, 616
Byrnes, Logan 106
Byron, Edward C. 296

Cabot, Sebastian 314
Cabot, Susan 206
The Cabot Connection 522
Cactus Flower 74, 522
Caesar and Cleopatra 594
Cage, Nicolas 453
Caged 211
Caged Fury 182
Cagney, James 143, 407, 455, 504, 505, 588, 596
Cahill, Barry 13
Cahill, Christine 13
Cahn, Edward L. 475
The Caine Mutiny 15, 453, 565
The Caine Mutiny Court-Martial 56, 155, 428, 534, 561
Calder, King 108, 525, 613
Calhoun, Rory 120, 144
California Dog Fight 373
The Californians 218
Call Me Bwana 22
Call Me Madam 491, 531
Call Me Mister 87, 168, 198, 202
Call Me Ziggy 565
Call Northside 777 148
Call Out the Marines 344
Calling Mr. Diamond 608
Calvert, John 376
Camelot 267
Cameron, Catherine 110
Cameron, Rod 108–*109*, 110–111, 608, 617
Cameron, Tony 110
Camille 549
Campanella, Joseph 141, 227
Campbell, Beverly 226, 228
Campbell, Bob 228
Campbell, Helen 65
Campbell, Louise 380
Campbell, Mollie 506, 507
Campbell, William 57
Can Can 299
Canada Carries On 524
Candelli, Stelio 367
Candida 259, 432, 460, 461
Candoli, Pete 123
The Candy Man 493
Canicule 358
Cannon 120
Cannonball 57
Cantinflas 169
Cantor, Eddie 455
The Cape Cod Follies 427
Capital News 74
Capone, Al 455, 510, 511
Capra, Frank 309, 509
Captain Corelli's Mandolin 453

630 Index

Captain from Castile 482
Captain Midnight 580, 581
Captain Midnight Makes General 581
Captain Scarlet and the Mysterions 238
Captains of the Clouds 407
Cardinal Richelieu 482
Cardinale, Claudia 42
Carefree 565
Carey, Charles 111
Carey, Charles, Jr. 111
Carey, Ellen 115
Carey, Gordon 111
Carey, Harry, Jr. 115
Carey, Harry, Sr. 115
Carey, Jeffrey 117
Carey, Linda 117
Carey, Lisa 114
Carey, Lisa-Ann 117
Carey, Lynn 114
Carey, Macdonald 111–*113*, 114–115, 155, 195, 613
Carey, Macdonald, Jr. 114
Carey, Olive 113, 115–116, 613
Carey, Paul 114
Carey, Philip 116–*117*, 118, 615
Carey, Sean 117
Carey, Shannon 117
Carey, Steve 114
Carey, Theresa 114
Carey, Timothy *220*
Carlisle, Mary *557*
Carlson, Christopher 120
Carlson, Henry Clay 118
Carlson, Richard 118–*119*, 120–121, 182, 273, 412, 516, 599, 612
Carlson, Richard Henry 120
Carlyle, Richard 121, 233, 372, 609
Carmen, Jewel 557
Carminati, Tullio 481
Carnegie Hall 333
Carney, Grace 121, 308, 616
Carnival Story 50, 415
The Carol Burnett Show 513
Caron, Leslie 299
Carr, John Dickson 304
Carradine, John 235, 411
Carrington, Eva 500
Carroll, Diahann 428
Carroll, Robert 122, 617
Carroll, Virginia 103
Carson, Jack 7, 407, 408, 409
Carson, Johnny 340
Carson, Selena 410
Carter, Gwendolyn 169
Carter, Lynne 542
Carver, Kathryn 389
Cary, Claiborne 332

Casablanca (film) 173, 376, 407, 455, 456, 531
Casablanca (TV series) 376, 531
Case, Carroll 243
A Case for P.C. 49 464
Case Histories of Scotland Yard 421, 422, 608
The Case of the Stuttering Bishop 596
The Cases of Eddie Ace 411
The Cases of Eddie Drake 244, 410, 411, 479, 480, 608
Casey Jones (play) 52
Casey Jones (TV series) 246
Cassavetes, Alexandra (Xan) 125, 487
Cassavetes, John 23, 122–*124*, 125–126, 128, 486, 487, 612
Cassavetes, Nicholas 122
Cassavetes, Nick 125, 487
Cassavetes, Zoe 125, 487
Cassel, Seymour 122
Castello, Louisa Mary 460
The Castilian 162
Castle, William 354
Castle in the Air 478
Castro, Fidel 457
Cat Ballou 357
Cat People 152
Cat Women of the Moon 294
Catacombs 367
Catch Me If You Can 169, 271
Cattle Empire 244
Caulfield, Joan 424
Cause for Alarm 534
The CBS radio Mystery Theater 251
CC and Company 506
Cebe 95
Celanese Theater 155
Celi, Teresa 424
Cellier, Antoinette 498
Centennial 146
Cesar's World 483
Chadney, Bill 7
The Challenge 200
Chamber of Horrors 432
Chamberlain, Richard 354, 362
Champagne Charlie 157, 589
Champion 7, 104, 131
Chandler, Jeff 402, 416
Chandler, Raymond 117, 615
Chanel, Lorraine 493
Chaney, Lon, Jr. 160, 181, 504
Chaney, Lon, Sr. 301, 504, 591
Chapeau Chinois 175
Chaplin, Charles 21, 22, 33, 387
Chaplin, Oona 22
Chapman, Lonny 126–127, 489, 612
Chapman, William Elmer 126
Chapman, Wyley Dean 126

Charasuchin, Allene 254
Charasuchin, Rosalie 254
Charasuchin, Sam 252
Charisse, Cyd 168
Charlie Ahearn and His Millionaires 8
Charlie Chan at Monte Carlo 283
Charlie Chan at the Opera 302
Charlie Girl 584
Charlie Wild Private Detective 333, 382, 608
Charley Varrick 565
Charley's Aunt 499, 583
Charlie's Angels 145, 254, 299
Charlot, André 395
The Charm School 582
Charrier, Jacques 280
Charteris, Leslie 152, 265, 267, 491
Chase 579
Chase, Borden 69
Chase, Edith Lindsey 401
Chatterton, Ruth 65
Cheer Up and Smile 418
Cher 5, 333
Chertok, Jack 241
Chevalier, Maurice 299
Chevrolet on Broadway 303
Chevrolet Teletheater 132, 253
Chevy Mystery Show 67
Cheyenne 105
Chicago 222
Chicken Every Sunday 352
Chico and the Man 5
A Child Is Waiting 123, 487
The Children Are Watching Us 186
The Chiltern Hundreds 499
Chin, Tsai 351
The Chisholms 446
The Chocolate Soldier 16
Christian, Hildy 462
Christian, Linda 424
Christian, Marc 417
Christie, Agatha 266, 283, 348
Christine Cromwell 42
A Christmas Carol 314
Christmas in Connecticut 408
Christmas in July 109
Christophsen, Lisbet (Betsy) 422
Chrome 417
Chu Chin Chow 592
The Church Mouse 265
Churchill, Sarah 497
Churchill, Winston 33, 37, 131, 497, 501
Churchill and the Generals 22
Ciannelli, Eduardo 123, *127*–129, 612
Ciannelli, Eduardo, Jr. 128
Ciannelli, Lewis 128
Circk, Minnie 242

The Circle of Chalk 591
The Cisco Kid 450
Citizen Kane 21, 137, 266, 501, 504, 527
City Assignment 608
The City Chap 454
City Detective 109, 608
City Hospital 488
City in Fear 290
Claire, Ina 533
Clarence 307
Clark, Dane 67, 129–*131*, 132–133, 236, 353, *354*, *369*, 392, 448, 608, 612, 618
Clarke, Gary 183
Clash by Night 17, 269
The Clemenceau Affair 185
Clerembard 176
Clift, Montgomery 92, 155
Climax 424, 469
The Climax 303
Clive of India 482
Cloak and Dagger 529
Cloudburst 444, 544
Clurman, Harold 431
Cobb, Lee J. 53, 72
The Cockeyed World 343
Code 3 450, 562, 598, 608
Codee, Ann 434
The Coffee Club 576
Coffin, Tristram 133–*135*, 245, 610
Cohan, George M. 381
Cohen, Larry 163, 467
Cohn, Harry 161, 272, 560
Colbert, Claudette 28, 197, 336, 396, 534
The Colbys 271
A Cold Wind in August 7, 354
Cole, Tina 228, 517, 619
Cole Younger Gunfighter 342
Colleano, Bonar 27
Collier, Lois 135–*136*, 137, 546, 608
Collins, Junius 137
Collins, Michael 64
Collins, Ray *93*, 94, 137–*138*, 615
Colman, Ronald 29, 70, 388, 492, 596
Colonel Humphrey Flack 291
Colonel March Investigates 304
Colonel March of Scotland Yard 303, *304*, 441, 478, 608
The Color of Love: Jacey's Story 487
Columbo 89, 124, 299
Columbo, Russ 9
Combat Leadership—The Ultimate Challenge 358
Come Back Little Sheba 126
Come On Up, Ring Twice 195
Come to the Stable 352

The Comedy of Terrors 304
Comes the Revelation 155
Command Decision 54, 192
Compton, Fay 259
Compton, John 138–139, 349, 609
Conan Doyle, Adrian 281
Conan Doyle, Sir Arthur 281, 360, 470, 617
Concerning Miss Marlowe 600, 601
The Confession 398
Confidential Report 21
Conflict 202, 601
Connery, Sean 59, 314
Connors, Dana 142
Connors, Matthew 142
Connors, Mike 94, 139–*141*, 142–143, 617
Conquest of Space 463
Conrad, Camille 146
Conrad, Chelsea 146
Conrad, Christian 145, 146
Conrad, Christy 146
Conrad, Joan 145, 146
Conrad, Kaja 146
Conrad, Nancy 146
Conrad, Robert 143–*144*, 145–147, 207, 208, 413, *442*, 443, *517*, 611
Conrad, Shane 145, 146
Conrad, Tammy Brandy 146
Conrad, William 375, 578
The Consul 600
Conte, Mark 149
Conte, Pasquale 147
Conte, Richard 100, 147–*149*, 150, 169, 186, *259*, 261, 470, 555, 602, 610
Conte, Ruth 149
Conte, Shirley 149
Conti, Italia 258
Conti, Tom 405
Conversation Piece 265, 490
Conway, Jack 559
Conway, Morgan 103
Conway, Muriel 151
Conway, Russ 150–*151*, 287, 596, 616
Conway, Tom 85, 151–*153*, 154, 237, 376, 490, 491, 612
Coogan, Richard 218
Cooke, Alistair 469
Cooke, James 523, 524
Cooper, Gary 42, 72, 329, 372, 387, 396, 444, 455, 531
Cooper, Gladys 99
Cooper, Jackie 48, 167, 308, 455
Cooper, Ray 226
Cooperman, Alvin 512
Coote, Robert 544
Copa, Maria 44

Copland, Ronda 286
Copley, Peter *350*
Le Corbeau 468
Corbett, Gretchen 605
Corday, Mara 182, 338, 339, 597
Corey, Bonnie Alice Elsie 156
Corey, Jeff 276
Corey, Jennifer Julia 156
Corey, Jonathan Wendell 156
Corey, Lucy Robin 156
Corey, Reverend Milton Rothwell
Corey, Wendell 42, 154–*156*, 157, 611
Corman, Roger 56, 80, 107, 139, 158, 182, 206, 226, 227, 243, 398
Cornell, Katharine 127, 233, 361
Coronado 9 109, 110, 608
Coronation Street 60
Corregidor 597
Le Corsaire 297
Cosa Nostra, An Arch Enemy of the FBI 604
Costello, Frank 456
Costello, Lou 456, 520
Costello, Pat 456
Cotsworth, Staats 372
Cotten, Joseph 112
Cotton, Jean Alice 17
Coulter, Judy Katt 248
The Count of Monte Cristo 343
Counterblast 204
Counterthrust 19, 20, 293, 608
The Country Girl 20, 132, 485
Court, Hazel *157*–159, 432, 499, 574, 610
The Court of Last Resort 50, 51, 56, 113, 608, 609
Courtin' Time 428
Courtland, Jerome 202
The Court-Martial of Billy Mitchell 42, 171, 372
Courtneidge, Cecily 223
Coward, Noel 160, 265
Cowboy in Africa 281
Cowl, Jane 343, 533
Cox, Constance 555
Coxe, George Harmon 121, 372
Cozzens, James Gould 603
Craft, Flora 5
Craig, Catherine 446
Craig Kennedy Criminologist 359, 587, 596, 597, 609
Crain, Jeanne 285, 415, 416
Cramer, Marjorie 538
Crane 462
Crank, Carrington Kendall 228
Crank, Cathleen 228
Crank, Fillmore 228
Crank, Fillmore (Smokey), Jr. 228

Crank, James 228
Crawford, Broderick 159–*161*, 162–164, 368, 611
Crawford, Christopher 163
Crawford, Joan 29, 61, 68, 69, 130, 197, 223, 368, 369, 408, 481, 534, 549
Crawford, Kelly 163
Crawford, Kim 163
Crawford, Lester 160
Crawford, Robert 295, 619
Crayne, Dani 290
Crazy with the Heat 91
The Creature from the Black Lagoon 119, 182
Creel, Claudia 347
Creel, Robert 347
Creeping Shadows 364
The Creeping Unknown 193
Cregar, Laird 91
Crime Club 271
Crime Does Not Pay 548
Crime Photographer 121, 233, 251, 371, 372, 401, 503, 609
Crime Squad 456
Crime with Father 325, 336, 609
Crimes of the Century 142
The Criminal Code 301
The Crimson Cult 304
Crisp, Beatrice 375
Cronyn, Hume 259
The Crooked Billet 360
Crosby, Bing 223, 227, 330, 444, 563
Crosby, Everett 444
Cross Current 402, 609
Cross Roads 45, 47
Crouse, Russell 41
The Crowded Sky 604
The Cruel Sea 260, 554
Cruikshank, Rufus 205
Crusader 313, 506, 609
Cruz, Penelope 453
Cruze, James 560
Cry of the City 148
Cry of the Hunted 534
Cukor, George 550
Culver, Roland 175
Cummings, Susan 327
Cummins, Peggy 175
The Curse of Frankenstein 158
Curtis, Dan 373
Curtis, Donald 30, 164–*165*, 166, 609
Curtis, Dorothy 165
Curtis, Tony 415, 416, 457
Cushing, Peter 157, 158
Cutler, Victor 426
The Cycle 552
Cyrano de Bergerac 384, 448
Czukor, Dr. Eugene 77

Czukor, Christina Eugenia 78
Czukor, Theodore Britton 78

Da 314
The D.A. 144, 579
The D.A.'s Man 138, 349, 609
Dabney, Augusta 448, 449
Dabney, Virginia 429
d'Abruzzo, Anthony 8
Da Costa, Morton 504
Dailey, Dan 58, 148, 166–*169*, 170, 186, 259, 261, 610
Dailey, Daniel, Sr. 166
Dailey, Dan, III 167, 170
Dailey, Irene 166, 170
Dale, Dana 263
Dale, Virginia 263
D'Allaire, Marie Anita Alexandrine 414
Dallas 35, 242, 599
Dalton, Timothy 271
Daly, Charles Percival 171
Daly, Cynthia Ann 171
Daly, David 171
Daly, Glynn 171
Daly, James *171*–172, 447, 554, 610
Daly, Mary Ellen 171
Daly, Pegeen 171
Daly, Timothy 171
Daly, Tyne 171
The Damned 112
The Damned Don't Cry 69
Dance Night 438
Dancers in the Dark 455
Dances with Wolves 326
Dancing Lady 29
Dancing Verselle Sisters 5
Dandridge, Dorothy 469
Danforth, Harold 138
Danger 392
Danger Man 593
Danger on the Air 596
Danger UXB 573
Dangerous Assignment 101, 102, 192, 538, 539, 609
Dangerous Crossing 468
Dangerous Exile 298
Dangerous to Know 592
Daniel, Dinah 212
Daniell, Henry 533
Daniels, Bebe 65
Daniely, Lisa *172*–173, 567, 612
Dannay, Frederic 61, 257, 352, 416, 607
Danova, Cesare 269, 432, *436*
Dantine, Helmut 173–174, 175, 617
Dantine, Niki *174*
Danton, Ray 457
Danziger, Edward 22, 237, 323
Danziger, Edward, Jr. 323

Danziger, Harry 22, 237
Danziger, Natasha 323
Darby's Rangers 105
Darin, Bobby 123
The Dark at the Top of the Stairs 445
Dark City 578
The Dark Corner 525
Dark Eyes 321
Dark Journey 99, 322
Dark of the Moon 256
Dark Rosaleen 52
Dark Victory 66
Darkness at Noon 313, 468
Darlan, Admiral 283
Darnell, Linda 9, 237
Daro un Milione 186
Darrow, Henry 289, 605
Darun, Rosine 176
A Date with Judy 509
Dateline Europe 553, 609
Dateline Hollywood 32
Daughter of the Dragon 591, *592*
Dauphin, Claude 114, *175*–177, 298, 615
Dauphin, Jean-Claude 176
Dauphin, Madeleine 175
Dauphin, Norma 114, 176
Davalos, Richard 362
Davenport, Marcia 600
David, Mack 144
David Copperfield 583
Davidson, Julia 426
Davidson, Norman 426
Davies, Hogan 179
Davies, Jessica 179
Davies, Rupert 177–*178*, 179, 274, 614
Davies, Timothy 179
Davis, Bette 61, 64, 65, 66, 69, 94, 131, 339, 390, 392, 393, 407, 534, 562
Davis, Jim 165
Davis, Nancy 557
Davis, Sammy, Jr. 330
Dawson, Elizabeth 401
Day, Doris 298, 330
The Day the Earth Stood Still 468
The Days of My Life 113
Days of Our Lives 10, 111, 113
Days of Wine and Roses 53
Dead End 130, 185, 375
Dead Pigeon 72
The Deadlier Sex 301
Deadline 527, 528, 609
Deadline for Action 609
The Deadly Companions 313
Dean, Basil 258
Dean, Erma 126
Dean, James 362, 371, 432
De Angelo, Carlo 431
Dear Octopus 583

Dear Phoebe 329
Dear Ruth 431
Dearden, Basil 261
Death of a Salesman 240, 269, 371
Death of a Scoundrel 67, 153, 491
Death Valley Days 374, 551
Death Wish 82
Debussey, Fleurette 263
Decameron Nights 298
De Carlo, Yvonne 109
Decker, Diana 179–*180*, 238, 613
de Cordova, Arturo 192
de Cordova, Frederick 228
Decoy 226, 227, 609
Dee, Frances 152
Deegan, Arthur 222
Deep Valley 131
The Defenders 529
DeForest, Marie 440
Degeneres, Ellen 271
de Grunwald, Anatole 280
de Havilland, Olivia 260, 407, 525
Dekker, Albert 227
Delbridge, Alice 42
De Leo, Lia 550
Delon, Alain 82
Del Rio, Dolores 343
The Delta Force 358
The Delta Force II 358
De Luxe 197
del Valle, Jaime 14
Demetre, Katherine 123
Demetrius and the Gladiators 468
DeMille, Cecil B. 52, 191, 223, 303, 346, 396, 444, 544
Deneau, Rita 402
Denison, Michael 2
Denning, Diana (Dee Dee) 181, 183
Denning, Richard 77, 142, 181–*182*, 183–185, 190, 437, 614
Dennis, Robert C. 483
The Dennis O'Keefe Show 212
Dennis the Menace 272
Denver, Bob 247
The Department 579
The Department of Queer Complainst 304
De Sales, Francis 182, 184–185, 614
The Desert Fox 469
Desert Fury 155
Desert Sands 461
The Desert Song 407
De Sica, Christian 187
De Sica, Manuel 187
De Sica, Vittorio 112, 148, 169, 185–*186*, 187–189, 230, *259*, 261, 610
The Desilu Westinghouse playhouse 510, 511

Désiree 468, 471
Desni, Tamara 498
Deslys, Gaby 418
The Desperate Hours 206, 224, 240, 325
Destination Moon 14
Destination Tokyo 15, 130, 448
Destry Rides Again 192
The Detective in Film 344
The Detective Story 41, 42, 349, 380, 382, 424, 564
The Detectives Starring Robert Taylor 18, 214, *549*, 550, 551, 556, 609, 619
Detective's Wife 29, 30, 164, 165, 609
De Toth, André 319
The Devil 301
The Devil and Daniel Webster 219
The Devil Bat 430
The Devil Is a Woman 482
Devil May Care 552
The Devil's Disciple 294
Devil's in Love 294
Devine, Andy 163
Devlin, Joe 103, 189–190, 610
Devon, Laura 317
Dewey, Thomas E. 296
Dewhurst, Colleen 227
De Wilton, Olive 305
Dexter, Maury 547
Dhu, Maura 6
The D.I. 340, 578
Diagnosis Murder 25, 141, 439
Diagnosis Unknown 432
Dial M for Murder 397
Dial 999 35, 36, 37, 324, 589, 590, 609
The Diamond 544
Dick and the Duchess 157, 158, 432, 499, 574, 609, 610
The Dick Powell Theater 313
Dick Powell's Zane Grey Theater 313
Dick Tracy (serial) 102
Dick Tracy (TV series) 102, 103, 189, 209, 239, 610
Dick Tracy's G-Men 102
Dick Tracy Returns 102
Dick Tracy vs. Crime Inc. 102
Dick Van Dyke and the Other Woman 404
The Dick Van Dyke Show 404, 437, 565
The Dickie Henderson Show 414
Dickinson, Angie 290
Dickinson, Thorold 280
Dickson, Carter 304, 608
Dietrich, Mai 402
Dietrich, Marlene 21, 192, 283, 387, 397, 455, 457, 482, 591
The Dinah Shore Show 520

Dinner at Eight 481, 560
Diplomacy 99
The Dirty Dozen 82, 124, 357, 385
The Dirty Dozen—Next Mission 358
Dishonorable Ladies 60
Disney, Walt 313, 314
Disraeli 99, ***100***
Disraeli, Sir Benjamin 99
The Distaff Side 212
Dive Bomber 520, 522
The Divorce of Lady X 467, 468
Dixon of Dock Green 324
Dmytryk, Edward 388, 389
Do Not Go Gentle Into That Good Night 199
Do You Want to Be an Actor? 181
D.O.A. 226
Dobbie, Edith 467, 471
Dobkin, Lawrence 32
Dr. Angelus 204
Dr. Broadway 112
Dr. Christian 112, 113
Dr. Kildare 220, 262, 354, 362
Dr. Simon Locke 5
Dr. Who 37, 572, 573
Doctor X 560
The Doctors 14
Dodd, Claire 546
Doer, Betty Reed 247
Dolin, Anton 592
Donahue, Marc Anthony 190
Donahue, Patricia 183, *190*–191, 617
Donahue, Sam 190
Donahue, Troy 106, 107, 144, 208, 517, 585, 619
Donath, Ludwig 227
Donlevy, Brian 101, 191–*193*, 194, 609
Donlevy, Judith Ann 193
Donlevy, Thomas Henry 191
The Donna Reed Show 439
Donovan, John 124
Donovan, General "Wild Bill" 462
Don't Make Waves 458
Doogie Howser M.D. 272
Doolittle, Franklin M., Sr. 341
Door with No Name 255, 475, 488, 588, 610
Doorway to Danger 64, 255, 488, 588, 610
The Doris Day Show 330
Dorne, Sandra 274
Dors, Diana 149, 180
Dorsey, Jimmy 122
Doubleday, Kay 503
Doucette, John 113, 194–196, 608, 613
The Doughgirls 383, 522

634 Index

Douglas, Gregory 196
Douglas, Kirk 7, 104, 131, 155, 156
Douglas, Lloyd C. 548
Douglas, Mary Helen 197
Douglas, Melvyn 77, 196–*198*, 199–200, 202, 561, 617
Douglas, Paul 17, 161
Douglas, Peter 196
Douglas, Robert 601
Douglas Fairbanks Presents 212
Down Three Dark Streets 161
Downtime 573
Doyle, David 254
Doyle, Len 200, 296, 614
Dozier, William 586
Dracula (film) 302
Dracula (play) 265
Dracula (TV) 299
Dracula vs. Frankenstein 420
Dragnet (film, 1954) 579
Dragnet (film, 1987) 579
Dragnet (TV series) 1, *11*, 14, 34, 92, 176, 211, 255, 292, 298, 340, 356, 440, 532, 576, *577*, 578, 579, 599, 610
Dragnet '69 (TV movie) 579
Dragon: The Bruce Lee Story 586
Drake, Alfred 16, 410
Drake, Jessica 201
Drake, Ken 201, 384, 615
Drake, Robert 201
Drake, Sylvie 201
Drake, Tom 568
Drango 280
Dream Girl 155, 240
Dressed to Kill 411
Dressler, Marie 569
Drew, John 360
Drew, Paula *201*, 344, 611
Drew, Wendy 201, 202, 463, 612
Driscoll, Bobby 248
Driscoll, Patricia 324
Drum Beat 80
Dubbins, Don 578
Dudley, Paul 462
Duffy, Henry 508
Duggan, Andrew 202–*203*, 204, 283, 337, *338*, 585, 608
Duggan, Edward Dean 202
Duggan, Melissa 203
Duggan, Nancy 203
Duggan, Richard 203
The Duke 145
Duke, Vera 134
The Duke in Darkness 91
The Dukes of Hazzard 450, 571
Dulcimer Street 478
Dullin, Charles 172
Du Maurier, Sir Gerald 99, 265, 360
The Dumb Girl of Portici 301

Duncan, Archie 204–*206*, 281, 617
Duncan, John George 204
Duning, George 378
Dunn, Jack 265
Dunn, James 206
Dunne, Irene 41, 197, 329, 548
Durant, Don 598
Durant, Heidi 598
Durant, Jeff 598
Durante, Jimmy 330, 454
Durbin, Deanna 41, 197, 388, 508, 509, 568
Durbridge, Francis 36
Durkin, Eleanor 85
Duryea, Dan 373
Dustin, Ruth 465
Dutoit, Mabel 118
Dyall, Valentine 36
Dynamite 52
Dynasty 89, 271, 331

Each Dawn I Die 452, 455
Each Pearl a Tear 10
Eagels, Jeanne 99
Earl Carroll Vanities 33
The Earl of Puddlestone 91
An Early Frost 487
Early to Bed 239
Earn Your Vacation 340
Earthquake 535
East of Eden 126, 362
East of Java 52
East of Sumatra 338
East of Suez 343
The East/West Game 125
Eastenders 476
Easter Parade 328
Eastwood, Clint 82
Easy Living 396
Eberhardt, Norma 114, 176
Ebsen, Buddy 327
The Eddie Capra Mysteries 385
Eddy, Nelson 407
The Eddy Duchin Story 504
Edeling, Betty 358
Eden, Eddie 180
Edge of Darkness 173
The Edge of Night 92, 233, 239
Edge of the City 123
Edmonson, Travis 504
Edwards, Blake 7, 287, 520, 521
Edwards, Dana 263
Edwards, Gus 418
Edwards, James 71
Edwards, Vince 340
Efird, Mary Mell 428, 429
The Egg and I 337
Eggers, Lillian 153
Egli, Joe 396
87th Precinct 487
Eisley, Amanda 208

Eisley, Anthony 143, 206–*207*, 208–209, 413, *442*, 443, 516, *517*, 611
Eisley, David 208
Eisley, Frederick, Sr. 206
Eisley, Jonathan 208
Eisley, Nancy 208
Ekberg, Anita 117
Ekdahl, Axennia Theresa 240
El Producto Cigars 346
The Eleventh Hour 42, 156
Elise, Jacqueline 37
Elisen, Colonel William 462
Ellery Queen (film series) 41, 61, 223
Ellery Queen (TV series) 12, 61, 62, 257, 564, 610
Ellery Queen's Penthouse Mystery 592
Elliott, Dick 103, 209, 210, 610
Elliott, Evan 210, 535, 611
Ellis, Herb 211, 577, 610
Ellwood, Adam 273
Ellwood, Craig 273
Ellwood, Erin 273
Ellwood, Jeffrey 273
Elphick, Jeanette 504
Elstree Calling 591
The Elusive Pimpernel 260
Elvey, Maurice 259
Emerald Point NAS 433
Emergency 579
Emergency Squad 164
Emerson, Hope *211*–212, 520, 570, 615
Emery, John 270
Emmerdale Farm 238
Empire 82
End of the River 421
End Station of the Damned 417
The Enemy Below 269
Enemy from Space 193
The Enforcer 501
Englebert, William, Jr. 479
Englebert, William, III 479, 480
English Without Tears 175
Englund, Adam 334
Englund, Brian 334
Englund, Dinah 334
Englund, George 334
Englund, George, Jr. 334
Englund, Morgan 334
Enter Arsene Lupin 322
Epple, Margaret Carol 538
Equus 171
Erickson, Leif 264
Erwin, Stuart 559
Essex, David 573
The Eternal Road 391, 447
Evans, Clifford 212–*213*, 214, 595, 617
Evans, David Hugh 212

Evans, Kenneth 212
Evans, Linda 290
Evans, Maurice 233, 306, 381, 447
The Eve of St. Mark 447
Everett, Chad 220
Everson, William K. 344
Every Man for Himself 561
Evil Town 558
Exiled 499
Exodus 328
The Exorcist 369
The Expendables 140
Experiment Perilous 66
The Eyes of Annie Jones 367

Fabares, Shelley 314
Fabian of Scotland Yard 498, 610
Fabian of the Yard *497*, 498, 610
Face of a Stranger 487
Faces 124
The Facts of Life 334
Fairbanks, Douglas, Jr. 213
Fairbanks, Douglas, Sr. 301, 591
Fairchild, William 185, 187
The Falcon (film series) 151, 152, 491
Falcon Crest 203, 483, 586
The Falcon's Brother 152, 491
Falk, Peter 32, 122, 124, 145, 227
Falkowski, Leonard 143
Fallen Angels 601
The Fallen Idol 259
Fallon, Tom 37
Fame Is the Spur 58
Family 79
The Family 148
Family Affair 314, 315, 380
Family Affairs 499
A Family in Blue 605
Family of Cops 82
A Family Upside Down 604
Fann, LaVelda 145, 146
Fanny 176
Fantasy Island 145, 517, 518
The Far Country 377
Faraday and Company 169
Farewell Friend 82
A Farewell to Arms (film, 1957) 186
A Farewell to Arms (play) 283
Farish, Margaret 56
The Farmer's Daughter 16, 53
Farnum, William 222
Farr, Lee 214, 550, 609
Farrell, Charles 42
Farrow, John 252
Farrow, Mia 124
Fashions in Love 387
Fate Is the Hunter 526
Father Damien—Leper Priest 290
Father Knows Best 504

Faulkner, William 68
Faust 406
Fawcett, Farrah 289
Faye, Alice 166, 457, 482
The FBI 30, 120, 142, 320, 323, 400, 471, 600, 603, 604
Fear Strikes Out 105
Fedderson, Don 228
Federal Men in Action 610
Feeley, Pamela 358
Feinsohn, Reba 600
Feldman, Charles K. 269, 322, 456
Feldshuh, Tovah 604
Fellini, Frederico 162
The Felony Squad 11
Felton, Norman 362
The Female Animal 416
Fernandez, Abel 214–*215*, 511, 618
Fernandez, Josie 215
Ferrer, José 384, 445, 448
Fessenden, James Atkins 226
Fibber McGee and Molly 569
Fiddler on the Roof 48
Field, Betty 155
Field, Lily 454
Fields, Benny 384
Fields, W.C. 403
Fifield, William 368, 370
The Fifth Season 123
The Fighting Lady 549
The File on Thelma Jordan 156
The Files of Jeffrey Jones 33, 134, 135, 244, 272, 273, 537, 610
Fina, Julia 147
The Final Conflict 158
Finch, Jon 367
Finian's Rainbow 516
Finnegan Begin Again 446
Fire Over Africa 112
The Firebrand 588
Firebrand of Florence 568
Fireside Theater 30, 67, 117
First Love 19, 508
First Monday in October 199
First Night 283
The First Nighter 563, 564
First You Cry 405
Fische, Ernestine 321
Fisher, Eddie 518
Fisher, Gail 141
Fisher, Joely 518, 519
Fisher, John Manard 29
Fisher, Tricia Leigh 518, 519
A Fistful of Dollars 82
Fitzgerald, F. Scott 534
Five Against the House 313
Five Fingers 86, 87, 268, 269, 270, 435, 436, 468, 610
Five Minutes That Can Change Your Life 165

Five Star Final 99
Flame of Love 591
Flame-Out 309
The Flame Within 265
Flamingo Road 68
Flash Gordon 254
Flavin, James 81, 215–217, 613
Flavin, William 216
Fleming, Arthur 217–*218*, 219, 612
Fleming, Becky 219
Fleming, Helene 62
Fleming, Rhonda 112
Fleming, Victor 62
Flesh and Blood 125
Flesh and the Spur 139
Flies in the Sun 99
Flight Command 549
Flint of the Flying Squad 497
Flipper 317
Florey, Robert 429, 456
Flothow, Rudolph 276, 420
Flower Drum Song 593
The Fly 268, 269
Flying Disc Men from Mars 136
The Flying Doctor 183
The Flying Scotsman 395
Flying Soldiers Show 444
Flying Tigers 218
Flynn, Errol 46, 525
Flynn, Gertrude 222
Foch, Nina 333
Fog Over Frisco 596
Folland, Gloria 20
Follies 30, 522
Follow the Boys 337
Follow Your Heart 475
Fonaroff, Nina 269
Fonda, Henry 19, 29, 376, 384, 455, 505
Fontaine, Joan 298, 525
Fontanne, Lynn 29, 127, 160, 171, 265, 427, 533, 591
The Fool 343
For Me and My Gal 167
For the People 126
For Those Who Think Young 505
Forbes, Bryan 261
Forbidden Planet 400
Ford, Glenn 148
Ford, John 115, 168, 268, 344, 419
The Ford Show 408
Ford Theater 17, 31, 53, 139, 198, 249, 534
Foreign Assignment 610
Foreign Correspondent 491
Foreign Intrigue 21, 171, 402, 432, 447, 497, 553, 554, 610
Foreman, Carl 261
Forrest, Leslie 174
The Forsyte Saga 595

Forsythe, Rosemary 290
Forty Carats 522
Forty Deuce 271
Forty Guns 533, 534
42nd Street (film) 65
42nd Street (stage musical) 424
Foster, Norman 501
Foster, Stephen 520
Foster, Susanna 303
Foulger, Byron 13
Four Boys and a Gun 219
Four for the Morgue 256
Four Frightened People 223
Four Guns to the Border 120
Four in a Jeep 384
The Four Just Men 58, 59, 100, 147, 148, 149, 166, 168, *169*, 185, 186, 187, 230, 231, 257, 258, *259*, 261, 310, 311, 555, 610
Four Star Jubilee 428, 534
Four Star playhouse 520
Fox, William 418
The Foxes of Harrow 532
Fraley, Oscar 510
Frances 90
Franciosa, Tony 513
Francis, Kay 65
Franciscus, Carla 221
Franciscus, James 87, 219–*220*, 221–222, 378, 380, 530, 614
Franciscus, Jamie 221
Franciscus, John 219, 221
Franciscus, John Allen 219
Franciscus, Julie 221
Franciscus, Kelly 221
Franciscus, Korie 221
Franey, Catherine 97
Frank, Geraldine 133
Frankenstein 301, 302
Frankenstein 1970 302
Franklin, Tom 552
Franz, Elizabeth 55
Fraso, Mary M. 308, 309
Frawley, William 408
Fredericks, Helena 323
Frederique, Berthe (Quique) 299
A Free Soul 196
Freeman, Leonard 512
Freeman-Turner, Charles 567
Freemantle, Margery (Peggy) 362
Freemantle, Admiral Sir Sydney 362
The French Atlantic Affair 39
The French Line 520
French Without Tears 77, 396
Frend, Charles 260
The Freshman 79
Freund, Karl 302
Friedman, Phil 130
From Failure to Success in Selling 49

From Hell It Came 20
From Here to Eternity 578
From the French 176
From This Day Forward 525
Fromkess, Leon 420
The Front Page (film, 1931) 388
The Front Page (play) 10, 216, 295, 307, 398, 427, 560
Front Page Detective 201, 291, 344, 610, 611
Frontier Gal 109
Frou Fro 418
Fu Manchu (film series) 235, 351
Fu Manchu (radio series) 563
Fu Manchu (TV pilot) 235
The Fugitive 57, 232, 286, 288, 289, 312, 419, 603
Full of Life 148
Fuller, George Michael 115
Fuller, Sam 357, 384, 509, 534
Fun for Your Money 8
The Furies 155
The Further Adventures of Ellery Queen 415, 416, 439, 564, 611
Further Outlook 490

Gabin, Jean 457
Gable, Clark 33, 276, 287, 388, 468, 550
Gabor, Eva 284
Gabor, Magda 493
Gabor, Zsa Zsa 153, 491, 493
Gahagan, Helen 196, 197, 198, 199
The Gallery of Mme. Liu-Tsong 590, 592, 593, 611
Galloway, Don 94
Gallows Glorious 212
Galsworthy, John 499
The Gambler and the Lady 132
Games People play 219
Gangbusters 339, 340, 475, 611
The Gangster 534
Gangway 467
Gann, Ernest K. 509
Garbo, Greta 52, 65, 197, 549
Garcia-Roady, Juan 39
Garcia-Roady, Laurent 39
Garcia-Roady, Serge 39
Garde, Colin 419
Gardella, Louis John 479
Garden, Mary 407
The Garden Murder Case 344
The Garden of the Finzi-Continis 187
Gardenia, Vincent 227
Gardner, Ava 329, 510
Gardner, Erle Stanley 50, 56, 57, 90, 92, 94, 541, 615
Garfield, John 8, 9, 129, 130, 143
Gargan, Ed 222
Gargan, Leslie Howard 222

Gargan, Patricia 222, 224
Gargan, William 222–*224*, 225, 273, 428, 464, 552, 561, 613, 614
Gargan, William (Barrie), Jr. 222
Gargan, William, Sr. 222, 224
Garland, Beverly 226–*227*, 228–229, 609
Garland, Judy 30, 123, 167
Garland, Richard 226, 228
The Garment Jungle 31
Garner, James 145
Garner, Shirley Colleen 149
Garrett, Betty 72
Garrick, John 592
Garrick, Rian *229*–230, 294, 613
Garson, Greer *41*, 42, 490
Garver, Kathy 314, 315
Garvey, Dora 341
Gastoni, Lisa 59, 187, 230–*231*, 610
Gates, Opal 579
Gauguin, Paul 97
The Gauntlet 448
Gay Falcon (story) 376
The Gay Falcon (film) 152
The Gay Sisters 67
Gaynor, Janet 119
The Gazebo 288
Gazzara, Ben 122, 124
G.E. True 578
Geas, Tom 540
Geller, Bruce 24, 141
Gendre, Henri 297
Gendre, Pierre 297
Gendre, Robert 297
General Electric 81
General Electric Theater 82, 148, 377, 585
General Hospital 13, 564
A Gentleman of Paris 328
Gentlewoman 427
George, Anthony 437, 511, 619
George, John 231–232, *235*, 607
George, Mareta Alice 463
The George Raft Casebook 456, 611
The George Raft Story 457
George Sanders Mystery Theater 492, 493, 611
Georgiade, Anastasia 232
Georgiade, Nick *215*, 232–*233*, 511, 618
Gerber, David 142
Gerolomi, Enzio 107
Gershung, Ted 270
Gershwin, George 8, 9
Gerstein, Rose 501
Getting Married 77
Ghetto 222
The Ghost of Yankee Doodle 119

The Ghoul 302
G. I. Hamlet 233
Giant 368, 369
Gibson, John 121, 233, 251, 372, 609
Gibson, Mel 460
Gide, André 298
Gielgud, Sir John 463, 583
The Gift of Love 510
Gigi 298, 299
Gilbert, Jane 278
Gilbert, Lewis 27
Gilbert and Sullivan 12
Gildersleeve's Bad Boy 248
Gill, Helen 243
Gilligan's Island 246, *247*
The Ginger Man 432
The Gingerbread Lady 30
Girl Crazy 537
The Girl in Room 13 193
The Girl of the Golden West 509
Girl on the Run 105, 601
Glaser, Barney 396
The Glass Menagerie 78, 415, 485
The Gleam 58
Gleason, Jackie 514
Gleason, James 99
Glockner, Eva 454
Gloria 125, *487*
Gluck, Alma 600
Glynis 17
Glynne, Renee 132
Go, Man, Go! 131
God Bless Dr. Shagetz 558
God Is My Co-Pilot 525
Goddard, Mark *18*, *549*, 551, 619
Goddard, Paulette 28, 112, *350*
The Goddess 72
The Godfather 128
The Godfather Part II 128
Gods of Lightning 52
Goettinger, Liselotte 440
Goff, Ivan 141
Gold 398
Gold, David 163
Gold, Lauren 163
Golden, George Fuller 115
Golden Boy 104, 130, 326, 553
Golden Earrings 397
The Golden Gate Murders 290
The Golden Girls 483
Goldfinger 59, 564
Goldstone, Nat 524
Goldwyn, Frances 319
Goldwyn, Sam 160, 191, 197, 319, 455, 548
Gomer-Lewis, Ethel 177
Gomer Pyle USMC 283
Gone with the Wind 66, 294
Gooch, Daphne 27
Gooch, Miranda 27
Gooch, Nicola 27

The Good Earth 592
The Good Humor Man 7
Good Morning Miss Dove 509
Good Neighbor Sam 140
Good News 328
The Good Old Summertime 12
Goodbye My Fancy 164
Goodman, Phoebe 258
Gorbachev, Mikhail 37
Gordon, Bruce 232–*233*, 234, 511, 607
Gordon, Don 540
Gordon, Glen 26, 231, 234–*235*, 236, 282, 347, 365, 607
Gordon, Noelle 47
Gore Vidal's Lincoln 405
The Gorgeous Hussy 197, 549
Gorky Park 358
Gough, Michael 477
Gould, Chester 102, 103
Gould, Deborah 331
The Governor and JJ 169
Gozier, Bernie 132, 236, 608
Grable, Betty 29, 166, 167, 168, 169, 458, 482
Grade, Lew 22
Graf, Bernice May 286, 287, 290
Graham, Ellie 290
Graham, Genine 590
Graham, Martha 269, 410
Grahame, Gloria 356
The Grand Duchess and the Waiter 387
Grand Jury 50, 51, 473, 529, 611
Granger, Farley 139
Granger, Stewart 119, 237
Grant, Cary 41, 70, 107, 182, 198, 203, 394, 445, 520, 564
Grant, Pres. U.S. 57, 144
The Grass Is Greener 583, 584
Grauman, Walter 511
Graves, Peter 25
Gray, Berkeley 153
Gray, Billy 468
Gray, Charles 262
Gray, Coleen 453
Gray, Deborah 238
Gray, Donald 27, 152, *180*, 236–*237*, 238, 274, 366, *367*, 461, 543, 544, 613, 616
Gray, Dulcie 47
Gray, Professor E. 548
Gray, Loretta 238
Gray, Lorna 69
Gray, Willoughby 572
The Gray Ghost 19, 20
Grayson, Kathryn 267
Grease 107
Great Catherine 262
The Great Escape 82
The Great Gatsby 62, 112, 219, 534

The Great Hotel Murder 344
The Great Jewel Robber 69
The Great Lie 66
The Great Man's Lady 192
The Great McGinty 192
The Great Missouri Raid 155
The Great Profile 388
The Great Ziegfeld 407
Greatest Heroes of the Bible 295
The Greatest Show on Earth 444
Greaza, Walter 223, 238–239, 613, 618
Greco, Buddy 290
The Greek Tycoon 221
Green, Harry 21, 22
Green, Sheila 238
Green Acres 74
The Green Archer 294
The Green Bay Tree 583
Green Dolphin Street 256
The Green Hornet 586
The Green Years 568
Greene, Angela 103, *239*–240, 610
Greene, Clarence 140
Greene, Graham 469
Greene, Lorne 178
Greene, Richard 304
The Greene Murder Case 475
Greenwood, Jack 421
Greenwood, Walter 212
Greer, Jane 91
Greetings 374
Gregory, James 240–*241*, 242, 612
Gregory, James Gillen 240
Gregory, Paul 361, 428
Greshler, Abby 288
Grey, Anne 365
Grey, Nan 596
Grey, Yvonne 193
Grey, Zane 294, 313
Griffin, Merv 107, 176
Griffith, Cynthia 48
Griffith, D.W. 10
Griffith, Kay 163
Griffith, Rachel Lee 559
Grimm, Maria 286
Grizzard, George 446
Grouch Club 211
Grouse in June 36
Grover, Loraine 219, 221
Growing Pains 410
Guadalcanal Diary 148
Guestwood Ho! 420
The Guilt of Janet Ames 450
Guilty as Hell 344
Guinan, Texas 454
The Guinea Pig 58
Guinness, Alec 204
Gulager, Clu 270, 555
Gunga Din 128

Gunn 7, 521
Gunnett, Laura Gail 580
The Guns of Zangara 513
Gunslinger 227
Gunsmoke (radio) 34, 440
Gunsmoke (TV) 270
Gutermuth, Deborah 290
Guthrie, Tyrone 310
Guys and Dolls 8, 9, 21, 22, 74, 169

Haavidsen, Mayme 383
Hackett, Marjorie 403
Hackett, Shelah 17
Hadley, Dale 243
Hadley, Reed 242–*243*, 244, 616
Hagen, Jean 383
Hagen, Uta 269
Haggerty, Don 33, 134, 244–*245*, 246, 272, 411, 479, 537, 608, 610
Hailey, Arthur 470
The Hairy Ape 44
Hale, Alan, Jr. 246–*247*, 248, *532*, 608
Hale, Alan, Sr. 130, 246
Hale, Barbara *93*, 94, 95, 96, 248–*249*, 250–251, 615
Hale, Jeanne 246
Hale, Juanita 248
Hale, Karen 246, 247
Hale, Luther Ezra 248
Hale, Willa Calvin 248
The Half Naked Truth 560
Halfway to Hell 475
Hall, Cliff 121, 251, 372, 609
Hall, Gita 535, 536
Hall, Juanita 593
Hall, Magdalen King 468
Halliday, Brett 183, 428
Hallmark Hall of Fame 171, 199
Halpen, Marjorie 29
The Halperin Brothers 407
Halsey, Brett 436
Hamill, Pete 458
Hamilton, Bruce 361
Hamlet (film) 100
Hamlet (play) 154, 171, 212, 233, 259, 360, 381, 463, 594
Hammerstein, Oscar, II 411
Hammett, Dashiell 320, 329, 382, 431, 608
Hammond, Earl 251–252, 308, 616
Handcuffs London 498
Handy Andy 548
Hangar 18 373
Hanging Judge 361
Hangman's Wharf 590
Hangmen Also Die 192
Hannah and Her Sisters 428
Hannen, Hermoine 213

Hannen, Nicholas 213
Hanson, June *266*, 267
The Happiest Millionaire 37
Happy Days (Fox revue) 344
Happy Days (TV series) 145, 437
Happy Go Lovely 482
The Happy Time 176, 298
Happy Town 209
Harbor Command 154, 155, 156, 611
Harbor Lights 9
Harbourmaster 24, 87, 210, 310, 349, 364, 534, 535, 582, 611
The Hard Way 407
Hardcastle and McCormick 314, 315
The Harder They Fall 529
Harding, Ann 197, 319
Harding, Grace 305
Hardly Working 530
Hardy, Thomas 281
Hargrove, Marion 601
Harker, Gordon 274
Harlan, Ella 597
Harlequinade 460
Harlow 140, 603
Harlow, John 36
Harper, Valerie 10
Harpers West One 477
Harris, Jonathan 252–*253*, 254–255, 467, 470, 617
Harris, Marion 481
Harris, Richard 254
Harris, Robert H. 50
Harris, Sam 66, 160
Harris, Stacy 64, *255*–256, 500, 610, 615
Harrison, Kathleen 157
Harrison, Rex 532
Harry O 289
Hart, Hillary 257
Hart, Lorenz 166, 167, 479
Hart, Mary 479, 480
Hart, Moss 112, 391, 423, 475, 485, 493
Hart, Richard 12, 61, 256–*257*, 607
Hart, Richard Lee 257
Hartman, Gretchen 246
Harts of the West 74
Harvest of Stars 361
Haskin, Byron 467
The Hasty Heart 351, 356
Hatch, Wilbur 511
Hatcher, Teri 228
The Hatchet Man 418
Hathaway, Henry 260, 262, 356
Haunts of the Very Rich 74
Have Gun Will Travel 234, 270, 541
Haver, June 525
Havers, Nigel 584

Havoc, June 509
Hawaii 413
Hawaii Five-O 51, 89, 183, 364, 413, 436, 463
Hawaiian Eye 143, *144*, 206, *207*, 208, 324, 413, *442*, 443, 516, *517*, 611, 619
Hawkins, Andrew 259, 260, 262
Hawkins, Caroline 260, 262
Hawkins, Florence 258
Hawkins, Gladys 258
Hawkins, Jack 148, 169, 186, 257–*259*, 260–263, 310, 554, 555, 583, 610
Hawkins, Nicholas 259, 262
Hawkins, Susan 258, 259, 260, 262
Hawkins, Thomas George 258
Hawkins, Tom 258
Hawks, Howard 260, 388, 455, 559
Hayden, Russell 134
Hayes, Annelle 525
Hayes, Bill 227
Hayes, Helen 410
Hayes, Margaret (Maggie) 263–*264*, 608
Hayward, Dana 267
Hayward, Louis 264–268, *266*, 613
Hayward, Susan 61, 468, 515
Hayworth, Rita 393, 501
He Walked By Night 576
Headline 526, 611
A Healing 518
Heaney, Gladys 420
Hearn, Martha 432
The Heart of Doris 360
Heart of Spain 321
Heart of the City 252, 611
Heartbeat 388
Heartland 314, 315
Hearts of the World 10
Heartsounds 405
Heaven with a Barbed Wire Fence 148
Hec Ramsey 579
Hecht, Ben 560
Heckscher, Betty 113, 114
Hedison, Albert David 268
Hedison, Alexandra Mary 271
Hedison, David 87, 268–*270*, 271–272, 435, *436*, 610
Hedison, Serena Rose 271
Heflin, Van 119, 510
Heggen, Thomas 505
Hell Below Zero 590
Hell in the Pacific 357
Hell-Ship Morgan 102
Heller in Pink Tights 344
Hellinger, Mark 40, 87, 378
Hell's House 53

Helm, Frances 314
Helmore, Evelyn Hope 305
Helmore, Tom 305
Hemingway, Ernest 357, 444
Hemingway's Adventures of a Young Man 169
Henderson, "Chuck" 272, 294, 613
Henderson, Dickie 413
Henderson, Edward 538
Hendry, Ian 59
Henie, Sonja 29, 287, 518
Hennesey 308
Henning, Charles 565
Henreid, Paul 65, 407
Henry, Gloria 245, 272–273, 610
Henry, Hank 8
Henry, O 482
Hensley, Pamela 95
Henson, Mildred 385
Hepburn, Audrey 604
Hepburn, Katharine 198, 550
Her Cardboard Lover 99
Her Jungle Love 396
Here Comes the Cavalry 562
Here's Love 521
Herman, Luba 502
Hernandez, Juano 69
Herrman, Bernard 468
Hersholt, Jean 112, 113
Hesse, Paul 6
Hesselberg, Edward G. 196
Heston, Charlton 220
Heyday 312
Heydrich, Reinhard 192
Heyerdahl, Thor 40
H.G. Wells' Invisible Man 611
Hi-Riders 385
Hickok, "Wild Bill" 242
Hicks, Patricia 572
Higgins, Liz 481
The High and the Mighty 23, 509
High Button Shoes 169
The High Cost of Loving 487
High Flight 397
High Mountain Rangers 145
High Noon 72
High Sierra 453, 455
High Sierra Search and Rescue 145
Higher and Higher 248
Highly Dangerous 131
Highway Patrol 37, 63, 110, 159, *161*, 162, 163, 563, 611
The Highwayman 267
Hill, Ona L. 96
Hill, Steven 25
Hillebrand, Fred 223, 273, 613
The Hills of Donegal 45
Hilton, James 321
Hindle, Art 95
The Hindu 304
Hines, Frazer 572

Hinton, Darby 274
Hinton, Ed 120, 273–274, 612
Hipple, George W. 352
His Brother's Wife 548
His Girl Friday 41
His Kind of Woman 91
His Majesty the American 301
Hiss and Tell 599
Hit the Deck 557
Hitchcock, Alfred 92, 112, 158, 298, 321, 384, 397, 460, 491, 529
The Hitch-Hiker 341, 541
Hitchy-Koo 12
Hitler, Adolf 501, 509, 594
Hitler's Madman 411
Hitower, Rosalind 196
Hobley, Macdonald 237
Hockstein, Jacob 529
Hofert, Elizabeth 167
Hoffman, Dustin 88
Hogan's Heroes 540
Holden, Jan 477
Holden, William 276, 384, 457, 576
Holiday 533
Holiday Camp 157
Holland, May Dell 479
Holliday, Judy 148, 161, 391, 509
Holliman, Earl 208
Holloway, Stanley 590
Hollywood Canteen 130, 520
Hollywood Hussar 592
Hollywood Offbeat 198, 199, 611
A Hollywood Revue 9
Hollywood Stadium Mystery 242
Holm, Sonia 274
Holt, Jack 102
Holt, Patrick 274–275, 613
Holt, Seth 416
Holtzer, Max 570
Home Before Dark 601
Home of the Brave 71, 341
Homicidal 354
Honey, Alice 204
Honey West 502
Honeymoon for Three 66
The Honeymooners 322
Hong, James 276–278, 420, 614
Hooker, Alice 20
Hoover, J. Edgar 603, 604
Hopalong Cassidy (film series) 294
Hopalong Cassidy Returns 475
Hope, Bob 22, 43, 518, 565
Hopkins, Miriam 66
Hopper, DeWolf 278
Hopper, DeWolf, Jr. 278
Hopper, Hedda 106, 278
Hopper, Joan 278
Hopper, William 92, *93*, 94, 278–279, 615

Horan, James 138
Horn, Edith Mary 499
Horsman, Patricia 281
Horwitz, Howie 106, 601
Hostile Witness 398
Hot Pepper 343
Hot Shots! (film) 74
Hot Shots (TV series) 89
Hot Shots!: Part Deux 74
Hotel (film) 470, 471
Hotel (TV series) 605
Hotpoint 404
House of Bamboo 509
House of Conley 44
House of Frankenstein 303
House of Rothschild 302
House of Strangers 148, 600
House of Wax (film) 319, 341
House of Wax (TV pilot) 432
The House on 92nd Street 242, 428
The House without a Key 419
How the West Was Won 361, 446
Howard, Ann 281
Howard, Fenella 281
Howard, Joe 525
Howard, Joyce 279
Howard, Ken 290, 315
Howard, Leslie 35, 96, 99, 212, 222, 223, 279, 280, 281, 360
Howard, Ronald 204, 279–*280*, 281–282, *350*, 351, 617
Howard, Sidney 71, 223
Howard, Steven 281
Howat, Clark 26, 235, 282, 365, 607
Howell, Arlene 282–283, 337, *338*, 608
Howell, Mary Lee 291
Hoy, Nancy 424
Huass, Dorothy 448
Hubbard, Jacqueline 143
Huber, Ethel 284
Huber, Harold 283–*284*, 611
Huber, Margaret 284
Hud 199
Hudson, Rock 252, 355, 369, 415, 416, 417, 510
Hudson's Bay 424
Huggins, Roy 288, 504, 601
Hugh-Kelly, Daniel 314, 315
Hughes, Howard 26, 30, 103
Hughes, Marie 519
Hugo, Victor 288
The Human Touch 204
Hume, Benita 492, 493
A Hundred Different Lives 362
Hunt, Marsha 156, 597
The Hunter 326, 423, 611
Hunter, Holly 487
Hunter, Ross 593
Huntley, Raymond 394

The Hurricane 361
Hurry Sundown 505
Husbands 124
Hush, Lizabeth 285, 384, 615
Hush Money 454
Huston, John 79, 176, 455
Hutchins, Will 402, 403, 451, 452, 505, 530
Hutchison, Frederick James Simpson 477
Huth, Harold 467
Hutton, Betty 384
Hyde-White, Wilfred 432, 470, 471
Hyman, B.D. 393
Hysterical Blindness 487

I Am a Camera 461
I Can Get It for You Wholesale 168
I Conquer the Sea 407
I Cover Times Square 283, 284, 611
I Do, I Do 446
I Led Three Lives (book) 120
I Led 3 Lives (TV series) 118, *119*, 120, 274, 412, 516, 599, 611, 612
I Love a Mystery 599
I Love Trouble 601
I Loved You Wednesday 294
I Married a Communist 541
I Married an Angel 167
I Never Sang for My Father 199, 362
I Shot Jesse James 242
I Spy 361, 362, 612
I Take This Woman 545
I Walk Alone 155
I Walked with a Zombie 152
I Want a Policeman 533
I Want to Live! 515
I Wanted Wings 580
I Was a Communist for the FBI 341
I Wonder Who's Kissing Her Now 525
I Won't play 130
Idiot's Delight 36, 361, 444, 560
Idol of Paris 468
I'll Be Seeing You 565
I'll Be Your Sweetheart 468
I'll Tell the World 562
I'm Almost Not Crazy 122
I'm the Law 453, 456, 457, 612
Imitation of Life 9
The Immoralist 298
The Immortal 69
Impact 592
In a Lonely Place 341
The In-Laws 125
In Old Arizona 343
In Old Chicago 191
In Search of My Father 281

In the Zone 360
In This Our Life 66, 407
Incendiary Blonde 192
The Incredible Mrs. Ritchie 487
The Incredible Shrinking Man 532
Independent Insurance Agents 95
The Indian Runner 82
Indiscretion 186
The Infernal Machine 71, 176
The Informer 395
Inge, William 384
Ingolia, Peter 516, 518
Ingram, Rex 231
Ingrim, Naomi 247
Inherit the Wind 199, 349
Inigo Pipkin 595
The Inn of the Sixth Happiness 574
Inness, Jean 293
Innocents in Paris 176
An Inspector Calls 478
Inspector Mark Saber—Homicide Squad 85, 151, 152, 153, 612
Inspector Morse 311
International Detective *218*, 219, 612
International Squadron 173
Internes Can't Take Money 61
The Interns 161
Interpol Calling 321, 322, 323, 476, *477*, 612
Intrigue 456
Intruder in the Dust 68
The Invaders 471
The Investigator 126, 489, 612
The Invisible Boy 400
The Invisible Man (1950's TV series) *172*, 567, 572, *573*, 612
The Invisible Man (1975 TV series) 522
The Invisible Monster 581
The Invisible Ray 302
Ireland, Jill 79, 80, 82, 83, 84
Iris 99
The Iron Glove 509
Ironside (TV movie pilot) 94
Ironside (TV series) 92, 94, 95, 97, 249, 348
Ironside in Paradise 96
Irving, Henry 301
Irving, Richard 109
Is Your Honeymoon Really Necessary? 179
Is Zat So? 99
Island in the Sun 469
Island of Desire 237
The Islander 143
Isle of the Dead 303
Istanbul 46
It Came from Beneath the Sea 165

It Came from Outer Space 119
It Conquered the World 227
It Couldn't Have Happened 352
It Happened in Brooklyn 329
It Happened One Sunday 36
It Should Happen to You 329
It Takes a Thief 55
It Took Nine Tailors 388
Italian Swiss Colony Wine Makers 531
It's a Great Feeling 408
It's a Living 557
It's a Pleasure 287
It's a Wonderful Life 309
It's Always Fair Weather 168
Ivanhoe 310
Ives, Burl 53

J for J 536
The Jack Albertson Comedy Hour 5
Jack and the Beanstalk 456
The Jack Carter Show Gravediggers of 1950: A Musical Extravaganza 482, 483
Jack the Ripper 259
Jackson, Charles 396
Jackson, Cornwall 92
Jackson, Gail Patrick 249
Jackson, Kate 228
Jacobs, W.W. 476
Jacqueline Bouvier Kennedy 221
Jacques, Hattie 574
Jagger, Dean 220
The Jail Diaries of Albee Sachs 477
James, Brian d'Arcy 317
James, Frank 155, 242
James, Harry 458
James, Jesse 155, 242
James Dean: Race with Destiny 142
James Michener Presents a South Pacific Adventure 50
Jane Eyre 152
Janis, Carlin 286
Janis, Christopher 286
Janis, Conrad 285–286, 463, 612
Janis, Elsie 418
Janis, Harriet 285
Janis, Sidney 285
Janssen, Dani 290
Janssen, David 24, 84, 89, 256, 286–*287*, 288–291, 312, 404, 557, 603, 616
Janssen, Diane 290
Janssen, Ellie 89, 290
Janssen, Eugene 287
Janssen, Jill 287, 290
Janssen, Kathy 290
Janssen, Teri 287, 290
Janus 176
Jarman, Claude, Jr. 69
Jason 148

Java Head 591, 592
The Jazz Singer 131, 307
JB 362
Jealousy 99
The Jean Arthur Show 149
Jefferson, Thomas 90
Jenkins, Roy 458
Jenks, Frank *291*–292, 344, 611
Jens, Salome 385
Jeopardy (film) 534
Jeopardy! (TV series) 219
Jergens, Diane 292–*293*, 608
Jerry Cotton (film series) 417
Jesse Hawkes 145
Jessel, George 222
The Jest 195
Jesus of Nazareth 37
Jet Jackson Flying Commando 580
Jewell, Isabel 561
Jezebel 66
Jimmy Hughes Rookie Cop 201, 285, 325, 463, 612
Joe Forrester 74
Joe Palooka 537
John Brown's Body 361
John Loves Mary 49, 333
Johnny Angel 456
Johnny Belinda 53
Johnny Concho 320
Johnny Cool 330
Johnny Eager 549
Johnny Guitar 368
Johnny Modero Pier 23 576
Johnny Ringo 598
Johnny Staccato 122, 123, 124, 127, 128, 520, 612
Johnny Two by Four 533
Johns, Glynis 17
Johnson, Andrew 130
Johnson, Arte 315
Johnson, Ida 566
Johnson, Van 510
The Joker Is Wild 226, 227
Jolly's Progress 155
Jolson, Al 131, 249, 307
Jolson Sings Again 249
The Jolson Story 131, 249
Jones, Alfred 395
Jones, Allan 407
Jones, Anissa 314
Jones, Buck 109, 134
Jones, Jennifer 53, 276
Jones, L.Q. 467
Jones, Mrs. Ruth 135
Jordan, Jim, Jr. 569
Jordan, Jim, Sr. 569
Jordan, Marion 569
Jory, Edwin 293
Jory, Jean 295
Jory, Jon 295
Jory, Victor 35, 230, 272, 293–*295*, 296, 383, 613

Jostyn, Jay 296–297, 571, 614
Jourdan, Louis 176, 297–*298*, 299–300, 615
Jourdan, Louis Henry, Jr. 299
Jourdan, Yvonne 297
Journey Into Fear 501
Journey Together 363
Journey's End 99, 258, 548, 583
Jowitt, Mary 595
Joyce, Nora 386
Judgment Day 341
Judy O'Connor 448
Julia 428
Julie 298
Julius Caesar 431, 443
The Jungle 109
The Jungle Book (film, 1942) 102
The Jungle Book (film, 1967) 493
Jungle Princess 396
Jungle Queen 136
Junior Miss 285, 463
Juno 318
Juno and the Paycock 204
Jurado, Katy 72
Just Jim 115
Just Joe 593
Just Off Broadway 476
Just Plain Bill 5
Just William's Luck 27
Justice (play) 499
Justice (TV series) 131, 132, 391, 392, 448, 612
Justice, Jack T. 563
Justice, William B., Sr. 562

The K-Guy 65
Kaiser, Ede 321
Kalmar, Harry 288
Kane, Irene 336
Kane, Walter 30
Kanin, Garson 176, 223, 391, 600
Kansas Pacific 242
Karas, Anton 470
Karen 183
Karloff, Boris 157, 158, 197, 235, 236, 300–*304*, 305–306, 430, 441, 478, 608
Karloff, Sara Jane 305
Karlson, Phil 510
Karnes, Robert 241, 306–307, 612
Karns, Katherine 309
Karns, Roscoe 122, 251, 307–*308*, *309*, 616
Karns, Todd 251, 308, *309*–310, 616
Katt, Barbara Willa Johanna 248
Katt, Laura Lee Juanita 248
Katt, William 248, 250
Katzman, Sam 408, 509
Kaufman, George S. 160, 493
Kaufman, Rita 345

Kaufmann, Barnaby 60
Kaufmann, Lottie 60
Kaufmann, Maurice 60
Kaz 433
Kazan, Elia 130, 148, 317
Keene, Mike 310, 535, 611
Keep America Beautiful 18
Keep the Home Fires Burning 101
Keighley, William 455
Keir, Andrew 261, 310–*311*, 312, 610
Keir, Andrew, Jr. 311
Keir, Deidre 311
Keir, Maureen 311
Keir, Sean 311
Keith, Barbara 314, 315
Keith, Betty 314, 315
Keith, Brian 312–*313*, 314–316, 334, 506, 609
Keith, Byron 107, 316, 337, 602, 616
Keith, Daisy 315
Keith, Michael 314, 315
Keith, Mimi 314, 315
Keith, Robert (1898–1966) 15, 312
Keith, Robert (b. 1970) 315
Keith, Rory 314, 315
Kelley, Barry 316–317, 608
Kelly, Brian 317–*318*, 408, 618
Kelly, Devon 317, 318
Kelly, Gene 167, 168
Kelly, Grace 397
Kelly, Hallie 317, 318
Kelly, Harry F. 317
Kemek 270
Kenlay, Joan 143, 146
Kennamer, Dr. Ruxford 458
Kennedy, Arthur 78, 248
Kennedy, Eunice 329
Kennedy, George 508
Kennedy, John F. 221, 328, 329, 330
Kennedy, Joseph 328, 329
Kennedy, Patricia 329, 330
Kenney, Mary Elizabeth Patricia 222, 224
Kent, Jean 100
Kerr, Deborah 119, 182, 212, 550
Kerr, Jean 470
Kesselring, Joseph 303
Key Largo 240
Keyes, Evelyn 322
Khan 120
Kid Galahad 7
Kidd, Michael 17, 168
Kiemast, Teresa 400
Kikune, Al 236
Kilbride, Percy 337
The Killer That Stalked New York 322
The Killer Who Wouldn't Die 142

642 Index

The Killers (film, 1946) 375
The Killers (film, 1964) 124, 357
Killers Kiss 336
The Killing of a Chinese Bookie 125
Kim 346
King, Dennis 557
King, Martin Luther 393
King, Nita Katt 248
The King and I 322, 371, 411
A King in New York 21, 22
King of Alcatraz 418, 444
King of Diamonds 162, 224
King of Hearts 333
King of the Khyber Rifles 468
King of the Rocketmen 134
King Soloman's Mines 119
Kingsley, Sidney 130, 564
Kingston, Lenore 564
Kingston: Confidential 95
Kinjite: Forbidden Subjects 554
Kinsella, Walter 223, 296, *318*, 613
Kirk, Phyllis *319*–321, *329*, 330, 540, 617
Kirkwood, Joe, Jr. 537
Kismet 364
Kiss and Tell 438
The Kiss Barrier 343
Kiss Me Deadly 333, 383, 384
Kiss Me Kate (film) 460
Kiss Me Kate (stage musical) 16, 411
Kiss of Death 192, 411, 485
Kiss the Girls and Make Them Die 140
Kitt, Freda Choy 376
Kitty Foyle 128, 407
Klee, Lawrence 14
Klugman, Jack 80
Knight, "Fuzzy" 109
Knives 125
Knots Landing 44
Knott, Frederick 397
Knute Rockne All American 596
Kolbe, Margaret 152, 490
Kolchak: The Night Stalker 373, 374
The Kolchak Papers 373
Koo, Wellington 591
Kookie, Kookie Lend Me Your Comb 106, 517
Kookie No More 107
Korda, Sir Alexander 102, 259, 260, 360, 361, 583
Korvin, Charles 321–*322*, 323, 476, *477*, 612
Koverman, Ida 548
Kraft Television Theater 18, 502
Kraines, Lois 114
Kramer, Stanley 7, 71, 72, 123, 323, 341, 388, 389, 576

The Kremlin Letter 493
Krieger, Shirley 149
Kubrick, Stanley 336, 384, 424
Kulek, Augusta 547
Kulp, Nancy 244

Labyrinth 22
LaCava, Paul 283
LaCentra, Peg 527
Ladd, Alan 112, 252, 444, 534
Ladd, Diane 227
Ladies in Retirement 267
Ladies Man 604
Lady Butterfly 12
The Lady Craved Excitement 310
Lady Do 481
Lady from Chungking *284*
The Lady from Shanghai 501
The Lady from the Sea 395
The Lady Gambles 444
Lady Godiva 416
Lady in Cement 149
Lady in the Dark 112, 495
Lady in the Iron Mask 246
Lady on a Train 41
Lady Windermere's Fan 371, 499
LaFarge, Francis 219
Laffan, Patricia 37
Lait, Jack 561
Lake, Veronica 444, 580
Lamarr, George 196
Lamarr, Hedy 66, 266, 416, 525, 545
Lamb, Robert 273
Lamont, Duncan 36, 323–*324*, 325, 609
Lamour, Dorothy 181, 396, 410, 444
Lancaster, Burt 123, 249
Lancer 203
Lanchester, Elsa 302
The Land Is Bright 353, 533
Land of the Pharoahs 260
Land Unknown 46
Landau, Juliet 26
Landau, Martin 24, *25*, 26
Landau, Susan 26
Landon, Judy 314
Landon, Michael 105, 143
Landres, Paul 81
Lane, Marjorie 193
Lane, Mike 302
Lane, Rusty 325, 336, 463, 609, 612
Lang, Fritz 192, 305, 356, 529
Langan, Glenn 30
Lansbury, Angela 429, 588
Lansing, Robert 88, 487
Laredo 117
The Lark 303
Larkin, John 497
Larkin, Margaret 542

Larsen, Erik 327
Larsen, Keith 326–327, 423, 611
Larsen, Kevin 327
Larsen, Trang 327
Larson, Susan 491
Lassie 214, 333
The Last Frontier 445
The Last Mile 444
The Last Picture Show 333
Last Rites 132
The Last Safari 262
The Last Starfighter 446
The Last Time I Saw Archie 578
The Last Voyage 510, 511
The Late Christopher Bean 371
Lau, Wesley 94, 619
Laugh That Off 222
Laughton, Charles 197, 223, 361, 395, 428
Launer, John 50
Laura 353
Laverick, June 269
Laverne and Shirley 145
Law, John Philip 505
Lawbreakers 356
Lawford, Christopher 329
Lawford, Deborah Gould 331
Lawford, Frances Sydney 329
Lawford, Mary Rowan 331
Lawford, Lady May 328
Lawford, Patricia Kennedy 329, 330
Lawford, Patricia Seaton 331
Lawford, Peter 319, 320, 327–*329*, 330–332, 540, 617
Lawford, Robin 329
Lawford, General Sir Sydney 328
Lawford, Victoria 329
The Lawless 112
The Lawless Years 241, 306, 612
Lawrence, Doreen 259, 262
Lawrence, Gertrude 112
Lawrence of Arabia 262
Lawson, Sarah 476
Leachman, Cloris 332–*333*, 334–335, 382, 431, 608
The League of Gentlemen 261
Lear, Norman 74
The Leather Jungle 366
Lee, Belinda 132, 298
Lee, Bruce 586
Lee, Christopher 157, 158, 235, 359
Lee, Manfred B. 61, 257, 352, 416, 607
Lee, Robert E. 57
Lee, Sammy 29
Lee: A Romance 358
Leeds, Barbara 391, 392
Leffingwell, Patricia 183
Le Gallienne, Eva 294, 447, 599

The Legend of Eli and Lottie Johl 581
The Legend of Prince Valiant 605
LeGrand-Nohain, Franc 175
Leigh, Vivien 99, 549
Leisen, Mitchell 112, 396, 397, 398
Le Maire, Charles 435
Lemmon, Jack 53
Lend Me a Tenor 424
Lennon, John 305
Leonard, Herbert B. 87, 88, 378
Leonard, Queenie 153
Leonard, Robert Z. 9
Leonard, Sheldon 253, 404
Lerner, Alan Jay 298
LeRoy, Mervyn 550
Leslie, Joan 407
Leslie, William 15, *335*–336, 613
Lesser, Ted 181
Letter from America 469
Letter from an Unknown Woman 298
Letters from an actor 463
Levin, Henry 450
Levine, Dr. Robert 405
Levinson, Richard 140
Levy, Jules 456
Lewin, Albert 491
Lewis, Hilda 582
Lewis, Jerry 502
Lewis, Lester 199
Lewis, Richard 313
Lewis, Robert 431
Lewis, Warren 80, 132
Lewton, Val 152, 303
Licence to Kill 271
Liebman, Ron 433
The Life and Legend of Wyatt Earp 245, 256, 324, 479
Life Begins at 8–40 191
The Life of Lewis Carroll 572
Life with Father 554
Life with Luigi 419, 420
Lifeboat 460
Light Up the Sky 423
The Lightin' Warrior 65
Lights Out 302
Lili Marlene 172
Liliom 371
Limehouse Blues 592
The Limping Man 72
Lincoln, Abraham 361
Linda Lovelace for President 472
Lindbergh, Jon 73
The Linden Tree 303
Lindsay, Howard 41, 160
Lindsay, Margaret 278, 481
The Lineup (film) 15
The Lineup (TV series) 13, 14, *15*, 16, 34, 335, 465, 466, 565, *566*, 571, 572, 612, 613

Link, William 140
Lisbon 397
Litel, John 153
The Little Foxes 119
The Little House on the Prairie 117
The Little Minister 574
Little Miss Marker 388
Little Nellie Kelly 557
The Little People 314
The Little Shop of Horrors 514
Live and Let Die 271
Lives of a Bengal Lancer 543
Livingston, Jerry 144
The Lizard on the Rock 261
Lloyd, Euan 190
Lloyd, Frank 394
Lloyd, Innes 572
The Lloyd Bridges Show 74
Lloyds of London 491
Lobbin, Peggy 325, 336, 609
Lock Up 113, 115, 195, 613
Lockhart, June 254
Lockridge, Frances 77, 182
Lockridge, Richard 77, 182
Lockwood, Margaret 131, 468, 583
Loder, John 365, 591, 592
Lodge, John 583
The Lodger 259
Loewe, Frederick 298
Loftin, Carey 510
Logan, Joshua 119, 357, 444, 486, 505, 600, 601
Logan, Robert 106, 107, 145, 602, 619
Loggia, Robert 551
Logue, Elizabeth (Betty) Ann 203
Lois & Clark—The New Adventures of Superman 228
Lolita 180
Lollobrigida, Gina 9, 186
Lombard, Carole 41, 223, 396, 455, 509
London, Julie 576, 577, 579
London, Steve 619
The Lone Wolf (radio) 402
The Lone Wolf (TV series) 266, 267, 613
The Lone Wolf and His Lady 460
The Lone Wolf Takes a Chance 71
The Loner 74
Long, Carey 338, 339
Long, Dale 336
Long, Gregory 338, 339
Long, Senator Huey 161
Long, Richard 202, 283, 316, 336–338, 339, *452*, 585, 602, 608, 616
Long, Stephen D. 336
Long, Valerie 338, 339
The Longest Day 106

Longstreet 219, 220, 378
Longstreet, Stephen 97
Look at Life 567
Look Back in Anger 27
Loraine, Denis 492
Lord, Jack 183, 413
Lord, Jeff 328
Lord, Phillips H. 296, 339–340, 611
Lord, Sofia M. 340
Lord Arthur Savile's Crime 281, 555
Lord Jim 262
Lord Love a Duck 7
Loren, Sophia 125, 187
The Loretta Young Show 416
Loring, Beatrice 53
Loring, Lynn 603
Lorna Doone 365
Lorre, Peter 29, 157, 158, 304, 424
Losey, Joseph 112
Loss, Joe 21
Lost in Space (film) 254
Lost in Space (TV series) 252, 253, 254, 471
Lost in Space Forever 254
Lost in Space: The Journey Home 254
Lost in Yonkers 369
The Lost Patrol 302
The Lost Weekend 394, 396, 397
The Lost World 270, 470
Louder Please 293
Loughery, Jackie 69, 340–*341*, 578, 579, 614
Louisiana Susie 336
Love Affair 182
The Love Boat 271, 409, 518
Love for Love 594
Love Happy 233
Love in the Tropics 239
Love Is a Many Splendored Thing 276
Love Life 50
Love of Life 475, 552
Love on the Dole 212
Love Story 394, 398
Love Streams 23, 125
The Love Suicide at Schofield Barracks 369
Love That Brute 482
Lovejoy, Frank 341–*342*, 343, 613, 614
Lovejoy, Judith 342
Lovejoy, Stephen 342
Lowe, Edmund 201, 291, 343–*344*, 345–346, 611
Lowe, Edward 343
Loy, Myrna 65, 320, 329, 423, 469
Luber, Bernard 457

Lubitsch, Ernst 197, 509
Lucky Boy 222
Lucky Nick Cain 453, 456
Luez, Laurette 235, *346*, 347, 607
Luft, John Michael 30
Luft, Sid 30
Lugosi, Bela 193, 302, 303, 430
Lugosi, Lillian Arch 193
Luiz, Francesca (Frances) 346
Luiz, Frank 346
Luke, Keye 302
Lulu 284
Luncheon at the Colony 264
Lunt, Alfred 127, 160, 171, 265, 427, 535, 591, 600
Lupino, Ida 19, 131, 173, 174, 267, 341, 407
Lupus, Peter 25
Lured 491
Lussier, Yvonne 110
Lust for Gold 448
Lustgarten, Edgar 421, 616
Lux Video Theater 7, 226, 278, 313
Luxury Liner (1933) 67
Luxury Liner (1948) 65, 66, 67
Lyles, A.C. 156, 506
Lynch, Ken 347–348, 434, 615
Lyon, Ben 468
Lyons, Gene 94, 348, 615
Lysistrata 211

M Squad 356, 357, 425, 613
MacArthur 605
MacArthur, Charles 560
MacArthur, James 469
Macbeth 226, 423
MacDonald, David 183
Macdonald, Elizabeth 111
MacDonald, Ross 314
MacGraw, Ali 398
Machine Gun Kelly 80, 82
Mack, Ted 504
Mack and Mabel 446
Mackenney, Julia Reid 155
The Mackenzie Raid 120
Mackenzie's Raiders 120
MacLaine, Shirley 299
MacMurray, Fred 109, 227, 228
The Macomber Affair 444
MacRae, Gordon 509
MacReady, George 448
The Mad Magician 432
Madame Bovary 298
Mme. Liu-Tsong 593, 613
Madigan's Millions 458
Madsen, Virginia 514
The Madwoman of Chaillot 252, 503
Maggie 78

The Magnificent Ambersons 137, 268
The Magnificent Dope 29
The Magnificent Obsession 548
The Magnificent Seven 82
Mahaffry, Marie 368
Mahoney, Jock 46
Maigret 178
Maigret and the Lady 178
Maigret at Bay 178
Mail Call 590
Main, Marjorie 337, 569
The Major and the Minor 396
Major Barbara 171
Make Like a Thief 337
Make Room for Daddy 380
Malden, Karl 514, 601
The Male Animal 445
Malice in Wonderland 331
Malone, Dorothy 8, 510
Malone, Nancy 87, 88, 619
Maloney, James 349, 408, 618
The Maltese Falcon 455
Mama Malone 349
Mame 446
Man Against Crime 1, 2, 30, 40, 41, 42, 164, 326, 342, 445, 540, 613
A Man Alone 397
The Man and the Challenge 416, 417
Man Behind the Badge 53, 613
The Man Behind the Door 386
A Man Called Adam 330
A Man Called Peter 408
A Man Called Sloane 145, 208
The Man Called X 534, 535, 613
A Man for All Seasons 234, 311
The Man from Colorado 450
The Man from Uncle 471
The Man I Love 9
The Man in the Iron Mask 265
Man of a Thousand Faces 504
Man of La Mancha 17, 74
Man of the World 521
Man on a Tightrope 36
The Man Who Came to Dinner (film) 562
The Man Who Came to Dinner (play) 254, 493, 533
The Man Who Could Work Miracles 491
The Man Who Shot Liberty Valance 357
The Man Who Wouldn't Talk 428
Man with a Camera 80, 81, 216, 531, 613
The Man with the Golden Arm 372
The Manchurian Candidate 240
Mancini, Henry 520, 521
Mandy 260

Manetti, Larry 143
Manhunt 35, 229, 230, 272, 293, 294, 295, 382, 383, 613, 619
Mankiewicz, Joseph L. 392
Mann, Abby 123
Mann, Anthony 112, 377, 445
Manning, Irene 408, 409
Mannix 140, 141
Mannix, Eddie 329
Manpower 455
Manulis, Martin 435
Manza, Catherine 349
Manza, Ralph 138, *349*–350, 609
Mara, Ratu Sir Kamisese 96
March, Fredric 36, 99
March of Time 244, 377, 527
Marcus Welby MD 522
Margie 30, 285
Marin, Edwin L. 456
Marino, Flora 10
Marion-Crawford, Charles 351
Marion-Crawford, Harold (father of Howard) 350
Marion-Crawford, Harold (son of Howard) 351
Marion-Crawford, Howard 281, *350*–351, 617
Maris, Herbert L. 113
Marjorie Morningstar 105
Mark Saber 21, 22, 27, 152, *180*, 237, 238, 274, 275, 366, *367*, 461, 545, 613
Markham 397, 398, 496, 613
Markham, Monte 94
Markle, Fletcher 369
Markle, John Lawrence 368, 370
Marlowe, Alona 345
Marlowe, Christian 353
Marlowe, Hugh 13, *352*–*353*, 354, 614
Marlowe, Hugh Michael 353
Marlowe, Jeffrey 353
Marlowe, June 345
Marlowe, Scott 7
Marriage Is a Private Affair 412
The Marriage Proposal 553
Marriott, Margaret 137
Marshall, Catherine 408
Marshall, Herbert 491, 534
Marshall, Joan 132, *354*–*355*, 608
Marshall, Reverend Peter 408
Marshall, Sidney 420
Marshall, William 398
Marshall, Zena 45
Marti, José 481
Marti, Maria Mantilla 481
Martin, Dean 241, 249, 330, 601
Martin, Quinn 88, 145, 288, 289, 437, 440, 510, 511, 513, 600, 603, 604
Martin, Ronald 280

Martin, Ross 144
Martin, Ruth 279
Martin, Stuart W. 240
Martin Kane Private Eye 1, 108, 222, 223, 224, 239, 273, 318, 380, 381, 428, 429, 496, 523, 524, 525, 552, 560, 561, 613
Martin Kane Private Investigator 224, 613
Marvin, Christopher 358
Marvin, Claudia 358
Marvin, Courtenay 358
Marvin, Cynthia 358
Marvin, Lamont Waltman 355, 356
Marvin, Lee 226, 313, 355–357, 358–359, 425, 571, 613
Marvin, Robert 355, 356
Marx, Groucho 276
Marx, Sam 329, 330
The Marx Brothers 160, 233
Mary (TV sitcom) 405
Mary (variety series) 405
Mary Had a Little 344
Mary, Mary 424, 470, 489
The Mary Tyler Moore Hour 405
The Mary Tyler Moore Show 333, 405
Mascalzoni 186
M*A*S*H 10, 472
The Mask 1, 391, 392, 448, 614
The Mask of Fu Manchu 302
Mason, James 36, 269, 467, 468, 469
Mason, Marilyn 220
Mason, Sydney 359, 597, 609
Mass Appeal 314
Massey, Anna 362, 363
Massey, Chester Daniel 359
Massey, Daniel 362, 363
Massey, Geoffrey 362, 363
Massey, Raymond 36, 303, 359–361, 362–363, 533, 560, 612
Massey, Vincent 359, 360
Matheson, Murray *349*, 363–364, 535, 611
Matheson, Richard 373
Mathias, Bob 34, 292
Matinée Theater (radio) 294
Matinée Theater (TV) 106, 267
Matthews, Lester 26, 235, 282, 364–*365*, 366, 607
Mature, Victor 411
Maubin, Maria 176
Maugham, Somerset 99, 259, 491, 583, 591
Maunder, Wayne 203
Maverick 39, 337, 504
The Maverick Queen 534
Maxwell, Jenny 143
Maxwell, John 50
Maxwell, Marilyn 329

Maxwell, Robert 57
May, Billy 88
May, Elaine 124
Mayer, Louis B. 52, 192, 329, 490, 548, 549
Mayfield, Mona 119, 120
Maynor, Asa 106
Mayo, Virginia 359
Maytime 14
Mazza, Buzz 510
McBain, Diane 143, 585, 602
McBain, Ed 487
McCallum, David 82, 522
McCallum, Mark 367
McCallum, Neil 22, 238, 366–*367*, 616
McCambridge, John Patrick 368
McCambridge, John Valerian 368
McCambridge, Mercedes 67, 132, 367–369, 370, 391, 393, 618
McCarthy, Senator Joseph 80, 303, 388
McCarthy, Kevin 449
McCleery, Albert 416, 439
McClelland, Donald 371, 609
McCloud 347
McClure, Kevin 538
McCord, Kent 63
McCormack, Patty 156
McCrea, Joel 396, 444
McCrudden, Lynn 43
McEwan, Nora 477, 478
McGaveran, Reid Delano Richardson 371
McGavin, Bogart 374
McGavin, Bridget 374
McGavin, Darren 90, 121, 251, 371–*372*, 373–375, 503, 609, 614
McGavin, Megan 374
McGavin, York 374
McGinley, Eleanor 516
McGrath, Margaret 471
McGraw, Charles 375–*376*, 377, 607
McGraw, Jill 376
McGuire, Dorothy 226
McHugh, Frances 566
McHugh, Jimmy 292
McIntire, Holly 378
McIntire, John 87, 219, 377–*378*, 379–380, 614
McIntire, Tim 378
McKendrick, Alexander 260
McKenna, Virginia 280
McKinley, William 314
McLaglen, Cyril 395
McLaglen, Victor 343, 344
McLeod, Catherine 116
McMahon, Horace *45*, 86, 87,

88, 219, 223, 378–*381*, 613, 614
McMahon, Kate 380
McMahon, Missy 380
McMahon, Thomas 380
McMaster, Iris 465
McMillan and Wife 158
McNair, Emily 605
McNamara, Maggie 298
Macnee, Patrick 39
McQuade, John 381–382, 431, 608
McVey, Patrick 263, 294, *382*–383, 426, 523, 525, 526, 568, 582, 608, 613
Meade, Betsy 463
A Medal for Benny 419
Medea 233
Medic 226, 506
Medical Center 171
Medina, Patricia 266
The Medium 600
Meeker, Dick 404
Meeker, Ralph 201, 285, 333, 383–*385*, 386, 534, 615
Meeker, Richard Carlton, Jr. 404, 405
Meet McGraw 342, 614
Meet Me in Las Vegas 168
Meet Mr. McNutley 397
Meet the Navy 413
Meet the People 5, 439
Megna, John 416
Mein Kampf—My Crimes 594
Meisner, Sandford 19, 147, 269
Melnick, Al 167
Melton, Sid 580
Memoirs of a Professional Cad 153, 492
Memories of Melody Lane 520
Memory of Love 415
The Men 576
Men of Darkness 595
Menjou, Adolphe 345, 386–*387*, 388–390, 617
Menjou, Harold 389
Menjou, Henry 386, 387
Menjou, Jean Adolph (Albert) 386
Menjou, Peter Adolphe 389
Mercader, Maria 187
The Merchant of Venice 196
Meredith, Burgess 130, 175, 485
Meredith, Charles 50
Merivale, Philip 91
Merlin, Jan 77, 303, 342
Merman, Ethel 119, 167, 168, 491
Merrell, Richard 401
Merrill, Barbara 392, 393
Merrill, Benjamin Gary 390
Merrill, Gary 171, 390–*391*, 392–394, 448, 612, 614

646 Index

Merrill, Jerry 390
Merrill, Margot 392, 393
Merrill, Michael 392, 393
Merry-Go-Round 283
The Merv Griffin Show 176
Mervyn, William 476
Meservey, Frank, Jr. 443
Meservey, Frank, Sr. 443, 446
Meshekoff, Michael 578
Mess Mates 205
Meteor 314
Metzger, Elsie 16
Mexican Manhunt 67
Meyer, Emile 15
Meyer, Harold Edward 286
Meyer, Stanley 578
Miami Undercover 62
Michael, Janet 66
Michael Shayne (film series) 427, 428, 430
Michael Shayne (TV series) 183, 190, 437
Michael Shayne, Private Detective 428
The Mickey Mouse Club 13
Mickey Spillane's Mike Hammer 90, 372, 614
Middle of the Night 24, 438, 486
The Middle Watch 499
Mid-Summer 371
A Midsummer Night's Dream 294, 501
Mifune, Toshiro 357
Mike Downstairs 132
Mikey and Nicky 124
Miles, Vera 115, 327
Milestone, Lewis 71, 330, 388
Milland, Daniel David 396, 399
Milland, Ray 77, 192, 394–*398*, 399–400, 444, 496, 613
Milland, Victoria Francesca 396, 399
Millar, Marjie 577
Millard, Eliza Sarah 300
Millard, Harry 270, 271
Miller, Anthony 401
Miller, Arthur 419
Miller, Carlyn 466
Miller, Esther 345
Miller, Glenn 29, 122, 161
Miller, Jean 281
Miller, Mandy 260
Miller, Marilyn 346
Miller, Mark 417
Miller, Marvin *400*–401, 495, 614
Miller, Melissa 401
The Millionaire 107, 400
Mills, Donna 290
Mills, Hayley 313
Mills, John 468
Mills, Juliet 338

Milner, Martin 63
Miltner, Anne Catherine 241
Minder on the Orient Express 37
Miner, Donald 401
Miner, Jan 372, 401–402, 609
Miner, Walter Curtis 401
Ministry of Fear 396
Minnie & Moskowitz 124
Minor Miracle 561
Minsky, Howard 398
Miracle in Milan 186
Miracle on 34th Street 521
The Miracle Worker 295
Mirisch, Walter 326
Les Misérables 288, 468
Misleading Lady 222
The Missiles of October 42
Mission: Impossible 24, *25*, 32, 89
Mississippi 597
Mr. and Mrs. North 77, 78, *182*, 185, 614
Mr. Belvedere 241
Mr. Big 533
Mr. Blandings Builds His Dream House 198
Mr. Broadway 8, 380, 521, 522
Mr. District Attorney 69, 200, 296, 340, 341, 561, 571, 614
Mr. Moto (film series) 427
Mr. Moto's Gamble 29
Mr. Novak 220
Mr. Roberts (film) 18, 504, 505
Mr. Roberts (stage) 18, 19, 63, 89, 90, 126, 206, 288, 303, 312, 313, 325, 384, 505, 520
Mr. Roberts (TV series) 505
Mr. Smith Goes to Washington 520
Mr. Wong (film series) 302
Mr. Wu 591
Mitchell, Cameron 467
Mitchell, Don 94
Mitchell, Guy 340
Mitchell, Mary Alice 163
Mitchell, Robert 310
Mitchum, Robert 53, 91, 214, 269, 375, 578
Mix, Tom 33
The Mob 161
Mobile One 579
Mobs Inc. 243
The Mod Father 18
The Mod Squad 18
Modini, Carlos 508
Mohr, Gerald *402*–403, 610
Mohr, Gerald, Sr. 402
Mon Gosse de Pere 387
Monash, Paul 510
The Monkey's Paw 476
Monroe, Marilyn 17, 168, 329, 346, 457, 518, 575
Monsarrat, Nicholas 260

Monsoon 415
Monster of the Island 304
A Month in the Country 269
The Moon and Sixpence 152, 491
The Moon Is Blue 423
Moon Over Burma 444
Moonrise 131
Moontide 103
Moor Barn 197
Moore, Demi 334
Moore, Elizabeth Tyler 403
Moore, George Tyler 403
Moore, John Tyler 403
Moore, Kieron 367, *497*
Moore, Mary Tyler 84, 287, 403–*404*, 404–406, 437, 616
Moore, Roger 267, 270, 271, 310, 398
Moore, Terry 269
Moran, Catherine 418
Moray, Helga 493
Morgan, Dennis 31, 32, 317, 349, 406–*408*, 409–410, 618
Morgan, Frank 389, 548
Morgan, Harry 532, 578, 579
Morgan, Helen 174
Morgan, James Irving 406
Morgan, Kristin 406
Morgan, Laura Andrina 96
Morgan, Rena 173
Morgan, Stanley 406
Morgan, Terence 100
Mori, Bridget 270
Morison, Patricia 244, *410*–412, 479, 608
Morison, William R. 410
Mork and Mindy 285
Morner, Dorothy 406
Morner, Frank 406
Morner, Kenneth 406
Morning Departure 469
Morning Star 529
Mornings at Seven 393
Morocco 387
Morris, Chester 427, 546
Morris, Ernie 238
Morris, Greg 25
Morrison, Captain William 523
Morrow, Patricia 120, *412*, 612
Morrow, Peggy Field 267
Morse, Barry 57, 288
Morse, Florence Pauline 581
The Mortal Storm 167, 508
Mortimer, Lee 561
Morton, Garry 140
Mossman, Doug 412–413, 611
Mossman, Heilee 413
Mossman, Judee 413
The Most Deadly Game 42
Most Wanted 513
The Moth 386
Mother Lode 197

Index

Mother Wore Tights 166, 167
Mother's Day 222
Move Over Mrs. Markham 60
Mowbray, Alan 291, 309
Moyzisch, L.C. 269, 468
Mrs. Miniver 173, 329
Mullen, Dorothy Ethelbert Hogan 171
Mulrooney, Grace 458
The Mummy 302
Mundy, Meg 42
Muni, Paul 70, 199, 455, 592
Murch, Alice Weston 31
Murder Ad-Lib 479
Murder by Proxy 131, 132
Murder in the Cathedral 421
Murder She Wrote 25, 132, 247, 428, 429, 518
Murphy, Alice 43
Murphy, Audie 510
Murphy, George 481
Murphy Brown 374
Murton, Jack 336
Murton, Lionel 413–*414*, 461, 615
The Music Man 72, 443, 445
Mutiny on the Bounty 461
My Adolescent Father 387
My Blue Heaven 168
My Boys Are Good Boys 385
My Dinner of Herbs 605
My Fair Lady 398, 522
My Favorite Husband 181, 424
My Favorite Story 388
My Heart's in the Higland 148
My Maryland 222
My Mother's Eyes 222
My Mother's Keeper 393
My Name Is Aquilon 319
My Outlaw Brother 509
My Sister and I 157
My Sister Eileen 19
My Three Sons 228
My Wild Irish Rose 408
Myra Breckenridge 278
The Mysteries of Chinatown 400, 495, 614
The Mysterious Doctor 365
Mystery Is My Business 352, 614
The Mystery of the Wax Museum 319
Mystery Theater 152, 614

Nader, George 414–*415*, 416–418, 439, 564, 611
Nader, George Garfield, Sr. 415
Naish, Carol Elaine 420
Naish, J. Carrol 178, *276*, 418–*419*, 420–421, 583, 614
Naish, Patrick Sarsfield 418
Naked City (TV series) 44, *45*, 86, 87, 88, 379, 380, 381, 614, 619
The Naked City (film) 87, 240, 381
The Naked City (TV series) 2, 44, 87, 219, 220, 377, 378, 380, 530, 614
The Naked Face 271
Naked Paradise 182
The Naked Spur 384
The Name of the Game 305, 513
Nanny and the Professor 338
Napier, Lois Mary Caird 422
Napier, Russell 421–*422*, 616
The Narrow Margin 375
Nash, Ogden 522
Nash at Nine 522
Nathanson, Nathalie Caroline 527
Native Son 375
The Natural 373
NBC Presents 202
NBC Repertory Theater 41
Neagle, Dame Anna 584
Neal, Mary Allen 486
Neal, Patricia 116, 383, 468
Nearest and Dearest 338
Neary, Colleen Rose 385
Nedell, Bernard 344
Negri, Pola 343
Negulesco, Jean 131, 415, 435, 469
Nelson, Barry 326, 422–*423*, 424–425, 470, 611
Nelson, Christine 452
Ness, Eliot 510
Ness, Elizabeth 512
Nettleton, Lois 227
Never Say Never 540
Never So Few 81, 330
Never Steal Anything Small 504
The New Adventures of Charlie Chan 178, 274, *276*, 418, *419*, 420, 583, 584, 614
The New Adventures of Ellery Queen 13, 352, 353, 614
The New Adventures of Martin Kane 224, 464, 465, 614
The New Adventures of Perry Mason 94, 132
The New Adventures of Sherlock Holmes 34
The New Avengers 37
New Faces 45
New Moon 68
New Orleans After Dark 256
New Orleans Police Department 614
The New Tightrope 140
New York Confidential 560, 561, 614
The Newcomers 573, 595

Newell, Mary Hope 171
Newhart 349
Newlan, Paul 356, 425–426, 613
Newman, Paul 143, 199, 384
News from America 527
Next of Kin 259
Ney, Richard 329
Nice Girl? 509
Nicholson, Jack 105, 424
Nielson, Tryge 422
Nigh, Jane *382*, *426*–427, 608
Night After Night 455
Night Beat 280
Night Court USA 296
Night Editor 223
Night Gallery 535
The Night Hank Williams Died 374
A Night in Monmartre 583
The Night of January 16th 155
Night of Mystery 475
Night of the Awk 155
Night of the Grizzly 244
The Night of the Iguana 362, 432, 571, *572*, 605
Night over Taos 446
Night Plane from Chungking 444
The Night Stalker 373
The Night Strangler 373
A Night to Remember 100
The Night Walker 549
Nightkill 221
Nightmare 192
1941 513
99 Ways to Cook Pasta 10
Ninotchka 197
Nitti, Frank 234, 511
Niven, David 398, 460, 482
Nixon, Richard 198
No Exit 175, 176
No Greater Love 183
No Highway 260
No Man of Her Own 50
No Medals 589
No More Ladies 197
No More Women 344
No Sad Songs for Me 155
No Time for Sergeants 424
No Time to Be Young 504
Noah's Ark 87
Nocturne 489
Nohain, Jean 175
Nolan, Christen Kathleen 64
Nolan, James Charles 427
Nolan, Jay Benedict 428
Nolan, Jeanette 377, 378
Nolan, John 64
Nolan, Lloyd 112, 223, 427–*429*, 430, 455, 534, 561, 613, 617
Nolan, Melinda Joyce 428, 430
Noonan, Mike 183
N.O.P.D. 255, 256, 500, 615

Index

The Norman Conquests 424
Normand, Mabel 387
Norris, Chuck 358
North, Jay 272
North by Northwest 564
North Sea Hijack 271
North to Alaska 106
North West Mounted Police 444
Northwest Passage (TV series) 326, 327
Northwest Passage: Rogers Rangers (film) 326
Norworth, Jack 408
Not as a Stranger 53
Not for Hire 201, 285, 383, 384, 385, 615
Not of This Earth 56, 227
Noustadt, Henrietta 402
Novack, Shelly 603
Novak, Kim 384
Novello, Ivor 99, 101, 259
Now Voyager 65
Nowhere to Go 415, 416
Nowhere to Run 289
The Number 132
Numkeena, Anthony 326
The Nurses 55, 529
Nuts 597
The Nutt House 334

Oakland, Simon 227
Oakley, Bob 136
Oberon, Merle 66, 322, 470, 471
Objective Burma! 525
Obligato 401
Obolensky, Princess Anne 38
Oboler, Arch 509
O'Brian, Hugh 73, 94
O'Brien, Edmond 226, 341
O'Brien, Erin 105
O'Brien, Pat 596
O'Brien, Willis 182
O'Bryen, Bill 259
Oceans Eleven 106, 149, 330
O'Connor, Carroll 145, 433
O'Connor, Donald 169
O'Connor, Maud 489
Octopussy 299
O'Day, Molly 454
The Odd Couple 169, 170
The Odd Man 476
Odd Man Out 36
Odets, Clifford 130, 155
Odongo 112
O'Donnell, Dolores 430
O'Donnell, Gene 430–431, 438, 607
Of Mice and Men 52, 130, 160, 541
Of Thee I Sing 12
Official Detective 502, 615
Oh Men! Oh Women! 72, 432

O'Hara, Maureen 77, 313, 416
O'Hara United States Treasury 120, 256, 289, 579
O'Keefe, Dennis 544
Oklahoma! 12, 509
Oland, Warner 235, 419, 588, 591
Olcott, Chauncey 408
The Old Dark House 197, 302, 360
The Old Lady Says No 371
The Old Maid 66, 77, 109
Oliver, Susan 393
Oliver Twist 94
Oliver's Story 398
Olivier, Laurence 27, 99, 100, 258, 591
Olson, Nancy 95
O'Malley, Pat 557
Omar Khayyam 469
Omnibus 123
O'Morrison, Kenny 431
O'Morrison, Kevin 382, 431–432, 608
O'Morrison, Sean E. 431
On a Clear Day You Can See Forever 299
On Approval 478
On Borrowed Time 303
On the Spot 591, 592
On the Town 461
On Your Toes 166
Once Around 487
Once Upon a Time in the West 82
Ondine 322
One by One 597
One Flew Over the Cuckoo's Nest 463
One Foot in Heaven 13
One Frightened Night 557
One Hundred and One Dalmatians 153
100 Men and a Girl 388
One Increasing Purpose 343
One Life to Live 117, 564
One Lifetime Is Not Enough 153
One Man's Family 368, 556, 564, 599
One More River 428
One More Time 330
199 Park Lane 476
One Sunday Afternoon 427
One Way Passage 66
O'Neal, Coke Wisdom 432
O'Neal, Michael 432, 433
O'Neal, Patrick 158, 432–434, 499, 574, 610
O'Neal, Ryan 398
O'Neal, Zelma 100
O'Neill, Eugene 132, 447
The Only Game In Town 424
Opening Night 125
Operation Cicero 269

Operation Cross Eagles 149
Operation Diamond 204
Operation Pacific 116
Ordinary People 405
Orphuls, Max 298
Orr, William T. 105, 442
Orrison, Jack 347, 434, 615
Orth, Frank 434–435, 546, 608
Osborn, Andrew 178
Osborne, Myrtle 447
OSS 413, 414, 459, 461, 462, 495, 615
O'Sullivan, Maureen 395
Othello 71, 259
The Other Side of the Wind 370
O'Toole, Peter 258, 262
Our Town 361
Our Very Own 319
Ouspenskaya, Maria 450
Out of a Blue Sky 222
Out West of Eighth 313
The Outer Limits 208
Outpost in Morocco 456
Outrage (film, 1950) 19
Outrage! (TV movie, 1986) 446
Outside Looking In 52
The Outsider 374
The Outsiders 311
Outward Bound 74
Over 21 116, 596
Overseas Adventure 171, 615
Owen, Reginald 591
Owen, William 196
Owen Marshall—Counselor-at-Law 120

Padlocks of 1927 454
La Padrona di Raggio di Luna 9
Page, Joy Ann 173
Page, Norman 212
Paige, Janis 521
Paint Your Wagon 203, 357
The Painted Veil 65
The Pajama Game 273
Pal, George 471, 564
Palm Springs Weekend 106
Palmer, P.K. 103
Palmolive 401
Palmy Days 455
Paluzzi, Luciana 86, 87, 269, 270, 435, 436–437, 610
Panic 130
Panic Button 140
Papa Piccolino 179
Paper Dolls 74
The Paradine Case 298
Paradise Bay 17
Paramor, Norrie 179
The Parent Trap 32, 313
Paris, Andrew 438
Paris, Jerry 183, 437–438, 511, 618

Paris, Ruth 438
Paris Precinct 175, 176, 298, 615
Parker, Don 276
Parker, Eleanor 550
Parker, Jennie 252
Parks, Larry 72, 249
Parks, Mary 191
Parrish, Judy *430*, 438, 607
Parry, Zale 73
Parson, Lindsley 67, 244
Parsonett, Marion 199
Parsons, Louella 106, 444
Parsons, Patrick 274
A Party for Lovers 431
Party Girl 550
Party Time at Club Roma 11
Passport to Danger 483, 615
Pasternak, Joe 168, 508, 568
Pastore, Senator John 289
Pat Novak for Hire 576
Paths of Glory 384
Patrick, Gail 92, 94, 249
Patrol Car 498, 615
Pattern for Murder 479
Patterns 202, 502
Patterson, Elizabeth 69
Patterson, Lee 585
The Patty Duke Show 330
Pavlova, Tatiana 185
Paxinou, Katina 21
Payment Deferred 395
Payment on Demand 534, 545
Payne, John 29, 571
Payne, Julie 571
Peace Comes to Peckham 179
Pearl, Jack 251
Pearson, Ben 470
Peary, Harold 248
Peck, Gregory 305, 444
Peckinpah, Sam 313
Peck's Bad Girl 156
Pendergast, Lester 160
Penn of Pennsylvania 212
A Penny for a Song 280
Pentagon Confidential 55, 473, 615
Pentagon USA 54, 55, 348, 473, 615
Pepe 169
Peppard, George 221, *349*, 364
Peppler, Maureen 117
The Perfect Marriage 294
Perfect Strangers 407
Perkins, Anthony 105
Perrini, Marina 508
The Perry Como Show 143, 207
Perry Mason 92, *93*, 94, 95, 96, 137, 138, 140, 153, 165, 248, *249*, 250, 276, *278*, 291, 383, *475*, 535, 541, *542*, 601, 615, 619
The Perry Mason Mysteries 250

Perry Mason Returns 95
Pers, Katherine 323
Pershing, General John 191
Personal Appearance Theater 565
Pete Kelly's Blues 207, 578
Peter Gunn 7, 48, 211, 212, 519, 520, *521*, 569, 570, 615
Peter Pan (film, 1924) 591
Peter Pan (film, 1953) 153
Peter Pan (play) 303, 371
Peters, Lyn 89
Peters, Susan 549
Peters, Sylvia 237
Petit, Pascale *497*
The Petrified Forest 402
Petry, Gedda 496
Peyton Place (film) 439
Peyton Place (TV series) 8, 15, 234, 256, 412
The Phantom of Hollywood 547
The Phantom of the Opera 303
Phantom of the Rue Morgue 176
The Phantom Pirate 509
The Phantom Stockman 504
The Phenix City Story 377
The Phil Silvers Show 18, 284, 496
Philbrick, Herbert A. 120, 611
Philco playhouse 448, 502
Philip Marlowe 117, 615
Philips, Caitlin Meg 439
Philips, Lee 416, 438–*439*, 564, 611
Phillips, Barney 439, 440, 577, 610
A Phoenix Too Frequent 269
Phone Call from a Stranger 392
Phyllis 334
Piazza, Ben 548
Piccadilly 591
Picerni, Paul *215*, 511, 619
Pichel, Irving 559
Pickford, Mary 525
The Pickwick Papers 351, 554
Picnic 206, 384
The Picture of Dorian Gray 491
Pidgeon, Walter 94, 152
Pied Piper Malone 312
Pierce, Jack 301, 302, 303, 508
Pilcer, Elsie 454
The Pilgrimage play 13, 293, 473
Pillar to Post 256
Pimpernel Smith 280
Pincus, Irving 257, 352
Pincus, Norman 257, 352
Pine, Joan 458
Pine, Virginia 458
Pink, Sidney 162, 533
Pink Tights 168
Pinza, Ezio 491
The Pipkins 595
Pirandello 322

The Pirate 6
Pirates of Capri 266
Pitfall 91
Pittman, Montgomery 601
A Place in the Sun 92
A Place of Our Own 368
Plain and Fancy 520
The Plainclothesman 347, 434, 615
Plaintiff in a Pretty Hat 583
Planet of the Apes 254
play of the Month 178
playhouse 90 53, 87, 199, 226, 394
The plaything 395
Plaza Suite 20, 169
Please Stand By 564
The Pleasure of Honesty 418
Pleshette, Suzanne 227
Plunkett, Patricia 567, 568
Plymouth Adventure 252
Poe, Edgar Allan 158, 396
Pohlmann, Eric 440–*441*, 442, 608
Pohlmann, Michael 440
Pohlmann, Steven 440
Point Blank 357
Point of Honor 60
Point Valaine 160, 265
Poitier, Sidney 123
Polanski, Roman 124
Police Academy 3 438
Police Story 74
Policewoman 227, 532
Policewoman Decoy 615
Pommy 280
Ponce, Poncie 143, 207, 208, *442*–443, 611
Pony Soldier 469
Poor Old Bill 328
Port Afrique 116
Port Charles 228
Port of Hell 131
Port Said 272
Porter, Cole 410, 411, 460
Portia Faces Life 432
Portrait in Black 593
Portrait of Alison 36
Powell, Dick 91, 117, 287, 313, 350
Powell, Eleanor 167
Powell, Jane *65*, 66, 416
Powell, William 320, 329, 423, 475
The Power 471
Power, Patia 443
Power, Tyrone 346, 361, 443, 468, 469, 482, 491, 510
The Power Game 213
Powers, Stefanie 290
Pratt, Edward 300
Prehistoric Women 347
Premature Burial 398
Preminger, Otto 505

650   Index

The President's Plane Is Missing 20
Presley, Elvis 7, 106, 588
Presley, Eunice 126
Prestidge, Mel 443, 611
Prestige 197
Preston, Margaret Janet 574
Preston, Robert 42, 72, 396, 443–*445*, 446–447, 613
Pretty Little Parlor 41
Pretty Woman 42
Préville, Anne 171, 447, 554, 610
Price, Vincent 80, 157, 158, 304, 319, 398
Pride of the Marines 130, 525
Pride of the Yankees 531
Priestley, J.B. 197, 302
Prince, Gorman 447
Prince, William 392, 447–*448*, 449, 612, 614
The Prince and the Showgirl 100, 575
Prince of Foxes 501
Prince Valiant 153, 469
Princess Turandot 592
Pringle, Jane 94
Prinze, Freddie 5
The Prisoner of Zenda 361
The Private Files of J. Edgar Hoover 163, 169
Private Lives 62, 299
Probation Officer 59
Producers Showcase 593
The Professionals 42, 357
Project UFO 579
Promised Land 334
Provenza, Paul 314
Pryor, Peggy 89
Psycho 354
PT 109 106
Public Defender 243, 615, 616
The Public Prosecutor 260
Pulitzer Prize playhouse 171, 445
Punches and Judy 160
Purdom, Edmund 267
Pursued 244
The Pursuers 266, 267
Pursuit of Happiness (TV series) 314
The Pursuit of Happiness (play) 341
Purviance, Edna 387
Pushover 116
Pygmalion 468
Pyle, Denver 449–*450*, 451, 562, 608
Pyle, Marilee 450
Pyle, "Skippy" 449
Pyle, Tippi 450
Pyle, Willis 449
Pyro 533

The Quality of Mercy 369
Quantrill, Charles 242
Quarles, Vicki 286
Quatermass and the Pit 100, 310, *311*
Queen Bee 534
Queen for a Day 374
Queen of Spades 280
Queen of the Nightclubs 454
The Queens Guards 362
The Queen's Husband 590
Quick Millions 454
The Quiet American 176
Quiet Please 19, 596
Quiet Please Murder 181, 479
Quincy 8, 10
Quinn, Anthony 338, 376, 455
Quinn, Louis 39, 451–*452*, 602, 611
Quo Vadis? 550

The Rack 155
Racket Squad 63, 242, 243, 616
Radio News Reel 36
The Radio Robot 427
Radio Shack 89
Raft, George 396, 411, 452–*453*, 464–459, 505, 592, 612
Ragged Army 427
Raid on Rommel 513
Rain 223
Raine, Norman Reilly 569
Raines, Ella 109
Rainey, Norman 410
The Rainmaker 72
Rains, Claude 88, 468, 470
The Rains Came 66, 468
The Rains of Ranchipur 468
Rainwater, Karolyn 20
Raisch, William 288
Raki, Laya *461*, 462
Ralston, Vera 110
Rambeau, Marjorie 307
Randall, Tony 462
Randell, Ernest B. 460
Randell, Norman 460
Randell, Ron 413, 459–*461*, 462–463, 615, 618
Random Harvest 157
Ranft, Conrad 454
The Rangers 579
Rangle River 294
Rank, J. Arthur 260, 274, 322
Rapper, Irving 67
Rathbone, Basil 152, 304
Rathgeber, Ralph Meeker 383
Ratoff, Gregory 123
Rattigan, Terence 175, 280
The Raven (film, 1935) 302
The Raven (film, 1963) 158, 304
Raw Deal 92
Rawhide 67, 245, 373

Rawlinson, Herbert 222
Ray, Fred Olen 271
Ray, Nicholas 368
Ray and Sharon Court's Hollywood Collectors' Convention 228, 586
The Ray Milland Show 397
Raymond Burr: A film, radio and Television Biography 96
The Razor's Edge 491
Rea, Ruth 443
Read, Barbara (aka. Reed) 173, 542
Reagan, Ronald 37, 142, 446, 532, 551, 557, 585, 596
The Real McCoys 138
Reap the Wild Wind 396, 444
Rear Gunner 130
Rear Window 92, 155
Rebecca 491
Rebel Without a Cause 278
The Red Buttons Show 319
The Red Lantern 590
Red Letter Day 554
Red Light 92
Redfield, Adam 463
Redfield, Henry Crittendon 463
Redfield, William (Billy) 285, 463–464, 612
Redford, Robert 405
Redgrave, Sir Michael 269
Reece, Brian 224, 464–*465*, 614
Reece, Christopher 465
Reece, Henry 464
Reece, Michael 465
Reece, Susan 465
Reed, Carol 21, 36, 259, 469, 583
Reed, Donna 439
Reed, Florence 418
Reed, Marshall 14, 15, 465–*466*, 467, 613
Reed, Robert 141, 271
Reed, Tracy 521
Reed, Walter George 465
Reeder, Colonel Russell 120
Reeve, Arthur B. 596
Reflections in a Golden Eye 314
Reform School Girl 105
Regehr, Duncan 605
The Rehearsal 530
Rehearsal for Murder 446
Reid, Frances 114
Reign of Terror 256
Reilly, Tommy 37
Reiner, Carl 404, 437
Reinhardt, Max 196
Reinhart, Alice 564
Remains to Be Seen 14
The Remarkable Andrew 192
Remember the Day 552
Remick, Lee 53
Remington Steele 605

Index 651

Renegades 293
Rennie, David 471
Rennie, James 467
Rennie, Joan 471
Rennie, Michael 94, 178, *253*, 467–*469*, 470–472, 617
Renoir, Jean 419
The Reporter 393
Repp, Stafford *472*–473, 617
The Return of Eliot Ness 513
The Return of Ironside 95
The Return of Jesse James 242
The Return of Sam McCloud 37
The Return of the Cisco Kid 482
Return of the Frog 274
Return of the Gunfighter 50
The Return of the Scarlet Pimpernel 99
Return to Peyton Place 256
Reunion in Vienna 427
Revlon 77
The Revlon Girl 77
The Reward 603
Reynolds, Burt 372, 373
Reynolds, Sheldon 21, 158, 171, 204, 280, 281, 351, 402, 432, 553
Reynolds, William 603
Rhapsody in Blue 9
Rhoda 10
Rice, Craig 561
Rice, Elmer 155
Rice, Jeff 373
The Rich Are Always with Us 65
Rich Man Poor Man Book I 398
Richard, Cliff 573
Richard Diamond Private Detective 24, 25, 84, 150, 151, 287, 288, 404, 516, 557, 616
Richard III 100
Richards, Addison 55, 348, *473*–475, 615
Richards, Ann (Addison's daughter) 473
Richards, Ann (actress) 192
Richards, Grant *475*–476, 488, 610
Richards, Patricia 473
Richards, Stephen 524, 525
Richardson, Sir Ralph 478
Richfield, Arabella 477
Richfield, Belinda 477
Richfield, Edwin 322, 476–*477*, 612
Richfield, Simon 477
Rickles, Dr. Nathan 30
Riddle, Nelson 512
Rider in the Rain 82
Riding with Buffalo Bill 465
Rietty, Robert 262
Rififi in Panama 457
The Righteous Are Bold 200

Riley, Mary Lou 142
Ring Around Elizabeth 450, 533
Rio Bravo 106
Rio Grande 419
Rio Rita 287
Rissone, Guiditta 186
Ritter, John 536
The River House Mystery 212
Riverboat 372, 373, 374
Roach, Hal, Jr. 243
Roach, Hal, Sr. 562
The Road West 535
Roadside 40, 356
Roar Like a Dove 478
Rob Roy 311
Robards, Jason 602, 603
Robbins, Harold 42, 267
The Robe 468
Robert Montgomery Presents 62, 77, 263
Robert Taylor's The Detectives 551. 616
Roberts, Ben 141
Roberts, Ewan 304, 477–479, 608
Roberts, Hobart K. 479
Roberts, John (b. 1950) 478
Roberts, John (b. 1920) 479
Roberts, Julia 487
Roberts, Lynne 244, 411, 479–*480*, 608
Roberts, Pernell 74
Robertson, Dale 69
Robinson, Ann 563
Robinson, Edward G. 99, 191, 418, 439, 453, 455, 457
Robinson, Joe 230
Robot Monster 416
Rocket to Stardom 442
Rocketship X-M 71
The Rockford Files 15, 110, 586
Rocky King Detective 616
Rocky King Inside Detective 121, 122, 251, 307, 308, *309*, 616
Rodgers, Richard 411, 479
Rodier, Esther 167
Roe, Thomas 492
Rogers, Charles 407
Rogers, Ginger *387*, 388, 396, 398, 407
Rogers, Judie 208
Rogers, Roy 326, 479
Rogers, Ward 119
Rogers, Will 548
Rogue Cop 452, 457, *486*
The Rogues 492
Rogue's Gallery 506
Rohmer, Sax 234, 235, 302, 607
Rolfe, Mary 49, 50, 51
Roman, Ruth 249
The Romance of Helen Trent 523
Romberg, Sigmund 407

Romeo and Juliet (film, 1936) 280
Romeo and Juliet (play) 212, 260
Romero, Cesar *86*, 109, 480–*483*, 484–485, 483, 615
Romero, Cesar Julio 481
Romero, Eddie 417
Romero, Maria 483, 484
Romero, Valerie Ann 317
Room for One More 202, 203
Rooney, Mickey 139
Roosevelt, Franklin Delano 42, 91, 198, 563
Roosevelt, Teddy 314
Roots 74, 111
Rose, Anna Perrott 203
Rose, Helen 320
The Rose Bowl Story 326
Rose Marie 222, 557
The Rose Tattoo 202
Rosemary's Baby 42, 124
Rosenbloom, Maxie 454
Rosmerholm 597
Ross, Anthony 485–*486*, 617
Ross, Betsy 56, 57
Rossen, Robert 161, 368
Rough Riders (miniseries) 314
Rough Riders (TV series) 546
Rourke, Mickey 290
Rouse, Russell 140
Route 66 302
Rowan, Dan 331
Rowan, Mary 331
Rowan and Martin's Laugh-In 331
Rowe, Ada 588
Rowlands, Edward Merwin 486
Rowlands, Gena 122, 124, 125, 486–*487*, 488, 527, 618
Roxie Hart 387
The Roy Rogers Show 80
Rubin, Robert 395
Rudley, Herbert 183
Rudolf, Carl 164
The Rugged Path 600
Ruggles, Charles 596
Rugolo, Pete 512
Ruick, Barbara 488
Ruick, Mel 475, 488–489, 588, 610
Rule, Janice 384
Rumba 455
Run, Buddy, Run 232, 234
A Run for Your Money 213
Run of the Arrow 384
Runaway Daughters 153
Russell, Jane 69, 520
Russell, Rosalind 41, 412
Rutherford, Ann 473
Rutherford, Blanche Sarah 35
Ruthless 266
Ryan, Helen 166

Ryan, Robert 10
The Ryan Girl 344

SA 7 616
Saber of London 22, 237, 366, 367, 543, 545, 616
Sabrina Fair 19, 155
The Sacred Flame 99
The Safecracker 397
Safford, Lucille 68
The Saga of Andy Burnette 202, 214
Sahara 71, 419
Sailor of Fortune 178
Sailors of Cattaro 130
Saint, Eva Marie 226
The Saint (film series) 152, 153, 190, 265, 266, 267, 270, 491
The Saint in New York 265
Saint Joan 258, 360
St. John, Howard 126, *489*, 612
St. John, Sidney 489
St. John, Toni 110
The Saint Strikes Back 134
The St. Valentine's Day Massacre 243
The Saint's Girl Friday 265, 266
Sakall, S.Z. 531
Salome Where She Danced 109
Saloon Bar 274
Salt and Pepper 330
Salute to France 175
Sam 579
Samish, Adrian 326
Sampson, Daisy Lei Aloha 315
Samson and Delilah 303, 544
Samuels, Hyman 479
Samuels, Peri Margaret 479, 480
San Demetrio London 36
San Francisco Beat 14, 616
San Francisco International Airport 74
San Quentin 91
Sand, George 411
Sanders, George 134, 151, 152, 153, 154, 266, 303, 376, 467, 470, 489–495, *493*, 611
Sanders, Henry 152, 490
Sanders, Margaret 152, 153, 490, 493
Sanders, Shari 354
Sanders, Steven 354
Sankey, Bill 58
The Santa Fé Trail 361, 407
Santa Fé Wine 347
Saperstein, Abe 131
Sargent, Joseph 220
Sartre, Jean-Paul 176
The Sash 311
Saunders, Gloria 400, *495*, 614
Saunders, Lanna 496

Saunders, Nicholas 223, 495–496, 613
Saunders, Theodore 496
Savage 535
The Savage Bees 604, 605
The Savage Innocents 593
Scanlan, Billy 408
Scarecrow and Mrs. King 25, 228, 526
The Scarf 368
Scarface 455
The Scarface Mob 437, 510
The Scarlet Pimpernel 99, 360, 478
Scarlet Street 322
Schary, Dore 42, 168, 457, 527, 597
Scheider, Roy 145
Scheimer, Lou 254
Schell, Maximilian 441
Schenck, Joseph 40
Schenck, Nicola 174
Schenck, Nicholas M. 174
Scherer, Amelia Rose 226
Schlitz playhouse of the Stars 69, 352
Schneider, Berno 391
The School for Scandal 462
Schreibman, Paul 136
Schroeder, Mildred 352
Schwitzer, Jack 340
Science Fiction Theater 13
Scotland Yard (play) 418
Scotland Yard (TV series) 421, 422, 616
Scotland Yard Inspector 482
Scott, Alice 415
Scott, George C. 446
Scott, Joyce Parker 311
Scott, Kathryn 557
Scott, Lizabeth 91
Scott, Randolph 355, 520
Scott, Simon 397, 496, 613
Scott, Sydna 497, 553–554, 610
Scott, Zachary 266
Scott-Gunn, Jeanne 351
Screaming Mimi 116
Screen actors Guild 50th Anniversary Celebration 334
The Sea Hawk 407
Sea Hunt 70, *71*, 72, 73, 74, 616
Sea of Grass 198
Seagal, Steven 433
Search 17
The Search 155
Search for Beauty 543
The Search for Bridey Murphy 267
The Searchers 115
Season in the Sun 485
Seaton, George 53
Seaton, Patricia 331
Sebastian, Don 479

Second Chance 214
The Second Greatest Sex 17, 415, 416
Secret Agent 467
Secret Agent X-9 71
Secret File USA 9, 616
The Secret Invasion 107
The Secret Six 40
See My Lawyer 391
Segal, Erich 398
Seinfeld 74
Self Made Lady 265
Sellers, Peter 199
Selznick, David O. 119, 297, 298, 305, 319, 527
Sennett, Mack 446
Separate Rooms 538
Sergeants 3 330
Serling, Rod 74, 535
Seton, Sir Alexander Hay 498
Seton, (Sir) Bruce *497*–499, 610
Seton, Sir Bruce Gordon 497
Seton, Christopher Bruce 498
Seven Angry Men 361
Seven Cities of Gold 468
Seven Days in May 202
Seven Sinners 344
The Seven Year Itch 464, 486
7th Heaven 228
The Seventh Victim 152
77 Sunset Strip 2, *39*, 104, 105, 106, 107, 143, 202, 206, 207, 316, 320, 337, 451, *452*, 503, 504, 505, 516, 600, 601, *602*, 603, 616, 619
The Sex Symbol 518
Sextette 455
Seyler, Athene 213
Shackelford, Lena 196
The Shadow 294
Shadow in the Sky 384
The Shadow Laughs 481
Shadow of a Doubt 112
Shadow of a Woman 174
Shadow of the Cloak 174, 617
Shadow of the Thin Man 423
Shadows 123
Shaleesh, Selma 18
Shame, Shame on the Bixby Boys 466
Shampoo 354
Shane 565
Shanghai Express 591
The Shanghai Gesture 418, 420
Shannon 417
Sharp, Mordaunt 582
Sharpe, Don 80, 81, 132, 520
Shatner, William 126
Shaw, George Bernard 171, 258, 360
Shaw, Irwin 283
Shaw, Robert 158

Shaw, Susan 27
Shaw, Victoria 504, 505
Shawkat, Alia 89
Shayne, Tamara 21
She 197
She Got What She Wanted 560
She Loves Me Not 160
She Married Her Boss 197
Shea, Margaret Elizabeth 427
Shearer, Norma 458
Sheehan, Winfield 455
Shelley, Mary 301
Shepherd, Jean 123
Shepley, Michael 432, *499*–*500*, 610
Shepley-Smith, Stancliffe 499
Sheridan, Ann 66, 408
Sheridan, Jack 420
Sheriff, R.C. 99
Sherlock Holmes (film series) 152, 411
Sherlock Holmes (radio) 152
Sherlock Holmes (TV series) 204, 205, 280, 281, *350*, 351, 617
Sherry! 493
Sherwood, Robert E. 123, 361, 549
She's De Lovely 125
Shiffrin, Bill 510
Shikles, Gail, Sr. 519
Shine, Dorothy 305
Shine On Harvest Moon 408
The Shining 424
The Shining Hour 360
Ship of Fools 323, 357
Shipman, Helena 312
Shirley, Anne 571
Shirley, Eve 454
Shirley Temple's Storybook 253
Shoeshine 186
The Shop at Sly Corner 303
The Shot in Question 205
The Show Off 560
Showboat 334
Showdown at Abilene 50
The Shrike 132
Shubert, J.J. 222
Siddons, Mrs. Sarah 274
The Siege of Pinchgut 367
Siegel, Bugsy 456
Siegel, Don 15, 23, 123, 124, 357
Siegel, Karen 211
Siegel, Sylvia 211
Sienkiewicz, Henry 550
Sierra, Margarita 585
The Silent Barrier 387
The Silent Gun 74
Silent Night, Lonely Night 74
Silliphant, Stirling 87, 219, 220, 380
Silver, Artie 442
The Silver Darlings 213

Silver Spurs 465
SilverTheater 61
The Silver Whistle 428
Silverman, Fred 289, 373
Silvers, Phil 5
Simenon, Georges 178
Simmons, Jean 468, 601
Simmonds, Dr. Mary 96
Simon, René 297
Simon, Simone 152
Simon, Sylvan S. 506
Simpson, Dorothy 70, 74, 75
Sinatra, Frank 7, 81, 149, 226, 227, 248, 299, 320, 328, 329, 330, 331, 457
Sing, Baby, Sing 388
Siodmark, Robert 462
Sir Francis Drake 100, 478
Sirgo, Joyce 500
Sirgo, Louis 255, 500–501, 615
Sirk, Douglas 510
Sitting Bull 419
Six Bridges to Cross 416
16 Fathoms Deep 71
Sixteen Reasons 517
The $64,000 Question 77
Skeets, Dr. Robert 593
Skelton, Red 457, 514
Sky Murder 152
Sky Raiders 596
Slander 529
Slattery's Hurricane 391
Sledge, John 256
A Slight Case of Murder 206
Sloan, Michael 95
Sloane, Erika 502
Sloane, Everett 368, 501–*502*, 503, 615
Sloane, Nathaniel 502
Sloane, Nathaniel I. 501
Sly Fox 446
Small, Edward 265
Smart, Ralph 567, 572
Smash-Up the Story of a Woman 61
Smiling Faces 211
Smith, Alexis 519, 520, 521, 522
Smith, Archie 372, 503, 609
Smith, Sir C. Aubrey 361
Smith, Dallas (Roger Smith's daughter) 504, 505
Smith, Dallas (Roger Smith's father) 503
Smith, Emma 576
Smith, Ethel 43
Smith, G. Dudley 44
Smith, Jaclyn 42, 221
Smith, Jordan 504, 505
Smith, Kent 94
Smith, Leone 503
Smith, Linda Louise 40
Smith, Maggie 416

Smith, Margaret 576
Smith, Minerva 90, 96, 97
Smith, Roger 39, 104, 105, 106, 316, 451, *452*, 503–*505*, 506, 601, 602, 616
Smith, Tracey 504, 505
Smith, Wilbur 398
The Smith Family 376
Smith-Peterson, Morton 555
Smithee, Allan 290
Smithy 460
Snafu 285
The Snake Pit 525
The Snark Was a Boodlum 342
The Sniper 388
Snow, C.P. 22, 95
Snyder, Joanna 293
So Big 65
So Evil My Love 394
So Well Remembered 119
Soapy Wash and Son 27
S.O.B. 522
Sofia 410
Soldano, Alexander 346
Soldano, Philip 346
A Soldier for Christmas 36
Soldier of Fortune 276, 468
Soloman, Michael 436
Solomon and Sheba 491
Soma, Linda 431
Some Like It Hot 457
Somebody Loves Me 384
Somebody Up There Likes Me 529
The Somerset Maugham Hour 583
Somerville, J. Baxter 574
Something for the Boys 426
Something to Talk About 487
The Son of Frankenstein 302
The Son of Monte Cristo 266
The Son of Robin Hood 269
Song 591
Song of Bernadette 53
Song of Russia 549
A Song to Remember 371
Song Without End 411
The Sonny Comedy Hour 604
The Sons of Katie Elder 241
Sorrell and Son 583
The Sorrowful Shore 115
Soule, Helen Vivian (Poppy) 305
Souls at Sea 452, 455
The Sound of Fury 72, 341
Soundings 205
Soussanin, Nicholas 495
South Pacific 491
The Southerner 419
Space, Arthur 313, 506–508, 609
Space, Charles Augustus 506
Space Academy 254
Space: 1999 25
Spain, Ella O. 562
Spalding, Loranda Stephanie 605

Spanish Lovers 582
Sparks, Cameron Michael 293
Sparks, Melinda Anne 293
Sparks, Randy 293
Spartacus 31, 375
Spawn of the North 452, 455
Spear, Eric 498
Special Agent 7 428, 429, 616, 617
The Speckled Band 360
Spelling, Aaron 605
Spencer, Rosemary Hall 38
Spielberg, Steven 186, 513, 535
Spillane, Mickey 372, 384
Spin of a Coin 457
The Spiral Staircase 66
Spofford 77, 199
Spread Eagle 594
The Spreading Dawn 343
Spring Again 541
Springfield Rifle 69
Springtime 591
Spurgeon, Lesley 11
The Square Ring 36
Squaring the Circle 391
The Squeaker 344
Staccato 122, 123, 124, 127, 128, 617
Stack, Charles Robert 514
Stack, Elizabeth Langford 514
Stack, James Langford 508
Stack, James L., Jr. 508
Stack, Robert 215, 437, 508–512, 513–515, 618
Stacy, James 203, 518
Stahl, John M. 548
Staiola, Enzo 453
Stalag 17 529
Staley, Joan 602, 619
Stallings, Laurence 343
Stallone, Sylvester 146
Stalmaster, Lynn 515–516, 608
Stamboul Quest 65
Standing, Sir Guy 394
Stanhope, Ruth 548, 551
Stanley, Richard 407
Stanwyck, Barbara 29, 50, 64, 65, 155, 337, 338, 408, 444, 533, 534, 548, 550
Star in the Night 596
The Star Spangled Girl 518
Star Stage 109
Stardust 107
Stars in Your Eyes 119, 167
Start Cheering 160
Starting from Scratch 517, 518
State of the Union 41
State Trooper 109, 110, 617
Statham, Mertie 49
Station West 91
Steel Against the Sky 520, 522
Steele, Dorothy Anderson 37

Stefan, Bud 516
Stefan, Virginia 120, 516, 612
Steffany, Michael 295, 619
Steiger, Rod 155, 371
Steinbeck, John 160
Step on a Crack 393
Sternberg, Maurice D. 527
Sterns, Elizabeth Regina 581
Steve Randall 198, 199, 617
Stevens, Arrelle 525, 526
Stevens, Connie 106, 143, 207, 208, 442, 516–517, 518–519, 611
Stevens, Craig 7, 8, 211, 380, 519–523, 615
Stevens, George 509
Stevens, Julie 523, 608
Stevens, K.T. 353
Stevens, Marc 526
Stevens, Mark 23, 223, 317, 382, 523–524, 525–527, 598, 608, 613
Stevens, Mark Richard 525, 526
Stevens, Stella 123
Stevens, Teddy 516
Stevenson, Adlai 42, 368
Stewart, James 92, 155, 192, 197, 309, 509
Stewart, Paul 249, 486, 527–528, 609, 618
Stock, Patricia 500
Stolen Babies 405
Stolen Harmony 427
A Stolen Life 131
Stone, Andrew L. 123, 298, 440, 510
Stone, Ezra 391
Stone, Harold J. 51, 528–529, 530, 611
Stone, Jennifer 530
Stone, Joan 530
Stone, Michael 530
Stone, Miriam 530
Stone, Robert 530
Stoney, Kevin 324
Storey, Ruth 149
Stories of the Century 165
Storm, Joan 52
Storm Operation 19
Stormier, Suzanne 495
Storrs, Suzanne 219, 530, 614
Story of a Woman 513
The Story of Dr. Wassell 346, 460
The Story of Louis Pasteur 596
The Story of Robin Hood and His Merrie Men 204
The Story of Temple Drake 222
Story Theater 525
Stossel, Eleanore 531
Stossel, Ludwig 81, 530–531, 613
Straight Shooting 513
Strange, Glenn 303
Strange as It May Seem 237

The Strange Awakening 230
Strange Bedfellows 77
The Strange Door 303
Strange Fruit 384
The Strange Woman 266
The Stranger (film, 1946) 316, 336
The Stranger (TV series) 122, 617
Strasberg, Lee 132, 401
Streamers 385
Street of Shadows 482
Street Scene 211, 401
The Street Singer 481
The Street with No Name 428, 509, 525
A Streetcar Named Desire 121, 337, 356, 524
Streets of Danger 617
Streets of Laredo 112
The Streets of San Francisco 14
Streisand, Barbara 597
Strictly Dishonorable 481
Strife 464
Strike Force 513
Strock, Herbert L. 161
Stryker of Scotland Yard 617
Stryker of the Yard 213, 594, 595, 617
Stuart, Gaynor 477
Stuart, Kathleen 27
Stuart, Randy 246, 532, 533, 608
Studio One 87, 112, 128, 319, 322, 418, 448
A Study in Scarlet 591
Stump the Stars 227
Sturges, John 534, 603
Sturges, Preston 192
The Subject Was Roses 5
Submarine D-1 160
Submarine Seahawk 47
Sudden Fear 139
Suez 37, 346
Sugarfoot 403, 517, 530
Sullavan, Margaret 155
Sullivan, Barry 87, 94, 210, 310, 364, 533–534, 535–537, 582, 611, 613
Sullivan, Cornelius Daniel 533
Sullivan, Ed 384
Sullivan, Jenny 536
Sullivan, John Cornelius 536
Sullivan, Patsy 536
Sully, Frank 33, 537–538, 610
Sumara, Désirée 536
Summer and Smoke 19
Summers, Dirk Wayne 354
Summertime 372
The Sun Also Rises 510
Sun Valley Serenade 29
Sunbeam 14
Sunday in New York 505

Index

Sundown Beach 333
Sunrise at Campobello *41*, 42
Sunset Boulevard 576
The Sunshine Boys 5, 314
Superdome 290
Surfside 6 202, 585
Surrender 40
The Survivors 42, 267
Susannah and the Elders 71
Suspense (film, 1946) 534
Suspense (TV series) 283, 423, 553
Suspicion (TV series) 281, 397
Susskind, David 22, 132, 392, 448
Sutherland, Annette 96, 97
Sutherland, A. Edward 218
Sutter's Gold 560
Swamp Fire 287
Swanson, Gloria 197
$weepstake$ 107
Sweet Peril 460
Sweet Stranger 428
Sweet Sue 405
The Swindle 162
Swing Your Lady 463
Swope, Herbert Bayard, Jr. 264, 435
Swope, Herbert Bayard (Rusty), III 264
Swope, Tracy Brooks 264
Sword of Freedom 267
Sykes 574
Sykes, Eric 574
Sylvester, William 36

Tabac, Maria 442
Tabor, Joan 163
Tafel, Suzanne 327
Taft, President Howard 70
Take Care of My Little Girl 415
Take It from Me 273
Take Me Along 398
Take Me High 573
Talbot, Cynthia 538
Talbot, David 538
Talbot, Florence 538
Talbot, Lyle 102, 192, 538–*539*, 540, 609
Talbot, Margaret 538
Talbot, Nicole 540
Talbot, Nita *540*–541, 617
Talbot, Olivia 540
Talbot, Stephen 538
A Tale of Two Cities (film, 1935) 596
A Tale of Two Cities (film, 1958) *324*
Tales from the Vienna Woods 441
Tales of the 77th Bengal Lancers 116
Tales of the Vikings 555

Talk of the Town 384
Tall, Dark and Handsome 482
The Tall Men 535
Tall Story 582, 585
Tallas, Greg 347
Talman, Ada B. 541
Talman, Barbie 542
Talman, Billy 542
Talman, Debbie 542
Talman, Lynda 542
Talman, Steve 542
Talman, Susan 542
Talman, Tim 542
Talman, Tom 541
Talman, William *93*, 94, 96, 341, 541–*542*, 543, 615
Talman, William, Sr. 541
The Tamarind Seed 262
The Taming of the Shrew 71, 447
Tamiroff, Akim 21
Tammy 597
Tandy, Jessica 258, 259, 260
Tangier Incident 67
Tani, Yoko 100
Tanner, Gordon *543*, 616
Tap Roots 303
Tapestry in Gray 197
Tapley, Colin 543–*544*, 545, 613, 616
Tarantino, Quentin 385
Target 388, 617
Targets 304
Tarleton, Alan 46
Tarnished Angels 510
Tashman, Lilyan 345
Taxi! (film, 1932) 455
Taxi (film, 1953) 123
Taylor, Bill 547
Taylor, Don 158, 159
Taylor, Elizabeth 299, 314, 329, 331, 417, 509
Taylor, Jonathan 158
Taylor, Jud 290
Taylor, Judy 547
Taylor, Kay 547
Taylor, Kent 136, 545–*546*, 547, 608
Taylor, Robert *18*, 197, 324, 423, *486*, 548–*549*, 550–552, 609, 616
Taylor, Rod 460
Taylor, Terry 550, 551
Taylor, Tessa 550, 551
Tchin Tchin 132
Tea and Sympathy 105
The Teahouse of the August Moon 252, 270, 414
Tear Gas Squad 407
Teasdale, Veree 389
The Telephone 600
Tele-Theater 294
The Telltale Clue 485, 617

Temple, Shirley 253, 388, 482, 565
Temptation 322
The Ten Commandments 165
Ten Gentlemen from West Point 103
Ten Little Indians 384
The Tender Trap 7
Tendler, Harriet 82
Tennessee Johnson 130
Teresa 55, 384
Terror in the Wax Museum 267
Terror Out of the Sky 604, 605
Terry and the Pirates 495
Terry-Thomas 555
Tetzlaff, Ted 248
The Texan 324
Texas Lady 534
The Texas Rangers 112, 427
Texasville 333
Thalberg, Irving 458
Thalberg, Irving, Jr. 458
Thank Your Lucky Stars 407
Thanks 334
The Thanksgiving Promise 74
That Certain Age 197
That Championship Season 44, 163
Thatcher, Heather 499
That'll Be the Day 573
Theater Hour 428
Theodora Goes Wild 197
There's Always Tomorrow 548
There's No Business Like Showbusiness 168, 169
Therese 294
They Drive By Night 455
They Knew What They Wanted 223
Thicker Than Water 338
The Thief 397
The Thief of Bagdad 591
Thiess, George 550
Thiess, Manuela 550
Thiess, Michael 550
Thiess, Ursula 415, 550, 551, 619
The Thin Man (film) 482
The Thin Man (radio) 564
The Thin Man (TV series) 5, 17, 24, 182, 190, 191, 319, 320, 328, *329*, 330, 472, 540, 550, 617
Things Are Looking Up 223
Things to Come 360, 361
The Third Day Comes 125
The Third Man 178, *253*, 467, 469, 470, 471, 617
Third Man on the Mountain 469
The Third Secret 446
13, East Street 274
13 Rue de l'Amour 299
13 Rue Madeleine 239, 588
The 13th Letter 468

656 Index

-30- 578
This Gun for Hire 444
This Is My Affair 548
This Is the Army 14, 136, 391, 485, 520
This Is the Life 532
This Love of Ours 322
This Man Dawson 17, 18, 617
This Savage Land 535
This Side of Innocence 341
This Woman Is Dangerous 69, 408
Thomas, Brandon 499
Thomas, Danny 380, 404
Thomas, Frank 223, 552, 553, 613
Thomas, Frankie, Jr. 552
Thomas, Jevan Brandon 499
The Thomas Crown Affair 89
Thompson, Marshall 72, 336
Thompson, Wallace (Wally) 6
Thor, Jerome 21, 497, 553–554, 610
Thorburn, June 59, 148, 554–555, 556, 610
Thorndike, Sybil 258
Thornton, Norma Nadine 19
Thoroughly Modern Millie 404
Thorpe, Jerry 511
Thorson, Russell 550, 551, *556*, 609
Those We Love 596
A Thousand Clowns 132
Three Coins in the Fountain 298, 435
Three Men on a Horse 200, 380
The Three Mesquiteers 136
Three plays of Love and Hate 125
The 3 Worlds of Gulliver 554, 555
Threepenny Opera 18
Thriller 304
Thunder Island 318
Thunderball 436
Thundercats 251
Thundering Jets 174
Tibbets, Col. Paul, Jr. 423, 550
A Ticket to Tomahawk 168
Tidbury, Don 237
Tidbury, Eldred 237, 543
Tierney, Lawrence 91
Tiger Bay 591
Tight Spot 72
Tightrope! 139, 140, 141, 617
'Til We Meet Again 66, 77
Till the Day I Die 130
Time for Love 283
A Time for Us 263
Time Lock 36
The Time of Your Life 200, 565
Time Out for Ginger 199
The Time, the Place and the Girl 408
The Time Tunnel 471, 599

Timetable 525
The Tin Star 377
Tinker, Grant 403, 404, 405
Tinsdell, Oliver 548
Tinsley, Katherine 389
Titanic 469
To Be or Not to Be 509
To Dorothy a Son 280
To Walk with Lions 60
Tobias, George 130
Tobruk 513
Today Is Ours 432
Today's FBI 142
Todd, Mike 287, 457, 585
Todd, Richard 408
Toler, Sidney 419, 588
The Toll of the Sea 591
Tom Corbett, Space Cadet 552
tom thumb 554, 555
Tomorrow Is Forever 66, 336
Tomorrow Never Comes 95
Tomorrow the World 41
Tone, Franchot 197, 601
Tonight at Samarkand 298
Tonight or Never 196, 197
Tony Rome 149
Too Late Blues 123
Too Late the Phalarope 534
Too Many Thieves 32
Too Scared to Scream 142
Toomey, Francis 556, 557
Toomey, Marie 556, 557
Toomey, Ord 556, 557
Toomey, Othelia 556
Toomey, Regis 287, 556–557, 558–559, 616
Toomey, Sarah 556
Top Secret USA 486, 487, 527, 528, 617, 618
Tors, Ivan 72, 73
Tory, Rosemary 353
La Tosca 343
Touch and Go 554
The Towering Inferno 254
Towers, Harry Alan 37, 224
Town Boy 40
Towne, Dorothy 579
Toy, Lee Gon 590, 593
Toy Story 2 254
Tracy, Lee 223, 428, 559–560, 561–562, 607, 613, 614
Tracy, Spencer 192, 198, 252, 326, 600
Tracy, William Lindsay 559
Trader Horn 115
Tradition . . . A Family at Christmas 518
The Traitor 561
The Transit of Venus 360
Trapper John M.D. 496
The Travels of Jamie McPheeters 82

Travers, Alfred *497*
Travis, Richard 450, *562–563*, 598, 608
Treasure Island 219, 463
Treasury Men in Action 239, 618
Tree, Sir Herbert Beerbohm 424
A Tree Grows in Brooklyn 428
Tremayne, Dolly 563
Tremayne, Joan 564, 565
Tremayne, Les 416, 439, *563–564*, 565, 611
Trevor, Claire 533
The Trial and Torture of Sir John Rampayne 262
The Trials of O'Brien 32
Triangle 47
Trinder, Tommy 589
Trio 468
Triola, Michelle 357, 571
Troughton, Patrick 572
Troup, Bobby 579
The Trout 522
Truffaut, François 21
Truscott-Jones, Elizabeth 395
Trust Me 25
Tubbs, Judith 208
Tucker: The Man and His Dream 74
Tugboat Annie 569
Tully, Nina 566
Tully, Tom 14, 15, 565–566, 613
Tumillo, Frances 8
Turner, Lana 9, 42, 329, 348, 439, 469, 534, 549, 602, 603
Turner, Stephen 573
Turner, Tim *172*, 566–568, *573*, 612
Tuttle, Laurene 488
12 Angry Men 55
Twelve O'Clock High (film) 88, 392
Twelve O'Clock High (TV series) 88, 89, 203
Twentieth Century 445
21st Precinct 502
21 Beacon Street 31, 32, 317, 349, 406, 408, 409, 618
26 Men 134
The Twilight Zone 535
Twin Peaks 271
Two Blind Mice 198
The Two Bouquets 410
Two Faced Woman 197
Two Faces West 35, 185
Two for the Seesaw 597
Two Guys from Milwaukee 408
Two Guys from Texas 408
Two Minute Warning 125
The Two Mrs. Carrolls 294
Two Seconds 283, 527
2,000 Women 21
2001: A Space Odyssey 37

Index   657

Two Tickets to London 195
Two Women 187
Two's Company 392
The Tycoon 585
Tyler, Beverly 568–*569*, 608
Typhoon 444

Ulmer, Edgar G. 266
Umberto D 186
Unconquered 303, 444
The Undeclared War 271
Under Pressure 344
Under Siege 433
Under Suspicion 65
Under the Yum Yum Tree 271
Undercurrent 550
Underground 95
Underwater Warrior 72
Uneasy Terms 468
Unhook the Stars 487
The Uninvited 396
Union Pacific 191, 444
Union Station 50
The Unknown Guest 294
Unsolved Mysteries 514
Untamed World 117
The Untouchables (film) 513
The Untouchables (TV series) 2, 214, *215*, 232, *233*, 234, 241, 437, 453, 508, 510, 511, *512*, 513, 618, 619
The Upper Hand 60
Upstairs Downstairs 584
Urecal, Minerva 520, *569*–571, 615
Uron, Joan 137
U.S. Border Patrol 580, 581, 618
U.S. Steel Hour 7, 42, 155

Vague, Vera 599
The Valachi Papers 82
Valentino, Rudolph 454, 481
Valerie, Joan 475, 476
Valery, Louise 257
Valinsky, Mary 80
Valley of Decision 600
Valley of the Dolls 89
Vanburgh, Dame Irene 583
Vance, Louis Joseph 267
Van Cleef, Lee 355
Van der Horck, Josephine 597
Van Doren, Mamie 415
Van Druten, John 258
Van Dusen, Grace 406
Van Dyke, Dick 404, 437
Van Dyke, W.S. 545
Van Eyck, Peter 21
Vanity Fare 334
Van Voorhis, Westbrook 132
Varnel, Max 238
Vaughn, Robert 290, 433
The Vault of Horror 590

La Vecchia Signora 186
Vedder, Lillian 406, 409
Vegas 535
The Veil 304
Velez, Lupe 345, 596
The Velvet Shotgun 285
Venable, Evelyn 546
Vendetta 367
Venus at Large 9
Vera Cruz 482
Veres, Margot 132
Verner, Anthony 573
The Very Thought of You 130
Victor/Victoria 446
Victoria Regina 410
Vidal, Gore 342, 561
Vidor, King 192
A View from the Bridge 419
The Vigilantes Return 201
Vila, Bob 285, 286
Villa, Pancho 191, 559
Village of the Damned 470
Vincent, Anna 359
The V.I.P.s 299
The Virginian (play) 301
The Virginian (TV series) 53, 378
The Vise 58, 237, 461, 618
Viva Villa! 559
Viva Zapata! 13
Voice of the Turtle 155, 353
Vola, Vicki 296, 571, 614
von Sternberg, Josef 482
Voodoo Island 304
Voodoo Man 593
Vosper, Margery 478
Voyage to the Bottom of the Sea 268, 270, 470
Vye, Mervyn 509
Vyner, Margaret 583, 584

Wagner, Robert 55, 143
Wagner, Wende 586
Wagon Train 26, 373, 378, 503
Wait Until Dark 60, 604
Waiting for Godot 5
Waiting for Lefty 130
Wake Island 112, 444
Walbridge, Mrs. J.L. 43
Wald, Jerry 130
Walk a Tightrope 367
A Walk in the Sun 71
Walk with Destiny 37
Walker, Clint 105, 244
Walker, Robert 585
Wall of Noise 385
Wallace, Edgar 148, 168, 186, 261, 591
Wallace, Julia 311
Wallace, Julie T. 311
Wallach, Eli 15

Wallis, Hal B. 65, 154, 155, 455, 456, 532
Wallis, Minna 65
Walper, Frances Elizabeth 365
Walsh, Dermot 157, 158
Walsh, Sally 158
Walter and Emily 316, 334
The Waltons 236
Waltz of the Toreadors 176, 199
Wang, James 590
War and Peace 178
War and Remembrance 42, 142
The War of the Worlds (film, 1953) 563, 564
War of the Worlds (radio) 137, 501, 527
War Song 222
Ward, Isabella 96, 97
Ward, Jeanette J. 278
Ward, Skip (James) 15, 571–572, 613
Warner, Jack (actor) 157
Warner, Jack L. (mogul) 66, 105, 106, 107, 131, 142, 376, 407, 408, 442, 455, 456, 457, 470, 471, 603
Warner, Jack Lionel 32
Warner, Nora 169
Warren, Robert Penn 161
Washington, Courtenay Davidge 355, 356
Washington, Ned 378
The Wasp Woman 206
Wasserman, Lew 290, 515
Waterloo Bridge 549, 550
Waterston, Sam 405
Watling, Debbie 172, 567, 572–*573*, 574, 612
Watling, Dilys 572
Watling, Giles 572
Watling, Jack 572
Watling, Nicola 572
Wattis, Cameron Tom 574
Wattis, Richard 432, *574*–576, 610
Waugh, Evelyn 99
Way Back Home 339
Way of a Sailor 395
Wayne, John 108, 116, 357, 385, 509, 548
We Refuse to Die 533
Weaver, Dennis 37
The Web 240
Webb, Clifton 252
Webb, Duncan 37
Webb, Jack *11*, 63, 87, 92, 107, 138, 144, 211, 255, 282, 289, 298, 340, 356, 440, 523, 526, 576–*577*, 578–580, 599, 602, 610
Webb, Jimmy 536
Webb, John Richard 580

Webb, Lisa 579
Webb, Patricia Gail 581
Webb, Richard *580*–581, 618
Webb, Richelle Regina 581
Webb, Samuel Chester 576
Webb, Stacy 579
Webber, Malvina Muriel (Mal) 395, 399
The Wedding of Lili Marlene 172
Wednesday's Child 552
Wee Willie Winkie 482
Weekend with Father 182
Weeks, Kim 83
Weinstein, Hannah 187, 205, 267, 303, 304
Weissmuller, Johnny 287, 358
Welch, Coleen 117
Welch, Raquel 22
Weld, Tuesday 7
We'll Meet Again 237
Welles, Orson 21, 130, 137, 336, 367, 368, 369, 370, 402, 469, 501, 527, 576
Wellman, Kitty 221
Wellman, William 105, 139, 191, 192, 221, 444, 509
Wells, H.G. 360, 361, 567
Wells, Mary K. 582, 608
Wendy and Me 517
Werbisek, Giselle 91
We're Not Dressing 396
Wesley 552
West, Adam *18*, 483, 551, 619
West, Mae 195, 455, 543
West, Roland 557
West of the Pecos 248
The West Wind 413, 586
Western Waters 119
The Westerner 313
Weston, Diana 60
Whale, James 99, 197, 301, 302
What a Way to Go! 153
What Every Woman Knows 205, 212
What Price Glory? (film) 343
What Price Glory? (play) 191, 192, 318, 343
What's Going On 62
What's My Line? 460
Wheatley, Alan *544*
Wheel of Fortune 107
When I Was Young 362
When My Baby Smiles at Me 167
When Radio Was 219
When the Smoke Hits the Fan 42
When Were You Born? 592
When Worlds Collide 13
Where Eagles Dare 37
Where Is Parsifal? 331
Where It's At 290
Where Love Has Gone 140
Where the Rainbow Ends 258

Where the Sidewalk Ends 520
While Parents Sleep 259
While the Sun Shines 237, 280, 460
Whiplash 129
Whispering Smith 444
The Whistle at Eaton Falls 72
Whistling in the Dark 485
Whitaker, Johnny 314, 315
Whitaker, Judith 367
Whitby, Gwynne 582
White, A. Norman 467
White, Jesse 452
White, Larry 567
White Cargo 347
The White Cliffs of Dover 329
White Oaks 119
White Tie and Tails 322
Whiteoaks 237
Whitman, Stuart 290
Whitney, Dorothy Ludington 362
Who Was That Lady I Saw You With? 207
Who's Afraid of Virginia Woolf 369
Whose Life Is It Anyway? 405
Why Me? 224
Wicked as They Come 116
The Wicked Lady 468
A Wicked Woman 548
Wide-Eyed in Babylon 398
Widmark, Richard 391, 525
Wilcox, Nina 535, 582, 611
Wild About Harry 604
Wild Boys of the Road 246
Wild Harvest 444
Wild Iris 487
The Wild Pair 74
The Wild, Wild West 143, 144, 156, 208
Wildcat 17
Wilde, Cornel 148, 326
Wilde, Oscar 491
Wilder, Billy 396, 457
Wilder, Thornton 361
Wilding, Michael 175
Wiley, Alice Nevin 156
Wiley, Hugh 302
Wiley, Jan *102*
The Will 260
Willard, Catherine 42
William, Warren 489
Williams, Bernard 585
Williams, Bill 94, 248, *249*, 250, 426, 437, 511
Williams, Emlyn 178
Williams, Frances 342
Williams, Grant 144, 207, 208, 532, 576, 619
Williams, Guy 253
Williams, Hugh 554, 582–*584*, 585, 614

Williams, Hugh D.A. 582
Williams, Hugo 584
Williams, Margaret 583, 584
Williams, Montana Laurena 305
Williams, Polly 584
Williams, Simon 584
Williams, Tennessee 362, 415, 485, 605
Williams, Van 202, 337, *338*, 413, 585–*586*, 587, 608
Williams, Vicki 586
The Willow Tree 592
Willson, Henry 139, 230
Willson, Meredith 445, 521
Wilson, Dina 587
Wilson, Lewis *587*, 597, 609
Wilson, Marjorie 335
Wilson, Michael G. 587
Wilson, Stanley 356
Wimbush, Mary 351
Winchell, Walter 283, 511, 560
Winchester '73 377
The Wind and the Lion 314
The Wind Cannot Read 100
The Window 248
The Winds of War 42
Windsor, Marie 109, 375, 456
Winged Victory 16, 391, 423, 475
Wings for the Eagle 407
Winona, Kim 326
Winter Soldier 321
Winternitz, Felix 588
Winters, Liane *218*
Winters, Roland 64, 419, 488, 587–*588*, 589, 610
Winterset 19, 127
Wire Service 65, 67, 104, 131, 132, 368, *369*, 618
Wise, Robert 468, 515
The Witch 212
With the Marines at Tarawa 266
Within These Gates 197
Within These Walls 525
Without Love 256
Without Warning 385
Witness for the Prosecution 348
Witney, William 102, 236, 242
Witty, John 36, *589*–590, 609
Witty, Jonathan 590
Witty, Sara-Jane 590
Witty, Susan 590
Wolf Larsen 535
The Wolf Man 41
Wolfe, Alma 128
Wolheim, Louis 388
Woman Bites Dog 341
Woman Chases Man 160
The Woman in Room 13 395
A Woman of Mystery 125
A Woman of Paris 387
Woman of the Town 533

A Woman Under the Influence 124, 487
The Woman Who Willed a Miracle 334
Woman with Red Hair 77
A Woman's Devotion 384
A Woman's Face 197
The Women 532
Women Must Dress 136
Women of All Nations 343
Won Ton Ton the Dog Who Saved Hollywood 409
Wonder Boy 380
Wong, Anna May (U.S. actress) 590–*592*, 593–594, 611
Wong, Anna May (British actress) 593
Wong, Mary 593
Wong, Richard 592, 593
Wong, Sam 590, 591, 592
Wong, Ying (Lulu) 593
Wood, Elizabeth Modini 508
Wood, Natalie 97, 105, 278, 601
Wood, Nina 350
Wood, Sam 353, 394, 407
Wood, Ward 141
Woodbridge, Arthur Knott 594
Woodbridge, George 213, *594–595*, 617
Woods, Conrad 597
Woods, Donald 150, 359, 587, 596–*597*, 598, 609
Woods, Linda 597
Woods, Mary Ellen 52
Woods, Thomas 52
Woodward, Joanne 384
Wookey, Karen Hale 247
Woolf, John 22
Woolrich, Cornell 248
The Woolworth Hour 597
World Crime Hunt 298, 618
The World of Carl Sandburg 393
The World of Suzie Wong 462
The World We Make 529

World Without End 352
Worth, Constance 66
Wouk, Herman 534
Wrather, Jack 322
Wray, Fay 455, 533
Wright, Luke Savin 379
Wright, Opal 579
Wright, Teresa 267
Wrightsman, Charlene 174
Written on the Wind 510
Wroe, Trudy 526, 598, 608
The Wrong Man 529
Wuthering Heights 583
Wyler, William 53, 260, 509
Wyman, Jane 53, 483, 557
Wymark, Patrick 213
Wymore, Patrice *602*
Wynn, Fred 562, 598–599, 608
Wynn, Marty 576
Wyse, Mrs. Helen Thomas 561

X-15 *404*
The X-Files 374

A Yank at Oxford 549, 574
A Yank in the RAF 103
A Yank on the Burma Road 423
Yankee Fable 533
Yarborough, Barton 440, 577, 599, 610
Yarborough, Joan 599
Yates, Herbert J. 479
Yellow Jack 71
The Yellow Jacket 582
Yes, My Darling Daughter 319
Yesterday, Today and Tomorrow 187
Yoder, Margot 132
York, Melanie 374
York, Susannah 290, 398
You Bet Your Life 276
You Can't Take It with You 179, 314
You Were Meant for Me 168

Young, Carleton 50
Young, Loretta 16, 53, 416, 418, 534
Young, Mary 239
Young, Robert 467, 514
Young, Terence 436
Young, Victoria 314, 315
Young and Dangerous 517
The Young and the Restless 271
Young Dr. Kildare 393
Young Dr. Malone 448
The Young in Heart 119
The Young Set 320
Young Woodley 258
Youngblood Hawk 106, 220
Your Witness 344
You're in the Army Now 557
You're in the Navy Now 80, 356

Zacharias, Rear Admiral Ellis M. 234
Zanuck, Darryl F. 29, 167, 455, 457, 468, 482, 491, 509
Zaremba, John 120, 599–600, 612
Zavattini, Cesare 186
Zerbe, Anthony 289
Ziegfeld Follies of 1931 251
Zimbalist, Efrem, Jr. 39, 104, 105, 107, 220, 316, 337, 451, *452*, 503, 504, 505, 600–*602*, 603–606, 616
Zimbalist, Efrem, Sr. 600
Zimbalist, Efrem, III 605
Zimbalist, Maria Virginia 600
Zimbalist, Nancy 605
Zimbalist, Sam 260
Zimbalist, Stephanie 600, 605
Zinneman, Fred 384
Ziv, Fred 72, 136, 161, 162
Zoo in Silesia 583
Zorro 253, 322, 605
Zorro's Fighting Legion 242
Zweig, Stefan 298